Programming Perl

Programming Perl

Second Edition

Larry Wall, Tom Christiansen,
and Randal L. Schwartz

with Stephen Potter

O'REILLY®

Beijing · Cambridge · Farnham · Köln · Paris · Sebastopol · Taipei · Tokyo

Programming Perl, Second Edition

by Larry Wall, Tom Christiansen, and Randal L. Schwartz, with Stephen Potter

Published by O'Reilly & Associates, Inc., 101 Morris Street, Sebastopol, CA 95472.

Editor, First Edition: Tim O'Reilly

Editor, Second Edition: Steve Talbott

Production Editor: Nicole Gipson Arigo

Printing History:

January 1991:	First Edition.
August 1991:	Minor corrections.
March 1992:	Minor corrections.
September 1996:	Second Edition.

ISBN: 1-56592-149-6   [1/00]
[M]

Table of Contents

Preface

Perl in a Nutshell

Perl is a language for getting your job done.

Of course, if your job is programming, you can get your job done with any "complete" computer language, theoretically speaking. But we know from experience that computer languages differ not so much in what they make *possible*, but in what they make *easy*. At one extreme, the so-called "fourth generation languages" make it easy to do some things, but nearly impossible to do other things. At the other extreme, certain well known, "industrial-strength" languages make it equally difficult to do almost everything.

Perl is different. In a nutshell, Perl is designed to make the easy jobs easy, without making the hard jobs impossible.

And what are these "easy jobs" that ought to be easy? The ones you do every day, of course. You want a language that makes it easy to manipulate numbers and text, files and directories, computers and networks, and especially programs. It should be easy to run external programs and scan their output for interesting tidbits. It should be easy to send those same tidbits off to other programs that can do special things with them. It should be easy to develop, modify, and debug your own programs too. And, of course, it should be easy to compile and run your programs, and do it portably, on any modern operating system.

Perl does all that, and a whole lot more.

Initially designed as a glue language for the UNIX operating system (or any of its myriad variants), Perl also runs on numerous other systems, including MS-DOS, VMS, OS/2, Plan 9, Macintosh, and any variety of Windows you care to mention. It is one of the most portable programming languages available today. To program C portably, you have to put in all those strange `#ifdef` markings for different operating systems. And to program a shell portably, you have to remember the syntax for each operating system's version of each command, and somehow find the least common denominator that (you hope) works everywhere. Perl happily avoids both of these problems, while retaining many of the benefits of both C and shell programming, with some additional magic of its own. Much of the explosive growth of Perl has been fueled by the hankerings of *former* UNIX programmers who wanted to take along with them as much of the "old country" as they could. For them, Perl is the portable distillation of UNIX culture, an oasis in the wilderness of "can't get there from here". On the other hand, it works in the other direction, too: Web programmers are often delighted to discover that they can take their scripts from a Windows machine and run them unchanged on their UNIX servers.

Although Perl is especially popular with systems programmers and Web developers, it also appeals to a much broader audience. The hitherto well-kept secret is now out: Perl is no longer just for text processing. It has grown into a sophisticated, general-purpose programming language with a rich software development environment complete with debuggers, profilers, cross-referencers, compilers, interpreters, libraries, syntax-directed editors, and all the rest of the trappings of a "real" programming language. (But don't let that scare you: nothing requires you to go tinkering under the hood.) Perl is being used daily in every imaginable field, from aerospace engineering to molecular biology, from computer-assisted design/computer-assisted manufacturing (CAD/CAM) to document processing, from database manipulation to client-server network management. Perl is used by people who are desperate to analyze or convert lots of data quickly, whether you're talking DNA sequences, Web pages, or pork belly futures. Indeed, one of the jokes in the Perl community is that the next big stock market crash will probably be triggered by a bug in a Perl script. (On the brighter side, any unemployed stock analysts will still have a marketable skill, so to speak.)

There are many reasons for the success of Perl. It certainly helps that Perl is freely available, and freely redistributable. But that's not enough to explain the Perl phenomenon, since many freeware packages fail to thrive. Perl is not just free; it's also fun. People feel like they can be creative in Perl, because they have freedom of expression: they get to choose what to optimize for, whether that's computer speed or programmer speed, verbosity or conciseness, readability or maintainability or reusability or portability or learnability or teachability. You can even optimize for obscurity, if you're entering an Obfuscated Perl contest.

Perl can give you all these degrees of freedom because it's essentially a language with a split personality. It's both a very simple language and a very rich language. It has taken good ideas from nearly everywhere, and installed them into an easy-to-use mental framework. To those who merely like it, Perl is the *Practical Extraction and Report Language*. To those who love it, Perl is the *Pathologically Eclectic Rubbish Lister*. And to the minimalists in the crowd, Perl seems like a pointless exercise in redundancy. But that's okay. The world needs a few reductionists (mainly as physicists). Reductionists like to take things apart. The rest of us are just trying to get it together.

Perl is in many ways a simple language. You don't have to know many special incantations to compile a Perl program—you can just execute it like a shell script. The types and structures used by Perl are easy to use and understand. Perl doesn't impose arbitrary limitations on your data—your strings and arrays can grow as large as they like (so long as you have memory), and they're designed to scale well as they grow. Instead of forcing you to learn new syntax and semantics, Perl borrows heavily from other languages you may already be familiar with (such as C, and *sed*, and *awk*, and English, and Greek). In fact, just about any programmer can read a well-written piece of Perl code and have some idea of what it does.

Most important, you don't have to know everything there is to know about Perl before you can write useful programs. You can learn Perl "small end first". You can program in Perl Baby-Talk, and we promise not to laugh. Or more precisely, we promise not to laugh any more than we'd giggle at a child's creative way of putting things. Many of the ideas in Perl are borrowed from natural language, and one of the best ideas is that it's okay to use a subset of the language as long as you get your point across. Any level of language proficiency is acceptable in Perl culture. We won't send the language police after you. A Perl script is "correct" if it gets the job done before your boss fires you.

Though simple in many ways, Perl is also a rich language, and there is much to be learned about it. That's the price of making hard things possible. Although it will take some time for you to absorb all that Perl can do, you will be glad that you have access to the extensive capabilities of Perl when the time comes that you need them. We noted above that Perl borrows many capabilities from the shells and C, but Perl also possesses a strict superset of *sed* and *awk* capabilities. There are, in fact, translators supplied with Perl to turn your old *sed* and *awk* scripts into Perl scripts, so you can see how the features you may already be familiar with correspond to those of Perl.

Because of that heritage, Perl was a rich language even when it was "just" a data-reduction language, designed for navigating files, scanning large amounts of text, creating and obtaining dynamic data, and printing easily formatted reports based on that data. But somewhere along the line, Perl started to blossom. It also became a language for filesystem manipulation, process management, database administration, client-server programming, secure programming, Web-based information management, and even for object-oriented and functional programming. These capabilities were not just slapped onto the side of Perl—each new capability works synergistically with the others, because Perl was designed to be a glue language from the start.

But Perl can glue together more than its own features. Perl is designed to be modularly extensible. Perl allows you to rapidly design, program, debug, and deploy applications, but it also allows you to easily extend the functionality of these applications as the need arises. You can embed Perl in other languages, and you can embed other languages in Perl. Through the module importation mechanism, you can use these external definitions as if they were built-in features of Perl. Object-oriented external libraries retain their object-orientedness in Perl.

Perl helps you in other ways too. Unlike a strictly interpreted language such as the shell, which compiles and executes a script one command at a time, Perl first compiles your whole program quickly into an intermediate format. Like any other compiler, it performs various optimizations, and gives you instant feedback on everything from syntax and semantic errors to library binding mishaps. Once Perl's compiler frontend is happy with your program, it passes off the intermediate code to the interpreter to execute (or optionally to any of several modular back ends that can emit C or bytecode.) This all sounds complicated, but the compiler and interpreter are quite efficient, and most of us find that the typical compile-run-fix cycle is measured in mere seconds. Together with Perl's many fail-soft characteristics, this quick turnaround capability makes Perl a language in which you really can do rapid prototyping. Then later, as your program matures, you can tighten the screws on yourself, and make yourself program with less flair but more discipline. Perl helps you with that too, if you ask nicely.

Perl also helps you to write programs more securely. While running in privileged mode, you can temporarily switch your identity to something innocuous before accessing system resources. Perl also guards against accidental security errors through a data tracing mechanism that automatically determines which data was derived from insecure sources and prevents dangerous operations before they can happen. Finally, Perl lets you set up specially protected compartments in which you can safely execute Perl code of dubious lineage, masking out dangerous operations. System administrators and CGI programmers will particularly welcome these features.

But, paradoxically, the way in which Perl helps you the most has almost nothing to do with Perl, and everything to do with the people who use Perl. Perl folks are, frankly, some of the most helpful folks on earth. If there's a religious quality to the Perl movement, then this is at the heart of it. Larry wanted the Perl community to function like a little bit of heaven, and he seems to have gotten his wish, so far. Please do your part to keep it that way.

Whether you are learning Perl because you want to save the world, or just because you are curious, or because your boss told you to, this handbook will lead you through both the basics and the intricacies. And although we don't intend to teach you how to program, the perceptive reader will pick up some of the art, and a little of the science, of programming. We will encourage you to develop the three great virtues of a programmer: *laziness, impatience*, and *hubris*. Along the way, we hope you find the book mildly amusing in some spots (and wildly amusing in others). And if none of this is enough to keep you awake, just keep reminding yourself that learning Perl will increase the value of your resume. So keep reading.

The Rest of This Book

Here's how the book is laid out:

Chapter 1, *An Overview of Perl*. Getting started is always hard to do. This chapter presents the fundamental ideas of Perl in an informal, curl-up-in-your-favorite-chair fashion. Not a full tutorial, it merely offers a quick jump-start, which may not serve everyone's need. *Learning Perl* (discussed in the next section) offers a more complete, carefully paced introduction to the language.

Chapter 2, *The Gory Details*. This chapter consists of an in-depth, no-holds-barred discussion of the guts of the language, from data types, variables, and objects to functions, subroutines, and modules, as well as special variables, control flow, and regular expressions. You'll gain a good sense of how the language works.

Chapter 3, *Functions*. Here you'll find an authoritative, reference-style description of Perl's built-in functions. The explanations cover function syntax, arguments, and general use.

Chapter 4, *References and Nested Data Structures*. References in Perl are analogous to pointers in C. This chapter tells you how to create references, how to get at the data they refer to, and how to build complex, nested data structures by using references. A tutorial and extensive examples guide you through the subtleties of the topic.

Chapter 5, *Packages, Modules, and Object Classes.* Packages give you a tool for namespace management, and library modules enable you to write reusable code. Together, packages and modules provide a basis for Perl's object-oriented facilities. In addition to explaining these matters, this chapter offers a brief refresher on object-oriented programming, illustrates how to treat built-in variables as objects, and provides some hints for good object-oriented design using Perl.

Chapter 6, *Social Engineering.* This chapter presents how Perl tries to cooperate with everything and everyone in the whole wide world, up to a point.

Chapter 7, *The Standard Perl Library.* This reference chapter describes all the library modules that come with the standard Perl distribution. These modules greatly extend the range of the language. Interfaces to standard database packages, tools for managing terminal input, mechanisms for loading code on the fly at run-time, mathematical packages, safe programming aids, and much else—it is well worth your time to browse through the brief listing of modules at the beginning of this chapter.

Chapter 8, *Other Oddments.* Leftovers worthy of a main meal: the Perl debugger, efficiency considerations, common mistakes, programming style, and a few historical and postmodernist notes.

Chapter 9, *Diagnostic Messages.* Special communications from Perl to you at particularly difficult moments—sometimes helpful, occasionally snide, and too often ignored. But never irrelevant.

Glossary. The words and definitions you'll find here aren't exactly what you'd expect in a normal glossary, but Perl is not really a normal language (nor are the authors of this book really normal authors, or normally real authors).

Additional Resources

Perl Manpages

The online manpages for Perl have been divided into separate sections so you can easily find what you are looking for without wading through hundreds of pages of text. Since the top-level manpage is simply called *perl*, the UNIX command "man perl" should take you to it.[*] That page in turn directs you to more specific pages. For example, "man perlre" will display the manpage for Perl's regular expressions. The perldoc command may work when the *man*(1) command won't, especially on module documentation that your system administrator may not have felt comfortable installing with the ordinary manpages. On the other hand, your system

---

[*] If you still get a humongous page when you do that, you're probably picking up the ancient Release 4 manpage. Check your MANPATH for archeological sites.

administrator may have installed the Perl documentation in hypertext markup language (HTML) format.

Usenet Newsgroups

The Perl newsgroups are a great, if sometimes cluttered, source of information about Perl. *comp.lang.perl.announce* is a moderated, low-traffic newsgroup for Perl-related announcements. These often deal with new version releases, bug fixes, new extensions and modules, and Frequently Asked Questions (FAQs).

The high-traffic *comp.lang.perl.misc* group discusses everything from technical issues to Perl philosophy to Perl games and Perl poetry. Like Perl itself, *comp.lang.perl.misc* is meant to be useful, and no question is too silly to ask.[*]

The *comp.lang.perl.tk* group discusses how to use the popular Tk toolkit from Perl. The *comp.lang.perl.modules* group is about the development and use of Perl modules, which are the best way to get reusable code. There may be other *comp.lang.perl.whatever* newsgroups by the time you read this; look around.

One other newsgroup you might want to check out, at least if you're doing CGI programming on the Web, is *comp.infosystems.www.authoring.cgi.* While it isn't strictly speaking a Perl group, most of the programs discussed there are written in Perl. It's the right place to go for Web-related Perl issues.

The Perl Homepage

If you have access to the World Wide Web, visit the Perl homepage at http://www.perl.com/perl/. It tells what's new in the Perl world, and contains source code and ports, documentation, third-party modules, the Perl bugs database, mailing list information, and more. This site also provides the CPAN multiplexer, described later.

Also check out http://www.perl.org/, which is the homepage of the Perl Institute, a non-profit organization dedicated to saving the world through serving the Perl community.

Frequently Asked Questions List

The Perl Frequently Asked Questions (FAQ) is a collection of questions and answers that often show up on *comp.lang.perl.misc.* In many respects it is a companion to the available books, explaining concepts that people may not have understood and maintaining up-to-date information about such things as the latest release level and the best place to get the Perl source.

---

[*] Of course, some questions are too silly to answer, especially those already answered in the FAQ.

There is also a metaFAQ, which answers supercommon questions. It has pointers to the current Perl distribution, various non-UNIX ports, and the full FAQ. There may be other FAQs you will find useful—for example, FAQs about non-UNIX ports, Web programming, or perltk.

Another FAQish sort of posting is the Perl Modules List, which keeps track of all the various existing and proposed modules that various folks have worked on, or will work on someday real soon now. Included are the email addresses of people to bug, and much free advice on module design. A must-read for people who don't want to reinvent either the buggy whip or the wheel.

The FAQs are periodically posted to *comp.lang.perl.announce*, and can also be found on the web at http://www.perl.com/perl/faq.

Bug Reports

In the unlikely event that you should encounter a bug that's in Perl proper and not just in your own program, you should try to reduce it to a minimal test case and then report it with the *perlbug* program that comes with Perl.

The Perl Distribution

Perl is distributed under either of two licenses (your choice). The first is the standard GNU Copyleft, which means briefly that if you can execute Perl on your system, you should have access to the full source of Perl for no additional charge. Alternately, Perl may also be distributed under the Artistic License, which some people find less threatening than the Copyleft (especially lawyers).

Within the Perl distribution, you will find some example programs in the *eg/* directory. You may also find other tidbits. Poke around in there on some rainy afternoon. Study the Perl source (if you're a C hacker with a masochistic streak). Look at the test suite. See how *Configure* determines whether you have the *mkdir*(2) system call. Figure out how Perl does dynamic loading of C modules. Or whatever else suits your fancy.

Other Books

Learning Perl by Randal Schwartz (published by O'Reilly & Associates) is a companion to *Programming Perl*. It is more of a tutorial, whereas this book is more of a reference. If the tutorial section of *Programming Perl* is too short or assumes too much about your background, try *Learning Perl* for a kinder, gentler introduction to the language. If you want to learn more about Perl's regular expressions, we suggest *Mastering Regular Expressions*, by Jeffrey E.F. Friedl (also published by O'Reilly & Associates).

The AWK Programming Language, by Aho, Kernighan, and Weinberger (published by Addison-Wesley), and *sed & awk*, by Dale Dougherty (published by O'Reilly & Associates), provide an essential background in such things as associative arrays, regular expressions, and the general worldview that gave rise to Perl. They also contain many examples that can be translated into Perl by the awk-to-perl translator *a2p* or by the sed-to-perl translator *s2p*. These translators won't produce idiomatic Perl, of course, but if you can't figure out how to imitate one of those examples in Perl, the translator output will give you a good place to start.

We also recommend Johan Vromans's convenient and thorough quick reference booklet, called *Perl 5 Desktop Reference*, published coincidentally by O'Reilly & Associates.

How to Get Perl

The main distribution point for Perl is the *Comprehensive Perl Archive Network*, or CPAN. This archive contains not only the source code, but also just about everything you could ever want that's Perl-related. CPAN is mirrored by dozens of sites all over the world, as well as a few down under. The main site is *ftp.funet.fi* (128.214.248.6). You can find a more local CPAN site by getting the file */pub/languages/perl/CPAN/MIRRORS* from *ftp.funet.fi*. Or you can use your Web browser to access the CPAN multiplex service at *www.perl.com*. Whenever you ask this Web server for a file starting with */CPAN/*, it connects you to a CPAN site, which it chooses by looking at your domain name. Here are some popular universal resource locators (URLs) out of CPAN:

```
http://www.perl.com/CPAN/
http://www.perl.com/CPAN/README.html
http://www.perl.com/CPAN/modules/
http://www.perl.com/CPAN/ports/
http://www.perl.com/CPAN/src/latest.tar.gz
```

The CPAN multiplex service tries to connect you to a local, fast machine on a large bandwidth hub. This doesn't always work, however, because domain names may not reflect network connections. For example, you might have a hostname ending in *.se* but you may actually be better connected to North America than to Sweden. If so, you can use the following URL to choose your own site:

```
http://www.perl.com/CPAN
```

Note the absence of a slash at the end of the URL. When you omit the trailing slash, the CPAN multiplexer presents a menu of CPAN mirrors from which you can select a site. It will remember your choice next time.

The following machines should have the Perl source code plus a copy of the CPAN mirror list—both available for anonymous FTP. (Try to use the machine names rather than the numbers, since the numbers may change.)

```
ftp.perl.com         199.45.129.30
ftp.cs.colorado.edu  131.211.80.17
ftp.cise.ufl.edu     128.227.162.34
ftp.funet.fi         128.214.248.6
ftp.cs.ruu.nl        131.211.80.17
```

The location of the top directory of the CPAN mirror differs on these machines, so look around once you get there. It's often something like */pub/perl/CPAN*.

Where the Files Are

Under the main CPAN directory, you'll see at least the following subdirectories:

- *authors*. This directory contains numerous subdirectories, one for each contributor of software. For example, if you wanted to find Lincoln Stein's great CGI module, and you knew for a fact that he wrote it, you could look in *authors/Lincoln_Stein*. If you didn't know he wrote it, you could look in the *modules* directory explained below.

- *doc*. A directory containing all manner of Perl documentation. This includes all official documentation (manpages) in several formats (such as ASCII text, HTML, PostScript, and Perl's native POD format), plus the FAQs and interesting supplementary documents.

- *modules*. This directory contains unbundled modules written in C, Perl, or both. Extensions allow you to emulate or access the functionality of other software, such as Tk graphical facilities, the UNIX curses library, and math libraries. They also give you a way to interact with databases (Oracle, Sybase, etc.), and to manage HTML files and CGI scripts.

- *ports*. This directory contains the source code and/or binaries for Perl ports to operating systems not directly supported in the standard distribution. These ports are the individual efforts of their respective authors, and may not all function precisely as described in this book. For example, none of the MS-DOS ports implement the **fork** function, for some reason.

- *scripts*. A collection of diverse scripts from all over the world. If you need to find out how to do something, or if you just want to see how other people write programs, check this out. The subdirectory *nutshell* contains the examples from this book. (You can also find these sources at the O'Reilly & Associates *ftp.oreilly.com* site, in */pub/examples/nutshell/programming_perl2/*.)

- *src.* Within this directory you will find the source for the standard Perl distribution. The current production release is always in the file that is called *src/latest.tar.gz,*[*] which as of this writing is a symbolic link to the file *src/5.0/perl5.003.tar.gz,* but will likely point to a higher version number by the time you read this. This very large file contains full source and documentation for Perl. Configuration and installation should be relatively straightforward on UNIX and UNIX-like systems, as well as VMS and OS/2.

Using Anonymous FTP

In the event you've never used anonymous FTP, here is a quick primer in the form of a sample session with comments. Text in bold typewriter font is what you should type; comments are in italics. The **%** represents your prompt, and should not be typed.

```
% ftp ftp.CPAN.org (ftp.CPAN.org is not a real site)
Connected to ftp.CPAN.org.
220 CPAN FTP server (Version wu-2.4(1) Fri Dec 1 00:00:00 EST 1995) ready.
Name (ftp.CPAN.org:CPAN): anonymous
331 Guest login ok, send your complete e-mail address as password.
Password: camel@nutshell.com (Use your user name and host here.)
230 Guest login ok, access restrictions apply.
ftp> cd pub/perl/CPAN/src
250 CWD command successful.
ftp> binary (You must specify binary transfer for compressed files.)
200 Type set to I.
ftp> get latest.tar.gz
200 PORT command successful.
150 Opening BINARY mode data connection for FILE.
226 Transfer complete.
         .
         .           (repeat this step for each file you want)
         .
ftp> quit
221 Goodbye.
%
```

Once you have the files, first unzip and untar them, and then configure, build, and install Perl:

```
% gunzip < latest.tar.gz | tar xvf -
% cd perl15.003       (Use actual directory name.)

Now either one of these next two lines:
% sh configure        (Lowercase "c" for automatic configuration)
% sh Configure        (Capital "C" for manual configuration)

% make                (Build all of Perl.)
```

---

[*] The trailing *.tar.gz* means that it's in the standard Internet format of a GNU-zipped, *tar* archive.

```
% make test         (Make sure it works.)
% make install      (You should be the superuser for this.)
```

Fetching modules

For retrieving and building unbundled Perl modules, the process is slightly different. Let's say you want to build and install a module named CoolMod. You'd first fetch it via *ftp*(1), or you could use your Web browser to access the module service from *http://www.perl.com/*, which always retrieves the most up-to-date version of a particular registered module. The address to feed your browser would be something like:

```
http://www.perl.com/cgi-bin/cpan_mod?module=CoolMod
```

Once you've gotten the file, do this:

```
% gunzip < CoolMod-2.34.tar.gz | tar xvf -
% cd CoolMod-2.34
% perl Makefile.PL   (Creates the real Makefile)

% make               (Build the whole module.)
% make test          (Make sure it works.)
% make install       (Probably should be the superuser)
```

When the CoolMod module has been successfully installed (it will be automatically placed in your system's Perl library path), your programs can use CoolMod, and you should be able to run *man CoolMod* (or maybe *perldoc CoolMod*) to read the module's documentation.

Conventions Used in This Book

Since we pretty much made them up as we went along to fit different circumstances, we describe them as we go along, too. In general, though, the names of files and UNIX utilities are printed in *italics*, the names of Perl functions, operators, and other keywords of the language are in **bold**, and examples or fragments of Perl code are in `constant width`, and generic code terms for which you must substitute particular values are in `italic constant width`. Data values are represented by `constant width` in roman quotes, which are not part of the value.

Acknowledgments

This work would not have been possible without the help of a lot of folks. We can't possibly name everyone here, and undoubtedly we've overlooked at least one major contributor; but here are at least some of the folks that we'd like to thank publicly and profusely for their contributions of verbiage and vitality: Ilya Zakharevich, Johan Vromans, Mike Stok, Lincoln Stein, Aaron Sherman, David Muir Sharnoff, Gurusamy Sarathy, Tony Sanders, Chip Salzenberg, Dean Roehrich,

Randy J. Ray, Hal Pomeranz, Tom Phoenix, Jon Orwant, Jeff Okamoto, Bill Middleton, Paul Marquess, John Macdonald, Andreas Koenig, Nick Ing-Simmons, Sharon Hopkins, Jarkko Hietaniemi, Felix Gallo, Hallvard B. Furuseth, Jeffrey Friedl, Chaim Frenkel, Daniel Faigin, Andy Dougherty, Tim Bunce, Mark Biggar, Malcolm Beattie, Graham Barr, Charles Bailey, and Kenneth Albanowski. Not necessarily in that order.

The authors would also like to thank all of their personal friends (and relations) for remaining their personal friends (and relations) throughout the long, wearisome process.

We'd like to express our special gratitude to Tim O'Reilly for encouraging authors to write the sort of books people might enjoy reading.

Thanks also to the staff at O'Reilly & Associates. Steve Talbott was the technical editor. Nicole Gipson Arigo was the production editor and project manager. Joseph Pomerance was the copyeditor, and Steven Kleinedler proofread the book. Kismet McDonough-Chan and Sheryl Avruch performed quality control checks. Seth Maislin wrote the index. Erik Ray, Ellen Siever, and Lenny Muellner worked with the tools to create the book. Nancy Priest and Mary Jane Walsh designed the interior book layout, and Edie Freedman and Hanna Dyer designed the front cover.

We'd Like to Hear from You

We have tested and verified all of the information in this book to the best of our ability, but you may find that features have changed (or even that we have made mistakes!). Please let us know about any errors you find, as well as your suggestions for future editions, by writing:

O'Reilly & Associates, Inc.
101 Morris Street
Sebastopol, CA 95472
1-800-998-9938 (in the US or Canada)
1-707-829-0515 (international/local)
1-707-829-0104 (FAX)

You can also send us messages electronically. To be put on the mailing list or request a catalog, send email to:

nuts@oreilly.com

To ask technical questions or comment on the book, send email to:

bookquestions@oreilly.com

1

An Overview of Perl

Getting Started

We think that Perl is an easy language to learn and use, and we hope to convince you that we're right. One thing that's easy about Perl is that you don't have to say much before you say what you want to say. In many programming languages, you have to declare the types, variables, and subroutines you are going to use before you can write the first statement of executable code. And for complex problems demanding complex data structures, this is a good idea. But for many simple, everyday problems, you would like a programming language in which you can simply say:

```
print "Howdy, world!\n";
```

and expect the program to do just that.

Perl is such a language. In fact, the example is a complete program,[*] and if you feed it to the Perl interpreter, it will print "Howdy, world!" on your screen.

And that's that. You don't have to say much *after* you say what you want to say, either. Unlike many languages, Perl thinks that falling off the end of your program is just a normal way to exit the program. You certainly *may* call the **exit** function explicitly if you wish, just as you *may* declare some of your variables and subroutines, or even *force* yourself to declare all your variables and subroutines. But it's your choice. With Perl you're free to do The Right Thing, however you care to define it.

---

[*] Or script, or application, or executable, or doohickey. Whatever.

1

There are many other reasons why Perl is easy to use, but it would be pointless to list them all here, because that's what the rest of the book is for. The devil may be in the details, as they say, but Perl tries to help you out down there in the hot place too. At every level, Perl is about helping you get from here to there with minimum fuss and maximum enjoyment. That's why so many Perl programmers go around with a silly grin on their face.

This chapter is an overview of Perl, so we're not trying to present Perl to the rational side of your brain. Nor are we trying to be complete, or logical. That's what the next chapter is for.* This chapter presents Perl to the *other* side of your brain, whether you prefer to call it associative, artistic, passionate, or merely spongy. To that end, we'll be presenting various views of Perl that will hopefully give you as clear a picture of Perl as the blind men had of the elephant. Well, okay, maybe we can do better than that. We're dealing with a camel here. Hopefully, at least one of these views of Perl will help get you over the hump.

Natural and Artificial Languages

Languages were first invented by humans, for the benefit of humans. In the annals of computer science, this fact has occasionally been forgotten.† Since Perl was designed (loosely speaking) by an occasional linguist, it was designed to work smoothly in the same ways that natural language works smoothly. Naturally, there are many aspects to this, since natural language works well at many levels simultaneously. We could enumerate many of these linguistic principles here, but the most important principle of language design is simply that easy things should be easy, and hard things should be possible. That may seem obvious, but many computer languages fail at one or the other.

Natural languages are good at both because people are continually trying to express both easy things and hard things, so the language evolves to handle both. Perl was designed first of all to evolve, and indeed it has evolved. Many people have contributed to the evolution of Perl over the years. We often joke that a camel is a horse designed by a committee, but if you think about it, the camel is pretty well adapted for life in the desert. The camel has evolved to be relatively self-sufficient.‡

---

* Vulcans (and like-minded humans) should skip this overview and go straight to Chapter 2, *The Gory Details*, for maximum information density. If, on the other hand, you're looking for a carefully paced tutorial, you should probably get Randal's nice book, *Learning Perl* (published by O'Reilly & Associates). But don't throw out this book just yet.

† More precisely, this fact has occasionally been remembered.

‡ On the other hand, the camel has not evolved to smell good. Neither has Perl.

Now when someone utters the word "linguistics", many people think of one of two things. Either they think of words, or they think of sentences. But words and sentences are just two handy ways to "chunk" speech. Either may be broken down into smaller units of meaning, or combined into larger units of meaning. And the meaning of any unit depends heavily on the syntactic, semantic, and pragmatic context in which the unit is located. Natural language has words of various sorts, nouns and verbs and such. If I say "dog" in isolation, you think of it as a noun, but I can also use the word in other ways. That is, a noun can function as a verb, an adjective or an adverb when the context demands it. If you dog a dog during the dog days of summer, you'll be a dog tired dogcatcher.*

Perl also evaluates words differently in various contexts. We will see how it does that later. Just remember that Perl is trying to understand what you're saying, like any good listener does. Perl works pretty hard to try to keep up its end of the bargain. Just say what you mean, and Perl will usually "get it". (Unless you're talking nonsense, of course—the Perl parser understands Perl a lot better than either English or Swahili.)

But back to nouns. A noun can name a particular object, or it can name a class of objects generically without specifying which one or ones are currently being referred to. Most computer languages make this distinction, only we call the particular thing a value and the generic one a variable. A value just exists somewhere, who knows where, but a variable gets associated with one or more values over its lifetime. So whoever is interpreting the variable has to keep track of that association. That interpreter may be in your brain, or in your computer.

Nouns

A variable is just a handy place to keep something, a place with a name, so you know where to find your special something when you come back looking for it later. As in real life, there are various kinds of places to store things, some of them rather private, and some of them out in public. Some places are temporary, and other places are more permanent. Computer scientists love to talk about the "scope" of variables, but that's all they mean by it. Perl has various handy ways of dealing with scoping issues, which you'll be happy to learn later when the time is right. Which is not yet. (Look up the adjectives "local" and "my" in Chapter 3, *Functions*, when you get curious.)

But a more immediately useful way of classifying variables is by what sort of data they can hold. As in English, Perl's primary type distinction is between singular and plural data. Strings and numbers are singular pieces of data, while lists of

---

* And you're probably dog tired of all this linguistics claptrap. But we'd like you to understand why Perl is different from the typical computer language, doggone it!

strings or numbers are plural. (And when we get to object-oriented programming, you'll find that an object looks singular from the outside, but may look plural from the inside, like a class of students.) We call a singular variable a *scalar*, and a plural variable an *array*. Since a string can be stored in a scalar variable, we might write a slightly longer (and commented) version of our first example like this:

```
$phrase = "Howdy, world!\n";          # Set a variable.
print $phrase;                         # Print the variable.
```

Note that we did not have to predefine what kind of variable $phrase is. The $ character tells Perl that phrase is a scalar variable, that is, one containing a singular value. An array variable, by contrast, would start with an @ character. (It may help you to remember that a $ is a stylized "S", for "scalar", while @ is a stylized "a", for "array".)

Perl has some other variable types, with unlikely names like "hash", "handle", and "typeglob". Like scalars and arrays, these types of variables are also preceded by funny characters.* For completeness, Table 1-1 lists all the funny characters you'll encounter.

Table 1-1: Variable Syntax

Type	Character	Example	Is a name for:
Scalar	$	$cents	An individual value (number or string)
Array	@	@large	A list of values, keyed by number
Hash	%	%interest	A group of values, keyed by string
Subroutine	&	&how	A callable chunk of Perl code
Typeglob	*	*struck	Everything named struck

Singularities

From our example, you can see that scalars may be assigned a new value with the = operator, just as in many other computer languages. Scalar variables can be assigned any form of scalar value: integers, floating-point numbers, strings, and even esoteric things like references to other variables, or to objects. There are many ways of generating these values for assignment.

---

* Some language purists point to these funny characters as a reason to abhor Perl. This is superficial. These characters have many benefits: Variables can be interpolated into strings with no additional syntax. Perl scripts are easy to read (for people who have bothered to learn Perl!) because the nouns stand out from verbs, and new verbs can be added to the language without breaking old scripts. (We told you Perl was designed to evolve.) And the noun analogy is not frivolous—there is ample precedent in various natural languages for requiring grammatical noun markers. It's how we think! (We think.)

As in the UNIX shell, you can use different quoting mechanisms to make different kinds of values. Double quotation marks (double quotes) do variable interpolation[*] and backslash interpretation,[†] while single quotes suppress both interpolation and interpretation. And backquotes (the ones leaning to the left) will execute an external program and return the output of the program, so you can capture it as a single string containing all the lines of output.

```
$answer = 42;                # an integer
$pi = 3.14159265;            # a "real" number
$avocados = 6.02e23;         # scientific notation
$pet = "Camel";              # string
$sign = "I love my $pet";    # string with interpolation
$cost = 'It costs $100';     # string without interpolation
$thence = $whence;           # another variable
$x = $moles * $avocados;     # an expression
$cwd = `pwd`;                # string output from a command
$exit = system("vi $x");     # numeric status of a command
$fido = new Camel "Fido";    # an object
```

Uninitialized variables automatically spring into existence as needed. Following the principle of least surprise, they are created with a null value, either "" or 0. Depending on where you use them, variables will be interpreted automatically as strings, as numbers, or as "true" and "false" values (commonly called Boolean values). Various operators expect certain kinds of values as parameters, so we will speak of those operators as "providing" or "supplying" a scalar context to those parameters. Sometimes we'll be more specific, and say it supplies a numeric context, a string context, or a Boolean context to those parameters. (Later we'll also talk about list context, which is the opposite of scalar context.) Perl will automatically convert the data into the form required by the current context, within reason. For example, suppose you said this:

```
$camels = '123';
print $camels + 1, "\n";
```

The original value of $camels is a string, but it is converted to a number to add 1 to it, and then converted back to a string to be printed out as 124. The newline, represented by "\n", is also in string context, but since it's already a string, no conversion is necessary. But notice that we had to use double quotes there—using single quotes to say '\n' would result in a two-character string consisting of a backslash followed by an "n", which is not a newline by anybody's definition.

---

[*] Sometimes called "substitution" by shell programmers, but we prefer to reserve that word for something else in Perl. So please call it interpolation. We're using the term in the textual sense ("this passage is a Gnostic interpolation") rather than in the mathematical sense ("this point on the graph is an interpolation between two other points").

[†] Such as turning \t into a tab, \n into a newline, \001 into a CTRL-A, and so on, in the tradition of many UNIX programs.

So, in a sense, double quotes and single quotes are yet another way of specifying context. The interpretation of the innards of a quoted string depends on which quotes you use. Later we'll see some other operators that work like quotes syntactically, but use the string in some special way, such as for pattern matching or substitution. These all work like double-quoted strings too. The *double-quote* context is the "interpolative" context of Perl, and is supplied by many operators that don't happen to resemble double quotes.

Pluralities

Some kinds of variables hold multiple values that are logically tied together. Perl has two types of multivalued variables: arrays and hashes. In many ways these behave like scalars. They spring into existence with nothing in them when needed. When you assign to them, they supply a *list* context to the right side of the assignment.

You'd use an array when you want to look something up by number. You'd use a hash when you want to look something up by name. The two concepts are complementary. You'll often see people using an array to translate month numbers into month names, and a corresponding hash to translate month names back into month numbers. (Though hashes aren't limited to holding only numbers. You could have a hash that translates month names to birthstone names, for instance.)

Arrays.   An *array* is an ordered list of scalars, accessed[*] by the scalar's position in the list. The list may contain numbers, or strings, or a mixture of both. (In fact, it could also contain references to other lists, but we'll get to that in Chapter 4, *References and Nested Data Structures*, when we're discussing multidimensional arrays.) To assign a list value to an array, you simply group the variables together (with a set of parentheses):

```
@home = ("couch", "chair", "table", "stove");
```

Conversely, if you use @home in a list context, such as on the right side of a list assignment, you get back out the same list you put in. So you could set four scalar variables from the array like this:

```
($potato, $lift, $tennis, $pipe) = @home;
```

These are called list assignments. They logically happen in parallel, so you can swap two variables by saying:

```
($alpha,$omega) = ($omega,$alpha);
```

---

* Or keyed, or indexed, or subscripted, or looked up. Take your pick.

As in C, arrays are zero-based, so while you would talk about the first through fourth elements of the array, you would get to them with subscripts 0 through 3.[*] Array subscripts are enclosed in square brackets [like this], so if you want to select an individual array element, you would refer to it as $home[*n*], where *n* is the subscript (one less than the element number) you want. See the example below. Since the element you are dealing with is a scalar, you always precede it with a $.

If you want to assign to one array element at a time, you could write the earlier assignment as:

```
$home[0] = "couch";
$home[1] = "chair";
$home[2] = "table";
$home[3] = "stove";
```

Since arrays are ordered, there are various useful operations that you can do on them, such as the stack operations, **push** and **pop**. A stack is, after all, just an ordered list, with a beginning and an end. Especially an end. Perl regards the end of your list as the top of a stack. (Although most Perl programmers think of a list as horizontal, with the top of the stack on the right.)

Hashes.   A *hash* is an unordered set of scalars, accessed[†] by some string value that is associated with each scalar. For this reason hashes are often called "associative arrays". But that's too long for lazy typists to type, and we talk about them so often that we decided to name them something short and snappy.[‡] The other reason we picked the name "hash" is to emphasize the fact that they're disordered. (They are, coincidentally, implemented internally using a hash-table lookup, which is why hashes are so fast, and stay so fast no matter how many values you put into them.) You can't **push** or **pop** a hash though, because it doesn't make sense. A hash has no beginning or end. Nevertheless, hashes are extremely powerful and useful. Until you start thinking in terms of hashes, you aren't really thinking in Perl.

Since the keys to a hash are not automatically implied by their position, you must supply the key as well as the value when populating a hash. You can still assign a list to it like an ordinary array, but each pair of items in the list will be interpreted as a key/value pair. Suppose you wanted to translate abbreviated day names to the corresponding full names. You could write the following list assignment.

---

[*] If this seems odd to you, just think of the subscript as an offset, that is, the count of how many array elements come before it. Obviously, the first element doesn't have any elements before it, and so has an offset of 0. This is how computers think. (We think.)

[†] Or keyed, or indexed, or subscripted, or looked up. Take your pick.

[‡] Presuming for the moment that we can classify *any* sort of hash as "snappy". Please pass the Tabasco.

```
%longday = ("Sun", "Sunday", "Mon", "Monday", "Tue", "Tuesday",
            "Wed", "Wednesday", "Thu", "Thursday", "Fri",
            "Friday", "Sat", "Saturday");
```

Because it is sometimes difficult to read a hash that is defined like this, Perl pro-vides the => (equal sign, greater than) sequence as an alternative separator to the comma. Using this syntax (and some creative formatting), it is easier to see which strings are the keys, and which strings are the associated values.

```
%longday = (
    "Sun" => "Sunday",
    "Mon" => "Monday",
    "Tue" => "Tuesday",
    "Wed" => "Wednesday",
    "Thu" => "Thursday",
    "Fri" => "Friday",
    "Sat" => "Saturday",
);
```

Not only can you assign a list to a hash, as we did above, but if you use a hash in list context, it'll convert the hash back to a list of key/value pairs, in a weird order. This is occasionally useful. More often people extract a list of just the keys, using the (aptly named) **keys** function. The key list is also unordered, but can easily be sorted if desired, using the (aptly named) **sort** function. More on that later.

Because hashes are a fancy kind of array, you select an individual hash element by enclosing the key in braces. So, for example, if you want to find out the value associated with Wed in the hash above, you would use $longday{"Wed"}. Note again that you are dealing with a scalar value, so you use $, not %.

Linguistically, the relationship encoded in a hash is genitive or possessive, like the word "of" in English, or like "'s". The wife *of* Adam is Eve, so we write:

```
$wife{"Adam"} = "Eve";
```

Verbs

As is typical of your typical imperative computer language, many of the verbs in Perl are commands: they tell the Perl interpreter to do something. On the other hand, as is typical of a natural language, the meanings of Perl verbs tend to mush off in various directions, depending on the context. A statement starting with a verb is generally purely imperative, and evaluated entirely for its side effects. We often call these verbs *procedures*, especially when they're user-defined. A fre-quently seen command (in fact, you've seen it already) is the **print** command:

```
print "Adam's wife is ", $wife{'Adam'}, ".\n";
```

This has the side effect of producing the desired output.

But there are other "moods" besides the imperative mood. Some verbs are for asking questions, and are useful in conditional statements. Other verbs translate their input parameters into return values, just as a recipe tells you how to turn raw ingredients into something (hopefully) edible. We tend to call these verbs *functions*, in deference to generations of mathematicians who don't know what the word "functional" means in natural language.

An example of a built-in function would be the exponential function:

```
$e = exp(1);   # 2.718281828459, or thereabouts
```

But Perl doesn't make a hard distinction between procedures and functions. You'll find the terms used interchangeably. Verbs are also sometimes called subroutines (when user-defined) or operators (when built-in). But call them whatever you like—they all return a value, which may or may not be a meaningful value, which you may or may not choose to ignore.

As we go on, you'll see additional examples of how Perl behaves like a natural language. But there are other ways to look at Perl too. We've already sneakily introduced some notions from mathematical language, such as addition and subscripting, not to mention the exponential function. But Perl is also a control language, a glue language, a prototyping language, a text-processing language, a list-processing language, and an object-oriented language. Among other things.

But Perl is also just a plain old computer language. And that's how we'll look at it next.

A Grade Example

Suppose you had a set of scores for each member of a class you are teaching. You'd like a combined list of all the grades for each student, plus their average score. You have a text file (imaginatively named *grades*) that looks like this:

```
Noël 25
Ben 76
Clementine 49
Norm 66
Chris 92
Doug 42
Carol 25
Ben 12
Clementine 0
Norm 66
...
```

You can use the following script to gather all their scores together, determine each student's average, and print them all out in alphabetical order. This program assumes, rather naively, that you don't have two Carols in your class. That is, if there is a second entry for Carol, the program will assume it's just another score for the first Carol (not to be confused with the first Noël).

By the way, the line numbers are not part of the program, any other resemblances to BASIC notwithstanding.

```
1  #!/usr/bin/perl
2
3  open(GRADES, "grades") or die "Can't open grades: $!\n";
4  while ($line = <GRADES>) {
5      ($student, $grade) = split(" ", $line);
6      $grades{$student} .= $grade . " ";
7  }
8
9  foreach $student (sort keys %grades) {
10     $scores = 0;
11     $total = 0;
12     @grades = split(" ", $grades{$student});
13     foreach $grade (@grades) {
14         $total += $grade;
15         $scores++;
16     }
17     $average = $total / $scores;
18     print "$student: $grades{$student}\tAverage: $average\n";
19 }
```

Now before your eyes cross permanently, we'd better point out that this example demonstrates a lot of what we've covered so far, plus quite a bit more that we'll explain presently. But if you let your eyes go just a little out of focus, you may start to see some interesting patterns. Take some wild guesses now as to what's going on, and then later on we'll tell you if you're right.

We'd tell you to try running it, but you may not know how yet.

How to Do It

Gee, right about now you're probably wondering how to run a Perl program. The short answer is that you feed it to the Perl language interpreter program, which coincidentally happens to be named *perl* (note the case distinction). The longer answer starts out like this: There's More Than One Way To Do It.[*]

The first way to invoke *perl* (and the way most likely to work on any operating system) is to simply call *perl* explicitly from the command line. If you are on a version of UNIX and you are doing something fairly simple, you can use the **-e**

---

[*] That's the Perl Slogan, and you'll get tired of hearing it, unless you're the Local Expert, in which case you'll get tired of saying it. Sometimes it's shortened to TMTOWTDI, pronounced "tim-toady". But you can pronounce it however you like. After all, TMTOWTDI.

switch (% in the following example represents a standard shell prompt, so don't type it):

```
% perl -e 'print "Hello, world!\n";'
```

On other operating systems, you may have to fiddle with the quotes some. But the basic principle is the same: you're trying to cram everything Perl needs to know into 80 columns or so.[*]

For longer scripts, you can use your favorite text editor (or any other text editor) to put all your commands into a file and then, presuming you named the script *gradation* (not to be confused with graduation), you'd say:

```
% perl gradation
```

You're still invoking the Perl interpreter explicitly, but at least you don't have to put everything on the command line every time. And you don't have to fiddle with quotes to keep the shell happy.

The most convenient way to invoke a script is just to name it directly (or click on it), and let the operating system find the interpreter for you. On some systems, there may be ways of associating various file extensions or directories with a particular application. On those systems, you should do whatever it is you do to associate the Perl script with the Perl interpreter. On UNIX systems that support the #! "shebang" notation (and most UNIX systems do, nowadays), you can make the first line of your script be magical, so the operating system will know which program to run. Put a line resembling[†] line 1 of our example into your program:

```
#!/usr/bin/perl
```

Then all you have to say is

```
% gradation
```

Of course, this didn't work because you forgot to make sure the script was executable (see the manpage for *chmod*(1))[‡] and in your PATH. If it isn't in your

---

[*] These types of scripts are often referred to as "one-liners". If you ever end up hanging out with other Perl programmers, you'll find that some of us are quite fond of creating intricate one-liners. Perl has occasionally been maligned as a write-only language because of these shenanigans.

[†] If *perl* isn't in */usr/bin*, you'll have to change the #! line accordingly.

[‡] Although Perl has its share of funny notations, this one must be blamed on UNIX. *chmod*(1) means you should refer to the manpage for the *chmod* command in section one of your UNIX manual. If you type either `man 1 chmod` or `man -s 1 chmod` (depending on your flavor of UNIX), you should be able to find out all the interesting information your system knows about the command *chmod*. (Of course, if your flavor of UNIX happens to be "Not UNIX!" then you'll need to refer to your system's documentation for the equivalent command, presuming you are so blessed. Your chief consolation is that, if an equivalent command does exist, it will have a much better name than *chmod*.)

PATH, you'll have to provide a complete filename so that the operating system knows how to find your script. Something like

```
% ../bin/gradation
```

Finally, if you are unfortunate enough to be on an ancient UNIX system that doesn't support the magic #! line, or if the path to your interpreter is longer than 32 characters (a built-in limit on many systems), you may be able to work around it like this:

```
#!/bin/sh -- # perl, to stop looping
eval 'exec /usr/bin/perl -S $0 ${1+"$@"}'
    if 0;
```

Some operating systems may require variants on this to deal with */bin/csh, DCL, COMMAND.COM,* or whatever happens to be your default command interpreter. Ask your Local Expert.

Throughout this book, we'll just use #!/usr/bin/perl to represent all these notions and notations, but you'll know what we really mean by it.

A random clue: when you write a test script, don't call your script *test*. UNIX systems have a built-in test command, which will likely be executed instead of your script. Try *try* instead.

A not-so-random clue: while learning Perl, and even after you think you know what you're doing, we suggest using the **-w** option, especially during development. This option will turn on all sorts of useful and interesting warning messages, not necessarily in that order. You can put the **-w** switch on the shebang line, like this:

```
#!/usr/bin/perl -w
```

Now that you know how to run your own Perl program (not to be confused with the *perl* program), let's get back to our example.

Filehandles

Unless you're using artificial intelligence to model a solipsistic philosopher, your program needs some way to communicate with the outside world. In lines 3 and 4 of our grade example you'll see the word GRADES, which exemplifies another of Perl's data types, the *filehandle*. A filehandle is just a name you give to a file, device, socket, or pipe to help you remember which one you're talking about, and to hide some of the complexities of buffering and such. (Internally, filehandles are similar to streams from a language like C++, or I/O channels from BASIC.)

Filehandles make it easier for you to get input from and send output to many different places. Part of what makes Perl a good glue language is that it can talk to many files and processes at once. Having nice symbolic names for various external objects is just part of being a good glue language.[*]

You create a filehandle and attach it to a file by using the **open** function. **open** takes two parameters: the filehandle and the filename you want to associate it with. Perl also gives you some predefined (and preopened) filehandles. STDIN is your program's normal input channel, while STDOUT is your program's normal output channel. And STDERR is an additional output channel so that your program can make snide remarks off to the side while it transforms (or attempts to transform) your input into your output.[†]

Since you can use the **open** function to create filehandles for various purposes (input, output, piping), you need to be able to specify which behavior you want. As you would do on the UNIX command line, you simply add characters to the filename.

```
open(SESAME, "filename");              # read from existing file
open(SESAME, "<filename");             #  (same thing, explicitly)
open(SESAME, ">filename");             # create file and write to it
open(SESAME, ">>filename");            # append to existing file
open(SESAME, "| output-pipe-command"); # set up an output filter
open(SESAME, "input-pipe-command |");  # set up an input filter
```

As you can see, the name you pick is arbitrary. Once opened, the filehandle SESAME can be used to access the file or pipe until it is explicitly closed (with, you guessed it, close(SESAME)), or the filehandle is attached to another file by a subsequent **open** on the same filehandle.[‡]

Once you've opened a filehandle for input (or if you want to use STDIN), you can read a line using the line reading operator, <>. This is also known as the angle operator, because of its shape. The angle operator encloses the filehandle

---

[*] Some of the other things that make Perl a good glue language are: it's 8-bit clean, it's embeddable, and you can embed other things in it via extension modules. It's concise, and networks easily. It's environmentally conscious, so to speak. You can invoke it in many different ways (as we saw earlier). But most of all, the language itself is not so rigidly structured that you can't get it to "flow" around your problem. It comes back to that TMTOWTDI thing again.

[†] These filehandles are typically attached to your terminal, so you can type to your program and see its output, but they may also be attached to files (and such). Perl can give you these predefined handles because your operating system already provides them, one way or another. Under UNIX, processes inherit standard input, output, and error from their parent process, typically a shell. One of the duties of a shell is to set up these I/O streams so that the child process doesn't need to worry about them.

[‡] Opening an already opened filehandle implicitly closes the first file, making it inaccessible to the filehandle, and opens a different file. You must be careful that this is what you really want to do. Sometimes it happens accidentally, like when you say open($handle,$file), and $handle happens to contain the null string. Be sure to set $handle to something unique, or you'll just open a new file on the null filehandle.

(<SESAME>) you want to read lines from.[*] An example using the STDIN filehandle to read an answer supplied by the user would look something like this:

```
print STDOUT "Enter a number: ";        # ask for a number
$number = <STDIN>;                       # input the number
print STDOUT "The number is $number\n";  # print the number
```

Did you see what we just slipped by you? What's the STDOUT doing in those **print** statements there? Well, that's one of the ways you can use an output filehandle. A filehandle may be supplied as the first argument to the **print** statement, and if present, tells the output where to go. In this case, the filehandle is redundant, because the output would have gone to STDOUT anyway. Much as STDIN is the default for input, STDOUT is the default for output. (In line 18 of our grade example, we left it out, to avoid confusing you up till now.)

We also did something else to trick you. If you try the above example, you may notice that you get an extra blank line. This happens because the read does not automatically remove the newline from your input line (your input would be, for example, "9\n"). For those times when you do want to remove the newline, Perl provides the **chop** and **chomp** functions. **chop** will indiscriminately remove (and return) the last character passed to it, while **chomp** will only remove the end of record marker (generally, "\n"), and return the number of characters so removed. You'll often see this idiom for inputting a single line:

```
chop($number = <STDIN>);    # input number and remove newline
```

which means the same thing as

```
$number = <STDIN>;          # input number
chop($number);              # remove newline
```

Operators

As we alluded to earlier, Perl is also a mathematical language. This is true at several levels, from low-level bitwise logical operations, up through number and set manipulation, on up to larger predicates and abstractions of various sorts. And as we all know from studying math in school, mathematicians love strange symbols. What's worse, computer scientists have come up with their own versions of these strange symbols. Perl has a number of these strange symbols too, but take heart, most are borrowed directly from C, FORTRAN, *sed*(1) or *awk*(1), so they'll at least be familiar to users of those languages.

---

[*] The empty angle operator, <>, will read lines from all the files specified on the command line, or STDIN, if none were specified. (This is standard behavior for many UNIX filter programs.)

Perl's built-in operators may be classified by number of operands into unary, binary, and trinary operators. They may be classified by whether they're infix operators or prefix operators. They may also be classified by the kinds of objects they work with, such as numbers, strings, or files. Later, we'll give you a table of all the operators, but here are some to get you started.

Arithmetic Operators

Arithmetic operators do exactly what you would expect from learning them in school. They perform some sort of mathematical function on numbers.

Table 1-2: Some Binary Arithmetic Operators

Example	Name	Result
$a + $b	Addition	Sum of $a and $b
$a * $b	Multiplication	Product of $a and $b
$a % $b	Modulus	Remainder of $a divided by $b
$a ** $b	Exponentiation	$a to the power of $b

Yes, we left subtraction and division out of Table 1-2. But we suspect you can figure out how they should work. Try them and see if you're right. (Or cheat and look in the index.) Arithmetic operators are evaluated in the order your math teacher taught you (exponentiation before multiplication, and multiplication before addition). You can always use parentheses to make it come out differently.

String Operators

There is also an "addition" operator for strings that does concatenation. Unlike some languages that confuse this with numeric addition, Perl defines a separate operator (.) for string concatenation:

```
$a = 123;
$b = 456;
print $a + $b;      # prints 579
print $a . $b;      # prints 123456
```

There's also a "multiply" operation for strings, also called the *repeat* operator. Again, it's a separate operator (**x**) to keep it distinct from numeric multiplication:

```
$a = 123;
$b = 3;
print $a * $b;      # prints 369
print $a x $b;      # prints 123123123
```

These string operators bind as tightly as their corresponding arithmetic operators. The repeat operator is a bit unusual in taking a string for its left argument but a number for its right argument. Note also how Perl is automatically converting from numbers to strings. You could have put all the literal numbers above in quotes, and it would still have produced the same output. Internally though, it would have been converting in the opposite direction (that is, from strings to numbers).

A couple more things to think about. String concatenation is also implied by the interpolation that happens in double-quoted strings. When you print out a list of values, you're also effectively concatenating strings. So the following three statements produce the same output:

```
print $a . ' is equal to ' . $b . "\n";    # dot operator
print $a, ' is equal to ', $b, "\n";       # list
print "$a is equal to $b\n";               # interpolation
```

Which of these you use in any particular situation is entirely up to you.

The **x** operator may seem relatively worthless at first glance, but it is quite useful at times, especially for things like this:

```
print "-" x $scrwid, "\n";
```

which draws a line across your screen, presuming your screen width is in `$scrwid`.

Assignment Operators

Although it's not exactly a mathematical operator, we've already made extensive use of the simple assignment operator, =. Try to remember that = means "gets set to" rather than "equals". (There is also a mathematical equality operator == that means "equals", and if you start out thinking about the difference between them now, you'll save yourself a lot of headache later.)

Like the operators above, assignment operators are binary infix operators, which means they have an operand on either side of the operator. The right operand can be any expression you like, but the left operand must be a valid *lvalue* (which, when translated to English, means a valid storage location like a variable, or a location in an array). The most common assignment operator is simple assignment. It determines the value of the expression on its right side, and sets the variable on the left side to that value:

```
$a = $b;
$a = $b + 5;
$a = $a * 3;
```

Notice the last assignment refers to the same variable twice; once for the computation, once for the assignment. There's nothing wrong with that, but it's a common enough operation that there's a shortcut for it (borrowed from C). If you say:

```
lvalue operator= expression
```

it is evaluated as if it were:

```
lvalue = lvalue operator expression
```

except that the lvalue is not computed twice. (This only makes a difference if evaluation of the lvalue has side effects. But when it *does* make a difference, it usually does what you want. So don't sweat it.)

So, for example, you could write the above as:

```
$a *= 3;
```

which reads "multiply $a by 3". You can do this with almost any binary operator in Perl, even some that you can't do it with in C:

```
$line .= "\n";   # Append newline to $line.
$fill x= 80;     # Make string $fill into 80 repeats of itself.
$val ||= "2";    # Set $val to 2 if it isn't already set.
```

Line 6 of our grade example contains two string concatenations, one of which is an assignment operator. And line 14 contains a +=.

Regardless of which kind of assignment operator you use, the final value is returned as the value of the assignment as a whole. (This is unlike, say, Pascal, in which assignment is a statement and has no value.) This is why we could say:

```
chop($number = <STDIN>);
```

and have it chop the final value of $number. You also frequently see assignment as the condition of a **while** loop, as in line 4 of our grade example.

Autoincrement and Autodecrement Operators

As if $variable += 1 weren't short enough, Perl borrows from C an even shorter way to increment a variable. The autoincrement and autodecrement operators simply add (or subtract) one from the value of the variable. They can be placed on either side of the variable, depending on when you want them to be evaluated (see Table 1-3).

Table 1–3: Unary Arithmetic Operators

Example	Name	Result
++$a, $a++	Autoincrement	Add 1 to $a
--$a, $a--	Autodecrement	Subtract 1 from $a

If you place one of the auto operators before the variable, it is known as a pre-incremented (pre-decremented) variable. Its value will be changed before it is referenced. If it is placed after the variable, it is known as a post-incremented (post-decremented) variable and its value is changed after it is used. For example:

```
$a = 5;        # $a is assigned 5
$b = ++$a;     # $b is assigned the incremented value of $a, 6
$c = $a--;     # $c is assigned 6, then $a is decremented to 5
```

Line 15 of our grade example increments the number of scores by one, so that we'll know how many scores we're averaging the grade over. It uses a post-increment operator ($scores++), but in this case it doesn't matter, since the expression is in a void context, which is just a funny way of saying that the expression is being evaluated only for the side effect of incrementing the variable. The value returned is being thrown away.[*]

Logical Operators

Logical operators, also known as "short-circuit" operators, allow the program to make decisions based on multiple criteria, without using nested conditionals. They are known as short-circuit because they skip evaluating their right argument if evaluating their left argument is sufficient to determine the overall value.

Perl actually has two sets of logical operators, a crufty old set borrowed from C, and a nifty new set of ultralow-precedence operators that parse more like people expect them to parse, and are also easier to read. (Once they're parsed, they behave identically though.) See Table 1-4 for examples of logical operators.

Table 1-4: Logical Operators

Example	Name	Result
$a && $b	And	$a if $a is false, $b otherwise
$a || $b	Or	$a if $a is true, $b otherwise
! $a	Not	True if $a is not true
$a and $b	And	$a if $a is false, $b otherwise
$a or $b	Or	$a if $a is true, $b otherwise
not $a	Not	True if $a is not true

Since the logical operators "short circuit" the way they do, they're often used to conditionally execute code. The following line (from our grade example) tries to open the file *grades*.

---

[*] The optimizer will notice this and optimize the post-increment into a pre-increment, because that's a little more efficient to execute. (You didn't need to know that, but we hoped it would cheer you up.)

```
open(GRADES, "grades") or die "Can't open file grades: $!\n";
```

If it opens the file, it will jump to the next line of the program. If it can't open the file, it will provide us with an error message and then stop execution.

Literally, the above message means "Open *grades* or die!" Besides being another example of natural language, the short-circuit operators preserve the visual flow. Important actions are listed down the left side of the screen, and secondary actions are hidden off to the right. (The $! variable contains the error message returned by the operating system—see "Special Variables" in Chapter 2). Of course, these logical operators can also be used within the more traditional kinds of conditional constructs, such as the **if** and **while** statements.

Comparison Operators

Comparison, or relational, operators tell us how two scalar values (numbers or strings) relate to each other. There are two sets of operators—one does numeric comparison and the other does string comparison. (In either case, the arguments will be "coerced" to have the appropriate type first.) Table 1-5 assumes $a and $b are the left and right arguments, respectively.

Table 1–5: Some Numeric and String Comparison Operators

Comparison	Numeric	String	Return Value
Equal	==	eq	True if $a is equal to $b
Not equal	!=	ne	True if $a is not equal to $b
Less than	<	lt	True if $a is less than $b
Greater than	>	gt	True if $a is greater than $b
Less than or equal	<=	le	True if $a not greater than $b
Comparison	<=>	cmp	0 if equal, 1 if $a greater, -1 if $b greater

The last pair of operators (<=> and cmp) are entirely redundant. However, they're incredibly useful in **sort** subroutines (see Chapter 3).[*]

File Test Operators

The file test operators allow you to test whether certain file attributes are set before you go and blindly muck about with the files. For example, it would be very nice to know that the file */etc/passwd* already exists before you go and open it as a new file, wiping out everything that was in there before. See Table 1-6 for examples of file test operators.

---

[*] Some folks feel that such redundancy is evil because it keeps a language from being minimalistic, or orthogonal. But Perl isn't an orthogonal language; it's a diagonal language. By which we mean that Perl doesn't force you to always go at right angles. Sometimes you just want to follow the hypotenuse of the triangle to get where you're going. TMTOWTDI is about shortcuts. Shortcuts are about efficiency.

Table 1-6: Some File Test Operators

Example	Name	Result
-e $a	Exists	True if file named in $a exists
-r $a	Readable	True if file named in $a is readable
-w $a	Writable	True if file named in $a is writable
-d $a	Directory	True if file named in $a is a directory
-f $a	File	True if file named in $a is a regular file
-T $a	Text File	True if file named in $a is a text file

Here are some examples:

```
-e "/usr/bin/perl" or warn "Perl is improperly installed\n";
-f "/vmunix" and print "Congrats, we seem to be running BSD Unix\n";
```

Note that a regular file is not the same thing as a text file. Binary files like */vmunix* are regular files, but they aren't text files. Text files are the opposite of binary files, while regular files are the opposite of irregular files like directories and devices.

There are a lot of file test operators, many of which we didn't list. Most of the file tests are unary Boolean operators: they take only one operand, a scalar that evaluates to a file or a filehandle, and they return either a true or false value. A few of them return something fancier, like the file's size or age, but you can look those up when you need them.

Control Structures

So far, except for our one large example, all of our examples have been completely linear; we executed each command in order. We've seen a few examples of using the short circuit operators to cause a single command to be (or not to be) executed. While you can write some very useful linear programs (a lot of CGI scripts fall into this category), you can write much more powerful programs if you have conditional expressions and looping mechanisms. Collectively, these are known as control structures. So you can also think of Perl as a control language.

But to have control, you have to be able to decide things, and to decide things, you have to know the difference between what's true and what's false.

What Is Truth?

We've bandied about the term truth,[*] and we've mentioned that certain operators return a true or a false value. Before we go any further, we really ought to explain

---

[*] Strictly speaking, this is not true.

exactly what we mean by that. Perl treats truth a little differently than most computer languages, but after you've worked with it awhile it will make a lot of sense. (Actually, we're hoping it'll make a lot of sense after you've read the following.)

Basically, Perl holds truths to be self-evident. That's a glib way of saying that you can evaluate almost anything for its truth value. Perl uses practical definitions of truth that depend on the type of thing you're evaluating. As it happens, there are many more kinds of truth than there are of nontruth.

Truth in Perl is always evaluated in a scalar context. (Other than that, no type coercion is done.) So here are the rules for the various kinds of values that a scalar can hold:

1. Any string is true except for `""` and `"0"`.

2. Any number is true except for 0.

3. Any reference is true.

4. Any undefined value is false.

Actually, the last two rules can be derived from the first two. Any reference (rule 3) points to something with an address, and would evaluate to a number or string containing that address, which is never 0. And any undefined value (rule 4) would always evaluate to 0 or the null string.

And in a way, you can derive rule 2 from rule 1 if you pretend that everything is a string. Again, no coercion is actually done to evaluate truth, but if a coercion to string *were* done, then any numeric value of 0 would simply turn into the string `"0"`, and be false. Any other number would not turn into the string `"0"`, and so would be true. Let's look at some examples so we can understand this better:

```
0            # would become the string "0", so false
1            # would become the string "1", so true
10 - 10      # 10-10 is 0, would convert to string "0", so false
0.00         # becomes 0, would convert to string "0", so false
"0"          # the string "0", so false
""           # a null string, so false
"0.00"       # the string "0.00", neither empty nor exactly "0", so true
"0.00" + 0   # the number 0 (coerced by the +), so false.
\$a          # a reference to $a, so true, even if $a is false
undef()      # a function returning the undefined value, so false
```

Since we mumbled something earlier about truth being evaluated in a scalar context, you might be wondering what the truth value of a list is. Well, the simple fact is, there *is* no operation in Perl that will return a list in a scalar context. They all return a scalar value instead, and then you apply the rules of truth to that scalar. So there's no problem, as long as you can figure out what any given operator will return in a scalar context.

The if and unless statements

We saw earlier how a logic operator could function as a conditional. A slightly more complex form of the logic operators is the **if** statement. The **if** statement evaluates a truth condition, and executes a block if the condition is true.

A block is one or more statements grouped together by a set of braces. Since the **if** statement executes a block, the braces are required by definition. If you know a language like C, you'll notice that this is different. Braces are optional in C if you only have a single line of code, but they are not optional in Perl.

```
if ($debug_level > 0) {
    # Something has gone wrong.  Tell the user.
    print "Debug: Danger, Will Robinson, danger!\n";
    print "Debug: Answer was '54', expected '42'.\n";
}
```

Sometimes, just executing a block when a condition is met isn't enough. You may also want to execute a different block if that condition *isn't* met. While you could certainly use two **if** statements, one the negation of the other, Perl provides a more elegant solution. After the block, **if** can take an optional second condition, called **else**, to be executed only if the truth condition is false. (Veteran computer programmers will not be surprised at this point.)

Other times, you may even have more than two possible choices. In this case, you'll want to add an **elsif** truth condition for the other possible choices. (Veteran computer programmers may well be surprised by the spelling of "elsif", for which nobody here is going to apologize. Sorry.)

```
if ($city eq "New York") {
    print "New York is northeast of Washington, D.C.\n";
}
elsif ($city eq "Chicago") {
    print "Chicago is northwest of Washington, D.C.\n";
}
elsif ($city eq "Miami") {
    print "Miami is south of Washington, D.C.  And much warmer!\n";
}
else {
    print "I don't know where $city is, sorry.\n";
}
```

The **if** and **elsif** clauses are each computed in turn, until one is found to be true or the **else** condition is reached. When one of the conditions is found to be true, its block is executed and all the remaining branches are skipped. Sometimes, you don't want to do anything if the condition is true, only if it is false. Using an empty **if** with an **else** may be messy, and a negated **if** may be illegible; it sounds weird to say "do something if not this is true". In these situations, you would use the **unless** statement.

```
unless ($destination eq $home) {
    print "I'm not going home.\n";
}
```

There is no "elsunless" though. This is generally construed as a feature.

Iterative (Looping) Constructs

Perl has four main iterative statement types: **while**, **until**, **for**, and **foreach**. These statements allow a Perl program to repeatedly execute the same code for different values.

The while and until statements

The **while** and **until** statements function similarly to the **if** and **unless** statements, in a looping fashion. First, the conditional part of the statement is checked. If the condition is met (if it is true for a **while** or false for an **until**) the block of the statement is executed.

```
while ($tickets_sold < 10000) {
    $available = 10000 - $tickets_sold;
    print "$available tickets are available.  How many would you like: ";
    $purchase = <STDIN>;
    chomp($purchase);
    $tickets_sold += $purchase;
}
```

Note that if the original condition is never met, the loop will never be entered at all. For example, if we've already sold 10,000 tickets, we might want to have the next line of the program say something like:

```
print "This show is sold out, please come back later.\n";
```

In our grade example earlier, line 4 reads:

```
while ($line = <GRADES>) {
```

This assigns the next line to the variable $line, and as we explained earlier, returns the value of $line so that the condition of the **while** statement can evaluate $line for truth. You might wonder whether Perl will get a false negative on blank lines and exit the loop prematurely. The answer is that it won't. The reason is clear, if you think about everything we've said. The line input operator leaves the newline on the end of the string, so a blank line has the value "\n". And you know that "\n" is not one of the canonical false values. So the condition is true, and the loop continues even on blank lines.

On the other hand, when we finally do reach the end of the file, the line input operator returns the undefined value, which always evaluates to false. And the loop terminates, just when we wanted it to. There's no need for an explicit test against the **eof** function in Perl, because the input operators are designed to work smoothly in a conditional context.

In fact, almost everything is designed to work smoothly in a conditional context. For instance, an array in a scalar context returns its length. So you often see:

```
while (@ARGV) {
    process(shift @ARGV);
}
```

The loop automatically exits when @ARGV is exhausted.

The for statement

Another iterative statement is the **for** loop. A **for** loop runs exactly like the **while** loop, but looks a good deal different. (C programmers will find it very familiar though.)

```
for ($sold = 0; $sold < 10000; $sold += $purchase) {
    $available = 10000 - $sold;
    print "$available tickets are available.  How many would you like: ";
    $purchase = <STDIN>;
    chomp($purchase);
}
```

The **for** loop takes three expressions within the loop's parentheses: an expression to set the initial state of the loop variable, a condition to test the loop variable, and an expression to modify the state of the loop variable. When the loop starts, the initial state is set and the truth condition is checked. If the condition is true, the block is executed. When the block finishes, the modification expression is executed, the truth condition is again checked, and if true, the block is rerun with the new values. As long as the truth condition remains true, the block and the modification expression will continue to be executed.

The foreach statement

The last of Perl's main iterative statements is the **foreach** statement. **foreach** is used to execute the same code for each of a known set of scalars, such as an array:

```
foreach $user (@users) {
    if (-f "$home{$user}/.nexrc") {
        print "$user is cool... they use a perl-aware vi!\n";
    }
}
```

In a **foreach** statement, the expression in parentheses is evaluated to produce a list. Then each element of the list is aliased to the loop variable in turn, and the block of code is executed once for each element. Note that the loop variable becomes a reference to the element itself, rather than a copy of the element. Hence, modifying the loop variable will modify the original array.

You find many more **foreach** loops in the typical Perl program than **for** loops, because it's very easy in Perl to generate the lists that **foreach** wants to iterate over. A frequently seen idiom is a loop to iterate over the sorted keys of a hash:

```
foreach $key (sort keys %hash) {
```

In fact, line 9 of our grade example does precisely that.

Breaking out: next and last

The **next** and **last** operators allow you to modify the flow of your loop. It is not at all uncommon to have a special case; you may want to skip it, or you may want to quit when you encounter it. For example, if you are dealing with UNIX accounts, you may want to skip the system accounts (like root or lp). The **next** operator would allow you to skip to the end of your current loop iteration, and start the next iteration. The **last** operator would allow you to skip to the end of your block, as if your test condition had returned false. This might be useful if you are, for example, looking for a specific account and want to quit as soon as you find it.

```
foreach $user (@users) {
    if ($user eq "root" or $user eq "lp") {
        next;
    }
    if ($user eq "special") {
        print "Found the special account.\n";
        # do some processing
        last;
    }
}
```

It's possible to break out of multi-level loops by labeling your loops and specifying which loop you want to break out of. Together with statement modifiers (another form of conditional we haven't talked about), this can make for very readable loop exits, if you happen to think English is readable:

```
LINE: while ($line = <ARTICLE>) {
    last LINE if $line eq "\n"; # stop on first blank line
    next LINE if $line =~ /^#/; # skip comment lines
    # your ad here
}
```

You may be saying, "Wait a minute, what's that funny ^# thing there inside the leaning toothpicks? That doesn't look much like English." And you're right. That's a pattern match containing a regular expression (albeit a rather simple one). And that's what the next section is about. Perl is above all a text processing language, and regular expressions are at the heart of Perl's text processing.

Regular Expressions

Regular expressions (aka regexps, regexes or REs) are used by many UNIX programs, such as *grep*, *sed* and *awk*,[*] editors like *vi* and *emacs*, and even some of the shells. A regular expression is a way of describing a set of strings without having to list all the strings in your set.

Regular expressions are used several ways in Perl. First and foremost, they're used in conditionals to determine whether a string matches a particular pattern. So when you see something that looks like /foo/, you know you're looking at an ordinary *pattern-matching* operator.

Second, if you can locate patterns within a string, you can replace them with something else. So when you see something that looks like s/foo/bar/, you know it's asking Perl to substitute "bar" for "foo", if possible. We call that the *substitution* operator.

Finally, patterns can specify not only where something is, but also where it isn't. So the **split** operator uses a regular expression to specify where the data isn't. That is, the regular expression defines the *delimiters* that separate the fields of data. Our grade example has a couple of trivial examples of this. Lines 5 and 12 each split strings on the space character in order to return a list of words. But you can split on any delimiter you can specify with a regular expression.

(There are various modifiers you can use in each of these contexts to do exotic things like ignore case when matching alphabetic characters, but these are the sorts of gory details that we'll cover in Chapter 2.)

The simplest use of regular expressions is to match a literal expression. In the case of the splits we just mentioned, we matched on a single space. But if you match on several characters in a row, they all have to match sequentially. That is, the pattern looks for a substring, much as you'd expect. Let's say we want to show all the lines of an HTML file that are links to other HTML files (as opposed to FTP links). Let's imagine we're working with HTML for the first time, and we're being a little naive yet. We know that these links will always have "http:" in them somewhere. We could loop through our file with this:[†]

---

[*] A good source of information on regular expression concepts is the Nutshell Handbook *sed & awk* by Dale Dougherty (O'Reilly & Associates). You might also keep an eye out for Jeffrey Friedl's forthcoming book, *Mastering Regular Expressions* (O'Reilly & Associates).

[†] This is very similar to what the UNIX command grep 'http:' file would do. On MS-DOS you could use the *find* command, but it doesn't know how to do more complicated regular expressions. (However, the misnamed *findstr* program of Windows NT does know about regular expressions.)

```
while ($line = <FILE>) {
    if ($line =~ /http:/) {
        print $line;
    }
}
```

Here, the =~ (pattern binding operator) is telling Perl to look for a match of the regular expression http: in the variable $line. If it finds the expression, the operator returns a true value and the block (a **print** command) is executed. By the way, if you don't use the =~ binding operator, then Perl will search a default variable instead of $line. This default space is really just a special variable that goes by the odd name of $_. In fact, many of the operators in Perl default to using the $_ variable, so an expert Perl programmer might write the above as:

```
while (<FILE>) {
    print if /http:/;
}
```

(Hmm, another one of those statement modifiers seems to have snuck in there. Insidious little beasties.)

This stuff is pretty handy, but what if we wanted to find all the links, not just the HTTP links? We could give a list of links, like "http:", "ftp:", "mailto:", and so on. But that list could get long, and what would we do when a new kind of link was added?

```
while (<FILE>) {
    print if /http:/;
    print if /ftp:/;
    print if /mailto:/;
    # What next?
}
```

Since regular expressions are descriptive of a set of strings, we can just describe what we are looking for: a number of alphabetic characters followed by a colon. In regular expression talk (Regexpese?), that would be /[a-zA-Z]+:/, where the brackets define a *character class*. The a-z and A-Z represent all alphabetic characters (the dash means the range of all characters between the starting and ending character, inclusive). And the + is a special character which says "one or more of whatever was before me". It's what we call a *quantifier*, meaning a gizmo that says how many times something is allowed to repeat. (The slashes aren't really part of the regular expression, but rather part of the pattern match operator. The slashes are acting like quotes that just happen to contain a regular expression.)

Because certain classes like the alphabetics are so commonly used, Perl defines special cases for them. See Table 1-7 for these special cases.

Table 1-7: Regular Expression Character Classes

Name	Definition	Code
Whitespace	[\t\n\r\f]	\s
Word character	[a-zA-Z_0-9]	\w
Digit	[0-9]	\d

Note that these match *single* characters. A \w will match any single word character, not an entire word. (Remember that + quantifier? You can say \w+ to match a word.) Perl also provides the negation of these classes by using the uppercased character, such as \D for a non-digit character.

(We should note that \w is not always equivalent to [a-zA-Z_0-9]. Some locales define additional alphabetic characters outside the ASCII sequence, and \w respects them.)

There is one other very special character class, written with a ".", that will match any character whatsoever.* For example, /a./ will match any string containing an "a" that is not the last character in the string. Thus it will match "at" or "am" or even "a+", but not "a", since there's nothing after the "a" for the dot to match. Since it's searching for the pattern anywhere in the string, it'll match "oasis" and "camel", but not "sheba". It matches "caravan" on the first "a". It could match on the second "a", but it stops after it finds the first suitable match, searching from left to right.

Quantifiers

The characters and character classes we've talked about all match single characters. We mentioned that you could match multiple "word" characters with \w+ in order to match an entire word. The + is one kind of quantifier, but there are others. (All of them are placed after the item being quantified.)

The most general form of quantifier specifies both the minimum and maximum number of times an item can match. You put the two numbers in braces, separated by a comma. For example, if you were trying to match North American phone numbers, /\d{7,11}/ would match at least seven digits, but no more than eleven digits. If you put a single number in the braces, the number specifies both the minimum and the maximum; that is, the number specifies the exact number of times the item can match. (If you think about it, all unquantified items have an implicit {1} quantifier.)

---

* Except that it won't normally match a newline. When you think about it, a "." doesn't normally match a newline in *grep*(1) either.

If you put the minimum and the comma but omit the maximum, then the maximum is taken to be infinity. In other words, it will match at least the minimum number of times, plus as many as it can get after that. For example, /\d{7}/ will only match a local (North American) phone number (7 digits), while /\d{7,}/ will match any phone number, even an international one (unless it happens to be shorter than 7 digits). There is no special way of saying "at most" a certain number of times. Just say /.{0,5}/, for example, to find at most five arbitrary characters.

Certain combinations of minimum and maximum occur frequently, so Perl defines special quantifiers for them. We've already seen +, which is the same as {1,}, or "at least one of the preceding item". There is also *, which is the same as {0,}, or "zero or more of the preceding item", and ?, which is the same as {0,1}, or "zero or one of the preceding item" (that is, the preceding item is optional).

There are a couple things about quantification that you need to be careful of. First of all, Perl quantifiers are by default *greedy*. This means that they will attempt to match as much as they can as long as the entire expression still matches. For example, if you are matching /\d+/ against "1234567890", it will match the entire string. This is something to especially watch out for when you are using ".", any character. Often, someone will have a string like:

```
spp:Fe+H2O=FeO2;H:2112:100:Stephen P Potter:/home/spp:/bin/tcsh
```

and try to match "spp:" with /.+:/. However, since the + quantifier is greedy, this pattern will match everything up to and including "/home/spp:". Sometimes you can avoid this by using a negated character class, that is, by saying /[^:]+:/, which says to match one or more non-colon characters (as many as possible), up to the first colon. It's that little caret in there that negates the sense of the character class.[*] The other point to be careful about is that regular expressions will try to match as *early* as possible. This even takes precedence over being greedy. Since scanning happens left-to-right, this means that the pattern will match as far left as possible, even if there is some other place where it could match longer. (Regular expressions are greedy, but they aren't into delayed gratification.) For example, suppose you're using the substitution command (s///) on the default variable space (variable $_, that is), and you want to remove a string of x's from the middle of the string. If you say:

```
$_ = "fred xxxxxxx barney";
s/x*//;
```

it will have absolutely no effect. This is because the x* (meaning zero or more "x" characters) will be able to match the "nothing" at the beginning of the string, since

---

[*] Sorry, we didn't pick that notation, so don't blame us. That's just how regular expressions are customarily written in UNIX culture.

the null string happens to be zero characters wide and there's a null string just sitting there plain as day before the "f" of "fred".[*]

There's one other thing you need to know. By default quantifiers apply to a single preceding character, so /bam{2}/ will match "bamm" but not "bambam". To apply a quantifier to more than one character, use parentheses. So to match "bambam", use the pattern /(bam){2}/.

Minimal Matching

If you were using an ancient version of Perl and you didn't want greedy matching, you had to use a negated character class. (And really, you were still getting greedy matching of a constrained variety.)

In modern versions of Perl, you can force nongreedy, minimal matching by use of a question mark after any quantifier. Our same username match would now be /.*?:/. That .*? will now try to match as few characters as possible, rather than as many as possible, so it stops at the first colon rather than the last.

Nailing Things Down

Whenever you try to match a pattern, it's going to try to match in every location till it finds a match. An *anchor* allows you to restrict where the pattern can match. Essentially, an anchor is something that matches a "nothing", but a special kind of nothing that depends on its surroundings. You could also call it a rule, or a constraint, or an assertion. Whatever you care to call it, it tries to match something of zero width, and either succeeds or fails. (If it fails, it merely means that the pattern can't match that particular way. The pattern will go on trying to match some other way, if there are any other ways to try.)

The special character string \b matches at a word boundary, which is defined as the "nothing" between a word character (\w) and a non-word character (\W), in either order. (The characters that don't exist off the beginning and end of your string are considered to be non-word characters.) For example,

```
/\bFred\b/
```

would match both "The Great Fred" and "Fred the Great", but would not match "Frederick the Great" because the "de" in "Frederick" does not contain a word boundary.

In a similar vein, there are also anchors for the beginning of the string and the end of the string. If it is the first character of a pattern, the caret (^) matches the "nothing" at the beginning of the string. Therefore, the pattern /^Fred/ would match

---

[*] Even the authors get caught by this from time to time.

"Frederick the Great" and not "The Great Fred", whereas /Fred^/ wouldn't match either. (In fact, it doesn't even make much sense.) The dollar sign ($) works like the caret, except that it matches the "nothing" at the end of the string instead of the beginning.[*]

So now you can probably figure out that when we said:

```
next LINE if $line =~ /^#/;
```

we meant "Go to the next iteration of LINE loop if this line happens to begin with a # character."

Backreferences

We mentioned earlier that you can use parentheses to group things for quantifiers, but you can also use parentheses to remember bits and pieces of what you matched. A pair of parentheses around a part of a regular expression causes whatever was matched by that part to be remembered for later use. It doesn't change what the part matches, so /\d+/ and /(\d+)/ will still match as many digits as possible, but in the latter case they will be remembered in a special variable to be backreferenced later.

How you refer back to the remembered part of the string depends on where you want to do it from. Within the same regular expression, you use a backslash followed by an integer. The integer corresponding to a given pair of parentheses is determined by counting left parentheses from the beginning of the pattern, starting with one. So for example, to match something similar to an HTML tag (like "<B>Bold</B>", you might use /<(.*?)>.*?<\/\1>/. This forces the two parts of the pattern to match the exact same string, such as the "B" above.

Outside the regular expression itself, such as in the replacement part of a substitution, the special variable is used as if it were a normal scalar variable named by the integer. So, if you wanted to swap the first two words of a string, for example, you could use:

```
s/(\S+)\s+(\S+)/$2 $1/
```

The right side of the substitution is really just a funny kind of double-quoted string, which is why you can interpolate variables there, including backreference variables. This is a powerful concept: interpolation (under controlled circumstances) is one of the reasons Perl is a good text-processing language. The other reason is the pattern matching, of course. Regular expressions are good for

---

[*] This is a bit oversimplified, since we're assuming here that your string contains only one line. ^ and $ are actually anchors for the beginnings and endings of lines rather than strings. We'll try to straighten this all out in Chapter 2 (to the extent that it can be straightened out).

picking things apart, and interpolation is good for putting things back together again. Perhaps there's hope for Humpty Dumpty after all.

List Processing

Much earlier in this chapter, we mentioned that Perl has two main contexts, scalar context (for dealing with singular things) and list context (for dealing with plural things). Many of the traditional operators we've described so far have been strictly scalar in their operation. They always take singular arguments (or pairs of singular arguments for binary operators), and always produce a singular result, even in a list context. So if you write this:

```
@array = (1 + 2, 3 - 4, 5 * 6, 7 / 8);
```

you know that the list on the right side contains exactly four values, because the ordinary math operators always produce scalar values, even in the list context provided by the assignment to an array.

However, other Perl operators can produce either a scalar or a list value, depending on their context. They just "know" whether a scalar or a list is expected of them. But how will you know that? It turns out to be pretty easy to figure out, once you get your mind around a few key concepts.

First, list context has to be provided by something in the "surroundings". In the example above, the list assignment provides it. If you look at the various syntax summaries scattered throughout Chapter 2 and Chapter 3, you'll see various operators that are defined to take a *LIST* as an argument. Those are the operators that *provide* a list context. Throughout this book, *LIST* is used as a specific technical term to mean "a syntactic construct that provides a list context". For example, if you look up **sort**, you'll find the syntax summary:

```
sort LIST
```

That means that **sort** provides a list context to its arguments.

Second, at compile time, any operator that takes a *LIST* provides a list context to each syntactic element of that *LIST*. So every top-level operator or entity in the *LIST* knows that it's supposed to produce the best list it knows how to produce. This means that if you say:

```
sort @guys, @gals, other();
```

then each of @guys, @gals, and other() knows that it's supposed to produce a list value.

Finally, at run-time, each of those *LIST* elements produces its list in turn, and then (this is important) all the separate lists are joined together, end to end, into a single list. And that squashed-flat, one-dimensional list is what is finally handed off to the function that wanted a *LIST* in the first place. So if @guys contains (Fred,Barney), @gals contains (Wilma,Betty), and the other() function returns the single-element list (Dino), then the *LIST* that sort sees is

    (Fred,Barney,Wilma,Betty,Dino)

and the *LIST* that **sort** returns is

    (Barney,Betty,Dino,Fred,Wilma)

Some operators produce lists (like **keys**), some consume them (like **print**), and some transform lists into other lists (like **sort**). Operators in the last category can be considered filters; only, unlike in the shell, the flow of data is from right to left, since list operators operate on their arguments passed in from the right. You can stack up several list operators in a row:

```
print reverse sort map {lc} keys %hash;
```

That takes the keys of %hash and returns them to the **map** function, which lower-cases all the keys by applying the **lc** operator to each of them, and passes them to the **sort** function, which sorts them, and passes them to the **reverse** function, which reverses the order of the list elements, and passes them to the **print** function, which prints them.

As you can see, that's much easier to describe in Perl than in English.

What You Don't Know Won't Hurt You (Much)

Finally, allow us to return once more to the concept of Perl as a natural language. Speakers of a natural language are allowed to have differing skill levels, to speak different subsets of the language, to learn as they go, and generally, to put the language to good use before they know the whole language. You don't know all of Perl yet, just as you don't know all of English. But that's Officially Okay in Perl culture. You can work with Perl usefully, even though we haven't even told you how to write your own subroutines yet. We've scarcely begun to explain how to view Perl as a system management language, or a rapid prototyping language, or a networking language, or an object-oriented language. We could write chapters about some of these things. (Come to think of it, we already did.)

But in the end, you must create your own view of Perl. It's your privilege as an artist to inflict the pain of creativity on yourself. We can teach you how *we* paint, but we can't teach you how *you* paint. There's More Than One Way To Do It.

Have the appropriate amount of fun.

2

The Gory Details

This chapter describes in detail the syntax and semantics of a Perl program. Individual Perl functions are described in Chapter 3, *Functions*, and certain specialized topics such as References and Objects are deferred to later chapters.

For the most part, this chapter is organized from small to large. That is, we take a bottom-up approach. The disadvantage is that you don't necessarily get the Big Picture before getting lost in a welter of details. But the advantage is that you can understand the examples as we go along. (If you're a top-down person, just turn the book over and read the chapter backward.)

Lexical Texture

Perl is, for the most part, a free-form language. The main exceptions to this are **format** declarations and quoted strings, because these are in some senses literals. Comments are indicated by the # character and extend to the end of the line.

Perl is defined in terms of the ASCII character set. However, string literals may contain characters outside of the ASCII character set, and the delimiters you choose for various quoting mechanisms may be any non-alphanumeric, non-whitespace character.

Whitespace is required only between tokens that would otherwise be confused as a single token. All whitespace is equivalent for this purpose. A comment counts as whitespace. Newlines are distinguished from spaces only within quoted strings, and in formats and certain line-oriented forms of quoting.

One other lexical oddity is that if a line begins with = in a place where a statement would be legal, Perl ignores everything from that line down to the next line that says =cut. The ignored text is assumed to be POD, or plain old documentation. (The Perl distribution has programs that will turn POD commentary into manpages, LaTeX, or HTML documents.)

Built-in Data Types

Computer languages vary in how many and what kinds of data types they provide at compile time. Unlike some commonly used languages that provide many types for similar kinds of values, Perl provides just a few built-in data types. (You can, however, define fancy dynamic types via the object-oriented features of Perl—see Chapter 5, *Packages, Modules, and Object Classes.*) Perl has three basic data types: *scalars*, *arrays* of scalars, and *hashes* of scalars, also known as *associative arrays*.

Scalars are the fundamental type from which more complicated structures are built. A scalar stores a single, simple value, typically a string or a number. Elements of this simple type can be combined into either of the two composite types. An *array* is an ordered list of scalars that you access with a numeric subscript (subscripts start at 0).[*] A *hash* is an unordered set of key/value pairs that you access using strings (keys) as subscripts, to look up the scalar value corresponding to a given key. Variables are always one of these three types. (Other than variables, Perl also has some partially hidden thingies called filehandles, directory handles, subroutines, typeglobs, and formats, which you can think of as data types.)

Terms

Now that we've talked about the kinds of data you can represent in Perl, we'd like to introduce you to the various kinds of terms you can use to pull that data into expressions. We'll use the technical term *term* when we want to talk in terms of these syntactic units. (Hmm, this could get confusing.) The first terms we'll talk about are *variables*.

Variables

There are variable types corresponding to each of the three data types we mentioned. Each of these is introduced (grammatically speaking) by what we call a "funny character". Scalar variables are always named with an initial $, even when referring to a scalar that is part of an array or hash. It works a bit like the English word "the". Thus, we have:

---

[*] As in C, all of Perl's indexing starts with zero. (A negative subscript counts from the end, though.) This applies to various substring and sublist operations as well as to regular subscripting.

Construct	Meaning
$days	Simple scalar value $days
$days[28]	29th element of array @days
$days{'Feb'}	"Feb" value from hash %days
$#days	Last index of array @days
$days->[28]	29th element of array pointed to by reference $days

Entire arrays or array slices (and also slices of hashes) are named with @, which works much like the words "these" or "those":

Construct	Meaning
@days	Same as ($days[0], $days[1], . . . $days[n])
@days[3, 4, 5]	Same as ($days[3], $days[4], $days[5])
@days[3..5]	Same as ($days[3], $days[4], $days[5])
@days{'Jan','Feb'}	Same as ($days{'Jan'},$days{'Feb'})

Entire hashes are named by %:

Construct	Meaning
%days	(Jan => 31, Feb => $leap ? 29 : 28, ...)

Any of these nine constructs may serve as an *lvalue*, that is, they specify a location that you could assign a value to, among other things.[*]

In addition, subroutine calls are named with an initial &, although this is optional when it's otherwise unambiguous (just as "do" is often redundant in English). Symbol table entries can be named with an initial *, but you don't really care about that yet.

Every variable type has its own namespace. You can, without fear of conflict, use the same name for a scalar variable, an array, or a hash (or, for that matter, a filehandle, a subroutine name, a label, or your pet llama). This means that $foo and @foo are two different variables. It also means that $foo[1] is an element of @foo, not a part of $foo. This may seem a bit weird, but that's okay, because it is weird.

Since variable names always start with $, @, or %, the reserved words can't conflict with variable names. But they can conflict with nonvariable identifiers, such as labels and filehandles, which don't have an initial funny character. Since reserved words are always entirely lowercase, we recommend that you pick label and filehandle names that do not appear all in lowercase. For example, you could say

---

[*] Assignment itself is an *lvalue* in certain contexts—see examples under s///, tr///, chop, and chomp in Chapter 3.

`open(LOG,'logfile')` rather than the regrettable `open(log,'logfile')`.[*] Using uppercase filehandles also improves readability and protects you from conflict with future reserved words.

Case *is* significant—`FOO`, `Foo` and `foo` are all different names. Names that start with a letter or underscore may be of any length (well, 255 characters, at least) and may contain letters, digits, and underscores. Names that start with a digit may only contain more digits. Names that start with anything else are limited to that one character (like **$?** or **$$**), and generally have a predefined significance to Perl. For example, just as in the Bourne shell, **$$** is the current process ID and **$?** the exit status of your last child process.

Sometimes you want to name something indirectly. It is possible to replace an alphanumeric name with an expression that returns a reference to the actual variable (see Chapter 4, *References and Nested Data Structures*).

Scalar Values

Whether it's named directly or indirectly, or is just a temporary value on a stack, a scalar always contains a single value. This value may be a number,[†] a string,[‡] or a reference to another piece of data. (Or there may be no value at all, in which case the scalar is said to be *undefined*.) While we might speak of a scalar as "containing" a number or a string, scalars are essentially typeless; there's no way to declare a scalar to be of type "number" or "string". Perl converts between the various subtypes as needed, so you can treat a number as a string or a string as a number, and Perl will do the Right Thing.[§]

While strings and numbers are interchangeable for nearly all intents and purposes, references are a bit different. They're strongly typed, uncastable[‖] pointers with built-in reference-counting and destructor invocation. You can use them to create

---

[*] Regrettable because `log` is a predefined function returning the base *e* logarithm of its argument, or of `$_` if its argument is missing, as it is in this case.

[†] Perl stores numbers as signed integers if possible, or as double-precision floating-point values in the machine's native format otherwise. Floating-point values are not infinitely precise. This is very important to remember, since comparisons like (10/3 == 1/3*10) tend to fail mysteriously.

[‡] Perl stores strings as sequences of bytes, with no arbitrary constraints on length or content. In human terms, you don't have to decide in advance how long your strings are going to get, and you can include any characters including null characters within your string.

[§] To convert from string to number, Perl uses C's *atof*(3) function. To convert from number to string, it does the equivalent of an *sprintf*(3) with a format of `"%.14g"` on most machines.

[‖] By which we mean that you can't, for instance, convert a reference to an array into a reference to a hash. References are not castable to other pointer types. However, if you use a reference as a number or a string, you will get a numeric or string value, which is guaranteed to retain the uniqueness of the reference even though the "referenceness" of the value is lost when the value is copied from the real reference. You can compare such values or test whether they are defined. But you can't do much else with the values, since there's no way to convert numbers or strings into references. In general this is not a problem, since Perl doesn't force you to do pointer arithmetic—or even allow it.

complex data types, including user-defined objects. But they're still scalars, for all that. See Chapter 4 for more on references.

Numeric literals

Numeric literals are specified in any of several customary[*] floating point or integer formats:

```
12345                # integer
12345.67             # floating point
6.02E23              # scientific notation
0xffff               # hexadecimal
0377                 # octal
4_294_967_296        # underline for legibility
```

Since Perl uses the comma as a list separator, you cannot use it to delimit the triples in a large number. To improve legibility, Perl does allow you to use an underscore character instead. The underscore only works within literal numbers specified in your program, not for strings functioning as numbers or data read from somewhere else. Similarly, the leading 0x for hex and 0 for octal work only for literals. The automatic conversion of a string to a number does not recognize these prefixes—you must do an explicit conversion[†] with the **oct** function (which works for hex-looking data, too, as it happens).

String literals

String literals are usually delimited by either single or double quotes. They work much like UNIX shell quotes: double-quoted string literals are subject to backslash and variable interpolation; single-quoted strings are not (except for \' and \\, so that you can put single quotes and backslashes into single-quoted strings).

You can also embed newlines directly in your strings; that is, they can begin and end on different lines. This is nice for many reasons, but it also means that if you forget a trailing quote, the error will not be reported until Perl finds another line containing the quote character, which may be much further on in the script. Fortunately, this usually causes an immediate syntax error on the same line, and Perl is then smart enough to warn you that you might have a runaway string.

Note that a single-quoted string must be separated from a preceding word by a space, since a single quote is a valid (though deprecated) character in an identifier; see Chapter 5.

---

* Customary in UNIX culture, that is. If you're from a different culture, welcome to ours!

† Sometimes people think Perl should convert all incoming data for them. But there are far too many decimal numbers with leading zeroes in the world to make Perl do this automatically. For example, the zip code for O'Reilly & Associates' office in Cambridge, MA is 02140. The postmaster would get upset if your mailing label program turned 02140 into 1120 decimal.

With double-quoted strings, the usual C-style backslash rules apply for inserting characters such as newline, tab, and so on. You may also specify characters in octal and hexadecimal, or as control characters:

Code	Meaning
\n	Newline
\r	Carriage return
\t	Horizontal tab
\f	Form feed
\b	Backspace
\a	Alert (bell)
\e	ESC character
\033	ESC in octal
\x7f	DEL in hexadecimal
\cC	Control-C

In addition, there are escape sequences to modify the case of subsequent characters, as with the substitution operator in the *vi* editor:

Code	Meaning
\u	Force next character to uppercase.
\l	Force next character to lowercase.
\U	Force all following characters to uppercase.
\L	Force all following characters to lowercase.
\Q	Backslash all following non-alphanumeric characters.
\E	End \U, \L, or \Q.

Besides the backslash escapes listed above, double-quoted strings are subject to *variable interpolation* of scalar and list values. This means that you can insert the values of certain variables directly into a string literal. It's really just a handy form of string concatenation. Variable interpolation may only be done for scalar variables, entire arrays (but not hashes), single elements from an array or hash, or slices (multiple subscripts) of an array or hash. In other words, you may only interpolate expressions that begin with $ or @, because those are the two characters (along with backslash) that the string parser looks for.[*] Although a complete hash specified with a % may not be interpolated into the string, single hash values and hash slices are okay, because they begin with $ and @ respectively.

---

[*] Inside strings a literal @ that is not part of an array or slice identifier must be escaped with a backslash (\@), or else a compilation error will result. See Chapter 9, *Diagnostic Messages*.

The following code segment prints out: "The price is $100."

```
$Price = '$100';             # not interpolated
print "The price is $Price.\n";   # interpolated
```

As in some shells, you can put braces around the identifier to distinguish it from following alphanumerics: `"How ${verb}able!"`. In fact, an identifier within such braces is forced to be a string, as is any single identifier within a hash subscript. For example:

```
$days{'Feb'}
```

can be written as:

```
$days{Feb}
```

and the quotes will be assumed automatically. But anything more complicated in the subscript will be interpreted as an expression.

Apart from the subscripts of interpolated array and hash variables, there are no multiple levels of interpolation. In particular, contrary to the expectations of shell programmers, backquotes do not interpolate within double quotes, nor do single quotes impede evaluation of variables when used within double quotes.

Pick your own quotes

While we usually think of quotes as literal values, in Perl they function more like operators, providing various kinds of interpolating and pattern matching capabilities. Perl provides the customary quote characters for these behaviors, but also provides a way for you to choose your quote character for any of them.

Customary	Generic	Meaning	Interpolates
' '	q//	Literal	No
" "	qq//	Literal	Yes
` `	qx//	Command	Yes
()	qw//	Word list	No
//	m//	Pattern match	Yes
s///	s///	Substitution	Yes
y///	tr///	Translation	No

Some of these are simply forms of "syntactic sugar" to let you avoid putting too many backslashes into quoted strings. Any non-alphanumeric, non-whitespace delimiter can be used in place of /.[*] If the delimiters are single quotes, no variable interpolation is done on the pattern. If the opening delimiter is a parenthesis,

---

[*] In particular, the newline and space characters are not allowed as delimiters. (Ancient versions of Perl allowed this.)

bracket, brace, or angle bracket, the closing delimiter will be the matching construct. (Embedded occurrences of the delimiters must match in pairs.) Examples:

```
$single = q!I said, "You said, 'She said it.'"!;
$double = qq(Can't we get some "good" $variable?);
$chunk_of_code = q {
    if ($condition) {
        print "Gotcha!";
    }
};
```

Finally, for two-string constructs like s/// and tr///, if the first pair of quotes is a bracketing pair, then the second part gets its own starting quote character, which needn't be the same as the first pair. So you can write things like s{foo}(bar) or tr[a-z][A-Z]. Whitespace is allowed between the two inner quote characters, so you could even write that last one as:

```
tr [a-z]
   [A-Z];
```

Or leave the quotes out entirely

A word that has no other interpretation in the grammar will be treated as if it were a quoted string. These are known as *barewords.*[*] For example:

```
@days = (Mon,Tue,Wed,Thu,Fri);
print STDOUT hello, ' ', world, "\n";
```

sets the array @days to the short form of the weekdays and prints hello world followed by a newline on STDOUT. If you leave the filehandle out, Perl tries to interpret hello as a filehandle, resulting in a syntax error. Because this is so error-prone, some people may wish to outlaw barewords entirely. If you say:

```
use strict 'subs';
```

then any bareword that would not be interpreted as a subroutine call produces a compile-time error instead. The restriction lasts to the end of the enclosing block. An inner block may countermand this by saying:

```
no strict 'subs';
```

Note that the bare identifiers in constructs like:

```
"${verb}able"
$days{Feb}
```

are not considered barewords, since they're allowed by explicit rule rather than by having "no other interpretation in the grammar".

---

[*] As with filehandles and labels, a bareword that consists entirely of lowercase letters risks conflict with future reserved words. If you use the **-w** switch, Perl will warn you about barewords.

Interpolating array values

Array variables are interpolated into double-quoted strings by joining all the elements of the array with the delimiter specified in the $" variable[*] (which is a space by default). The following are equivalent:

```
$temp = join($",@ARGV);
print $temp;

print "@ARGV";
```

Within search patterns (which also undergo double-quotish interpolation) there is a bad ambiguity: Is /$foo[bar]/ to be interpreted as /${foo}[bar]/ (where [bar] is a character class for the regular expression) or as /${foo[bar]}/ (where [bar] is the subscript to array @foo)? If @foo doesn't otherwise exist, then it's obviously a character class. If @foo exists, Perl takes a good guess about [bar], and is almost always right.[†] If it does guess wrong, or if you're just plain paranoid, you can force the correct interpretation with braces as above. Even if you're merely prudent, it's probably not a bad idea.

"Here" documents

A line-oriented form of quoting is based on the shell's *here-document* syntax.[‡] Following a << you specify a string to terminate the quoted material, and all lines following the current line down to the terminating string are quoted. The terminating string may be either an identifier (a word), or some quoted text. If quoted, the type of quote you use determines the treatment of the text, just as in regular quoting. An unquoted identifier works like double quotes. There must be no space between the << and the identifier. (If you insert a space, it will be treated as a null identifier, which is valid but deprecated, and matches the first blank line—see the first Hurrah! example below.) The terminating string must appear by itself (unquoted and with no surrounding whitespace) on the terminating line.

```
    print <<EOF;    # same as earlier example
The price is $Price.
EOF

    print <<"EOF";  # same as above, with explicit quotes
The price is $Price.
EOF
```

---

[*] $LIST_SEPARATOR if you use the English library module. See Chapter 7, *The Standard Perl Library*.

[†] The guesser is too boring to describe in full, but basically takes a weighted average of all the things that look like character classes (a-z, \w, initial ^) versus things that look like expressions (variables or reserved words).

[‡] It's line-oriented in the sense that delimiters are lines rather than characters. The starting delimiter is the current line, and the terminating delimiter is a line consisting of the string you specify.

```
    print <<'EOF';     # single-quoted quote
All things (e.g. a camel's journey through
A needle's eye) are possible, it's true.
But picture how the camel feels, squeezed out
In one long bloody thread, from tail to snout.
                            -- C.S. Lewis
EOF

    print << x 10;     # print next line 10 times
The camels are coming!  Hurrah!  Hurrah!

    print <<"" x 10;   # the preferred way to write that
The camels are coming!  Hurrah!  Hurrah!

    print <<'EOC';     # execute commands
echo hi there
echo lo there
EOC

    print <<"dromedary", <<"camelid"; # you can stack them
I said bactrian.
dromedary
She said llama.
camelid
```

Just don't forget that you have to put a semicolon on the end to finish the statement, as Perl doesn't know you're not going to try to do this:

```
print <<ABC
179231
ABC
    + 20;   # prints 179251
```

Other literal tokens

Two special literals are `__LINE__` and `__FILE__`, which represent the current line number and filename at that point in your program. They may only be used as separate tokens; they will not be interpolated into strings. In addition, the token `__END__` may be used to indicate the logical end of the script before the actual end of file. Any following text is ignored, but may be read via the DATA filehandle.

The `__DATA__` token functions similarly to the `__END__` token, but opens the DATA filehandle within the current package's namespace, so that **required** files can each have their own DATA filehandles open simultaneously. For more information, see Chapter 5.

Context

Until now we've seen a number of terms that can produce scalar values. Before we can discuss terms further, though, we must come to terms with the notion of *context*.

Scalar and list context

Every operation[*] that you invoke in a Perl script is evaluated in a specific context, and how that operation behaves may depend on the requirements of that context. There are two major contexts: *scalar* and *list*. For example, assignment to a scalar variable evaluates the right-hand side in a scalar context, while assignment to an array or a hash (or slice of either) evaluates the right-hand side in a list context. Assignment to a list of scalars would also provide a list context to the right-hand side.

You will be miserable until you learn the difference between scalar and list context, because certain operators know which context they are in, and return lists in contexts wanting a list, and scalar values in contexts wanting a scalar. (If this is true of an operation, it will be mentioned in the documentation for that operation.) In computer lingo, the functions are *overloaded* on the type of their return value. But it's a very simple kind of overloading, based only on the distinction between singular and plural values, and nothing else.

Other operations *supply* the list contexts to their operands, and you can tell which ones they are because they all have LIST in their syntactic descriptions. Generally it's quite intuitive.[†] If necessary, you can force a scalar context in the middle of a LIST by using the **scalar** function. (Perl provides no way to force a list context in a scalar context, because anywhere you would want a list context it's already provided by the LIST of some controlling function.)

Scalar context can be further classified into string context, numeric context, and don't-care context. Unlike the scalar versus list distinction we just made, operations never know which scalar context they're in. They simply return whatever kind of scalar value they want to, and let Perl translate numbers to strings in string context, and strings to numbers in numeric context. Some scalar contexts don't care whether a string or number is returned, so no conversion will happen. (This happens, for example, when you are assigning the value to another variable. The new variable just takes on the same subtype as the old value.)

---

[*] Here we use the term "operation" loosely to mean either an operator or a term. The two concepts fuzz into each other when you start talking about functions that parse like terms but look like unary operators.

[†] Note, however, that the list context of a LIST can propagate down through subroutine calls, so it's not always obvious by inspection whether a given simple statement is going to be evaluated in a scalar or list context. The program can find out its context within a subroutine by using the **wantarray** function.

Boolean context

One special scalar context is called *Boolean context*. Boolean context is simply any place where an expression is being evaluated to see whether it's true or false. We sometimes write true and false when we mean the technical definition that Perl uses: a scalar value is true if it is not the null string or the number 0 (or its string equivalent, "0"). References are always true.

A Boolean context is a don't-care context in the sense that it never causes any conversions to happen (at least, no conversions beyond what scalar context would impose).

We said that a null string is false, but there are actually two varieties of null scalars: defined and undefined. Boolean context doesn't distinguish between defined and undefined scalars. Undefined null scalars are returned when there is no real value for something, such as when there was an error, or at end of file, or when you refer to an uninitialized variable or element of an array. An undefined null scalar may become defined the first time you use it as if it were defined, but prior to that you can use the **defined** operator to determine whether the value is defined or not. (The return value of **defined** is always defined, but not always true.)

Void context

Another peculiar kind of scalar context is the *void* context. This context not only doesn't care what the return value is, it doesn't even *want* a return value. From the standpoint of how functions work, it's no different from an ordinary scalar context, but if you use the **-w** command-line switch, the Perl compiler will warn you if you use an expression with no side effects in a place that doesn't want a value, such as in a statement that doesn't return a value. For example, if you use a string as a statement:

```
"Camel Lot";
```

you may get a warning like this:

```
Useless use of a constant in void context in myprog line 123;
```

Interpolative context

We mentioned that double-quoted literal strings do backslash interpretation and variable interpolation, but the interpolative context (often called "double-quote context") applies to more than just double-quoted strings. Some other double-quotish constructs are the generalized backtick operator qx//, the pattern match operator m//, and the substitution operator s///. In fact, the substitution operator does interpolation on its left side before doing a pattern match, and then does interpolation on its right side each time the left side matches.

The interpolative context only happens inside quotes, or things that work like quotes, so perhaps it's not fair to call it a context in the same sense as scalar and list context. (Then again, maybe it is.)

List Values and Arrays

Now that we've talked about context, we can talk about list values, and how they behave in context. List values are denoted by separating individual values by commas (and enclosing the list in parentheses where precedence requires it):

```
(LIST)
```

In a list context, the value of the list literal is all the values of the list in order. In a scalar context, the value of a list literal is the value of the final element, as with the C comma operator, which always throws away the value on the left and returns the value on the right. (In terms of what we discussed earlier, the left side of the comma operator provides a void context.) For example:

```
@stuff = ("one", "two", "three");
```

assigns the entire list value to array @stuff, but:

```
$stuff = ("one", "two", "three");
```

assigns only the value three to variable $stuff. The comma operator knows whether it is in a scalar or a list context. An actual array variable also knows its context. In a list context, it would return its entire contents, but in a scalar context it returns only the length of the array (which works out nicely if you mention the array in a conditional). The following assigns to $stuff the value 3:

```
@stuff = ("one", "two", "three");
$stuff = @stuff;        # $stuff gets 3, not "three"
```

Until now we've pretended that *LIST*s are just lists of literals. But in fact, any expressions that return values may be used within lists. The values so used may either be scalar values or list values. *LIST*s do automatic interpolation of sublists. That is, when a *LIST* is evaluated, each element of the list is evaluated in a list context, and the resulting list value is interpolated into *LIST* just as if each individual element were a member of *LIST*. Thus arrays lose their identity in a *LIST*. The list:

```
(@foo,@bar,&SomeSub)
```

contains all the elements of @foo, followed by all the elements of @bar, followed by all the elements returned by the subroutine named SomeSub when it's called in a list context. You can use a reference to an array if you do not want it to interpolate. See Chapter 4, yet again.

The null list is represented by (). Interpolating it in a list has no effect. Thus, ((), (), ()) is equivalent to (). Similarly, interpolating an array with no elements is the same as if no array had been interpolated at that point.

You may place an optional comma at the end of any list value. This makes it easy to come back later and add more elements.

```
@numbers = (
    1,
    2,
    3,
);
```

Another way to specify a literal list is with the **qw** (quote words) syntax we mentioned earlier. This construct is equivalent to splitting a single-quoted string on whitespace. For example:

```
@foo = qw(
    apple       banana      carambola
    coconut     guava       kumquat
    mandarin    nectarine   peach
    pear        persimmon   plum
);
```

(Note that those parentheses are behaving as quote characters, not ordinary parentheses. We could just as easily have picked angle brackets or braces or slashes.)

A list value may also be subscripted like a normal array. You must put the list in parentheses (real ones) to avoid ambiguity. Examples:

```
# Stat returns list value.
$modification_time = (stat($file))[9];

# SYNTAX ERROR HERE.
$modification_time = stat($file)[9];  # OOPS, FORGOT PARENS

# Find a hex digit.
$hexdigit = ('a','b','c','d','e','f')[$digit-10];

# A "reverse comma operator".
return (pop(@foo),pop(@foo))[0];
```

Lists may be assigned to if and only if each element of the list is legal to assign to:

```
($a, $b, $c) = (1, 2, 3);

($map{red}, $map{green}, $map{blue}) = (0x00f, 0x0f0, 0xf00);
```

List assignment in a scalar context returns the number of elements produced by the expression on the right side of the assignment:

```
$x = ( ($foo,$bar) = (7,7,7) );        # set $x to 3, not 2
$x = ( ($foo,$bar) = f() );            # set $x to f()'s return count
```

This is handy when you want to do a list assignment in a Boolean context, since most list functions return a null list when finished, which when assigned produces a 0, which is interpreted as false. The final list element may be an array or a hash:

```
($a, $b, @rest) = split;
my ($a, $b, %rest) = @arg_list;
```

You can actually put an array or hash anywhere in the list you assign to, but the first one in the list will soak up all the values, and anything after it will get an undefined value. This may be useful in a **local** or **my**, where you probably want the arrays initialized to be empty anyway.

You may find the number of elements in the array @days by evaluating @days in a scalar context, such as:

```
@days + 0;      # implicitly force @days into a scalar context
scalar(@days)   # explicitly force @days into a scalar context
```

Note that this only works for arrays. It does not work for list values in general. A comma-separated list evaluated in a scalar context will return the last value, like the C comma operator.

Closely related to the scalar evaluation of @days is $#days. This will return the subscript of the last element of the array, or one less than the length, since there is (ordinarily) a 0th element.[*] Assigning to $#days changes the length of the array. Shortening an array by this method destroys intervening values. You can gain some measure of efficiency by pre-extending an array that is going to get big. (You can also extend an array by assigning to an element that is off the end of the array.) You can truncate an array down to nothing by assigning the null list () to it.[†] The following two statements are equivalent:

```
@whatever = ();
$#whatever = -1;
```

And the following is always true:[‡]

```
scalar(@whatever) == $#whatever + 1;
```

---

[*] For historical reasons, the special variable $[can be used to change the array base. Its use is not recommended, however. In fact, this is the last we'll even mention it. Just don't use it.

[†] In the current version of Perl, re-extending a truncated array does not recover the values in the array. (It did in earlier versions.)

[‡] Unless you've diddled the deprecated $[variable. Er, *this* is the last time we'll mention it . . .

Hashes (Associative Arrays)

As we indicated previously, a hash is just a funny kind of array in which you look values up using key strings instead of numbers. It defines associations between keys and values, so hashes are often called associative arrays.

There really isn't any such thing as a hash literal in Perl, but if you assign an ordinary list to a hash, each pair of values in the list will be taken to indicate one key/value association:

```
%map = ('red',0x00f,'green',0x0f0,'blue',0xf00);
```

This has the same effect as:

```
%map = ();              # clear the hash first
$map{red}   = 0x00f;
$map{green} = 0x0f0;
$map{blue}  = 0xf00;
```

It is often more readable to use the => operator between key/value pairs. The => operator is just a synonym for a comma, but it's more visually distinctive, and it also quotes any bare identifiers to the left of it (just like the identifiers in braces above), which makes it nice for initializing hash variables:

```
%map = (
    red   => 0x00f,
    green => 0x0f0,
    blue  => 0xf00,
);
```

or for initializing anonymous hash references to be used as records:

```
$rec = {
    witch => 'Mable the Merciless',
    cat   => 'Fluffy the Ferocious',
    date  => '10/31/1776',
};
```

or for using call-by-named-parameter to invoke complicated functions:

```
$field = $query->radio_group(
                NAME      => 'group_name',
                VALUES    => ['eenie','meenie','minie'],
                DEFAULT   => 'meenie',
                LINEBREAK => 'true',
                LABELS    => \%labels,
            );
```

But we're getting ahead of ourselves. Back to hashes.

You can use a hash variable (`%hash`) in a list context, in which case it interpolates all the key/value pairs into the list. But just because the hash was initialized in a particular order doesn't mean that the values come back in that order. Hashes are implemented internally using hash tables for speedy lookup, which means that the order in which entries are stored is dependent on the nature of the hash function used to calculate positions in the hash table, and not on anything interesting. So the entries come back in a seemingly random order. (The two elements of each key/value pair come out in the right order, of course.) For examples of how to arrange for an output ordering, see the **keys** entry in Chapter 3, or DB_BTREE description in the DB_File documentation in Chapter 7.

If you evaluate a hash variable in a scalar context, it returns a value that is true if and only if the hash contains any key/value pairs. (If there are any key/value pairs, the value returned is a string consisting of the number of used buckets and the number of allocated buckets, separated by a slash. This is pretty much only useful to find out whether Perl's (compiled in) hashing algorithm is performing poorly on your data set. For example, you stick 10,000 things in a hash, but evaluating `%HASH` in scalar context reveals "1/8", which means only one out of eight buckets has been touched, and presumably that one bucket contains all 10,000 of your items. This isn't supposed to happen.)

Typeglobs and Filehandles

Perl uses an internal type called a *typeglob* to hold an entire symbol table entry. The type prefix of a typeglob is a `*`, because it represents all types. This used to be the preferred way to pass arrays and hashes by reference into a function, but now that we have real references, this mechanism is seldom needed.

Typeglobs (or references thereto) are still used for passing or storing filehandles. If you want to save away a filehandle, do it this way:

```
$fh = *STDOUT;
```

or perhaps as a real reference, like this:

```
$fh = \*STDOUT;
```

This is also the way to create a local filehandle. For example:

```
sub newopen {
    my $path = shift;
    local *FH;  # not my!
    open (FH, $path) || return undef;
    return *FH;
}
$fh = newopen('/etc/passwd');
```

See the **open** entry in Chapter 3 and the FileHandle module in Chapter 7, for how to generate new filehandles.

But the main use of typeglobs nowadays is to alias one symbol table entry to another symbol table entry. If you say:

```
*foo = *bar;
```

it makes everything named "foo" a synonym for every corresponding thing named "bar". You can alias just one of the variables in a typeglob by assigning a reference instead:

```
*foo = \$bar;
```

makes $foo an alias for $bar, but doesn't make @foo an alias for @bar, or %foo an alias for %bar. Aliasing variables like this may seem like a silly thing to want to do, but it turns out that the entire module export/import mechanism is built around this feature, since there's nothing that says the symbol you're aliasing has to be in your namespace. See Chapter 4 and Chapter 5 for more discussion on typeglobs.

Input Operators

There are several input operators we'll discuss here because they parse as terms. In fact, sometimes we call them pseudo-literals because they act like quoted strings in many ways. (Output operators like **print** parse as list operators and are discussed in Chapter 3.)

Command input (backtick) operator

First of all, we have the command input operator, also known as the backticks operator, because it looks like this:

```
$info = `finger $user`;
```

A string enclosed by backticks (grave accents) first undergoes variable interpolation just like a double-quoted string. The result of that is then interpreted as a command by the shell, and the output of that command becomes the value of the pseudo-literal. (This is modeled after a similar operator in some of the UNIX shells.) In scalar context, a single string consisting of all the output is returned. In list context, a list of values is returned, one for each line of output. (You can set $/ to use a different line terminator.)

The command is executed each time the pseudo-literal is evaluated. The numeric status value of the command is saved in $? (see the section "Special Variables" later in this chapter for the interpretation of $?). Unlike the *csh* version of this command, no translation is done on the return data—newlines remain newlines. Unlike any of the shells, single quotes do not hide variable names in the command from interpretation. To pass a $ through to the shell you need to hide it with a backslash. The $user in our example above is interpolated by Perl, not by the shell. (Because the command undergoes shell processing, see Chapter 6, *Social Engineering*, for security concerns.)

The generalized form of backticks is qx// (for "quoted execution"), but the operator works exactly the same way as ordinary backticks. You just get to pick your quote characters.

Line input (angle) operator

The most heavily used input operator is the line input operator, also known as the angle operator. Evaluating a filehandle in angle brackets (<STDIN>, for example) yields the next line from the associated file. (The newline is included, so according to Perl's criteria for truth, a freshly input line is always true, up until end of file, at which point an undefined value is returned, which is false.) Ordinarily you would assign the input value to a variable, but there is one situation where an automatic assignment happens. If and only if the line input operator is the only thing inside the conditional of a **while** loop, the value is automatically assigned to the special variable $_. The assigned value is then tested to see whether it is defined. (This may seem like an odd thing to you, but you'll use the construct in almost every Perl script you write.) Anyway, the following lines are equivalent to each other:

```
while (defined($_ = <STDIN>)) { print $_; }   # the long way
while (<STDIN>) { print; }                     # the short way
for (;<STDIN>;) { print; }                     # while loop in disguise
print $_ while defined($_ = <STDIN>);          # long statement modifier
print while <STDIN>;                           # short statement modifier
```

Remember that this special magic requires a **while** loop. If you use the input operator anywhere else, you must assign the result explicitly if you want to keep the value:

```
if (<STDIN>)        { print; }   # WRONG, prints old value of $_
if ($_ = <STDIN>) { print; }   # okay
```

The filehandles STDIN, STDOUT, and STDERR are predefined and pre-opened.* Additional filehandles may be created with the **open** function. See the **open** entry in Chapter 3 for details on this. Some object modules also create object references that can be used as filehandles. See the FileHandle module in Chapter 7.

---

* The filehandles stdin, stdout, and stderr will also work except in packages, where they would be interpreted as local identifiers rather than global. They're only there for compatibility with very old scripts, so use the uppercase versions.

In the **while** loops above, we were evaluating the line input operator in a scalar context, so it returned each line separately. However, if you use it in a list context, a list consisting of all the remaining input lines is returned, one line per list element. It's easy to make a *large* data space this way, so use this feature with care:

```
$one_line = <MYFILE>;   # Get first line.
@all_lines = <MYFILE>;  # Get the rest of the lines.
```

There is no **while** magic associated with the list form of the input operator, because the condition of a **while** loop is always a scalar context (as is any conditional).

Using the null filehandle within the angle operator is special and can be used to emulate the command-line behavior of typical UNIX filter programs such as *sed* and *awk*. When you read lines from <>, it magically gives you all the lines from all the files mentioned on the command line. If no files were mentioned, it gives you standard input instead, so your program is easy to insert into the middle of a pipeline of processes.

Here's how it works: the first time <> is evaluated, the **@ARGV** array is checked, and if it is null, $ARGV[0] is set to "–", which when opened gives you standard input. The **@ARGV** array is then processed as a list of filenames. The loop:

```
while (<>) {
    ...                         # code for each line
}
```

is equivalent to the following Perl-like pseudocode:

```
@ARGV = ('-') unless @ARGV;
while ($ARGV = shift) {
    open(ARGV, $ARGV) or warn "Can't open $ARGV: $!\n";
    while (<ARGV>) {
        ...                 # code for each line
    }
}
```

except that it isn't so cumbersome to say, and will actually work. It really does shift array **@ARGV** and put the current filename into variable $ARGV. It also uses filehandle **ARGV** internally—<> is just a synonym for <ARGV>, which is magical. (The pseudocode above doesn't work because it treats <ARGV> as non-magical.)

You can modify **@ARGV** before the first <> as long as the array ends up containing the list of filenames you really want. Line numbers ($.) continue as if the input were one big happy file. (But see the example under **eof** for how to reset line numbers on each file.)

If you want to set **@ARGV** to your own list of files, go right ahead. If you want to pass switches into your script, you can use one of the Getopts modules or put a loop on the front like this:

```
while ($_ = $ARGV[0], /^-/) {
    shift;
    last if /^--$/;
    if (/^-D(.*)/) { $debug = $1 }
    if (/^-v/)     { $verbose++  }
    ...                # other switches
}
while (<>) {
    ...                # code for each line
}
```

The <> symbol will return false only once. If you call it again after this it will assume you are processing another **@ARGV** list, and if you haven't set **@ARGV**, it will input from STDIN.

If the string inside the angle brackets is a scalar variable (for example, <$foo>), then that variable contains the name of the filehandle to input from, or a reference to the same. For example:

```
$fh = \*STDIN;
$line = <$fh>;
```

Filename globbing operator

You might wonder what happens to a line input operator if you put something fancier inside the angle brackets. What happens is that it mutates into a different operator. If the string inside the angle brackets is anything other than a filehandle name or a scalar variable (even if there are just extra spaces), it is interpreted as a filename pattern to be "globbed".[*] The pattern is matched against the files in the current directory (or the directory specified as part of the glob pattern), and the filenames so matched are returned by the operator. As with line input, the names are returned one at a time in scalar context, or all at once in list context. In fact, the latter usage is more prevalent. You generally see things like:

```
my @files = <*.html>;
```

As with other kinds of pseudo-literals, one level of variable interpolation is done first, but you can't say <$foo> because that's an indirect filehandle as explained earlier. (In older versions of Perl, programmers would insert braces to force interpretation as a filename glob: <${foo}>. These days, it's considered cleaner to call

---

[*] This has nothing to do with the previously mentioned typeglobs, other than that they both use the * character in a wildcard fashion. The * character has the nickname "glob" when used like this. With typeglobs you're globbing symbols with the same name from the symbol table. With a filename glob, you're doing wildcard matching on the filenames in a directory, just as the various shells do.

the internal function directly as `glob($foo)`, which is probably the right way to have invented it in the first place.)

Whether you use the **glob** function or the old angle-bracket form, the globbing operator also does **while** magic like the line input operator, and assigns the result to $_. For example:

```
while (<*.c>) {
    chmod 0644, $_;
}
```

is equivalent to:

```
open(FOO, "echo *.c | tr -s ' \t\r\f' '\\012\\012\\012\\012'|");
while (<FOO>) {
    chop;
    chmod 0644, $_;
}
```

In fact, it's currently implemented that way, more or less. (Which means it will not work on filenames with spaces in them unless you have *csh*(1) on your machine.) Of course, the shortest way to do the above is:

```
chmod 0644, <*.c>;
```

Because globbing invokes a subshell, it's often faster to call **readdir** yourself and just do your own **grep** on the filenames. Furthermore, due to its current implementation of using a shell, the **glob** routine may get "`Arg list too long`" errors (unless you've installed *tcsh*(1) as */bin/csh*).

A glob evaluates its (embedded) argument only when it is starting a new list. All values must be read before it will start over. In a list context this isn't important, because you automatically get them all anyway. In a scalar context, however, the operator returns the next value each time it is called, or a false value if you've just run out. Again, false is returned only once. So if you're expecting a single value from a glob, it is much better to say:

```
($file) = <blurch*>;   # list context
```

than to say:

```
$file = <blurch*>;     # scalar context
```

because the former slurps all the matched filenames and resets the operator, while the latter will alternate between returning a filename and returning false.

It you're trying to do variable interpolation, it's definitely better to use the **glob** operator, because the older notation can cause people to become confused with the indirect filehandle notation. But with things like this, it begins to become apparent that the borderline between terms and operators is a bit mushy:

```
@files = glob("$dir/*.[ch]");    # call glob as function
@files = glob $some_pattern;     # call glob as operator
```

We left the parentheses off of the second example to illustrate that **glob** can be used as a *unary* operator; that is, a prefix operator that takes a single argument. The **glob** operator is an example of a *named unary operator*, which is just one of the kinds of operators we'll talk about in the section "Operators" later in this chapter. But first we're going to talk about pattern matching operations, which also parse like terms but operate like operators.

Pattern Matching

The two main pattern matching operators are m//, the match operator, and s///, the substitution operator. There is also a **split** operator, which takes an ordinary match operator as its first argument but otherwise behaves like a function, and is therefore documented in Chapter 3.

Although we write m// and s/// here, you'll recall that you can pick your own quote characters. On the other hand, for the m// operator only, the m may be omitted if the delimiters you pick are in fact slashes. (You'll often see patterns written this way, for historical reasons.)

Now that we've gone to all the trouble of enumerating these weird, quote-like operators, you might wonder what it is we've gone to all the trouble of quoting. The answer is that the string inside the quotes specifies a *regular expression*. We'll discuss regular expressions in the next section, because there's a lot to discuss.

The matching operations can have various modifiers, some of which affect the interpretation of the regular expression inside:

Modifier	Meaning
i	Do case-insensitive pattern matching.
m	Treat string as multiple lines (^ and $ match internal \n).
s	Treat string as single line (^ and $ ignore \n, but . matches \n).
x	Extend your pattern's legibility with whitespace and comments.

These are usually written as "the /x modifier", even though the delimiter in question might not actually be a slash. In fact, any of these modifiers may also be embedded within the regular expression itself using the (? . . .) construct. See the section "Regular Expression Extensions" later in this chapter.

The /x modifier itself needs a little more explanation. It tells the regular expression parser to ignore whitespace that is not backslashed or within a character class. You can use this modifier to break up your regular expression into (slightly) more readable parts. The # character is also treated as a metacharacter introducing a comment, just as in ordinary Perl code. Taken together, these features go a long way toward making Perl a readable language.

Regular Expressions

The regular expressions used in the pattern matching and substitution operators are syntactically similar to those used by the UNIX *egrep* program. When you write a regular expression, you're actually writing a grammar for a little language. The regular expression interpreter (which we'll call the Engine) takes your grammar and compares it to the string you're doing pattern matching on. If some portion of the string can be parsed as a sentence of your little language, it says "yes". If not, it says "no".

What happens after the Engine has said "yes" depends on how you invoked it. An ordinary pattern match is usually used as a conditional expression, in which case you don't care *where* it matched, only *whether* it matched. (But you can also find out where it matched if you need to know that.) A substitution command will take the part that matched and replace it with some other string of your choice. And the **split** operator will return (as a list) all the places your pattern didn't match.

Regular expressions are powerful, packing a lot of meaning into a short space. They can therefore be quite daunting if you try to intuit the meaning of a large regular expression as a whole. But if you break it up into its parts, and if you know how the Engine interprets those parts, you can understand any regular expression.

The regular expression bestiary

Before we dive into the rules for interpreting regular expressions, let's take a look at some of the things you'll see in regular expressions. First of all, you'll see literal strings. Most characters[*] in a regular expression simply match themselves. If you string several characters in a row, they must match in order, just as you'd expect. So if you write the pattern match:

```
/Fred/
```

you can know that the pattern won't match unless the string contains the substring "Fred" somewhere.

---

[*] In this section we are misusing the term "character" to mean "byte". So far, Perl only knows about byte-sized characters, but this will change someday, at which point "character" will be a more appropriate word.

Other characters don't match themselves, but are *metacharacters*. (Before we explain what metacharacters do, we should reassure you that you can always match such a character literally by putting a backslash in front of it. For example, backslash is itself a metacharacter, so to match a literal backslash, you'd backslash the backslash: \\.) The list of metacharacters is:

```
\ | ( ) [ { ^ $ * + ? .
```

We said that backslash turns a metacharacter into a literal character, but it does the opposite to an alphanumeric character: it turns the literal character into a sort of metacharacter or sequence. So whenever you see a two-character sequence:

```
\b \D \t \3 \s
```

you'll know that the sequence matches something strange. A \b matches a word boundary, for instance, while \t matches an ordinary tab character. Notice that a word boundary is zero characters wide, while a tab character is one character wide. Still, they're alike in that they both assert that something is true about a particular spot in the string. Most of the things in a regular expression fall into the class of assertions, including the ordinary characters that simply assert that they match themselves. (To be precise, they also assert that the next thing will match one character later in the string, which is why we talk about the tab character being "one character wide". Some assertions eat up some of the string as they match, and others don't. But we usually reserve the term "assertion" for the zero-width assertions. We'll call these assertions with nonzero width *atoms*.) You'll also see some things that aren't assertions. Alternation is indicated with a vertical bar:

```
/Fred|Wilma|Barney|Betty/
```

That means that any of those strings can trigger a match. Grouping of various sorts is done with parentheses, including grouping of alternating substrings within a longer regular expression:

```
/(Fred|Wilma|Pebbles) Flintstone/
```

Another thing you'll see are what we call quantifiers. They say how many of the previous thing should match in a row. Quantifiers look like:

```
* + ? *? {2,5}
```

Quantifiers only make sense when attached to atoms, that is, assertions that have width. Quantifiers attach only to the previous atom, which in human terms means they only quantify one character. So if you want to match three copies of "moo" in a row, you need to group the "moo" with parentheses, like this:

```
/(moo){3}/
```

That will match "moomoomoo". If you'd said /moo{3}/, it would only have matched "moooo".

Since patterns are processed as double-quoted strings, the normal double-quoted interpolations will work. (See "String Literals" earlier in this chapter.) These are applied before the string is interpreted as a regular expression. One caveat though: any $ immediately followed by a vertical bar, closing parenthesis, or the end of the string will be interpreted as an end-of-line assertion rather than a variable interpolation. So if you say:

```
$foo = "moo";
/$foo$/;
```

it's equivalent to saying:

```
/moo$/;
```

You should also know that interpolating variables into a pattern slows down the pattern matcher considerably, because it feels it needs to recompile the pattern each time through, since the variable might have changed.

The rules of regular expression matching

Now that you've seen some regular expressions, we'll lay out the rules that the Engine uses to match your pattern against the string. The Perl Engine uses a non-deterministic finite-state automaton (NFA) to find a match. That just means that it keeps track of what it has tried and what it hasn't, and when something doesn't pan out, it backs up and tries something else. This is called *backtracking*. The Perl Engine is capable of trying a million things at one spot, then giving up on all those, backing up to within one choice of the beginning, and trying the million things again at a different spot. If you're cagey, you can write efficient patterns that don't do a lot of silly backtracking.

The order of the rules below specifies which order the Engine tries things. So when someone trots out a stock phrase like "left-most, longest match", you'll know that overall Perl prefers left-most over longest. But the Engine doesn't realize it's preferring anything at that level. The global preferences result from a lot of localized choices. The Engine thinks locally and acts globally.

Rule 1. The Engine tries to match as far left in the string as it can, such that the entire regular expression matches under Rule 2.

In order to do this, its first choice is to start just before the first character (it could have started anywhere), and to try to match the entire regular expression at that point. The regular expression matches if and only if Engine reaches the end of the regular expression before it runs off the end of the string. If it matches, it quits immediately—it doesn't keep looking for a "better" match, even though the regular expression could match in many different ways. The match only has to reach the end of the regular expression; it doesn't have to reach the end of the string, unless there's an assertion in the regular expression that says it must. If it exhausts all possibilities at the first position, it realizes that its very first choice was wrong, and proceeds to its second choice. It goes to the second position in the string (between the first and second characters), and tries all the possibilities again. If it succeeds, it stops. If it fails, it continues on down the string. The pattern match as a whole doesn't fail until it has tried to match the entire regular expression at every position in the string, including after the last character in the string.

Note that the positions it's trying to match at are *between* the characters of the string. This rule sometimes surprises people when they write a pattern like /x*/ that can match zero or more x's. If you try the pattern on a string like "fox", it will match the null string before the "f" in preference to the "x" that's later in the string. If you want it to match one or more x's, you need to tell it that by using /x+/ instead. See the quantifiers under Rule 5.

A corollary to this rule is that any regular expression that can match the null string is guaranteed to match at the leftmost position in the string.

Rule 2. For this rule, the whole regular expression is regarded as a set of alternatives (where the degenerate case is just a set with one alternative). If there are two or more alternatives, they are syntactically separated by the | character (usually called a vertical bar). A set of alternatives matches a string if any of the alternatives match under Rule 3. It tries the alternatives left-to-right (according to their position in the regular expression), and stops on the first match that allows successful completion of the entire regular expression. If none of the alternatives matches, it backtracks to the Rule that invoked this Rule, which is usually Rule 1, but could be Rule 4 or 6. That rule will then look for a new position at which to apply Rule 2.

If there's only one alternative, then it either it matches or doesn't, and the rule still applies. (There's no such thing as zero alternatives, because a null string can always match something of zero width.)

Rule 3. Any particular alternative matches if every item in the alternative matches sequentially according to Rules 4 and 5 (such that the entire regular expression can be satisfied). An item consists of either an assertion, which is covered in Rule 4, or a quantified atom, which is covered by Rule 5. Items that have choices on how to match are given "pecking order" from left to right. If the items cannot be matched in order, the Engine backtracks to the next alternative under Rule 2.

Items that must be matched sequentially aren't separated in the regular expression by anything syntactic—they're merely juxtaposed in the order they must match. When you ask to match /^foo/, you're actually asking for four items to be matched one after the other. The first is a zero-width assertion, and the other three are ordinary letters that must match themselves, one after the other.

The left-to-right pecking order means that in a pattern like:

```
/x*y*/
```

x gets to pick one way to match, and then y tries all its ways. If that fails, then x gets to pick its second choice, and make y try all of its ways again. And so on. The items to the right vary faster, to borrow a phrase from multi-dimensional arrays.

Rule 4. An assertion must match according to this table. If the assertion does not match at the current position, the Engine backtracks to Rule 3 and retries higher-pecking-order items with different choices.

Assertion	Meaning
^	Matches at the beginning of the string (or line, if /m used)
$	Matches at the end of the string (or line, if /m used)
\b	Matches at word boundary (between \w and \W)
\B	Matches except at word boundary
\A	Matches at the beginning of the string
\Z	Matches at the end of the string
\G	Matches where previous m//g left off
(?= . . .)	Matches if engine would match . . . next
(?! . . .)	Matches if engine wouldn't match . . . next

The $ and \Z assertions can match not only at the end of the string, but also one character earlier than that, if the last character of the string happens to be a newline.

The positive (?= . . .) and negative (?! . . .) lookahead assertions are zero-width themselves, but assert that the regular expression represented above by . . . would (or would not) match at this point, were we to attempt it. In fact, the Engine does attempt it. The Engine goes back to Rule 2 to test the subexpression, and then wipes out any record of how much string was eaten, returning only the success or failure of the subexpression as the value of the assertion. We'll show you some examples later.

Rule 5. A quantified atom matches only if the atom itself matches some number of times allowed by the quantifier. (The atom is matched according to Rule 6.) Different quantifiers require different numbers of matches, and most of them allow a range of numbers of matches. Multiple matches must all match in a row, that is, they must be adjacent within the string. An unquantified atom is assumed to have a quantifier requiring exactly one match. Quantifiers constrain and control matching according to the table below. If no match can be found at the current position for any allowed quantity of the atom in question, the Engine backtracks to Rule 3 and retries higher-pecking-order items with different choices.

Quantifiers are:

Maximal	Minimal	Allowed Range
$\{n,m\}$	$\{n,m\}?$	Must occur at least *n* times but no more than *m* times
$\{n,\}$	$\{n,\}?$	Must occur at least *n* times
$\{n\}$	$\{n\}?$	Must match exactly *n* times
*	*?	0 or more times (same as $\{0,\}$)
+	+?	1 or more times (same as $\{1,\}$)
?	??	0 or 1 time (same as $\{0,1\}$)

If a brace occurs in any other context, it is treated as a regular character. *n* and *m* are limited to integral values less than 65,536.

If you use the $\{n\}$ form, then there is no choice, and the atom must match exactly that number of times or not at all. Otherwise, the atom can match over a range of quantities, and the Engine keeps track of all the choices so that it can backtrack if necessary. But then the question arises as to which of these choices to try first. One could start with the maximal number of matches and work down, or the minimal number of matches and work up.

The quantifiers in the left column above try the biggest quantity first. This is often called "greedy" matching. To find the greediest match, the Engine doesn't actually count down from the maximum value, which after all could be infinity. What actually happens in this case is that the Engine first counts up to find out how many atoms it's possible to match in a row in the current string, and then it remembers all the shorter choices and starts out from the longest one. This could fail, of course, in which case it backtracks to a shorter choice.

If you say /.*foo/, for example, it will try to match the maximal number of "any" characters (represented by the dot) clear out to the end of the line before it ever tries looking for "foo", and then when the "foo" doesn't match there (and it can't, because there's not enough room for it at the end of the string), the Engine will back off one character at a time until it finds a "foo". If there is more than one "foo" in the line, it'll stop on the last one, and throw away all the shorter choices it could have made.

By placing a question mark after any of the greedy quantifiers, they can be made to choose the smallest quantity for the first try. So if you say /.*?foo/, the .*? first tries to match 0 characters, then 1 character, then 2, and so on until it can match the "foo". Instead of backtracking backward, it backtracks forward, so to speak, and ends up finding the first "foo" on the line instead of the last.

Rule 6. Each atom matches according to its type, listed below. If the atom doesn't match (or doesn't allow a match of the rest of the regular expression), the Engine backtracks to Rule 5 and tries the next choice for the atom's quantity.

Atoms match according to the following types:

- A regular expression in parentheses, (. . .), matches whatever the regular expression (represented by . . .) matches according to Rule 2. Parentheses therefore serve as a grouping operator for quantification. Parentheses also have the side effect of remembering the matched substring for later use in a *backreference* (to be discussed later). This side effect can be suppressed by using (?: . . .) instead, which has only the grouping semantics—it doesn't store anything in $1, $2, and so on.

- A "." matches any character except \n. (It also matches \n if you use the /s modifier.) The main use of dot is as a vehicle for a minimal or maximal quantifier. A .* matches a maximal number of don't-care characters, while a .*? matches a minimal number of don't-care characters. But it's also sometimes used within parentheses for its width: /(..):(..):(..)/ matches three colon-separated fields, each of which is two characters long.

- A list of characters in square brackets (called a *character class*) matches any one of the characters in the list. A caret at the front of the list causes it to match only characters that are *not* in the list. Character ranges may be indicated using the a-z notation. You may also use any of \d, \w, \s, \n, \r, \t, \f, or \nnn, as listed below. A \b means a backspace in a character class. You may use a backslash to protect a hyphen that would otherwise be interpreted as a range delimiter. To match a right square bracket, either backslash it or place it first in the list. To match a caret, *don't* put it first. Note that most other metacharacters lose their meta-ness inside square brackets. In particular, it's meaningless to specify alternation in a character class, since the characters are interpreted individually. For example, [fee|fie|foe] means the same thing as [feio|].

- A backslashed letter matches a special character or character class:

Code	Matches
\a	Alarm (beep)
\n	Newline
\r	Carriage return
\t	Tab
\f	Formfeed
\e	Escape
\d	A digit, same as [0-9]
\D	A nondigit

Code	Matches
\w	A word character (alphanumeric), same as [a-zA-Z_0-9]
\W	A nonword character
\s	A whitespace character, same as [\t\n\r\f]
\S	A non-whitespace character

Note that \w matches a character of a word, not a whole word. Use \w+ to match a word.

- A backslashed single-digit number matches whatever the corresponding parentheses actually matched (except that \0 matches a null character). This is called a *backreference* to a substring. A backslashed multi-digit number such as \10 will be considered a backreference if the pattern contains at least that many substrings prior to it, and the number does not start with a 0. Pairs of parentheses are numbered by counting left parentheses from the left.

- A backslashed two- or three-digit octal number such as \033 matches the character with the specified value, unless it would be interpreted as a backreference.

- A backslashed x followed by one or two hexadecimal digits, such as \x7f, matches the character having that hexadecimal value.

- A backslashed c followed by a single character, such as \cD, matches the corresponding control character.

- Any other backslashed character matches that character.

- Any character not mentioned above matches itself.

The fine print

As mentioned above, \1, \2, \3, and so on, are equivalent to whatever the corresponding set of parentheses matched, counting opening parentheses from left to right. (If the particular pair of parentheses had a quantifier such as * after it, such that it matched a series of substrings, then only the last match counts as the backreference.) Note that such a backreference matches whatever actually matched for the subpattern in the string being examined; it's not just a shorthand for the rules of that subpattern. Therefore, (0|0x)\d*\s\1\d* will match "0x1234 0x4321", but not "0x1234 01234", since subpattern 1 actually matched "0x", even though the rule 0|0x could potentially match the leading 0 in the second number.

Outside of the pattern (in particular, in the replacement of a substitution operator) you can continue to refer to backreferences by using $ instead of \ in front of the number. The variables $1, $2, $3 ... are automatically localized, and their scope (and that of **$`**, **$&**, and **$'** below) extends to the end of the enclosing block or **eval** string, or to the next successful pattern match, whichever comes first. (The \1 notation sometimes works outside the current pattern, but should not be relied upon.) $+ returns whatever the last bracket match matched. **$&** returns the entire matched string. **$`** returns everything before the matched string.[*] **$'** returns everything after the matched string. For more explanation of these magical variables (and for a way to write them in English), see the section "Special Variables" at the end of this chapter.

You may have as many parentheses as you wish. If you have more than nine pairs, the variables **$10**, **$11**, ... refer to the corresponding substring. Within the pattern, \10, \11, and so on, refer back to substrings if there have been at least that many left parentheses before the backreference. Otherwise (for backward compatibility) \10 is the same as \010, a backspace, and \11 the same as \011, a tab. And so on. (\1 through \9 are always backreferences.)

Examples:

```
s/^([^ ]+) +([^ ]+)/$2 $1/;    # swap first two words

/(\w+)\s*=\s*\1/;              # match "foo = foo"

/.{80,}/;                      # match line of at least 80 chars

/^(\d+\.?\d*|\.\d+)$/;         # match valid number

if (/Time: (..):(..):(..)/) { # pull fields out of a line
        $hours   = $1;
        $minutes = $2;
        $seconds = $3;
}
```

Hint: instead of writing patterns like /(...)(..)(.....)/, use the **unpack** function. It's more efficient.

A word boundary (\b) is defined as a spot between two characters that has a \w on one side of it and a \W on the other side of it (in either order), counting the imaginary characters off the beginning and end of the string as matching a \W. (Within character classes \b represents backspace rather than a word boundary.)

---

* In the case of something like s/pattern/length($`)/eg, which does multiple replacements if the pattern occurs multiple times, the value of $` does not include any modifications done by previous replacement iterations. To get the other effect, say:

```
1 while s/pattern/length($`)/e;
```

For example, to change all tabs to the corresponding number of spaces, you could say:

```
1 while s/\t+/' ' x (length($&) * 8 - length($`) % 8)/e;
```

Normally, the ^ character is guaranteed to match only at the beginning of the string, the $ character only at the end (or before the newline at the end), and Perl does certain optimizations with the assumption that the string contains only one line. Embedded newlines will not be matched by ^ or $. However, you may wish to treat a string as a multi-line buffer, such that the ^ will also match after any newline within the string, and $ will also match before any newline. At the cost of a little more overhead, you can do this by using the /m modifier on the pattern match operator. (Older programs did this by setting $*, but this practice is now deprecated.) \A and \Z are just like ^ and $ except that they won't match multiple times when the /m modifier is used, while ^ and $ will match at every internal line boundary. To match the actual end of the string, not ignoring newline, you can use \Z(?!\n). There's an example of a negative lookahead assertion.

To facilitate multi-line substitutions, the . character never matches a newline unless you use the /s modifier, which tells Perl to pretend the string is a single line—even if it isn't. (The /s modifier also overrides the setting of $*, in case you have some (badly behaved) older code that sets it in another module.) In particular, the following leaves a newline on the $_ string:

```
$_ = <STDIN>;
s/.*(some_string).*/$1/;
```

If the newline is unwanted, use any of these:

```
s/.*(some_string).*/$1/s;
s/.*(some_string).*\n/$1/;
s/.*(some_string)[^\0]*/$1/;
s/.*(some_string)(.|\n)*/$1/;

chop; s/.*(some_string).*/$1/;
/(some_string)/ && ($_ = $1);
```

Note that all backslashed metacharacters in Perl are alphanumeric, such as \b, \w, and \n. Unlike some regular expression languages, there are no backslashed symbols that aren't alphanumeric. So anything that looks like \\, \(, \), \<, \>, \{, or \} is always interpreted as a literal character, not a metacharacter. This makes it simple to quote a string that you want to use for a pattern but that you are afraid might contain metacharacters. Just quote all the non-alphanumeric characters:

```
$pattern =~ s/(\W)/\\$1/g;
```

You can also use the built-in **quotemeta** function to do this. An even easier way to quote metacharacters right in the match operator is to say:

```
/$unquoted\Q$quoted\E$unquoted/
```

Remember that the first and last alternatives (before the first | and after the last one) tend to gobble up the other elements of the regular expression on either side, out to the ends of the expression, unless there are enclosing parentheses. A common mistake is to ask for:

    /^fee|fie|foe$/

when you really mean:

    /^(fee|fie|foe)$/

The first matches "fee" at the beginning of the string, or "fie" anywhere, or "foe" at the end of the string. The second matches any string consisting solely of "fee" or "fie" or "foe".

Regular expression extensions

Perl defines a consistent extension syntax for regular expressions. You've seen some of them already. The syntax is a pair of parentheses with a question mark as the first thing within the parentheses.[*] The character after the question mark gives the function of the extension. Several extensions are already supported:

(?#text)
> A comment. The text is ignored. If the **/x** switch is used to enable whitespace formatting, a simple # will suffice.

(?: . . .)
> This groups things like "(...)" but doesn't make backreferences like "(...)" does. So:
>
>   split(/\b(?:a|b|c)\b/)
>
> is like:
>
>   split(/\b(a|b|c)\b/)
>
> but doesn't actually save anything in **$1**, which means that the first **split** doesn't spit out extra delimiter fields as the second one does.

(?= . . .)
> A zero-width positive lookahead assertion. For example, /\w+(?=\t)/ matches a word followed by a tab, without including the tab in **$&**.

(?! . . .)
> A zero-width negative lookahead assertion. For example /foo(?!bar)/ matches any occurrence of "foo" that isn't followed by "bar". Note, however, that lookahead and lookbehind are *not* the same thing. You cannot use this for lookbehind: /(?!foo)bar/ will not find an occurrence of "bar" that is preceded by something that is not "foo". That's because the (?!foo) is just saying

_____

[*] This was a syntax error in older versions of Perl. If you try to use this and have problems, upgrade to the newest version.

that the next thing cannot be "foo"—and it's not, it's a "bar", so "foobar" will match. You would have to do something like /(?!foo)...bar/ for that. We say "like" because there's the case of your "bar" not having three characters before it. You could cover that this way: /(?:(?!foo)...|^.{0, 2})bar/. Sometimes it's still easier just to say:

```
if (/bar/ and $` !~ /foo$/)
```

(?imsx)

One or more embedded pattern-match modifiers. This is particularly useful for patterns that are specified in a table somewhere, some of which want to be case-sensitive, and some of which don't. The case-insensitive ones merely need to include (?i) at the front of the pattern. For example:

```
# hardwired case insensitivity
$pattern = "buffalo";
if ( /$pattern/i )

# data-driven case insensitivity
$pattern = "(?i)buffalo";
if ( /$pattern/ )
```

We chose to use the question mark for this (and for the new minimal matching construct) because (1) question mark is pretty rare in older regular expressions, and (2) whenever you see one, you should stop and *question* exactly what is going on. That's psychology.

Pattern-Matching Operators

Now that we've got all that out of the way, here finally are the quotelike operators (er, terms) that perform pattern matching and related activities.

m/*PATTERN*/gimosx

/*PATTERN*/gimosx

This operator searches a string for a pattern match, and in a scalar context returns true (1) or false (""). If no string is specified via the =~ or !~ operator, the $_ string is searched. (The string specified with =~ need not be an lvalue—it may be the result of an expression evaluation, but remember the =~ binds rather tightly, so you may need parentheses around your expression.)

Modifiers are:

Modifier	Meaning
g	Match globally, that is, find all occurrences.
i	Do case-insensitive pattern matching.
m	Treat string as multiple lines. *(continued)*

Modifier	Meaning
o	Only compile pattern once.
s	Treat string as single line.
x	Use extended regular expressions.

If / is the delimiter then the initial m is optional. With the m you can use any pair of non-alphanumeric, non-whitespace characters as delimiters. This is particularly useful for matching filenames that contain "/", thus avoiding LTS (leaning tooth-pick syndrome).

PATTERN may contain variables, which will be interpolated (and the pattern recompiled) every time the pattern search is evaluated. (Note that $) and $| will not be interpolated because they look like end-of-line tests.) If you want such a pattern to be compiled only once, add a /o after the trailing delimiter. This avoids expensive run-time recompilations, and is useful when the value you are interpolating won't change during execution. However, mentioning /o constitutes a promise that you won't change the variables in the pattern. If you do change them, Perl won't even notice.

If the *PATTERN* evaluates to a null string, the last successfully executed regular expression not hidden within an inner block (including **split**, **grep**, and **map**) is used instead.

If used in a context that requires a list value, a pattern match returns a list consisting of the subexpressions matched by the parentheses in the pattern—that is, (**$1**, **$2**, **$3** ...). (The variables are also set.) If the match fails, a null list is returned. If the match succeeds, but there were no parentheses, a list value of (1) is returned.

Examples:

```
# case insensitive matching
open(TTY, '/dev/tty');
<TTY> =~ /^y/i and foo();      # do foo() if they want it

# pulling a substring out of a line
if (/Version: *([0-9.]+)/) { $version = $1; }

# avoiding Leaning Toothpick Syndrome
next if m#^/usr/spool/uucp#;

# poor man's grep
$arg = shift;
while (<>) {
    print if /$arg/o;        # compile only once
}

# get first two words and remainder as a list
if (($F1, $F2, $Etc) = ($foo =~ /^\s*(\S+)\s+(\S+)\s*(.*)/))
```

This last example splits $foo into the first two words and the remainder of the line, and assigns those three fields to $F1, $F2, and $Etc. The conditional is true if any variables were assigned, that is, if the pattern matched. Usually, though, one would just write the equivalent **split**:

```
if (($F1, $F2, $Etc) = split(' ', $foo, 3))
```

The **/g** modifier specifies global pattern matching—that is, matching as many times as possible within the string. How it behaves depends on the context. In a list context, it returns a list of all the substrings matched by all the parentheses in the regular expression. If there are no parentheses, it returns a list of all the matched strings, as if there were parentheses around the whole pattern.

In a scalar context, **m//g** iterates through the string, returning true each time it matches, and false when it eventually runs out of matches. (In other words, it remembers where it left off last time and restarts the search at that point. You can find the current match position of a string using the **pos** function—see Chapter 3.) If you modify the string in any way, the match position is reset to the beginning. Examples:

```
# list context--extract three numeric fields from uptime command
($one,$five,$fifteen) = (`uptime` =~ /(\d+\.\d+)/g);

# scalar context--count sentences in a document by recognizing
# sentences ending in [.!?], perhaps with quotes or parens on
# either side.  Observe how dot in the character class is a literal
# dot, not merely any character.
$/ = "";  # paragraph mode
while ($paragraph = <>) {
    while ($paragraph =~ /[a-z]['")]*[.!?]+['")]*\s/g) {
        $sentences++;
    }
}
print "$sentences\n";

# find duplicate words in paragraphs, possibly spanning line boundaries.
#   Use /x for space and comments, /i to match the both 'is'
#   in "Is is this ok?", and use /g to find all dups.
$/ = "";         # paragrep mode again
while (<>) {
    while ( m{
                \b           # start at a word boundary
                (\w\S+)      # find a wordish chunk
                (
                    \s+      # separated by some whitespace
                    \1       # and that chunk again
                ) +          # repeat ad lib
                \b           # until another word boundary
             }xig
         )
    {
```

```
            print "dup word '$1' at paragraph $.\n";
        }
    }
```

?PATTERN?

> This is just like the */PATTERN/* search, except that it matches only once between calls to the **reset** operator. This is a useful optimization when you only want to see the first occurrence of something in each file of a set of files, for instance. Only **??** patterns local to the current package are reset.

This usage is vaguely deprecated, and may be removed in some future version of Perl. Most people just bomb out of the loop when they get the match they want.

*s/PATTERN/REPLACEMENT/*egimosx

> This operator searches a string for *PATTERN*, and if found, replaces that match with the *REPLACEMENT* text and returns the number of substitutions made, which can be more than one with the **/g** modifier. Otherwise it returns false (0).

If no string is specified via the =~ or !~ operator, the **$_** variable is searched and modified. (The string specified with =~ must be a scalar variable, an array element, a hash element, or an assignment to one of those, that is, an lvalue.)

If the delimiter you choose happens to be a single quote, no variable interpolation is done on either the *PATTERN* or the *REPLACEMENT*. Otherwise, if the *PATTERN* contains a $ that looks like a variable rather than an end-of-string test, the variable will be interpolated into the *PATTERN* at run-time. If you want the *PATTERN* compiled only once, when the variable is first interpolated, use the **/o** option. If the *PATTERN* evaluates to a null string, the last successfully executed regular expression is used instead. The *REPLACEMENT* pattern also undergoes variable interpolation, but it does so each time the *PATTERN* matches, unlike the *PATTERN*, which just gets interpolated once when the operator is evaluated. (The *PATTERN* can match multiple times in one evaluation if you use the **/g** option below.)

Modifiers are:

Modifier	Meaning
e	Evaluate the right side as an expression.
g	Replace globally, that is, all occurrences.
i	Do case-insensitive pattern matching.
m	Treat string as multiple lines.
o	Only compile pattern once.
s	Treat string as single line.
x	Use extended regular expressions.

Any non-alphanumeric, non-whitespace delimiter may replace the slashes. If single quotes are used, no interpretation is done on the replacement string (the /e modifier overrides this, however). If the *PATTERN* is contained within naturally paired delimiters (such as parentheses), the *REPLACEMENT* has its own pair of delimiters, which may or may not be the same ones used for *PATTERN*—for example, s(foo)(bar) or s<foo>/bar/. A /e will cause the replacement portion to be interpreted as a full-fledged Perl expression instead of as a double-quoted string. (It's kind of like an **eval**, but its syntax is checked at compile-time.)

Examples:

```
# don't change wintergreen
s/\bgreen\b/mauve/g;

# avoid LTS with different quote characters
$path =~ s(/usr/bin)(/usr/local/bin);

# interpolated pattern and replacement
s/Login: $foo/Login: $bar/;

# modifying a string "en passant"
($foo = $bar) =~ s/this/that/;

# counting the changes
$count = ($paragraph =~ s/Mister\b/Mr./g);

# using an expression for the replacement
$_ = 'abc123xyz';
s/\d+/$&*2/e;               # yields 'abc246xyz'
s/\d+/sprintf("%5d",$&)/e;  # yields 'abc  246xyz'
s/\w/$& x 2/eg;             # yields 'aabbcc  224466xxyyzz'

# how to default things with /e
s/%(.)/$percent{$1}/g;        # change percent escapes; no /e
s/%(.)/$percent{$1} || $&/ge; # expr now, so /e
s/^=(\w+)/&pod($1)/ge;        # use function call

# /e's can even nest; this will expand simple embedded variables in $_
s/(\$\w+)/$1/eeg;

# delete C comments
$program =~ s {
    /\*     # Match the opening delimiter.
    .*?     # Match a minimal number of characters.
    \*/     # Match the closing delimiter.
} []gsx;

# trim white space
s/^\s*(.*?)\s*$/$1/;

# reverse 1st two fields
s/([^ ]*) *([^ ]*)/$2 $1/;
```

Note the use of $ instead of \ in the last example. Some people get a little too used to writing things like:

```
$pattern =~ s/(\W)/\\\1/g;
```

This is grandfathered for the right-hand side of a substitution to avoid shocking the *sed* addicts, but it's a dirty habit to get into.[*] That's because in PerlThink, the right-hand side of a s/// is a double-quoted string. In an ordinary double-quoted string, \1 would mean a control-A, but for s/// the customary UNIX meaning of \1 is kludged in. (The lexer actually translates it to **$1** on the fly.) If you start to rely on that, however, you get yourself into trouble if you then add an **/e** modifier:

```
s/(\d+)/ \1 + 1 /eg;    # a scalar reference plus one?
```

Or if you try to do:

```
s/(\d+)/\1000/;          # "\100" . "0" == "@0"?
```

You can't disambiguate that by saying \{1}000, whereas you *can* fix it with ${1}000. Basically, the operation of interpolation should not be confused with the operation of matching a backreference. Certainly, interpolation and matching mean two different things on the *left* side of the s///.

Occasionally, you can't just use a **/g** to get all the changes to occur, either because the substitutions have to happen right-to-left, or because you need the length of $` to change between matches. In this case you can usually do what you want by calling the substitution repeatedly. Here are two common cases:

```
# put commas in the right places in an integer
1 while s/(\d)(\d\d\d)(?!\d)/$1,$2/;

# expand tabs to 8-column spacing
1 while s/\t+/' ' x (length($&)*8 - length($`)%8)/e;
```

tr/*SEARCHLIST*/*REPLACEMENTLIST*/cds
y/*SEARCHLIST*/*REPLACEMENTLIST*/cds

Strictly speaking, this operator doesn't belong in a section on pattern matching because it doesn't use regular expressions. Rather, it scans a string character by character, and replaces all occurrences of the characters found in the *SEARCHLIST* with the corresponding character in the *REPLACEMENTLIST*. It returns the number of characters replaced or deleted. If no string is specified via the =~ or !~ operator, the $_ string is translated. (The string specified with =~ must be a scalar variable, an array element, or an assignment to one of those, that is, an lvalue.) For *sed* devotees, **y** is provided as a synonym for **tr///**. If the *SEARCHLIST* is contained within naturally paired delimiters (such as

---

[*] Or to not get out of, depending on how you look at it.

parentheses), the *REPLACEMENTLIST* has its own pair of delimiters, which may or may not be naturally paired ones—for example, tr[A-Z][a-z] or tr(+-*/)/ABCD/.

Modifiers:

Modifier	Meaning
c	Complement the *SEARCHLIST*.
d	Delete found but unreplaced characters.
s	Squash duplicate replaced characters.

If the /c modifier is specified, the *SEARCHLIST* character set is complemented; that is, the effective search list consists of all the characters *not* in *SEARCHLIST*. If the /d modifier is specified, any characters specified by *SEARCHLIST* but not given a replacement in *REPLACEMENTLIST* are deleted. (Note that this is slightly more flexible than the behavior of some **tr///** programs, which delete anything they find in the *SEARCHLIST*, period.) If the /s modifier is specified, sequences of characters that were translated to the same character are squashed down to a single instance of the character.

If the /d modifier is used, the *REPLACEMENTLIST* is always interpreted exactly as specified. Otherwise, if the *REPLACEMENTLIST* is shorter than the *SEARCHLIST*, the final character is replicated until it is long enough. If the *REPLACEMENTLIST* is null, the *SEARCHLIST* is replicated. This latter is useful for counting characters in a class or for squashing character sequences in a class.

Examples:

```
$ARGV[1] =~ tr/A-Z/a-z/;        # canonicalize to lower case

$cnt = tr/*/*/;                 # count the stars in $_

$cnt = $sky =~ tr/*/*/;         # count the stars in $sky

$cnt = tr/0-9//;                # count the digits in $_

tr/a-zA-Z//s;                   # bookkeeper -> bokeper

($HOST = $host) =~ tr/a-z/A-Z/;

tr/a-zA-Z/ /cs;                 # change non-alphas to single space

tr [\200-\377]
   [\000-\177];                 # delete 8th bit
```

If multiple translations are given for a character, only the first one is used:

```
tr/AAA/XYZ/
```

will translate any A to X.

Note that because the translation table is built at compile time, neither the *SEARCH-LIST* nor the *REPLACEMENTLIST* are subject to double quote interpolation. That means that if you want to use variables, you must use an **eval**:

```
eval "tr/$oldlist/$newlist/";
die $@ if $@;

eval "tr/$oldlist/$newlist/, 1" or die $@;
```

One more note: if you want to change your text to uppercase or lowercase, it's better to use the \U or \L sequences in a double-quoted string, since they will pay attention to locale information, but `tr/a-z/A-Z/` won't.

Operators

The terms of an expression often need to be combined and modified in various ways, and that's what operators are for. The tightness with which operators bind is controlled by the *precedence* of the operators. Perl operators have the following associativity and precedence, listed from highest precedence to lowest.[*]

Associativity	Operators
Left	Terms and list operators (leftward)
Left	->
Nonassociative	++ --
Right	**
Right	! ~ \ and unary + and -
Left	=~ !~
Left	* / % x
Left	+ - .
Left	<< >>
Nonassociative	Named unary operators
Nonassociative	< > <= >= lt gt le ge
Nonassociative	== != <=> eq ne cmp
Left	&
Left	| ^
Left	&&
Left	||

---

[*] Classic Camel readers will note that we reversed this table from the old edition. The higher precedence operators are now higher on the page, which makes some kind of metaphorical sense.

Associativity	Operators
Nonassociative	.. ...
Right	?:
Right	= += -= *= and so on
Left	, =>
Nonassociative	List operators (rightward)
Right	not
Left	and
Left	or xor

It may seem like there are too many precedence levels. Well, you're right, there are. Fortunately, there are two things going for you here. First, the precedence levels as they're defined usually follow your intuition, presuming you're not psychotic. And second, if you're merely neurotic, you can always put in extra parentheses to relieve your anxiety.

Note that any operators borrowed from C keep the same precedence relationship with each other, even where C's precedence is slightly screwy. (This makes learning Perl easier for C folks.)

In the following sections, these operators are covered in precedence order. With very few exceptions, these all operate on scalar values only, not list values. We'll mention the exceptions as they come up.

Terms and List Operators (Leftward)

Any *term* is of highest precedence in Perl. These include variables, quote and quotelike operators, any expression in parentheses, and any function whose arguments are parenthesized. Actually, there aren't really any functions in this sense, just list operators and unary operators behaving as functions because you put parentheses around their arguments. These operators are all covered in Chapter 3.

Now, listen carefully. Here are a couple of rules that are very important and simplify things greatly, but may occasionally produce counterintuitive results for the unwary. If any list operator (such as **print**) or any named unary operator (such as **chdir**) is followed by a left parenthesis as the next token on the same line,[*] the operator and its arguments within parentheses are taken to be of highest precedence, just like a normal function call. The rule is: If it *looks* like a function call, it is a function call. You can make it look like a non-function by prefixing the arguments with a unary plus, which does absolutely nothing, semantically speaking—it doesn't even convert the argument to numeric.

---

[*] And we nearly had you convinced Perl was a free-form language.

For example, since | | has lower precedence than **chdir**, we get:

```
chdir $foo       || die;      # (chdir $foo) || die
chdir($foo)      || die;      # (chdir $foo) || die
chdir ($foo)     || die;      # (chdir $foo) || die
chdir +($foo)    || die;      # (chdir $foo) || die
```

but, because * has higher precedence than **chdir**, we get:

```
chdir $foo * 20;             # chdir ($foo * 20)
chdir($foo) * 20;            # (chdir $foo) * 20
chdir ($foo) * 20;           # (chdir $foo) * 20
chdir +($foo) * 20;          # chdir ($foo * 20)
```

Likewise for numeric operators:

```
rand 10 * 20;               # rand (10 * 20)
rand(10) * 20;              # (rand 10) * 20
rand (10) * 20;             # (rand 10) * 20
rand +(10) * 20;            # rand (10 * 20)
```

In the absence of parentheses, the precedence of list operators such as **print**, **sort**, or **chmod** is either very high or very low depending on whether you look at the left side of the operator or the right side of it. (That's what the "Leftward" is doing in the title of this section.) For example, in:

```
@ary = (1, 3, sort 4, 2);
print @ary;          # prints 1324
```

the commas on the right of the **sort** are evaluated before the **sort**, but the commas on the left are evaluated after. In other words, a list operator tends to gobble up all the arguments that follow it, and then act like a simple term with regard to the preceding expression. Note that you have to be careful with parentheses:

```
# These evaluate exit before doing the print:
print($foo, exit);  # Obviously not what you want.
print $foo, exit;   # Nor is this.

# These do the print before evaluating exit:
(print $foo), exit; # This is what you want.
print($foo), exit;  # Or this.
print ($foo), exit; # Or even this.
```

Also note that:

```
print ($foo & 255) + 1, "\n";    # prints ($foo & 255)
```

probably doesn't do what you expect at first glance. Fortunately, mistakes of this nature generally produce warnings like "Useless use of addition in a void context" when you use the **-w** command-line switch.

Also parsed as terms are the do {} and eval {} constructs, as well as subroutine and method calls, the anonymous array and hash composers [] and {}, and the anonymous subroutine composer sub {}.

The Arrow Operator

Just as in C and C++, -> is an infix dereference operator. If the right side is either a [. . .] or { . . . } subscript, then the left side must be either a hard or symbolic reference to an array or hash (or a location capable of holding a hard reference, if it's an lvalue (assignable)). More on this in Chapter 4.

Otherwise, the right side must be a method name or a simple scalar variable containing the method name, and the value of the left side must either be an object (a blessed reference) or a class name (that is, a package name). See Chapter 5.

Autoincrement and Autodecrement

The ++ and -- operators work as in C. That is, if placed before a variable, they increment or decrement the variable before returning the value, and if placed after, they increment or decrement the variable after returning the value. For example, $a++ increments the value of scalar variable $a, returning the value *before* it performs the increment. Similarly, --$b{(/(\w+)/)[0]} decrements the element of the hash %b indexed by the first "word" in the default search variable ($_) and returns the value *after* the decrement.[*]

The autoincrement operator has a little extra built-in magic to it. If you increment a variable that is numeric, or that has ever been used in a numeric context, you get a normal increment. If, however, the variable has only been used in string contexts since it was set, and has a value that is not null and matches the pattern /^[a-zA-Z]*[0-9]*$/, the increment is done as a string, preserving each character within its range, with carry:

```
print ++($foo = '99');      # prints '100'
print ++($foo = 'a0');      # prints 'a1'
print ++($foo = 'Az');      # prints 'Ba'
print ++($foo = 'zz');      # prints 'aaa'
```

The autodecrement operator, however, is not magical.

---

[*] OK, so that wasn't exactly fair. We just wanted to make sure you were paying attention. Here's how that expression works. First the pattern match finds the first word in $_ using the regular expression \w+. The parentheses around that causes the word to be returned as a single-element list value, because the pattern match is in a list context. The list context is supplied by the list slice operator, (. . .)[0], which returns the first (and only) element of the list. That value is then used as the key for the hash, and the hash entry (value) is decremented and returned. In general, when confronted with a complex expression, analyze it from the inside out to see what order things happen in.

Exponentiation

Binary ** is the exponentiation operator. Note that it binds even more tightly than unary minus, so -2**4 is -(2**4), not (-2)**4. The operator is implemented using C's *pow*(3) function, which works with doubles internally. It calculates using logarithms, which means that it works with fractional powers, but you sometimes get results that aren't as exact as a straight multiplication would produce.

Ideographic Unary Operators

Most unary operators just have names (see "Named Unary and File Test Operators" below), but some operators are deemed important enough to merit their own special symbolic representation. Most of these operators seem to have something to do with negation. Blame the mathematicians.

Unary ! performs logical negation, that is, "not". See also **not** for a lower precedence version of this. The value of a negated operation is 1 if the operand is false (numeric 0, string "0", null string, or undefined); otherwise, the value is that of the null string.

Unary - performs arithmetic negation if the operand is numeric. If the operand is an identifier, a string consisting of a minus sign concatenated with the identifier is returned. Otherwise, if the string starts with a plus or minus, a string starting with the opposite sign is returned. One effect of these rules is that -bareword is equivalent to "-bareword". This is most useful for Tk and CGI programmers.

Unary ~ performs bitwise negation, that is, 1's complement. For example, on a 32-bit machine, ~123 is 4294967172. But you knew that already.

(What you perhaps didn't know is that if the argument to ~ happens to be a string instead of a number, a string of identical length is returned, but with all the bits of the string complemented. This is a fast way to flip a lot of bits all at once. See also the bitwise logical operators, which also have stringish variants.)

Unary + has no semantic effect whatsoever, even on strings. It is syntactically useful for separating a function name from a parenthesized expression that would otherwise be interpreted as the complete list of function arguments. (See examples above under the section "Terms and List Operators".)

Unary \ creates a reference to whatever follows it (see Chapter 4). Do not confuse this behavior with the behavior of backslash within a string, although both forms do convey the notion of protecting the next thing from interpretation. This resemblance is not entirely accidental.

The \ operator may also be used on a parenthesized list value in a list context, in which case it returns references to each element of the list.

Binding Operators

Binary =~ binds a scalar expression to a pattern match, substitution, or translation. These operations search or modify the string $_ by default. The binding operator makes those operations work on some other string instead. The argument on the right is the search pattern, substitution, or translation. The left argument is what is supposed to be searched, substituted, or translated instead of the default $_. The return value indicates the success of the operation. If the right argument is an expression rather than a search pattern, substitution, or translation, it is interpreted as a search pattern at run-time. That is, $_ =~ $pat is equivalent to $_ =~ /$pat/. This is less efficient than an explicit search, since the pattern must be compiled every time the expression is evaluated. (But /$pat/o doesn't recompile it because of the /o modifier.)

Binary !~ is just like =~ except the return value is negated in the logical sense. The following expressions are functionally equivalent:

```
$string !~ /pattern/
not $string =~ /pattern/
```

We said that the return value indicates success, but there are many kinds of success. Substitutions return the number of successful substitutions, as do translations. (In fact, the translation operator is often used to count characters.) Since any non-zero result is true, it all works out. The most spectacular kind of true value is a list value: in a list context, pattern matches can return substrings matched by the parentheses in the pattern. But again, according to the rules of list assignment, the list assignment itself will return true if anything matched and was assigned, and false otherwise. So you sometimes see things like:

```
if ( ($k,$v) = $string =~ m/(\w+)=(\w*)/ ) {
    print "KEY $k VALUE $v\n";
}
```

Let's pick that apart. The =~ binds $string to the pattern match on the right, which is scanning for occurrences of things that look like *KEY=VALUE* in your string. It's in a list context because it's on the right side of a list assignment. If it matches, it does a list assignment to $k and $v. The list assignment itself is in a scalar context, so it returns 2, the number of values on the right side of the assignment. And 2 happens to be true, since our scalar context is also a Boolean context. When the match fails, no values are assigned, which returns 0, which is false.

Multiplicative Operators

Perl provides the C-like operators * (multiply), / (divide), and % (modulus). The *
and / work exactly as you might expect, multiplying or dividing their two
operands. Division is done in floating-point, unless you've used the integer library
module.

The % operator converts its operands to integers before finding the remainder
according to integer division. For the same operation in floating-point, you may
prefer to use the fmod( ) function from the POSIX module (see Chapter 7).

Binary **x** is the repetition operator. In scalar context, it returns a concatenated
string consisting of the left operand repeated the number of times specified by the
right operand.

```
print '-' x 80;                 # print row of dashes

print "\t" x ($tab/8), ' ' x ($tab%8);      # tab over
```

In list context, if the left operand is a list in parentheses, the **x** works as a list replicator rather than a string replicator. This is useful for initializing all the elements of
an array of indeterminate length to the same value:

```
@ones = (1) x 80;           # a list of 80 1's
@ones = (5) x @ones;        # set all elements to 5
```

Similarly, you can also use **x** to initialize array and hash slices:

```
@keys = qw(perls before swine);
@hash{@keys} = ("") x @keys;
```

If this mystifies you, note that @keys is being used both as a list on the left side of
the assignment, and as a scalar value (returning the array length) on the right side
of the assignment. The above has the same effect on %hash as:

```
$hash{perls}  = "";
$hash{before} = "";
$hash{swine}  = "";
```

Additive Operators

Strangely enough, Perl also has the customary + (addition) and – (subtraction)
operators. Both operators convert their arguments from strings to numeric values if
necessary, and return a numeric result.

Additionally, Perl provides a string concatenation operator ".". For example:

```
$almost = "Fred" . "Flintstone";    # returns FredFlintstone
```

Note that Perl does not place a space between the strings being concatenated. If you want the space, or if you have more than two strings to concatenate, you can use the **join** operator, described in Chapter 3. Most often, though, people do their concatenation implicitly inside a double-quoted string:

```
$fullname = "$firstname $lastname";
```

Shift Operators

The bit-shift operators (<< and >>) return the value of the left argument shifted to the left (<<) or to the right (>>) by the number of bits specified by the right argument. The arguments should be integers. For example:

```
1 << 4;    # returns 16
32 >> 4;   # returns 2
```

Named Unary and File Test Operators

Some of "functions" described in Chapter 3 are really unary operators, including:

–X (file tests)	gethostbyname	localtime	rmdir
alarm	getnetbyname	log	scalar
caller	getpgrp	lstat	sin
chdir	getprotobyname	my	sleep
chroot	glob	oct	sqrt
cos	gmtime	ord	srand
defined	goto	quotemeta	stat
delete	hex	rand	uc
do	int	readlink	ucfirst
eval	lc	ref	umask
exists	lcfirst	require	undef
exit	length	reset	
exp	local	return	

These are all unary operators, with a higher precedence than some of the other binary operators. For example:

```
sleep 4 | 3;
```

does not sleep for 7 seconds; it sleeps for 4 seconds, and then takes the return value of **sleep** (typically zero) and ORs that with 3, as if the expression were parenthesized as:

```
(sleep 4) | 3;
```

Compare this with:

```
print 4 | 3;
```

which *does* take the value of 4 ORed with 3 before printing it (7 in this case), as if it were written:

```
print (4 | 3);
```

This is because **print** is a list operator, not a simple unary operator. Once you've learned which operators are list operators, you'll have no trouble telling them apart. When in doubt, you can always use parentheses to turn a named unary operator into a function. Remember, if it looks like a function, it is a function.

Another funny thing about named unary operators is that many of them default to $_ if you don't supply an argument. However, if the thing following the named unary operator looks like it might be the start of an argument, Perl will get confused. When the next character in your program is one of the following characters, the Perl tokener returns different token types depending on whether a term or operator is expected:

Char	Operator	Term
+	Addition	Unary plus
–	Subtraction	Unary minus
*	Multiplication	`*typeglob`
/	Division	`/pattern/`
<	Less than, left shift	`<HANDLE>`, `<<END`
.	Concatenation	`.3333`
?	?:	`?pattern?`
%	Modulo	`%assoc`
&	`&`, `&&`	`&subroutine`

So a typical boo-boo is:

```
next if length < 80;
```

in which the < looks to the parser like the beginning of the <> input symbol (a term) instead of the "less than" (an operator) you were thinking of. There's really no way to fix this, and still keep Perl pathologically eclectic. If you're so incredibly lazy that you cannot bring yourself to type the two characters $_, then say one of these instead:

```
next if length() < 80;
next if (length) < 80;
next if 80 > length;
next unless length >= 80;
```

A file test operator is a unary operator that takes one argument, either a filename or a filehandle, and tests the associated file to see if something is true about it. If the argument is omitted, it tests $_, except for -t, which tests STDIN. Unless otherwise documented, it returns 1 for true and "" for false, or the undefined value if the file doesn't exist. The operator may be any of the following:

Operator	Meaning
-r	File is readable by effective uid/gid.
-w	File is writable by effective uid/gid.
-x	File is executable by effective uid/gid.
-o	File is owned by effective uid.
-R	File is readable by real uid/gid.
-W	File is writable by real uid/gid.
-X	File is executable by real uid/gid.
-O	File is owned by real uid.
-e	File exists.
-z	File has zero size.
-s	File has non-zero size (returns size).
-f	File is a plain file.
-d	File is a directory.
-l	File is a symbolic link.
-p	File is a named pipe (FIFO).
-S	File is a socket.
-b	File is a block special file.
-c	File is a character special file.
-t	Filehandle is opened to a tty.
-u	File has setuid bit set.
-g	File has setgid bit set.
-k	File has sticky bit set.
-T	File is a text file.
-B	File is a binary file (opposite of -T).
-M	Age of file (at startup) in days since modification.
-A	Age of file (at startup) in days since last access.
-C	Age of file (at startup) in days since inode change.

The interpretation of the file permission operators -r, -R, -w, -W, -x, and -X is based solely on the mode of the file and the user and group IDs of the user. There may be other reasons you can't actually read, write, or execute the file, such as

Andrew File System (AFS) access control lists. Also note that for the superuser, -r, -R, -w, and -W always return 1, and -x, and -X return 1 if any execute bit is set in the mode. Scripts run by the superuser may thus need to do a **stat** in order to determine the actual mode of the file, or temporarily set the uid to something else. Example:

```
while (<>) {
    chomp;
    next unless -f $_;       # ignore "special" files
    ...
}
```

Note that -s/a/b/ does not do a negated substitution. Saying -exp($foo) still works as expected, however—only single letters following a minus are interpreted as file tests.

The -T and -B switches work as follows. The first block or so of the file is examined for odd characters such as strange control codes or characters with the high bit set. If too many odd characters (>30%) are found, it's a -B file, otherwise it's a -T file. Also, any file containing null in the first block is considered a binary file. If -T or -B is used on a filehandle, the current input (standard I/O or "stdio") buffer is examined rather than the first block of the file. Both -T and -B return true on a null file, or on a file at EOF (end of file) when testing a filehandle. Because you have to read a file to do the -T test, on most occasions you want to use a -f against the file first, as in:

```
next unless -f $file && -T _;
```

If any of the file tests (or either the **stat** or **lstat** operators) are given the special filehandle consisting of a solitary underline, then the *stat* structure of the previous file test (or **stat** operator) is used, thereby saving a system call. (This doesn't work with -t, and you need to remember that **lstat** and -l will leave values in the *stat* structure for the symbolic link, not the real file.)[*] Example:

```
print "Can do.\n" if -r $a || -w _ || -x _;

stat($filename);
print "Readable\n" if -r _;
print "Writable\n" if -w _;
print "Executable\n" if -x _;
print "Setuid\n" if -u _;
print "Setgid\n" if -g _;
print "Sticky\n" if -k _;
print "Text\n" if -T _;
print "Binary\n" if -B _;
```

---

[*] Likewise, -l _ will always be false after a normal **stat**.

File ages for –M, –A, and –C are returned in days (including fractional days) since the time when the script started running. (This time is stored in the special variable $^T.) Thus, if the file changed after the script started, you would get a negative time. Note that most times (86,399 out of 86,400, on average) are fractional, so testing for equality with an integer without using the **int** function is usually futile. Examples:

```
next unless -M $file > .5;     # files older than 12 hours
&newfile if -M $file < 0; ·    # file is newer than process
&mailwarning if int(-A) == 90; # file ($_) accessed 90 days ago today
```

To reset the script's start time to the current time, change $^T as follows:

```
$^T = time;
```

Relational Operators

Perl has two classes of relational operators. One class operates on numeric values, and the other class operates on string values. To repeat the table given in the overview:

Numeric	String	Meaning
>	gt	Greater than
>=	ge	Greater than or equal to
<	lt	Less than
<=	le	Less than or equal to

These operators return 1 for true, and `""` for false. String comparisons are based on the ASCII collating sequence, and unlike in some languages, trailing spaces count in the comparison. Note that relational operators are non-associating, which means that $a < $b < $c is a syntax error.

Equality Operators

The equality operators are much like the relational operators.

Numeric	String	Meaning
==	eq	Equal to
!=	ne	Not equal to
<=>	cmp	Comparison, with signed result

The equal and not-equal operators return 1 for true, and `""` for false (just as the relational operators do). The <=> and **cmp** operators return -1 if the left operand is less than the right operand, 0 if they are equal, and +1 if the left operand is greater than the right. Although these appear to be very similar to the relational operators, they do have a different precedence level, so $a < $b <=> $c < $d is syntactically valid.

For reasons that are apparent to anyone who has seen *Star Wars*, the <=> operator is known as the "spaceship" operator.

Bitwise Operators

Like C, Perl has bitwise AND, OR, and XOR (exclusive OR) operators: &, |, and ^. Note from the table at the start of this section that bitwise-AND has a higher precedence. These operators work differently on numeric values than they do on strings. (This is one of the few places where Perl cares about the difference.) If either operand is a number (or has been used as a number), then both operands are converted to type integer, and the bitwise operation is performed between the two integers. These integers are guaranteed to be at least 32 bits long, but may be 64 bits on some machines. The point is that there's an arbitrary limit imposed by the machine's architecture.

If both operands are strings (and have not been used as numbers since being set), these operators do bitwise operations between corresponding bits from the two strings. In this case, there's no arbitrary limit, since strings aren't arbitrarily limited in size. If one string is longer than the other, the shorter string is considered to have a sufficient number of 0 bits on the end to make up the difference.

For example, if you AND together two strings:

```
"123.45" & "234.56"
```

you get another string:

```
"020.44"
```

But if you AND together a string and a number:

```
"123.45" & 234.56
```

The string is first converted to a number, giving:

```
123.45 & 234.56
```

The numbers are then converted to integer:

```
123 & 234
```

which evaluates to 106.

Note that all bit strings are true (unless they come out to being the string "0"). This means that tests of the form:

```
if ( "fred" & "\1\2\3\4" ) { ... }
```

would need to be written instead as:

```
if ( ("fred" & "\1\2\3\4") =~ /[^\0]/ ) { ... }
```

C-style Logical (Short Circuit) Operators

Like C, Perl provides the && (logical AND) and || (logical OR) operators. They evaluate from left to right (with && having slightly higher precedence than ||) testing the truth of the statement. These operators are known as short-circuit operators because they determine the truth of the statement by evaluating the fewest number of operands possible. For example, if the left operand of an && operator is false, the right operand is never evaluated because the result of the operator is false regardless of the value of the right operand.

Example	Name	Result
$a && $b	And	$a if $a is false, $b otherwise
$a || $b	Or	$a if $a is true, $b otherwise

Such short circuits are not only time savers, but are frequently used to control the flow of evaluation. For example, an oft-appearing idiom in Perl programs is:

```
open(FILE, "somefile") || die "Cannot open somefile: $!\n";
```

In this case, Perl first evaluates the **open** function. If the value is true (because *somefile* was successfully opened), the execution of the **die** function is unnecessary, and is skipped. You can read this literally as "Open some file or die!"

The || and && operators differ from C's in that, rather than returning 0 or 1, they return the last value evaluated. This has the delightful result that you can select the first of a series of values that happens to be true. Thus, a reasonably portable way to find out the home directory might be:

```
$home = $ENV{HOME}
     || $ENV{LOGDIR}
     || (getpwuid($<))[7]
     || die "You're homeless!\n";
```

Perl also provides lower precedence **and** and **or** operators that are more readable and don't force you to use parentheses as much. They also short-circuit.

Range Operator

The .. range operator is really two different operators depending on the context. In a list context, it returns a list of values counting (by ones) from the left value to the right value. This is useful for writing `for (1..10)` loops and for doing slice operations on arrays.[*]

In a scalar context, .. returns a Boolean value. The operator is bi-stable, like an electronic flip-flop, and emulates the line-range (comma) operator of *sed*, *awk*, and various editors. Each scalar .. operator maintains its own Boolean state. It is false as long as its left operand is false. Once the left operand is true, the range operator stays true until the right operand is true, *after* which the range operator becomes false again. (The operator doesn't become false until the next time it is evaluated. It can test the right operand and become false on the same evaluation as the one where it became true (the way *awk*'s range operator behaves), but it still returns true once. If you don't want it to test the right operand until the next evaluation (which is how *sed*'s range operator works), just use three dots (. . .) instead of two.) The right operand is not evaluated while the operator is in the false state, and the left operand is not evaluated while the operator is in the true state.

The precedence is a little lower than || and &&. The value returned is either the null string for false, or a sequence number (beginning with 1) for true. The sequence number is reset for each range encountered. The final sequence number in a range has the string "E0" appended to it, which doesn't affect its numeric value, but gives you something to search for if you want to exclude the endpoint. You can exclude the beginning point by waiting for the sequence number to be greater than 1. If either operand of scalar .. is a numeric literal, that operand is evaluated by comparing it to the $. variable, which contains the current line number for your input file. Examples:

As a scalar operator:

```
if (101 .. 200) { print; }  # print 2nd hundred lines
next line if (1 .. /^$/);    # skip header lines
s/^/> / if (/^$/ .. eof());  # quote body
```

---

[*] Be aware that under the current implementation, a temporary array is created, so you'll burn a *lot* of memory if you write something like this:

```
for (1 .. 1_000_000) {
    # code
}
```

As a list operator:

```
for (101 .. 200) { print; }        # prints 101102...199200
@foo = @foo[0 .. $#foo];           # an expensive no-op
@foo = @foo[ -5 .. -1];            # slice last 5 items
```

The range operator (in a list context) makes use of the magical autoincrement algorithm if the operands are strings.[*] So you can say:

```
@alphabet = ('A' .. 'Z');
```

to get all the letters of the alphabet, or:

```
$hexdigit = (0 .. 9, 'a' .. 'f')[$num & 15];
```

to get a hexadecimal digit, or:

```
@z2 = ('01' .. '31');  print $z2[$mday];
```

to get dates with leading zeros. You can also say:

```
@combos = ('aa' .. 'zz');
```

to get all combinations of two lowercase letters. However, be careful of something like:

```
@bigcombos = ('aaaaaa' .. 'zzzzzz');
```

since that will require lots of memory. More precisely, it'll need space to store 308,915,776 scalars. Let's hope you allocated a *large* swap partition. Perhaps you should consider an iterative approach instead.

Conditional Operator

Trinary ?: is the conditional operator, just as in C. It works as:

```
TEST_EXPR ? IF_TRUE_EXPR : IF_FALSE_EXPR
```

much like an if-then-else, except that it can safely be embedded within other operations and functions. If the `TEST_EXPR` is true, only the `IF_TRUE_EXPR` is evaluated, and the value of that expression becomes the value of the entire expression. Otherwise, only the `IF_FALSE_EXPR` is evaluated, and its value becomes the value of the entire expression.

```
printf "I have %d dog%s.\n", $n,
       ($n == 1) ? "" : "s";
```

---

[*] If the final value specified is not in the sequence that the magical increment would produce, the sequence goes until the next value would be longer than the final value specified.

Scalar or list context propagates downward into the second or third argument, whichever is selected. (The first argument is always in scalar context, since it's a conditional.)

```
$a = $ok ? $b : $c;   # get a scalar
@a = $ok ? @b : @c;   # get an array
$a = $ok ? @b : @c;   # get a count of elements in one of the arrays
```

You can assign to the conditional operator[*] if both the second and third arguments are legal lvalues (meaning that you can assign to them), provided that both are scalars or both are lists (or Perl won't know which context to supply to the right side of the assignment):

```
($a_or_b ? $a : $b) = $c;   # sets either $a or $b to equal $c
```

Assignment Operators

Perl recognizes the C assignment operators, as well as providing some of its own. There are quite a few of them:

```
=     **=    +=    *=    &=    <<=    &&=
      -=    /=    |=    >>=    ||=
      .=    %=    ^=
            x=
```

Each operator requires an lvalue (a variable or array element) on the left side, and some expression on the right side. For the simple assignment operator, =, the value of the expression is stored into the designated variable. For the other operators, Perl evaluates the expression:

```
$var OP= $value
```

as if it were written:

```
$var = $var OP $value
```

except that $var is evaluated only once. Compare the following two operations:

```
$var[$a++] += $value;              # $a is incremented once
$var[$a++] = $var[$a++] + $value;  # $a is incremented twice
```

Unlike in C, the assignment operator produces a valid lvalue. Modifying an assignment is equivalent to doing the assignment and then modifying the variable that was assigned to. This is useful for modifying a copy of something, like this:

---

[*] This is not necessarily guaranteed to contribute to the readability of your program. But it can be used to create some cool entries in an Obfuscated Perl contest.

```
($tmp = $global) += $constant;
```

which is the equivalent of:

```
$tmp = $global + $constant;
```

Likewise:

```
($a += 2) *= 3;
```

is equivalent to:

```
$a += 2;
$a *= 3;
```

That's not actually very useful, but you often see this idiom:

```
($new = $old) =~ s/foo/bar/g;
```

In all cases, the value of the assignment is the new value of the variable. Since assignment operators associate right-to-left, this can be used to assign many variables the same value, as in:

```
$a = $b = $c = 0;
```

which assigns 0 to $c, and the result of that (still 0) to $b, and the result of that (*still* 0) to $a.

List assignment may be done only with the plain assignment operator, =. In a list context, list assignment returns the list of new values just as scalar assignment does. In a scalar context, list assignment returns the number of values that were available on the right side of the assignment, as we mentioned earlier in "List Values and Arrays". This makes it useful for testing functions that return a null list when they're "unsuccessful", as in:

```
while (($key, $value) = each %gloss) { ... }

next unless ($dev, $ino, $mode) = stat $file;
```

Comma Operators

Binary "," is the comma operator. In a scalar context it evaluates its left argument, throws that value away, then evaluates its right argument and returns that value. This is just like C's comma operator. For example:

```
$a = (1, 3);
```

assigns 3 to $a. Do not confuse the scalar context use with the list context use. In a list context, it's just the list argument separator, and inserts both its arguments into the *LIST*. It does not throw any values away.

For example, if you change the above to:

```
@a = (1, 3);
```

you are constructing a two-element list, while:

```
atan2(1, 3);
```

is calling the function **atan2** with two arguments.

The => digraph is mostly just a synonym for the comma operator. It's useful for documenting arguments that come in pairs. It also forces any identifier to the left of it to be interpreted as a string.

List Operators (Rightward)

The right side of a list operator governs all the list operator's arguments, which are comma separated, so the precedence of list operators is looser than comma if you're looking to the right.

Logical and, or, not, and xor

As more readable alternatives to &&, ||, and !, Perl provides the **and**, **or** and **not** operators. The behavior of these operators is identical—in particular, they short-circuit the same way.[*]

The precedence of these operators is much lower, however, so you can safely use them after a list operator without the need for parentheses:

```
unlink "alpha", "beta", "gamma"
        or gripe(), next LINE;
```

With the C-style operators that would have to be written like this:

```
unlink("alpha", "beta", "gamma")
        || (gripe(), next LINE);
```

There is also a logical **xor** operator that has no exact counterpart in C or Perl, since the other XOR operator (^) works on bits. The best equivalent for $a xor $b is perhaps !$a != !$b.[†] This operator can't short-circuit either, since both sides must be evaluated.

---

[*] Obviously the unary **not** doesn't short circuit, just as ! doesn't.

[†] One could also write !$a ^ !$b or even $a ? !$b : !!$b, of course. The point is that both $a and $b have to evaluate to true or false in a Boolean context, and the existing bitwise operator doesn't provide a Boolean context.

C Operators Missing from Perl

Here is what C has that Perl doesn't:

unary &

> The address-of operator. Perl's \ operator (for taking a reference) fills the same ecological niche, however:
>
> $ref_to_var = \$var;
>
> But references are much safer than addresses.

unary *

> The dereference-address operator. Since Perl doesn't have addresses, it doesn't need to dereference addresses. It does have references though, so Perl's variable prefix characters serve as dereference operators, and indicate type as well: $, @, % and &. Oddly enough, there actually is a * dereference operator, but since * is the funny character indicating a typeglob, you wouldn't use it the same way.

(TYPE)

> The typecasting operator. Nobody likes to be typecast anyway.

Statements and Declarations

A Perl program consists of a sequence of declarations and statements. A declaration may be placed anywhere a statement may be placed, but it has its primary (or only) effect at compile time. (Some declarations do double duty as ordinary statements, while others are totally transparent at run-time.) After compilation, the main sequence of statements is executed just once, unlike in *sed* and *awk* scripts, where the sequence of statements is executed for each input line. While this means that you must explicitly loop over the lines of your input file (or files), it also means you have much more control over which files and which lines you look at.[*] Unlike many high-level languages, Perl requires only subroutines and report formats to be explicitly declared. All other user-created objects spring into existence with a null or 0 value unless they are defined by some explicit operation such as assignment.[†]

You *may* declare your variables though, if you like. You may even make it an error to use an undeclared variable. This kind of discipline is fine, but you have to declare that you want the discipline. (This seems appropriate, somehow.) See **use strict** in the section on "Pragmas" later in this chapter.

---

[*] Actually, I'm lying—it is possible to do an implicit loop with either the **-n** or **-p** command-line switch. It's just not the mandatory default like it is in *sed* and *awk*.

[†] The **-w** command-line switch will warn you about using undefined values.

Simple Statements

A simple statement is an expression evaluated for its side effects. Every simple statement must end in a semicolon, unless it is the final statement in a block. In this case, the semicolon is optional (but strongly encouraged in any multiline block, since you may eventually add another line).

Even though some operators (like eval {} and do {}) look like compound statements, they aren't. True, they allow multiple statements on the inside, but that doesn't count. From the outside those statements are just terms in an expression, and thus need an explicit semicolon if used as the last item in a statement.

Any simple statement may optionally be followed by a single modifier, just before the terminating semicolon (or block ending). The possible modifiers are:

```
if EXPR
unless EXPR
while EXPR
until EXPR
```

The **if** and **unless** modifiers work pretty much as you'd expect if you speak English:

```
$trash->take('out') if $you_love_me;
shutup() unless $you_want_me_to_leave;
```

The **while** and **until** modifiers evaluate repeatedly as long as the modifier is true:

```
$expression++ while -e "$file$expression";
kiss('me') until $I_die;
```

The **while** and **until** modifiers also have the usual while-loop semantics (conditional evaluated first), except when applied to a do {} (or to the now-deprecated do-SUBROUTINE statement), in which case the block executes once before the conditional is evaluated. This is so that you can write loops like:

```
do {
    $line = <STDIN>;
    ...
} until $line eq ".\n";
```

See the **do** entry in Chapter 3. Note also that the loop-control statements described later will not work in this construct, since modifiers don't take loop labels. Sorry. You can always wrap another block around it to do that sort of thing. Or write a real loop with multiple loop-control commands inside. Speaking of real loops, we'll talk about compound statements next.

Compound Statements

A sequence of statements that defines a scope is called a *block*. Sometimes a block is delimited by the file containing it (in the case of either a "**required**" file, or the program as a whole), and sometimes it's delimited by the extent of a string (in the case of an **eval**). But generally, a block is delimited by braces ({}). When we mean a block with braces, we'll use the term *BLOCK*.

Compound statements are built out of expressions and *BLOCK*s. The expressions are built out of the terms and operators we've already discussed. In our syntax diagrams, we'll use the word *EXPR* to indicate a place where you can use an expression.

The following conditionals and loops may be used to control flow:

```
if (EXPR) BLOCK
if (EXPR) BLOCK else BLOCK
if (EXPR) BLOCK elsif (EXPR) BLOCK ...
if (EXPR) BLOCK elsif (EXPR) BLOCK ... else BLOCK

LABEL while (EXPR) BLOCK
LABEL while (EXPR) BLOCK continue BLOCK

LABEL for (EXPR; EXPR; EXPR) BLOCK

LABEL foreach VAR (LIST) BLOCK
LABEL foreach VAR (LIST) BLOCK continue BLOCK

LABEL BLOCK
LABEL BLOCK continue BLOCK
```

Note that unlike in C and Pascal, these are defined in terms of *BLOCK*s, not statements. This means that the braces are required—no dangling statements allowed. If you want to write conditionals without braces there are several other ways to do it. The following all do the same thing:

```
if (!open(FOO, $foo)) { die "Can't open $foo: $!"; }

die "Can't open $foo: $!" unless open(FOO, $foo);

open(FOO, $foo) or die "Can't open $foo: $!";       # FOO or bust!

open(FOO, $foo) ? 'hi mom' : die "Can't open $foo: $!";
                    # a bit exotic, that last one
```

Your readers would tend to prefer the third of those under most circumstances.

If Statements

The **if** statement is straightforward. Since *BLOCKS* are always bounded by braces, there is never any ambiguity about which **if** an **else** or an **elsif** goes with. In any particular sequence of **if**/**elsif**/**else** *BLOCKS*, only the first one that has a true condition will be executed. If none of them is true, then the **else** *BLOCK*, if there is any, is executed.

If you use **unless** in place of **if**, the sense of the test is reversed. That is:

```
unless ($OS_ERROR) ...
```

is equivalent to:[*]

```
if (not $OS_ERROR) ...
```

Loop Statements

All compound loop statements have an optional *LABEL*. If present, the label consists of an identifier followed by a colon. It's customary to make the label upper case to avoid potential conflict with reserved words, and so it stands out better. (But don't use BEGIN or END!)

While statements

The **while** statement repeatedly executes the block as long as the *EXPR* is true. If the word **while** is replaced by the word **until**, the sense of the test is reversed. The conditional is still tested before the first iteration, though.

The **while** statement has an optional extra block on the end called a **continue** block. This is a block that is executed every time the block is continued, either by falling off the end of the first block, or by an explicit loop-control command that goes to the next iteration. The **continue** block is not heavily used in practice, but it's in there so we can define the **for** loop rigorously. So let's do that.

For loops

The C-style **for** loop has three semicolon-separated expressions within its parentheses. These three expressions function respectively as the initialization, the condition, and the re-initialization expressions of the loop. (All three expressions are optional, and the condition, if omitted, is assumed to be true.) The **for** loop can be defined in terms of the corresponding **while** loop.

---

[*] $OS_ERROR is the same as $! if you use English.

Thus, the following:

```
for ($i = 1; $i < 10; $i++) {
    ...
}
```

is the same as:

```
$i = 1;
while ($i < 10) {
    ...
}
continue {
    $i++;
}
```

(Defining the **for** loop in terms of a **continue** block allows us to preserve the correct semantics even when the loop is continued via a **next** statement. This is unlike C, in which there is no way to write the exact equivalent of a continued **for** loop without chicanery.)

If you want to iterate through two variables simultaneously, just separate the parallel expressions with commas:

```
for ($i = 0, $bit = 1; $mask & $bit; $i++, $bit <<= 1) {
    print "Bit $i is set\n";
}
```

Besides the normal array index looping, **for** can lend itself to many other interesting applications. There doesn't even have to be an explicit loop variable. Here's one example that avoids the problem you get into if you explicitly test for end-of-file on an interactive file descriptor, causing your program to appear to hang.

```
$on_a_tty = -t STDIN && -t STDOUT;
sub prompt { print "yes? " if $on_a_tty }
for ( prompt(); <STDIN>; prompt() ) {
    # do something
}
```

One final application for the **for** loop results from the fact that all three expressions are optional. If you do leave all three expressions out, you have written an "infinite" loop in a way that is customary in the culture of both Perl and C:

```
for (;;) {
    ...
}
```

If the notion of infinite loops bothers you, we should point out that you can always terminate such a loop from the inside with an appropriate loop-control command. Of course, if you're writing the code to control a cruise missile, you may not actually need to write a loop exit. The loop will be terminated automatically at the appropriate moment.[*]

Foreach loops

The **foreach** loop iterates over a list value and sets the control variable (*VAR*) to be each element of the list in turn:

```
foreach VAR (LIST) {
    ...
}
```

The variable is implicitly local to the loop and regains its former value upon exiting the loop. If the variable was previously declared with **my**, that variable instead of the global one is used, but it's still localized to the loop.

The **foreach** keyword is actually a synonym for the **for** keyword, so you can use **foreach** for readability or **for** for brevity. If *VAR* is omitted, **$_** is used. If *LIST* is an actual array (as opposed to an expression returning a list value), you can modify each element of the array by modifying *VAR* inside the loop. That's because the **foreach** loop index variable is an implicit alias for each item in the list that you're looping over. Our first two examples modify an array in place:

```
for (@ary) { s/ham/turkey/ }           # substitution

foreach $elem (@elements) {            # multiply by 2
    $elem *= 2;
}

for $count (10,9,8,7,6,5,4,3,2,1,'BOOM') { # do a countdown
    print $count, "\n"; sleep(1);
}

for $count (reverse 'BOOM', 1..10) {   # same thing
    print $count, "\n"; sleep(1);
}

for $item (split /:[\\\n:]*/, $TERMCAP) {   # any LIST expression
    print "Item: $item\n";
}

foreach $key (sort keys %hash) {       # sorting keys
    print "$key => $hash{$key}\n";
}
```

That last one is the canonical way to print out the values of a hash in sorted order.

Note that there is no way with **foreach** to tell where you are in a list. You can compare adjacent elements by remembering the previous one in a variable, but

---

[*] That is, the fallout from the loop tends to occur automatically.

sometimes you just have to break down and write an ordinary **for** loop with subscripts. That's what **for** is there for, after all.

Here's how a C programmer might code up a particular algorithm in Perl:

```
for ($i = 0; $i < @ary1; $i++) {
    for ($j = 0; $j < @ary2; $j++) {
        if ($ary1[$i] > $ary2[$j]) {
            last; # can't go to outer :-(
        }
        $ary1[$i] += $ary2[$j];
    }
    # this is where that last takes me
}
```

Whereas here's how a Perl programmer more comfortable with list processing might do it:

```
WID: foreach $this (@ary1) {
    JET: foreach $that (@ary2) {
        next WID if $this > $that;
        $this += $that;
    }
}
```

See how much easier this is? It's cleaner, safer, and faster. It's cleaner because it's less noisy. It's safer because if code gets added between the inner and outer loops later on, the new code won't be accidentally executed: **next** explicitly iterates the other loop rather than merely terminating the inner one. And it's faster because Perl executes a **foreach** statement more rapidly than it would the equivalent **for** loop because the elements are accessed directly instead of through subscripting.

Like the **while** statement, the **foreach** statement can also take a **continue** block.

We keep dropping hints about **next**, but now we're going to explain it.

Loop control

We mentioned that you can put a *LABEL* on a loop to give it a name. The loop's *LABEL* identifies the loop for the loop-control commands **next**, **last**, and **redo**. The *LABEL* names the loop as a whole, not just the top of the loop. Hence, a loop-control command referring to the loop doesn't actually "go to" the loop label itself. As far as the computer is concerned, the label could just as easily have been placed at the end of the loop. But people like things labeled at the top, for some reason.

Loops are typically named for the item the loop is processing on each iteration. This interacts nicely with the loop-control commands, which are designed to read like English when used with an appropriate label and a statement modifier. The

archetypical loop processes lines, so the archetypical loop label is `LINE:`, and the
archetypical loop-control command is something like this:

```
next LINE if /^#/;        # discard comments
```

The syntax for the loop-control commands is:

```
last LABEL
next LABEL
redo LABEL
```

The *LABEL* is optional, and if omitted, the loop-control command refers to the
innermost enclosing loop. If you want to break out more than one level, though,
you must use a *LABEL*. You may have as many loop-control commands in a loop as
you like.[*]

The **last** command is like the `break` statement in C (as used in loops); it immediately exits the loop in question. The **continue** block, if any, is not executed. The
following example bombs out of the loop on the first blank line:

```
LINE: while (<STDIN>) {
    last LINE if /^$/;      # exit when done with header
    ...
}
```

The **next** command is like the `continue` statement in C; it skips the rest of the current iteration and starts the next iteration of the loop. If there is a **continue** *BLOCK*
on the loop, it is always executed just before the conditional is about to be evaluated again, just like the third part of a C-style **for** loop. Thus it can be used to
increment a loop variable, even when a particular iteration of the loop has been
interrupted by a **next**:

```
LINE: while (<STDIN>) {
    next LINE if /^#/;      # skip comments
    next LINE if /^$/;      # skip blank lines
    ...
} continue {
    $count++;
}
```

The **redo** command restarts the loop block without evaluating the conditional
again. The **continue** block, if any, is not executed. This command is normally used
by programs that want to lie to themselves about what was just input.

---

[*] In the early days of structured programming, some people insisted that loops and subroutines have
only one entry and one exit. The one-entry notion is still a good idea, but the one-exit notion has led
people to write a lot of unnatural code. Much of programming consists of traversing decision trees. A
decision tree naturally starts with a single trunk but ends with many leaves. Write your code with the
number of loop exits (and function returns) that is natural to the problem you're trying to solve. If
you've declared your local variables with reasonable scopes, things will automatically get cleaned up at
the appropriate moment, whichever way you leave the block.

Suppose you are processing a file like */etc/termcap*. If your input line ends with a backslash to indicate continuation, skip ahead and get the next record.

```
while (<>) {
    chomp;
    if (s/\\$//) {
        $_ .= <>;
        redo;
    }
    # now process $_
}
```

which is Perl shorthand for the more explicitly written version:

```
LINE: while ($line = <ARGV>) {
    chomp($line);
    if ($line =~ s/\\$//) {
        $line .= <ARGV>;
        redo LINE;
    }
    # now process $line
}
```

One more point about loop-control commands. You may have noticed that we are not calling them "statements". That's because they aren't statements, though they can be used for statements. (This is unlike C, where break and continue are allowed *only* as statements.) You can almost think of them as unary operators that just happen to cause a change in control flow. So you can use them anywhere it makes sense to use them in an expression. In fact, you can even use them where it doesn't make sense. One sometimes sees this coding error:

```
open FILE, $file
    or warn "Can't open $file: $!\n", next FILE;   # WRONG
```

The intent is fine, but the next FILE is being parsed as one of the arguments to **warn**, which is a list operator. So the **next** executes before the **warn** gets a chance to emit the warning. In this case, it's easily fixed by turning the **warn** list operator into the **warn** function call with some suitably situated parentheses:

```
open FILE, $file
    or warn("Can't open $file: $!\n"), next FILE;   # okay
```

Bare Blocks and Case Structures

A *BLOCK* by itself (labeled or not) is semantically equivalent to a loop that executes once. Thus you can use **last** to leave the block or **redo** to restart the block.[*] Note

---

[*] For reasons that may (or may not) become clear upon reflection, a **next** also exits the once-through block. There is a slight difference, however, in that a **next** will execute a **continue** block, while a **last** won't.

that this is not true of the blocks in eval {}, sub {}, or do {} commands, which
are not loop blocks and cannot be labeled. They can't be labeled because they're
just terms in an expression. Loop control commands may only be used on true
loops, just as the **return** command may only be used within a subroutine or **eval**.
But you can always introduce an extra set of braces to give yourself a bare block,
which counts as a loop.

The bare block is particularly nice for doing case structures (multiway switches).

```
SWITCH: {
    if (/^abc/) { $abc = 1; last SWITCH; }
    if (/^def/) { $def = 1; last SWITCH; }
    if (/^xyz/) { $xyz = 1; last SWITCH; }
    $nothing = 1;
}
```

There is no official switch statement in Perl, because there are already several
ways to write the equivalent. In addition to the above, you could write: [*]

```
SWITCH: {
    $abc = 1, last SWITCH if /^abc/;
    $def = 1, last SWITCH if /^def/;
    $xyz = 1, last SWITCH if /^xyz/;
    $nothing = 1;
}
```

or:

```
SWITCH: {
    /^abc/ && do { $abc = 1; last SWITCH; };
    /^def/ && do { $def = 1; last SWITCH; };
    /^xyz/ && do { $xyz = 1; last SWITCH; };
    $nothing = 1;
}
```

or, formatted so it stands out more as a "proper" switch statement:

```
SWITCH: {
    /^abc/      && do {
                    $abc = 1;
                    last SWITCH;
                 };
    /^def/      && do {
                    $def = 1;
                    last SWITCH;
                 };
```

---

[*] This code is actually not as strange as it looks once you realize that you can use loop-control operators within an expression. That's just the normal scalar (C-style) comma operator between the assignment and the **last**. It evaluates the assignment for its side-effect, and then exits the loop in question,
which happens to be a bare block named SWITCH.

```
    /^xyz/        && do {
                        $xyz = 1;
                        last SWITCH;
                };
    $nothing = 1;
}
```

or:

```
SWITCH: {
    /^abc/      and $abc = 1, last SWITCH;
    /^def/      and $def = 1, last SWITCH;
    /^xyz/      and $xyz = 1, last SWITCH;
    $nothing = 1;
}
```

or even, horrors:

```
if     (/^abc/) { $abc = 1 }
elsif (/^def/) { $def = 1 }
elsif (/^xyz/) { $xyz = 1 }
else            { $nothing = 1 }
```

You might think it odd to write a loop over a single value, but a common idiom for a switch statement is to use **foreach**'s aliasing capability to make a temporary assignment to $_ for convenient matching:

```
for ($some_ridiculously_long_variable_name) {
    /In Card Names/    and do { push @flags, '-e'; last; };
    /Anywhere/         and do { push @flags, '-h'; last; };
    /In Rulings/       and do {              last; };
    die "unknown value for form variable where: `$where'";
}
```

Notice how the **last** commands in that example ignore the do {} blocks, which aren't loops, and exit the main loop instead.

Goto

Although not for the faint of heart (or the pure of heart, for that matter), Perl does support a **goto** command. There are three forms: goto *LABEL*, goto *EXPR*, and goto *&NAME*.

The goto *LABEL* form finds the statement labeled with *LABEL* and resumes execution there. It may not be used to go inside any construct that requires initialization, such as a subroutine or a **foreach** loop. It also can't be used to go into a construct that is optimized away. It can be used to go almost anywhere else within the current block or one you were called from, including out of subroutines, but it's usually better to use some other construct. The author of Perl has never felt the need to use this form of **goto** (in Perl, that is—C is another matter).

The goto *EXPR* form is just a generalization of goto *LABEL*. It expects the expression to return a label name, whose location obviously has to be resolved dynamically by the interpreter. (Don't expect this to work in compiled Perl.) This allows for computed gotos per FORTRAN, but isn't necessarily recommended if you're optimizing for maintainability:

```
goto ("FOO", "BAR", "GLARCH")[$i];
```

In almost all cases like this, it's usually a far, far better idea to use the structured control flow mechanisms of **next**, **last**, or **redo** instead of resorting to a **goto**. For certain applications, a hash of function pointers or the catch-and-throw pair of **eval** and **die** for exception processing can also be prudent approaches.

The goto *&NAME* form is highly magical, and quite different from an ordinary **goto**. It substitutes a call to the named subroutine for the currently running subroutine. This is used by AUTOLOAD subroutines that wish to load another subroutine and then pretend that the other subroutine had been called in the first place. After the **goto**, not even **caller** will be able to tell that this routine was called first. See Chapter 3 for a discussion of **caller** and Chapter 7 for AutoLoader.

Global Declarations

Subroutine and format declarations are global declarations. No matter where you place them, they declare global thingies (actually, package thingies, but packages are global) that are visible from everywhere. Global declarations can be put anywhere a statement can, but have no effect on the execution of the primary sequence of statements—the declarations take effect at compile time. Typically the declarations are put at the beginning or the end of your program, or off in some other file. However, if you're using lexically scoped private variables created with **my**, you'll want to make sure your format or subroutine definition is within the same block scope as the **my** if you expect to be able to access those private variables.*

Formats are bound to a filehandle and accessed implicitly via the **write** function. For more on formats, see "Formats" later in this chapter.

Subroutines are generally accessed directly, but don't actually have to be defined before calls to them can be compiled. The difference between a subroutine definition and a mere declaration is that the definition supplies a *BLOCK* containing the code to be executed, while the declaration doesn't. A subroutine definition can function as a declaration if the subroutine hasn't previously been declared.

---

* For esoteric reasons related to closures, lexicals, and the **foreach** aliasing mechanism, these **my** variables must not be the index variable of a **foreach** loop, because any named subroutine or format will only have been compiled with the first binding.

Declaring a subroutine allows a subroutine name to be used as if it were a list operator from that point forward in the compilation. You can declare a subroutine without defining it by just saying:

```
sub myname;
$me = myname $0            or die "can't get myname";
```

Note that it functions as a list operator, though, not as a unary operator, so be careful to use **or** instead of ||. The || binds too tightly to use after a list operator (at least, not without using extra parentheses to turn the list operator back into a function call).[*] You also need to define the subroutine at some point, or you'll get an error at run-time indicating that you've called an undefined subroutine.

Subroutine definitions can be loaded from other files with the **require** statement, but there are two problems with that. First, the other file will typically insert the subroutine names into a package (a namespace) of its own choosing, not your package. Second, a **require** happens at run-time, so the declaration occurs too late to serve as a declaration in the file invoking the **require**.

A more useful way to pull in declarations and definitions is via the **use** declaration, which essentially performs a **require** at compile time and then lets you import declarations into your own namespace. Because it is importing names into your own (global) package at compile time, this aspect of **use** can be considered a kind of global declaration. See Chapter 5 for details on this.

Scoped Declarations

Like global declarations, lexically scoped declarations have an effect at the time of compilation. Unlike global declarations, lexically scoped declarations have an effect only from the point of the declaration to the end of the innermost enclosing block. That's why we call them lexically scoped, though perhaps "textually scoped" would be more accurate, since lexical scoping has nothing to do with lexicons. But computer scientists the world around know what "lexically scoped" means, so we perpetuate the usage here.

We mentioned that some aspects of **use** could be considered global declarations, but there are other aspects that are lexically scoped. In particular, **use** is not only used to perform symbol importation but also to implement various magical *pragmas* (compiler hints). Most such pragmas are lexically scoped, including the use strict vars pragma that forces you to use lexically declared variables. See the section "Pragmas" below.

---

[*] Alternately, turn the subroutine into a unary operator with a prototype. But we haven't talked about that yet.

A **package** declaration, oddly enough, is lexically scoped, despite the fact that a package is a global entity. But a **package** declaration merely declares the identity of the default package for the rest of the enclosing block. Undeclared, unqualified variable names will be looked up in that package. In a sense, a package isn't declared at all, but springs into existence when you refer to a variable that belongs in the package. It's all very Perlish.

The most frequently seen form of lexically scoped declaration is the declaration of **my** variables. A related form of scoping known as *dynamic scoping* applies to **local** variables, which are really global variables in disguise. If you refer to a variable that has not been declared, its visibility is global by default, and its lifetime is forever. A variable used at one point in your program is accessible from anywhere else in the program.[*] If this were all there were to the matter, Perl programs would quickly become unwieldy as they grew in size. Fortunately, you can easily create private variables using **my**, and semi-private values of global variables using **local**. A **my** or a **local** declares the listed variables (in the case of **my**), or the values of the listed global variables (in the case of **local**), to be confined to the enclosing block, subroutine, **eval**, or file. If more than one variable is listed, the list must be placed in parentheses. All listed elements must be legal lvalues. (For **my** the constraints are even tighter: the elements must be simple scalar, array, or hash variables, and nothing else.) Here are some examples of declarations of lexically scoped variables:

```
my $name = "fred";
my @stuff = ("car", "house", "club");
my ($vehicle, $home, $tool) = @stuff;
```

(These declarations also happen to perform an initializing assignment at run-time.)

A **local** variable is *dynamically scoped*, whereas a **my** variable is *lexically scoped*. The difference is that any dynamic variables are also visible to functions called from within the block in which those variables are declared. Lexical variables are not. They are totally hidden from the outside world, including any called subroutines (even if it's the same subroutine called from itself or elsewhere—every instance of the subroutine gets its own copy of the variables).[†] In either event, the variable (or local value) disappears when the program exits the lexical scope in which the **my** or **local** finds itself. By and large, you should prefer to use **my** over

---

[*] To reiterate, even apparently global variables aren't really global—they're actually *package variables*. These work a bit like C's file static variables, or C++'s class static variables. Packages are used by libraries, modules, and classes to store their own private data so it doesn't conflict with data in your main program. If you see someone write `$Some::stuff` or `$Some'stuff`, they're using the `$stuff` scalar variable from the package `Some`. See Chapter 5.

[†] An **eval**, however, can see the lexical variables of the scope it is being evaluated in, so long as the names aren't hidden by declarations within the **eval** itself. Likewise, any anonymous subroutine (closure) created within the scope will also see such lexical variables. See Chapter 4 for more on closures.

local because it's faster and safer. But you have to use **local** if you want to temporarily change the value of an existing global variable, such as any of the special variables listed at the end of this chapter. Only alphanumeric identifiers may be lexically scoped. We won't talk much more about the semantics of **local** here. See **local** in Chapter 3 for more information.

Syntactically, **my** and **local** are simply modifiers (adjectives) on an lvalue expression. When you assign to a modified lvalue, the modifier doesn't change whether the lvalue is viewed as a scalar or a list. To figure how the assignment will work, just pretend that the modifier isn't there. So:

```
my ($foo) = <STDIN>;
my @FOO = <STDIN>;
```

both supply a list context to the right-hand side, while:

```
my $foo = <STDIN>;
```

supplies a scalar context.

The **my** binds more tightly (with higher precedence) than the comma does. The following only declares one variable because the list following **my** is not enclosed in parentheses:

```
my $foo, $bar = 1;
```

This has the same effect as:

```
my $foo;
$bar = 1;
```

(You'll get a warning about the mistake if you use **-w**.)

The declared variable is not introduced (is not visible) until after the current statement. Thus:

```
my $x = $x;
```

can be used to initialize the new inner $x with the value of the old outer $x. (Not that we recommend this style.) On the other hand, the expression:

```
my $x = 123 and $x == 123
```

is false unless the old $x just happened to have the value 123.

Declaring a lexical variable of a particular name hides any previously declared lexical variable of the same name. It also hides any unqualified global variable of the same name, but you can always get to the global variable by explicitly qualifying it with the name of the package the global is in.

For example:

```
$PackageName::varname
```

A statement sequence may contain declarations of lexically scoped variables, but apart from declaring variable names, the declarations act like ordinary statements, and each of them is elaborated within the sequence of statements as if it were an ordinary statement.

Pragmas

Many languages allow you to give hints to the compiler. In Perl these hints are conveyed to the compiler with the **use** declaration. Some of the pragmas are:

```
use integer
use strict
use lib
use sigtrap
use subs
use vars
```

All the Perl pragmas are described in Chapter 7, but we'll talk about some of the more useful ones here.

By default, Perl assumes that it must do much of its arithmetic in floating point. But by saying:

```
use integer;
```

you may tell the compiler that it's okay to use integer operations from here to the end of the enclosing block. An inner block may countermand this by saying:

```
no integer;
```

which lasts until the end of that inner block.

Some users may wish to encourage the use of lexical variables. As an aid to catching implicit references to package variables, if you say:

```
use strict 'vars';
```

then any variable reference from there to the end of the enclosing block must either refer to a lexical variable, or must be fully qualified with the package name. A compilation error results otherwise. An inner block may countermand this with:

```
no strict 'vars'
```

You can also turn on strict checking of symbolic references and barewords with this pragma. Often people say **use strict;** to turn on all three strictures.

Subroutines and variables that are imported from other modules have special privileges in Perl. Imported subroutines can *override* many built-in operators, and imported variables are exempt from use strict 'vars', since importation is considered a form of declaration. Sometimes you want to confer these privileges on your own subroutines and variables. You can do this with:

```
use subs qw(&read &write);
```

and:

```
use vars qw($fee $fie $foe $foo @sic);
```

Finally, Perl searches for modules in a standard list of locations. You need to be able to add to that list at compile time, because when you **use** modules they're loaded at compile time, and adding to the list at run-time would be too late. So you can put:

```
use lib "/my/own/lib/directory";
```

at the front of your program to do this. Note that these last three pragmas all modify global structures, and can therefore have effects outside of the current lexical scope.

Subroutines

Like many languages, Perl provides for user-defined subroutines. (We'll also call them *functions*, but functions are the same thing as subroutines in Perl.) These subroutines may be defined anywhere in the main program, loaded in from other files via the **do**, **require**, or **use** keywords, or even generated on the fly using **eval**. You can generate anonymous subroutines, accessible only through references. You can even call a subroutine indirectly using a variable containing either its name or a reference to the routine.

To declare a subroutine, use one of these forms:

```
sub NAME;              # A "forward" declaration.
sub NAME (PROTO);      # Ditto, but with prototype.
```

To declare and define a subroutine, use one of these forms:

```
sub NAME BLOCK         # A declaration and a definition.
sub NAME (PROTO) BLOCK # Ditto, but with prototype.
```

To define an anonymous subroutine or closure at run-time, use a statement like:

```
$subref = sub BLOCK;
```

To import subroutines defined in another package, say:

```
use PACKAGE qw(NAME1 NAME2 NAME3...);
```

To call subroutines directly:

```
NAME(LIST);             # & is optional with parentheses.
NAME LIST;              # Parens optional if predeclared/imported.
&NAME;                  # Passes current @_ to subroutine.
```

To call subroutines indirectly (by name or by reference):

```
&$subref(LIST);         # & is not optional on indirect call.
&$subref;               # Passes current @_ to subroutine.
```

The Perl model for passing data into and out of a subroutine is simple: all function parameters are passed as one single, flat list of scalars, and multiple return values are likewise returned to the caller as one single, flat list of scalars. As with any *LIST*, any arrays or hashes passed in these lists will interpolate their values into the flattened list, losing their identities—but there are several ways to get around this, and the automatic list interpolation is frequently quite useful. Both parameter lists and return lists may contain as many or as few scalar elements as you'd like (though you may put constraints on the parameter list using prototypes). Indeed, Perl is designed around this notion of *variadic* functions (those taking any number of arguments), unlike C, where they're sort of grudgingly kludged in so that you can call *printf*(3).

Now, if you're going to design a language around the notion of passing varying numbers of arbitrary arguments, you'd better make it easy to process those arbitrary lists of arguments. In the interests of dealing with the function parameters as a list, any arguments passed to a Perl routine come in as the array @_. If you call a function with two arguments, those would be stored in $_[0] and $_[1]. Since @_ is an array, you can use any array operations you like on the parameter list. (This is an area where Perl is *more* orthogonal than the typical computer language.) The array @_ is a local array, but its values are implicit references to the actual scalar parameters. Thus you can modify the actual parameters if you modify the corresponding element of @_. (This is rarely done, however, since it's so easy to return interesting values in Perl.)

The return value of the subroutine (or of any other block, for that matter) is the value of the last expression evaluated. Or you may use an explicit **return** statement to specify the return value and exit the subroutine from any point in the subroutine. Either way, as the subroutine is called in a scalar or list context, so also is the final expression of the routine evaluated in the same scalar or list context.

Perl does not have named formal parameters, but in practice all you do is assign the contents of @_ to a **my** list, which serves nicely for a list of formal parameters. But you don't have to, which is the whole point of the @_ array.

For example, to calculate a maximum, the following routine just iterates over @_ directly:

```
sub max {
    my $max = shift(@_);
    foreach $foo (@_) {
        $max = $foo if $max < $foo;
    }
    return $max;
}
$bestday = max($mon,$tue,$wed,$thu,$fri);
```

Here's a routine that ignores its parameters entirely, since it wants to keep a global lookahead variable:

```
# Get a line, combining continuation lines that start with whitespace

sub get_line {
    my $thisline = $LOOKAHEAD;
    LINE: while ($LOOKAHEAD = <STDIN>) {
        if ($LOOKAHEAD =~ /^[ \t]/) {
            $thisline .= $LOOKAHEAD;
        }
        else {
            last LINE;
        }
    }
    $thisline;
}

$LOOKAHEAD = <STDIN>;        # get first line
while ($_ = get_line()) {
    ...
}
```

Use list assignment to a private list to name your formal arguments:

```
sub maybeset {
    my($key, $value) = @_;
    $Foo{$key} = $value unless $Foo{$key};
}
```

This also has the effect of turning call-by-reference into call-by-value (to borrow some fancy terms from computer science), since the assignment copies the values.

Here's an example of *not* naming your formal arguments, so that you can modify your actual arguments:

```
upcase_in($v1, $v2);  # this changes $v1 and $v2
sub upcase_in {
    for (@_) { tr/a-z/A-Z/ }
}
```

You aren't allowed to modify constants in this way, of course. If an argument were actually a literal and you tried to change it, you'd take an exception (presumably fatal, possibly career-threatening). For example, this won't work:

```
upcase_in("frederick");
```

It would be much safer if the `upcase_in()` function were written to return a copy of its parameters instead of changing them in place:

```
($v3, $v4) = upcase($v1, $v2);
sub upcase {
    my @parms = @_;
    for (@parms) { tr/a-z/A-Z/ }
    # wantarray checks whether we were called in list context
    return wantarray ? @parms : $parms[0];
}
```

Notice how this (unprototyped) function doesn't care whether it was passed real scalars or arrays. Perl will see everything as one big, long, flat `@_` parameter list. This is one of the ways where Perl's simple argument-passing style shines. The `upcase` function will work perfectly well without changing the `upcase` definition even if we feed it things like this:

```
@newlist   = upcase(@list1, @list2);
@newlist   = upcase( split /:/, $var );
```

Do not, however, be tempted to do this:

```
(@a, @b)   = upcase(@list1, @list2);   # WRONG
```

Why not? Because, like the flat incoming parameter list, the return list is also flat. So all you have managed to do here is store everything in `@a` and make `@b` an empty list. See the later section on "Passing References" for alternatives.

The official name of a subroutine includes the `&` prefix. A subroutine may be called using the prefix, but the `&` is usually optional, and so are the parentheses if the subroutine has been predeclared. (Note, however, that the `&` is not optional when you're just naming the subroutine, such as when it's used as an argument to **defined** or **undef**, or when you want to generate a reference to a named subroutine by saying `$subref = \&name`. Nor is the `&` optional when you want to do an indirect subroutine call with a subroutine name or reference using the `&$subref()` or `&{$subref}()` constructs. See Chapter 4 for more on that.)

Subroutines may be called recursively. If a subroutine is called using the & form, the argument list is optional, and if omitted, no @_ array is set up for the subroutine: the @_ array of the calling routine at the time of the call is visible to called subroutine instead. This is an efficiency mechanism that new users may wish to avoid.

```
&foo(1,2,3);    # pass three arguments
foo(1,2,3);     # the same

foo();          # pass a null list
&foo();         # the same

&foo;           # foo() gets current args, like foo(@_) !!
foo;            # like foo() if sub foo pre-declared, else bareword "foo"
```

Not only does the & form make the argument list optional, but it also disables any prototype checking on the arguments you do provide. This is partly for historical reasons, and partly for having a convenient way to cheat if you know what you're doing. See the section on "Prototypes" later in this chapter.

Any variables you use in the function that aren't declared private are global variables. For more on creating private variables, see **my** in Chapter 3.

Passing Symbol Table Entries (Typeglobs)

Note that the mechanism described in this section was originally the only way to simulate pass-by-reference in older versions of Perl. While it still works fine in modern versions, the new reference mechanism is generally easier to work with. See below.

Sometimes you don't want to pass the value of an array to a subroutine but rather the name of it, so that the subroutine can modify the global copy of it rather than working with a local copy. In Perl you can refer to all objects of a particular name by prefixing the name with a star: *foo. This is often known as a *typeglob*, since the star on the front can be thought of as a wildcard match for all the funny prefix characters on variables and subroutines and such.

When evaluated, a typeglob produces a scalar value that represents all the objects of that name, including any scalar, array, or hash variable, and also any filehandle, format, or subroutine. When assigned to, a typeglob sets up its own name to be an alias for whatever typeglob value was assigned to it. For example:

```
sub doubleary {
    local(*someary) = @_;
    foreach $elem (@someary) {
        $elem *= 2;
    }
}
```

```
doubleary(*foo);
doubleary(*bar);
```

Note that scalars are already passed by reference, so you can modify scalar arguments without using this mechanism by referring explicitly to $_[0], and so on. You can modify all the elements of an array by passing all the elements as scalars, but you have to use the * mechanism (or the equivalent reference mechanism described below) to **push**, **pop**, or change the size of an array. It will certainly be faster to pass the typeglob (or reference) than to push a bunch of scalars onto the argument stack only to pop them all back off again.

Even if you don't want to modify an array, this mechanism is useful for passing multiple arrays in a single *LIST*, since normally the *LIST* mechanism will flatten all the list values so that you can't extract out the individual arrays.

Passing References

If you want to pass more than one array or hash into or out of a function and have them maintain their integrity, then you're going to want to use an explicit pass-by-reference. Before you do that, you need to understand references as detailed in Chapter 4. This section may not make much sense to you otherwise. But hey, you can always look at the pictures.

Here are a few simple examples. First, let's pass in several arrays to a function and have it **pop** each of them, returning a new list of all their former last elements:

```
@tailings = popmany ( \@a, \@b, \@c, \@d );

sub popmany {
    my $aref;
    my @retlist = ();
    foreach $aref ( @_ ) {
        push @retlist, pop @$aref;
    }
    return @retlist;
}
```

Here's how you might write a function that returns a list of keys occurring in all the hashes passed to it:

```
@common = inter( \%foo, \%bar, \%joe );
sub inter {
    my ($k, $href, %seen); # locals
    foreach $href (@_) {
        while ( ($k) = each %$href ) {
            $seen{$k}++;
        }
    }
    return grep { $seen{$_} == @_ } keys %seen;
}
```

So far, we're just using the normal list return mechanism. What happens if you want to pass or return a hash? Well, if you're only using one of them, or you don't mind them concatenating, then the normal calling convention is OK, although a little expensive.

Where people get into trouble is here:

```
(@a, @b) = func(@c, @d);
```

or here:

```
(%a, %b) = func(%c, %d);
```

That syntax simply won't work. It just sets @a or %a and clears @b or %b. Plus the function doesn't get two separate arrays or hashes as arguments: it gets one long list in @_, as always.

If you can arrange for the function to receive references as its parameters and return them as its return results, it's cleaner code, although not so nice to look at. Here's a function that takes two array references as arguments, returning the two array references ordered according to how many elements they have in them:

```
($aref, $bref) = func(\@c, \@d);
print "@$aref has more than @$bref\n";
sub func {
    my ($cref, $dref) = @_;
    if (@$cref > @$dref) {
        return ($cref, $dref);
    } else {
        return ($dref, $cref);
    }
}
```

It turns out that you can actually mix the typeglob approach with the reference approach, like this:

```
(*a, *b) = func(\@c, \@d);
print "@a has more than @b\n";
sub func {
    local (*c, *d) = @_;
    if (@c > @d) {
        return (\@c, \@d);
    } else {
        return (\@d, \@c);
    }
}
```

Here we're using the typeglobs to do symbol table aliasing. It's a tad subtle, though, and also won't work if you're using **my** variables, since only globals (well, and **locals**) are in the symbol table. When you assign a reference to a typeglob like that, only the one element from the typeglob (in this case, the array element) is aliased, instead of all the similarly named elements, since the reference knows what it's referring to.

If you're passing around filehandles, you can usually just use the bare typeglob, like *STDOUT, but references to typeglobs work even better because they still behave properly under use strict 'refs'. For example:

```
splutter(\*STDOUT);
sub splutter {
    my $fh = shift;
    print $fh "her um well a hmmm\n";
}

$rec = get_rec(\*STDIN);
sub get_rec {
    my $fh = shift;
    return scalar <$fh>;
}
```

If you're planning on generating new filehandles, see the **open** entry in Chapter 3 for an example using the FileHandle module.

Prototypes

As of the 5.003 release of Perl, you can declare your subroutines to take arguments just like many of the built-ins, that is, with certain constraints on the number and types of arguments. For instance, if you declare:

```
sub mypush (\@@)
```

then mypush takes arguments exactly like **push** does. The declaration of the function to be called must be visible at compile time. The prototype only affects the interpretation of new-style calls to the function, where new-style is defined as "not using the & character". In other words, if you call it like a built-in function, then it behaves like a built-in function. If you call it like an old-fashioned subroutine, then it behaves like an old-fashioned subroutine. It naturally falls out from this rule that prototypes have no influence on subroutine references like \&foo or on indirect subroutine calls like &{$subref}.

Method calls are not influenced by prototypes either. This is because the function to be called is indeterminate at compile-time, depending as it does on inheritance, which is dynamically determined in Perl.

Since the intent is primarily to let you define subroutines that work like built-in commands, here are the prototypes for some other functions that parse almost exactly like the corresponding built-ins. (Note that the "my" on the front of each is just part of the name we picked, and has nothing to do with Perl **my** operator. You can name your prototyped functions anything you like—we just picked our names to parallel the built-in functions.)

Declared as	Called as
sub mylink ($$)	mylink $old, $new
sub myvec ($$$)	myvec $var, $offset, 1
sub myindex ($$;$)	myindex &getstring, "substr"
sub mysyswrite ($$$;$)	mysyswrite $buf, 0, length($buf) - $off, $off
sub myreverse (@)	myreverse $a,$b,$c
sub myjoin ($@)	myjoin ":",$a,$b,$c
sub mypop (\@)	mypop @array
sub mysplice (\@$$@)	mysplice @array,@array,0,@pushme
sub mykeys (\%)	mykeys %{$hashref}
sub myopen (*;$)	myopen HANDLE, $name
sub mypipe (**)	mypipe READHANDLE, WRITEHANDLE
sub mygrep (&@)	mygrep { /foo/ } $a,$b,$c
sub myrand ($)	myrand 42
sub mytime ()	mytime

Any backslashed prototype character (shown between parentheses in the left column above) represents an actual argument (exemplified in the right column) that absolutely must start with that character. Just as the first argument to **keys** must start with %, so too must the first argument to mykeys.

Unbackslashed prototype characters have special meanings. Any unbackslashed @ or % eats all the rest of the actual arguments, and forces list context. (It's equivalent to *LIST* in a syntax diagram.) An argument represented by $ forces scalar context on it. An & requires an anonymous subroutine (which, if passed as the first argument, does not require the "sub" keyword or a subsequent comma). And a * does whatever it has to do to turn the argument into a reference to a symbol table entry. It's typically used for filehandles.

A semicolon separates mandatory arguments from optional arguments. (It would be redundant before @ or %, since lists can be null.)

Note how the last three examples above are treated specially by the parser. mygrep is parsed as a true list operator, myrand is parsed as a true unary operator with unary precedence the same as **rand**, and mytime is truly argumentless, just like **time**.

That is, if you say:

```
mytime +2;
```

you'll get `mytime() + 2`, not `mytime(2)`, which is how it would be parsed without the prototype, or with a unary prototype.

The interesting thing about `&` is that you can generate new syntax with it:

```
sub try (&$) {
    my($try,$catch) = @_;
    eval { &$try };
    if ($@) {
        local $_ = $@;
        &$catch;
    }
}
sub catch (&) { shift }

try {
    die "phooey";
} catch {
    /phooey/ and print "unphooey\n";
};
```

This prints "unphooey". What happens is that `try` is called with two arguments, the anonymous function `{die "phooey";}` and the return value of the `catch` function, which in this case is nothing but its own argument, the entire block of yet another anonymous function. Within `try`, the first function argument is called while protected within an **eval** block to trap anything that blows up. If something does blow up, the second function is called with a local version of the global `$_` variable set to the raised exception.[*] If this all sounds like pure gobbledygook, you'll have to read about **die** and **eval** in Chapter 3, and then go check out anonymous functions in Chapter 4.

And here's a reimplementation of the **grep** operator (the built-in one is more efficient, of course):

```
sub mygrep (&@) {
    my $coderef = shift;
    my @result;
    foreach $_ (@_) {
        push(@result, $_) if &$coderef;
    }
    @result;
}
```

---

[*] Yes, there are still unresolved issues having to do with the visibility of `@_`. We're ignoring that question for the moment. (But note that if we make `@_` lexically scoped someday, those anonymous subroutines can act like closures. (Gee, is this sounding a little Lispish? (Nevermind.)))

Some folks would prefer to see full alphanumeric prototypes. Alphanumerics have been intentionally left out of prototypes for the express purpose of someday adding named, formal parameters. (Maybe.) The current mechanism's main goal is to let module writers provide better diagnostics for module users. Larry feels that the notation is quite understandable to Perl programmers, and that it will not intrude greatly upon the meat of the module, nor make it harder to read. The line noise is visually encapsulated into a small pill that's easy to swallow.

One note of caution. It's probably best to put prototypes on new functions, not retrofit prototypes onto older ones. That's because you must be especially careful about silently imposing a different context. Suppose, for example, you decide that a function should take just one parameter, like this:

```
sub func ($) {
    my $n = shift;
    print "you gave me $n\n";
}
```

and someone has been calling it with an array or expression returning a single-element list:

```
func(@foo);
func( split /:/ );
```

Then you've just supplied an implicit **scalar** in front of their argument, which can be more than a bit surprising. The old @foo that used to hold one thing doesn't get passed in. Instead, 1 (the number of elements in @foo) is now passed to func. And the **split** gets called in a scalar context and starts scribbling on your @_ parameter list.

But if you're careful, you can do a lot of neat things with prototypes. This is all very powerful, of course, and should only be used in moderation to make the world a better place.

Formats

Perl has a mechanism to help you generate simple, formatted reports and charts. It can keep track of things like how many lines on a page, what page you're on, when to print page headers, and so on. Keywords are borrowed from FORTRAN: **format** to declare and **write** to execute; see the relevant entries in Chapter 3. Fortunately, the layout is much more legible, more like the PRINT USING statement of BASIC. Think of it as a poor man's *nroff*(1). (If you know *nroff,* that may not sound like a recommendation.)

Formats, like packages and subroutines, are declared rather than executed, so they may occur at any point in your program. (Usually it's best to keep them all together.) They have their own namespace apart from all the other types in Perl. This means that if you have a function named "Foo", it is not the same thing as a format named "Foo". However, the default name for the format associated with a given filehandle is the same as the name of the filehandle. Thus, the default format for STDOUT is named "STDOUT", and the default format for filehandle TEMP is named "TEMP". They just look the same. They really aren't.

Output record formats are declared as follows:

```
format NAME =
FORMLIST
.
```

If *NAME* is omitted, format STDOUT is defined. *FORMLIST* consists of a sequence of lines, each of which may be of one of three types:

- A comment, indicated by putting a # in the first column.

- A "picture" line giving the format for one output line.

- An argument line supplying values to plug into the previous picture line.

Picture lines are printed exactly as they look, except for certain fields that substitute values into the line.[*] Each substitution field in a picture line starts with either @ (at) or ^ (caret). These lines do not undergo any kind of variable interpolation. The @ field (not to be confused with the array marker @) is the normal kind of field; the other kind, the ^ field, is used to do rudimentary multiline text-block filling. The length of the field is indicated by padding out the field with multiple <, >, or | characters to specify, respectively, left justification, right justification, or centering. If the variable would exceed the width specified, it is truncated.

As an alternate form of right justification, you may also use # characters (after an initial @ or ^, and with an optional ".") to specify a numeric field. This way you can line up the decimal points. If any value supplied for these fields contains a newline, only the text up to the newline is printed. Finally, the special field @* can be used for printing multi-line, non-truncated values; it should generally appear on a picture line by itself.

The values are specified on the following line in the same order as the picture fields. The expressions providing the values should be separated by commas. The expressions are all evaluated in a list context before the line is processed, so a single list expression could produce multiple list elements. The expressions may be

---

[*] Even those fields maintain the integrity of the columns you put them in, however. There is nothing in a picture line that can cause fields to grow or shrink or shift back and forth. The columns you see are sacred in a WYSIWYG sense.

spread out to more than one line if enclosed in braces. If so, the opening brace must be the first token on the first line.

Picture fields that begin with ^ rather than @ are treated specially. With a # field, the field is blanked out if the value is undefined. For other field types, the caret enables a kind of fill mode. Instead of an arbitrary expression, the value supplied must be a scalar variable name that contains a text string. Perl puts as much text as it can into the field, and then chops off the front of the string so that the next time the variable is referenced, more of the text can be printed. (Yes, this means that the variable itself is altered during execution of the **write** call, and is not preserved. Use a scratch variable if you want to preserve the original value.) Normally you would use a sequence of fields in a vertical stack to print out a block of text. You might wish to end the final field with the text " . . . ", which will appear in the output if the text was too long to appear in its entirety. You can change which characters are legal to "break" on (or after) by changing the variable $: (that's $FORMAT_LINE_BREAK_CHARACTERS if you're using the English module) to a list of the desired characters.

Using ^ fields can produce variable-length records. If the text to be formatted is short, just repeat the format line with the ^ field in it a few times. If you just do this for short data you'd end up getting a few blank lines. To suppress lines that would end up blank, put a ~ (tilde) character anywhere in the line. (The tilde itself will be translated to a space upon output.) If you put a second tilde contiguous to the first, the line will be repeated until all the text in the fields on that line have been printed. (This works because the ^ fields chew up the strings they print. But if you use a field of the @ variety in conjunction with two tildes, the expression you supply had better not give the same value every time forever! Use a **shift**, or some other operator with a side effect that exhausts the set of values.)

Top-of-form processing is by default handled by a format with the same name as the current filehandle with "_TOP" concatenated to it. It's triggered at the top of each page. See **write** in Chapter 3.

Examples:

```
# a report on the /etc/passwd file
format STDOUT_TOP =
                        Passwd File
Name                Login   Office   Uid   Gid Home
-------------------------------------------------------------------
.

format STDOUT =
@<<<<<<<<<<<<<<<<<<< @|||||||  @<<<<<<@>>>> @>>>> @<<<<<<<<<<<<<<<<<<
$name,              $login,  $office,$uid,$gid, $home
.

# a report from a bug report form
```

```
format STDOUT_TOP =
                       Bug Reports
@<<<<<<<<<<<<<<<<<<<<<<<    @|||        @>>>>>>>>>>>>>>>>>>>>>>>
$system,                   $%,         $date
----------------------------------------------------------------------
.

format STDOUT =
Subject: @<<<<<<<<<<<<<<<<<<<<<<<<<<<<<<<<<<<<<<<<<<<<<<<<<<<<<<<
         $subject
Index: @<<<<<<<<<<<<<<<<<<<<<<<<<<< ^<<<<<<<<<<<<<<<<<<<<<<<<<<<<<<
       $index,                      $description
Priority: @<<<<<<<<< Date: @<<<<<<< ^<<<<<<<<<<<<<<<<<<<<<<<<<<<<<<
          $priority,      $date,    $description
From: @<<<<<<<<<<<<<<<<<<<<<<<<<<<<< ^<<<<<<<<<<<<<<<<<<<<<<<<<<<<<<
      $from,                         $description
Assigned to: @<<<<<<<<<<<<<<<<<<<<<< ^<<<<<<<<<<<<<<<<<<<<<<<<<<<<<<
             $programmer,            $description
~                                    ^<<<<<<<<<<<<<<<<<<<<<<<<<<<<<<
                                     $description
~                                    ^<<<<<<<<<<<<<<<<<<<<<<<<<<<<<<
                                     $description
~                                    ^<<<<<<<<<<<<<<<<<<<<<<<<<<<<<<
                                     $description
~                                    ^<<<<<<<<<<<<<<<<<<<<<<<<<<<<<<
                                     $description
~                                    ^<<<<<<<<<<<<<<<<<<<<<<<<<<<<...
                                     $description
.
```

It is possible to intermix **print**s with **write**s on the same output channel, but you'll
have to handle the **$-** special variable ($FORMAT_LINES_LEFT if you're using the
English module) yourself.

Format Variables

The current format name is stored in the variable **$~** ($FORMAT_NAME), and the current top-of-form format name is in **$^** ($FORMAT_TOP_NAME). The current output page
number is stored in **$%** ($FORMAT_PAGE_NUMBER), and the number of lines on the
page is in **$=** ($FORMAT_LINES_PER_PAGE). Whether to autoflush output on this han-
dle is stored in **$|** ($OUTPUT_AUTOFLUSH). The string to be output before each top of
page (except the first) is stored in **$^L** ($FORMAT_FORMFEED). These variables are set
on a per-filehandle basis, so you'll need to **select** the filehandle associated with a
format in order to affect its format variables.

```
select((select(OUTF),
        $~ = "My_Other_Format",
        $^ = "My_Top_Format"
       )[0]);
```

Pretty ugly, eh? It's a common idiom though, so don't be too surprised when you
see it. You can at least use a temporary variable to hold the previous filehandle

(this is a much better approach in general, because not only does legibility improve, but you now have an intermediary statement in the code to stop on when you're single-stepping the debugger):

```
$ofh = select(OUTF);
$~ = "My_Other_Format";
$^ = "My_Top_Format";
select($ofh);
```

If you use the English module, you can even read the variable names:

```
use English;
$ofh = select(OUTF);
$FORMAT_NAME      = "My_Other_Format";
$FORMAT_TOP_NAME = "My_Top_Format";
select($ofh);
```

But you still have those funny calls to **select**. So just use the FileHandle module. Now you can access these special variables using lowercase method names instead:

```
use FileHandle;
OUTF->format_name("My_Other_Format");
OUTF->format_top_name("My_Top_Format");
```

Much better!

Since the values line following your picture line may contain arbitrary expressions (for @ fields, not ^ fields), you can farm out more sophisticated processing to other functions, like **sprintf** or one of your own. For example, to insert commas into a number:

```
format Ident =
    @<<<<<<<<<<<<<<<
    commify($n)
.
```

To get a real @, ~, or ^ into the field, do this:

```
format Ident =
I have an @ here.
       "@"
.
```

To center a whole line of text, do something like this:

```
format Ident =
@|||||||||||||||||||||||||||||||||||||||||||||||||||||||||||||||||||||||
                    "Some text line"
.
```

The > field-length indicator ensures that the text will be right-justified within the field, but the field as a whole occurs exactly where you show it occurring. There is no built-in way to say "float this field to the right-hand side of the page, however wide it is." You have to specify where it goes relative to the left margin. The truly desperate can generate their own format on the fly, based on the current number of columns, and then **eval** it:

```
$format  = "format STDOUT = \n"
          . '^' . '<' x $cols . "\n"
          . '$entry' . "\n"
          . "\t^" . "<" x ($cols-8) . "~~\n"
          . '$entry' . "\n"
          . ".\n";
print $format if $Debugging;
eval $format;
die $@ if $@;
```

The most important line there is probably the **print**. What the **print** would print out looks something like this:

```
format STDOUT =
^<<<<<<<<<<<<<<<<<<<<<<<<<<<<<<<<<<<<<<<<<<<<<<<<<<<<<<<
$entry
     ^<<<<<<<<<<<<<<<<<<<<<<<<<<<<<<<<<<<<<<<<<<<<<<~~
$entry
.
```

Here's a little program that's somewhat like *fmt*(1):

```
format =
^<<<<<<<<<<<<<<<<<<<<<<<<<<<<<<<<<<<<<<<<<<<< ~~
$_


.

$/ = "";
while (<>) {
    s/\s*\n\s*/ /g;
    write;
}
```

Footers

While `$FORMAT_TOP_NAME` contains the name of the current header format, there is no corresponding mechanism to automatically do the same thing for a footer. Not knowing how big a format is going to be until you evaluate it is one of the major problems. It's on the TODO list.

Here's one strategy: If you have a fixed-size footer, you can get footers by checking `$FORMAT_LINES_LEFT` before each **write** and then **print** the footer yourself if necessary.

Here's another strategy; open a pipe to yourself, using open(MESELF, "|-") (see the **open** entry in Chapter 3) and always **write** to MESELF instead of STDOUT. Have your child process postprocess its STDIN to rearrange headers and footers however you like. Not very convenient, but doable.

Accessing Formatting Internals

For low-level access to the formatting mechanism, you may use **formline** and access $^A (the $ACCUMULATOR variable) directly. (Formats essentially compile into a sequence of calls to **formline**.) For example:

```
$str = formline <<'END', 1,2,3;
@<<<  @|||  @>>>
END

print "Wow, I just stored '$^A' in the accumulator!\n";
```

Or to make an **swrite()** subroutine which is to **write** as **sprintf** is to **printf**, do this:

```
use Carp;
sub swrite {
    croak "usage: swrite PICTURE ARGS" unless @_;
    my $format = shift;
    $^A = "";
    formline($format,@_);
    return $^A;
}

$string = swrite(<<'END', 1, 2, 3);
Check me out
@<<<  @|||  @>>>
END
print $string;
```

Lexical variables (declared with **my**) are not visible within a format unless the format is declared within the scope of the lexical variable.

Special Variables

The following names have special meaning to Perl. Most of the punctuational names have reasonable mnemonics, or analogs in one of the shells. Nevertheless, if you wish to use the long variable names, just say:

```
use English;
```

at the top of your program. This will alias all the short names to the long names in the current package. Some of them even have medium names, generally borrowed from *awk*(1).

A few of these variables are considered read-only. This means that if you try to assign to this variable, either directly, or indirectly through a reference, you'll raise a run-time exception.

Regular Expression Special Variables

There are several variables that are associated with regular expressions and pattern matching. Except for **$*** they are always local to the current block, so you never need to mention them in a **local**. (And **$*** is deprecated, so you never need to mention it at all.)

$*digit*

> Contains the text matched by the corresponding set of parentheses in the last pattern matched, not counting patterns matched in nested blocks that have been exited already. (Mnemonic: like *digit*.) These variables are all read-only.

$&
$MATCH

> The string matched by the last successful pattern match, not counting any matches hidden within a block or **eval** enclosed by the current block. (Mnemonic: like & in some editors.) This variable is read-only.

$`
$PREMATCH

> The string preceding whatever was matched by the last successful pattern match not counting any matches hidden within a block or **eval** enclosed by the current block. (Mnemonic: ` often precedes a quoted string.) This variable is read-only.

$'
$POSTMATCH

> The string following whatever was matched by the last successful pattern match not counting any matches hidden within a block or **eval** enclosed by the current block. (Mnemonic: ' often follows a quoted string.) Example:

```
$_ = 'abcdefghi';
/def/;
print "$`:$&:$'\n";        # prints abc:def:ghi
```

> This variable is read-only.

$+

$LAST_PAREN_MATCH

The last bracket matched by the last search pattern. This is useful if you don't know which of a set of alternative patterns matched. For example:

```
/Version: (.*)|Revision: (.*)/ && ($rev = $+);
```

(Mnemonic: be positive and forward looking.) This variable is read-only.

$*

$MULTILINE_MATCHING

Use of **$*** is now deprecated, and is allowed only for maintaining backwards compatibility with older versions of Perl. Use **/m** (and maybe **/s**) in the regular expression match instead.

Set to 1 to do multi-line matching within a string, 0 to tell Perl that it can assume that strings contain a single line for the purpose of optimizing pattern matches. Pattern matches on strings containing multiple newlines can produce confusing results when **$*** is 0. Default is 0. (Mnemonic: * matches multiple things.) Note that this variable only influences the interpretation of ^ and $. A literal newline can be searched for even when **$*** == 0.

Per-Filehandle Special Variables

These variables never need to be mentioned in a **local** because they always refer to some value pertaining to the currently selected output filehandle—each filehandle keeps its own set of values. When you **select** another filehandle, the old filehandle keeps whatever values it had in effect, and the variables now reflect the values of the new filehandle.

To go a step further and avoid **select** entirely, these variables that depend on the currently selected filehandle may instead be set by calling an object method on the FileHandle object. (Summary lines below for this contain the word *HANDLE*.) First you must say:

```
use FileHandle;
```

after which you may use either:

> *method HANDLE EXPR*

or:

> *HANDLE->method(EXPR)*

Each of the methods returns the old value of the FileHandle attribute. The methods each take an optional *EXPR*, which if supplied specifies the new value for the

FileHandle attribute in question. If not supplied, most of the methods do nothing to the current value, except for `autoflush`, which will assume a 1 for you, just to be different.

`$|`
`$OUTPUT_AUTOFLUSH`
`autoflush` *HANDLE EXPR*

> If set to nonzero, forces an *fflush* (3) after every **write** or **print** on the currently selected output channel. (This is called "command buffering". Contrary to popular belief, setting this variable does not turn off buffering.) Default is 0, which on many systems means that STDOUT will default to being line buffered if output is to the terminal, and block buffered otherwise. Setting this variable is useful primarily when you are outputting to a pipe, such as when you are running a Perl script under *rsh* and want to see the output as it's happening. This has no effect on input buffering. If you have a need to flush a buffer immediately after setting `$|`, you may simply `print ""`; rather than waiting for the next **print** to flush it. (Mnemonic: when you want your pipes to be piping hot.)

`$%`
`$FORMAT_PAGE_NUMBER`
`format_page_number` *HANDLE EXPR*

> The current page number of the currently selected output channel. (Mnemonic: `%` is page number in *nroff.*)

`$=`
`$FORMAT_LINES_PER_PAGE`
`format_lines_per_page` *HANDLE EXPR*

> The current page length (printable lines) of the currently selected output channel. Default is 60. (Mnemonic: = has horizontal lines.)

`$-`
`$FORMAT_LINES_LEFT`
`format_lines_left` *HANDLE EXPR*

> The number of lines left on the page of the currently selected output channel. (Mnemonic: `lines_on_page` - `lines_printed`.)

`$~`
`$FORMAT_NAME`
`format_name` *HANDLE EXPR*

> The name of the current report format for the currently selected output channel. Default is name of the filehandle. (Mnemonic: takes a turn after `$^`.)

$^
$FORMAT_TOP_NAME
format_top_name *HANDLE EXPR*

The name of the current top-of-page format for the currently selected output channel. Default is name of the filehandle with _TOP appended. (Mnemonic: points to top of page.)

Global Special Variables

There are quite a few variables that are global in the fullest sense—they mean the same thing in every package. If you want a private copy of one of these, you must localize it in the current block.

$_
$ARG

The default input and pattern-searching space. These pairs are equivalent:

```
while (<>) {...}    # only equivalent in while!
while (defined($_ = <>)) {...}

/^Subject:/
$_ =~ /^Subject:/

tr/a-z/A-Z/
$_ =~ tr/a-z/A-Z/

chop
chop($_)
```

Here are the places where Perl will assume $_ even if you don't use it:

- Various unary functions, including functions like **ord** and **int**, as well as all the file tests (-f, -d) except for -t, which defaults to STDIN.

- Various list functions like **print** and **unlink**.

- The pattern-matching operations m//, s///, and tr/// when used without an =~ operator.

- The default iterator variable in a **foreach** loop if no other variable is supplied.

- The implicit iterator variable in the **grep** and **map** functions.

- The default place to put an input record when a <FH> operation's result is tested by itself as the sole criterion of a **while** test. Note that outside of a **while** test, this will not happen.

Mnemonic: underline is the underlying operand in certain operations.

$.

$INPUT_LINE_NUMBER

$NR

> The current input line number of the last filehandle that was read. An explicit close on the filehandle resets the line number. Since <> never does an explicit close, line numbers increase across **ARGV** files (but see examples under **eof** in Chapter 3). Localizing **$.** has the effect of also localizing Perl's notion of the last read filehandle. (Mnemonic: many programs use "." to mean the current line number.)

$/

$INPUT_RECORD_SEPARATOR

$RS

> The input record separator, newline by default. It works like *awk*'s RS variable, and, if set to the null string, treats blank lines as delimiters. You may set it to a multi-character string to match a multi-character delimiter. Note that setting it to "\n\n" means something slightly different than setting it to "", if the file contains consecutive blank lines. Setting it to "" will treat two or more consecutive blank lines as a single blank line. Setting it to "\n\n" means Perl will blindly assume that the next input character belongs to the next paragraph, even if it's a third newline. (Mnemonic: / is used to delimit line boundaries when quoting poetry.)

```
undef $/;
$_ = <FH>;              # whole file now here
s/\n[ \t]+/ /g;
```

$,

$OUTPUT_FIELD_SEPARATOR

$OFS

> The output field separator for the **print** operator. Ordinarily the **print** operator simply prints out the comma separated fields you specify. In order to get behavior more like *awk*, set this variable as you would set *awk*'s OFS variable to specify what is printed between fields. (Mnemonic: what is printed when there is a "," in your **print** statement.)

$\

$OUTPUT_RECORD_SEPARATOR

$ORS

> The output record separator for the **print** operator. Ordinarily the **print** operator simply prints out the comma-separated fields you specify, with no trailing newline or record separator assumed. In order to get behavior more like *awk*, set this variable as you would set *awk*'s ORS variable to specify what is printed at the end of the **print**. (Mnemonic: you set $\ instead of adding "\n" at the end of the print. Also, it's just like /, but it's what you get "back" from Perl.)

`$"`

`$LIST_SEPARATOR`

This is like `$,` above except that it applies to list values interpolated into a double-quoted string (or similar interpreted string). Default is a space. (Mnemonic: obvious, I think.)

`$;`

`$SUBSCRIPT_SEPARATOR`

`$SUBSEP`

The subscript separator for multi-dimensional array emulation. If you refer to a hash element as:

        `$foo{$a,$b,$c}`

it really means:

        `$foo{join($;, $a, $b, $c)}`

But don't put:

        `@foo{$a,$b,$c}       # a slice--note the @`

which means:

        `($foo{$a},$foo{$b},$foo{$c})`

Default is `"\034"`, the same as SUBSEP in *awk*. Note that if your keys contain binary data there might not be any safe value for `$;`. (Mnemonic: comma— the syntactic subscript separator—is a semi-semicolon. Yeah, I know, it's pretty lame, but `$,` is already taken for something more important.)

This variable is for maintaining backward compatibility, so consider using "real" multi-dimensional arrays now.

`$^L`

`$FORMAT_FORMFEED`

`format_formfeed` *HANDLE EXPR*

What a format outputs to perform a formfeed. Default is `"\f"`.

`$:`

`$FORMAT_LINE_BREAK_CHARACTERS`

`format_line_break_characters` HANDLE EXPR

The current set of characters after which a string may be broken to fill continuation fields (starting with ^) in a format. Default is `" \n-"`, to break on whitespace or hyphens. (Mnemonic: a colon in poetry is a part of a line.)

$^A
$ACCUMULATOR

The current value of the **write** accumulator for **format** lines. A format contains **formline** commands that put their result into $^A. After calling its format, **write** prints out the contents of $^A and empties. So you never actually see the contents of $^A unless you call **formline** yourself and then look at it.

$#
$OFMT

Use of $# is now deprecated and is allowed only for maintaining backwards compatibility with older versions of Perl. You should use **printf** instead. $# contains the output format for printed numbers. This variable is a half-hearted attempt to emulate *awk*'s OFMT variable. There are times, however, when *awk* and Perl have differing notions of what is in fact numeric. Also, the initial value is approximately %.14g rather than %.6g, so you need to set $# explicitly to get *awk*'s value. (Mnemonic: # is the number sign. Better yet, just forget it.)

$?
$CHILD_ERROR

The status returned by the last pipe close, backtick (` `` `) command, or **system** operator. Note that this is the status word returned by the *wait*(2) system call, so the exit value of the subprocess is actually ($? >> 8). Thus on many systems, ($? & 255) gives which signal, if any, the process died from, and whether there was a core dump. (Mnemonic: similar to *sh* and *ksh*.)

$!
$OS_ERROR
$ERRNO

If used in a numeric context, yields the current value of the errno variable (identifying the last system call error) in the currently executing *perl*, with all the usual caveats. (This means that you shouldn't depend on the value of $! to be anything in particular unless you've gotten a specific error return indicating a system error.) If used in a string context, yields the corresponding system error string. You can assign to $! in order to set errno, if, for instance, you want $! to return the string for error *n*, or you want to set the exit value for the **die** operator. (Mnemonic: What just went bang?)

$@
$EVAL_ERROR

The Perl syntax error message from the last **eval** command. If null, the last **eval** was parsed and executed correctly (although the operations you invoked may have failed in the normal fashion). (Mnemonic: Where was the syntax error "at"?)

Note that warning messages are not collected in this variable. You can, however, set up a routine to process warnings by setting $SIG{__WARN__} below.

$$

$PROCESS_ID

$PID

The process number of the Perl running this script. (Mnemonic: same as shells.)

$<

$REAL_USER_ID

$UID

The real user ID (uid) of this process. (Mnemonic: it's the uid you came *from*, if you're running setuid.)

$>

$EFFECTIVE_USER_ID

$EUID

The effective uid of this process. Example:

```
$< = $>;            # set real to effective uid
($<,$>) = ($>,$<);  # swap real and effective uid
```

(Mnemonic: it's the uid you went *to*, if you're running setuid.) Note: **$<** and **$>** can only be swapped on machines supporting *setreuid*(2). And sometimes not even then.

$(

$REAL_GROUP_ID

$GID

The real group ID (gid) of this process. If you are on a machine that supports membership in multiple groups simultaneously, gives a space-separated list of groups you are in. The first number is the one returned by *getgid*(1), and the subsequent ones by *getgroups*(2), one of which may be the same as the first number. (Mnemonic: parentheses are used to *group* things. The real gid is the group you *left*, if you're running setgid.)

$)

$EFFECTIVE_GROUP_ID

$EGID

The effective gid of this process. If you are on a machine that supports membership in multiple groups simultaneously, **$)** gives a space-separated list of groups you are in. The first number is the one returned by *getegid*(2), and the subsequent ones by *getgroups*(2), one of which may be the same as the first number. (Mnemonic: parentheses are used to *group* things. The effective gid is the group that's *right* for you, if you're running setgid.)

Note: $<, $>, $(, and $) can only be set on machines that support the corresponding system set-id routine. $(and $) can only be swapped on machines supporting *setregid*(2). Because Perl doesn't currently use *initgroups*(2), you can't set your group vector to multiple groups.

`$0`
`$PROGRAM_NAME`

Contains the name of the file containing the Perl script being executed. Assigning to **$0** attempts to modify the argument area that the *ps*(1) program sees. This is more useful as a way of indicating the current program state than it is for hiding the program you're running. But it doesn't work on all systems. (Mnemonic: same as *sh* and *ksh*.)

`$[`   The index of the first element in an array, and of the first character in a substring. Default is 0, but you could set it to 1 to make Perl behave more like *awk* (or FORTRAN) when subscripting and when evaluating the **index** and **substr** functions. (Mnemonic: [begins subscripts.)

Assignment to **$[** is now treated as a compiler directive, and cannot influence the behavior of any other file. Its use is discouraged.

`$]`
`$PERL_VERSION`

Returns the version + patchlevel / 1000. It can be used to determine at the beginning of a script whether the Perl interpreter executing the script is in the right range of versions. Example:

```
warn "No checksumming!\n" if $] < 3.019;
die "Must have prototyping available\n" if $] < 5.003;
```

(Mnemonic: Is this version of Perl in the right bracket?)

`$^D`
`$DEBUGGING`

The current value of the debugging flags. (Mnemonic: value of **-D** switch.)

`$^F`
`$SYSTEM_FD_MAX`

The maximum system file descriptor, ordinarily 2. System file descriptors are passed to *exec*ed processes, while higher file descriptors are not. Also, during an **open**, system file descriptors are preserved even if the **open** fails. (Ordinary file descriptors are closed before the **open** is attempted, and stay closed if the **open** fails.) Note that the close-on-exec status of a file descriptor will be decided according to the value of **$^F** at the time of the **open**, not the time of the *exec*.

$^H

> This variable contains internal compiler hints enabled by certain pragmatic modules. Hint: ignore this and use the pragmata.

$^I
$INPLACE_EDIT

> The current value of the inplace-edit extension. Use **undef** to disable inplace editing. (Mnemonic: value of –i switch.)

$^O
$OSNAME

> This variable contains the name of the operating system the current Perl binary was compiled for. It's intended as a cheap alternative to pulling it out of the Config module.

$^P
$PERLDB

> The internal flag that the debugger clears so that it doesn't debug itself. You could conceivably disable debugging yourself by clearing it.

$^T
$BASETIME

> The time at which the script began running, in seconds since the epoch (the beginning of 1970, for UNIX systems). The values returned by the –M, –A, and –C filetests are based on this value.

$^W
$WARNING

> The current value of the warning switch, either true or false. (Mnemonic: the value is related to the –w switch.)

$^X
$EXECUTABLE_NAME

> The name that the Perl binary itself was executed as, from C's `argv[0]`.

$ARGV

> Contains the name of the current file when reading from <ARGV>.

Global Special Arrays

The following arrays and hashes are global. Just like the special global scalar variables, they refer to package main no matter when they are referenced. The following two statements are exactly the same:

```
print "@INC\n";
print "@main::INC\n";
```

@ARGV

The array containing the command-line arguments intended for the script. Note that $#ARGV is generally the number of arguments minus one, since $ARGV[0] is the first argument, not the command name. See **$0** for the command name.

@INC

The array containing the list of places to look for Perl scripts to be evaluated by the do EXPR, **require**, or **use** constructs. It initially consists of the arguments to any -I command-line switches, followed by the default Perl libraries, such as:

```
/usr/local/lib/perl5/$ARCH/$VERSION
/usr/local/lib/perl5
/usr/local/lib/perl5/site_perl
/usr/local/lib/perl5/site_perl/$ARCH
```

followed by ".", to represent the current directory. If you need to modify this list at run-time, you should use the lib module in order to also get the machine-dependent library properly loaded:

```
use lib '/mypath/libdir/';
use SomeMod;
```

@F The array into which the input lines are split when the **-a** command-line switch is given. If the **-a** option is not used, this array has no special meaning. (This array is actually only @main::F, and not in all packages at once.)

%INC

The hash containing entries for the filename of each file that has been included via **do** or **require**. The key is the filename you specified, and the value is the location of the file actually found. The **require** command uses this array to determine whether a given file has already been included.

%ENV

The hash containing your current environment. Setting a value in **%ENV** changes the environment for child processes:

```
$ENV{PATH} = "/bin:/usr/bin";
```

To remove something from your environment, make sure to use **delete** instead of **undef**.

Note that processes running as a *crontab* entry inherit a particularly impoverished set of environment variables. Also note that you should set $ENV{PATH}, $ENV{SHELL}, and $ENV{IFS} if you are running as a setuid script. See Chapter 8, *Other Oddments*, for more on security and setuid issues.

%SIG

The hash used to set signal handlers for various signals. Example:

```
sub handler {        # 1st argument is signal name
    local($sig) = @_;
    print "Caught a SIG$sig--shutting down\n";
    close(LOG);
    exit(0);
}

$SIG{INT} = 'handler';
$SIG{QUIT} = 'handler';
...
$SIG{INT} = 'DEFAULT';    # restore default action
$SIG{QUIT} = 'IGNORE';    # ignore SIGQUIT
```

The %**SIG** array only contains values for the signals actually set within the Perl script. Here are some other examples:

```
$SIG{PIPE} = Plumber;      # SCARY!!
$SIG{PIPE} = "Plumber";    # just fine, assumes main::Plumber
$SIG{PIPE} = \&Plumber;    # just fine; assume current Plumber
$SIG{PIPE} = Plumber();    # oops, what did Plumber() return??
```

The example marked SCARY!! is problematic because it's a bareword, which means sometimes it's a string representing the function, and sometimes it's going to call the subroutine right then and there! Best to be sure and quote it or take a reference to it. Certain internal hooks can also be set using the %**SIG** hash. The routine indicated by $SIG{__WARN__} is called when a warning message is about to be printed. The warning message is passed as the first argument. The presence of a __WARN__ hook causes the ordinary printing of warnings to STDERR to be suppressed. You can use this to save warnings in a variable, or turn warnings into fatal errors, like this:

```
local $SIG{__WARN__} = sub { die $_[0] };
eval $proggie;
```

The routine indicated by $SIG{__DIE__} is called when a fatal exception is about to be thrown. The error message is passed as the first argument. When a __DIE__ hook routine returns, the exception processing continues as it would have in the absence of the hook, unless the hook routine itself exits via a **goto**, a loop exit, or a **die**. The __DIE__ handler is explicitly disabled during the call, so that you yourself can then call the real **die** from a __DIE__ handler. (If it weren't disabled, the handler would call itself recursively forever.) The case is similar for __WARN__.

Global Special Filehandles

The following filehandles (except for DATA) always refer to `main::FILEHANDLE`.

ARGV

    The special filehandle that iterates over command line filenames in **@ARGV**. Usually written as the null filehandle in <>.

STDERR

    The special filehandle for standard error in any package.

STDIN

    The special filehandle for standard input in any package.

STDOUT

    The special filehandle for standard output in any package.

DATA

    The special filehandle that refers to anything following the __END__ token in the file containing the script. Or, the special filehandle for anything following the __DATA__ token in a required file, as long as you're reading data in the same package that the __DATA__ was found in.

_ (underline)

    The special filehandle used to cache the information from the last **stat**, **lstat**, or **file** test operator.

3

Functions

This chapter describes each of the Perl functions. They're presented one by one in alphabetical order. (Well, actually, some related functions are presented in pairs, or even threes or fours. This is usually the case when the Perl functions simply make UNIX system calls or C library calls. In such cases, the presentation of the Perl function matches up with the corresponding UNIX manpage organization.)

Each function description begins with a brief presentation of the syntax for that function. Parameters in *ALL_CAPS* represent placeholders for actual expressions, as described in the body of the function description. Some parameters are optional; the text describes the default values used when the parameter is not included.

The functions described in this chapter can serve as terms in an expression, along with literals and variables. (Or you can think of them as prefix operators. We call them operators half the time anyway.) Some of these operators, er, functions take a *LIST* as an argument. Such a list can consist of any combination of scalar and list values, but any list values are interpolated as a sequence of scalar values; that is, the overall argument *LIST* remains a single-dimensional list value. (To interpolate an array as a single element, you must explicitly create and interpolate a reference to the array instead.) Elements of the *LIST* should be separated by commas (or by =>, which is just a funny kind of comma). Each element of the *LIST* is evaluated in a list context.

The functions described in this chapter may be used either with or without parentheses around their arguments. (The syntax descriptions omit the parentheses.) If you use the parentheses, the simple (but occasionally surprising) rule is this: if it looks like a function, it is a function, and precedence doesn't matter. Otherwise it's a list operator or unary operator, and precedence does matter. And whitespace between the function and its left parenthesis doesn't count—so you need to be careful sometimes:

```
print 1+2+3;        # Prints 6.
print(1+2) + 3;     # Prints 3.
print (1+2)+3;      # Also prints 3!
print +(1+2)+3;     # Prints 6.
print ((1+2)+3);    # Prints 6.
```

If you run Perl with the **-w** switch it can warn you about this. For example, the third line above produces:

```
print (...) interpreted as function at - line 3.
Useless use of integer addition in void context at - line 3.
```

Some of the *LIST* operators impose special semantic significance on the first element or two of the list. For example, the **chmod** function requires that the first element of the list be the new permission to apply to the files listed in the remaining elements. Syntactically, however, the argument to **chmod** is really just a *LIST*, and you could say:

```
unshift @array,0644;
chmod @array;
```

which is the same as:

```
chmod 0644, @array;
```

In these cases, the syntax summary at the top of the section mentions only the bare *LIST*, and any special initial arguments are documented in the description.

On the other hand, if the syntax summary lists any arguments before the *LIST*, those arguments are syntactically distinguished (not just semantically distinguished), and may impose syntactic constraints on the actual arguments you pass to the function when you call it. For instance, the first argument to the **push** function must be an array name. (You may also put such syntactic constraints on your own subroutine declarations by the use of prototypes. See "Prototypes" in Chapter 2, *The Gory Details*.)

Many of these operations are based directly on the C library's functions. If so, we do not attempt to duplicate the UNIX system documentation for that function, but refer you directly to the manual page. Such references look like this: "See *getlogin*(3)." The number in parentheses tells you which section of the UNIX manual normally contains the given entry. If you can't find a manual page (manpage for short) for a particular C function on your system, it's likely that the corresponding Perl function is unimplemented. For example, not all systems implement *socket*(2) calls. If you're running in the MS-DOS world, you may have *socket* calls, but you won't have *fork*(2). (You probably won't have manpages either, come to think of it.)

Occasionally you'll find that the documented C function has more arguments than the corresponding Perl function. The missing arguments are almost always things that Perl already knows, such as the length of the previous argument, so you needn't supply them in Perl. Any remaining disparities are due to different ways Perl and C specify their filehandles and their success/failure values.

For functions that can be used in either scalar or list context, non-abortive failure is generally indicated in a scalar context by returning the undefined value, and in a list context by returning the null list. Successful execution is generally indicated by returning a value that will evaluate to true (in context).

Remember the following rule: *there is no general rule for converting a list into a scalar!*

Many operators can return a list in list context. Each such operator knows whether it is being called in scalar or list context, and in scalar context returns whichever sort of value it would be most appropriate to return. Some operators return the length of the list that would have been returned in list context. Some operators return the first value in the list. Some operators return the last value in the list. Some operators return the "other" value, when something can be looked up either by number or by name. Some operators return a count of successful operations. In general, Perl operators do exactly what you want, unless you want consistency.

Perl Functions by Category

Here are Perl's functions and function-like keywords, arranged by category. Some functions appear under more than one heading.

Scalar manipulation
> chomp, chop, chr, crypt, hex, index, lc, lcfirst, length, oct, ord, pack, q//, qq//, reverse, rindex, sprintf, substr, tr///, uc, ucfirst, y///

Regular expressions and pattern matching
> m//, pos, quotemeta, s///, split, study

Numeric functions
> abs, atan2, cos, exp, hex, int, log, oct, rand, sin, sqrt, srand

Array processing
> pop, push, shift, splice, unshift

List processing
> grep, join, map, qw//, reverse, sort, unpack

Hash processing
> delete, each, exists, keys, values

Input and output
> binmode, close, closedir, dbmclose, dbmopen, die, eof, fileno, flock, format, getc, print, printf, read, readdir, rewinddir, seek, seekdir, select (ready file descriptors), syscall, sysread, syswrite, tell, telldir, truncate, warn, write

Fixed-length data and records
> pack, read, syscall, sysread, syswrite, unpack, vec

Filehandles, files, and directories
> chdir, chmod, chown, chroot, fcntl, glob, ioctl, link, lstat, mkdir, open, opendir, readlink, rename, rmdir, select (ready file descriptors), select (output filehandle), stat, symlink, sysopen, umask, unlink, utime

Flow of program control
> caller, continue, die, do, dump, eval, exit, goto, last, next, redo, return, sub, wantarray

Scoping
> caller, import, local, my, package, use

Miscellaneous
> defined, dump, eval, formline, local, my, reset, scalar, undef, wantarray

Processes and process groups
> alarm, exec, fork, getpgrp, getppid, getpriority, kill, pipe, qx//, setpgrp, setpriority, sleep, system, times, wait, waitpid

Library modules
> do, import, no, package, require, use

Classes and objects
> bless, dbmclose, dbmopen, package, ref, tie, tied, untie, use

Low-level socket access
> accept, bind, connect, getpeername, getsockname, getsockopt, listen, recv, send, setsockopt, shutdown, socket, socketpair

System V interprocess communication
> msgctl, msgget, msgrcv, msgsnd, semctl, semget, semop, shmctl, shmget, shmread, shmwrite

Fetching user and group information
> endgrent, endhostent, endnetent, endpwent, getgrent, getgrgid, getgrnam, getlogin, getpwent, getpwnam, getpwuid, setgrent, setpwent

Fetching network information

> endprotoent, endservent, gethostbyaddr, gethostbyname, gethostent, getnetbyaddr, getnetbyname, getnetent, getprotobyname, getprotobynumber, getprotoent, getservbyname, getservbyport, getservent, sethostent, setnetent, setprotoent, setservent

Time

> gmtime, localtime, time, times

Perl Functions in Alphabetical Order

/PATTERN/

> /PATTERN/
> m/PATTERN/

The match operator. See "Regular Expressions" in Chapter 2.

?PATTERN?

> ?PATTERN?

This is just like the /PATTERN/ search, except that it matches only once between calls to **reset**, so it finds only the first occurrence of something rather than all occurrences. (In other words, the operator works repeatedly until it actually matches something, then it turns itself off until you explicitly turn it back on with **reset**.) This may be useful (and efficient) if you want to see only the first occurrence of the pattern in each file of a set of files. Note that m?? is equivalent to ??.

The **reset** operator will only reset instances of ?? that were compiled in the same package that it was.

abs

> abs VALUE

This function returns the absolute value of its argument (or $_ if omitted).

accept

> accept NEWSOCKET, GENERICSOCKET

This function does the same thing as the **accept** system call—see *accept*(2). It is used by server processes that wish to accept socket connections from clients. Execution is suspended until a connection is made, at which time the NEWSOCKET filehandle is opened and attached to the newly made connection. The function returns the connected address if the call succeeded, false otherwise (and puts the error code into $!). *GENERICSOCKET* must be a filehandle already opened via the **socket** operator and bound to one of the server's network addresses. For example:

```
unless ($peer = accept NS, S) {
    die "Can't accept a connection: $!\n";
}
```

See also the example in the section "Sockets" in Chapter 6, *Social Engineering*.

alarm

```
alarm EXPR
```

This function sends a SIGALRM signal to the executing Perl program after *EXPR* seconds. On some older systems, alarms go off at the "top of the second," so, for instance, an **alarm** 1 may go off anywhere between 0 to 1 second from now, depending on when in the current second it is. An **alarm** 2 may go off anywhere from 1 to 2 seconds from now. And so on. For better resolution, you may be able to use **syscall** to call the *itimer* routines that some UNIX systems support. Or you can use the timeout feature of the **select** function.

Each call disables the previous timer, and an argument of 0 may be supplied to cancel the previous timer without starting a new one. The return value is the number of seconds remaining on the previous timer.

atan2

```
atan2 Y, X
```

This function returns the arctangent of Y/X in the range $-\pi$ to π. A quick way to get an approximate value of π is to say:

```
$pi = atan2(1,1) * 4;
```

For the tangent operation, you may use the POSIX::tan() function, or use the familiar relation:

```
sub tan { sin($_[0]) / cos($_[0]) }
```

bind

```
bind SOCKET, NAME
```

This function does the same thing as the **bind** system call—see *bind*(2). It attaches an address (a name) to an already opened socket specified by the *SOCKET* filehandle. The function returns true if it succeeded, false otherwise (and puts the error code into $!). *NAME* should be a packed address of the proper type for the socket.

```
bind S, $sockaddr or die "Can't bind address: $!\n";
```

See also the example in the section "Sockets" in Chapter 6.

binmode

```
binmode FILEHANDLE
```

This function arranges for the file to be treated in binary mode on operating systems that distinguish between binary and text files. It should be called after the **open** but before any I/O is done on the filehandle. The only way to reset binary mode on a filehandle is to reopen the file.

On systems that distinguish binary mode from text mode, files that are read in text mode have \r\n sequences translated to \n on input and \n translated to \r\n on output. **binmode** has no effect under UNIX or Plan9. If *FILEHANDLE* is an expression, the value is taken as the name of the filehandle. The following example shows how a Perl script might prepare to read a word processor file with embedded control codes:

```
open WP, "$file.wp" or die "Can't open $file.wp: $!\n";
binmode WP;
while (read WP, $buf, 1024) {...}
```

bless

```
bless REF, CLASSNAME
bless REF
```

This function looks up the item pointed to by reference *REF* and tells the item that it is now an object in the *CLASSNAME* package—or the current package if no *CLASS-NAME* is specified, which is often the case. It returns the reference for convenience, since a **bless** is often the last thing in a constructor function. (Always use the two-argument version if the constructor doing the blessing might be inherited by a derived class. In such cases, the class you want to bless your object into will normally be found as the first argument to the constructor in question.) See "Objects" in Chapter 5, *Packages, Modules, and Object Classes* for more about the blessing (and blessings) of objects.

caller

```
caller EXPR
caller
```

This function returns information about the stack of current subroutine calls. Without an argument it returns the package name, filename, and line number that the currently executing subroutine was called from:

```
($package, $filename, $line) = caller;
```

With an argument it evaluates *EXPR* as the number of stack frames to go back before the current one. It also reports some additional information.

```
$i = 0;
while (($pack, $file, $line, $subname, $hasargs, $wantarray) = caller($i++)) {
    ...
}
```

Furthermore, when called from within the DB package, **caller** returns more detailed information: it sets the list variable @DB::args to be the arguments passed in the given stack frame.

chdir

```
chdir EXPR
```

This function changes the working directory to *EXPR*, if possible. If *EXPR* is omitted, it changes to the home directory. The function returns 1 upon success, 0 otherwise (and puts the error code into $!).

```
chdir "$prefix/lib" or die "Can't cd to $prefix/lib: $!\n";
```

The following code can be used to move to the user's home directory, one way or another:

```
$ok = chdir($ENV{"HOME"} || $ENV{"LOGDIR"} || (getpwuid($<))[7]);
```

Alternately, taking advantage of the default, you could say this:

```
$ok = chdir() || chdir((getpwuid($<))[7]);
```

See also the Cwd module, described in Chapter 7, *The Standard Perl Library*, which lets you keep track of your current directory.

chmod

```
chmod LIST
```

This function changes the permissions of a list of files. The first element of the list must be the numerical mode, as in *chmod*(2). (When using nonliteral mode data, you may need to convert an octal string to a decimal number using the **oct** function.) The function returns the number of files successfully changed. For example:

```
$cnt = chmod 0755, 'file1', 'file2';
```

will set $cnt to 0, 1, or 2, depending on how many files got changed (in the sense that the operation succeeded, not in the sense that the bits were different afterward). Here's a more typical usage:

```
chmod 0755, @executables;
```

If you need to know which files didn't allow the change, use something like this:

```
@cannot = grep {not chmod 0755, $_} 'file1', 'file2', 'file3';
die "$0: could not chmod @cannot\n" if @cannot;
```

This idiom makes use of the **grep** function to select only those elements of the list for which the **chmod** function failed.

chomp

```
chomp VARIABLE
chomp LIST
chomp
```

This is a slightly safer version of **chop** (see below) in that it removes only any line ending corresponding to the current value of $/, and not just any last character. Unlike **chop**, **chomp** returns the number of characters deleted. If $/ is empty (in paragraph mode), **chomp** removes all trailing newlines from the selected string (or strings, if chomping a *LIST*).

chop

```
chop VARIABLE
chop LIST
chop
```

This function chops off the last character of a string and returns the character chopped. The **chop** operator is used primarily to remove the newline from the end of an input record, but is more efficient than s/\n$//. If *VARIABLE* is omitted, the function chops the $_ variable. For example:

```
while (<PASSWD>) {
    chop;   # avoid \n on last field
    @array = split /:/;
    ...
}
```

If you chop a *LIST*, each string in the list is chopped:

```
@lines = `cat myfile`;
chop @lines;
```

You can actually chop anything that is an lvalue, including an assignment:

```
chop($cwd = `pwd`);
chop($answer = <STDIN>);
```

Note that this is different from:

```
$answer = chop($tmp = <STDIN>);  # WRONG
```

which puts a newline into $answer, because **chop** returns the character chopped, not the remaining string (which is in $tmp). One way to get the result intended here is with **substr**:

```
$answer = substr <STDIN>, 0, -1;
```

But this is more commonly written as:

```
chop($answer = <STDIN>);
```

To chop more than one character, use **substr** as an lvalue, assigning a null string. The following removes the last five characters of $caravan:

```
substr($caravan, -5) = "";
```

The negative subscript causes **substr** to count from the end of the string instead of the beginning.

chown

```
chown LIST
```

This function changes the owner (and group) of a list of files. The first two elements of the list must be the *numerical* uid and gid, in that order. The function returns the number of files successfully changed. For example:

```
$cnt = chown $uid, $gid, 'file1', 'file2';
```

will set $cnt to 0, 1, or 2, depending on how many files got changed (in the sense that the operation succeeded, not in the sense that the owner was different afterward). Here's a more typical usage:

```
chown $uid, $gid, @filenames;
```

Here's a subroutine that looks everything up for you, and then does the **chown**:

```
sub chown_by_name {
    local($user, $pattern) = @_;
    chown((getpwnam($user))[2,3], glob($pattern));
```

```
}

&chown_by_name("fred", "*.c");
```

Notice that this forces the group of each file to be the gid fetched from the *passwd* file. An alternative is to pass a -1 for the gid, which leaves the group of the file unchanged.

On most systems, you are not allowed to change the ownership of the file unless you're the superuser, although you should be able to change the group to any of your secondary groups. On insecure systems, these restrictions may be relaxed, but this is not a portable assumption.

chr

```
chr NUMBER
```

This function returns the character represented by that *NUMBER* in the character set. For example, chr(65) is "A" in ASCII. To convert multiple characters, use pack("C*", *LIST*) instead.

chroot

```
chroot FILENAME
```

This function does the same operation as the **chroot** system call—see *chroot*(2). If successful, *FILENAME* becomes the new root directory for the current process—the starting point for pathnames beginning with "/". This directory is inherited across *exec* calls and by all subprocesses. There is no way to undo a **chroot**. Only the superuser can use this function. Here's some code that approximates what many FTP servers do:

```
chroot +(getpwnam('ftp'))[7]
    or die "Can't do anonymous ftp: $!\n";
```

close

```
close FILEHANDLE
```

This function closes the file, socket, or pipe associated with the filehandle. You don't have to close *FILEHANDLE* if you are immediately going to do another **open** on it, since the next **open** will close it for you. (See **open**.) However, an explicit **close** on an input file resets the line counter ($.), while the implicit close done by **open** does not. Also, closing a pipe will wait for the process executing on the pipe to complete (in case you want to look at the output of the pipe afterward), and it prevents the script from exiting before the pipeline is finished.[*] Closing a pipe explicitly also puts the status value of the command executing on the pipe into $?. For example:

```
open OUTPUT, '|sort >foo';      # pipe to sort
...                             # print stuff to output
close OUTPUT;                    # wait for sort to finish
die "sort failed" if $?;        # check for sordid sort
open INPUT, 'foo';              # get sort's results
```

FILEHANDLE may be an expression whose value gives the real filehandle name. It may also be a reference to a filehandle object returned by some of the newer object-oriented I/O packages.

closedir

```
closedir DIRHANDLE
```

This function closes a directory opened by **opendir**. See the examples under **readdir**.

connect

```
connect SOCKET, NAME
```

This function does the same thing as the **connect** system call—see *connect*(2). The function initiates a connection with another process that is waiting at an *accept*(2). The function returns true if it succeeded, false otherwise (and puts the error code into $!). *NAME* should be a packed network address of the proper type for the socket. For example:

```
connect S, $destadd
    or die "Can't connect to $hostname: $!\n";
```

To disconnect a socket, either **close** or **shutdown**. See also the example in the section "Sockets" in Chapter 6.

cos

```
cos EXPR
```

This function returns the cosine of *EXPR* (expressed in radians). For example, the following script will print a cosine table of angles measured in degrees:

---

[*] Note, however, that a *dup*'ed pipe is treated as an ordinary filehandle, and **close** will not wait for the child on that filehandle. You have to wait for the child by closing the filehandle on which it was originally opened.

```
# Here's the lazy way of getting degrees-to-radians.

$pi = atan2(1,1) * 4;
$piover180 = $pi/180;

# Print table.

for ($_ = 0; $_ <= 90; $_++) {
    printf "%3d %7.5f\n", $_, cos($_ * $piover180);
}
```

For the inverse cosine operation, you may use the POSIX::acos() function, or use this relation:

```
sub acos { atan2( sqrt(1 - $_[0] * $_[0]), $_[0] ) }
```

crypt

```
crypt PLAINTEXT, SALT
```

This function encrypts a string exactly in the manner of *crypt*(3). This is useful for checking the password file for lousy passwords.[*] Only the guys wearing white hats are allowed to do this.

To see whether a typed-in password $guess matches the password $pass obtained from a file (such as */etc/passwd*), try something like the following:

```
if (crypt($guess, $pass) eq $pass) {
    # guess is correct
}
```

Note that there is no easy way to decrypt an encrypted password apart from guessing. Also, truncating the salt to two characters is a waste of CPU time, although the manpage for *crypt*(3) would have you believe otherwise.

Here's an example that makes sure that whoever runs this program knows their own password:

```
$pwd = (getpwuid ($<))[1];
$salt = substr $pwd, 0, 2;

system "stty -echo";
print "Password: ";
chop($word = <STDIN>);
print "\n";
system "stty echo";

if (crypt($word, $salt) ne $pwd) {
    die "Sorry...\n";
} else {
```

---

[*] What you really want to do is prevent people from adding the bad passwords in the first place.

```
    print "ok\n";
}
```

Of course, typing in your own password to whoever asks for it is unwise.

The **crypt** function is unsuitable for encrypting large quantities of data. Find a library module for PGP (or something like that) for something like that.

dbmclose

```
dbmclose HASH
```

This function breaks the binding between a DBM file and a hash.

This function is actually just a call to **untie** with the proper arguments, but is provided for backward compatibility with older versions of Perl.

dbmopen

```
dbmopen HASH, DBNAME, MODE
```

This binds a DBM file to a hash (that is, an associative array). (DBM stands for Data Base Management, and consists of a set of C library routines that allow random access to records via a hashing algorithm.) *HASH* is the name of the hash (with a %). *DBNAME* is the name of the database (without the .dir or .pag extension). If the database does not exist, and a valid *MODE* is specified, the database is created with the protection specified by *MODE* (as modified by the umask). To prevent creation of the database if it doesn't exist, you may specify a *MODE* of **undef**, and the function will return a false value if it can't find an existing database. If your system supports only the older DBM functions, you may have only one **dbmopen** in your program.

Values assigned to the hash prior to the **dbmopen** are not accessible.

If you don't have write access to the DBM file, you can only read the hash variables, not set them. If you want to test whether you can write, either use file tests or try setting a dummy array entry inside an **eval**, which will trap the error.

Note that functions such as **keys** and **values** may return huge list values when used on large DBM files. You may prefer to use the **each** function to iterate over large DBM files. This example prints out the mail aliases on a system using *sendmail*:

```
dbmopen %ALIASES, "/etc/aliases", 0666
    or die "Can't open aliases: $!\n";

while (($key,$val) = each %ALIASES) {
    print $key, ' = ', $val, "\n";
}
dbmclose %ALIASES;
```

Hashes bound to DBM files have the same limitations as DBM files, in particular the restrictions on how much you can put into a bucket. If you stick to short keys and values, it's rarely a problem. Another thing you should bear in mind is that many existing DBM databases contain null-terminated keys and values because they were set up with C programs in mind. The B News history file and the old *sendmail* aliases file are examples. Just use `"$key\0"` instead of `$key`.

There is currently no built-in way to lock generic DBM files. Some would consider this a bug. The DB_File module does provide locking at the granularity of the entire file, however. See the documentation on that module in Chapter 7 for details.

This function is actually just a call to **tie** with the proper arguments, but is provided for backward compatibility with older versions of Perl.

defined

```
defined EXPR
```

This function returns a Boolean value saying whether *EXPR* has a real value or not. A scalar that contains no valid string, numeric, or reference value is known as the undefined value, or **undef** for short. Many operations return the undefined value under exceptional conditions, such as end of file, uninitialized variable, system error, and such. This function allows you to distinguish between an undefined null string and a defined null string when you're using operators that might return a real null string.

You may also check to see whether arrays, hashes, or subroutines have been allocated any memory yet. Arrays and hashes are allocated when you first put something into them, whereas subroutines are allocated when a definition has been successfully parsed. Using **defined** on the predefined special variables is not guaranteed to produce intuitive results.

Here is a fragment that tests a scalar value from a hash:

```
print if defined $switch{'D'};
```

When used on a hash element like this, **defined** only tells you whether the value is defined, not whether the key has an entry in the hash table. It's possible to have an undefined scalar value for an existing hash key. Use **exists** to determine whether the hash key exists.

In the next example we use the fact that some operations return the undefined value when you run out of data:

```
print "$val\n" while defined($val = pop(@ary));
```

The same thing goes for error returns from system calls:

```
die "Can't readlink $sym: $!"
    unless defined($value = readlink $sym);
```

Since symbol tables for packages are stored as hashes (associative arrays), it's possible to check for the existence of a package like this:

```
die "No XYZ package defined" unless defined %XYZ::;
```

Finally, it's possible to avoid blowing up on nonexistent subroutines:

```
sub saymaybe {
    if (defined &say) {
        say(@_);
    }
    else {
        warn "Can't say";
    }
}
```

See also **undef**.

delete

```
delete EXPR
```

This function deletes the specified key and associated value from the specified hash. (It doesn't delete a file. See **unlink** for that.) Deleting from $ENV{} modifies the environment. Deleting from a hash that is bound to a (writable) DBM file deletes the entry from the DBM file.

The following naïve example inefficiently deletes all the values of a hash:

```
foreach $key (keys %HASH) {
    delete $HASH{$key};
}
```

(It would be faster to use the **undef** command on the whole hash.) *EXPR* can be arbitrarily complicated as long as the final operation is a hash key lookup:

```
delete $ref->[$x][$y]{$key};
```

For normal hashes, the **delete** function happens to return the value (not the key) that was deleted, but this behavior is not guaranteed for tied hashes, such as those bound to DBM files.

To test whether a hash element has been deleted, use **exists**.

die

>   die *LIST*

Outside of an **eval**, this function prints the concatenated value of *LIST* to STDERR and exits with the current value of **$!** (errno). If **$!** is 0, it exits with the value of ($? >> 8) (which is the status of the last reaped child from a **system**, **wait**, **close** on a pipe, or `command`). If ($? >> 8) is 0, it exits with 255. If *LIST* is unspecified, the current value of the **$@** variable is propagated, if any. Otherwise the string "Died" is used as the default.

Equivalent examples:

>   die "Can't cd to spool: $!\n" unless chdir '/usr/spool/news';

>   chdir '/usr/spool/news' or die "Can't cd to spool: $!\n"

(The second form is generally preferred, since the important part is the **chdir**.)

Within an **eval**, the function sets the **$@** variable equal to the error message that would have been produced otherwise, and aborts the **eval**, which then returns the undefined value. The **die** function can thus be used to raise named exceptions that can be caught at a higher level in the program. See the section on the **eval** function later in this chapter.

If the final value of *LIST* does not end in a newline, the current script filename, line number, and input line number (if any) are appended to the message, as well as a newline. Hint: sometimes appending ", stopped" to your message will cause it to make better sense when the string "at scriptname line 123" is appended. Suppose you are running script *canasta*:

>   die "/etc/games is no good";
>   die "/etc/games is no good, stopped";

which produces, respectively:

>   /etc/games is no good at canasta line 123.
>   /etc/games is no good, stopped at canasta line 123.

If you want your own error messages reporting the filename and linenumber, use the _ _FILE_ _ and _ _LINE_ _ special tokens:

>   die '"', _ _FILE_ _, '"', line ', _ _LINE_ _, ", phooey on you!\n";

This produces output like:

>   "canasta", line 38, phooey on you!

See also **exit** and **warn**.

do

```
do BLOCK
do SUBROUTINE(LIST)
do EXPR
```

The do *BLOCK* form executes the sequence of commands in the *BLOCK*, and returns the value of the last expression evaluated in the block. When modified by a loop modifier, Perl executes the *BLOCK* once before testing the loop condition. (On other statements the loop modifiers test the conditional first.)

The do *SUBROUTINE(LIST)* is a deprecated form of a subroutine call. See "Subroutines" in Chapter 2.

The do *EXPR* form uses the value of *EXPR* as a filename and executes the contents of the file as a Perl script. Its primary use is (or rather was) to include subroutines from a Perl subroutine library, so that:

```
do 'stat.pl';
```

is rather like:

```
eval `cat stat.pl`;
```

except that it's more efficient, more concise, keeps track of the current filename for error messages, and searches all the directories listed in the @INC array. (See the section on "Special Variables" in Chapter 2.) It's the same, however, in that it does reparse the file every time you call it, so you probably don't want to do this inside a loop.

Note that inclusion of library modules is better done with the **use** and **require** operators, which also do error checking and raise an exception if there's a problem.

dump

```
dump LABEL
dump
```

This function causes an immediate core dump. Primarily this is so that you can use *undump*(1) to turn your core dump into an executable binary after having initialized all your variables at the beginning of the program. (The *undump* program is not supplied with the Perl distribution, and is not even possible on some architectures. There are hooks in the code for using the GNU unexec() routine as an alternative. Other methods may be supported in the future.) When the new binary is executed it will begin by executing a goto LABEL (with all the restrictions that **goto** suffers). Think of the operation as a **goto** with an intervening core dump and reincarnation. If *LABEL* is omitted, the function arranges for the program to restart from the top. Please note that any files opened at the time of the dump will not be open any more when the program is reincarnated, with possible confusion resulting on the part of Perl. See also the **-u** command-line switch. For example:

```
#!/usr/bin/perl
use Getopt::Std;
use MyHorridModule;
%days = (
    Sun => 1,
    Mon => 2,
    Tue => 3,
    Wed => 4,
    Thu => 5,
    Fri => 6,
    Sat => 7,
);

dump QUICKSTART if $ARGV[0] eq '-d';

QUICKSTART:
Getopts('f:');
...
```

This startup code does some slow initialization code, and then calls the **dump** function to take a snapshot of the program's state. When the dumped version of the program is run, it bypasses all the startup code and goes directly to the QUICK-START label. If the original script is invoked without the **-d** switch, it just falls through and runs normally.

If you're looking to use **dump** to speed up your program, check out the discussion of efficiency matters in Chapter 8, *Other Oddments*, as well the Perl native-code compiler in Chapter 6. You might also consider autoloading, which at least makes it *appear* to run faster.

each

    each *HASH*

This function returns a two-element list consisting of the key and value for the next value of a hash. With successive calls to **each** you can iterate over the entire hash. Entries are returned in an apparently random order. When the hash is entirely read, a null list is returned (which, when used in a list assignment, produces a false value). The next call to **each** after that will start a new iteration. The iterator can be reset either by reading all the elements from the hash, or by calling the **keys** function in scalar context. You must not add elements to the hash while iterating over it, although you are permitted to use **delete**. In a scalar context, **each** returns just the key, but watch out for false keys.

There is a single iterator for each hash, shared by all **each**, **keys**, and **values** function calls in the program. This means that after a **keys** or **values** call, the next **each** call will start again from the beginning. The following example prints out your environment like the *printenv*(1) program, only in a different order:

```
while (($key,$value) = each %ENV) {
    print "$key=$value\n";
}
```

See also **keys** and **values**.

eof

```
eof FILEHANDLE
eof()
eof
```

This function returns true if the next read on *FILEHANDLE* will return end of file, or if *FILEHANDLE* is not open. *FILEHANDLE* may be an expression whose value gives the real filehandle name. An **eof** without an argument returns the end-of-file status for the last file read. Empty parentheses () may be used in connection with the combined files listed on the command line. That is, inside a while (<>) loop eof() will detect the end of only the last of a group of files. Use eof(ARGV) or eof (without the parentheses) to test *each* file in a while (<>) loop. For example, the following code inserts dashes just before the last line of the *last* file:

```
while (<>) {
    if (eof()) {
        print "-" x 30, "\n";
    }
    print;
}
```

On the other hand, this script resets line numbering on *each* input file:

```
while (<>) {
    print "$.\t$_";
    if (eof) {          # Not eof().
        close ARGV;     # reset $.
    }
}
```

Like "$" in a *sed* program, **eof** tends to show up in line number ranges. Here's a script that prints lines from /pattern/ to end of each input file:

```
while (<>) {
    print if /pattern/ .. eof;
}
```

Here, the flip-flop operator (..) evaluates the regular expression match for each line. Until the pattern matches, the operator returns false. When it finally matches, the operator starts returning true, causing the lines to be printed. When the **eof** operator finally returns true (at the end of the file being examined), the flip-flop operator resets, and starts returning false again.

Note that the **eof** function actually reads a byte and then pushes it back on the input stream with *ungetc*(3), so it is not very useful in an interactive context. In fact, experienced Perl programmers rarely use **eof**, since the various input operators already behave quite nicely in **while**-loop conditionals. See the example in the description of **foreach** in Chapter 2.

eval

```
eval EXPR
eval BLOCK
```

The value expressed by *EXPR* is parsed and executed as though it were a little Perl program. It is executed in the context of the current Perl program, so that any variable settings remain afterward, as do any subroutine or format definitions. The code of the **eval** is treated as a block, so any locally scoped variables declared within the **eval** last only until the **eval** is done. (See **local** and **my**.) As with any code in a block, a final semicolon is not required. If *EXPR* is omitted, the operator evaluates $_.

The value returned from an **eval** is the value of the last expression evaluated, just as with subroutines. Similarly, you may use the **return** operator to return a value from the middle of the **eval**. If there is a syntax error or run-time error (including any produced by the **die** operator), **eval** returns the undefined value and puts the error message in $@. If there is no error, $@ is guaranteed to be set to the null string, so you can test it reliably afterward for errors.

Here's a statement that assigns an element to a hash chosen at run-time:

```
eval "\$$arrayname{\$key} = 1";
```

(You can accomplish that more simply with soft references—see "Symbolic References" in Chapter 4, *References and Nested Data Structures.*) And here is a simple Perl shell:

```
while (<>) { eval; print $@; }
```

Since **eval** traps otherwise-fatal errors, it is useful for determining whether a particular feature (such as **socket** or **symlink**) is implemented. In fact, **eval** is the way to do all exception handling in Perl. If the code to be executed doesn't vary, you should use the `eval` *BLOCK* form to trap run-time errors; the code in the block is compiled only once rather than on each execution, yielding greater efficiency. The error, if any, is still returned in $@. Examples:

```
# make divide-by-zero non-fatal
eval { $answer = $a / $b; }; warn $@ if $@;

# same thing, but less efficient
eval '$answer = $a / $b'; warn $@ if $@;

# a compile-time error (not trapped)
eval { $answer = };

# a run-time error
eval '$answer =';   # sets $@
```

Here, the code in the *BLOCK* has to be valid Perl code to make it past the compilation phase. The code in the string doesn't get examined until run-time, and so doesn't cause an error until run-time.

With an **eval** you should be careful to remember what's being looked at when:

```
eval $x;          # CASE 1
eval "$x";        # CASE 2

eval '$x';        # CASE 3
eval { $x };      # CASE 4

eval "\$$x++";    # CASE 5
$$x++;            # CASE 6
```

Cases 1 and 2 above behave identically: they run the code contained in the variable $x. (Case 2 has misleading double quotes, making the reader wonder what else might be happening, when nothing is. The contents of $x would in any event have to be converted to a string for parsing.) Cases 3 and 4 likewise behave in the same way: they run the code $x, which does nothing at all except return the value of $x. (Case 4 is preferred since the expression doesn't need to recompiled each time.) Case 5 is a place where normally you *would* like to use double quotes to let you interpolate the variable name, except that in this particular situation you can just use symbolic references instead, as in case 6.

A frequently asked question is how to set up an exit routine. One common way is to use an END block. But you can also do it with an **eval**, like this:

```
#!/usr/bin/perl

eval <<'EndOfEval'; $start = __LINE__;
    .
    .               # your ad here
    .
EndOfEval
```

```
# Cleanup

unlink "/tmp/myfile$$";
$@ && ($@ =~ s/\(eval \d+\) at line (\d+)/$0 .
    " line " . ($1+$start)/e, die $@);
exit 0;
```

Note that the code supplied for an **eval** might not be recompiled if the text hasn't changed. On the rare occasions when you want to force a recompilation (because you want to reset a .. operator, for instance), you could say something like this:

```
eval $prog . '#' . ++$seq;
```

exec

```
exec LIST
```

This function terminates the currently running Perl script by executing another program in place of itself. If there is more than one argument in *LIST* (or if *LIST* is an array with more than one value) the function calls C's *execvp*(3) routine with the arguments in *LIST*. This bypasses any shell processing of the command. If there is only one scalar argument, the argument is checked for shell metacharacters. If metacharacters are found, the entire argument is passed to "/bin/sh -c" for parsing.[*] If there are no metacharacters, the argument is split into words and passed directly to *execvp*(3) in the interests of efficiency, since this bypasses all the overhead of shell processing. Ordinarily **exec** never returns—if it does return, it always returns false, and you should check $! to find out what went wrong. Note that **exec** (and **system**) do not flush your output buffer, so you may need to enable command buffering by setting $| on one or more filehandles to avoid lost output. This statement runs the *echo* program to print the current argument list:

```
exec 'echo', 'Your arguments are: ', @ARGV;
```

This example shows that you can **exec** a pipeline:

```
exec "sort $outfile | uniq"
    or die "Can't do sort/uniq: $!\n";
```

The UNIX *execv*(3) call provides the ability to tell a program the name it was invoked as. This name might have nothing to do with the name of the program you actually gave the operating system to run. By default, Perl simply replicates the first element of *LIST* and uses it for both purposes. If, however, you don't really want to execute the first argument of *LIST*, but you want to lie to the program you are executing about its own name, you can do so. Put the real name of

---

[*] Under UNIX, that is. Other operating systems may use other command interpreters.

the program you want to run into a variable and then put that variable out in front of the *LIST* *without* a comma, kind of like a filehandle for a **print** statement. (This always forces interpretation of the *LIST* as a multi-valued list, even if there is only a single scalar in the list.) Then the first element of *LIST* will be used only to mislead the executing program as to its name. For example:

```
$shell = '/bin/csh';
exec $shell '-sh', @args;     # pretend it's a login shell
die "Couldn't execute csh: $!\n";
```

You can also replace the simple scalar holding the program name with a block containing arbitrary code, which simplifies the above example to:

```
exec {'/bin/csh'} '-sh', @args; # pretend it's a login shell
```

exists

```
exists EXPR
```

This function returns true if the specified hash key exists in its hash, even if the corresponding value is undefined.

```
print "Exists\n" if exists $hash{$key};
print "Defined\n" if defined $hash{$key};
print "True\n" if $hash{$key};
```

A hash element can only be true if it's defined, and can only be defined if it exists, but the reverse doesn't necessarily hold true in either case.

EXPR can be arbitrarily complicated as long as the final operation is a hash key lookup:

```
if (exists $ref->[$x][$y]{$key}) { ... }
```

exit

```
exit EXPR
```

This function evaluates *EXPR* and exits immediately with that value. Here's a fragment that lets a user exit the program by typing x or X:

```
$ans = <STDIN>;
exit 0 if $ans =~ /^[Xx]/;
```

If *EXPR* is omitted, the function exits with 0 status. You shouldn't use **exit** to abort a subroutine if there's any chance that someone might want to trap whatever error happened. Use **die** instead, which can be trapped by an **eval**.

exp

```
exp EXPR
```

This function returns *e* to the power of *EXPR*. If *EXPR* is omitted, it gives `exp($_)`. To do general exponentiation, use the `**` operator.

fcntl

```
fcntl FILEHANDLE, FUNCTION, SCALAR
```

This function calls UNIX's *fcntl*(2) function. (*fcntl* stands for "file control".) You'll probably have to say:

```
use Fcntl;
```

first to get the correct function definitions. *SCALAR* will be read and/or written depending on the *FUNCTION*—a pointer to the string value of *SCALAR* will be passed as the third argument of the actual *fcntl* call. (If *SCALAR* has no string value but does have a numeric value, that value will be passed directly rather than a pointer to the string value.)

The return value of **fcntl** (and **ioctl**) is as follows:

System call returns	Perl returns
-1	undefined value
0	string "0 but true"
anything else	that number

Thus Perl returns true on success and false on failure, yet you can still easily determine the actual value returned by the operating system:

```
$retval = fcntl(...) or $retval = -1;
printf "System returned %d\n", $retval;
```

Here, even the string "0 but true" prints as 0, thanks to the `%d` format.

For example, since Perl always sets the close-on-exec flag for file descriptors above 2, if you wanted to pass file descriptor 3 to a subprocess, you might want to clear the flag like this:

```
use Fcntl;
open TTY,"+>/dev/tty" or die "Can't open /dev/tty: $!\n";
fileno TTY == 3 or die "Internal error: fd mixup";
fcntl TTY, &F_SETFL, 0
    or die "Can't clear the close-on-exec flag: $!\n";
```

fcntl will produce a fatal error if used on a machine that doesn't implement *fcntl*(2). On machines that do implement it, you can do such things as modify the close-on-exec flags, modify the non-blocking I/O flags, emulate the *lockf*(3) function, and arrange to receive the SIGIO signal when I/O is pending. You might even have record-locking facilities.

fileno

```
fileno FILEHANDLE
```

This function returns the file descriptor for a filehandle. (A *file descriptor* is a small integer, unlike the filehandle, which is a symbol.) It returns **undef** if the handle is not open. It's useful for constructing bitmaps for **select**, and for passing to certain obscure system calls if *syscall*(2) is implemented. It's also useful for double-checking that the **open** function gave you the file descriptor you wanted—see the example under **fcntl**.

If *FILEHANDLE* is an expression, its value is taken to represent a filehandle, either indirectly by name, or directly as a reference to a filehandle object.

A caution: don't count on the association of a Perl filehandle and a numeric file descriptor throughout the life of the program. If a file has been closed and reopened, the file descriptor may change. Filehandles STDIN, STDOUT, and STDERR start with file descriptors of 0, 1, and 2 (the UNIX standard convention), but even they can change if you start closing and opening them with wild abandon. But you can't get into trouble with 0, 1, and 2 as long as you always reopen immediately after closing, since the basic rule on UNIX systems is to pick the lowest available descriptor, and that'll be the one you just closed.

flock

```
flock FILEHANDLE, OPERATION
```

This function calls *flock*(2) on *FILEHANDLE*. See the manual page for *flock*(2) for the definition of *OPERATION*. Invoking **flock** will produce a fatal error if used on a machine that doesn't implement *flock*(2) or emulate it through some other locking mechanism. Here's a mailbox appender for some BSD-based systems:

```
$LOCK_SH = 1;
$LOCK_EX = 2;
$LOCK_NB = 4;
$LOCK_UN = 8;

sub lock {
    flock MBOX, $LOCK_EX;
    # and, in case someone appended
    # while we were waiting...
    seek MBOX, 0, 2;
```

```
    }

    sub unlock {
        flock MBOX, $LOCK_UN;
    }

    open MBOX, ">>/usr/spool/mail/$ENV{'USER'}"
        or die "Can't open mailbox: $!";

    lock();
    print MBOX $msg, "\n\n";
    unlock();
```

Note that **flock** is unlikely to work on a file being accessed through a network file system.

fork

```
    fork
```

This function does a *fork*(2) call. If it succeeds, the function returns the child pid to the parent process and 0 to the child process. (If it fails, it returns the undefined value to the parent process. There is no child process.) Note that unflushed buffers remain unflushed in both processes, which means you may need to set $| on one or more filehandles earlier in the program to avoid duplicate output.

A nearly bulletproof way to launch a child process while checking for "cannot fork" errors would be:

```
    FORK: {
        if ($pid = fork) {
            # parent here
            # child process pid is available in $pid
        } elsif (defined $pid) { # $pid is zero here if defined
            # child here
            # parent process pid is available with getppid
        } elsif ($! =~ /No more process/) {
            # EAGAIN, supposedly recoverable fork error
            sleep 5;
            redo FORK;
        } else {
            # weird fork error
            die "Can't fork: $!\n";
        }
    }
```

These precautions are not necessary on operations which do an implicit *fork*(2), such as **system**, backquotes, or opening a process as a filehandle, because Perl automatically retries a fork on a temporary failure in these cases. Be very careful to end the child code with an **exit**, or your child may inadvertently leave the conditional and start executing code intended only for the parent process.

If you **fork** your child processes, you'll have to **wait** on their zombies when they die. See the **wait** function for examples of doing this.

The **fork** function is unlikely to be implemented on any operating system not resembling UNIX, unless it purports POSIX compliance.

format

```
format NAME =
    picture line
    value list
    ...
.
```

Declares a named sequence of picture lines (with associated values) for use by the **write** function. If *NAME* is omitted, the name defaults to STDOUT, which happens to be the default format name for the STDOUT filehandle. Since, like a **sub** declaration, this is a global declaration that happens at compile time, any variables used in the value list need to be visible at the point of the format's declaration. That is, lexically scoped variables must be declared earlier in the file, while dynamically scoped variables merely need to be set in the routine that calls **write**. Here's an example (which assumes we've already calculated $cost and $quantity):

```
my $str = "widget";          # A lexically scoped variable.

format Nice_Output =
Test: @<<<<<<<< @||||| @>>>>>
      $str,     $%,    '$' . int($num)
.

$~ = "Nice_Output";          # Select our format.
local $num = $cost * $quantity;   # Dynamically scoped variable.

write;
```

Like filehandles, format names are identifiers that exist in a symbol table (package) and may be fully qualified by package name. Within the typeglobs of a symbol table's entries, formats reside in their own namespace, which is distinct from filehandles, directory handles, scalars, arrays, hashes, or subroutines. Like those other six types, however, a format named Whatever would also be affected by a **local** on the *Whatever typeglob. In other words, a format is just another gadget contained in a typeglob, independent of the other gadgets.

The "Formats" section in Chapter 2 contains numerous details and examples of their use. The "Per Filehandle Special Variables" and "Global Special Variables" sections in Chapter 2 describe the internal format-specific variables, and the English and FileHandle modules in Chapter 7 provide easier access to them.

formline

```
formline PICTURE, LIST
```

This is an internal function used by formats, although you may also call it. It formats a list of values according to the contents of *PICTURE*, placing the output into the format output accumulator, $^A. Eventually, when a **write** is done, the contents of $^A are written to some filehandle, but you could also read $^A yourself and then set $^A back to "". Note that a format typically does one **formline** per line of form, but the **formline** function itself doesn't care how many newlines are embedded in the *PICTURE*. This means that the ~ and ~~ tokens will treat the entire *PICTURE* as a single line. You may therefore need to use multiple formlines to implement a single record-format, just like the format compiler.

Be careful if you put double quotes around the picture, since an @ character may be taken to mean the beginning of an array name. **formline** always returns true. See "Formats" in Chapter 2 for other examples.

getc

```
getc FILEHANDLE
getc
```

This function returns the next byte from the input file attached to *FILEHANDLE*. At end-of-file, it returns a null string. If *FILEHANDLE* is omitted, the function reads from STDIN. This operator is very slow, but is occasionally useful for single-character, buffered input from the keyboard. This does *not* enable single-character input. For unbuffered input, you have to be slightly more clever, in an operating-system-dependent fashion. Under UNIX you might say this:

```
if ($BSD_STYLE) {
    system "stty cbreak </dev/tty >/dev/tty 2>&1";
} else {
    system "stty", "-icanon", "eol", " ......";
}

$key = getc;

if ($BSD_STYLE) {
    system "stty -cbreak </dev/tty >/dev/tty 2>&1";
} else {
    system "stty", "icanon", "eol", "^@"; # ASCII NUL
}
print "\n";
```

This code puts the next character typed on the terminal in the string $key. If your *stty* program has options like cbreak, you'll need to use the code where $BSD_STYLE is true, otherwise, you'll need to use the code where it is false. Determining the options for *stty* is left as an exercise to the reader.

The POSIX module in Chapter 7 provides a more portable version of this using the
POSIX::getattr() function. See also the TERM::ReadKey module from your nearest
CPAN site.

getgrent

```
getgrent
setgrent
endgrent
```

These functions do the same thing as their like-named system library routines—
see *getgrent*(3). These routines iterate through your */etc/group* file (or its moral
equivalent coming from some server somewhere). The return value from **getgrent**
in list context is:

```
($name, $passwd, $gid, $members)
```

where $members contains a space-separated list of the login names of the members
of the group. To set up a hash for translating group names to gids, say this:

```
while (($name, $passwd, $gid) = getgrent) {
    $gid{$name} = $gid;
}
```

In scalar context, **getgrent** returns only the group name.

getgrgid

```
getgrgid GID
```

This function does the same thing as *getgrgid*(3): it looks up a group file entry by
group number. The return value in list context is:

```
($name, $passwd, $gid, $members)
```

where $members contains a space-separated list of the login names of the members
of the group. If you want to do this repeatedly, consider caching the data in a
hash (associative array) using **getgrent**.

In scalar context, **getgrgid** returns only the group name.

getgrnam

```
getgrnam NAME
```

This function does the same thing as *getgrnam*(3): it looks up a group file entry
by group name. The return value in list context is:

```
($name, $passwd, $gid, $members)
```

where $members contains a space-separated list of the login names of the members of the group. If you want to do this repeatedly, consider slurping the data into a hash (associative array) using **getgrent**.

In scalar context, **getgrnam** returns only the numeric group ID.

gethostbyaddr

        gethostbyaddr ADDR, ADDRTYPE

This function does the same thing as *gethostbyaddr*(3): it translates a packed binary network address to its corresponding names (and alternate addresses). The return value in list context is:

        ($name, $aliases, $addrtype, $length, @addrs)

where @addrs is a list of packed binary addresses. In the Internet domain, each address is four bytes long, and can be unpacked by saying something like:

        ($a, $b, $c, $d) = unpack('C4', $addrs[0]);

In scalar context, **gethostbyaddr** returns only the host name. See the section on "Sockets" in Chapter 6 for another approach.

gethostbyname

        gethostbyname NAME

This function does the same thing as *gethostbyname*(3): it translates a network hostname to its corresponding addresses (and other names). The return value in list context is:

        ($name, $aliases, $addrtype, $length, @addrs)

where @addrs is a list of raw addresses. In the Internet domain, each address is four bytes long, and can be unpacked by saying something like:

        ($a, $b, $c, $d) = unpack('C4', $addrs[0]);

In scalar context, **gethostbyname** returns only the host address. See the section on "Sockets" in Chapter 6 for another approach.

gethostent

        gethostent
        sethostent STAYOPEN
        endhostent

These functions do the same thing as their like-named system library routines— see *gethostent*(3).

They iterate through your */etc/hosts* file and return each entry one at a time. The return value from **gethostent** is:

```
($name, $aliases, $addrtype, $length, @addrs)
```

where @addrs is a list of raw addresses. In the Internet domain, each address is four bytes long, and can be unpacked by saying something like:

```
($a, $b, $c, $d) = unpack('C4', $addrs[0]);
```

Scripts that use these routines should not be considered portable. If a machine uses a nameserver, it would interrogate most of the Internet to try to satisfy a request for all the addresses of every machine on the planet. So these routines are unimplemented on such machines.

getlogin

```
getlogin
```

This function returns the current login from */etc/utmp*, if any. If null, use **getpwuid**. For example:

```
$login = getlogin || (getpwuid($<))[0] || "Intruder!!";
```

getnetbyaddr

```
getnetbyaddr ADDR, ADDRTYPE
```

This function does the same thing as *getnetbyaddr*(3): it translates a network address to the corresponding network name or names. The return value in list context is:

```
($name, $aliases, $addrtype, $net)
```

In scalar context, **getnetbyaddr** returns only the network name.

getnetbyname

```
getnetbyname NAME
```

This function does the same thing as *getnetbyname*(3): it translates a network name to its corresponding network address. The return value in list context is:

```
($name, $aliases, $addrtype, $net)
```

In scalar context, **getnetbyname** returns only the network address.

getnetent

```
getnetent
setnetent STAYOPEN
endnetent
```

These functions do the same thing as their like-named system library routines—see *getnetent*(3). They iterate through your */etc/networks* file, or moral equivalent. The return value in list context is:

```
($name, $aliases, $addrtype, $net)
```

In scalar context, **getnetent** returns only the network name.

getpeername

```
getpeername SOCKET
```

This function returns the packed socket address of other end of the *SOCKET* connection. For example:

```
use Socket;
$hersockaddr = getpeername SOCK;
($port, $heraddr) = unpack_sockaddr_in($hersockaddr);
$herhostname = gethostbyaddr($heraddr, AF_INET);
$herstraddr = inet_ntoa($heraddr);
```

getpgrp

```
getpgrp PID
```

This function returns the current process group for the specified *PID* (use a *PID* of 0 for the current process). Invoking **getpgrp** will produce a fatal error if used on a machine that doesn't implement *getpgrp*(2). If *PID* is omitted, the function returns the process group of the current process (the same as using a *PID* of 0). On systems implementing this operator with the POSIX *getpgrp*(2) system call, *PID* must be omitted or, if supplied, must be 0.

getppid

```
getppid
```

This function returns the process ID of the parent process. On the typical UNIX system, if your parent process ID changes to 1, your parent process has died and you've been adopted by the *init* program.

getpriority

```
getpriority WHICH, WHO
```

This function returns the current priority for a process, a process group, or a user. See *getpriority*(2). Invoking **getpriority** will produce a fatal error if used on a machine that doesn't implement *getpriority*(2). For example, to get the priority of the current process, use:

```
$curprio = getpriority(0, 0);
```

getprotobyname

```
getprotobyname NAME
```

This function does the same thing as *getprotobyname*(3): it translates a protocol name to its corresponding number. The return value in list context is:

```
($name, $aliases, $protocol_number)
```

In scalar context, **getprotobyname** returns only the protocol number.

getprotobynumber

```
getprotobynumber NUMBER
```

This function does the same thing as *getprotobynumber*(3): it translates a protocol number to its corresponding name. The return value in list context is:

```
($name, $aliases, $protocol_number)
```

In scalar context, **getprotobynumber** returns only the protocol name.

getprotoent

```
getprotoent
setprotoent STAYOPEN
endprotoent
```

These functions do the same thing as their like-named system library routines— see *getprotent*(3). The return value from **getprotoent** is:

```
($name, $aliases, $protocol_number)
```

In scalar context, **getprotoent** returns only the protocol name.

getpwent

```
getpwent
setpwent
endpwent
```

These functions do the same thing as their like-named system library routines—see *getpwent*(3). They iterate through your */etc/passwd* file (or its moral equivalent coming from some server somewhere). The return value in list context is:

```
($name, $passwd, $uid, $gid, $quota, $comment, $gcos, $dir, $shell)
```

Some machines may use the quota and comment fields for other purposes, but the remaining fields will always be the same. To set up a hash for translating login names to uids, say this:

```
while (($name, $passwd, $uid) = getpwent) {
    $uid{$name} = $uid;
}
```

In scalar context, **getpwent** returns only the username.

getpwnam

```
getpwnam NAME
```

This function does the same thing as *getpwnam*(3): it translates a username to the corresponding *passwd* file entry. The return value in list context is:

```
($name, $passwd, $uid, $gid, $quota, $comment, $gcos, $dir, $shell)
```

If you want to do this repeatedly, consider caching the data in a hash (associative array) using **getpwent**.

In scalar context, **getpwnam** returns only the numeric user ID.

getpwuid

```
getpwuid UID
```

This function does the same thing as *getpwuid*(3): it translates a numeric user id to the corresponding *passwd* file entry. The return value in list context is:

```
($name, $passwd, $uid, $gid, $quota, $comment, $gcos, $dir, $shell)
```

If you want to do this repeatedly, consider slurping the data into a hash using **getpwent**.

In scalar context, **getpwuid** returns the username.

getservbyname

```
getservbyname NAME, PROTO
```

This function does the same thing as *getservbyname*(3): it translates a service (port) name to its corresponding port number. *PROTO* is a protocol name such as "tcp". The return value in list context is:

```
($name, $aliases, $port_number, $protocol_name)
```

In scalar context, **getservbyname** returns only the service port number.

getservbyport

```
getservbyport PORT, PROTO
```

This function does the same thing as *getservbyport*(3): it translates a service (port) number to its corresponding names. *PROTO* is a protocol name such as "tcp". The return value in list context is:

```
($name, $aliases, $port_number, $protocol_name)
```

In scalar context, **getservbyport** returns only the service port name.

getservent

```
getservent
setservent STAYOPEN
endservent
```

These functions do the same thing as their like-named system library routines— see *getservent*(3). They iterate through the */etc/services* file or its equivalent. The return value in list context is:

```
($name, $aliases, $port_number, $protocol_name)
```

In scalar context, **getservent** returns only the service port name.

getsockname

```
getsockname SOCKET
```

This function returns the packed sockaddr address of this end of the *SOCKET* connection. (And why wouldn't you know your own address already? Because you might have bound an address containing wildcards to the generic socket before doing an **accept**. Or because you might have been passed a socket by your parent process—for example, *inetd*.)

```
use Socket;
$mysockaddr = getsockname(SOCK);
($port, $myaddr) = unpack_sockaddr_in($mysockaddr);
```

getsockopt

```
getsockopt SOCKET, LEVEL, OPTNAME
```

This function returns the socket option requested, or the undefined value if there is an error. See **setsockopt** for more.

glob

```
glob EXPR
```

This function returns the value of *EXPR* with filename expansions such as a shell would do. (If *EXPR* is omitted, $_ is globbed instead.) This is the internal function implementing the <*> operator, except that it may be easier to type this way. For example, compare these two:

```
@result = map { glob($_) } "*.c", "*.c,v";

@result = map <${_}>, "*.c", "*.c,v";
```

The **glob** function is not related to the Perl notion of typeglobs, other than that they both use a * to represent multiple items.

gmtime

```
gmtime EXPR
```

This function converts a time as returned by the **time** function to a 9-element list with the time correct for the Greenwich time zone (aka GMT, or UTC, or even Zulu in certain cultures, not including the Zulu culture, oddly enough). Typically used as follows:

```
($sec,$min,$hour,$mday,$mon,$year,$wday,$yday,$isdst) =
        gmtime(time);
```

All list elements are numeric, and come straight out of a struct tm (that's a C programming structure—don't sweat it). In particular this means that $mon has the range 0..11, $wday has the range 0..6, and the year has had 1,900 subtracted from it. (You can remember which ones are 0-based because those are the ones you're always using as subscripts into 0-based arrays containing month and day names.) If *EXPR* is omitted, it does gmtime(time). For example, to print the current month in London:

```
$london_month = (qw(Jan Feb Mar Apr May Jun
        Jul Aug Sep Oct Nov Dec))[(gmtime)[4]];
```

The Perl library module Time::Local contains a subroutine, timegm(), that can convert in the opposite direction.

In scalar context, **gmtime** returns a *ctime*(3)-like string based on the GMT time value.

goto

```
goto LABEL
goto EXPR
goto &NAME
```

goto *LABEL* finds the statement labeled with *LABEL* and resumes execution there. It may not be used to go into any construct that requires initialization, such as a subroutine or a **foreach** loop. It also can't be used to go into a construct that is optimized away. It can be used to go almost anywhere else within the dynamic scope,[*] including out of subroutines, but for that purpose it's usually better to use some other construct such as **last** or **die**. The author of Perl has never felt the need to use this form of **goto** (in Perl, that is—C is another matter).

Going to even greater heights of orthogonality (and depths of idiocy), Perl allows goto *EXPR*, which expects *EXPR* to evaluate to a label name, whose scope is *guaranteed* to be unresolvable until run-time since the label is unknown when the statement is compiled. This allows for computed gotos per FORTRAN, but isn't necessarily recommended[†] if you're optimizing for maintainability:

```
goto +("FOO", "BAR", "GLARCH")[$i];
```

goto *&NAME* is highly magical, substituting a call to the named subroutine for the currently running subroutine. This is used by AUTOLOAD subroutines that wish to load another subroutine and then pretend that this subroutine—and not the original one—had been called in the first place (except that any modifications to @_ in the original subroutine are propagated to the replacement subroutine). After the **goto**, not even **caller** will be able to tell that the original routine was called first.

grep

```
grep EXPR, LIST
grep BLOCK LIST
```

This function evaluates *EXPR* or *BLOCK* in a Boolean context for each element of *LIST*, temporarily setting $_ to each element in turn. In list context, it returns a list of those elements for which the expression is true. (The operator is named after a beloved UNIX program that extracts lines out of a file that match a particular pattern. In Perl the expression is often a pattern, but doesn't have to be.) In scalar context, **grep** returns the number of times the expression was true.

---

[*] This means that if it doesn't find the label in the current routine, it looks back through the routines that called the current routine for the label, thus making it nearly impossible to maintain your program.

[†] Understatement is reputed to be funny, so we thought we'd try one here.

Presuming @all_lines contains lines of code, this example weeds out comment lines:

```
@code_lines = grep !/^#/, @all_lines;
```

Since $_ is a reference into the list value, altering $_ will modify the elements of the original list. While this is useful and supported, it can occasionally cause bizarre results if you aren't expecting it. For example:

```
@list = qw(barney fred dino wilma);
@greplist = grep { s/^[bfd]// } @list;
```

@greplist is now "arney", "red", "ino", but @list is now "arney", "red", "ino", "wilma"! Caveat Programmor.

See also **map**. The following two statements are functionally equivalent:

```
@out = grep { EXPR } @in;
@out = map { EXPR ? $_ : () } @in
```

hex

```
hex EXPR
```

This function interprets *EXPR* as a hexadecimal string and returns the equivalent decimal value. (To interpret strings that might start with 0 or 0x see **oct**.) If *EXPR* is omitted, it interprets $_. The following code sets $number to 4,294,906,560:

```
$number = hex("ffff12c0");
```

To do the inverse function, use:

```
sprintf "%lx", $number;        # (That's an ell, not a one.)
```

import

```
import CLASSNAME LIST
import CLASSNAME
```

There is no built-in **import** function. It is merely an ordinary class method defined (or inherited) by modules that wish to export names to another module through the **use** operator. See **use** for details.

index

```
index STR, SUBSTR, POSITION
index STR, SUBSTR
```

This function returns the position of the first occurrence of *SUBSTR* in *STR*. The *POSITION*, if specified, says where to start looking. Positions are based at 0 (or whatever you've set the $[variable to—but don't do that). If the substring is not

found, the function returns one less than the base, ordinarily -1. To work your
way through a string, you might say:

```
$pos = -1;
while (($pos = index($string, $lookfor, $pos)) > -1) {
    print "Found at $pos\n";
    $pos++;
}
```

int

```
int EXPR
```

This function returns the integer portion of *EXPR*. If *EXPR* is omitted, it uses $_. If
you're a C programmer, you'll often forget to use **int** in conjunction with division,
which is a floating-point operation in Perl:

```
$average_age = 939/16;       # yields 58.6875 (58 in C)
$average_age = int 939/16;   # yields 58
```

ioctl

```
ioctl FILEHANDLE, FUNCTION, SCALAR
```

This function implements the *ioctl*(2) system call. You'll probably have to say:

```
require "ioctl.ph";
    # probably /usr/local/lib/perl/ioctl.ph
```

first to get the correct function definitions. If *ioctl.ph* doesn't exist or doesn't have
the correct definitions you'll have to roll your own, based on your C header files
such as *<sys/ioctl.h>*. (The Perl distribution includes a script called *h2ph* to help
you do this, but it's non-trivial.) *SCALAR* will be read and/or written depending on
the *FUNCTION*—a pointer to the string value of *SCALAR* will be passed as the third
argument of the actual *ioctl*(2) call. (If *SCALAR* has no string value but does have a
numeric value, that value will be passed directly rather than a pointer to the string
value.) The **pack** and **unpack** functions are useful for manipulating the values of
structures used by **ioctl**. The following example sets the erase character to DEL on
many UNIX systems (see the POSIX module in Chapter 7 for a slightly more
portable interface):

```
require 'ioctl.ph';
$getp = &TIOCGETP or die "NO TIOCGETP";
$sgttyb_t = "ccccs";          # 4 chars and a short
if (ioctl STDIN, $getp, $sgttyb) {
    @ary = unpack $sgttyb_t, $sgttyb;
    $ary[2] = 127;
    $sgttyb = pack $sgttyb_t, @ary;
    ioctl STDIN, &TIOCSETP, $sgttyb
```

```
        or die "Can't ioctl TIOCSETP: $!";
}
```

The return value of **ioctl** (and **fcntl**) is as follows:

System call returns	Perl returns
-1	undefined value
0	string "0 but true"
anything else	that number

Thus Perl returns true on success and false on failure, yet you can still easily determine the actual value returned by the operating system:

```
$retval = ioctl(...) or $retval = -1;
printf "System returned %d\n", $retval;
```

Calls to **ioctl** should not be considered portable. If, say, you're merely turning off echo once for the whole script, it's much more portable (and not much slower) to say:

```
system "stty -echo";   # Works on most UNIX boxen.
```

Just because you *can* do something in Perl doesn't mean you *ought* to. To quote the Apostle Paul, "Everything is permissible—but not everything is beneficial."

join

```
join EXPR, LIST
```

This function joins the separate strings of *LIST* into a single string with fields separated by the value of *EXPR*, and returns the string. For example:

```
$_ = join ':', $login,$passwd,$uid,$gid,$gcos,$home,$shell;
```

To do the opposite, see **split**. To join things together into fixed-position fields, see **pack**.

The most efficient way to concatenate many strings together is to **join** them with a null string.

keys

```
keys HASH
```

This function returns a list consisting of all the keys of the named hash. The keys are returned in an apparently random order, but it is the same order as either the

values or **each** function produces (assuming that the hash has not been modified between calls). Here is yet another way to print your environment:

```
@keys = keys %ENV;
@values = values %ENV;
while (@keys) {
    print pop(@keys), '=', pop(@values), "\n";
}
```

or how about sorted by key:

```
foreach $key (sort keys %ENV) {
    print $key, '=', $ENV{$key}, "\n";
}
```

To sort a hash by value, you'll need to provide a comparison function. Here's a descending numeric sort of a hash by its values:

```
foreach $key (sort { $hash{$b} <=> $hash{$a} } keys %hash) {
    printf "%4d %s\n", $hash{$key}, $key;
}
```

Note that using **keys** on a hash bound to a largish DBM file will produce a largish list, causing you to have a largish process. You might prefer to use the **each** function in this case, which will iterate over the hash entries one-by-one without slurping them all into a single gargantuan list.

In scalar context, **keys** returns the number of elements of the hash (and resets the **each** iterator). However, to get this information for tied hashes, including DBM files, Perl must still walk the entire hash, so it's not very efficient in that case.

kill

```
kill LIST
```

This function sends a signal to a list of processes. The first element of the list must be the signal to send. You may use a signal name in quotes (without a SIG on the front). The function returns the number of processes successfully signaled. If the signal is negative, the function kills process groups instead of processes. (On System V, a negative process number will also kill process groups, but that's not portable.) Examples:

```
$cnt = kill 1, $child1, $child2;
kill 9, @goners;
kill 'STOP', getppid;  # Can *so* suspend my login shell...
```

last

```
last LABEL
last
```

The **last** command is like the **break** statement in C (as used in loops); it immediately exits the loop in question. If the *LABEL* is omitted, the command refers to the innermost enclosing loop. The **continue** block, if any, is not executed.

```
LINE: while (<STDIN>) {
    last LINE if /^$/; # exit when done with header
    # rest of loop here
}
```

lc

```
lc EXPR
```

This function returns a lowercased version of *EXPR* (or **$_** if omitted). This is the internal function implementing the \L escape in double-quoted strings. POSIX *setlocale*(3) settings are respected.

lcfirst

```
lcfirst EXPR
```

This function returns a version of *EXPR* (or **$_** if omitted) with the first character lowercased. This is the internal function implementing the \l escape in double-quoted strings. POSIX *setlocale*(3) settings are respected.

length

```
length EXPR
```

This function returns the length in bytes of the scalar value *EXPR*. If *EXPR* is omitted, the function returns the length of **$_**, but be careful that the next thing doesn't look like the start of an *EXPR*, or the tokener will get confused. When in doubt, always put in parentheses.

Do not try to use **length** to find the size of an array or hash. Use `scalar @array` for the size of an array, and `scalar keys %hash` for the size of a hash. (The `scalar` is typically dropped when redundant, which is typical.)

link

```
link OLDFILE, NEWFILE
```

This function creates a new filename linked to the old filename. The function returns 1 for success, 0 otherwise (and puts the error code into $!). See also **sym-**

link later in this chapter. This function is unlikely to be implemented on non-UNIX systems.

listen

```
listen SOCKET, QUEUESIZE
```

This function does the same thing as the *listen*(2) system call. It tells the system that you're going to be accepting connections on this socket and that the system can queue the number of waiting connections specified by *QUEUESIZE*. Imagine having call-waiting on your phone, with up to five callers queued. (Gives me the willies!) The function returns true if it succeeded, false otherwise (and puts the error code into $!). See the section "Sockets" in Chapter 6.

local

```
local EXPR
```

This operator declares one or more global variables to have locally scoped values within the innermost enclosing block, subroutine, **eval**, or file. If more than one variable is listed, the list must be placed in parentheses, because the operator binds more tightly than comma. All the listed variables must be legal lvalues, that is, something you could assign to. This operator works by saving the current values of those variables on a hidden stack and restoring them upon exiting the block, subroutine, or **eval**, or file. After the **local** is executed, but before the scope is exited, any called subroutines will see the local, inner value, not the previous, outer value, because the variable is still a global variable, despite having a localized value. The technical term for this is "dynamic scoping".

The *EXPR* may be assigned to if desired, which allows you to initialize your local variables. (If no initializer is given, all scalars are initialized to the undefined value and all arrays and hashes to empty.) Commonly, this is used to name the formal arguments to a subroutine. As with ordinary assignment, if you use parentheses around the variables on the left (or if the variable is an array or hash), the expression on the right is evaluated in list context. Otherwise the expression on the right is evaluated in scalar context.

Here is a routine that executes some random piece of code that depends on $i running through a range of numbers. Note that the scope of $i propagates into the **eval** code.

```
&RANGEVAL(20, 30, '$foo[$i] = $i');

sub RANGEVAL {
    local($min, $max, $thunk) = @_;
    local $result = "";
    local $i;
```

```
    # Presumably $thunk makes reference to $i

    for ($i = $min; $i < $max; $i++) {
        $result .= eval $thunk;
    }

    $result;
}
```

This code demonstrates how to make a temporary modification to a global array:

```
if ($sw eq '-v') {
    # init local array with global array
    local @ARGV = @ARGV;
    unshift @ARGV, 'echo';
    system @ARGV;
}
# @ARGV restored
```

You can also temporarily modify hashes:

```
# temporarily add a couple of entries to the %digits hash
if ($base12) {
    # (NOTE: not claiming this is efficient!)
    local(%digits) = (%digits, T => 10, E => 11);
    parse_num();
}
```

But you probably want to be using **my** instead, because **local** isn't really what most people think of as local. See the section on **my** later.

localtime

```
localtime EXPR
```

This function converts the value returned by **time** to a nine-element list with the time corrected for the local time zone. It's typically used as follows:

```
($sec,$min,$hour,$mday,$mon,$year,$wday,$yday,$isdst) =
        localtime(time);
```

All list elements are numeric, and come straight out of a struct tm. (That's a bit of C programming lingo—don't worry about it.) In particular this means that $mon has the range 0..11, $wday has the range 0..6, and the year has had 1,900 subtracted from it. (You can remember which ones are 0-based because those are the ones you're always using as subscripts into 0-based arrays containing month and day names.) If *EXPR* is omitted, it does localtime(time). For example, to get the name of the current day of the week:

```
$thisday = (Sun,Mon,Tue,Wed,Thu,Fri,Sat)[(localtime)[6]];
```

The Perl library module Time::Local contains a subroutine, `timelocal()`, that can convert in the opposite direction.

In scalar context, **localtime** returns a *ctime*(3)-like string based on the localtime value. For example, the *date* command can be emulated with:

```
perl -e 'print scalar localtime'
```

See also POSIX::strftime() in Chapter 7 for a more fine-grained approach to formatting times.

log

```
log EXPR
```

This function returns logarithm (base *e*) of *EXPR*. If *EXPR* is omitted, the function returns the logarithm of $_.

lstat

```
lstat EXPR
```

This function does the same thing as the **stat** function, but if the last component of the filename is a symbolic link, stats a symbolic link instead of the file the symbolic link points to. (If symbolic links are unimplemented on your system, a normal **stat** is done instead.)

map

```
map BLOCK LIST
map EXPR, LIST
```

This function evaluates the *BLOCK* or *EXPR* for each element of *LIST* (locally setting $_ to each element) and returns the list value composed of the results of each such evaluation. It evaluates *BLOCK* or *EXPR* in a list context, so each element of *LIST* may produce zero, one, or more elements in the returned value. These are all flattened into one list. For instance:

```
@words = map { split ' ' } @lines;
```

splits a list of lines into a list of words. Often, though, there is a one-to-one mapping between input values and output values:

```
@chars = map chr, @nums;
```

translates a list of numbers to the corresponding characters. And here's an example of a one-to-two mapping:

```
%hash = map { genkey($_), $_ } @array;
```

which is just a funny functional way to write this:

```
%hash = ();
foreach $_ (@array) {
    $hash{genkey($_)} = $_;
}
```

See also **grep**. **map** differs from **grep** in that **map** returns a list consisting of the results of each successive evaluation of *EXPR*, whereas **grep** returns a list consisting of each value of *LIST* for which *EXPR* evaluates to true.

mkdir

```
mkdir FILENAME, MODE
```

This function creates the directory specified by *FILENAME*, with permissions specified by the numeric *MODE* (as modified by the current umask). If it succeeds it returns 1, otherwise it returns 0 and sets $! (from the value of errno).

If *mkdir*(2) is not built in to your C library, Perl emulates it by calling the *mkdir*(1) program. If you are creating a long list of directories on such a system it will be more efficient to call the *mkdir* program yourself with the list of directories to avoid starting zillions of subprocesses.

msgctl

```
msgctl ID, CMD, ARG
```

This function calls the *msgctl*(2) system call. See *msgctl*(2) for details. If *CMD* is &IPC_STAT, then *ARG* must be a variable that will hold the returned msqid_ds structure. The return value works like **ioctl**'s: the undefined value for error, "0 but true" for zero, or the actual return value otherwise. On error, it puts the error code into $!. Before calling, you should say:

```
require "ipc.ph";
require "msg.ph";
```

This function is available only on machines supporting System V IPC, which turns out to be far fewer than those supporting sockets.

msgget

> msgget *KEY, FLAGS*

This function calls the System V IPC *msgget*(2) system call. See *msgget*(2) for details. The function returns the message queue ID, or the undefined value if there is an error. On error, it puts the error code into $!. Before calling, you should say:

```
require "ipc.ph";
require "msg.ph";
```

This function is available only on machines supporting System V IPC.

msgrcv

> msgrcv *ID, VAR, SIZE, TYPE, FLAGS*

This function calls the *msgrcv*(2) system call to receive a message from message queue ID into variable *VAR* with a maximum message size of *SIZE*. See *msgrcv*(2) for details. When a message is received, the message type will be the first thing in *VAR*, and the maximum length of *VAR* is *SIZE* plus the size of the message type. The function returns true if successful, or false if there is an error. On error, it puts the error code into $!. Before calling, you should say:

```
require "ipc.ph";
require "msg.ph";
```

This function is available only on machines supporting System V IPC.

msgsnd

> msgsnd *ID, MSG, FLAGS*

This function calls the *msgsnd*(2) system call to send the message *MSG* to the message queue *ID*. See *msgsnd*(2) for details. *MSG* must begin with the long integer message type. You can create a message like this:

```
$msg = pack "L a*", $type, $text_of_message;
```

The function returns true if successful, or false if there is an error. On error, it puts the error code into $!. Before calling, you should say:

```
require "ipc.ph";
require "msg.ph";
```

This function is available only on machines supporting System V IPC.

my

```
my EXPR
```

This operator declares one or more private variables to exist only within the inner-most enclosing block, subroutine, **eval**, or file. If more than one variable is listed, the list must be placed in parentheses, because the operator binds more tightly than comma. Only simple scalars or complete arrays and hashes may be declared this way. The variable name may not be package qualified, because package variables are all global, and private variables are not related to any package. Unlike **local**, this operator has nothing to do with global variables, other than hiding any other variable of the same name from view within its scope. (A global variable can always be accessed through its package-qualified form, however.) A private variable is not visible until the statement *after* its declaration. Subroutines called from within the scope of such a private variable cannot see the private variable unless the subroutine is also textually declared within the scope of the variable. The technical term for this is "lexical scoping", so we often call these "lexical variables". In C culture they're called "auto" variables, since they're automatically allocated and deallocated at scope entry and exit.

The EXPR may be assigned to if desired, which allows you to initialize your lexical variables. (If no initializer is given, all scalars are initialized to the undefined value and all arrays and hashes to empty arrays.) As with ordinary assignment, if you use parentheses around the variables on the left (or if the variable is an array or hash), the expression on the right is evaluated in list context. Otherwise the expression on the right is evaluated in scalar context. You can name your formal subroutine parameters with a list assignment, like this:

```
my ($friends, $romans, $countrymen) = @_;
```

Be careful not to omit the parentheses indicating list assignment, like this:

```
my $country = @_;   # right or wrong?
```

This assigns the length of the array (that is, the number of the subroutine's arguments) to the variable, since the array is being evaluated in scalar context. You can profitably use scalar assignment for a formal parameter though, as long as you use the **shift** operator. In fact, since object methods are passed the object as the first argument, many such method subroutines start off like this:

```
sub simple_as {
    my $self = shift;    # scalar assignment
    my ($a,$b,$c) = @_; # list assignment
    ...
}
```

new

```
new CLASSNAME LIST
new CLASSNAME
```

There is no built-in **new** function. It is merely an ordinary constructor method (subroutine) defined (or inherited) by the *CLASSNAME* module to let you construct objects of type *CLASSNAME*. Most constructors are named "new", but only by convention, just to delude C++ programmers into thinking they know what's going on.

next

```
next LABEL
next
```

The **next** command is like the **continue** statement in C: it starts the next iteration of the loop designated by *LABEL*:

```
LINE: while (<STDIN>) {
    next LINE if /^#/;      # discard comments
    ...
}
```

Note that if there were a **continue** block in this example, it would execute immediately following the invocation of **next**. When *LABEL* is omitted, the command refers to the innermost enclosing loop.

no

```
no Module LIST
```

See the **use** operator, which **no** is the opposite of, kind of.

oct

```
oct EXPR
```

This function interprets *EXPR* as an octal string and returns the equivalent decimal value. (If *EXPR* happens to start off with 0x, it is interpreted as a hex string instead.) The following will handle decimal, octal, and hex in the standard notation:

```
$val = oct $val if $val =~ /^0/;
```

If *EXPR* is omitted, the function interprets $_. To perform the inverse function on octal numbers, use:

```
$oct_string = sprintf "%lo", $number;
```

open

```
open FILEHANDLE, EXPR
open FILEHANDLE
```

This function opens the file whose filename is given by *EXPR*, and associates it with *FILEHANDLE*. If *EXPR* is omitted, the scalar variable of the same name as the *FILEHANDLE* must contain the filename. (And you must also be careful to use "or die" after the statement rather than "|| die", because the precedence of || is higher than list operators like **open**.) *FILEHANDLE* may be a directly specified filehandle name, or an expression whose value will be used for the filehandle. The latter is called an indirect filehandle. If you supply an undefined variable for the indirect filehandle, Perl will not automatically fill it in for you—you have to make sure the expression returns something unique, either a string specifying the actual filehandle name, or a filehandle object from one of the object-oriented I/O packages. (A filehandle object is unique because you call a constructor to generate the object. See the example later in this section.)

After the filehandle is determined, the filename string is processed. First, any leading and trailing whitespace is removed from the string. Then the string is examined on both ends for characters specifying how the file is to be opened. (By an amazing coincidence, these characters look just like the characters you'd use to indicate I/O redirection to the Bourne shell.) If the filename begins with < or nothing, the file is opened for input. If the filename begins with >, the file is truncated and opened for output. If the filename begins with >>, the file is opened for appending. (You can also put a + in front of the > or < to indicate that you want both read and write access to the file.) If the filename begins with |, the filename is interpreted as a command to which output is to be piped, and if the filename ends with a |, the filename is interpreted as command which pipes input to us. You may not have an **open** command that pipes both in and out, although the IPC::Open2 and IPC::Open3 library routines give you a close equivalent. See the section "Bidirectional Communication" in Chapter 6.

Any pipe command containing shell metacharacters is passed to */bin/sh* for execution; otherwise it is executed directly by Perl. The filename "-" refers to STDIN, and ">-" refers to STDOUT. **open** returns non-zero upon success, the undefined value otherwise. If the **open** involved a pipe, the return value happens to be the process ID of the subprocess.

If you're unfortunate enough to be running Perl on a system that distinguishes between text files and binary files (modern operating systems don't care), then you should check out **binmode** for tips for dealing with this. The key distinction between systems that need **binmode** and those that don't is their text file formats. Systems like UNIX and Plan9 that delimit lines with a single character, and that encode that character in C as '\n', do not need **binmode**. The rest need it.

Here is some code that shows the relatedness of a filehandle and a variable of the same name:

```
$ARTICLE = "/usr/spool/news/comp/lang/perl/misc/38245";
open ARTICLE or die "Can't find article $ARTICLE: $!\n";
while (<ARTICLE>) {...
```

Append to a file like this:

```
open LOG, '>>/usr/spool/news/twitlog'; # ('log' is reserved)
```

Pipe your data from a process:

```
open ARTICLE, "caesar <$article |";    # decrypt article with rot13
```

Here < does not indicate that Perl should open the file for input, because < is not the first character of *EXPR*. Rather, the concluding | indicates that input is to be piped from caesar <$article (from the program *caesar*, which takes *$article* as its standard input). The < is interpreted by the subshell that Perl uses to start the pipe, because < is a shell metacharacter.

Or pipe your data to a process:

```
open EXTRACT, "|sort >/tmp/Tmp$$";    # $$ is our process number
```

In this next example we show one way to do recursive opens, via indirect filehandles. The files will be opened on filehandles fh01, fh02, fh03, and so on. Because $input is a local variable, it is preserved through recursion, allowing us to close the correct file before we return.

```
# Process argument list of files along with any includes.

foreach $file (@ARGV) {
    process($file, 'fh00');
}

sub process {
    local($filename, $input) = @_;
    $input++;                 # this is a string increment
    unless (open $input, $filename) {
        print STDERR "Can't open $filename: $!\n";
        return;
    }
    while (<$input>) {       # note the use of indirection
        if (/^#include "(.*)"/) {
            process($1, $input);
            next;
        }
        ...                   # whatever
    }
    close $input;
}
```

You may also, in the Bourne shell tradition, specify an *EXPR* beginning with >&, in which case the rest of the string is interpreted as the name of a filehandle (or file descriptor, if numeric) which is to be duped and opened.[*] You may use & after >, >>, <, +>, +>>, and +<. The mode you specify should match the mode of the original filehandle. Here is a script that saves, redirects, and restores STDOUT and STDERR:

```
#!/usr/bin/perl
open SAVEOUT, ">&STDOUT";
open SAVEERR, ">&STDERR";

open STDOUT, ">foo.out" or die "Can't redirect stdout";
open STDERR, ">&STDOUT" or die "Can't dup stdout";

select STDERR; $| = 1;      # make unbuffered
select STDOUT; $| = 1;      # make unbuffered

print STDOUT "stdout 1\n";  # this propagates to
print STDERR "stderr 1\n";  # subprocesses too

close STDOUT;
close STDERR;

open STDOUT, ">&SAVEOUT";
open STDERR, ">&SAVEERR";

print STDOUT "stdout 2\n";
print STDERR "stderr 2\n";
```

If you specify <&=*N*, where *N* is a number, then Perl will do an equivalent of C's *fdopen*(3) of that file descriptor; this is more parsimonious with file descriptors than the dup form described earlier. (On the other hand, it's more dangerous, since two filehandles may now be sharing the same file descriptor, and a close on one filehandle may prematurely close the other.) For example:

```
open FILEHANDLE, "<&=$fd";
```

If you open a pipe to or from the command "-" (that is, either |- or -|), then an implicit fork is done, and the return value of **open** is the pid of the child within the parent process, and 0 within the child process. (Use defined($pid) in either the parent or child to determine whether the **open** was successful.) The filehandle behaves normally for the parent, but input and output to that filehandle is piped from or to the STDOUT or STDIN of the child process. In the child process the filehandle isn't opened—I/O happens from or to the new STDIN or STDOUT. Typically this is used like the normal piped **open** when you want to exercise more control over just how the pipe command gets executed, such as when you are running

---

[*] The word "dup" is UNIX-speak for "duplicate". We're not really trying to dupe you. Trust us.

setuid, and don't want to have to scan shell commands for metacharacters. The
following pairs are equivalent:

```
open FOO, "|tr '[a-z]' '[A-Z]'";
open FOO, "|-" or exec 'tr', '[a-z]', '[A-Z]';

open FOO, "cat -n file|";
open FOO, "-|" or exec 'cat', '-n', 'file';
```

Explicitly closing any piped filehandle causes the parent process to wait for the
child to finish, and returns the status value in $?. On any operation which may do
a fork, unflushed buffers remain unflushed in both processes, which means you
may need to set $| on one or more filehandles to avoid duplicate output (and
then do output to flush them).

Filehandles STDIN, STDOUT, and STDERR remain open following an exec. Other filehandles do not. (However, on systems supporting the **fcntl** function, you may
modify the close-on-exec flag for a filehandle. See **fcntl** earlier in this chapter. See
also the special $^F variable.)

Using the constructor from the FileHandle module, described in Chapter 7, you
can generate anonymous filehandles which have the scope of whatever variables
hold references to them, and automatically close whenever and however you
leave that scope:

```
use FileHandle;
...
sub read_myfile_munged {
    my $ALL = shift;
    my $handle = new FileHandle;
    open $handle, "myfile" or die "myfile: $!";
    $first = <$handle> or return ();      # Automatically closed here.
    mung $first or die "mung failed";     # Or here.
    return $first, <$handle> if $ALL;     # Or here.
    $first;                               # Or here.
}
```

In order to open a file with arbitrary weird characters in it, it's necessary to protect
any leading and trailing whitespace, like this:

```
$file =~ s#^(\s)#./$1#;
open (FOO, "< $file\0");
```

But we've never actually seen anyone use that in a script...

If you want a real C *open*(2), then you should use the **sysopen** function. This is
another way to protect your filenames from interpretation. For example:

```
use FileHandle;
sysopen HANDLE, $path, O_RDWR|O_CREAT|O_EXCL, 0700
    or die "sysopen $path: $!";
```

```
HANDLE->autoflush(1);
HANDLE->print("stuff $$\n");
seek HANDLE, 0, 0;
print "File contains: ", <HANDLE>;
```

See **seek** for some details about mixing reading and writing.

opendir

```
opendir DIRHANDLE, EXPR
```

This function opens a directory named *EXPR* for processing by **readdir**, **telldir**, **seekdir**, **rewinddir**, and **closedir**. The function returns true if successful. Directory handles have their own namespace separate from filehandles.

ord

```
ord EXPR
```

This function returns the numeric ASCII value of the first character of *EXPR*. If *EXPR* is omitted, it uses $_. The return value is always unsigned. If you want a signed value, use unpack('c', *EXPR*). If you want all the characters of the string converted to a list of numbers, use unpack('C*', *EXPR*) instead.

pack

```
pack TEMPLATE, LIST
```

This function takes a list of values and packs it into a binary structure, returning the string containing the structure. The *TEMPLATE* is a sequence of characters that gives the order and type of values, as follows:

Character	Meaning
a	An ASCII string, will be null padded
A	An ASCII string, will be space padded
b	A bit string, low-to-high order (like **vec**( ))
B	A bit string, high-to-low order
c	A signed char value
C	An unsigned char value
d	A double-precision float in the native format
f	A single-precision float in the native format
h	A hexadecimal string, low nybble first
H	A hexadecimal string, high nybble first
i	A signed integer value
I	An unsigned integer value
l	A signed long value
L	An unsigned long value *(continued)*

Character	Meaning
n	A short in "network" (big-endian) order
N	A long in "network" (big-endian) order
p	A pointer to a string
P	A pointer to a structure (fixed-length string)
s	A signed short value
S	An unsigned short value
v	A short in "VAX" (little-endian) order
V	A long in "VAX" (little-endian) order
u	A uuencoded string
x	A null byte
X	Back up a byte
@	Null-fill to absolute position

Each character may optionally be followed by a number which gives a repeat count. Together the character and the repeat count make a field specifier. Field specifiers may be separated by whitespace, which will be ignored. With all types except "a" and "A", the **pack** function will gobble up that many values from the *LIST*. Saying "*" for the repeat count means to use however many items are left. The "a" and "A" types gobble just one value, but pack it as a string of length *count*, padding with nulls or spaces as necessary. (When unpacking, "A" strips trailing spaces and nulls, but "a" does not.) Real numbers (floats and doubles) are in the native machine format only; due to the multiplicity of floating formats around, and the lack of a standard network representation, no facility for interchange has been made. This means that packed floating-point data written on one machine may not be readable on another—even if both use IEEE floating-point arithmetic (as the endian-ness of the memory representation is not part of the IEEE spec). Also, Perl uses doubles internally for all numeric calculation, and converting from double to float to double will lose precision; that is, `unpack("f", pack("f",$num))` will not in general equal $num.

This first pair of examples packs numeric values into bytes:

```
$out = pack "cccc", 65, 66, 67, 68;     # $out eq "ABCD"
$out = pack "c4", 65, 66, 67, 68;       # same thing
```

This does a similar thing, with a couple of nulls thrown in:

```
$out = pack "ccxxcc", 65, 66, 67, 68;   # $out eq "AB\0\0CD"
```

Packing your shorts doesn't imply that you're portable:

```
$out = pack "s2", 1, 2;    # "\1\0\2\0" on little-endian
                           # "\0\1\0\2" on big-endian
```

On binary and hex packs, the count refers to the number of bits or nybbles, not the number of bytes produced:

```
$out = pack "B32", "01010000011001010111001001101100";
$out = pack "H8", "5065726c";    # both produce "Perl"
```

The length on an "a" field applies only to one string:

```
$out = pack "a4", "abcd", "x", "y", "z";    # "abcd"
```

To get around that limitation, use multiple specifiers:

```
$out = pack "aaaa", "abcd", "x", "y", "z";    # "axyz"
$out = pack "a" x 4, "abcd", "x", "y", "z";    # "axyz"
```

The "a" format does null filling:

```
$out = pack "a14", "abcdefg";    # "abcdefg\0\0\0\0\0\0\0"
```

This template packs a C struct tm record (at least on some systems):

```
$out = pack "i9pl", gmtime, $tz, $toff;
```

The same template may generally also be used in the **unpack** function. If you want to join variable length fields with a delimiter, use the **join** function.

Note that, although all of our examples use literal strings as templates, there is no reason you couldn't pull in your templates from a disk file. You could, in fact, build an entire relational database system around this function.

package

package *NAMESPACE*

This is not really a function, but a declaration that says that the rest of the innermost enclosing block, subroutine, **eval** or file belongs to the indicated namespace. (The scope of a **package** declaration is thus the same as the scope of a **local** or **my** declaration.) All subsequent references to unqualified global identifiers will be resolved by looking them up in the declared package's symbol table. A **package** declaration affects only global variables—including those you've used **local** on— but not lexical variables created with **my**.

Typically you would put a **package** declaration as the first thing in a file that is to be included by the **require** or **use** operator, but you can put one anywhere that a statement would be legal. When defining a class or a module file, it is customary to name the package the same name as the file, to avoid confusion. (It's also customary to name such packages beginning with a capital letter, because lowercase modules are by convention interpreted as pragmas.)

You can switch into a given package in more than one place; it merely influences which symbol table is used by the compiler for the rest of that block. (If it sees another **package** declaration at the same level, the new one overrides the previous one.) Your main program is assumed to start with a package main declaration.

You can refer to variables and filehandles in other packages by qualifying the identifier with the package name and a double colon: $Package::Variable. If the package name is null, the main package as assumed. That is, $::sail is equivalent to $main::sail.

The symbol table for a package is stored in a hash with a name ending in a double colon. The main package's symbol table is named %main:: for example. So the package symbol *main::sail can also be accessed as $main::{"sail"}.

See "Packages" in Chapter 5, for more information about packages, modules, and classes. See **my** in Chapter 3, *Functions*, for other scoping issues.

pipe

>   pipe *READHANDLE, WRITEHANDLE*

Like the corresponding system call, this function opens a pair of connected pipes—see *pipe*(2). This call is almost always used right before a **fork**, after which the pipe's reader should close *WRITEHANDLE*, and the writer close *READHANDLE*. (Otherwise the pipe won't indicate EOF to the reader when the writer closes it.) Note that if you set up a loop of piped processes, deadlock can occur unless you are very careful. In addition, note that Perl's pipes use standard I/O buffering, so you may need to set $| on your *WRITEHANDLE* to flush after each output command, depending on the application—see **select** (*output filehandle*).

See also the section on "Pipes" in Chapter 6.

pop

>   pop *ARRAY*
>   pop

This function treats an array like a stack—it pops and returns the last value of the array, shortening the array by 1. If *ARRAY* is omitted, the function pops @**ARGV** (in the main program), or @_ (in subroutines). It has the same effect as:

```
$tmp = $ARRAY[$#ARRAY--];
```

or:

```
$tmp = splice @ARRAY, -1;
```

If there are no elements in the array, **pop** returns the undefined value. See also **push** and **shift**. If you want to pop more than one element, use **splice**.

Note that **pop** requires its first argument to be an array, not a list. If you just want the last element of a list, use this:

```
(something_returning_a_list)[-1]
```

pos

> pos *SCALAR*

Returns the location in *SCALAR* where the last m//g search over *SCALAR* left off. It returns the offset of the character *after* the last one matched. (That is, it's equivalent to length($`) + length($&).) This is the offset where the next m//g search on that string will start. Remember that the offset of the beginning of the string is 0. For example:

```
$grafitto = "fee fie foe foo";
while ($grafitto =~ m/e/g) {
    print pos $grafitto, "\n";
}
```

prints 2, 3, 7, and 11, the offsets of each of the characters following an "e". The **pos** function may be assigned a value to tell the next m//g where to start:

```
$grafitto = "fee fie foe foo";
pos $grafitto = 4;  # Skip the fee, start at fie
while ($grafitto =~ m/e/g) {
        print pos $grafitto, "\n";
}
```

This prints only 7 and 11. (Thank heaven.) The regular expression assertion, \G, matches only at the location currently specified by **pos** for the string being searched.

print

> print *FILEHANDLE LIST*
> print *LIST*
> print

This function prints a string or a comma-separated list of strings. The function returns 1 if successful, 0 otherwise. *FILEHANDLE* may be a scalar variable name (unsubscripted), in which case the variable contains either the name of the actual filehandle or a reference to a filehandle object from one of the object-oriented filehandle packages. *FILEHANDLE* may also be a block that returns either kind of value:

```
print { $OK ? "STDOUT" : "STDERR" } "stuff\n";
print { $iohandle[$i] } "stuff\n";
```

Note that if *FILEHANDLE* is a variable and the next token is a term, it may be misinterpreted as an operator unless you interpose a **+** or put parentheses around the arguments. For example:

```
print $a - 2;    # prints $a - 2 to default filehandle (usually STDOUT)
print $a (- 2);  # prints -2 to filehandle specified in $a
print $a -2;     # ditto (weird parsing rules :-)
```

If *FILEHANDLE* is omitted, the function prints to the currently selected output filehandle, initially STDOUT. To set the default output filehandle to something other than STDOUT use the select(*FILEHANDLE*) operation.[*] If *LIST* is also omitted, prints **$_**. Note that, because **print** takes a *LIST*, anything in the *LIST* is evaluated in list context, and any subroutine that you call will likely have one or more of its own internal expressions evaluated in list context. Thus, when you say:

```
print OUT <STDIN>;
```

it is not going to print out the next line from standard input, but all the rest of the lines from standard input up to end-of-file, since that's what <STDIN> returns in list context. Also, remembering the if-it-looks-like-a-function-it-is-a-function rule, be careful not to follow the **print** keyword with a left parenthesis unless you want the corresponding right parenthesis to terminate the arguments to the **print**—interpose a **+** or put parens around all the arguments:

```
print (1+2)*3, "\n";      # WRONG
print +(1+2)*3, "\n";     # ok
print ((1+2)*3, "\n");    # ok
```

printf

```
printf FILEHANDLE FORMAT LIST
printf FORMAT LIST
```

This function prints a formatted string to *FILEHANDLE* or, if omitted, the currently selected output filehandle, initially STDOUT. The first item in the *LIST* must be a string that says how to format the rest of the items. This is similar to the C library's *printf*(3) and *fprintf*(3) function, except that the ***** field width specifier is not supported. The function is equivalent to:

```
print FILEHANDLE sprintf LIST
```

See **print** and **sprintf**. The description of **sprintf** includes the list of acceptable specifications for the format string.

Don't fall into the trap of using a **printf** when a simple **print** would do. The **print** is more efficient, and less error prone.

---

[*] Thus, STDOUT isn't really the default filehandle for **print**. It's merely the default default filehandle.

push

```
push ARRAY, LIST
```

This function treats *ARRAY* as a stack, and pushes the values of *LIST* onto the end of *ARRAY*. The length of *ARRAY* increases by the length of *LIST*. The function returns this new length. The **push** function has the same effect as:

```
foreach $value (LIST) {
    $ARRAY[++$#ARRAY] = $value;
}
```

or:

```
splice @ARRAY, @ARRAY, 0, LIST;
```

but is more efficient (for both you and your computer). You can use **push** in combination with **shift** to make a fairly time-efficient shift register or queue:

```
for (;;) {
    push @ARRAY, shift @ARRAY;
    ...
}
```

See also **pop** and **unshift**.

q/STRING/

```
q/STRING/
qq/STRING/
qx/STRING/
qw/STRING/
```

Generalized quotes. See Chapter 2.

quotemeta

```
quotemeta EXPR
```

This function returns the value of *EXPR* (or **$_** if not specified) with all non-alphanumeric characters backslashed. This is the internal function implementing the \Q escape in interpolative contexts (including double-quoted strings, backticks, and patterns).

rand

```
rand EXPR
rand
```

This function returns a random fractional number between 0 and the value of *EXPR*. (*EXPR* should be positive.) If *EXPR* is omitted, the function returns a value between 0 and 1 (including 0, but excluding 1). See also **srand**.

To get an integral value, combine this with **int**, as in:

```
$roll = int(rand 6) + 1;        # $roll is now an integer between 1 and 6
```

read

```
read FILEHANDLE, SCALAR, LENGTH, OFFSET
read FILEHANDLE, SCALAR, LENGTH
```

This function attempts to read *LENGTH* bytes of data into variable *SCALAR* from the specified *FILEHANDLE*. The function returns the number of bytes actually read, 0 at end-of-file. It returns the undefined value on error. *SCALAR* will be grown or shrunk to the length actually read. The *OFFSET*, if specified, says where in the variable to start putting bytes, so that you can do a read into the middle of a string.

To copy data from filehandle FROM into filehandle TO, you could say:

```
while (read FROM, $buf, 16384) {
    print TO $buf;
}
```

Note that the opposite of **read** is simply a **print**, which already knows the length of the string you want to write, and can write a string of any length.

Perl's **read** function is actually implemented in terms of standard I/O's *fread*(3) function, so the actual *read*(2) system call may read more than *LENGTH* bytes to fill the input buffer, and *fread*(3) may do more than one system *read*(2) in order to fill the buffer. To gain greater control, specify the real system call using **sysread**. Calls to **read** and **sysread** should not be intermixed unless you are into heavy wizardry (or pain).

readdir

```
readdir DIRHANDLE
```

This function reads directory entries from a directory handle opened by **opendir**. In scalar context, this function returns the next directory entry, if any, otherwise an undefined value. In list context, it returns all the rest of the entries in the directory, which will of course be a null list if there are none. For example:

```
opendir THISDIR, "." or die "serious dainbramage: $!";
@allfiles = readdir THISDIR;
closedir THISDIR;
print "@allfiles\n";
```

prints all the files in the current directory on one line. If you want to avoid the "."
and ".." entries, use this instead:

```
@allfiles = grep !/^\.\.?$/, readdir THISDIR;
```

And to avoid all `.*` files (like the *ls* program):

```
@allfiles = grep !/^\./, readdir THISDIR;
```

To get just text files, say this:

```
@textfiles = grep -T, readdir THISDIR;
```

But watch out on that last one, because the result of **readdir** needs to have the
directory part glued back on if it's not the current directory—like this:

```
opendir THATDIR, $thatdir;
@text_of_thatdir = grep -T, map "$thatdir/$_", readdir THATDIR;
closedir THATDIR;
```

readlink

```
readlink EXPR
```

This function returns the name of a file pointed to by a symbolic link. *EXPR* should
evaluate to a filename, the last component of which is a symbolic link. If it is not a
symbolic link, or if symbolic links are not implemented, or if some system error
occurs, the undefined value is returned, and you should check the error code in
`$!`. If *EXPR* is omitted, the function uses `$_`.

Be aware that the returned symlink may be relative to the location you specified.
For instance, you may say:

```
readlink "/usr/local/src/express/yourself.h"
```

and **readlink** might return:

```
../express.1.23/includes/yourself.h
```

which is not directly usable as a filename unless your current directory happens to
be `/usr/local/src/express`.

recv

```
recv SOCKET, SCALAR, LEN, FLAGS
```

This function receives a message on a socket. It attempts to receive *LENGTH* bytes
of data into variable *SCALAR* from the specified *SOCKET* filehandle. The function
returns the address of the sender, or the undefined value if there's an error. *SCALAR*
will be grown or shrunk to the length actually read. The function takes the same
flags as *recv*(2). See the section "Sockets" in Chapter 6.

redo

```
redo LABEL
redo
```

The **redo** command restarts a loop block without evaluating the conditional again. The **continue** block, if any, is not executed. If the *LABEL* is omitted, the command refers to the innermost enclosing loop. This command is normally used by programs that wish to deceive themselves about what was just input:

```
# A loop that joins lines continued with a backslash.
LINE: while (<STDIN>) {
    if (s/\\\n$// and $nextline = <STDIN>) {
        $_ .= $nextline;
        redo LINE;
    }
    print;  # or whatever...
}
```

ref

```
ref EXPR
```

The **ref** operator returns a true value if *EXPR* is a reference, the null string otherwise. The value returned depends on the type of thing the reference is a reference to. Built-in types include:

```
REF
SCALAR
ARRAY
HASH
CODE
GLOB
```

If the referenced object has been blessed into a package, then that package name is returned instead. You can think of **ref** as a "typeof" operator.

```
if (ref($r) eq "HASH") {
    print "r is a reference to a hash.\n";
}
elsif (ref($r) eq "Hump") {
    print "r is a reference to a Hump object.\n";
}
elsif (not ref $r) {
    print "r is not a reference at all.\n";
}
```

See Chapter 4 for more details.

rename

```
rename OLDNAME, NEWNAME
```

This function changes the name of a file. It returns 1 for success, 0 otherwise (and puts the error code into $!). It will not work across filesystem boundaries. If there is already a file named *NEWNAME*, it will be destroyed.

require

```
require EXPR
require
```

This function asserts a dependency of some kind on its argument. (If *EXPR* is not supplied, $_ is used as the argument.)

If the argument is a string, this function includes and executes the Perl code found in the separate file whose name is given by the string. This is similar to performing an **eval** on the contents of the file, except that **require** checks to see that the library file has not been included already. (It can thus be used to express file dependencies without worrying about duplicate compilation.) The function also knows how to search the include path stored in the @INC array (see the section "Special Variables" in Chapter 2).

This form of the **require** function behaves much like this subroutine:

```
sub require {
    my($filename) = @_;
    return 1 if $INC{$filename};
    my($realfilename, $result);
    ITER: {
        foreach $prefix (@INC) {
            $realfilename = "$prefix/$filename";
            if (-f $realfilename) {
                $result = eval `cat $realfilename`;
                last ITER;
            }
        }
        die "Can't find $filename in \@INC";
    }
    die $@ if $@;
    die "$filename did not return true value" unless $result;
    $INC{$filename} = $realfilename;
    return $result;
}
```

Note that the file must return true as the last value to indicate successful execution of any initialization code, so it's customary to end such a file with 1; unless you're sure it'll return true otherwise.

This operator differs from the now somewhat obsolete do *EXPR* operator in that the file will not be included again if it was included previously with either a **require** or do *EXPR* command, and any difficulties will be detected and reported as fatal errors (which may be trapped by use of **eval**). The **do** command does know how to do the @INC path search, however.

If **require**'s argument is a number, the version number of the currently executing Perl binary (as known by $]) is compared to *EXPR*, and if smaller, execution is immediately aborted. Thus, a script that requires Perl version 5.003 can have as its first line:

```
require 5.003;
```

and earlier versions of Perl will abort.

If **require**'s argument is a package name (see **package**), **require** assumes an automatic .pm suffix, making it easy to load standard modules. This is like **use**, except that it happens at run-time, not compile time, and the **import** routine is not called. For example, to pull in Socket.pm without introducing any symbols into the current package, say this:

```
require Socket; # instead of "use Socket;"
```

However, one can get the same effect with the following, which has the advantage of giving a compile-time warning if Socket.pm can't be located:

```
use Socket ();
```

reset

```
reset EXPR
reset
```

This function is generally used at the top of a loop or in a **continue** block at the end of a loop, to clear global variables or reset ?? searches so that they work again. The expression is interpreted as a list of single characters (hyphens are allowed for ranges). All scalar variables, arrays, and hashes beginning with one of those letters are reset to their pristine state. If the expression is omitted, one-match searches (?*PATTERN*?) are reset to match again. The function resets variables or searches for the current package only. It always returns 1.

To reset all "x" variables, say this:

```
reset 'X';
```

To reset all lowercase variables, say this:

```
reset 'a-z';
```

Lastly, to just reset ?? searches, say:

```
reset;
```

Note that resetting "A-Z" is not recommended since you'll wipe out your **ARGV**, **INC**, **ENV**, and **SIG** arrays.

Lexical variables (created by **my**) are not affected. Use of **reset** is vaguely deprecated.

return

```
return EXPR
```

This function returns from a subroutine (or **eval**) with the value specified. (In the absence of an explicit **return**, the value of the last expression evaluated is returned.) Use of **return** outside of a subroutine or **eval** is verboten, and results in a fatal error. Note also that an **eval** cannot do a **return** on behalf of the subroutine that called the **eval**.

The supplied expression will be evaluated in the context of the subroutine invocation. That is, if the subroutine was called in a scalar context, *EXPR* is also evaluated in scalar context. If the subroutine was invoked in a list context, then *EXPR* is also evaluated in list context, and can return a list value. A return with no argument returns the undefined value in scalar context, and a null list in list context. The context of the subroutine call can be determined from within the subroutine by using the (misnamed) **wantarray** function.

reverse

```
reverse LIST
```

In list context, this function returns a list value consisting of the elements of *LIST* in the opposite order. This is fairly efficient because it just swaps the pointers around. The function can be used to create descending sequences:

```
for (reverse 1 .. 10) { ... }
```

Because of the way hashes flatten into lists when passed to (non-hash-aware) functions, **reverse** can also be used to invert a hash, presuming the values are unique:

```
%barfoo = reverse %foobar;
```

In scalar context, the function concatenates all the elements of *LIST* together and then returns the reverse of that, character by character.

A small hint: reversing a list sorted earlier by a user-defined function can sometimes be achieved more easily by simply sorting in the opposite direction in the first place.

rewinddir

```
rewinddir DIRHANDLE
```

This function sets the current position to the beginning of the directory for the **readdir** routine on *DIRHANDLE*. The function may not be available on all machines that support **readdir**.

rindex

```
rindex STR, SUBSTR, POSITION
rindex STR, SUBSTR
```

This function works just like **index** except that it returns the position of the last occurrence of *SUBSTR* in *STR* (a reverse **index**). The function returns $[-1 if not found. Since $[is almost always 0 nowadays, the function almost always returns -1. *POSITION*, if specified, is the rightmost position that may be returned. To work your way through a string backward, say:

```
$pos = length $string;
while (($pos = rindex $string, $lookfor, $pos) >= 0) {
    print "Found at $pos\n";
    $pos--;
}
```

rmdir

```
rmdir FILENAME
```

This function deletes the directory specified by *FILENAME* if it is empty. If it succeeds, it returns 1, otherwise it returns 0 and puts the error code into $!. If FILE-NAME is omitted, the function uses $_.

s///

```
s///
```

The substitution operator. See "Pattern Matching Operators" in Chapter 2.

scalar

```
scalar EXPR
```

This pseudo-function may be used within a *LIST* to force *EXPR* to be evaluated in scalar context when evaluation in list context would produce a different result.

For example:

```
local($nextvar) = scalar <STDIN>;
```

prevents <STDIN> from reading all the lines from standard input before doing the assignment, since assignment to a **local** list provides a list context. (Without the use of **scalar** in this example, the first line from <STDIN> would still be assigned to $nextvar, but the subsequent lines would be read and thrown away. This is because the assignment is being made to a list—one that happens to be able to receive only a single, scalar value.)

Of course, a simpler way with less typing would be to simply leave the parentheses off, thereby changing the list context to a scalar one:

```
local $nextvar = <STDIN>;
```

Since a **print** function is a *LIST* operator, you have to say:

```
print "Length is ", scalar(@ARRAY), "\n";
```

if you want the length of @ARRAY to be printed out.

One never needs to force evaluation in a list context, because any operation that wants a list already provides a list context to its list arguments for free. So there's no **list** function corresponding to **scalar**.

seek

```
seek FILEHANDLE, OFFSET, WHENCE
```

This function positions the file pointer for *FILEHANDLE*, just like the *fseek*(3) call of standard I/O. The first position in a file is at offset 0, not offset 1, and offsets refer to byte positions, not line numbers. (In general, since line lengths vary, it's not possible to access a particular line number without examining the whole file up to that line number, unless all your lines are known to be of a particular length, or you've built an index that translates line numbers into byte offsets.) *FILEHANDLE* may be an expression whose value gives the name of the filehandle or a reference to a filehandle object. The function returns 1 upon success, 0 otherwise. For handiness, the function can calculate offsets from various file positions for you. The value of *WHENCE* specifies which file position your *OFFSET* is relative to: 0, the beginning of the file; 1, the current position in the file; or 2, the end of the file. *OFFSET* may be negative for a *WHENCE* of 1 or 2.

One interesting use for this function is to allow you to follow growing files, like this:

```
for (;;) {
    while (<LOG>) {
        ...                 # Process file.
```

```
    }
    sleep 15;
    seek LOG,0,1;        # Reset end-of-file error.
}
```

The final **seek** clears the end-of-file error without moving the pointer. If that
doesn't work (depending on your C library's standard I/O implementation), then
you may need something more like this:

```
for (;;) {
    for ($curpos = tell FILE; $_ = <FILE>; $curpos = tell FILE) {
        # search for some stuff and put it into files
    }
    sleep $for_a_while;
    seek FILE, $curpos, 0;
}
```

Similar strategies could be used to remember the **seek** addresses of each line in an
array.

seekdir

```
seekdir DIRHANDLE, POS
```

This function sets the current position for the **readdir** routine on *DIRHANDLE*. *POS*
must be a value returned by **telldir**. This function has the same caveats about possible directory compaction as the corresponding system library routine. The function may not be implemented everywhere that **readdir** is. It's certainly not
implemented where **readdir** isn't.

select (output filehandle)

```
select FILEHANDLE
select
```

For historical reasons, there are two **select** operators that are totally unrelated to
each other. See the next section for the other one. This **select** operator returns the
currently selected output filehandle, and if *FILEHANDLE* is supplied, sets the current
default filehandle for output. This has two effects: first, a **write** or a **print** without a
filehandle will default to this *FILEHANDLE*. Second, special variables related to output will refer to this output filehandle. For example, if you have to set the same
top-of-form format for more than one output filehandle, you might do the following:

```
select REPORT1;
$^ = 'MyTop';
select REPORT2;
$^ = 'MyTop';
```

But note that this leaves `REPORT2` as the currently selected filehandle. This could be construed as antisocial, since it could really foul up some other routine's **print** or **write** statements. Properly written library routines leave the currently selected filehandle the same on exit as it was upon entry. To support this, *FILEHANDLE* may be an expression whose value gives the name of the actual filehandle. Thus, you can save and restore the currently selected filehandle:

```
my $oldfh = select STDERR; $| = 1; select $oldfh;
```

or (being bizarre and obscure):

```
select((select(STDERR), $| = 1)[0])
```

This example works by building a list consisting of the returned value from `select(STDERR)` (which selects `STDERR` as a side effect) and `$| = 1` (which is always 1), but sets autoflushing on the now-selected `STDERR` as a side effect. The first element of that list (the previously selected filehandle) is now used as an argument to the outer **select**. Bizarre, right? That's what you get for knowing just enough Lisp to be dangerous.

However, now that we've explained all that, we should point out that you rarely need to use this form of **select** nowadays, because most of the special variables you would want to set have object-oriented wrapper methods to do it for you. So instead of setting `$|` directly, you might say:

```
use FileHandle;
STDOUT->autoflush(1);
```

And the earlier format example might be coded as:

```
use FileHandle;
REPORT1->format_top_name("MyTop");
REPORT2->format_top_name("MyTop");
```

select (ready file descriptors)

```
select RBITS, WBITS, EBITS, TIMEOUT
```

The four-argument **select** operator is totally unrelated to the previously described operator. This operator is for discovering which (if any) of your file descriptors are ready to do input or output, or to report an exceptional condition. (This helps you avoid having to do polling.) It calls the *select*(2) system call with the bitmasks you've specified, which you can construct using **fileno** and **vec**, like this:

```
$rin = $win = $ein = "";
vec($rin, fileno(STDIN), 1) = 1;
vec($win, fileno(STDOUT), 1) = 1;
$ein = $rin | $win;
```

If you want to **select** on many filehandles you might wish to write a subroutine:

```
sub fhbits {
    my @fhlist = @_;
    my $bits;
    for (@fhlist) {
        vec($bits, fileno($_), 1) = 1;
    }
    return $bits;
}
$rin = fhbits(qw(STDIN TTY MYSOCK));
```

If you wish to use the same bitmasks repeatedly (and it's more efficient if you do), the usual idiom is:

```
($nfound, $timeleft) =
    select($rout=$rin, $wout=$win, $eout=$ein, $timeout);
```

Or to block until any file descriptor becomes ready:

```
$nfound = select($rout=$rin, $wout=$win, $eout=$ein, undef);
```

The `$wout=$win` trick works because the value of an assignment is its left side, so `$wout` gets clobbered first by the assignment, and then by the **select**, while `$win` remains unchanged.

Any of the bitmasks can also be **undef**. The timeout, if specified, is in seconds, which may be fractional. (A timeout of 0 effects a poll.) Not many implementations are capable of returning the `$timeleft`. If not, they always return `$timeleft` equal to the supplied `$timeout`.

One use for **select** is to sleep with a finer resolution than **sleep** allows. To do this, specify **undef** for all the bitmasks. So, to sleep for (at least) 4.75 seconds, use:

```
select undef, undef, undef, 4.75;
```

(On some non-UNIX systems this may not work, and you may need to fake up at least one bitmask for a valid descriptor that won't ever be ready.)

Mixing buffered I/O (like **read** or **<HANDLE>**) with four-argument **select** is asking for trouble. Use **sysread** instead.

semctl

    semctl *ID, SEMNUM, CMD, ARG*

This function calls the System V IPC system call *semctl*(2). If CMD is &IPC_STAT or &GETALL, then ARG must be a variable which will hold the returned semid_ds structure or semaphore value array. The function returns like **ioctl**: the undefined value for error, "0 but true" for zero, or the actual return value otherwise. On error, it puts the error code into $!. Before calling, you should say:

```
require "ipc.ph";
require "sem.ph";
```

This function is available only on machines supporting System V IPC.

semget

```
semget KEY, NSEMS, SIZE, FLAGS
```

This function calls the System V IPC system call *semget*(2). The function returns the semaphore ID, or the undefined value if there is an error. On error, it puts the error code into $!. Before calling, you should say:

```
require "ipc.ph";
require "sem.ph";
```

This function is available only on machines supporting System V IPC.

semop

```
semop KEY, OPSTRING
```

This function calls the System V IPC system call *semop*(2) to perform semaphore operations such as signaling and waiting. *OPSTRING* must be a packed array of semop structures. You can make each **semop** structure by saying pack("s*", $sem-num, $semop, $semflag). The number of semaphore operations is implied by the length of *OPSTRING*. The function returns true if successful, or false if there is an error. On error, it puts the error code into $!. Before calling, you should say:

```
require "ipc.ph";
require "sem.ph";
```

The following code waits on semaphore $semnum of semaphore id $semid:

```
$semop = pack "s*", $semnum, -1, 0;
die "Semaphore trouble: $!\n" unless semop $semid, $semop;
```

To signal the semaphore, simply replace –1 with 1.

This function is available only on machines supporting System V IPC.

send

```
send SOCKET, MSG, FLAGS, TO
send SOCKET, MSG, FLAGS
```

This function sends a message on a socket. It takes the same flags as the system call of the same name—see *send*(2). On unconnected sockets you must specify a destination to send *TO*, in which case **send** works like *sendto*(2). The function returns the number of bytes sent, or the undefined value if there is an error. On error, it puts the error code into $!.

(Some non-UNIX systems improperly treat sockets as different objects than ordinary file descriptors, with the result that you must always use **send** and **recv** on sockets rather than the handier standard I/O operators.)

setpgrp

```
setpgrp PID, PGRP
```

This function sets the current process group (pgrp) for the specified *PID* (use a *PID* of 0 for the current process). Invoking **setpgrp** will produce a fatal error if used on a machine that doesn't implement *setpgrp*(2). Beware: some systems will ignore the arguments you provide and always do `setpgrp(0, $$)`. Fortunately, those are the arguments one usually provides. (For better portability (by some definition), use the `setpgid()` function in the POSIX module, or if you're really just trying to daemonize your script, consider the `POSIX::setsid()` function as well.)

setpriority

```
setpriority WHICH, WHO, PRIORITY
```

This function sets the current priority for a process, a process group, or a user. See *setpriority*(2). Invoking **setpriority** will produce a fatal error if used on a machine that doesn't implement *setpriority*(2). To "nice" your process down by four units (the same as executing your program with *nice*(1)), try:

```
setpriority 0, 0, getpriority(0, 0) + 4;
```

The interpretation of a given priority may vary from one operating system to the next.

setsockopt

```
setsockopt SOCKET, LEVEL, OPTNAME, OPTVAL
```

This function sets the socket option requested. The function returns undefined if there is an error. *OPTVAL* may be specified as **undef** if you don't want to pass an argument. A common option to set on a socket is SO_REUSEADDR, to get around the problem of not being able to bind to a particular address while the previous TCP connection on that port is still making up its mind to shut down. That would look like this:

```
use Socket;
...
setsockopt(MYSOCK, SOL_SOCKET, SO_REUSEADDR, 1)
        or warn "Can't do setsockopt: $!\n";
```

shift

```
shift ARRAY
shift
```

This function shifts the first value of the array off and returns it, shortening the array by 1 and moving everything down. (Or up, or left, depending on how you visualize the array list.) If there are no elements in the array, the function returns the undefined value. If ARRAY is omitted, the function shifts **@ARGV** (in the main program), or @_ (in subroutines). See also **unshift, push, pop,** and **splice**. The **shift** and **unshift** functions do the same thing to the left end of an array that **pop** and **push** do to the right end.

shmctl

```
shmctl ID, CMD, ARG
```

This function calls the System V IPC system call, *shmctl*(2). If CMD is &IPC_STAT, then ARG must be a variable which will hold the returned shmid_ds structure. The function returns like **ioctl**: the undefined value for error, "0 but true" for zero, or the actual return value otherwise. On error, it puts the error code into $!. Before calling, you should say:

```
require "ipc.ph";
require "shm.ph";
```

This function is available only on machines supporting System V IPC.

shmget

```
shmget KEY, SIZE, FLAGS
```

This function calls the System V IPC system call, *shmget*(2). The function returns the shared memory segment ID, or the undefined value if there is an error. On error, it puts the error code into $!. Before calling, you should say:

```
require "ipc.ph";
require "shm.ph";
```

This function is available only on machines supporting System V IPC.

shmread

```
shmread ID, VAR, POS, SIZE
```

This function reads from the shared memory segment ID starting at position POS for size SIZE (by attaching to it, copying out, and detaching from it). VAR must be a variable that will hold the data read. The function returns true if successful, or false if there is an error. On error, it puts the error code into $!. This function is available only on machines supporting System V IPC.

shmwrite

```
shmwrite ID, STRING, POS, SIZE
```

This function writes to the shared memory segment ID starting at position *POS* for size *SIZE* (by attaching to it, copying in, and detaching from it). If *STRING* is too long, only *SIZE* bytes are used; if *STRING* is too short, nulls are written to fill out *SIZE* bytes. The function returns true if successful, or false if there is an error. On error, it puts the error code into $!. This function is available only on machines supporting System V IPC.

shutdown

```
shutdown SOCKET, HOW
```

This function shuts down a socket connection in the manner indicated by *HOW*. If *HOW* is 0, further receives are disallowed. If *HOW* is 1, further sends are disallowed. If *HOW* is 2, everything is disallowed.

(If you came here trying to figure out how to shut down your system, you'll have to execute an external program to do that. See **system**.)

sin

```
sin EXPR
```

Sorry, there's nothing wicked about this operator. It merely returns the sine of *EXPR* (expressed in radians). If *EXPR* is omitted, it returns sine of $_.

For the inverse sine operation, you may use the POSIX::asin() function, or use this relation:

```
sub asin { atan2($_[0], sqrt(1 - $_[0] * $_[0])) }
```

sleep

```
sleep EXPR
sleep
```

This function causes the script to sleep for *EXPR* seconds, or forever if no *EXPR*. It may be interrupted by sending the process a SIGALRM. The function returns the number of seconds actually slept. On some systems, the function sleeps till the "top of the second," so, for instance, a `sleep` 1 may sleep anywhere from 0 to 1 second, depending on when in the current second you started sleeping. A `sleep` 2 may sleep anywhere from 1 to 2 seconds. And so on. If available, the **select** (ready file descriptors) call can give you better resolution. You may also be able to use **syscall** to call the *getitimer*(2) and *setitimer*(2) routines that some UNIX systems support.

socket

```
socket SOCKET, DOMAIN, TYPE, PROTOCOL
```

This function opens a socket of the specified kind and attaches it to filehandle *SOCKET. DOMAIN, TYPE,* and *PROTOCOL* are specified the same as for *socket*(2). Before using this function, your program should contain the line:

```
use Socket;
```

This gives you the proper constants. The function returns true if successful. See the examples in the section "Sockets" in Chapter 6.

socketpair

```
socketpair SOCKET1, SOCKET2, DOMAIN, TYPE, PROTOCOL
```

This function creates an unnamed pair of sockets in the specified domain, of the specified type. *DOMAIN, TYPE,* and *PROTOCOL* are specified the same as for *socketpair*(2). If *socketpair*(2) is unimplemented, invoking this function yields a fatal error. The function returns true if successful.

This function is typically used just before a **fork**. One of the resulting processes should close *SOCKET1*, and the other should close *SOCKET2*. You can use these sockets bidirectionally, unlike the filehandles created by the **pipe** function.

sort

```
sort SUBNAME LIST
sort BLOCK LIST
sort LIST
```

This function sorts the *LIST* and returns the sorted list value. By default, it sorts in standard string comparison order (undefined values sorting before defined null strings, which sort before everything else). *SUBNAME,* if given, is the name of a subroutine that returns an integer less than, equal to, or greater than 0, depending on how the elements of the list are to be ordered. (The handy <=> and `cmp` operators can be used to perform three-way numeric and string comparisons.) In the interests of efficiency, the normal calling code for subroutines is bypassed, with the following effects: the subroutine may not be a recursive subroutine, and the two elements to be compared are passed into the subroutine not via @_ but as **$a** and **$b** (see the examples below). The variables **$a** and **$b** are passed by reference, so don't modify them in the subroutine. *SUBNAME* may be a scalar variable name (unsubscripted), in which case the value provides the name of (or a reference to) the actual subroutine to use. In place of a *SUBNAME*, you can provide a *BLOCK* as an anonymous, in-line sort subroutine.

To do an ordinary numeric sort, say this:

```
sub numerically { $a <=> $b; }
@sortedbynumber = sort numerically 53,29,11,32,7;
```

To sort in descending order, simply reverse the $a and $b. To sort a list value by some associated value, use a hash lookup in the sort routine:

```
sub byage {
    $age{$a} <=> $age{$b};
}
@sortedclass = sort byage @class;
```

As an extension of that notion, you can cascade several different comparisons using the handy comparison operators, which work nicely for this because when they return 0 they fall through to the next case. The routine below sorts to the front of the list those people who are first richer, then taller, then younger, then less alphabetically challenged. We also put a final comparison between $a and $b to make sure the ordering is always well defined.

```
sub prospects {
    $money{$b} <=> $money{$a}
        or
    $height{$b} <=> $height{$a}
        or
    $age{$a} <=> $age{$b}
        or
    $lastname{$a} cmp $lastname{$b}
        or
    $a cmp $b;
}
@sortedclass = sort prospects @class;
```

To sort fields without regard to case, say:

```
@sorted = sort { lc($a) cmp lc($b) } @unsorted;
```

And finally, note the equivalence of the two ways to sort in reverse:

```
sub backwards { $b cmp $a; }
@harry = qw(dog cat x Cain Abel);
@george = qw(gone chased yz Punished Axed);
```

```
print sort @harry;              # prints AbelCaincatdogx
print sort backwards @harry;    # prints xdogcatCainAbel
print reverse sort @harry;      # prints xdogcatCainAbel
print sort @george, "to", @harry;  # Remember, it's one LIST.
         # prints AbelAxedCainPunishedcatchaseddoggonetoxyz
```

Do not declare **$a** and **$b** as lexical variables (with **my**). They are package globals (though they're exempt from the usual restrictions on globals when you're using **use strict**). You do need to make sure your sort routine is in the same package though, or qualify $a and $b with the package name of the caller.

One last caveat. Perl's **sort** is implemented in terms of C's *qsort*(3) function. Some *qsort*(3) versions will dump core if your sort subroutine provides inconsistent ordering of values.

splice

```
splice ARRAY, OFFSET, LENGTH, LIST
splice ARRAY, OFFSET, LENGTH
splice ARRAY, OFFSET
```

This function removes the elements designated by *OFFSET* and *LENGTH* from an array, and replaces them with the elements of *LIST*, if any. The function returns the elements removed from the array. The array grows or shrinks as necessary. If *LENGTH* is omitted, the function removes everything from *OFFSET* onward. The following equivalences hold (assuming $[is 0):

Direct Method	Splice Equivalent
push(@a, $x, $y)	splice(@a, $#a+1, 0, $x, $y)
pop(@a)	splice(@a, -1)
shift(@a)	splice(@a, 0, 1)
unshift(@a, $x, $y)	splice(@a, 0, 0, $x, $y)
$a[$x] = $y	splice(@a, $x, 1, $y);

The **splice** function is also handy for carving up the argument list passed to a subroutine. For example, assuming list lengths are passed before lists:

```
sub list_eq {        # compare two list values
    my @a = splice(@_, 0, shift);
    my @b = splice(@_, 0, shift);
    return 0 unless @a == @b;        # same len?
    while (@a) {
        return 0 if pop(@a) ne pop(@b);
    }
    return 1;
}
if (list_eq($len, @foo[1..$len], scalar(@bar), @bar)) { ... }
```

It would probably be cleaner just to use references for this, however.

split

```
split /PATTERN/, EXPR, LIMIT
split /PATTERN/, EXPR
split /PATTERN/
split
```

This function scans a string given by EXPR for delimiters, and splits the string into a list of substrings, returning the resulting list value in list context, or the count of substrings in scalar context. The delimiters are determined by repeated pattern matching, using the regular expression given in PATTERN, so the delimiters may be of any size, and need not be the same string on every match. (The delimiters are not ordinarily returned, but see below.) If the PATTERN doesn't match at all, **split** returns the original string as a single substring. If it matches once, you get two substrings, and so on.

If LIMIT is specified and is not negative, the function splits into no more than that many fields (though it may split into fewer if it runs out of delimiters). If LIMIT is negative, it is treated as if an arbitrarily large LIMIT has been specified. If LIMIT is omitted, trailing null fields are stripped from the result (which potential users of **pop** would do well to remember). If EXPR is omitted, the function splits the $_ string. If PATTERN is also omitted, the function splits on whitespace, /\s+/, after skipping any leading whitespace.

Strings of any length can be split:

```
@chars = split //, $word;
@fields = split /:/, $line;
@words = split ' ', $paragraph;
@lines = split /^/m, $buffer;
```

A pattern capable of matching either the null string or something longer than the null string (for instance, a pattern consisting of any single character modified by a * or ?) will split the value of EXPR into separate characters wherever it is the null string that produces the match; non-null matches will skip over occurrences of the delimiter in the usual fashion. (In other words, a pattern won't match in one spot more than once, even if it matched with a zero width.) For example:

```
print join ':', split / */, 'hi there';
```

produces the output "h:i:t:h:e:r:e". The space disappears because it matched as part of the delimiter. As a trivial case, the null pattern // simply splits into separate characters (and spaces do not disappear).

The *LIMIT* parameter is used to split only part of a string:

```
($login, $passwd, $remainder) = split /:/, $_, 3;
```

We encourage you to split to lists of names like this in order to make your code self-documenting. (For purposes of error checking, note that $remainder would be undefined if there were fewer than three fields.) When assigning to a list, if *LIMIT* is omitted, Perl supplies a *LIMIT* one larger than the number of variables in the list, to avoid unnecessary work. For the split above, *LIMIT* would have been 4 by default, and $remainder would have received only the third field, not all the rest of the fields. In time-critical applications it behooves you not to split into more fields than you really need.

We said earlier that the delimiters are not returned, but if the *PATTERN* contains parentheses, then the substring matched by each pair of parentheses is included in the resulting list, interspersed with the fields that are ordinarily returned. Here's a simple case:

```
split /([-,])/, "1-10,20";
```

produces the list value:

```
(1, '-', 10, ',', 20)
```

With more parentheses, a field is returned for each pair, even if some of the pairs don't match, in which case undefined values are returned in those positions. So if you say:

```
split /(-)|(,)/, "1-10,20";
```

you get the value:

```
(1, '-', undef, 10, undef, ',', 20)
```

The */PATTERN/* argument may be replaced with an expression to specify patterns that vary at run-time. (To do run-time compilation only once, use /$variable/o.) As a special case, specifying a space " " will split on whitespace just as **split** with no arguments does. Thus, split(" ") can be used to emulate *awk*'s default behavior, whereas split(/ /) will give you as many null initial fields as there are leading spaces. (Other than this special case, if you supply a string instead of a regular expression, it'll be interpreted as a regular expression anyway.)

The following example splits an RFC-822 message header into a hash containing $head{Date}, $head{Subject}, and so on. It uses the trick of assigning a list of pairs to a hash, based on the fact that delimiters alternate with delimited fields. It makes use of parentheses to return part of each delimiter as part of the returned list value. Since the **split** pattern is guaranteed to return things in pairs by virtue of containing one set of parentheses, the hash assignment is guaranteed to receive a list consisting of key/value pairs, where each key is the name of a header field. (Unfortunately this technique loses information for multiple lines with the same key field, such as Received-By lines. Ah, well. . . .)

```
$header =~ s/\n\s+/ /g;        # Merge continuation lines.
%head = ('FRONTSTUFF', split /^([-\w]+):/m, $header);
```

The following example processes the entries in a UNIX *passwd* file. You could leave out the **chop**, in which case $shell would have a newline on the end of it.

```
open PASSWD, '/etc/passwd';
while (<PASSWD>) {
    chop;          # remove trailing newline
    ($login, $passwd, $uid, $gid, $gcos, $home, $shell) =
            split /:/;
    ...
}
```

The inverse of **split** is performed by **join** (except that **join** can only join with the same delimiter between all fields). To break apart a string with fixed-position fields, use **unpack**.

sprintf

```
sprintf FORMAT, LIST
```

This function returns a string formatted by the usual **printf** conventions. The *FOR-MAT* string contains text with embedded field specifiers into which the elements of *LIST* are substituted, one per field. Field specifiers are roughly of the form:

```
%m.nx
```

where the *m* and *n* are optional sizes whose interpretation depends on the type of field, and *x* is one of:

Code	Meaning
c	Character
d	Decimal integer
e	Exponential format floating-point number
f	Fixed point format floating-point number
g	Compact format floating-point number
ld	Long decimal integer
lo	Long octal integer
lu	Long unsigned decimal integer
lx	Long hexadecimal integer
o	Octal integer
s	String
u	Unsigned decimal integer

Code	Meaning
x	Hexadecimal integer
X	Hexadecimal integer with upper-case letters

The various combinations are fully documented in the manpage for *printf(3)*, but we'll mention that m is typically the minimum length of the field (negative for left justified), and n is precision for exponential formats and the maximum length for other formats. Padding is typically done with spaces for strings and zeroes for numbers. The * character as a length specifier is not supported. But, you can easily get around this by including the length expression directly into *FORMAT*, as in:

```
$width = 20; $value = sin 1.0;
foreach $precision (0..($width-2)) {
    $output_arr[$precision] = sprintf "%${width}.${precision}f", $value;
}
```

sqrt

```
sqrt EXPR
sqrt
```

This function returns the square root of *EXPR*. If *EXPR* is omitted, it returns the square root of $_. For other roots such as cube roots, you can use the ** operator to raise something to a fractional power.[*]

srand

```
srand EXPR
```

This function sets the random number seed for the **rand** operator. If *EXPR* is omitted, it does srand(time), which is pretty predictable, so don't use it for security-type things, such as random password generation. Try something like this instead:[†]

```
srand( time() ^ ($$ + ($$ << 15)) );
```

---

[*] Don't try either of these approaches with negative numbers, as that poses a slightly more complex problem.

[†] Frequently called programs (like CGI scripts) that simply use

```
time ^ $$
```

for a seed can fall prey to the mathematical property that

```
a^b == (a+1)^(b+1)
```

one-third of the time. If you're particularly concerned with this, see the Math::TrulyRandom module in CPAN.

Of course, you'd need something much more random than that for serious crypto-graphic purposes, since it's easy to guess the current time. Checksumming the compressed output of one or more rapidly changing operating system status pro-grams is the usual method. For example:

```
srand (time ^ $$ ^ unpack "%32L*", `ps axww | gzip`);
```

Do *not* call **srand** multiple times in your program unless you know exactly what you're doing and why you're doing it. The point of the function is to "seed" the **rand** function so that **rand** can produce a different sequence each time you run your program. Just do it once at the top of your program, or you won't get ran-dom numbers out of **rand**!

stat

```
stat FILEHANDLE
stat EXPR
```

This function returns a 13-element list giving the statistics for a file, either the file opened via *FILEHANDLE*, or named by *EXPR*. It's typically used as follows:

```
($dev,$ino,$mode,$nlink,$uid,$gid,$rdev,$size,
    $atime,$mtime,$ctime,$blksize,$blocks)
        = stat $filename;
```

Not all fields are supported on all filesystem types. Here are the meanings of the fields:

Field	Meaning
dev	Device number of filesystem
ino	Inode number
mode	File mode (type and permissions)
nlink	Number of (hard) links to the file
uid	Numeric user ID of file's owner
gid	Numeric group ID of file's owner
rdev	The device identifier (special files only)
size	Total size of file, in bytes
atime	Last access time since the epoch
mtime	Last modify time since the epoch
ctime	Inode change time (NOT creation time!) since the epoch
blksize	Preferred blocksize for file system I/O
blocks	Actual number of blocks allocated

$dev and $ino, taken together, uniquely identify a file. The $blksize and $blocks are likely defined only on BSD-derived filesystems. The $blocks field (if defined) is reported in 512-byte blocks. Note that $blocks*512 can differ greatly from $size for files containing unallocated blocks, or "holes", which aren't counted in $blocks.

If **stat** is passed the special filehandle consisting of an underline, no actual *stat*(2) is done, but the current contents of the stat structure from the last **stat** or **stat**-based file test (the –x operators) are returned.

The following example first stats $file to see whether it is executable. If it is, it then pulls the device number out of the existing stat structure and tests it to see whether it looks like a Network File System (NFS). Such filesystems tend to have negative device numbers.

```
if (-x $file and ($d) = stat(_) and $d < 0) {
    print "$file is executable NFS file\n";
}
```

Hint: if you need only the size of the file, check out the –s file test operator, which returns the size in bytes directly. There are also file tests that return the ages of files in days.

study

```
study SCALAR
study
```

This function takes extra time to study *SCALAR* ($_ if unspecified) in anticipation of doing many pattern matches on the string before it is next modified. This may or may not save time, depending on the nature and number of patterns you are searching on, and on the distribution of character frequencies in the string to be searched—you probably want to compare run-times with and without it to see which runs faster. Those loops that scan for many short constant strings (including the constant parts of more complex patterns) will benefit most. If all your pattern matches are constant strings, anchored at the front, **study** won't help at all, because no scanning is done. You may have only one **study** active at a time—if you study a different scalar the first is "unstudied".

The way **study** works is this: a linked list of every character in the string to be searched is made, so we know, for example, where all the "k" characters are. From each search string, the rarest character is selected, based on some static frequency tables constructed from some C programs and English text. Only those places that contain this rarest character are examined.

For example, here is a loop that inserts index-producing entries before any line containing a certain pattern:

```
while (<>) {
    study;
    print ".IX foo\n" if /\bfoo\b/;
    print ".IX bar\n" if /\bbar\b/;
    print ".IX blurfl\n" if /\bblurfl\b/;
    ...
    print;
}
```

In searching for /\bfoo\b/, only those locations in $_ that contain "f" will be looked at, because "f" is rarer than "o". In general, this is a big win except in pathological cases. The only question is whether it saves you more time than it took to build the linked list in the first place.

If you have to look for strings that you don't know until run-time, you can build an entire loop as a string and **eval** that to avoid recompiling all your patterns all the time. Together with setting **$/** to input entire files as one record, this can be very fast, often faster than specialized programs like *fgrep*. The following scans a list of files (@files) for a list of words (@words), and prints out the names of those files that contain a match:

```
$search = 'while (<>) { study;';
foreach $word (@words) {
    $search .= "++\$seen{\$ARGV} if /\\b$word\\b/;\n";
}
$search .= "}";
@ARGV = @files;
undef $/;                    # slurp each entire file
eval $search;                # this screams
die $@ if $@;                # in case eval failed
$/ = "\n";                   # put back to normal input delim
foreach $file (sort keys(%seen)) {
    print $file, "\n";
}
```

sub

```
sub NAME BLOCK
sub NAME
sub BLOCK

sub NAME PROTO BLOCK
sub NAME PROTO
sub PROTO BLOCK
```

The first two of these are not really operators, but rather they declare the existence of named subroutines, which is why the syntax includes a *NAME*, after all. (As declarations, they return no value.) The first one additionally defines the subroutine with a *BLOCK*, which contains the code for the subroutine. The second one (the one without the *BLOCK*) is just a forward declaration, that is, a declaration that introduces the subroutine name without defining it, with the expectation that the real definition will come later. (This is useful because the parser treats a word specially if it knows it's a user-defined subroutine. You can call such a subroutine as if it were a list operator, for instance.)

The third form really *is* an operator, in that it can be used within expressions to generate an anonymous subroutine at run-time. (More specifically, it returns a reference to an anonymous subroutine, since you can't talk about something anonymous without some kind of reference to it.) If the anonymous subroutine refers to any lexical variables declared outside its *BLOCK*, it functions as a *closure*, which means that different calls to the same **sub** operator will do the bookkeeping necessary to keep the correct "version" of each such lexical variable in sight for the life of the closure, even if the original scope of the lexical variable has been destroyed.

The final three forms are identical to the first three, except that they also supply a prototype that lets you specify how calls to your subroutine should be parsed and analyzed, so you can make your routines act more like some of Perl's built-in functions. See "Subroutines" in Chapter 2 and "Anonymous Subroutines" in Chapter 4 for more details.

substr

```
substr EXPR, OFFSET, LENGTH
substr EXPR, OFFSET
```

This function extracts a substring out of the string given by *EXPR* and returns it. The substring is extracted starting at *OFFSET* characters from the front of the string. (Note: if you've messed with $[, the beginning of the string isn't at 0, but since you haven't messed with it (have you?), it is.) If *OFFSET* is negative, the substring starts that far from the end of the string instead. If *LENGTH* is omitted, everything to the end of the string is returned. If *LENGTH* is negative, the length is calculated to leave that many characters off the end of the string. Otherwise, *LENGTH* indicates the length of the substring to extract, which is sort of what you'd expect.

You can use **substr** as an lvalue (something to assign to), in which case *EXPR* must also be a legal lvalue. If you assign something shorter than the length of your substring, the string will shrink, and if you assign something longer than the length, the string will grow to accommodate it. To keep the string the same length you may need to pad or chop your value using **sprintf** or the **x** operator.

To prepend the string `"Larry"` to the current value of `$_`, use:

```
substr($_, 0, 0) = "Larry";
```

To instead replace the first character of `$_` with `"Moe"`, use:

```
substr($_, 0, 1) = "Moe";
```

and finally, to replace the last character of `$_` with `"Curly"`, use:

```
substr($_, -1, 1) = "Curly";
```

These last few examples presume you haven't messed with the value of $[. You haven't, have you? Good.

symlink

```
symlink OLDFILE, NEWFILE
```

This function creates a new filename symbolically linked to the old filename. The function returns 1 for success, 0 otherwise. On systems that don't support symbolic links, it produces a fatal error at run-time. To check for that, use **eval** to trap the potential error:

```
$can_symlink = (eval { symlink("", ""); }, $@ eq "");
```

Or use the Config module. Be careful if you supply a relative symbolic link, since it'll be interpreted relative to the location of the symbolic link itself, not your current working directory.

See also **link** and **readlink** earlier in this chapter.

syscall

```
syscall LIST
```

This function calls the system call specified as the first element of the list, passing the remaining elements as arguments to the system call. (Many of these are now more readily available through the POSIX module, and others.) The function produces a fatal error if *syscall*(2) is unimplemented. The arguments are interpreted as follows: if a given argument is numeric, the argument is passed as a C integer. If not, a pointer to the string value is passed. You are responsible for making sure the string is long enough to receive any result that might be written into it. Otherwise you're looking at a coredump. If your integer arguments are not literals and have never been interpreted in a numeric context, you may need to add 0 to them to force them to look like numbers. (See the following example.)

This example calls the *setgroups*(2) system call to add to the group list of the current process. (It will only work on machines that support multiple group membership.)

```
require 'syscall.ph';
syscall &SYS_setgroups, @groups+0, pack("i*", @groups);
```

Note that you may have to run *h2ph* as indicated in the Perl installation instructions for *syscall.ph* to exist. Some systems may require a **pack** template of "s*" instead. Best of all, the **syscall** function assumes the size equivalence of the C types int, long, and char*.

Try not to think of **syscall** as the epitome of portability.

sysopen

```
sysopen FILEHANDLE, FILENAME, MODE
sysopen FILEHANDLE, FILENAME, MODE, PERMS
```

This function opens the file whose filename is given by *FILENAME*, and associates it with *FILEHANDLE*. If *FILEHANDLE* is an expression, its value is used as the name of (or reference to) the filehandle. This function calls *open*(2) with the parameters *FILENAME*, *MODE*, *PERMS*.

The possible values and flag bits of the *MODE* parameter are system-dependent; they are available via the Fcntl library module. However, for historical reasons, some values are universal: zero means read-only, one means write-only, and two means read/write.

If the file named by *FILENAME* does not exist and **sysopen** creates it (typically because *MODE* includes the O_CREAT flag), then the value of *PERMS* specifies the permissions of the newly created file. If *PERMS* is omitted, the default value is 0666, which allows read and write for all. This default is reasonable: see **umask**.

The FileHandle module described in Chapter 7 provides a more object-oriented approach to **sysopen**. See also **open** earlier in this chapter.

sysread

```
sysread FILEHANDLE, SCALAR, LENGTH, OFFSET
sysread FILEHANDLE, SCALAR, LENGTH
```

This function attempts to read *LENGTH* bytes of data into variable *SCALAR* from the specified *FILEHANDLE* using *read*(2). The function returns the number of bytes actually read, or 0 at EOF. It returns the undefined value on error. *SCALAR* will be grown or shrunk to the length actually read. The *OFFSET*, if specified, says where in the string to start putting the bytes, so that you can read into the middle of a string that's being used as a buffer. For an example, see **syswrite**. You should be prepared to handle the problems (like interrupted system calls) that standard I/O normally handles for you. Also, do not mix calls to **read** and **sysread** on the same filehandle unless you are into heavy wizardry (and/or pain).

system

```
system LIST
```

This function executes any program on the system for you. It does exactly the same thing as **exec** *LIST* except that it does a **fork** first, and then, after the exec, it waits for the exec'd program to complete. That is (in non-UNIX terms), it runs the program for you, and returns when it's done, unlike **exec**, which never returns (if it succeeds). Note that argument processing varies depending on the number of arguments, as described for **exec**. The return value is the exit status of the program as returned by the *wait*(2) call. To get the actual exit value, divide by 256. (The lower 8 bits are set if the process died from a signal.) See **exec**.

Because **system** and backticks block SIGINT and SIGQUIT, killing the program they're running with one of those signals doesn't actually interrupt your program.

```
@args = ("command", "arg1", "arg2");
system(@args) == 0
        or die "system @args failed: $?"
```

Here's a more elaborate example of analyzing the return value from **system** on a UNIX system to check for all possibilities, including for signals and coredumps.

```
$rc = 0xffff & system @args;
printf "system(%s) returned %#04x: ", "@args", $rc;
if ($rc == 0) {
    print "ran with normal exit\n";
}
elsif ($rc == 0xff00) {
    print "command failed: $!\n";
}
elsif (($rc & 0xff) == 0) {
    $rc >>= 8;
    print "ran with non-zero exit status $rc\n";
}
else {
    print "ran with ";
    if ($rc &   0x80) {
        $rc &= ~0x80;
        print "coredump from ";
    }
    print "signal $rc\n"
}
$ok = ($rc == 0);
```

syswrite

```
syswrite FILEHANDLE, SCALAR, LENGTH, OFFSET
syswrite FILEHANDLE, SCALAR, LENGTH
```

This function attempts to write *LENGTH* bytes of data from variable *SCALAR* to the specified *FILEHANDLE* using *write*(2). The function returns the number of bytes actually written, or the undefined value on error. You should be prepared to handle the problems that standard I/O normally handles for you, such as partial writes. The *OFFSET*, if specified, says where in the string to start writing from, in case you're using the string as a buffer, for instance, or you need to recover from a partial write. To copy data from filehandle FROM into filehandle TO, use something like:

```
$blksize = (stat FROM)[11] || 16384;  # preferred block size?
while ($len = sysread FROM, $buf, $blksize) {
    if (!defined $len) {
        next if $! =~ /^Interrupted/;
        die "System read error: $!\n";
    }
    $offset = 0;
    while ($len) {          # Handle partial writes.
        $written = syswrite TO, $buf, $len, $offset;
        die "System write error: $!\n"
            unless defined $written;
        $len -= $written;
        $offset += $written;
    }
}
```

Do not mix calls to (**print** or **write**) and **syswrite** on the same filehandle unless you are into heavy wizardry.

tell

```
tell FILEHANDLE
tell
```

This function returns the current file position (in bytes, 0-based) for *FILEHANDLE*. This value is typically fed to the **seek** function at some future time to get back to the current position. *FILEHANDLE* may be an expression whose value gives the name of the actual filehandle, or a reference to a filehandle object. If *FILEHANDLE* is omitted, the function returns the position of the file last read. File positions are only meaningful on regular files. Devices, pipes, and sockets have no file position.

See **seek** for an example.

telldir

    telldir *DIRHANDLE*

This function returns the current position of the **readdir** routines on *DIRHANDLE*. This value may be given to **seekdir** to access a particular location in a directory. The function has the same caveats about possible directory compaction as the corresponding system library routine. This function may not be implemented everywhere that **readdir** is. Even if it is, no calculation may be done with the return value. It's just an opaque value, meaningful only to **seekdir**.

tie

    tie *VARIABLE*, *CLASSNAME*, *LIST*

This function binds a variable to a package class that will provide the implementation for the variable. *VARIABLE* is the name of the variable to be tied. *CLASSNAME* is the name of a class implementing objects of an appropriate type. Any additional arguments are passed to the "new" method of the class (meaning TIESCALAR, TIEARRAY, or TIEHASH). Typically these are arguments such as might be passed to the *dbm_open*(3) function of C, but this is package dependent. The object returned by the "new" method is also returned by the **tie** function, which can be useful if you want to access other methods in *CLASSNAME*. (The object can also be accessed through the **tied** function.) So, a class for tying a hash to an ISAM implementation might provide an extra method to traverse a set of keys sequentially (the "S" of ISAM), since your typical DBM implementation can't do that.

Note that functions such as **keys** and **values** may return huge list values when used on large objects like DBM files. You may prefer to use the **each** function to iterate over such. For example:

```
use NDBM_File;
tie %ALIASES, "NDBM_File", "/etc/aliases", 1, 0
    or die "Can't open aliases: $!\n";
while (($key,$val) = each %ALIASES) {
    print $key, ' = ', $val, "\n";
}
untie %ALIASES;
```

A class implementing a hash should provide the following methods:

```
TIEHASH $class, LIST
DESTROY $self
FETCH $self, $key
STORE $self, $key, $value
DELETE $self, $key
EXISTS $self, $key
FIRSTKEY $self
NEXTKEY $self, $lastkey
```

A class implementing an ordinary array should provide the following methods:

```
TIEARRAY $classname, LIST
DESTROY $self
FETCH $self, $subscript
STORE $self, $subscript, $value
```

(As of this writing, other methods are still being designed. Check the online documentation for additions.)

A class implementing a scalar should provide the following methods:

```
TIESCALAR $classname, LIST
DESTROY $self
FETCH $self,
STORE $self, $value
```

See "Using Tied Variables" in Chapter 5 for detailed discussion of all these methods. Unlike **dbmopen**, the **tie** function will not **use** or **require** a module for you—you need to do that explicitly yourself. See the DB_File and Config modules for interesting **tie** implementations.

tied

```
tied VARIABLE
```

This function returns a reference to the object underlying *VARIABLE* (the same value that was originally returned by the **tie** call which bound the variable to a package.) It returns the undefined value if *VARIABLE* isn't tied to a package. So, for example, you can use:

```
ref tied %hash
```

to find out which package your hash is currently tied to. (Presuming you've forgotten.)

time

```
time
```

This function returns the number of non-leap seconds since January 1, 1970, UTC.[*] The returned value is suitable for feeding to **gmtime** and **localtime**, and for comparison with file modification and access times returned by **stat**, and for feeding to **utime**—see the examples under **utime**.

---

[*] Also known as the "epoch", not to be confused with the "epic", which is about the making of UNIX. (Other operating systems may have a different epoch, not to mention a different epic.)

times

```
times
```

This function returns a four-element list giving the user and system CPU times, in seconds (possibly fractional), for this process and the children of this process.

```
($user, $system, $cuser, $csystem) = times;
```

For example, to time the execution speed of a section of Perl code:

```
$start = (times)[0];
...
$end = (times)[0];
printf "that took %.2f CPU seconds\n", $end - $start;
```

tr///

```
tr///
y///
```

This is the translation operator, which is like the one in the UNIX *sed* program, only better, in everybody's humble opinion. See Chapter 2.

truncate

```
truncate FILEHANDLE, LENGTH
truncate EXPR, LENGTH
```

This function truncates the file opened on *FILEHANDLE*, or named by *EXPR*, to the specified length. The function produces a fatal error if *truncate*(2) or an equivalent isn't implemented on your system. (You can always truncate a file by copying the front of it, if you have the disk space.)

uc

```
uc EXPR
```

This function returns an uppercased version of *EXPR* (or $_ if *EXPR* is omitted). This is the internal function implementing the \U escape in double-quoted strings. POSIX *setlocale*(3) settings are respected.

ucfirst

```
ucfirst EXPR
```

This function returns a version of *EXPR* (or $_ if *EXPR* is omitted) with the first character uppercased, that is, capitalized. This is the internal function implementing the \u escape in double-quoted strings. POSIX *setlocale*(3) settings are respected.

To force initial caps, and everything else lowercase, use:

```
ucfirst lc $word
```

which is equivalent to `"\u\L$word"`.

umask

```
umask EXPR
umask
```

This function sets the umask for the process and returns the old one. (The umask tells UNIX which permission bits to disallow when creating a file.) If *EXPR* is omitted, the function merely returns the current umask. For example, to ensure that the "other" bits are turned on, and the "user" bits are turned off, try something like:

```
umask((umask() & 077) | 7);
```

undef

```
undef EXPR
undef
```

This function undefines the value of *EXPR*, which must be an lvalue. Use only on a scalar value, an entire array or hash, or a subroutine name (using the & prefix). Any storage associated with the object will be recovered for reuse (though not returned to the system, for most versions of UNIX). The **undef** function will probably not do what you expect on most special variables.

The function always returns the undefined value. This is useful because you can omit the *EXPR*, in which case nothing gets undefined, but you still get an undefined value that you could, for instance, return from a subroutine to indicate an error. Here are some uses of **undef** as a unary operator:

```
undef $foo;
undef $bar{'blurfl'};
undef @ary;
undef %assoc;
undef &mysub;
```

Without an argument, **undef** is just used for its value:

```
return (wantarray ? () : undef) if $they_blew_it;
select(undef, undef, undef, $naptime);
```

You may use **undef** as a placeholder on the left side of a list assignment, in which case the corresponding value from the right side is simply discarded. Apart from that, you may not use **undef** as an lvalue.

unlink

```
unlink LIST
```

This function deletes a list of files.* If *LIST* is omitted, it unlinks the file given in $_. The function returns the number of files successfully deleted. Some sample commands:

```
$cnt = unlink 'a', 'b', 'c';
unlink @goners;
unlink <*.bak>;
```

Note that **unlink** will not delete directories unless you are superuser and the –U flag is supplied to Perl. Even if these conditions are met, be warned that unlinking a directory can inflict Serious Damage on your filesystem. Use **rmdir** instead.

Here's a very simple *rm* command with very simple error checking:

```
#!/usr/bin/perl
@cannot = grep {not unlink} @ARGV;
die "$0: could not unlink @cannot\n" if @cannot;
```

unpack

```
unpack TEMPLATE, EXPR
```

This function does the reverse of **pack**: it takes a string (*EXPR*) representing a data structure and expands it out into a list value, returning the list value. (In a scalar context, it can be used to unpack a single value.) The *TEMPLATE* has much the same format as in the **pack** function—it specifies the order and type of the values to be unpacked. (See **pack** for a more detailed description of *TEMPLATE*.)

Here's a subroutine that does (some of) **substr**, only slower:

```
sub substr {
    my($what, $where, $howmuch) = @_;
    if ($where < 0) {
        $where = -$where;
        return unpack "\@* X$where a$howmuch", $what;
    }
    else {
        return unpack "x$where a$howmuch", $what;
    }
}
```

---

* Actually, under UNIX, it removes the directory entries that refer to the real files. Since a file may be referenced (linked) from more than one directory, the file isn't actually removed until the last reference to it is removed.

and then there's:

```
sub signed_ord { unpack "c", shift }
```

Here's a complete *uudecode* program:

```
#!/usr/bin/perl
$_ = <> until ($mode,$file) = /^begin\s*(\d*)\s*(\S*)/;
open(OUT,"> $file") if $file ne "";
while (<>) {
    last if /^end/;
    next if /[a-z]/;
    next unless int((((ord() - 32) & 077) + 2) / 3) ==
                int(length() / 4);
    print OUT unpack "u", $_;
}
chmod oct $mode, $file;
```

In addition, you may prefix a field with %*number* to indicate that you want it to return a *number*-bit checksum of the items instead of the items themselves. Default is a 16-bit checksum. For example, the following computes the same number as the System V *sum* program:

```
undef $/;
$checksum = unpack ("%32C*", <>) % 32767;
```

The following efficiently counts the number of set bits in a bit vector:

```
$setbits = unpack "%32b*", $selectmask;
```

Here's a simple MIME decoder:

```
while (<>) {
  tr#A-Za-z0-9+/##cd;             # remove non-base64 chars
  tr#A-Za-z0-9+/# -_#;            # convert to uuencoded format
  $len = pack("c", 32 + 0.75*length);   # compute length byte
  print unpack("u", $len . $_);   # uudecode and print
}
```

unshift

```
unshift ARRAY, LIST
```

This function does the opposite of a **shift**. (Or the opposite of a **push**, depending on how you look at it.) It prepends *LIST* to the front of the array, and returns the new number of elements in the array:

```
unshift @ARGV, '-e', $cmd unless $ARGV[0] =~ /^-/;
```

untie

```
untie VARIABLE
```

Breaks the binding between a variable and a package. See **tie**.

use

```
use Module LIST
use Module
```

The **use** declaration imports some semantics into the current package from the named module, generally by aliasing certain subroutine or variable names into your package. It is exactly equivalent to the following:

```
BEGIN { require Module; import Module LIST; }
```

The **BEGIN** forces the **require** and **import** to happen at compile time. The **require** makes sure the module is loaded into memory if it hasn't been yet. The **import** is not a built-in—it's just an ordinary static method call into the package named by *Module* to tell the module to import the list of features back into the current package. The module can implement its import method any way it likes, though most modules just choose to derive their import method via inheritance from the Exporter class that is defined in the Exporter module. See Chapter 5 for more information.

If you don't want your namespace altered, explicitly supply an empty list:

```
use Module ();
```

That is exactly equivalent to the following:

```
BEGIN { require Module; }
```

Because this is a wide-open interface, pragmas (compiler directives) are also implemented this way. Currently implemented pragmas include:

```
use integer;
use diagnostics;
use sigtrap qw(SEGV BUS);
use strict  qw(subs vars refs);
```

These pseudomodules typically import semantics into the current block scope, unlike ordinary modules, which import symbols into the current package. (The latter are effective through the end of the file.)

There's a corresponding declaration, **no**, that "unimports" any meanings originally imported by **use**, but that have since become, er, unimportant:

```
no integer;
no strict 'refs';
```

See Chapter 7 for a list of standard modules and pragmas.

utime

```
utime LIST
```

This function changes the access and modification times on each file of a list of files. The first two elements of the list must be the *numerical* access and modification times, in that order. The function returns the number of files successfully changed. The inode change time of each file is set to the current time. Here's an example of a *touch* command:

```
#!/usr/bin/perl
$now = time;
utime $now, $now, @ARGV;
```

and here's a more sophisticated *touch* command with a bit of error checking:

```
#!/usr/bin/perl
$now = time;
@cannot = grep {not utime $now, $now, $_} @ARGV;
die "$0: Could not touch @cannot.\n" if @cannot;
```

The standard *touch* command will actually create missing files, something like this:

```
$now = time;
foreach $file (@ARGV) {
    utime $now, $now, $file
        or open TMP, ">>$file"
        or warn "Couldn't touch $file: $!\n";
}
```

To read the times from existing files, use **stat**.

values

```
values HASH
```

This function returns a list consisting of all the values of the named hash. The values are returned in an apparently random order, but it is the same order as either the **keys** or **each** function would produce on the same hash. To sort the hash by its values, see the example under **keys**. Note that using **values** on a hash that is bound to a humongous DBM file is bound to produce a humongous list, causing you to have a humongous process, leaving you in a bind. You might prefer to use the **each** function, which will iterate over the hash entries one by one without slurping them all into a single gargantuan (that is, humongous) list.

vec

```
vec EXPR, OFFSET, BITS
```

This function treats a string (the value of *EXPR*) as a vector of unsigned integers, and returns the value of the element specified by *OFFSET* and *BITS*. The function may also be assigned to, which causes the element to be modified. The purpose of the function is to provide very compact storage of lists of small integers. The integers may be very small—vectors can hold numbers that are as small as one bit, resulting in a bitstring.

The *OFFSET* specifies how many elements to skip over to find the one you want. *BITS* is the number of bits per element in the vector, so each element can contain an unsigned integer in the range $0..(2**BITS)-1$. *BITS* must be one of 1, 2, 4, 8, 16, or 32. As many elements as possible are packed into each byte, and the ordering is such that vec($vectorstring,0,1) is guaranteed to go into the lowest bit of the first byte of the string. To find out the position of the byte in which an element is going to be put, you have to multiply the *OFFSET* by the number of elements per byte. When *BITS* is 1, there are eight elements per byte. When *BITS* is 2, there are four elements per byte. When *BITS* is 4, there are two elements (called nybbles) per byte. And so on.

Regardless of whether your machine is big-endian or little-endian, vec($foo, 0, 8) always refers to the first byte of string $foo. See **select** for examples of bitmaps generated with **vec**.

Vectors created with **vec** can also be manipulated with the logical operators |, &, ^, and ~, which will assume a bit vector operation is desired when the operands are strings.

A bit vector (*BITS* == *1*) can be translated to or from a string of 1s and 0s by supplying a b* template to **unpack** or **pack**. Similarly, a vector of nybbles (*BITS* == *4*) can be translated with an h* template.

wait

```
wait
```

This function waits for a child process to terminate and returns the pid of the deceased process, or -1 if there are no child processes. The status is returned in $?. If you get zombie child processes, you should be calling this function, or **waitpid**. A common strategy to avoid such zombies is:

```
$SIG{CHLD} = sub { wait };
```

If you expected a child and didn't find it, you probably had a call to **system**, a close on a pipe, or backticks between the **fork** and the **wait**. These constructs also do a *wait*(2) and may have harvested your child process. Use **waitpid** to avoid this problem.

waitpid

```
waitpid PID, FLAGS
```

This function waits for a particular child process to terminate and returns the pid when the process is dead, or -1 if there are no child processes, or 0 if the *FLAGS* specify non-blocking and the process isn't dead yet. The status of the dead process is returned in $?. To get valid flag values say this:

```
use POSIX "sys_wait_h";
```

On systems that implement neither the *waitpid*(2) nor *wait4*(2) system call, *FLAGS* may be specified only as 0. In other words, you can wait for a specific *PID*, but you can't do it in non-blocking mode.

wantarray

```
wantarray
```

This function returns true if the context of the currently executing subroutine is looking for a list value. The function returns false if the context is looking for a scalar. Here's a typical usage, demonstrating an "unsuccessful" return:

```
return wantarray ? () : undef;
```

See also **caller**. This function should really have been named "wantlist", but we named it back when list contexts were still called array contexts.

warn

```
warn LIST
```

This function produces a message on STDERR just like **die**, but doesn't try to exit or throw an exception. For example:

```
warn "Debug enabled" if $debug;
```

If the message supplied is null, the message "Something's wrong" is used. As with **die**, a message not ending with a newline will have file and line number information automatically appended. The **warn** operator is unrelated to the –w switch.

write

```
write FILEHANDLE
write
```

This function writes a formatted record (possibly multi-line) to the specified file-handle, using the format associated with that filehandle—see the section "Formats" in Chapter 2. By default the format for a filehandle is the one having the same name as the filehandle. However, the format for a filehandle may be changed by saying:

```
use FileHandle;
HANDLE->format_name("NEWNAME");
```

Top-of-form processing is handled automatically: if there is insufficient room on the current page for the formatted record, the page is advanced by writing a form feed, a special top-of-page format is used to format the new page header, and then the record is written. The number of lines remaining on the current page is in variable $-, which can be set to 0 to force a new page on the next **write**. (You may need to **select** the filehandle first.) By default the name of the top-of-page format is the name of the filehandle with "_TOP" appended, but the format for a file-handle may be changed by saying:

```
use FileHandle;
HANDLE->format_top_name("NEWNAME_TOP");
```

If *FILEHANDLE* is unspecified, output goes to the current default output filehandle, which starts out as STDOUT but may be changed by the **select** operator. If the *FILE-HANDLE* is an expression, then the expression is evaluated to determine the actual *FILEHANDLE* at run-time.

Note that **write** is *not* the opposite of **read**. Use **print** for simple string output. If you looked up this entry because you wanted to bypass standard I/O, see **syswrite**.

y///

```
y///
```

The translation operator, also known as tr///. See Chapter 2.

4

References and Nested Data Structures

For both practical and philosophical reasons, Perl has always been biased in favor of flat, linear data structures. And for many problems, this is exactly what you want. But occasionally you need to set up something just a little more complicated and hierarchical. Under older versions of Perl you could construct complex data structures indirectly by using **eval** or typeglobs.

Suppose you wanted to build a simple table (two-dimensional array) showing vital statistics—say, age, eye color, and weight—for a group of people. You could do this by first creating an array for each individual:

```
@john = (47, "brown", 186);
@mary = (23, "hazel", 128);
@bill = (35, "blue", 157);
```

and then constructing a single, additional array consisting of the names of the other arrays:

```
@vitals = ('john', 'mary', 'bill');
```

Unfortunately, actually using this table as a two-dimensional data structure is cumbersome. To change John's eyes to "red" after a night on the town, you'd have to say something like:

```
$vitals = $vitals[0];
eval "\$${vitals}[1] = 'red'";
```

A much more efficient (but not more readable) way to do the same thing is to use a typeglob assignment to temporarily alias one symbol table entry to another:

```
local(*array) = $vitals[0];   # Alias *array to *john.
$array[1] = 'red';            # Actually sets $john[1].
```

Alternatively, you could avoid the symbol table altogether by doing everything with a set of parallel hash arrays, emulating pointers symbolically by doing key lookups in the appropriate hash. Finally, you could define all your structures operationally, using **pack** and **unpack**, or **join** and **split**.

So even though you could use a variety of techniques to emulate pointers and data structures, all of them could get to be unwieldy. To be sure, Perl still supports these older mechanisms, since they remain quite useful for simple problems. But now Perl also supports *references*.

What Is a Reference?

In the preceding example using **eval**, $vitals[0] had the value 'john'. That is, it happened to contain a string that was also the name for another variable. You could say that the first variable *referred* to the second. We will speak of this sort of reference as a *symbolic* reference. You can think of it as analogous to symbolic links in UNIX filesystems. Perl now provides some simplified mechanisms for using symbolic references; in particular, the need for an **eval** or a typeglob assignment in our example disappears. See "Symbolic References" later in this chapter.

The other kind of reference is the *hard* reference.* A hard reference refers not to the name of another variable (which is just a container for a value) but rather to an actual value, some internal glob of data, which we will call a "thingy", in honor of that thingy that hangs down in the back of your throat. (You may also call it a "referent", if you prefer to live a joyless existence.) Suppose, for example, that you create a hard reference to the thingy contained in the variable @array. This hard reference and the thingy it refers to will continue to exist even after @array goes out of scope. Only when the reference count of the thingy itself goes to zero is the thingy actually destroyed.

To put it another way, a Perl variable lives in a symbol table and holds one hard reference to its underlying thingy (which may be a simple thingy like a number, or a complex thingy like an array or hash, but there's still only one reference from the variable to the value). There may be other hard references to the same thingy, but if so, the variable doesn't know (or care) about them. A symbolic reference names another variable, so there's always a named location involved, but a hard

---

* If you like, you can think of hard references as real references, and symbolic references as fake references. It's like the difference between real friendship and mere name-dropping.

reference just points to a thingy. It doesn't know (or care) whether there are any other references to the thingy, or whether any of those references are through variables. Hence, a hard reference can refer to an anonymous thingy. All such anonymous thingies are accessed through hard references. But the converse is not necessarily true—just because something has a hard reference to it doesn't necessarily mean it's anonymous. It might have another reference through a named variable. (It can even have more than one name, if it is aliased with typeglobs.)

To *reference* a variable, in the terminology of this chapter, is to create a hard reference to the thingy underlying the variable. (There's a special operator to do this creative act.) The hard reference so created is simply a scalar value, which behaves in all familiar contexts just like any other scalar value should. To *dereference* this scalar value is to use it to refer back to the original thingy, as you must do when reading or writing to the thingy. Both referencing and dereferencing occur only when you invoke certain explicit mechanisms; no implicit referencing or dereferencing occurs in Perl.* †

Any scalar may hold a hard reference, and such a reference may point to any data structure. Since arrays and hashes contain scalars, you can build arrays of arrays, arrays of hashes, hashes of arrays, arrays of hashes and functions, and so on.

Keep in mind, though, that Perl arrays and hashes are internally one-dimensional. They can only hold scalar values (strings, numbers, and references). When we use a phrase like "array of arrays", we really mean "array of references to arrays". But since that's the only way to implement an array of arrays in Perl, it follows that the shorter, less accurate phrase is not so inaccurate as to be false, and therefore should not be totally despised, unless you're into that sort of thing.

Creating Hard References

There are several ways to compose references, most of which we will describe before explaining how to use (dereference) the resulting references.

The Backslash Operator

You can create a reference to any named variable or subroutine by using the unary backslash operator. (You may also use it on an anonymous scalar value.) This works much like the & (address-of) operator in C.

---

* Actually, a function with a prototype *can* use implicit pass-by-reference if explicitly declared that way. If so, then the caller of the function doesn't need to know he's passing a reference, but you still have to dereference it explicitly within the function. See Chapter 2, *The Gory Details*.

† Actually, to be perfectly honest, there's also some mystical automatic dereferencing when you use certain kinds of filehandles, but that's for backward compatibility, and is transparent to the casual user.

Here are some examples:

```
$scalarref = \$foo;
$constref  = \186_282.42;
$arrayref  = \@ARGV;
$hashref   = \%ENV;
$code_ref  = \&handler;
$globref   = \*STDOUT;
```

The Anonymous Array Composer

You can create a reference to an anonymous array by using brackets:

```
$arrayref = [1, 2, ['a', 'b', 'c']];
```

Here we've composed a reference to an anonymous array of three elements whose final element is a reference to another anonymous array of three elements.

These square brackets work like this only where the Perl parser is expecting a term in an expression, and should not be confused with the brackets that are functioning as operators when used to subscript an array (though there is an obvious mnemonic association with arrays). Square brackets inside a quoted string do not result in the interpolation of a reference to an anonymous array. Rather, such brackets become literal elements in the string. (However, if you're interpolating something into the string, and the expression defining the interpolation contains brackets, they have their normal meaning within the expression, since they are, after all, in an expression.)

Note that taking a reference to an enumerated list is not the same as using brackets—instead it's treated as a shorthand for creating a list of references:

```
@list = (\$a, \$b, \$c);
@list = \($a, $b, $c);     # same thing!
```

The Anonymous Hash Composer

You can create a reference to an anonymous hash by using braces:

```
$hashref = {
    'Adam'  => 'Eve',
    'Clyde' => 'Bonnie',
};
```

The values above are literal strings; variables and expressions would work as well. Also, for the values (but not the keys) of the hash, you can freely mix anonymous hash and array composers to produce as complicated a structure as you want.

These braces work like this only where the Perl parser is expecting a term in an expression, and should not be confused with the braces that are functioning as operators when used to subscript a hash (though there is an obvious mnemonic association with hashes). Braces inside a quoted string do not result in the interpolation of a reference to an anonymous hash. Rather, such braces become literal elements in the string. (However, the same caveat about interpolating expressions applies to braces as it does to brackets.)

Since braces are also used for several other things including *BLOCK*s, you may occasionally have to disambiguate braces at the beginning of a statement by putting a + or a **return** in front so that Perl realizes the opening brace isn't starting a *BLOCK*. For example, if you wanted a function to make a new hash and return a reference to it, you have these options:

```
sub hashem {        { @_ } }   # silently WRONG
sub hashem {       +{ @_ } }   # ok
sub hashem { return { @_ } }   # ok
```

The Anonymous Subroutine Composer

You can create a reference to an anonymous subroutine by using **sub** without a subroutine name:

```
$coderef = sub { print "Boink!\n" };
```

Note the presence of the semicolon, which is required here to terminate the expression. (It wouldn't be required after the declaration of a named subroutine.) A nameless **sub** {} is not so much a declaration as it is an operator—like do {} or eval {}—except that the code inside isn't executed immediately. Instead, it just generates a reference to the code and returns that. However, no matter how many times you execute the line shown above, $coderef will still refer to the same anonymous subroutine.[*]

Object Constructors

Subroutines can also return references. That may sound trite, but sometimes you are *supposed* to use a subroutine to create a reference rather than creating the reference yourself. In particular, special subroutines called *constructors* return references to objects. An object is simply a special kind of thingy that happens to know which class it's associated with. Constructors know how to create that association. They do so by taking an ordinary thingy and turning it into an object (which remains a thingy even while it's also being an object). The operator that a constructor uses to do this is called **bless**, so we can speak of an object as a blessed

---

[*] But see later about closures. Even though there's only one anonymous subroutine, there may be several copies of the lexical variables in use by the subroutine, depending on when the subroutine reference was generated.

thingy. Constructors are customarily named `new()`, but don't have to be. They're usually called in one of two ways:

```
$objref = new Doggie Tail => 'short', Ears => 'long';
    # same as
$objref = Doggie->new(Tail => 'short', Ears => 'long');
```

See Chapter 5, *Packages, Modules, and Object Classes*, for a discussion of Perl objects.

Filehandle Referencers

References to filehandles can be created by taking a reference to a typeglob. This is currently the best way to pass named filehandles into or out of subroutines, or to store them in larger data structures.

```
splutter(\*STDOUT);
sub splutter {
    my $fh = shift;
    print $fh "her um well a hmmm\n";
}

$rec = get_rec(\*STDIN);
sub get_rec {
    my $fh = shift;
    return scalar <$fh>;
}
```

However, if you don't need to refer to existing named filehandles, you should consider using one of the newer, object-oriented library modules that provide filehandle objects via a constructor (see the previous section). In either case, you won't use filehandle names directly, but rather you'll use scalars (as above) to hold a reference to something that will (one way or another) be interpreted as a filehandle. As we admitted earlier, there is some implicit dereferencing magic going on here.

Implicit Creation of References

A final method for creating references is not really a method at all. References of an appropriate type simply spring into existence if you dereference them in a context that assumes they exist. This is extremely useful, and is also What You Expect. This topic is covered in the next section.

Using Hard References

Just as there are numerous ways to create references, there are also several ways to use, or dereference, a reference.

Using a Variable as a Variable Name

Anywhere you might ordinarily put an alphanumeric identifier as part of a variable or subroutine name, you can just replace the identifier with a simple scalar variable containing a reference of the correct type. For example:

```
$foo        = "two humps";
$scalarref  = \$foo;
$camel_model = $$scalarref;  # $camel_model is now "two humps"
```

Here are various dereferences:

```
$bar = $$scalarref;
push(@$arrayref, $filename);
$$arrayref[0] = "January";
$$hashref{"KEY"} = "VALUE";
&$coderef(1,2,3);
print $globref "output\n";
```

It's important to understand that we are specifically not dereferencing `$arrayref[0]` or `$hashref{"KEY"}` there. The dereferencing of the scalar variable happens before any array or hash lookups. To dereference anything more complicated than a simple scalar variable, you must use one of the next two methods described below. However, "simple scalars" can include an identifier that itself uses this first method recursively. Therefore, the following prints "howdy":

```
$refrefref = \\\"howdy";
print $$$$refrefref;
```

You can think of the dollar signs as executing right to left.

Using a BLOCK as a Variable Name

The second way is just like the first, except using a *BLOCK* instead of a variable. Anywhere you'd put an alphanumeric identifier as part of a variable or subroutine name, you can replace the identifier with a *BLOCK* returning a reference of the correct type. In other words, the previous examples could also be handled like this:

```
$bar = ${$scalarref};
push(@{$arrayref}, $filename);
${$arrayref}[0] = "January";
${$hashref}{"KEY"} = "VALUE";
&{$coderef}(1,2,3);
```

Admittedly, it's silly to use the braces in these simple cases, but the *BLOCK* can contain any arbitrary expression. In particular, it can contain subscripted expressions.

In the following example, $dispatch{$index} is assumed to contain a reference to a subroutine. The example invokes the subroutine with three arguments.

```
&{ $dispatch{$index} }(1, 2, 3);
```

Using the Arrow Operator

For references to arrays or hashes, a third method of dereferencing the reference involves the use of the -> infix operator. This is a form of syntactic sugar that makes it easier to get at individual array or hash elements, especially when the reference expression is complicated. Each of these trios is equivalent, corresponding to the three notations we've introduced. (We've inserted some spaces to line up equivalent elements.)

```
$  $arrayref  [0] = "January";        #1
${ $arrayref }[0] = "January";        #2
   $arrayref->[0] = "January";        #3

$  $hashref  {KEY} = "F#major";       #1
${ $hashref }{KEY} = "F#major";       #2
   $hashref->{KEY} = "F#major";       #3
```

You can see from this example that the first $ is missing from the third notation. It is, however, implied, and since it is implied, the notation can only be used to reference scalar values, not slices. But just as with the second notation, you can use any expression to the left of the ->, including another dereference, because arrow operators associate left to right:

```
print $array[3]->{"English"}->[0];
```

Note that $array[3] and $array->[3] are not the same. The first is talking about the fourth element of @array, while the second one is talking about the fourth element of the (possibly anonymous) array whose reference is contained in $array.

Suppose now that $array[3] is undefined. The following statement is still legal:

```
$array[3]->{"English"}->[0] = "January";
```

This is one of those cases mentioned earlier in which references spring into existence when used in an lvalue context. Supposing $array[3] to have been undefined, it's automatically defined with a hash reference so that we can look up {"English"} in it. Once that's done, $array[3]->{"English"} will automatically get defined with an array reference so that we can look up [0] in it. But this only happens when you're trying to create an element. Nothing would spring into existence if you were just trying to print out the value. You'd just get the undefined value out of it.

One more shortcut here. The arrow is optional between brace- or bracket-enclosed subscripts, so you can shrink the above code down to:

```
$array[3]{"English"}[0] = "January";
```

Which, in the case of ordinary arrays, gives you multi-dimensional arrays just like C's arrays:

```
$answer[$x][$y][$z] += 42;
```

Well, okay, not *entirely* like C's arrays. For one thing, C doesn't know how to grow its arrays on demand, while Perl does. Also, there are similar constructs in the two languages that parse differently. In Perl, the following two statements do the same thing:

```
$listref->[2][2] = "hello";    # pretty clear
$$listref[2][2] = "hello";     # a bit confusing
```

This second of these statements may disconcert the C programmer, who is accustomed to using *a[i] to mean "what's pointed to by the *i* th element of a". But in Perl, the five prefix dereferencers ($ @ * % &) effectively bind more tightly than the subscripting braces or brackets.* Therefore, it is $$listref and not $listref[$i] that is taken to be a reference to an array. If you want the C notion, you either have to write ${$listref[$i]} to force the $listref[$i] to get evaluated before the leading $ dereferencer, or you have to use the -> notation:

```
$listref[$i]->[$j] = "hello";
```

Using Object Methods

If a reference happens to be a reference to an object (a blessed thingy, that is), then there are probably methods to access the innards of the object, and you should probably stick to those methods unless you're writing the class package that defines the object's methods. (Such a package is allowed to treat the object as a mere thingy when it wants to.) In other words, be nice, and don't violate the object's encapsulation without a very good reason. Perl does not enforce encapsulation. We are not totalitarians here. We do expect some basic civility, however.

Other Tricks You Can Do with Hard References

You can use the **ref** operator to determine what type of thingy a reference is pointing to. Think of **ref** as a "typeof" operator that returns true if its argument is a ref-

---

* But not because of operator precedence. The funny characters in Perl are not operators in that sense. The grammar simply prohibits anything more complicated than a simple variable or block from following the initial funny character, for various funny reasons.

erence and false otherwise. The value returned depends on the type of thing referenced. Built-in types include:

```
REF
SCALAR
ARRAY
HASH
CODE
GLOB
```

If you simply use a hard reference in a string context, it'll be converted to a string containing both the type and the address: SCALAR(0x1fc0e). (The reverse conversion cannot be done, since reference count information has been lost.)

You can use the **bless** operator to associate a referenced thingy with a package functioning as an object class. When you do this, **ref** will return that package name instead of the internal type. An object reference used in a string context returns a string with both the external and internal types, along with the address: MyType=HASH(0x20d10). See Chapter 5 for more details about objects.

Since the dereference syntax always indicates the kind of reference desired, a typeglob can be used the same way a reference can, despite the fact that a typeglob contains multiple thingies of various types. So ${*foo} and ${\$foo} both refer to the same scalar variable. The latter is more efficient though.

Here's a trick for interpolating the value of a subroutine call into a string:

```
print "My sub returned @{[ mysub(1,2,3) ]} that time.\n";
```

It works like this. At compile time, when the @{ . . . } is seen within the double-quoted string, it's parsed as a block that will return a reference. Within the block, there are square brackets that will create a reference to an anonymous array from whatever is in the brackets. So at run-time, mysub(1,2,3) is called, and the results are loaded into an anonymous array, a reference to which is then returned within the block. That array reference is then immediately dereferenced by the surrounding @{ . . . }, and the array value is interpolated into the double-quoted string just as an ordinary array would be. This chicanery is also useful for arbitrary expressions, such as:

```
print "That yields @{[ $n + 5 ]} widgets\n";
```

Be careful though. The inside of the square brackets is supplying a list context to its expression. In this case it doesn't matter, although it's possible that the above call to mysub() might care. When it does matter, a similar trick can be done with a scalar reference. It just isn't quite as pretty:

```
print "That yields ${ \($n + 5) } widgets.";
```

Closures

Earlier we talked about creating anonymous subroutines with a nameless sub {}. Since anonymous subroutines have to be generated someplace within your code (in order to generate the reference that you poke into some variable), such routines can be thought of as coming into existence at run-time. (That is, they have a time of generation as well as a location of definition.) Because of this fact, anonymous subroutines can act as *closures* with respect to **my** variables—that is, with respect to variables visible lexically within the current scope. Closure is a notion out of the Lisp world that says if you define an anonymous function in a particular lexical context at a particular moment, it pretends to run in that context even when it's called outside of the context. In other words, you are guaranteed to get the same copy of a lexical variable, even though many other instances of the same lexical variable may have been created before or since. This gives you a way to pass arguments to a subroutine when you define it as well as when you call it. It's useful for setting up little bits of code to run later, such as callbacks.

You can also think of closures as a way to write a subroutine template without using **eval**. The lexical variables are like parameters to fill in the template.

Here's a small example of how closures work:

```perl
sub newprint {
    my $x = shift;
    return sub { my $y = shift; print "$x, $y!\n"; };
}
$h = newprint("Howdy");
$g = newprint("Greetings");

# Time passes...

&$h("world");
&$g("earthlings");
```

This prints:

```
Howdy, world!
Greetings, earthlings!
```

Note in particular how $x continues to refer to the value passed into newprint() despite the fact that the **my** $x has seemingly gone out of scope by the time the anonymous subroutine runs. That's what closures are all about.

This method only applies to **my** variables. Global variables work as they always worked (since they're neither created nor destroyed the way lexical variables are).

By and large, closures are not something you need to trouble yourself about. When you do need them, they just sorta do what you expect.[*]

Perl doesn't provide member pointers like C++ does, but you can get a similar effect using a closure. Suppose you want a pointer to a method for a particular object. You can remember both the object and the method as lexical variables bound to a closure:

```
sub get_method_ref {
    my ($self, $method) = @_;
    return sub { return $self->$method(@_) };
}
$dog_wag = get_method_ref($dog, 'wag');
&$dog_wag("tail");   # Calls $dog->wag('tail').
```

Symbolic References

What happens if you try to dereference a value that is not a hard reference? The value is then treated as a *symbolic reference*. That is, the reference (which still has a scalar value) is interpreted as a string. That string is taken to be the *name* of a variable, rather than a direct link to a (possibly anonymous) thingy.

Here is how it works:

```
$name = "bam";
$$name = 1;                      # Sets $bam
${$name} = 2;                    # Sets $bam
${$name x 2} = 3;                # Sets $bambam
$name->[0] = 4;                  # Sets $bam[0]
@$name = ();                     # Clears @bam
&$name();                        # Calls &bam() (as in prior versions of Perl)
$pkg = "THAT";                   #   (Don't use "package" or "pack"!)
${"${$pkg}::$name"} = 5;         # Sets $THAT::bam without eval
```

This is very powerful, and slightly dangerous, in that it's possible to intend (with the utmost sincerity) to use a hard reference, and accidentally use a symbolic reference instead. To protect against that, you can say:

```
use strict 'refs';
```

and then only hard references will be allowed for the rest of the enclosing block. An inner block may countermand that decree with:

```
no strict 'refs';
```

It is important to note the difference between the following two lines of code:

---

[*] Always presuming you expect the right thing, of course.

```
${identifier};    # same as $identifier
${"identifier"};  # also $identifier, but treated as symbolic reference
```

Because the second form is treated as a symbolic reference, it will generate an error under use strict 'refs'.

Only package variables are visible to symbolic references. Lexical variables (declared with **my**) aren't in a package symbol table, and thus are invisible to this mechanism. For example:

```
local $value = "10";
{
    my $value = "20";
    print ${"value"};
}
```

This will print "10", not "20". Remember that **local** affects package variables, which are all global to the package.

Braces, Brackets, and Quoting

In the previous section we pointed out that ${identifier} is not treated as a symbolic reference. Now you might wonder how this interacts with reserved words. The short answer is, it doesn't. Despite the fact that **push** is a reserved word, these two statements:

```
$push = "pop on ";
print "${push}over";
```

print out "pop on over". The reason is that, historically, this use of braces is how UNIX shells have delimited a variable name from subsequent alphanumeric text that would otherwise be interpreted as part of the variable name. It's how many people expect variable interpolation to work, so we made it work the same way in Perl. But with Perl, the notion extends further and applies to any braces used in generating references, whether or not they're inside quotes. This means that:

```
print ${push} . 'over';
```

or even:

```
print ${ push } . 'over';
```

will also print "pop on over", even though the braces are outside of double quotes. The same rule applies to any identifier that is used for subscripting a hash. So, instead of writing:

```
$hash{ "aaa" }{ "bbb" }{ "ccc" }
```

you can just write:

```
$hash{ aaa }{ bbb }{ ccc }
```

and not worry about whether the subscripts are reserved words. In the rare event that you do wish to do something like:

```
$hash{ shift }
```

you can force interpretation as a reserved word by adding anything that makes it more than a mere identifier:

```
$hash{ shift() }
$hash{ +shift }
$hash{ shift @_ }
```

The **-w** switch will warn you if it interprets a reserved word as a string, since you may have *meant* the reserved word. (That's why we recommend you use `${pkg}` instead of `${package}` or `${pack}`, since you'll avoid some warnings that way.)

Hard References Don't Work as Hash Keys

Consistent with the foregoing, hash keys are stored internally as strings.[*] If you try to store a hard reference as a key in a hash, the key value will be converted into a string:

```
$x{ \$a } = $a;
($key, $value) = each %x;
print $$key;    # WRONG
```

We mentioned earlier that you can't convert a string back to a hard reference. So if you try to dereference `$key`, which contains a mere string, it won't do a hard dereference, but rather a symbolic dereference, and since you probably don't have a variable named `SCALAR(0x1fc0e)`, you won't accomplish what you're attempting. You might want to do something more like:

```
$r = \@a;
$x{ $r } = $r;
```

And then at least you can use the hash *value*, which will be a hard reference, instead of the key, which won't.

Although you can't store a hard reference as a key, if you use a hard reference in a string context, it *is* guaranteed to produce a unique string, since the address of the reference is included as part of the resulting string. So you can in fact use a hard reference as a unique hash key. You just can't dereference it later.

---

[*] They're also stored externally as strings, such as when you put them into a DBM file. In fact, DBM files *require* that their keys (and values) be strings.

A Brief Tutorial: Manipulating Lists of Lists

There are many kinds of nested data structures. The simplest kind to build is a list of lists (also called an array of arrays, or a multi-dimensional array). It's reasonably easy to understand, and almost everything that applies here will also be applicable to the fancier data structures.

Composition and Access

Here's how to put together a two-dimensional array value:

```
# assign to an array a list of list references
@LoL = (
        [ "fred", "barney" ],
        [ "george", "jane", "elroy" ],
        [ "homer", "marge", "bart" ],
);

print $LoL[2][2];   # prints "bart"
```

The overall list is enclosed by parentheses, not brackets. That's because you're assigning a list to an array. If you didn't want the result to be a list, but rather a reference to an array, then you would use brackets on the outside:

```
# assign to a scalar variable a reference to a list of list references
$ref_to_LoL = [
    [ "fred", "barney", "pebbles", "bambam", "dino", ],
    [ "homer", "bart", "marge", "maggie", ],
    [ "george", "jane", "elroy", "judy", ],
];

print $ref_to_LoL->[2][2];   # prints "elroy"
```

$ref_to_LoL is a reference to an array, whereas @LoL is an array proper. The parentheses (indicating a list) have changed to brackets (indicating the creation of a reference to an array). Unlike C, Perl doesn't allow you to freely interchange arrays with references to arrays. This is a feature.

Remember that there is an implied -> between every pair of adjacent braces or brackets. Therefore these two lines:

```
$LoL[2][2]
$ref_to_LoL->[2][2]
```

are equivalent to these two lines:

```
$LoL[2]->[2]
$ref_to_LoL->[2]->[2]
```

There is, however, no implied -> before the first pair of brackets, which is why the dereference of $ref_to_LoL requires the ->.

Growing Your Own

Now those big list assignments are well and good for creating a fixed data structure, but what if you want to calculate each element on the fly, or otherwise build the structure piecemeal?

First, let's look at reading a data structure in from a file. We'll assume that there's a flat file in which each line is a row of the structure, and each word an element. Here's how to proceed:

```
while (<>) {
    @tmp = split;
    push @LoL, [ @tmp ];
}
```

You can also load the array from a function:

```
for $i ( 1 .. 10 ) {
    @tmp = somefunc($i);
    $LoL[$i] = [ @tmp ];
}
```

Of course, you don't need to name the temporary array:

```
while (<>) {
    push @LoL, [ split ];
}
```

and:

```
for $i ( 1 .. 10 ) {
    $LoL[$i] = [ somefunc($i) ];
}
```

You also don't have to use **push**. You could keep track of where you are in the array, and assign each line of the file to the appropriate row of the array:

```
my (@LoL, $i, $line);
for $i ( 0 .. 10 ) { # just first 11 lines
    $line = <>;
    $LoL[$i] = [ split ' ', $line ];
}
```

Simplifying, you can avoid the assignment of the line to a mediating variable:

```
my (@LoL, $i);
for $i ( 0 .. 10 ) { # just first 11 lines
    $LoL[$i] = [ split ' ', <> ];
}
```

In general, you should be leery of using potential list functions like <> in a scalar context without explicitly stating such. The following example would be clearer to the casual reader:

```
my (@LoL, $i);
for $i ( 0 .. 10 ) { # just first 11 lines
    $LoL[$i] = [ split ' ', scalar(<>) ];
}
```

If you want a $ref_to_LoL variable as a reference to an array, do something like:

```
my $ref_to_LoL;
while (<>) {
    push @$ref_to_LoL, [ split ];
}
```

So much for adding new rows to the list of lists. What about adding new columns? If you're just dealing with matrices, it's often easiest to use simple assignment:

```
for $x (1 .. 10) {
    for $y (1 .. 10) {
        $LoL[$x][$y] = func($x, $y);
    }
}

for $x ( 3, 7, 9 ) {
    $LoL[$x][20] += func2($x);
}
```

It doesn't matter whether the subscripted elements of @LoL are already there or not; Perl will gladly create them for you, setting intervening elements to the undefined value as need be. If you just want to append to a row, you have to do something a bit funnier looking:

```
# add new columns to an existing row
push @{ $LoL[0] }, "wilma", "betty";
```

Notice that this wouldn't work:

```
push $LoL[0], "wilma", "betty";   # WRONG!
```

In fact, that wouldn't even compile, because the argument to **push** must be a real array, not just a reference to an array. Therefore, the first argument absolutely must begin with an @ character. What comes after the @ is somewhat negotiable.

Access and Printing

Now it's time to print your data structure. If you only want one element, do this:

```
print $LoL[0][0];
```

If you want to print the whole thing, though, you can't just say:

```
print @LoL;          # WRONG
```

because you'll get references listed, and Perl will never automatically dereference thingies for you. Instead, you have to roll yourself a loop or two. The following code prints the whole structure, using the shell-style **for** construct to loop through the outer set of subscripts:

```
for $array_ref ( @LoL ) {
    print "\t [ @$array_ref ],\n";
}
```

Beware of the brackets. In this and the following example, the (non-subscripting) brackets do not indicate the creation of a reference. The brackets occur inside a quoted string, not in a place where a term is expected, and therefore lose their special meaning. They are just part of the string that **print** outputs.

If you want to keep track of subscripts, you might do this:

```
for $i ( 0 .. $#LoL ) {
    print "\t element $i is [ @{$LoL[$i]} ],\n";
}
```

or maybe even this (notice the inner loop):

```
for $i ( 0 .. $#LoL ) {
    for $j ( 0 .. $#{$LoL[$i]} ) {
        print "element $i $j is $LoL[$i][$j]\n";
    }
}
```

As you can see, things are getting a bit complicated. That's why sometimes it's easier to use a temporary variable on your way through:

```
for $i ( 0 .. $#LoL ) {
    $aref = $LoL[$i];
    for $j ( 0 .. $#{$aref} ) {
        print "element $i $j is $aref->[$j]\n";
    }
}
```

But that's still a bit ugly. How about this:

```
for $i ( 0 .. $#LoL ) {
    $aref = $LoL[$i];
    $n = @$aref - 1;
    for $j ( 0 .. $n ) {
        print "element $i $j is $aref->[$j]\n";
    }
}
```

Slices

If you want to get at a slice (part of a row) in a multi-dimensional array, you're going to have to do some fancy subscripting. That's because, while we have a nice synonym for a single element via the pointer arrow, no such convenience exists for slices. However, you can always write a loop to do a slice operation.

Here's how to create a one-dimensional slice of one subarray of a two-dimensional array, using a loop. We'll assume a list-of-lists variable (rather than a reference to a list of lists):

```
@part = ();
$x = 4;
for ($y = 7; $y < 13; $y++) {
    push @part, $LoL[$x][$y];
}
```

That same loop could be replaced with a slice operation:

```
@part = @{ $LoL[4] } [ 7..12 ];
```

If you want a *two-dimensional slice*, say, with $x running from 4..8 and $y from 7..12, here's one way to do it:

```
@newLoL = ();
for ($startx = $x = 4; $x <= 8; $x++) {
    for ($starty = $y = 7; $y <= 12; $y++) {
        $newLoL[$x - $startx][$y - $starty] = $LoL[$x][$y];
    }
}
```

In this example, the individual values within each subarray of @newLoL are assigned one by one, taken from the appropriate locations in @LoL. An alternative is to create anonymous arrays, each consisting of a desired slice of a subarray of @LoL, and then put references to these anonymous arrays into @newLoL. So we are writing references into @newLoL (subscripted once, so to speak) instead of subarray values into a twice-subscripted @newLol. This method eliminates the innermost loop:

```
for ($x = 4; $x <= 8; $x++) {
    push @newLoL, [ @{ $LoL[$x] } [ 7..12 ] ];
}
```

Of course, if you do this very often, you should probably write a subroutine called something like extract_rectangle().

Common Mistakes

As mentioned previously, every array or hash in Perl is implemented in one dimension. "Multi-dimensional" arrays, too, are one-dimensional, but the values in this one-dimensional array are references to other data structures. If you print these values out without dereferencing them, you will get the references rather than the data referenced. For example, these two lines:

```
@LoL = ( [2, 3], [4, 5, 7], [0] );
print "@LoL";
```

result in:

```
ARRAY(0x83c38) ARRAY(0x8b194) ARRAY(0x8b1d0)
```

On the other hand, this line:

```
print $LoL[1][2];
```

yields 7 as output.

Perl dereferences your variables only when you employ one of the dereferencing mechanisms. But remember that `$LoL[1][2]` is just a convenient way to write `$LoL[1]->[2]`, which in turn is a convenient way to write `${$LoL[1]}[2]`. Indeed, you could write all your dereferencing operations with braces, but that would be uglier than ugly. Use the syntactic sugar Perl provides to sweeten your program.

`@LoL` was defined as an array whose values happened to be references. Here's a similar-looking, but very different case:

```
my $listref = [
    [ "fred", "barney", "pebbles", "bambam", "dino", ],
    [ "homer", "bart", "marge", "maggie", ],
    [ "george", "jane", "elroy", "judy", ],
];

print $listref[2][2];    # WRONG!
```

Here, `$listref` is not an array, but a scalar variable *referring* to an array—in this case, referring to an anonymous, multi-dimensional array, the one created by the outer brackets. Therefore, to print `elroy` in this example, we should have said:

```
print $listref->[2][2];
```

By contrast, `$listref[2]` in the erroneous **print** statement is the second element in a not-yet-declared array. If you ask to

```
use strict 'vars'; # or just use strict
```

then the use of the undeclared array will be flagged as an error at compile time.

In constructing an array of arrays, remember to take a reference for the daughter arrays. Otherwise, you will just create an array containing the element counts of the daughter arrays, like this:

```
for $i (1..10) {
    @list = somefunc($i);
    $LoL[$i] = @list;       # WRONG!
}
```

Here @list is being accessed in a scalar context, and therefore yields a count of its elements, which is assigned to $LoL[$i]. The proper way to take the reference will be shown in a moment.

Another common error involves taking a reference to the same memory location over and over again:

```
for $i (1..10) {
    @list = somefunc($i);
    $LoL[$i] = \@list;      # WRONG!
}
```

Every reference generated by the second line of the **for** loop is the same, namely, a reference to the single array @list. Yes, this array is being given a different set of values on each pass through the loop, but when everything is said and done, $LoL contains a set of identical references to the same array, which now holds the last set of values that were assigned to it.

Here's a more successful approach:

```
for $i (1..10) {
    @list = somefunc($i);
    $LoL[$i] = [ @list ];
}
```

The brackets make a reference to a new array with a *copy* of what's in @list at the time of the assignment.

A similar result—though much more difficult to read—would be produced by:

```
for $i (1..10) {
    @list = somefunc($i);
    @{$LoL[$i]} = @list;
}
```

Since $LoL[$i] needs to be a reference, the reference springs into existence. Then, the preceding @ dereferences this new reference, with the result that the values of @list are assigned (in list context) to the array referenced by $LoL[$i]. For clarity's sake, you might wish to avoid this construct.

But there *is* a situation in which you might use it. Suppose @LoL is already an array of references to arrays. That is, suppose you had made assignments like:

```
$LoL[3] = \@original_list;
```

And now suppose that you want to change @original_list (that is, you want to change the fourth row of $LoL) so that it refers to the elements of @list. This code will work:

```
@{$LoL[3]} = @list;
```

In this case, the reference itself does not change, but the elements of the array being referred to do. You need to be aware, however, that this approach overwrites the values of @original_list.

Finally, the following dangerous-looking code actually works fine:

```
for $i (1..10) {
    my @list = somefunc($i);
    $LoL[$i] = \@list;
}
```

That's because the **my** variable is created afresh each time through the loop. So even though it looks as though you stored the same variable reference each time, you actually did not. This is a subtle distinction, but the technique can produce more efficient code, at the risk of misleading less enlightened programmers. It's more efficient because there's no copy in the final assignment. On the other hand, if you have to copy the values anyway (which the first assignment above is doing), then you might as well use the copy implied by the brackets and avoid the temporary variable:

```
for $i (1..10) {
    $LoL[$i] = [ somefunc($i) ];
}
```

In summary:

```
$LoL[$i] = [ @list ];   # safest, sometimes fastest
$LoL[$i] = \@list;       # fast but risky, depends on my-ness of list
@{ $LoL[$i] } = @list;   # too tricky for most uses
```

Data Structure Code Examples

Once you've mastered creating and using multi-dimensional arrays (lists of lists), you'll want to be able to make more complex data structures. If you're looking for C structures or Pascal records, you won't find any special reserved words in Perl to set these up for you. What you get instead is a more flexible system.[*] Perl has just two ways of organizing data: either as ordered lists stored in arrays and accessed by position, or as unordered key/value pairs stored in hashes and accessed by name.

---

[*] If your idea of a record structure is less flexible than this, or if you'd like to provide your users with something more opaque and rigid, then you can use the object-oriented features detailed in Chapter 5.

The best way to represent a record in Perl is using a hash reference, but how you choose to organize such records will vary. You may wish to keep an ordered list of these records around that you can look up by number, in which case you'd use an array to store the records (hash references). But you might wish to look up the records by name, in which case you'd store them in another hash. You could even do both at once: the array and the hash could each hold references to the same records, which are after all just anonymous hash thingies, and each one can have as many references to it as you want, within reason.[*]

In the following sections you will find code examples detailing how to compose, generate, access, and print out each of five data structures. The first four examples are straightforward homogeneous combinations of arrays and hashes, while the last one demonstrates how to use a less regular data structure. These examples, presented with little comment, assume that you have already familiarized yourself with the earlier explanations set forth in this chapter.

Arrays of Arrays

Use an array of arrays when you want a basic two-dimensional matrix. One application might include making a list of all the hosts on your network, but each of these hosts would have several possible aliases. Another might be a list of daily menus, each of which would itself be a list of foods served in it. For our example, we'll keep several lists of famous television characters, all stored together in one large list of lists.

Composition of an array of arrays

```
@LoL = (
    [ "fred", "barney" ],
    [ "george", "jane", "elroy" ],
    [ "homer", "marge", "bart" ],
);
```

Generation of an array of arrays

```
# reading from a file
while ( <> ) {
    push @LoL, [ split ];
}

# calling a function
for $i ( 1 .. 10 ) {
    $LoL[$i] = [ somefunc($i) ];
}
```

---

[*] Where reason is defined as 2**32 references, minus one. That's probably sufficient for most folks.

```
# using temp vars
for $i ( 1 .. 10 ) {
    @tmp = somefunc($i);
    $LoL[$i] = [ @tmp ];
}

# add to an existing row
push @{ $LoL[0] }, "wilma", "betty";
```

Access and printing of an array of arrays

```
# one element
$LoL[0][0] = "Fred";

# another element
$LoL[1][1] =~ s/(\w)/\u$1/;

# print the whole thing with refs
for $array_ref ( @LoL ) {
    print "\t [ @$array_ref ],\n";
}

# print the whole thing with indices
for $i ( 0 .. $#LoL ) {
    print "\t [ @{$LoL[$i]} ],\n";
}

# print the whole thing one at a time
for $i ( 0 .. $#LoL ) {
    for $j ( 0 .. $#{$LoL[$i]} ) {
        print "element $i $j is $LoL[$i][$j]\n";
    }
}
```

Hashes of Arrays

Use a hash of arrays when you want to look up each array by a particular string rather than merely by an index number. In our example of television characters, rather than merely looking up the list of names by the zeroth show, the first show, and so on, we'll set it up so we can look up the cast list according to the name of the show.

Because our outer data structure is a hash, we've lost all ordering of its contents. That means when you print it out, you can't predict the order things will come out. You can call the **sort** function and print its result if you'd like a particular output order.

Composition of a hash of arrays

```
# we customarily omit quotes when keys are identifiers
%HoL = (
    flintstones    => [ "fred", "barney" ],
    jetsons        => [ "george", "jane", "elroy" ],
    simpsons       => [ "homer", "marge", "bart" ],
);
```

Generation of a hash of arrays

```
# reading from file with the following format:
# flintstones: fred barney wilma dino
while ( <> ) {
    next unless s/^(.*?):\s*//;
    $HoL{$1} = [ split ];
}
```

```
# reading from file; more temporary variables
# flintstones: fred barney wilma dino
while ( $line = <> ) {
    ($who, $rest) = split /:\s*/, $line, 2;
    @fields = split ' ', $rest;
    $HoL{$who} = [ @fields ];
}
```

```
# calling a function that returns an array
for $group ( "simpsons", "jetsons", "flintstones" ) {
    $HoL{$group} = [ get_family($group) ];
}
```

```
# likewise, but using temporary variables
for $group ( "simpsons", "jetsons", "flintstones" ) {
    @members = get_family($group);
    $HoL{$group} = [ @members ];
}
```

```
# append new members to an existing family
push @{ $HoL{flintstones} }, "wilma", "betty";
```

Access and printing of a hash of arrays

```
# one element
$HoL{flintstones}[0] = "Fred";
```

```
# another element
$HoL{simpsons}[1] =~ s/(\w)/\u$1/;
```

```
# print the whole thing
foreach $family ( keys %HoL ) {
    print "$family: @{ $HoL{$family} }\n";
}
```

```
# print the whole thing with indices
foreach $family ( keys %HoL ) {
    print "$family: ";
    foreach $i ( 0 .. $#{ $HoL{$family} } ) {
        print " $i = $HoL{$family}[$i]";
    }
}
print "\n";

# print the whole thing sorted by number of members
foreach $family ( sort { @{$HoL{$b}} <=> @{$HoL{$a}} } keys %HoL ) {
    print "$family: @{ $HoL{$family} }\n"
}
# print the whole thing sorted by number of members and name
foreach $family ( sort { @{$HoL{$b}} <=> @{$HoL{$a}} } keys %HoL ) {
    print "$family: ", join(", ", sort @{ $HoL{$family} }), "\n";
}
```

Arrays of Hashes

An array of hashes is called for when you have a bunch of records that you'd like
to access sequentially, but each record itself contains key/value pairs. These arrays
tend to be used less frequently than the other homogeneous data structures.

Composition of an array of hashes

```
@LoH = (
    {
        lead    => "fred",
        friend  => "barney",
    },
    {
        lead    => "george",
        wife    => "jane",
        son     => "elroy",
    },
    {
        lead    => "homer",
        wife    => "marge",
        son     => "bart",
    },
);
```

Generation of an array of hashes

```
# reading from file
# format: lead=fred friend=barney
while ( <> ) {
    $rec = {};
    for $field ( split ) {
        ($key, $value) = split /=/, $field;
        $rec->{$key} = $value;
    }
    push @LoH, $rec;
}
```

```
# reading from file
# format: lead=fred friend=barney
# no temp
while ( <> ) {
    push @LoH, { split /[\s=]+/ };
}

# calling a function that returns a key,value array, like
# "lead","fred","daughter","pebbles"
while ( %fields = getnextpairset() ) {
    push @LoH, { %fields };
}

# likewise, but using no temp vars
while (<>) {
    push @LoH, { parsepairs($_) };
}

# add key/value to an element
$LoH[0]{pet} = "dino";
$LoH[2]{pet} = "santa's little helper";
```

Access and printing of an array of hashes

```
# one element
$LoH[0]{lead} = "fred";

# another element
$LoH[1]{lead} =~ s/(\w)/\u$1/;

# print the whole thing with refs
for $href ( @LoH ) {
    print "{ ";
    for $role ( keys %$href ) {
        print "$role=$href->{$role} ";
    }
    print "}\n";
}

# print the whole thing with indices
for $i ( 0 .. $#LoH ) {
    print "$i is { ";
    for $role ( keys %{ $LoH[$i] } ) {
        print "$role=$LoH[$i]{$role} ";
    }
    print "}\n";
}

# print the whole thing one at a time
for $i ( 0 .. $#LoH ) {
    for $role ( keys %{ $LoH[$i] } ) {
        print "element $i $role is $LoH[$i]{$role}\n";
    }
}
```

Hashes of Hashes

A multi-dimensional hash is the most flexible of Perl's homogeneous structures. It's like building up a record that itself contains other records. At each level you index into the hash with a string (quoted if it contains spaces). Remember, however, that the key/value pairs in the hash won't come out in any particular order. You must do your own sorting if the order matters.

Composition of a hash of hashes

```
%HoH = (
    flintstones => {
        lead      => "fred",
        pal       => "barney",
    },
    jetsons => {
        lead      => "george",
        wife      => "jane",
        "his boy" => "elroy",   # key quotes needed
    },
    simpsons => {
        lead      => "homer",
        wife      => "marge",
        kid       => "bart",
    },
);
```

Generation of a hash of hashes

```
# reading from file
# flintstones: lead=fred pal=barney wife=wilma pet=dino
while ( <> ) {
    next unless s/^(.*?):\s*//;
    $who = $1;
    for $field ( split ) {
        ($key, $value) = split /=/, $field;
        $HoH{$who}{$key} = $value;
    }
}

# reading from file; more temporary variables
while ( <> ) {
    next unless s/^(.*?):\s*//;
    $who = $1;
    $rec = {};
    $HoH{$who} = $rec;
    for $field ( split ) {
        ($key, $value) = split /=/, $field;
        $rec->{$key} = $value;
    }
}

# calling a function that returns a key,value for the inner hash
for $group ( "simpsons", "jetsons", "flintstones" ) {
```

```
        $HoH{$group} = { get_family($group) };
    }

    # likewise, but using temporary variables
    for $group ( "simpsons", "jetsons", "flintstones" ) {
        %members = get_family($group);
        $HoH{$group} = { %members };
    }

    # calling a function that returns the outer hash, including
    # references to the created inner hashes
    sub hash_families {
        my @ret;
        foreach $group ( @_ ) {
            push @ret, $group, { get_family($group) };
        }
        @ret;
    }
    %HoH = hash_families( "simpsons", "jetsons", "flintstones" );

    # append new members to an existing family
    %new_folks = (
        wife => "wilma",
        pet  => "dino";
    );
    for $what (keys %new_folks) {
        $HoH{flintstones}{$what} = $new_folks{$what};
    }
```

Access and printing of a hash of hashes

```
    # one element
    $HoH{flintstones}{wife} = "wilma";

    # another element
    $HoH{jetsons}{'his boy'} =~ s/(\w)/\u$1/;

    # print the whole thing
    foreach $family ( keys %HoH ) {
        print "$family: ";
        foreach $role ( keys %{ $HoH{$family} } ) {
            print "$role=$HoH{$family}{$role} ";
        }
        print "\n";
    }

    # print the whole thing, using temporaries
    while ( ($family,$roles) = each %HoH ) {
        print "$family: ";
        while ( ($role,$person) = each %$roles ) {  # using each precludes sorting
            print "$role=$person ";
        }
        print "\n";
    }
```

```perl
# print the whole thing somewhat sorted
foreach $family ( sort keys %HoH ) {
    print "$family: ";
    foreach $role ( sort keys %{ $HoH{$family} } ) {
        print "$role=$HoH{$family}{$role} ";
    }
    print "\n";
}

# print the whole thing sorted by number of members
foreach $family ( sort { keys %{$HoH{$a}} <=> keys %{$HoH{$b}} } keys %HoH ) {
    print "$family: ";
    foreach $role ( sort keys %{ $HoH{$family} } ) {
        print "$role=$HoH{$family}{$role} ";
    }
    print "\n";
}

# establish a sort order (rank) for each role
$i = 0;
for ( qw(lead wife son daughter pal pet) ) { $rank{$_} = ++$i }

# now print the whole thing sorted by number of members
foreach $family ( sort { keys %{$HoH{$a}} <=> keys %{$HoH{$b}} } keys %HoH ) {
    print "$family: ";

    # and print these according to rank order
    foreach $role ( sort { $rank{$a} <=> $rank{$b} } keys %{ $HoH{$family} } ) {
        print "$role=$HoH{$family}{$role} ";
    }
    print "\n";
}
```

More Elaborate Records

Those were simple, two-level, homogeneous data structures: each element contains the same kind of thingy as all the other elements do. It certainly doesn't have to be that way. Any element can hold any kind of scalar, which means that it could be a string, a number, or a reference to anything at all, including more exotic things than just array or hash references, such as references to named or anonymous functions or opaque objects. The only thing you can't do is to put more than one kind of thingy into a given scalar simultaneously. If you find yourself trying to do that, it's a signal that you need to establish an array or hash at the next lower level to handle the different types of thingy you're trying to overlay.

Below you will find code examples designed to illustrate all the possible kinds of things you might want to keep in a record. For our base structure, we'll use a hash reference. The keys are uppercase strings, a convention sometimes employed when the hash is being used as a specific record type rather than as a more generic associative array.

Composition of more elaborate records

This shows how to create and use a record whose fields are of many sorts:

```
$rec = {
    TEXT       => $string,
    SEQUENCE   => [ @old_values ],
    LOOKUP     => { %some_table },
    THATCODE   => \&some_function,
    THISCODE   => sub { $_[0] ** $_[1] },
    HANDLE     => \*STDOUT,
};

print $rec->{TEXT};

print $rec->{SEQUENCE}[0];
$last = pop @{ $rec->{SEQUENCE} };

print $rec->{LOOKUP}{"key"};
($first_k, $first_v) = each %{ $rec->{LOOKUP} };

# no difference calling named or anonymous subs
$answer = &{ $rec->{THATCODE} }($arg);
$answer = &{ $rec->{THISCODE} }($arg1, $arg2);

# must have extra braces on indirect object slot
print { $rec->{HANDLE} } "a string\n";

use FileHandle;
$rec->{HANDLE}->autoflush(1);
$rec->{HANDLE}->print("a string\n");
```

Composition of more elaborate records

```
%TV = (
    flintstones => {
        series   => "flintstones",
        nights   => [ qw(monday thursday friday) ],
        members  => [
            { name => "fred",    role => "lead", age  => 36, },
            { name => "wilma",   role => "wife", age  => 31, },
            { name => "pebbles", role => "kid",  age  =>  4, },
        ],
    },

    jetsons      => {
        series   => "jetsons",
        nights   => [ qw(wednesday saturday) ],
        members  => [
            { name => "george", role => "lead", age  => 41, },
            { name => "jane",   role => "wife", age  => 39, },
            { name => "elroy",  role => "kid",  age  =>  9, },
        ],
    },
```

```
    simpsons    => {
        series  => "simpsons",
        nights  => [ qw(monday) ],
        members => [
            { name => "homer", role => "lead", age => 34, },
            { name => "marge", role => "wife", age => 37, },
            { name => "bart",  role => "kid",  age => 11, },
        ],
    },
);
```

Generation of a hash of complex records

Because Perl is quite good at parsing complex data structures, you might just put
your data declarations in a separate file as regular Perl code and then load them in
with **do** or **require**. See Chapter 3, *Functions*, for details on those functions.

```
# here's a piece by piece build up
$rec = {};
$rec->{series} = "flintstones";
$rec->{nights} = [ find_days() ];

@members = ();
# assume this file is in field=value syntax
while (<>) {
    %fields = split /[\s=]+/;
    push @members, { %fields };
}
$rec->{members} = [ @members ];

# now remember the whole thing
$TV{ $rec->{series} } = $rec;
```

You can use extra pointer fields to avoid duplicate data. For example, you might
want a "kids" field included in a person's record. This could be a reference to a
list consisting of references to the kids' own records. That way you avoid the
update problems that result from having the same data in two places.

```
foreach $family (keys %TV) {
    my $rec = $TV{$family}; # temp pointer
    @kids = ();
    for $person ( @{$rec->{members}} ) {
        if ($person->{role} =~ /kid|son|daughter/) {
            push @kids, $person;
        }
    }
    # REMEMBER: $rec and $TV{$family} point to same data!!
    $rec->{kids} = [ @kids ];
}
# you copied the array, but the array itself contains pointers to
# uncopied objects. this means that if you make bart get older via

$TV{simpsons}{kids}[0]{age}++;
```

```
# then this would also change here
print $TV{simpsons}{members}[2]{age};

# because $TV{simpsons}{kids}[0] and $TV{simpsons}{members}[2]
# both point to the same underlying anonymous hash table

# print the whole thing
foreach $family ( keys %TV ) {
    print "the $family";
    print " is on during @{ $TV{$family}{nights} }\n";
    print "its members are:\n";
    for $who ( @{ $TV{$family}{members} } ) {
        print " $who->{name} ($who->{role}), age $who->{age}\n";
    }
    print "it turns out that $TV{$family}{'lead'} has ";
    print scalar ( @{ $TV{$family}{kids} } ), " kids named ";
    print join (", ", map { $_->{name} } @{ $TV{$family}{kids} } );
    print "\n";
}
```

5

Packages, Modules, and Object Classes

This chapter, more than any other in this book, is about Laziness, Impatience, and Hubris—because this chapter is about good software design.

We've all fallen into the trap of using cut-and-paste when we should have chosen to define a higher-level abstraction, if only just a loop or subroutine.[*] To be sure, some folks have gone to the opposite extreme of defining ever-growing mounds of higher-level abstractions when they should have used cut-and-paste.[†] Generally, though, most of us need to think about using more abstraction rather than less.

(Caught somewhere in the middle are the people who have a balanced view of how much abstraction is good, but who jump the gun on writing their own abstractions when they should be reusing existing code.)[‡]

Whenever you're tempted to do any of these things, you need to sit back and think about what will do the most good for you and your neighbor over the long haul. If you're going to pour your creative energies into a lump of code, why not make the world a better place while you're at it? (Even if you're only aiming for the program to *succeed*, you need to make sure it fits its ecological niche.)

The first step toward ecologically sustainable programming is simply: don't litter in the park. When you write a chunk of code, think about giving the code its own namespace, so that your variables and functions don't clobber anyone else's, or vice versa. A namespace is a bit like your home, where you're allowed to be as messy as you like, as long as you keep your external interface to other citizens

---

[*] This is a form of False Laziness.

[†] This is a form of False Hubris.

[‡] You guessed it, this is False Impatience. But if you're determined to reinvent the wheel, at least try to invent a better one.

moderately civil. In Perl, a namespace is called a *package*. Packages provide the fundamental building block upon which the higher-level concepts of modules and classes are constructed.

Like the notion of "home", the notion of "package" is a bit nebulous. Packages are independent of files. You can have many packages in a single file, or a single package that spans several files, just as your home could be one part of a larger building, if you live in an apartment, or could comprise several buildings, if your name happens to be Queen Elizabeth. But the usual size of a home is one building, and the usual size of a package is one file. Perl has some special help for people who want to put one package in one file, as long as you're willing to name the file with the same name as the package and give your file an extension of ".*pm*", which is short for "perl module". The *module* is the unit of reusability in Perl. Indeed, the way you *use* a module is with the **use** command, which is a compiler directive that controls the importation of functions and variables from a module. Every example of **use** you've seen until now has been an example of module reuse.

Object classes are another concept built on the package concept. The concept of classes therefore cuts across the concepts of files and modules. But the typical class is nevertheless implemented with a module. (If you're starting to get the feeling that much of Perl culture is governed by mere convention, then you're starting to get the right feeling, civilly speaking. The trend over the last 20 years or so has been to design computer languages that enforce a state of paranoia. You're expected to program every module as if it were in a state of siege. Certainly there are some feudal cultures where this is appropriate, but not all cultures are like this. In Perl culture, by contrast, you're expected to stay out of someone's home because you weren't invited in, not because there are bars[*] on the windows.)

Anyway, back to classes. When you **use** a module that implements a class, you're benefiting from the direct reuse of the software that implements that module. But with object classes you can get the additional benefits of *indirect* software reuse when the class you're using turns around and reuses other classes that it gets some characteristics from. But this is not primarily a book about object-oriented methodology, and we're not here to convert you into a raving object-oriented zealot, even if you want to be converted. There are already plenty of books out there for that. Perl's philosophy of object-oriented design fits right in with Perl's philosophy of everything else: use object-oriented design where it makes sense, and avoid it where it doesn't. Your call.

---

[*] But Perl provides some bars if you want them, too. See the Safe module in Chapter 7, *The Standard Perl Library*, for instance.

As we mentioned in the previous chapter, object-oriented programming in Perl is accomplished through use of references that happen to refer to thingies that know which class they're associated with. In fact, now that you know about references, you know almost everything hard about objects. The rest of it just "lays under the fingers", as a violinist would say. You will need to practice a little, though.

In this chapter we will discuss creation and use of packages, modules, and classes. Then we will review some of the essentials of object-oriented programming, explain how references become objects, and illustrate how these objects are manipulated as members of one or more classes. We'll also tell you how to **tie** ordinary variables into object classes to turn them into magical variables.

Packages

Perl provides a mechanism to protect different sections of code from inadvertently tampering with each other's variables. In fact, apart from certain magical variables, there's really no such thing as a global variable in Perl. Code is always compiled in the *current package*. The initial current package is package main, but at any time you can switch the current package to another one using the **package** declaration. The current package determines which symbol table is used for name lookups (for names that aren't otherwise package-qualified). The notion of "current package" is both a compile-time and run-time concept. Most name lookups happen at compile-time, but run-time lookups happen when symbolic references are dereferenced, and also when new bits of code are parsed under **eval**. In particular, **eval** operations know which package they were invoked in, and propagate that package inward as the current package of the evaluated code. (You can always switch to a different package within the **eval** string, of course, since an **eval** string counts as a block, as does a file loaded in with **do**, **require**, or **use**.)

The scope of a **package** declaration is from the declaration itself through the end of the innermost enclosing block (or until another **package** declaration at the same level, which hides the earlier one). All subsequent identifiers (except those declared with **my**, or those qualified with a different package name) will be placed in the symbol table belonging to the package. Typically, you would put a **package** declaration as the first declaration in a file to be included by **require** or **use**. But again, that's by convention. You can put a **package** declaration anywhere you can put a statement. You could even put it at the end of a block, in which case it would have no effect whatsoever. You can switch into a package in more than one place; it merely influences which symbol table is used by the compiler for the rest of that block. (This is how a given package can span more than one file.)

You can refer to identifiers[*] in other packages by prefixing ("qualifying") the identifier with the package name and a double colon: $Package::Variable. If the package name is null, the main package is assumed. That is, $::sail is equivalent to $main::sail.[†] (The old package delimiter was a single quote, which produced things like $main'sail and $'sail. But a double colon is now the preferred delimiter, in part because it's more readable to humans, and in part because it's more readable to *emacs* macros. It also gives C++ programmers a warm feeling.)

Packages may be nested inside other packages: $OUTER::INNER::var. This implies nothing about the order of name lookups, however. There are no fallback symbol tables. All undeclared symbols are either local to the current package, or must be fully qualified from the outer package name down. For instance, there is nowhere within package OUTER that $INNER::var refers to $OUTER::INNER::var. It would treat package INNER as a totally separate global package. Similarly, every **package** declaration must declare a complete package name. No package name ever assumes any kind of implied "prefix", even if (seemingly) declared within the scope of some other package declaration.

Only identifiers (names starting with letters or underscore) are stored in the current package's symbol table. All other symbols are kept in package main, including all the magical punctuation-only variables like $! and $_. In addition, the identifiers STDIN, STDOUT, STDERR, ARGV, ARGVOUT, ENV, INC, and SIG are forced to be in package main even when used for purposes other than their built-in ones. Furthermore, if you have a package called m, s, y, or tr, then you can't use the qualified form of an identifier as a filehandle because it will be interpreted instead as a pattern match, a substitution, or a translation. Using uppercase package names avoids this problem.

Assignment of a string to **%SIG** assumes the signal handler specified is in the main package, if the name assigned is unqualified. Qualify the signal handler name if you want to have a signal handler in a package, or don't use a string at all: assign a typeglob or a function reference instead:

```
$SIG{QUIT} = "quit_catcher";     # implies "main::quit_catcher"
$SIG{QUIT} = *quit_catcher;      # forces current package's sub
$SIG{QUIT} = \&quit_catcher;     # forces current package's sub
$SIG{QUIT} = sub { print "Caught SIGQUIT\n" };  # anonymous sub
```

---

[*] By identifiers, we mean the names used as symbol table keys to access scalar variables, array variables, hash variables, functions, file or directory handles, and formats. Syntactically speaking, labels are also identifiers, but they aren't put into a particular symbol table; rather, they are attached directly to the statements in your program. Labels may not be package qualified.

[†] To clear up another bit of potential confusion, in a variable name like $main::sail, we use the term "identifier" to talk about main and sail, but not main::sail. We call that a variable name instead, because an identifier may not contain a colon. The definition of an identifier is lexical, in that an identifier is a token that matches the pattern /^[A-Za-z_][A-Za-z_0-9]*$/.

See **my** and **local** in Chapter 3, *Functions*, for other scoping issues. See the "Signals" section in Chapter 6, *Social Engineering*, for more on signal handlers.

Symbol Tables

The symbol table for a package happens to be stored in a hash whose name is the same as the package name with two colons appended. The main symbol table's name is thus `%main::`, or `%::` for short, since package main is the default. Likewise, the symbol table for the nested package we mentioned earlier is named `%OUTER::INNER::`. As it happens, the main symbol table contains all other top-level symbol tables, including itself, so `%OUTER::INNER::` is also `%main::OUTER::INNER::`.

When we say that a symbol table "contains" another symbol table, we mean that it contains a reference to the other symbol table. Since package main is a top-level package, it contains a reference to itself, with the result that `%main::` is the same as `%main::main::`, and `%main::main::main::`, and so on, ad infinitum. It's important to check for this special case if you write code to traverse all symbol tables.

The keys in a symbol table hash are the identifiers of the symbols in the symbol table. The values in a symbol table hash are the corresponding typeglob values. So when you use the `*name` typeglob notation, you're really just accessing a value in the hash that holds the current package's symbol table. In fact, the following have the same effect, although the first is potentially more efficient because it does the symbol table lookup at compile time:

```
local *somesym = *main::variable;
local *somesym = $main::{"variable"};
```

Since a package is a hash, you can look up the keys of the package, and hence all the variables of the package. Try this:

```
foreach $symname (sort keys %main::) {
    local *sym = $main::{$symname};
    print "\$$symname is defined\n" if defined $sym;
    print "\@$symname is defined\n" if defined @sym;
    print "\%$symname is defined\n" if defined %sym;
}
```

Since all packages are accessible (directly or indirectly) through package main, you can visit every package variable in the program, using code written in Perl. The Perl debugger does precisely that when you ask it to dump all your variables.

Assignment to a typeglob performs an aliasing operation; that is,

```
*dick = *richard;
```

causes everything accessible via the identifier `richard` to also be accessible via the symbol `dick`. If you only want to alias a particular variable or subroutine, assign a reference instead:

```
*dick = \$richard;
```

This makes `$richard` and `$dick` the same variable, but leaves `@richard` and `@dick` as separate arrays. Tricky, eh?

This mechanism may be used to pass and return cheap references into or from subroutines if you don't want to copy the whole thing:

```
%some_hash = ();
*some_hash = fn( \%another_hash );
sub fn {
    local *hashsym = shift;
    # now use %hashsym normally, and you
    # will affect the caller's %another_hash
    my %nhash = (); # populate this hash at will
    return \%nhash;
}
```

On return, the reference will overwrite the hash slot in the symbol table specified by the `*some_hash` typeglob. This is a somewhat sneaky way of passing around references cheaply when you don't want to have to remember to dereference variables explicitly. It only works on package variables though, which is why we had to use **local** there instead of **my**.

Another use of symbol tables is for making "constant" scalars:

```
*PI = \3.14159265358979;
```

Now you cannot alter `$PI`, which is probably a good thing, all in all.

When you do that assignment, you're just replacing one reference within the typeglob. If you think about it sideways, the typeglob itself can be viewed as a kind of hash, with entries for the different variable types in it. In this case, the keys are fixed, since a typeglob can contain exactly one scalar, one array, one hash, and so on. But you can pull out the individual references, like this:

```
*pkg::sym{SCALAR}       # same as \$pkg::sym
*pkg::sym{ARRAY}        # same as \@pkg::sym
*pkg::sym{HASH}         # same as \%pkg::sym
*pkg::sym{CODE}         # same as \&pkg::sym
*pkg::sym{GLOB}         # same as \*pkg::sym
*pkg::sym{FILEHANDLE}   # internal filehandle, no direct equivalent
*pkg::sym{NAME}         # "sym" (not a reference)
*pkg::sym{PACKAGE}      # "pkg" (not a reference)
```

This is primarily used to get at the internal filehandle reference, since the other internal references are already accessible in other ways. But we thought we'd generalize it because it looks kind of pretty. Sort of. You probably don't need to remember all this unless you're planning to write a Perl debugger. So let's get back to the topic of writing good software.

Package Constructors and Destructors: BEGIN and END

Two special subroutine definitions that function as package constructors and destructors[*] are the BEGIN and END routines. The **sub** is optional for these routines.

A BEGIN subroutine is executed as soon as possible, that is, the moment it is completely defined, even before the rest of the containing file is parsed. You may have multiple BEGIN blocks within a file—they will execute in order of definition. Because a BEGIN block executes immediately, it can pull in definitions of subroutines and such from other files in time to be visible during compilation of the rest of the file. This is important because subroutine declarations change how the rest of the file will be parsed. At the very least, declaring a subroutine allows it to be used as a list operator, without parentheses. And if the subroutine is declared with a prototype, then calls to that subroutine may be parsed like any of several built-in functions (depending on which prototype is used).

An END subroutine, by contrast, is executed as *late* as possible, that is, when the interpreter is being exited, even if it is exiting as a result of a **die** function, or from an internally generated exception such as you'd get when you try to call an undefined function. (But not if it's is being blown out of the water by a signal—you have to trap that yourself (if you can).)[†] You may have multiple END blocks within a file—they will execute in reverse order of definition; that is: last in, first out (LIFO). That is so that related BEGINs and ENDs will nest the way you'd expect, if you pair them up.

When you use the **-n** and **-p** switches to Perl, BEGIN and END work just as they do in *awk*(1), as a degenerate case. For example, the output order of colors if you run the following program is red, green, and blue:

```
die "green\n";
END   { print "blue\n" }
BEGIN { print "red\n" }
```

Just as **eval** provides a way to get compilation behavior during run-time, so too BEGIN provides a way to get run-time behavior during compilation. But note that the compiler must execute BEGIN blocks even if you're just checking syntax with

---

[*] Strictly speaking, these aren't constructors and destructors, but initializers and finalizers. And strictly speaking, packages aren't objects. But strictly speaking, we don't speak strictly around here too often.

[†] See the sigtrap pragmatic module described in Chapter 7 for an easy way to do this. For general information on signal handling, see "Signals" in Chapter 6.

the −c switch. By symmetry, END blocks are also executed when syntax checking. Your END blocks should not assume that any or all of your main code ran. (They shouldn't do this in any event, since the interpreter might exit early from an exception.) This is not a bad problem in general. At worst, it means you should test the "definedness" of a variable before doing anything rash with it. In particular, before saying something like:

```
system "rm -rf '$dir'"
```

you should always check that $dir contains something meaningful, whether or not you're doing it in an END block. Caveat destructor.

Autoloading

Normally you can't call a subroutine that isn't defined. However, if there is a subroutine named AUTOLOAD in the undefined subroutine's package (or in the case of an object method, in the package of any of the object's base classes), then the AUTOLOAD subroutine is called with the same arguments as would have been passed to the original subroutine. The fully qualified name of the original subroutine magically appears in the package-global $AUTOLOAD variable, in the same package as the AUTOLOAD routine.

Most AUTOLOAD routines will load a definition for the undefined subroutine in question using **eval** or **require**, then execute that subroutine using a special form of **goto** that erases the stack frame of the AUTOLOAD routine without a trace.

The standard AutoSplit module is a tool used by module writers to help split their modules into separate files (with filenames ending in *.al*), each holding one routine. The files are placed in the *auto/* directory of the Perl library. These files can then be loaded on demand by the standard AutoLoader module. A similar approach is taken by the SelfLoader module, except that it autoloads functions from the file's own DATA area (which is less efficient in some ways and more efficient in others). Autoloading of Perl functions is analogous to dynamic loading of compiled C functions, except that autoloading (as practiced by AutoLoader and SelfLoader) is done at the granularity of the function call, whereas dynamic loading (as practiced by the DynaLoader module) is done at the granularity of the complete module, and will usually link in many C or C++ functions all at once. (See also the AutoLoader, SelfLoader, and DynaLoader modules in Chapter 7.)

But an AUTOLOAD routine can also just emulate the routine and never define it. For example, let's pretend that any function that isn't defined should just call **system** with its arguments. All you'd do is this:

```
sub AUTOLOAD {
    my $program = $AUTOLOAD;
    $program =~ s/.*:://;   # trim package name
```

```
        system($program, @_);
}
date();
who('am', 'i');
ls('-l');
```

In fact, if you predeclare the functions you want to call that way, you don't even need the parentheses:

```
use subs qw(date who ls);
date;
who "am", "i";
ls "-l";
```

A more complete example of this is the standard Shell module described in Chapter 7, which can treat undefined subroutine calls as calls to programs.

Modules

A module is just a reusable package that is defined in a library file whose name is the same as the name of the package (with a *.pm* on the end). A module may provide a mechanism for exporting some of its symbols into the symbol table of any other package using it. Or it may function as a class definition and make its operations available implicitly through method calls on the class and its objects, without explicitly exporting any symbols. Or it can do a little of both.

Most exporter modules rely on the customary exportation semantics supplied by the Exporter module. For example, to create an exporting module called Fred, create a file called *Fred.pm* and put this at the start of it:

```
package     Fred;
require     Exporter;
@ISA      = qw(Exporter);
@EXPORT   = qw(func1 func2);
@EXPORT_OK = qw($sally @listabob %harry func3);
```

Then go on to declare and use your variables and functions without any qualifications. See the Exporter module documentation in Chapter 7 for further information on the mechanics and style issues in module creation.

Perl modules are included in your program by saying:

```
use Module;
```

or:

```
use Module LIST;
```

This preloads Module at compile time, and then imports from it the symbols you've requested, either implicitly or explicitly. If you do not supply a list of symbols in a *LIST*, then the list from the module's @EXPORT array is used. (And if you do supply a *LIST*, all your symbols should be mentioned in either @EXPORT or @EXPORT_OK, or an error will result.) The two declarations above are exactly equivalent to:

```
BEGIN {
    require "Module.pm";
    Module->import();
}
```

or:

```
BEGIN {
    require "Module.pm";
    Module->import(LIST);
}
```

(We said that the first example above defaults to using the module's @EXPORT list, but that is a bit of a fib. It does this if the module uses the standard Exporter semantics. But a module can do anything it jolly well pleases when you do an import, since **use** just calls the ordinary import() method for the module, as above, and that method can be defined to do anything. Well, almost anything.)

Sometimes you might not wish to import anything from a module that exports things by default. As a special case, you can say:

```
use Module ();
```

which is exactly equivalent to

```
BEGIN { require "Module.pm"; }
```

Note that any initialization code in the Module is still run, as it would be for an ordinary **require**. It's only the **import** that is suppressed. If you really don't care whether the module is pulled in at compile-time or run-time, you can just say:

```
require Module;
```

This is slightly preferred over **require "Module.pm";** because it introduces Module as a package, which can clarify certain error messages that the parser might emit.

All Perl module files have the extension *.pm*. Both **use** and **require** will assume this (as well as the quotes) so that you don't have to spell out "Module.pm". This helps to differentiate new modules from the *.pl* and *.ph* files used by prior versions of Perl. Module names are also capitalized unless they're functioning as pragmas. Pragmas are in effect compiler directives, and such modules are sometimes called "pragmatic modules"—or even "pragmata" if you're a classicist.

Because the **use** declaration (in any form) implies a BEGIN block, the module is loaded (and any executable initialization code in it run) as soon as the **use** declaration is compiled, *before* the rest of the file is compiled. This is how **use** is able to function as a pragma mechanism to change the compiler's behavior, and also how modules are able to declare subroutines that are then visible as (unqualified) list operators for the rest of the current file. If, on the other hand, you invoke **require** instead of **use**, you must explicitly qualify any invocation of routines within the required package.

```
require Cwd;    # make Cwd:: accessible with qualification
$here = Cwd::getcwd();

use Cwd;        # import names from Cwd:: -- no qualification necessary
$here = getcwd();
```

In general, **use** is recommended over **require** because you get your error messages sooner. But **require** is useful for pulling in modules lazily at run-time.

Perl packages may be nested inside other packages, so we can have package names containing "::". But such compound names don't work well as filenames on many systems. Therefore, if a module's name is, say, Text::Soundex, then its definition is actually found in the library file *Text/Soundex.pm* (or whatever the equivalent pathname is on your system).

Perl modules always load a *.pm* file, but there may also be dynamically linked executables or autoloaded subroutine definitions associated with the module. If so, these will be entirely transparent to the user of the module. It is the responsibility of the *.pm* file to load (or arrange to autoload) any additional functionality. The POSIX module happens to do both dynamic loading and autoloading, but the user can just say

```
use POSIX;
```

to get it all.

Access to Modules

Perl does not patrol private/public borders within its modules—unlike languages such as C++, Ada, and Modula-17, Perl isn't infatuated with enforced privacy. As we mentioned at the beginning of the chapter, a Perl module would prefer that you stayed out of its living room because you weren't invited, not because it has a shotgun.

The module and its user have a contract, part of which is common law and part of which is written. Part of the common law contract is that a module doesn't pollute any namespace it wasn't asked to pollute. The written contract for the module (that is, the documentation) may make other provisions. But then, having read the written contract, you presumably know that when you say:

```
use RedefineTheWorld;
```

you're redefining the world, and you're willing to take the consequences. The next section talks about one way to redefine parts of the world.

Overriding Built-in Functions

Many built-in functions may be *overridden*, although (like knocking holes in your walls) you should only try this occasionally and for good reason. Typically, this might be done by a package attempting to emulate missing built-in functionality on a non-UNIX system. (Do not confuse overriding with *overloading*, which adds additional object-oriented meanings to built-in operators, but doesn't override much of anything. See the discussion of the overload module in Chapter 7 for more on that.)

Overriding may be done only by importing the name from a module—ordinary predeclaration isn't good enough. To be perfectly forthcoming, it's the assignment of a code reference to a typeglob that triggers the override, as in *open = \&myopen, which is how importing of functions is implemented. Furthermore, the assignment must occur in some other package; this makes unintentional overriding through typeglob aliasing more difficult. However, if you really want to do your own overriding, don't despair, because the subs pragma lets you predeclare subroutines via the import syntax, and these names may then override the built-in ones:

```
use subs qw(chdir chroot chmod chown);
chdir $somewhere;
sub chdir { ... }
```

Library modules should not in general export built-in names like **open** or **chdir** as part of their default @EXPORT list, since these names may sneak into someone else's namespace and change the semantics unexpectedly. Instead, if the module adds the name to the @EXPORT_OK list, then it's possible for users to import the name explicitly, but not implicitly. That is, they could say

```
use Module 'open';
```

and it would import the **open** override, but if they said

```
use Module;
```

they would get the default imports without the overrides.

The original versions of the built-in functions are always accessible via the CORE pseudopackage. Therefore, CORE::chdir() will always be the version that Perl was compiled with, even if the regular **chdir** function has been overridden.

Objects

First of all, you need to understand packages and modules as previously described in this chapter. You also need to know what references and referenced thingies are in Perl; see Chapter 4, *References and Nested Data Structures*, for that.

It's also helpful to understand a little about object-oriented programming (OOP), so in the next section we'll give you a little course on OOL (object-oriented lingo).

Brief Refresher on Object-Oriented Programming

An *object* is a data structure with a collection of behaviors. We generally speak of behaviors as being performed by the object directly, sometimes to the point of anthropomorphizing the object. For example, we might say that a rectangle "knows" how to display itself on the screen, or "knows" how to compute its own area.

An object gets its behaviors by being an *instance* of a *class*. The class defines *methods* that apply to all objects belonging to that class, called *instance methods*.

The class will also likely include instance-independent methods, called *class methods.** Some class methods create new objects of the classes, and are called *constructor methods* (such as "create a new rectangle with width 10 and height 5"). Other class methods might perform operations on many objects collectively ("display all rectangles"), or provide other necessary operations ("read a rectangle from this file").

A class may be defined so as to *inherit* both class and instance methods from *parent classes*, also known as *base classes*. This allows a new class to be created that is similar to an existing class, but with added behaviors. Any method invocation that is not found in a particular class will be searched for in the parent classes automatically. For example, a rectangle class might inherit some common behaviors from a generic polygon class.

While you might know the particular implementation of an object, generally you should treat the object as a black box. All access to the object should be obtained through the published interface via the provided methods. This allows the implementation to be revised, as long as the interface remains frozen (or at least, upward compatible). By published interface, we mean the written documentation

---

* Or sometimes *static methods*.

describing how to use a particular class. (Perl does not have an explicit interface facility apart from this. You are expected to exercise common sense and common decency.)

Objects of different classes may be held in the same variable at different times. When a method is invoked on the contents of the variable, the proper method for the object's class gets selected automatically. If, for example, the draw( ) method is invoked on a variable that holds either a rectangle or a circle, the method actually used depends on the current nature of the object to which the variable refers. For this to work, however, the methods for drawing circles and rectangles must both be called draw( ).

Admittedly, there's a lot more to objects than this, and a lot of ways to find out more. But that's not our purpose here. So, on we go.

Perl's Objects

Here are three simple definitions that you may find reassuring:

- An *object* is simply a referenced thingy that happens to know which class it belongs to.

- A *class* is simply a package that happens to provide methods to deal with objects.

- A *method* is simply a subroutine that expects an object reference (or a package name, for class methods) as its first argument.

We'll cover these points in more depth now.

An Object Is Simply a Referenced Thingy

Perl doesn't provide any special syntax for constructors. A constructor is merely a subroutine that returns a reference to a thingy that it has blessed into a class, generally the class in which the subroutine is defined. The constructor does this using the built-in **bless** function, which marks a thingy as belonging to a particular class. It takes either one or two arguments: the first argument is a regular hard reference to any kind of thingy, and the second argument (if present) is the package that will own the thingy. If no second argument is supplied, the current package is assumed. Here is a typical constructor:

```
package Critter;
sub new { return bless {}; }
```

The {} composes a reference to an empty anonymous hash. The **bless** function takes that hash reference and tells the thingy it references that it's now a member of the class Critter, and returns the reference. The same thing can be accomplished more explicitly this way:

```
sub new {
    my      $obref = {};        # ref to empty hash
    bless   $obref;             # make it an object in this class
    return $obref;              # return it
}
```

Once a reference has been blessed into a class, you can invoke the class's instance methods upon it. For example:

```
$circle->draw();
```

We'll discuss method invocation in more detail below.

Sometimes constructors call other methods in the class as part of the construction. Here we'll call an _initialize() method, which may be in the current package or in one of the classes (packages) that this class inherits from. The leading underscore is an oft-used convention indicating that the function is private, that is, to be used only by the class itself. This result can also be achieved by omitting the function from the published documentation for that class.

```
sub new {
    my $self = {}
    bless $self;
    $self->_initialize();
    return $self;
}
```

If you want your constructor method to be (usefully) inheritable, then you must use the two-argument form of **bless**. That's because, in Perl, methods execute in the context of the original base class rather than in the context of the derived class. For example, suppose you have a Polygon class that had a new() method as a constructor. This would work fine when called as Polygon->new(). But then you decide to also have a Square class, which inherits methods from the Polygon class. The only way for that constructor to build an object of the proper class when it is called as Square->new() is by using the two-argument form of **bless**, as in the following example:

```
sub new {
    my $class = shift;
    my $self = {};
    bless $self, $class;        # bless $self into the designated class
    $self->_initialize();       # in case there's more work to do
    return $self;
}
```

Within the class package, methods will typically deal with the reference as an ordinary (unblessed) reference to a thingy. Outside the class package, the reference should generally be treated as an opaque value that may only be accessed through the class's methods. (Mutually consenting classes may of course do whatever they like with each other, but even that doesn't necessarily make it right.)

A constructor may re-bless a referenced object currently belonging to another class, but then the new class is responsible for all cleanup later. The previous blessing is forgotten, as an object may only belong to one class at a time. (Although of course it's free to inherit methods from many classes.)

A clarification: Perl objects are blessed. References are not. Thingies know which package they belong to. References do not. The **bless** operator simply uses the reference in order to find the thingy. Consider the following example:

```
$a = {};                # generate reference to hash
$b = $a;                # reference assignment (shallow)
bless $b, Mountain;
bless $a, Fourteener;
print "\$b is a ", ref($b), "\n";
```

This reports $b as being a member of class `Fourteener`, not a member of class `Mountain`, because the second blessing operates on the underlying thingy that $a refers to, not on the reference itself. Thus is the first blessing forgotten.

A Class Is Simply a Package

Perl doesn't provide any special syntax for class definitions. You just use a package as a class by putting method definitions into the class.

Within each package a special array called `@ISA` tells Perl where else to look for a method if it can't find the method in that package. This is how Perl implements inheritance. Each element of the `@ISA` array is just the name of another package that happens to be used as a class. The packages are recursively searched (depth first) for missing methods, in the order that packages are mentioned in `@ISA`. This means that if you have two different packages (say, `Mom` and `Dad`) in a class's `@ISA`, Perl would first look for missing methods in `Mom` and all of her ancestor classes before going on to search through `Dad` and his ancestors. Classes accessible through `@ISA` are known as *base classes* of the current class, which is itself called the *derived class.*[*]

If a missing method is found in one of the base classes, Perl internally caches that location in the current class for efficiency, so the next time it has to find the

---

[*] Instead of "base class" and "derived class", some OOP literature uses *superclass* for the more generic classes and *subclass* for the more specific ones. Confusing the issue further, some literature uses "base class" to mean a "most super" superclass. That's not what we mean by it.

method, it doesn't have to look so far. Changing @ISA or defining new subroutines invalidates this cache and causes Perl to do the lookup again.

If a method isn't found but an AUTOLOAD routine is found, then that routine is called on behalf of the missing method, with that package's $AUTOLOAD variable set to the fully qualified method name.

If neither a method nor an AUTOLOAD routine is found in @ISA, then one last, desperate try is made for the method (or an AUTOLOAD routine) in the special predefined class called UNIVERSAL. This package does not initially contain any definitions (although see CPAN for some), but you may place your "last-ditch" methods there. Think of it as a global base class from which all other classes implicitly derive.

If that method still doesn't work, Perl finally gives up and complains by raising an exception.

Perl classes do only method inheritance. Data inheritance is left up to the class itself. By and large, this is not a problem in Perl, because most classes model the attributes of their object using an anonymous hash. All the object's data fields (termed "instance variables" in some languages) are contained within this anonymous hash instead of being part of the language itself. This hash serves as its own little namespace to be carved up by the various classes that might want to do something with the object. For example, if you want an object called $user_info to have a data field named age, you can simply access $user_info->{age}. No declarations are necessary. See the section on "Instance Variables" under "Some Hints About Object Design" later in this chapter.

A Method Is Simply a Subroutine

Perl doesn't provide any special syntax for method definition. (It does provide a little syntax for method invocation, though. More on that later.) A method expects its first argument to indicate the object or package it is being invoked on.

Class methods

A *class method* expects a class (package) name as its first argument. (The class name isn't blessed; it's just a string.) These methods provide functionality for the class as a whole, not for any individual object instance belonging to the class. Constructors are typically written as class methods. Many class methods simply ignore their first argument, since they already know what package they're in, and don't care what package they were invoked via. (These aren't necessarily the same, since class methods follow the inheritance tree just like ordinary instance methods.)

Another typical use for class methods might be to look up an object by some nick-name in a global registry:

```
sub find {
    my ($class, $nickname) = @_;
    return $objtable{$nickname};
}
```

Instance methods

An *instance method* expects an object reference[*] as its first argument. Typically it shifts the first argument into a private variable (often called $self or $this depending on the cultural biases of the programmer), and then it uses the variable as an ordinary reference:

```
sub display {
    my $self = shift;
    my @keys;
    if (@_ == 0) {                      # no further arguments
        @keys = sort keys(%$self);
    } else {
        @keys = @_;                     # use the ones given
    }
    foreach $key (@keys) {
        print "\t$key => $self->{$key}\n";
    }
}
```

Despite being counterintuitive to object-oriented novices, it's a good idea *not* to check the type of object that caused the instance method to be invoked. If you do, it can get in the way of inheritance.

Dual-nature methods

Because there is no language-defined distinction between definitions of class methods and instance methods (nor arbitrary functions, for that matter), you could actually have the same method work for both purposes. It just has to check whether it was passed a reference or not. Suppose you want a constructor that can figure out its class from either a classname or an existing object. Here's an example of the two uses of such a method:

```
$ob1  = StarKnight->new();
$luke = $ob1->new();
```

Here's how such a method might be defined. We use the **ref** function to find out the type of the object the method was called on so our new object can be blessed

---

[*] By which we mean simply an ordinary hard reference that happens to point to an object thingy. Remember that the reference itself doesn't know or care whether its thingy is blessed.

into that class. If **ref** returns false, then our $self argument isn't an object, so it must be a class name.

```
package StarKnight;
sub new {
    my $self  = shift;
    my $type  = ref($self) || $self;
    return bless {}, $type;
}
```

Method Invocation

Perl supports two different syntactic forms for explicitly invoking class or instance methods.[*] Unlike normal function calls, method calls always receive, as their first parameter, the appropriate class name or object reference upon which they were invoked.

The first syntax form looks like this:

METHOD CLASS_OR_INSTANCE LIST

Since this is similar to using the filehandle specification with **print** or **printf**, and also similar to English sentences like "Give the dog the bone," we'll call it the *indirect object* form. To look up an object with the class method **find**, and to print out some of its attributes with the instance method **display**, you could say this:

```
$fred = find Critter "Fred";
display $fred 'Height', 'Weight';
```

The indirect object form allows a *BLOCK* returning an object (or class) in the indirect object slot, so you can combine these into one statement:

```
display { find Critter "Fred" } 'Height', 'Weight';
```

The second syntax form looks like this:

CLASS_OR_INSTANCE->METHOD(LIST)

This second syntax employs the -> notation. It is sometimes called the *object-oriented* syntax. The parentheses are required if there are any arguments, because this form can't be used as a list operator, although the first form can.

```
$fred = Critter->find("Fred");
$fred->display('Height', 'Weight');
```

---

[*] Methods may also be called implicitly due to object destructors, tied variables, or operator overloading. Properly speaking, none of these is a function invocation. Rather, Perl uses the information presented via the syntax to determine which function to call. Operator overloading is implemented by the standard overload module as described separately in Chapter 7.

Or, you can put the above in only one statement, like this:

```
Critter->find("Fred")->display('Height', 'Weight');
```

There are times when one syntax is more readable, and times when the other syntax is more readable. The indirect object syntax is less cluttered, but it has the same ambiguity as ordinary list operators. If there is an open parenthesis following the class or object, then the matching close parenthesis terminates the list of arguments. Thus, the parentheses of

```
new Critter ('Barney', 1.5, 70);
```

are assumed to surround all the arguments of the method call, regardless of what comes afterward. Therefore, saying

```
new Critter ('Bam' x 2), 1.4, 45;
```

would be equivalent to

```
Critter->new('Bam' x 2), 1.4, 45;
```

which is unlikely to do what you want since the 1.4 and 45 are not being passed to the new() routine.

There may be occasions when you need to specify which class's method to use. In that case, you *could* call your method as an ordinary subroutine call, being sure to pass the requisite first argument explicitly:

```
$fred = MyCritter::find("Critter", "Fred");
MyCritter::display($fred, 'Height', 'Weight');
```

However, this does not do any inheritance. If you merely want to specify that Perl should start looking for a method in a particular package, use an ordinary method call, but qualify the method name with the package like this:

```
$fred = Critter->MyCritter::find("Fred");
$fred->MyCritter::display('Height', 'Weight');
```

If you're trying to control where the method search begins and you're executing in the class package itself, then you may use the SUPER pseudoclass, which says to start looking in your base class's @ISA list without having to explicitly name it:

```
$self->SUPER::display('Height', 'Weight');
```

The SUPER construct is meaningful only when used *inside* the class methods; while writers of class modules can employ SUPER in their own code, people who merely use class objects cannot.

Sometimes you want to call a method when you don't know the method name ahead of time. You can use the arrow form, replacing the method name with a simple scalar variable (not an expression or indexed aggregate) containing the method name:

```
$method = $fast ? "findfirst" : "findbest";
$fred->$method(@args);
```

We mentioned that the object-oriented notation is less syntactically ambiguous than the indirect object notation, even though the latter is less cluttered. Here's why: An indirect object is limited to a name, a scalar variable, or a *BLOCK*.[*] (If you try to put anything more complicated in that slot, it will not be parsed as you expect.) The left side of -> is not so limited. This means that A and B below are equivalent to each other, and C and D are also equivalent, but A and B differ from C and D:

```
A: method $obref->{fieldname}
B: (method $obref)->{fieldname}

C: $obref->{fieldname}->method()
D: method {$obref->{fieldname}}
```

In A and B, the method applies to `$obref`, which must yield a hash reference with `"fieldname"` as a key. In C and D the method applies to `$obref->{fieldname}`, which must evaluate to an object appropriate for the method.

Destructors

When the last reference to an object goes away, the object is automatically destroyed. (This may even be after you exit, if you've stored references in global variables.) If you want to capture control just before the object is freed, you may define a DESTROY method in your class. It will automatically be called at the appropriate moment, and you can do any extra cleanup you desire. (Perl does the memory management cleanup for you automatically.)

Perl does not do nested destruction for you. If your constructor re-blessed a reference from one of your base classes, your DESTROY method may need to call DESTROY for any base classes that need it. But this only applies to re-blessed objects; an object reference that is merely *contained* within the current object—as, for example, one value in a larger hash—will be freed and destroyed automatically. This is one of the reasons why containership via mere aggregation (sometimes called a "has-a" relationship) is often cleaner and clearer than inheritance (an "is-a" relationship). In other words, often you really only need to store one object

---

[*] Attentive readers will recall that this is precisely the same list of syntactic items that are allowed after a funny character to indicate a variable dereference—for example, @ary, @$aryref, or @{$aryref}.

inside another directly instead of employing inheritance, which can add unnecessary complexity.

Method Autoloading

After Perl has vainly looked through an object's class package and the packages of its base classes to find a method, it also checks for an AUTOLOAD routine in each package before concluding that the method can't be found. One could use this property to provide an interface to the object's data fields (instance variables) without writing a separate function for each. Consider the following code:

```
use Person;
$him = new Person;
$him->name("Jason");
$him->age(23);
$him->peers( ["Norbert", "Rhys", "Phineas"] );
printf "%s is %d years old.\n", $him->name, $him->age;
print "His peers are: ", join(", ", @{$him->peers}), ".\n";
```

The Person class implements a data structure containing three fields: name, age, and peers. Instead of accessing the objects' data fields directly, you use supplied methods to do so. To set one of these fields, call a method of that name with an argument of the value the field should be set to. To retrieve one of the fields without setting it, call the method without an argument. Here's the code that does that:

```
package Person;
use Carp;        # see Carp.pm in Chapter 7

my %fields = (
    name        => undef,
    age         => undef,
    peers       => undef,
);

sub new {
    my $that  = shift;
    my $class = ref($that) || $that;
    my $self  = {
        %fields,
    };
    bless $self, $class;
    return $self;
}

sub AUTOLOAD {
    my $self = shift;
    my $type = ref($self) || croak "$self is not an object";
    my $name = $AUTOLOAD;
    $name =~ s/.*://;    # strip fully-qualified portion
    unless (exists $self->{$name} ) {
```

```
            croak "Can't access '$name' field in object of class $type";
    }
    if (@_) {
        return $self->{$name} = shift;
    } else {
        return $self->{$name};
    }
}
```

As you see, there isn't really a method named `name()`, `age()`, or `peers()` to be found anywhere. The AUTOLOAD routine takes care of all of these. This class is a fairly generic implementation of something analogous to a C structure. A more complete implementation of this notion can be found in the Class::Template module contained on CPAN. The Alias module found there may also prove useful for simplifying member access.[*]

A Note on Garbage Collection

High-level languages typically allow the programmers to dispense with worrying about deallocating memory when they're done using it. This automatic reclamation process is known as *garbage collection*. For most purposes, Perl uses a fast and simple, reference-based garbage collection system. One serious concern is that unreachable memory with a non-zero reference count will normally not get freed. Therefore, saying this is a bad idea:

```
    {                   # make $a and $b point to each other
        my($a, $b);
        $a = \$b;
        $b = \$a;
    }
```

or more simply:

```
    {                   # make $a point to itself
        my $a;
        $a = \$a;
    }
```

When a block is exited, its **my** variables are normally freed up. But their internal reference counts can never go to zero, because the variables point at each other or themselves. This is circular reference. No one outside the block can reach them, which makes them useless. But even though they *should* go away, they can't. When building recursive data structures, you'll have to break the self-reference yourself explicitly if you don't care to cause a memory leak.

---

[*] CPAN is the Comprehensive Perl Archive Network, as described in the Preface.

For example, here's a self-referential node such as one might use in a sophisticated tree structure:

```perl
sub new_node {
    my $self = shift;
    my $class = ref($self) || $self;
    my $node = {};
    $node->{LEFT} = $node->{RIGHT} = $node;
    $node->{DATA} = [ @_ ];
    return bless $node, $class;
}
```

If you create nodes like this, they (currently)[*] won't ever go away unless you break the circular references yourself.

Well, almost never.

When an interpreter thread finally shuts down (usually when your program exits), then a complete pass of garbage collection is performed, and everything allocated by that thread gets destroyed. This is essential to support Perl as an embedded or a multithreadable language. When a thread shuts down, all its objects must be properly destructed, and all its memory has to be reclaimed. The following program demonstrates Perl's multi-phased garbage collection:

```perl
#!/usr/bin/perl
package Subtle;

sub new {
    my $test;
    $test = \$test;    # Create a self-reference.
    warn "CREATING " . \$test;
    return bless \$test;
}

sub DESTROY {
    my $self = shift;
    warn "DESTROYING $self";
}

package main;

warn "starting program";
{
    my $a = Subtle->new;
    my $b = Subtle->new;
    $$a = 0;                # Break this self-reference, but not the other.
```

---

[*] In other words, this behavior is not to be construed as a feature, and you shouldn't depend on it. Someday, Perl may have a full mark-and-sweep style garbage collection as in Lisp or Scheme. If that happens, it will properly clean up memory lost to unreachable circular data.

```
        warn "leaving block";
    }

    warn "just exited block";
    warn "time to die...";
    exit;
```

When run as */tmp/try*, the following output is produced:

```
starting program at /tmp/try line 18.
CREATING SCALAR(0x8e5b8) at /tmp/try line 7.
CREATING SCALAR(0x8e57c) at /tmp/try line 7.
leaving block at /tmp/try line 23.
DESTROYING Subtle=SCALAR(0x8e5b8) at /tmp/try line 13.
just exited block at /tmp/try line 26.
time to die... at /tmp/try line 27.
DESTROYING Subtle=SCALAR(0x8e57c) during global destruction.
```

Notice that "global destruction" in the last line? That's the thread garbage collector reaching the unreachable.

Objects are always destructed even when regular references aren't, and in fact are destructed in a separate pass before ordinary references. This is an attempt to prevent object destructors from using references that have themselves been destructed. Plain references are (currently) only garbage collected if the "destruct level" is greater than 0, which is usually only true when Perl is invoked as an embedded interpreter. You can test the higher levels of global destruction in the regular Perl executable by setting the PERL_DESTRUCT_LEVEL environment variable (presuming the -DDEBUGGING option was enabled at Perl build time).

Using Tied Variables

In older versions of Perl, a user could call **dbmopen** to tie a hash to a UNIX DBM file. Whenever the hash was accessed, the database file on disk (really just a hash, not a full relational database) would be magically[*] read from or written to. In modern versions of Perl, you can bind any ordinary variable (scalar, array, or hash) to an implementation class by using **tie**. (The class may or may not implement a DBM file.) You can break this association with **untie**.

The **tie** function creates the association by creating an object internally to represent the variable to the class. If you have a tied variable, but want to get at the underlying object, there are two ways to do it. First, the **tie** function returns a ref-

---

[*] In this case, magically means "transparently doing something very complicated". You know the old saying—any technology sufficiently advanced is indistinguishable from a Perl script.

erence to the object. But if you didn't bother to store that object reference anywhere, you could still retrieve it using the **tied** function.

```
$object = tie VARIABLE, CLASSNAME, LIST
untie VARIABLE
$object = tied VARIABLE
```

The **tie** function binds the variable to the class package that provides the methods for that variable. Once this magic has been performed, accessing a tied variable automatically triggers method calls in the proper class. All the complexity of the class is hidden behind magic method calls. The method names are predetermined, since they're called implicitly from within the innards of Perl. These names are in ALL CAPS, which is a convention in Perl culture that indicates that the routines are called implicitly rather than explicitly—just like BEGIN, END, and DESTROY. And AUTOLOAD too, for that matter.

You can almost think of **tie** as a funny kind of **bless**, except that it blesses a bare variable instead of a thingy reference, and takes extra parameters, like a constructor. That's because it actually does call a constructor internally. (That's one of the magic methods we mentioned.) This constructor is passed the *CLASSNAME* you specified, as well as any additional arguments you supply in the *LIST*. It is not passed the *VARIABLE*, however. The only way the constructor can tell which kind of *VARIABLE* is being tied is by knowing its own method name. This is not the customary constructor name, new, but rather one of TIESCALAR, TIEARRAY, or TIEHASH. (You can likely figure out which name goes with which variable type.) The constructor just returns an object reference in the normal fashion, and doesn't worry about whether it was called from **tie**—which it may not have been, since you can call these methods directly if you like. (Indeed, if you've tied your variable to a class that provides other methods not accessible through the variable, you *must* call the other methods directly yourself, via the object reference. These extra methods might provide services like file locking or other forms of transaction protection.)

As in any constructor, these constructors must **bless** a reference to a thingy and return it as the implementation object. The thingy inside the implementation object doesn't have to be of the same type as the variable you're tying to. It does have to be a properly blessed object, though. See the example below on tied arrays, which uses a hash object to hold information about an array.

The **tie** function will not **use** or **require** a module for you—you must do that explicitly yourself. (On the other hand, the **dbmopen** emulator function will, for backward compatibility, attempt to use one or another DBM implementation. But you can preempt its selection with an explicit **use**, provided the module you **use** is one of the modules in **dbmopen**'s list of modules to try. See the AnyDBM_File module in Chapter 7 for a fuller explanation.)

Tying Scalars

A class implementing a tied scalar must define the following methods: TIESCALAR, FETCH, STORE, and possibly DESTROY. These routines will be invoked implicitly when you **tie** a variable (TIESCALAR), read a tied variable (FETCH), or assign a value to a tied variable (STORE). The DESTROY method is called (as always) when the last reference to the object disappears. (This may or may not happen when you call **untie**, which destroys the reference used by the tie, but doesn't destroy any outstanding references you may have squirreled away elsewhere.) The FETCH and STORE methods are triggered when you access the variable that's been tied, not the object it's been tied to. If you have a handle on the object (either returned by the initial **tie** or retrieved later via **tied**), you can access the underlying object yourself without automatically triggering its FETCH or STORE methods.

Let's look at each of these methods in turn, using as our example an imaginary class called Nice.* Variables tied to this class are scalars containing process priorities, and each such variable is implicitly associated with an object that contains a particular process ID, such the ID of the currently running process or of the parent process. (Presumably you'd name your variables to remind you which process you're referring to.) Variables are tied to the class this way:

```
use Nice;      # load the Nice.pm module

tie $his_speed, 'Nice', getppid();
tie $my_speed,  'Nice', $$;
```

Once the variables have been tied, their previous contents are no longer accessible. The internally forged connection between the variable and the object takes precedence over ordinary variable semantics.

For example, let's say you copy a variable that's been tied:

```
$speed = $his_speed;
```

Instead of reading the value in the ordinary fashion from the $his_speed scalar variable, Perl implicitly calls the FETCH method on the associated underlying object. It's as though you'd written this:

```
$speed = (tied $his_speed)->FETCH();
```

Or if you'd captured the object returned by the **tie**, you could simply use that reference instead of the **tied** function, as in the following sample code.

---

* UNIX priorities are associated with the word "nice" because they're inverted from what you'd expect. Higher priorities run slower, hence are "nicer" to other processes. A more portable module might prefer a less UNIX-centric name like Priority. But if we were writing this class for the Perl library, we'd probably call it Tie::Priority or some such, to fit the library's hierarchical naming scheme. Not everything can be a top-level class, or things will get rather confused. Not to mention people.

```
$myobj = tie $my_speed, 'Nice', $$;
$speed = $my_speed;        # through the implicit interface
$speed = $myobj->FETCH(); # same thing, explicitly
```

You can use $myobj to call methods other than the implicit ones, such as those provided by the DB_File class (see Chapter 7). However, one normally minds one's own business and leaves the underlying object alone, which is why you often see the return value from **tie** ignored. You can still get at it if you need it later.

That's the external view of it. For our implementation, we'll use the BSD::Resource class (found in CPAN, but not included with Perl) to access the PRIO_PROCESS, PRIO_MIN, and PRIO_MAX constants from your system. Here's the preamble of our class, which we will put into a file named *Nice.pm*:

```
package Nice;
use Carp;                # Propagates error messages nicely.
use BSD::Resource;       # Use these hooks into the OS.
use strict;              # Enforce some discipline on ourselves,
use vars '$DEBUG';       # but exempt $DEBUG from discipline.
```

The Carp module provides methods carp(), croak(), and confess(), which we'll use in various spots below. As usual, see Chapter 7 for more about Carp.

The use strict would ordinarily disallow the use of unqualified package variables like $DEBUG, but we then declared the global with use vars, so it's exempt. Otherwise we'd have to say $Nice::DEBUG everywhere. But it is a global, and other modules can turn on debugging in our module by setting $Nice::DEBUG to some other value before using our module.

TIESCALAR *CLASSNAME, LIST*

The TIESCALAR method of the class (that is, the class package, but we're going to stop reminding you of that) is implicitly invoked whenever **tie** is called on a scalar variable. The *LIST* contains any optional parameters needed to properly initialize an object of the given class. (In our example, there is only one parameter, the process ID.) The method is expected to return an object, which may or may not contain an anonymous scalar as its blessed thingy. In our example, it does.

```
sub TIESCALAR {
    my $class = shift;
    my $pid   = shift;

    $pid ||= $$;                    # arg of 0 defaults to my process

    if ($pid =~ /\D/) {
        carp "Nice::TIESCALAR got non-numeric pid $pid" if $^W;
        return undef;
    }
```

```
      unless (kill 0, $pid) {   # EPERM or ERSCH, no doubt
          carp "Nice::TIESCALAR got bad pid $pid: $!" if $^W;
          return undef;
      }

      return bless \$pid, $class;
  }
```

Recall that the statement with the ||= operator is just shorthand for

```
  $pid = $pid || $$;      # set if not set
```

We say the object contains an anonymous scalar, but it doesn't really become anonymous until my $pid goes out of scope, since that's the variable we're generating a reference to when we bestow the blessing. When returning a reference to an array or hash, one could use the same approach by employing a lexically scoped array or hash variable, but usually people just use the anonymous array or hash composers, [] and {}. There is no similar composer for anonymous scalars.

On the subject of subterfuge, the **kill** isn't really killing the process. On most UNIX systems, a signal 0 merely checks to see whether the process is there.

This particular **tie** class has chosen to return an error value rather than raise an exception if its constructor fails. Other classes may not wish to be so forgiving. (In any event, the **tie** itself will throw an exception when the constructor fails to return an object. But you get more error messages this way, which many folks seem to prefer.) This routine checks the global variable **$^W** (which reflects Perl's **-w** flag) to see whether to emit its extra bit of noise.

But for all that, it's an ordinary constructor, and doesn't know it's being called from **tie**. It just suspects it strongly.

FETCH *THIS*

This method is triggered every time the tied variable is accessed (that is, read). It takes no arguments beyond a reference to the object that is tied to the variable. (The FETCH methods for arrays and hashes do, though.) Since in this case we're just using a scalar thingy as the tied object, a simple scalar dereference, $$self, allows the method to get at the real value stored in its object. In the example below, that real value is the process ID to which we've tied our variable.

```
  sub FETCH {
      my $self = shift;       # ref to scalar

      confess "wrong type" unless ref $self;
      croak "too many arguments" if @_;

      my $nicety;
      local $! = 0;           # preserve errno
```

```
        $nicety = getpriority(PRIO_PROCESS, $$self);
        if ($!) { croak "getpriority failed: $!" }
        return $nicety;
    }
```

This time we've decided to blow up (raise an exception) if the **getpriority** function fails—there's no place for us to return an error otherwise, and it's probably the right thing to do.

Note the absence of a $ on PRIO_PROCESS. That's really a subroutine call into BSD::Resource that returns the appropriate constant to feed back into **getpriority**. The PRIO_PROCESS declaration was imported by the **use** declaration. And that's why there's no $ on the front of it—it's not a variable. (If you had put a $, the **use strict** would have caught it for you as an unqualified global.)

STORE *THIS, VALUE*

This method is triggered every time the tied variable is set (assigned). The first argument, *THIS*, is again a reference to the object associated with the variable, and *VALUE* is the value the user is assigning to the variable.

```
    sub STORE {
        my $self = shift;
        my $new_nicety = shift;

        confess "wrong type" unless ref $self;
        croak "too many arguments" if @_;

        if ($new_nicety < PRIO_MIN) {
            carp sprintf
              "WARNING: priority %d less than minimum system priority %d",
                    $new_nicety, PRIO_MIN if $^W;
            $new_nicety = PRIO_MIN;
        }

        if ($new_nicety > PRIO_MAX) {
            carp sprintf
              "WARNING: priority %d greater than maximum system priority %d",
                    $new_nicety, PRIO_MAX if $^W;
            $new_nicety = PRIO_MAX;
        }

        unless (defined setpriority(PRIO_PROCESS, $$self, $new_nicety)) {
            confess "setpriority failed: $!";
        }
        return $new_nicety;
    }
```

There doesn't appear to be anything worth explaining there, except maybe that we return the new value because that's what an assignment returns.

DESTROY *THIS*

This method is triggered when the object associated with the tied variable needs to be destructed (usually only when it goes out of scope). As with other object classes, such a method is seldom necessary, since Perl deallocates the moribund object's memory for you automatically. Here, we'll use a DESTROY method for debugging purposes only.

```
sub DESTROY {
    my $self = shift;
    confess "wrong type" unless ref $self;
    carp "[ Nice::DESTROY pid $$self ]" if $DEBUG;
}
```

That's about all there is to it. Actually, it's more than all there is to it, since we've done a few nice things here for the sake of completeness, robustness, and general aesthetics (or lack thereof). Simpler TIESCALAR classes are certainly possible.

Tying Arrays

A class implementing a tied ordinary array must define the following methods: TIEARRAY, FETCH, STORE, and perhaps DESTROY.

Tied arrays are incomplete. There are, as yet, no defined methods to deal with $#ARRAY access (which is hard, since it's an lvalue), nor with the other obvious array functions, like **push**, **pop**, **shift**, **unshift**, and **splice**. This means that a tied array doesn't behave like an untied one. You can't even determine the length of the array. But if you use the tied arrays only for simple read and write access you'll be OK. These restrictions will be removed in a future release.

For the purpose of this discussion, we will implement an array whose indices are fixed at its creation. If you try to access anything beyond those bounds, you will cause an exception.

```
require Bounded_Array;
tie @ary, 'Bounded_Array', 2;    # maximum allowable subscript is 2
$| = 1;
for $i (0 .. 10) {
    print "setting index $i: ";
    $ary[$i] = 10 * $i;          # should raise exception on 3
    print "value of element $i now $ary[$i]\n";
}
```

The preamble code for the class is as follows:

```
package Bounded_Array;
use Carp;
use strict;
```

TIEARRAY *CLASSNAME, LIST*

This is the constructor for the class. That means it is expected to return a blessed reference through which the new array (probably an anonymous array reference) will be accessed.

In our example, just to demonstrate that you don't really have to use an array thingy, we'll choose a hash thingy to represent our object. A hash works out well as a generic record type: the {BOUND} field will store the maximum bound allowed, and the {ARRAY} field will hold the true array reference. Anyone outside the class who tries to dereference the object returned (doubtless thinking it an array reference), will blow up. This just goes to show that you should respect an object's privacy (unless you're well acquainted and committed to maintaining a good relationship for the rest of your life).

```
sub TIEARRAY {
    my $class = shift;
    my $bound = shift;

    confess "usage: tie(\@ary, 'Bounded_Array', max_subscript)"
        if @_ or $bound =~ /\D/;

    return bless {
        BOUND => $bound,
        ARRAY => [],
    }, $class;
}
```

In this case we have used the anonymous hash composer rather than a lexically scoped variable that goes out of scope. We also used the array composer within the hash composer.

FETCH *THIS, INDEX*

This method will be triggered every time an individual element in the tied array is accessed (read). It takes one argument beyond its self reference: the index we're trying to fetch. (The index is an integer, but just because the caller thinks of it as a mundane integer doesn't mean you have to do anything "linear" with it. You could use it to seed a random number generator, for instance, or process it with a hash function to do a random lookup in a hash table.)

Here we use list assignment rather than **shift** to process the method arguments. TMTOWTDI.

```
sub FETCH {
    my ($self, $idx) = @_;
    if ($idx > $self->{BOUND}) {
        confess "Array OOB: $idx > $self->{BOUND}";
    }
    return $self->{ARRAY}[$idx];
}
```

As you may have noticed, the names of the FETCH, STORE, and DESTROY methods are the same for all tied classes, even though the constructors differ in name (TIESCALAR versus TIEARRAY). While in theory you could have the same class servicing several tied types, in practice this becomes cumbersome, and it's easiest to simply write them with one type per class.

STORE *THIS, INDEX, VALUE*

This method will be triggered every time an element in the tied array is set (written). It takes two arguments beyond its self reference: the index at which we're trying to store something and the value we're trying to put there. For example:

```
sub STORE {
    my ($self, $idx, $value) = @_;
    if ($idx > $self->{BOUND} ) {
        confess "Array OOB: $idx > $self->{BOUND}";
    }
    return $self->{ARRAY}[$idx] = $value;
}
```

DESTROY *THIS*

This method will be triggered when the tied object needs to be deallocated. As with the scalar tie class, this is almost never needed in a language that does its own storage allocation, so this time we'll just leave it out.

The code we presented at the beginning of this section attempts several out-of-bounds accesses. It will therefore generate the following output:

```
setting index 0: value of element 0 now 0
setting index 1: value of element 1 now 10
setting index 2: value of element 2 now 20
setting index 3: Array OOB: 3 > 2 at Bounded_Array.pm line 39
        Bounded_Array::FETCH called at testba line 12
```

Tying Hashes

For historical reasons, hashes have the most complete and useful **tie** implementation. A class implementing a tied associative array must define various methods. TIEHASH is the constructor. FETCH and STORE access the key/value pairs. EXISTS reports whether a key is present in the hash, and DELETE deletes one. CLEAR empties the hash by deleting all the key/value pairs. FIRSTKEY and NEXTKEY implement the **keys** and **each** built-in functions to iterate over all the keys. And DESTROY (if defined) is called when the tied object is deallocated.

If this seems like a lot, then feel free to inherit most of these methods from the standard Tie::Hash module, redefining only the interesting ones. See the Tie::Hash module documentation in Chapter 7 for details.

Remember that Perl distinguishes a key not existing in the hash from a key that exists with an undefined value. The two possibilities can be tested with the **exists** and **defined** functions, respectively.

Because functions like **keys** and **values** may return huge array values when used on large hashes (like tied DBM files), you may prefer to use the **each** function to iterate over such. For example:

```
# print out B-news history file offsets
use NDBM_File;
tie(%HIST, 'NDBM_File', '/usr/lib/news/history', 1, 0);
while (($key,$val) = each %HIST) {
    print $key, ' = ', unpack('L',$val), "\n";
}
untie(%HIST);
```

(But does anyone run B-news any more?)

Here's an example of a somewhat peculiar tied hash class: it gives you a hash representing a particular user's dotfiles (that is, files whose names begin with a period). You index into the hash with the name of the file (minus the period) and you get back that dotfile's contents. For example:

```
use DotFiles;
tie %dot, "DotFiles";
if ( $dot{profile} =~ /MANPATH/ or
     $dot{login}   =~ /MANPATH/ or
     $dot{cshrc}   =~ /MANPATH/    )
{
    print "you've set your manpath\n";
}
```

Here's another way to use our tied class:

```
# third argument is name of user whose dot files we will tie to
tie %him, 'DotFiles', 'daemon';
foreach $f ( keys %him ) {
    printf "daemon dot file %s is size %d\n",
        $f, length $him{$f};
}
```

In our DotFiles example we implement the object as a regular hash containing several important fields, of which only the {CONTENTS} field will be what the user thinks of as the real hash. Here are the fields:

USER

   Whose dot files this object represents

HOME

> Where those dotfiles live

CLOBBER

> Whether we are allowed to change or remove those dot files

CONTENTS

> The hash of dotfile names and content mappings

Here's the start of *DotFiles.pm*:

```
package DotFiles;
use Carp;
sub whowasi { (caller(1))[3] . '()' }
my $DEBUG = 0;
sub debug { $DEBUG = @_ ? shift : 1 }
```

For our example, we want to be able to emit debugging information to help in
tracing during development. We also keep one convenience function around internally to help print out warnings; whowasi() returns the name of the function that
called the current function (whowasi()'s "grandparent" function).

Here are the methods for the DotFiles tied hash.

TIEHASH *CLASSNAME, LIST*

> This is the constructor for the class. That means it is expected to return a
> blessed reference through which the new object may be accessed. Again, the
> user of the tied class probably has little need of the object. It's Perl itself that
> needs the returned object so that it can magically call the right methods when
> the tied variable is accessed.

> Here's the constructor:

```
sub TIEHASH {
    my $self = shift;
    my $user = shift || $>;
    my $dotdir = shift || "";

    croak "usage: @{[&whowasi]} [USER [DOTDIR]]" if @_;

    $user = getpwuid($user) if $user =~ /^\d+$/;
    my $dir = (getpwnam($user))[7]
            or croak "@{[&whowasi]}: no user $user";
    $dir .= "/$dotdir" if $dotdir;

    my $node = {
        USER        => $user,
        HOME        => $dir,
        CONTENTS    => {},
        CLOBBER     => 0,
    };
```

```
opendir DIR, $dir
        or croak "@{[&whowasi]}: can't opendir $dir: $!";
foreach $dot ( grep /^\./ && -f "$dir/$_", readdir(DIR)) {
    $dot =~ s/^\.//;
    $node->{CONTENTS}{$dot} = undef;
}
closedir DIR;

return bless $node, $self;
}
```

It's probably worth mentioning that if you're going to filetest the return values returned by that **readdir**, you'd better prepend the directory in question (as we do). Otherwise, since no **chdir** was done, you'd test the wrong file.

FETCH *THIS, KEY*

This method will be triggered every time an element in the tied hash is accessed (read). It takes one argument beyond its self reference: the key whose value we're trying to fetch. The key is a string, and you can do anything you like with it (consistent with its being a string).

Here's the fetch for our DotFiles example.

```
sub FETCH {
    carp &whowasi if $DEBUG;
    my $self = shift;
    my $dot = shift;
    my $dir = $self->{HOME};
    my $file = "$dir/.$dot";

    unless (exists $self->{CONTENTS}->{$dot} || -f $file) {
        carp "@{[&whowasi]}: no $dot file" if $DEBUG;
        return undef;
    }

    # Implement a cache.
    if (defined $self->{CONTENTS}->{$dot}) {
        return $self->{CONTENTS}->{$dot};
    } else {
        return $self->{CONTENTS}->{$dot} = `cat $dir/.$dot`;
    }
}
```

This function was easy to write by having it call the UNIX *cat*(1) command, but it would be more portable (and somewhat more efficient) to open the file ourselves. On the other hand, since dot files are a UNIXy concept, we're not that concerned.

STORE *THIS, KEY, VALUE*

This method will be triggered every time an element in the tied hash is set (written). It takes two arguments beyond its self reference: the key under which we're storing the value and the value we're putting there.

Here in our DotFiles example we won't let users overwrite a file without first calling the `clobber()` method on the original object reference returned by **tie**.

```
sub STORE {
    carp &whowasi if $DEBUG;
    my $self = shift;
    my $dot = shift;
    my $value = shift;
    my $file = $self->{HOME} . "/.$dot";

    croak "@{[&whowasi]}: $file not clobberable"
        unless $self->{CLOBBER};

    open(F, "> $file") or croak "can't open $file: $!";
    print F $value;
    close(F);
}
```

If they want to clobber something, they can say:

```
$ob = tie %daemon_dots, 'daemon';
$ob->clobber(1);
$daemon_dots{signature} = "A true daemon\n";
```

But there's also the **tied** function, so they could alternatively set `clobber` using:

```
tie %daemon_dots, 'daemon';
tied(%daemon_dots)->clobber(1);
```

The `clobber` method is simply:

```
sub clobber {
    my $self = shift;
    $self->{CLOBBER} = @_ ? shift : 1;
}
```

DELETE *THIS, KEY*

This method is triggered when we remove an element from the hash, typically by using the **delete** function. Again, we'll be careful to check whether the user really wants to clobber files.

```
sub DELETE   {
    carp &whowasi if $DEBUG;

    my $self = shift;
    my $dot = shift;
    my $file = $self->{HOME} . "/.$dot";
    croak "@{[&whowasi]}: won't remove file $file"
        unless $self->{CLOBBER};
```

```
        delete $self->{CONTENTS}->{$dot};
        unlink $file or carp "@{[&whowasi]}: can't unlink $file: $!";
    }
```

CLEAR *THIS*

This method is triggered when the whole hash is to be cleared, usually by assigning the empty list to it.

In our example, that would remove all the user's dotfiles! It's such a dangerous thing that we'll require CLOBBER to be set higher than 1 before this can happen.

```
    sub CLEAR {
        carp &whowasi if $DEBUG;
        my $self = shift;
        croak "@{[&whowasi]}: won't remove all dotfiles for $self->{USER}"
            unless $self->{CLOBBER} > 1;
        my $dot;
        foreach $dot ( keys %{$self->{CONTENTS}}) {
            $self->DELETE($dot);
        }
    }
```

EXISTS *THIS, KEY*

This method is triggered when the user invokes the **exists** function on a particular hash. In our example, we'll look at the {CONTENTS} hash element to find the answer:

```
    sub EXISTS   {
        carp &whowasi if $DEBUG;
        my $self = shift;
        my $dot = shift;
        return exists $self->{CONTENTS}->{$dot};
    }
```

FIRSTKEY *THIS*

This method is triggered when the user begins to iterate through the hash, such as with a **keys** or **each** call. By calling **keys** in a scalar context, we reset its internal state to ensure that the next **each** used in the **return** statement will get the first key.

```
    sub FIRSTKEY {
        carp &whowasi if $DEBUG;
        my $self = shift;
        my $a    = keys %{$self->{CONTENTS}};
        return scalar each %{$self->{CONTENTS}};
    }
```

NEXTKEY *THIS, LASTKEY*

This method is triggered during a **keys** or **each** iteration. It has a second argument which is the last key that has been accessed. This is useful if the NEXTKEY method needs to know its previous state to calculate the next state.

For our example, we are using a real hash to represent the tied hash's data, except that this hash is stored in the hash's CONTENTS field instead of in the hash itself. So we can just rely on Perl's **each** iterator:

```
sub NEXTKEY {
    carp &whowasi if $DEBUG;
    my $self = shift;
    return scalar each %{ $self->{CONTENTS} }
}
```

DESTROY *THIS*

This method is triggered when a tied hash's object is about to be deallocated. You don't really need it except for debugging and extra cleanup. Here's a very simple function:

```
sub DESTROY {
    carp &whowasi if $DEBUG;
}
```

Some Hints About Object Design

In this section we present a collection of tricks, hints, and code examples derived from various sources. We hope to whet your curiosity about such things as the use of instance variables and the mechanics of object and class relationships. You can ignore these things when you're merely using a class, but when you're implementing a class, you have to pay more attention to what you're doing, and why.

You needn't feel bound by the particular styles and idioms you see here, but you should be thinking about the underlying principles.

Object-Oriented Scaling Tips

The following guidelines will help you design a class that can be transparently used as a base class by another class.

1. Do not attempt to verify that the type of $self is the class you're in. That'll break if the class is inherited, when the type of $self is valid but its package isn't what you expect. See rule 5.

    ```
    package Some_Class;
    sub some_method {
        my $self = shift;
        unless (ref($self) eq "Some_Class") {          # WRONG
            croak "I'm not a Some_Class anymore!";
        }
        unless (ref $self) {                           # better
            croak "bad method call";
        }
    }
    ```

2. If an object-oriented (->) or indirect-object syntax was used, then the object is probably the correct type and there's no need to become paranoid about it. Perl isn't a paranoid language anyway. If people subvert the object-oriented or indirect-object syntax by calling a method directly as an ordinary function, or vice versa, then they probably know what they're doing and you should let them do it.

3. Use the two-argument form of **bless**. Let a derived class (subclass) use your constructor. See the section on "Inheriting a Constructor".

4. The derived class is allowed to know things about its immediate base class (superclass); the base class is allowed to know nothing about a derived class.

5. Don't be trigger-happy with inheritance, which should generally be used to represent only the "is-a" relationship. One of the "has-a" relationships (implying some sort of aggregation) is often more appropriate. See the later sections on "Containment", "Implementation", and "Delegation".

6. The object is the namespace. Make package globals accessible via the object. That means you should include a reference to any package data inside the object somewhere, instead of having the method guess where to look for it. See the section on "Class Context and the Object".

7. Indirect-object syntax is certainly less noisy, but it is also prone to ambiguities which can cause difficult-to-find bugs. Allow people to use the sure-thing object-oriented syntax, even if you don't like it. On the other hand, allow people to use the indirect-object syntax when it increases clarity. Don't impose artificial house rules in either direction.

8. Do not use the ordinary subroutine call syntax on a method. You're going to be bitten someday. Someone might move that method into a base class and your code will be broken. On top of that, you're feeding the paranoia mentioned in rule 2.

9. Don't assume you know the home package of a method. You're making it difficult for someone to override that method. See the later section "Thinking of Code Reuse".

Instance Variables

An anonymous array or anonymous hash can be used to hold instance variables. (The hashes fare better in the face of inheritance.) We'll also show you some nice interactions with named parameters.

```
package HashInstance;

sub new {
    my $type   = shift;
```

```
    my %params = @_;
    my $self    = {};
    $self->{High} = $params{High};
    $self->{Low}  = $params{Low};
    return bless $self, $type;
}

package ArrayInstance;

sub new {
    my $type    = shift;
    my %params  = @_;
    my $self     = [];
    $self->[0] = $params{Left};
    $self->[1] = $params{Right};
    return bless $self, $type;
}

package main;

$a = HashInstance->new( High => 42, Low => 11 );
print "High=$a->{High}\n";
print "Low=$a->{Low}\n";

$b = ArrayInstance->new( Left => 78, Right => 40 );
print "Left=$b->[0]\n";
print "Right=$b->[1]\n";
```

This demonstrates how object references act like ordinary references if you use them like ordinary references, as you often do within the class definitions. Strictly speaking, we're cheating here on the principle of *encapsulation* when we dereference $a and $b outside of their class definitions. But hey, the classes didn't provide access methods, so there's a bit of blame on both sides.

Besides, most of the rest of these examples cheat too.

Scalar Instance Variables

An anonymous scalar can be used when only one instance variable is needed.

```
package ScalarInstance;

sub new {
    my $type = shift;
    my $self;
    $self = shift;
    return bless \$self, $type;
}

package main;

$a = ScalarInstance->new( 42 );
print "a=$$a\n";
```

Instance Variable Inheritance

This example demonstrates how one might inherit instance variables from a base class for inclusion in the new class. This requires calling the base class's constructor and adding one's own instance variables to the new object. Note that you're pretty much forced to use a hash if you want to do inheritance, since you can't have a reference to multiple types at the same time. A hash allows you to extend your object's little namespace in arbitrary directions, unlike an array, which can only be extended at the end. So, for example, your base class might use the first five elements of your array, but the various derived classes might start fighting over who owns the sixth element. So use a hash instead, like this:

```perl
package Base;

sub new {
    my $type = shift;
    my $self = {};
    $self->{buz} = 42;
    return bless $self, $type;
}

package Derived;
@ISA = qw( Base );

sub new {
    my $type = shift;
    my $self = Base->new;
    $self->{biz} = 11;
    return bless $self, $type;
}

package main;

$a = Derived->new;
print "buz = ", $a->{buz}, "\n";
print "biz = ", $a->{biz}, "\n";
```

You still have to be careful that two derived classes don't pick the same name in the object's namespace, but that's an easier problem than trying to make the same array element hold different values simultaneously.

Containment (the "Has-a" Relationship)

The following demonstrates how one might implement the "contains" relationship between objects. This is closely related to the "uses" relationship we show later.

```perl
package Inner;

sub new {
    my $type = shift;
```

```
    my $self = {};
    $self->{buz} = 42;
    return bless $self, $type;
}


package Outer;

sub new {
    my $type = shift;
    my $self = {};
    $self->{Inner} = Inner->new;
    $self->{biz} = 11;
    return bless $self, $type;
}


package main;

$a = Outer->new;
print "buz = ", $a->{Inner}->{buz}, "\n";
print "biz = ", $a->{biz}, "\n";
```

Overriding Base Class Methods

The following example demonstrates how to override a base class method within
a derived class, and then call the overridden method anyway. The SUPER pseudoclass allows the programmer to call an overridden base class (superclass) method
without actually knowing where that method is defined.[*]

```
package Buz;
sub goo { print "here's the goo\n" }

package Bar;
@ISA = qw( Buz );
sub google { print "google here\n" }

package Baz;
sub mumble { print "mumbling\n" }

package Foo;
@ISA = qw( Bar Baz );

sub new {
    my $type = shift;
    return bless [], $type;
}
sub grr { print "grumble\n" }
sub goo {
    my $self = shift;
```

---

[*] This is not to be confused with the mechanism mentioned earlier for overriding Perl's built-in functions, which aren't object methods, and so aren't overridden by inheritance. You call overridden built-
ins via the pseudopackage CORE rather than the pseudopackage SUPER.

```
    $self->SUPER::goo();
}
sub mumble {
    my $self = shift;
    $self->SUPER::mumble();
}
sub google {
    my $self = shift;
    $self->SUPER::google();
}

package main;

$foo = Foo->new;
$foo->mumble;
$foo->grr;
$foo->goo;
$foo->google;
```

Implementation (the "Uses" Relationship)

This example demonstrates an interface for the SDBM_File class. This creates a "uses" relationship between our class and the SDBM_File class.

```
package MyDBM;

require SDBM_File;
require Tie::Hash;
@ISA = qw( Tie::Hash );

sub TIEHASH {
    my $type = shift;
    my $ref  = SDBM_File->new(@_);
    return bless {dbm => $ref}, $type;
}
sub FETCH {
    my $self = shift;
    my $ref  = $self->{dbm};
    $ref->FETCH(@_);
}
sub STORE {
    my $self = shift;
    if (defined $_[0]){
        my $ref = $self->{dbm};
        $ref->STORE(@_);
    } else {
        die "Cannot STORE an undefined key in MyDBM\n";
    }
}

package main;
use Fcntl qw( O_RDWR O_CREAT );
```

```
tie %foo, "MyDBM", "sdbmfile1", O_RDWR|O_CREAT, 0640;
$foo{Fred} = 123;
print "foo-Fred = $foo{Fred}\n";

tie %bar, "MyDBM", "sdbmfile2", O_RDWR|O_CREAT, 0640;
$bar{Barney} = 456;
print "bar-Barney = $bar{Barney}\n";
```

Thinking of Code Reuse

When we think of code reuse, we often fall into the habit of thinking that new code will always reuse old code. But one strength of object-oriented languages is the ease with which old code can use new code, as long as you don't introduce spurious relationships that mess things up. The following examples will demonstrate first how one can hinder code reuse and then how one can promote code reuse.

This first example illustrates a class that uses a fully qualified method call to access the "private" method BAZ(). We'll show that it is impossible to override the BAZ() method.

```
package FOO;

sub new {
    my $type = shift;
    return bless {}, $type;
}
sub bar {
    my $self = shift;
    $self->FOO::private::BAZ;
}

package FOO::private;

sub BAZ {
    print "in BAZ\n";
}

package main;

$a = FOO->new;
$a->bar;
```

Now we try to override the BAZ() method. We would like FOO::bar() to call GOOP::BAZ(), but this cannot happen because FOO::bar() explicitly calls FOO::private::BAZ().

```
package FOO;

sub new {
    my $type = shift;
```

```
        return bless {}, $type;
    }
    sub bar {
        my $self = shift;
        $self->FOO::private::BAZ;
    }

    package FOO::private;

    sub BAZ {
        print "in BAZ\n";
    }

    package GOOP;
    @ISA = qw( FOO );
    sub new {
        my $type = shift;
        return bless {}, $type;
    }

    sub BAZ {
        print "in GOOP::BAZ\n";
    }

    package main;

    $a = GOOP->new;
    $a->bar;
```

To create reusable code we must modify class FOO, flattening class FOO::private. The next example shows a reusable class FOO which allows the method GOOP::BAZ() to be used in place of FOO::BAZ().

```
    package FOO;

    sub new {
        my $type = shift;
        return bless {}, $type;
    }
    sub bar {
        my $self = shift;
        $self->BAZ;
    }

    sub BAZ {
        print "in BAZ\n";
    }

    package GOOP;
    @ISA = qw( FOO );

    sub new {
        my $type = shift;
        return bless {}, $type;
```

```
    }
sub BAZ {
    print "in GOOP::BAZ\n";
}

package main;

$a = GOOP->new;
$a->bar;
```

The moral of the story is that generic interfaces are by nature not very private. Some languages go to great lengths to define various levels of privacy. Perl goes to great lengths not to.

Class Context and the Object

Use the object to solve package and class context problems. Everything a method needs should be available via the object or should be passed as a parameter to the method.

A class will sometimes have static or global data to be used by the methods. A derived class may want to override that data and replace it with new data. When this happens, the base class may not know how to find the new copy of the data.

This problem can be solved by using the object to define the context of the method. Let the method look in the object for a reference to the data. The alternative is to force the method to go hunting for the data ("Is it in my class, or in a derived class? Which derived class?"), and this can be inconvenient and will lead to hackery. It is better to just let the object tell the method where the data is located.

```
package Bar;

%fizzle = ( Password => 'XYZZY' );

sub new {
    my $type = shift;
    my $self = {};
    $self->{fizzle} = \%fizzle;
    return bless $self, $type;
}

sub enter {
    my $self = shift;

    # Don't try to guess if we should use %Bar::fizzle
    # or %Foo::fizzle.  The object already knows which
    # we should use, so just ask it.
    #
    my $fizzle = $self->{fizzle};
```

```
    print "The word is ", $fizzle->{Password}, "\n";
}

package Foo;
@ISA = qw( Bar );

%fizzle = ( Password => 'Rumple' );

sub new {
    my $type = shift;
    my $self = Bar->new;
    $self->{fizzle} = \%fizzle;
    return bless $self, $type;
}

package main;

$a = Bar->new;
$b = Foo->new;
$a->enter;
$b->enter;
```

Inheriting a Constructor

An inheritable constructor should use the two-argument form of **bless**, which
allows blessing directly into a specified class. Notice in this example that the
object will be a BAR not a FOO, even though the constructor is in class FOO.

```
package FOO;

sub new {
    my $type = shift;
    my $self = {};
    return bless $self, $type;
}

sub baz {
    print "in FOO::baz()\n";
}

package BAR;
@ISA = qw(FOO);

sub baz {
    print "in BAR::baz()\n";
}

package main;

$a = BAR->new;
$a->baz;
```

Delegation (the "Passes-the-Buck-to" Relationship)

Some classes, such as SDBM_File, cannot be effectively subclassed because they create foreign objects. Such a class can be extended with some sort of aggregation technique such as the "uses" relationship mentioned earlier in this chapter. Or you can use delegation.

The following example demonstrates delegation using an AUTOLOAD function to perform message-forwarding. This allows the MyDBM object to behave exactly like an SDBM_File object without having to predefine all the possible methods that might be invoked. As usual, the MyDBM class can still modify the behavior by adding custom FETCH and STORE methods, since the AUTOLOAD is only invoked on missing methods.

```perl
package MyDBM;

require SDBM_File;
require Tie::Hash;
@ISA = qw(Tie::Hash);

sub TIEHASH {
    my $type = shift;
    my $ref = SDBM_File->new(@_);
    return bless {delegate => $ref}, $type;
}

sub AUTOLOAD {
    my $self = shift;

    # The Perl interpreter places the name of the
    # message in a variable called $AUTOLOAD.

    # DESTROY messages should never be propagated.
    return if $AUTOLOAD =~ /::DESTROY$/;

    # Remove the package name.
    $AUTOLOAD =~ s/^MyDBM:://;

    # Pass the message to the delegate.
    $self->{delegate}->$AUTOLOAD(@_);
}

package main;
use Fcntl qw( O_RDWR O_CREAT );

tie %number, "MyDBM", "oddnumbers", O_RDWR|O_CREAT, 0666;
$number{beast} = 666;
```

As we say on the Net, "Hope this helps."

6

Social Engineering

Languages have different personalities. You can classify computer languages by how introverted or extroverted they are; for instance, Icon and Lisp are stay-at-home languages, while Tcl and the various shells are party animals. Self-sufficient languages prefer to compete with other languages, while social languages prefer to cooperate with other languages. As usual, Perl tries to do both.

So this chapter is about relationships. Until now we've looked inward at the competitive nature of Perl, but now we need to look outward and see the cooperative nature of Perl. If we really mean what we say about Perl being a glue language, then we can't just talk about glue; we have to talk about the various kinds of things you can glue together. A glob of glue by itself isn't very interesting.

Perl doesn't just glue together other computer languages. It also glues together command line interpreters, operating systems, processes, machines, devices, networks, databases, institutions, cultures, Web pages, GUIs, peers, servers, and clients, not to mention people like system administrators, users, and of course, hackers, both naughty and nice. In fact, Perl is rather competitive about being cooperative.

So this chapter is about Perl's relationship with everything in the world. Obviously, we can't talk about everything in the world, but we'll try.

Cooperating with Command Interpreters

It is fortunate that Perl grew up in the UNIX world—that means its invocation syntax works pretty well under the command interpreters of other operating systems too. Most command interpreters know how to deal with a list of words as arguments, and don't care if an argument starts with a minus sign. There are, of course, some sticky spots where you'll get fouled up if you move from one system to another. You can't use single quotes under MS-DOS as you do under UNIX, for instance. And on systems like VMS, some wrapper code has to jump through hoops to emulate UNIX I/O redirection. Once you get past those issues, however, Perl treats its switches and arguments much the same on any operating system.

Even when you don't have a command interpreter, *per se*, it's easy to execute a Perl script from another program, such as the *inet* daemon or a CGI server. Not only can such a server pass arguments in the ordinary way, but it can also pass in information via environment variables and (under UNIX at least) inherited file descriptors. Even more exotic argument-passing mechanisms may be encapsulated in a module that can be brought into the Perl script via a simple **use** directive.

Command Processing

Perl parses command-line switches in the standard fashion.[*] That is, it expects any switches (words beginning with a minus) to come first on the command line. After that comes the name of the script (usually), followed by any additional arguments (often filenames) to be passed into the script. Some of these additional arguments may be switches, but if so, they must be processed by the script, since Perl gives up parsing switches as soon as it sees a non-switch, or the special "--" switch that terminates switch processing.

Perl gives you some flexibility in how you supply your program. For small, quick-and-dirty jobs, you can program Perl entirely from the command line. For larger, more permanent jobs, you can supply a Perl script as a separate file. Perl looks for the script to be specified in one of three ways:

1. Specified line by line via -e switches on the command line.

2. Contained in the file specified by the first filename on the command line. (Note that systems supporting the #! shebang notation invoke interpreters this way on your behalf.)

3. Passed in implicitly via standard input. This only works if there are no file-name arguments; to pass arguments to a standard-input script you must explic-itly specify a "-" for the script name. For example, under UNIX:

    ```
    echo "print 'Hello, world'" | perl -
    ```

    With methods 2 and 3, Perl starts parsing the input file from the beginning, unless you've specified a -x switch, in which case it scans for the first line starting with #! and containing the word "perl", and starts there instead. This

---

[*] Presuming you agree that UNIX is both standard and fashionable.

is useful for running a script embedded in a larger message. (In this case you might indicate the end of the script using the __END__ token.)

Whether or not you use -x, the #! line is always examined for switches as the line is being parsed. Thus, if you're on a machine that only allows one argument with the #! line, or worse, doesn't even recognize the #! line as special, you still can get consistent switch behavior regardless of how Perl was invoked, even if -x was used to find the beginning of the script.

WARNING   Because many versions of UNIX silently chop off kernel interpretation of the #! line after 32 characters, some switches may be passed in on the command line, and some may not; you could even get a "-" without its letter, if you're not careful. You probably want to make sure that all your switches fall either before or after that 32-character boundary. Most switches don't actually care if they're processed redundantly, but getting a "-" instead of a complete switch could cause Perl to try to execute standard input instead of your script. And a partial -I switch could also cause odd results. Of course, if you're not on a UNIX system, you're guaranteed not to have this problem.

Parsing of the switches on the #! line starts wherever "perl" is mentioned in the line. The sequences "-*" and "- " are specifically ignored for the benefit of *emacs* users, so that, if you're so inclined, you can say:

```
#!/bin/sh -- # -*- perl -*- -p
eval 'exec perl -S $0 ${1+"$@"}'
    if 0;
```

and Perl will see only the -p switch. The fancy "-*- perl -*-" gizmo tells *emacs* to start up in Perl mode; you don't need it if you don't use *emacs*. The -S mess is explained below.

If the #! line does *not* contain the word "perl", the program named after the #! is executed instead of the Perl interpreter. For example, suppose you have an ordinary Bourne shell script out there that says:

```
#!/bin/sh
echo "I am a shell script"
```

If you feed that file to Perl, then Perl will run */bin/sh* for you. This is slightly bizarre, but it helps people on machines that don't recognize #!, because—by setting their SHELL environmental variable—they can tell a program (such as a mailer) that their shell is */usr/bin/perl*, and Perl will then dispatch the program to the correct interpreter for them, even though their kernel is too stupid to do so. Classify it as a strange form of cooperation.

But back to Perl scripts that are really Perl scripts. After locating your script, Perl compiles the entire script to an internal form. If any compilation errors arise, execution of the script is not attempted (unlike the typical shell script, which might run partway through before finding a syntax error). If the script is syntactically correct, it is executed. If the script runs off the end without hitting an **exit** or **die** operator, an implicit exit(0) is provided to indicate successful completion.

Switches

A single-character switch with no argument may be combined (bundled) with the following switch, if any.

```
#!/usr/bin/perl -spi.bak     # same as -s -p -i.bak
```

Switches are also known as options, or flags. Perl recognizes these switches:

- -   Terminates switch processing, even if the next argument starts with a minus. It has no other effect.

-0[*octnum*]

Specifies the record separator ($/) as an octal number. If *octnum* is not present, the null character is the separator. Other switches may precede or follow the octal number. For example, if you have a version of *find*(1) that can print filenames terminated by the null character, you can say this:

```
find . -name '*.bak' -print0 | perl -n0e unlink
```

The special value 00 will cause Perl to slurp files in paragraph mode, equivalent to setting the $/ variable to "". The value 0777 will cause Perl to slurp files whole since there is no legal ASCII character with that value. This is equivalent to undefining the $/ variable.

-a

Turns on autosplit mode when used with a **-n** or **-p**. An implicit **split** command to the @F array is done as the first thing inside the implicit **while** loop produced by the **-n** or **-p**. So:

```
perl -ane 'print pop(@F), "\n";'
```

is equivalent to:

```
while (<>) {
    @F = split(' ');
    print pop(@F), "\n";
}
```

A different field delimiter may be specified using **-F**.

-c

Causes Perl to check the syntax of the script and then exit without executing it. Actually, it will execute any **BEGIN** blocks and **use** directives, since these are considered to occur before the execution of your program. It also executes any **END** blocks, in case they need to clean up something that happened in a corresponding **BEGIN** block. The switch is more or less equivalent to having an exit(0) as the first statement in your program.

-d

Runs the script under the Perl debugger. See "The Perl Debugger" in Chapter 8, *Other Oddments.*

-d:*foo*

Runs the script under the control of a debugging or tracing module installed in the Perl library as Devel::*foo.* For example, -d:DProf executes the script using the Devel::DProf profiler. See also the debugging section in Chapter 8.

-D*number*

-D*list*

Sets debugging flags. (This only works if debugging is compiled into your version of Perl via the -DDEBUGGING C compiler switch.) You may specify either a number that is the sum of the bits you want, or a list of letters. To watch how it executes your script, for instance, use –D14 or –Dslt. Another nice value is –D1024 or –Dx, which lists your compiled syntax tree. And –D512 or –Dr displays compiled regular expressions. The numeric value is available internally as the special variable $^D. Here are the assigned bit values:

Bit	Letter	Meaning
1	p	Tokenizing and parsing
2	s	Stack snapshots
4	l	Label stack processing
8	t	Trace execution
16	o	Object method Lookup
32	c	String/numeric conversions
64	P	Print preprocessor command for –P
128	m	Memory allocation
256	f	Format processing
512	r	Regular expression processing
1,024	x	Syntax tree dump
2,048	u	Tainting checks
4,096	L	Memory leaks (not supported any more)
8,192	H	Hash dump - - usurps values()
16,384	X	Scratchpad allocation
32,768	D	Cleaning up

-e *commandline*

> May be used to enter one or more lines of script. If **-e** is used, Perl will not look for a script filename in the argument list. The **-e** argument is treated as if it ends with a newline, so multiple **-e** commands may be given to build up a multi-line script. (Make sure to use semicolons where you would in a normal program.) Just because **-e** supplies a newline on each argument doesn't mean you have to use multiple **-e** switches—if your shell supports multi-line quoting, you may pass a multi-line script as one **-e** argument, just as *awk*(1) scripts are typically passed.

-F*pattern*

> Specifies the pattern to split on if **-a** is also in effect. The pattern may be surrounded by //, "" or ' ', otherwise it will be put in single quotes. (Remember that to pass quotes through a shell, you have to quote the quotes.)

-h

> Prints a summary of Perl's command-line options.

-i[*extension*]

> Specifies that files processed by the <> construct are to be edited in-place. It does this by renaming the input file, opening the output file by the original name, and selecting that output file as the default for **print** statements. The extension, if supplied, is added to the name of the old file to make a backup copy. If no extension is supplied, no backup is made. From the shell, saying:

```
$ perl -p -i.bak -e "s/foo/bar/; ... "
```

> is the same as using the script:

```
#!/usr/bin/perl -pi.bak
s/foo/bar/;
```

> which is equivalent to:

```
#!/usr/bin/perl
while (<>) {
    if ($ARGV ne $oldargv) {
        rename($ARGV, $ARGV . '.bak');
        open(ARGVOUT, ">$ARGV");
        select(ARGVOUT);
        $oldargv = $ARGV;
    }
    s/foo/bar/;
}
continue {
    print;          # this prints to original filename
}
select(STDOUT);
```

> except that the **-i** form doesn't need to compare $ARGV to $oldargv to know when the filename has changed. It does, however, use ARGVOUT for the

selected filehandle. Note that STDOUT is restored as the default output filehandle after the loop. You can use **eof** without parentheses to locate the end of each input file, in case you want to append to each file, or reset line numbering (see the examples of **eof** in Chapter 3, *Functions*).

-Idirectory

Directories specified by **-I** are prepended to **@INC**, which holds the search path for modules. **-I** also tells the C preprocessor where to search for include files. The C preprocessor is invoked with **-P**; by default it searches */usr/include* and */usr/lib/perl*. Unless you're going to be using the C preprocessor (and almost no one does any more), you're better off using the **use lib** directive within your script.

-l[octnum]

Enables automatic line-end processing. It has two effects: first, it automatically **chomp**s the line terminator when used with **-n** or **-p**, and second, it sets **$** to the value of *octnum* so any print statements will have a line terminator of ASCII value *octnum* added back on. If *octnum* is omitted, sets **$** to the current value of **$/**, typically newline. So, to trim lines to 80 columns, say this:

```
perl -lpe 'substr($_, 80) = ""'
```

Note that the assignment **$** = **$/** is done when the switch is processed, so the input record separator can be different from the output record separator if the **-l** switch is followed by a **-0** switch:

```
gnufind / -print0 | perl -ln0e 'print "found $_" if -p'
```

This sets **$** to newline and later sets **$/** to the null character. (Note that 0 would have been interpreted as part of the **-l** switch had it followed the **-l** directly. That's why we bundled the **-n** switch between them.)

-m[-]module

-M[-]module

-M[-]' module ...'

-[mM][-]module=arg[,arg] ...

-mmodule

Executes **use** *module*() before executing your script.

-Mmodule

Executes **use** *module* before executing your script. The command is formed by mere interpolation, so you can use quotes to add extra code after the module name, for example, **-M'module qw(foo bar)'**. If the first character after the **-M** or **-m** is a minus (-), then the **use** is replaced with **no**.

A little built-in syntactic sugar means you can also say –mmodule=foo,bar or
–Mmodule=foo,bar as a shortcut for –M'module qw(foo bar)'. This avoids the
need to use quotes when importing symbols. The actual code generated by
–Mmodule=foo,bar is:

```
use module split(/,/, q{foo, bar})
```

Note that the = form removes the distinction between –m and –M.

–n

Causes Perl to assume the following loop around your script, which makes it
iterate over filename arguments rather as *sed –n* or *awk* do:

```
LINE:
while (<>) {
    ...                      # your script goes here
}
```

Note that the lines are not printed by default. See **-p** to have lines printed.
Here is an efficient way to delete all files older than a week, assuming you're
on UNIX:

```
find . -mtime +7 -print | perl -nle unlink
```

This is faster than using the *–exec* switch of *find*(1) because you don't have to
start a process on every filename found. By an amazing coincidence, BEGIN
and END blocks may be used to capture control before or after the implicit
loop, just as in *awk*.

–p

Causes Perl to assume the following loop around your script, which makes it
iterate over filename arguments rather as *sed* does:

```
LINE:
while (<>) {
    ...                      # your script goes here
} continue {
    print;
}
```

Note that the lines are printed automatically. To suppress printing use the **-n**
switch. A **-p** overrides a **-n** switch. By yet another amazing coincidence, BEGIN
and END blocks may be used to capture control before or after the implicit
loop, just as in *awk*.

–P

Causes your script to be run through the C preprocessor before compilation
by Perl. (Since both comments and *cpp*(1) directives begin with the # character, you should avoid starting comments with any words recognized by the C
preprocessor such as "if", "else" or "define".)

-s

Enables some rudimentary switch parsing for switches on the command line after the script name but before any filename arguments or "- -" switch terminator. Any switch found there is removed from **@ARGV**, and a variable of the same name as the switch is set in the Perl script. No switch bundling is allowed, since multi-character switches are allowed. The following script prints "true" if and only if the script is invoked with a -xyz switch.

```
#!/usr/bin/perl -s
if ($xyz) { print "true\n"; }
```

If the switch in question is followed by an equals sign, the variable is set to whatever follows the equals sign in that argument. The following script prints "true" if and only if the script is invoked with a -xyz=abc switch.

```
#!/usr/bin/perl -s
if ($xyz eq 'abc') { print "true\n"; }
```

-S

Makes Perl use the PATH environment variable to search for the script (unless the name of the script starts with a slash). Typically this is used to emulate #! startup on machines that don't support #!, in the following manner:

```
#!/usr/bin/perl
eval "exec /usr/bin/perl -S $0 $*"
        if $running_under_some_shell;
```

The system ignores the first line and feeds the script to */bin/sh*, which proceeds to try to execute the Perl script as a shell script. The shell executes the second line as a normal shell command, and thus starts up the Perl interpreter. On some systems $0 doesn't always contain the full pathname, so -S tells Perl to search for the script if necessary. After Perl locates the script, it parses the lines and ignores them because the variable $running_under_some_shell is never true. A better construct than $* would be ${1+"$@"}, which handles embedded spaces and such in the filenames, but doesn't work if the script is being interpreted by *csh*. In order to start up *sh* rather than *csh*, some systems have to replace the #! line with a line containing just a colon, which Perl will politely ignore. Other systems can't control that, and need a totally devious construct that will work under any of *csh*, *sh*, or *perl*, such as the following:

```
eval '(exit $?0)' && eval 'exec /usr/bin/perl -S $0 ${1+"$@"}'
    & eval 'exec /usr/bin/perl -S $0 $argv:q'
            if 0;
```

Yes, it's ugly, but so are the systems that work[*] this way.

---

[*] We use the term advisedly.

-T

> Forces "taint" checks to be turned on so you can test them. Ordinarily these checks are done only when running setuid or setgid. It's a good idea to turn them on explicitly for programs run on another's behalf, such as CGI programs. See "Cooperating with Strangers" later in this chapter.

-u

> Causes Perl to dump core after compiling your script. You can then take this core dump and turn it into an executable file by using the *undump* program (not supplied). This speeds startup at the expense of some disk space (which you can minimize by stripping the executable). If you want to execute a portion of your script before dumping, use Perl's **dump** operator instead. Note: availability of *undump* is platform specific; it may not be available for a specific port of Perl.

-U

> Allows Perl to do unsafe operations. Currently the only "unsafe" operations are the unlinking of directories while running as superuser, and running setuid programs with fatal taint checks turned into warnings.

-v

> Prints the version and patchlevel of your Perl executable.

-V

> Prints a summary of the major Perl configuration values and the current value of @INC.

-V:*name*

> Prints to STDOUT the value of the named configuration variable.

-w

> Prints warnings about identifiers that are mentioned only once, and scalar variables that are used before being set. Also warns about redefined subroutines, and references to undefined filehandles or filehandles opened read-only that you are attempting to write on. Also warns you if you use a non-number as though it were a number, or if you use an array as though it were a scalar, or if your subroutines recurse more than 100 deep, and innumerable other things. See every entry labeled (W) in Chapter 9, *Diagnostic Messages*.

-x*directory*

> Tells Perl to extract a script that is embedded in a message. Leading garbage will be discarded until the first line that starts with #! and contains the string "perl". Any meaningful switches on that line after the word "perl" will be applied. If a directory name is specified, Perl will switch to that directory before running the script. The **-x** switch only controls the disposal of leading

garbage. The script must be terminated with __END__ or __DATA__ if there is trailing garbage to be ignored. (The script can process any or all of the trailing garbage via the DATA filehandle if desired.)

Cooperating with Other Processes

Processes have almost as many ways of communicating as people do. But the difficulties of interprocess communication (IPC) should not be underestimated. It doesn't do you any good to listen for verbal cues when your friend is using only body language. Likewise, two processes can communicate only when they agree on the method of communication, and on the conventions built on top of that method. These layered conventions often gain the weight of "methodhood" themselves, so you'll sometimes hear people talking about *stacks* of communication methods. We can't hope to cover all the methods used in the world today, but we'll discuss some of the methods most commonly used in Perl.

The IPC facilities of Perl range from the very simple to the very complex. Which facility you want to use depends on the complexity of the information to be communicated. The simplest kind of information is, in a sense, no information at all, but just the awareness that a particular event has happened at a particular point in time. In Perl, these events are communicated via a signal mechanism modeled on the UNIX signal system.

At the other extreme, the socket facilities of Perl allow you to communicate with any other process on the Internet using any mutually supported protocol you like. Naturally, this freedom comes at a price: you have to go through a number of steps to set up the connections and make sure you're talking the same language as the process on the other end, which may in turn require you to adhere to any number of other strange customs, depending on the cultural conventions at work. To be protocoligorically correct, you might even be required to speak a language like HTML, or Java, or Perl. Horrors.

Sandwiched in between are some facilities intended primarily for communicating between processes on the same machine. These include pipes, FIFOs, and the various System V IPC calls.

Signals

Perl uses a simple signal handling model: the %SIG hash contains references (either symbolic or hard) to user-defined signal handlers. When an event transpires, the handler corresponding to that event is called with one argument containing the name of the signal that triggered it. In order to send a signal to another process, you use the **kill** function. If that process has installed a signal handler, it can execute code when you send the signal, but there's no way to get a return value (other than knowing that the signal was successfully sent).

We've classified this facility as a form of IPC, but in fact, signals can come from various sources, not just other processes. A signal might come from another process, or from your own process, or it might be generated when the user at the keyboard types a particular sequence like CTRL-C or CTRL-Z, or it might be manufactured by the kernel when special events transpire, such as when a child process is exiting, or when your process is running out of stack space, or hitting a file size limit.[*] But your own process can't easily distinguish among these cases. A signal is like a package that arrives mysteriously on your doorstep with no return address. You'd best open it carefully.

For example, to unpack an interrupt signal, set up a handler like this:

```
sub catch_zap {
    my $signame = shift;
    $shucks++;
    die "Somebody sent me a SIG$signame!";
}
$SIG{INT} = 'catch_zap';   # could fail outside of package main
$SIG{INT} = \&catch_zap;   # best strategy
```

Notice how all we do in the signal handler is set a global variable and then raise an exception with **die**. We try to avoid anything more complicated than that, because on most systems the C library is not re-entrant. Signals are delivered asynchronously, so calling any **print** functions (or even anything that needs to *malloc*(3) more memory) could in theory trigger a memory fault and subsequent core dump if you were already in a related C library routine when the signal was delivered. (Even the **die** routine is a bit unsafe unless the process is executing within an **eval**, which suppresses the I/O from **die**, which keeps it from calling the C library. Probably.)

The operating system thinks of signals as numbers rather than names. To find the names of the signals, you can use the **kill -l** command on your system (if you're running UNIX). Or you can retrieve them from Perl's Config module; the following snippet sets up two arrays: a **@signame** array indexed by number to get the signal name, and a **%signo** hash indexed by name to get the signal number:

```
use Config;
defined $Config{sig_name} or die "No sigs?";
$i = 0;     # Config prepends fake 0 signal called "ZERO".
foreach $name (split(' ', $Config{sig_name})) {
```

---

[*] Nevertheless, these are all examples of cooperation with *something*, even if it's not another process. Certainly, you tend to get more accomplished when you cooperate with your operating system.

```
        $signo{$name} = $i;
        $signame[$i] = $name;
        $i++;
    }
```

So to check whether signal 17 and SIGALRM are the same, you could do this:

```
    print "signal #17 = $signame[17]\n";
    if ($signo{ALRM}) {
        print "SIGALRM is $signo{ALRM}\n";
    }
```

You may also choose to assign either of the strings 'IGNORE' or 'DEFAULT' as the handler, in which case Perl will try to discard the signal or do the default thing. Some signals can be neither trapped nor ignored, such as the KILL and STOP signals. You can temporarily ignore other signals by using a **local** signal handler assignment, which goes out of effect once your block is exited. (Remember, though, that **local** values are inherited by functions called from within that block.)

```
    sub precious {
        local $SIG{INT} = 'IGNORE';
        &more_functions;
    }
    sub more_functions {
        # interrupts still ignored, for now...
    }
```

Sending a signal to a negative process ID means that you send the signal to the entire UNIX process-group. This code sends a hang-up signal to all processes in the current process group except for the current process itself:

```
    {
        local $SIG{HUP} = 'IGNORE';
        kill HUP => -$$;    # snazzy form of: kill('HUP', -$$)
    }
```

Another interesting signal to send is signal number 0. This doesn't actually affect the other process, but instead checks whether it's alive or has changed its UID. That is, it checks whether it's legal to send a signal, without actually sending one.

```
    unless (kill 0 => $kid_pid) {
        warn "something wicked happened to $kid_pid";
    }
```

Another cute trick is to employ anonymous functions for simple signal handlers:

```
    $SIG{INT} = sub { die "\nOutta here!\n" };
```

Because it's a subroutine without a name, this approach can be problematic for complicated handlers that need to reinstall themselves. That's because Perl's signal mechanism was historically based on the *signal*(3) function from the C library. On some systems, this function was broken; that is, it behaved in the unreliable

System V way rather than the reliable BSD (and POSIX) fashion. This meant that you had to reinstall the signal handler each time it got called.[*] You also had to manually restart interrupted system calls. Careful programmers tend to write self-referential handlers that reinstall themselves:

```
sub REAPER {
    $waitedpid = wait;
    $SIG{CHLD} = \&REAPER;   # loathe sysV
}
$SIG{CHLD} = \&REAPER;
# now do something that forks...
```

or, somewhat more elaborately:[†]

```
use POSIX "sys_wait_h";
sub REAPER {
    $SIG{CHLD} = \&REAPER;   # loathe sysV, dream of real POSIX
    my $child;
    while ($child = waitpid(-1, WNOHANG)) {
        $Kid_Status{$child} = $?;
    }
}
$SIG{CHLD} = \&REAPER;
# do something that forks...
```

And if you're writing code to behave the same way everywhere, even on rather old systems, it all gets more complex yet. Loops with blocking system calls (like <FILE> or **accept**) need additional logic to handle system calls that return failure for silly reasons, such as when your SIGCHLD handler triggers and you reap a moribund child process.

Fortunately, you shouldn't have to do that much any more. That's because whenever possible, Perl now uses the reliable *sigaction*(2) function from POSIX. If you know you're running on a system that supports *sigaction*(2), you won't have to reinstall your handlers, and a lot of other things will work out better, too. For example, "slow" system calls (ones that can block, like **read**, <STDIN>, **wait**, and **accept**) will restart automatically now if they get interrupted by a signal. This is generally construed to be a feature.

You check whether you have the more rigorous POSIX-style signal behavior by accessing the Config module, described in Chapter 7, *The Standard Perl Library*.

```
use Config;
print "Hurray!\n" if $Config{d_sigaction};
```

---

[*] If you were lucky. The old signal behavior had a race condition whereby you couldn't guarantee that you could reset your handler in time before the next signal came in, which is why it was changed.

[†] Although it seems unlikely that you would have POSIX WNOHANG **waitpid** behavior while lacking proper POSIX signals.

This will tell you whether you have reliable system calls that don't need to be reinstalled, but it won't tell you whether they're restartable. Perl doesn't provide that information in its Config module, but you could check out your system's C *signal.h* include file directly:

```
egrep 'S[AV]_(RESTART|INTERRUPT)' /usr/include/*/signal.h
```

On some older SysV systems, a simple but nonportable hack for avoiding zombies was to set $SIG{CHLD} to 'IGNORE'. This approach does not work on systems with *sigaction*(2). Instead, the best way to avoid zombies on POSIX systems is to use the REAPER() function above.

You can also use signals to impose time limits on long-running operations. If you're on a UNIX system (or any other system that supports the ALRM signal), you can ask the kernel to send your process an ALRM at some point in the future:

```
eval {
    local $SIG{ALRM} = sub { die "alarm clock restart" };
    alarm 10;        # schedule alarm in 10 seconds
    flock(FH, 2);    # a "write" lock that may block
    alarm 0;         # cancel the alarm
};
if ($@ and $@ !~ /alarm clock restart/) { die }
```

eval and **die** provide a convenient mechanism for aborting the **flock** if it hangs.

For more complex signal handling, see the POSIX module in Chapter 7. This module provides an object-oriented approach to signals that gives you complete access to low-level system behavior.

Pipes

A *pipe* is a unidirectional I/O channel that can transfer a stream of bytes from one process to another. They come in both named and nameless varieties. You may be more familiar with nameless pipes, so we'll talk about those first.

Anonymous pipes

Perl's **open** function opens a pipe instead of a file when you append or prepend a pipe symbol to the second argument to **open**. This turns the rest of the argument into a command, which will be interpreted as a process (or set of processes) to pipe a stream of data either into or out of. Here's how to start up a child process that you intend to write to:

```
open SPOOLER, "| cat -v | lpr -h 2>/dev/null"
                or die "can't fork: $!";
local $SIG{PIPE} = sub { die "spooler pipe broke" };
print SPOOLER "stuff\n";
close SPOOLER or die "bad spool: $! $?";
```

This example is actually starting up two processes, the first of which (running *cat*) we print to directly. The second process (running *lpr*) then receives the output of the first process. In shell programming this is often called a *pipeline*. A pipeline can have as many processes in a row as you like.

And here's how to start up a child process that you intend to read from:

```
open STATUS, "netstat -an 2>&1 |"
                or die "can't fork: $!";
while (<STATUS>) {
    next if /^(tcp|udp)/;
    print;
}
close STATUS or die "bad netstat: $! $?";
```

You can open a pipeline for input just as you can for output, but we don't show it in this example.

You might have noticed that you can use backticks to accomplish the same effect as opening a pipe for reading:

```
print grep { !/^(tcp|udp)/ } `netstat -an 2>&1`;
die "bad netstat" if $?;
```

While this is true, it's often more efficient to process the file one line or record at a time, because then Perl doesn't have to read the whole thing into memory at once. It also gives you finer control of the whole operation, letting you kill off the child process early if you like.

Be careful to check the return values of both **open** and **close**. (If you're writing to a pipe, you should also be prepared to handle the PIPE signal, which is sent to you if the process on the other end dies before you're done sending to it.) The reason you need to check both the **open** and the **close** has to do with an idiosyncrasy of UNIX in how piped commands are started up. When you do the **open**, your process forks a child process that is in charge of executing the command you gave it. The *fork*(2) system call, if successful, returns immediately within the parent process, and the parent script leaves the **open** function successfully, even though the child process may not have even run yet. By the time the child process actually tries to run the command, it's already a separately scheduled process. So if it fails to execute the command, it has no easy way to communicate the fact back to the **open** statement, which may have already exited successfully in the parent. The way the disaster is finally communicated back to the parent is the same way that any other disaster in the child process is communicated back: namely, the exit status of the child process is harvested by the parent process when it eventually does a *wait*(2) system call. But this happens in the **close** function, not the **open** function. And that's why you have to check the return value of your **close** function. Whew.

Talking to yourself

Another approach to IPC is to make your program talk to itself, in a manner of speaking. Actually, your process talks to a forked copy of itself. It works much like the piped open we talked about in the last section, except that the child process continues executing your script instead of trying to execute some other command.

To represent this to the **open** function, you use a pseudo-command consisting of a minus. So the second argument to **open** looks like either "-|" or "|-", depending on whether you want to pipe from yourself or to yourself. The **open** function returns the child's process ID in the parent process, but 0 in the child process. Another asymmetry is that the filehandle is used only in the parent process. The child's end of the pipe is hooked to either STDIN or STDOUT as appropriate. That is, if you open a pipe *to* minus, you can write to the filehandle you opened and your kid will find it in his STDIN. If you open a pipe *from* minus, you can read from the filehandle you opened whatever your kid writes to her STDOUT.

This is useful for safely opening a file when running under an assumed UID or GID, for example:

```
use English;
my $sleep_count = 0;

do {
    $pid = open(KID_TO_WRITE, "|-");
    unless (defined $pid) {
        warn "cannot fork: $!";
        die "bailing out" if $sleep_count++ > 6;
        sleep 10;
    }
} until defined $pid;

if ($pid) {  # parent
    print KID_TO_WRITE @some_data;
    close(KID_TO_WRITE) or warn "kid exited $?";
}
else {       # child
    ($EUID, $EGID) = ($UID, $GID); # suid progs only
    open (FILE, "> /safe/file")
                    or die "can't open /safe/file: $!";
    while (<STDIN>) {
        print FILE; # child's STDIN is parent's KID
    }
    exit;  # don't forget this
}
```

Another common use for this construct is to bypass the shell when you want to open a pipe from a command. You might want to do this for security reasons, because you don't want the shell interpreting any metacharacters in the filenames you're trying to pass to the command. We give an example of this later in the chapter—see "Cleaning Up Your Path".

Note that these operations are full UNIX forks, which means they may not be correctly implemented on alien systems. Additionally, these are not true multithreading. If you'd like to learn more about threading, see CPAN.

Bidirectional communication

While pipes work reasonably well for unidirectional communication, what about bidirectional communication? The obvious thing you'd like to do doesn't actually work:

```
open(PROG_FOR_READING_AND_WRITING, "| some program |")   # WRONG!
```

and if you forget to use the **-w** switch, then you'll miss out entirely on the diagnostic message:

```
Can't do bidirectional pipe at myprog line 3.
```

The **open** function won't allow this because it's rather error prone unless you know what you're doing, and can easily result in deadlock, which we'll explain later. But if you really want to do it, you can use the standard IPC::Open2 library module to attach two pipes to a subprocess's STDIN and STDOUT. There's also an IPC::Open3 module for tridirectional I/O (allowing you to catch your child's STDERR), but this requires an awkward **select** loop and doesn't allow you to use normal Perl input operations.

If you look at the source, you'll see that Open2 uses low-level primitives like **pipe** and **exec** to create all the connections. While it might have been slightly more efficient to use **socketpair**, it would have been even less portable. As it is, the Open2 and Open3 modules are unlikely to work anywhere except on a UNIX system, or some other system purporting to be POSIX compliant.

Here's an example using IPC::Open2::open2():

```
use FileHandle;
use IPC::Open2;
$pid = open2( \*Reader, \*Writer, "cat -u -n" );
Writer->autoflush();     # This is default, actually.
print Writer "stuff\n";
$got = <Reader>;
```

The problem with this in general is that UNIX buffering is really going to ruin your day. Even though your Writer filehandle is autoflushed, and the process on the other end will get your data in a timely manner, you can't usually do anything to force it to actually give it back to you in a similarly quick fashion. In this particular case we can, since (on some systems) the *cat* program has a **-u** option to make it do unbuffered output. But very few UNIX commands are designed to operate well over pipes, so this seldom works unless you yourself wrote the program on the other end of the double-ended pipe.

A partial solution to this is to use the *Comm.pl* library (not a standard module—see CPAN). It uses pseudo-ttys to make your program behave more reasonably, at least on those machines that force standard output to do line-buffering:

```perl
require 'Comm.pl';
$ph = open_proc('cat -n');
for (1..10) {
    print $ph "a line\n";
    print "got back ", scalar <$ph>;
}
```

This way you don't have to have control over the source code of the program you're using.

Named pipes

A named pipe (often called a FIFO) is an old UNIX mechanism for setting up pipes between unrelated processes. The names in question exist in the filesystem, which is just a funny way to say that you can put a special file in the filesystem that has another process behind it instead of a disk.

To create a named pipe, use the UNIX command *mknod*(1) or, on some systems, *mkfifo*(1). These commands may not be in your normal execution path.

```perl
# system() return value is backwards, so "and" not "or"
#
$ENV{PATH} .= ":/etc:/usr/etc";
if (      system('mknod', $path, 'p')
       and system('mkfifo', $path) )
{
    die "mk{nod,fifo} $path failed";
}
```

A FIFO is convenient when you want to connect a process to an unrelated one. When you open a FIFO, the program will block until there's something on the other end.

For example, let's say you'd like to have your *.signature* file be a named pipe that has a Perl program on the other end. Now every time any program (like a mailer, newsreader, finger program, and so on) tries to read from that file, the reading program will block and your program will supply the new signature. We'll use the pipe-checking file test, **-p**, to find out whether anyone (or anything) has accidentally removed our FIFO.

```
chdir; # go home
$FIFO = '.signature';
$ENV{PATH} .= ":/etc:/usr/games";

while (1) {
    unless (-p $FIFO) {
        unlink $FIFO;
        system('mknod', $FIFO, 'p')
            && die "can't mknod $FIFO: $!";
    }

    # next line blocks until there's a reader
    open (FIFO, "> $FIFO") or die "can't write $FIFO: $!";
    print FIFO "John Smith (smith\@host.org)\n", `fortune -s`;
    close FIFO;
    sleep 1;    # to avoid dup sigs
}
```

If that last comment seems opaque to you, consider how often the *fortune* program changes its current fortune.

Note that a FIFO in an NFS partition won't transfer data across your network.

System V IPC

Although System V IPC is pretty ancient, it still has some valid uses. But you can't use System V shared memory (or the more modern *mmap*(2) system call, for that matter) to share a variable among several processes. That's because Perl would reallocate your string when you weren't wanting it to. Instead, Perl uses a read/write notion.

Here's a small example showing shared memory usage:

```
$IPC_PRIVATE = 0;
$IPC_RMID = 0;
$size = 2000;
$key = shmget($IPC_PRIVATE, $size , 0777 );
die unless defined $key;

$message = "Message #1";
shmwrite($key, $message, 0, 60 ) or die "shmwrite: $!";
shmread($key,$buff,0,60) or die "shmread: $!";

print $buff,"\n";

print "deleting $key\n";
shmctl($key ,$IPC_RMID, 0) or die "shmctl: $!";
```

Here's an example of a semaphore:

```
$IPC_KEY = 1234;
$IPC_RMID = 0;
$IPC_CREATE = 0001000;
```

```
$key = semget($IPC_KEY, $nsems, 0666 | $IPC_CREATE );
die if !defined($key);
print "$key\n";
```

Put this code in a separate file so that more than one process can **require** and run it. Call the file *take*:

```
# create a semaphore

$IPC_KEY = 1234;
$key = semget($IPC_KEY, 0, 0 );
die if !defined($key);

$semnum = 0;
$semflag = 0;

# 'take' semaphore
# wait for semaphore to be zero
$semop = 0;
$opstring1 = pack("sss", $semnum, $semop, $semflag);

# Increment the semaphore count
$semop = 1;
$opstring2 = pack("sss", $semnum, $semop,  $semflag);
$opstring = $opstring1 . $opstring2;

semop($key,$opstring) or die "semop: $!";
```

Put this code in a separate file to be run in more than one process. Call this file *give*:

```
# 'give' the semaphore
# run this in the original process and you will see
# that the second process continues

$IPC_KEY = 1234;
$key = semget($IPC_KEY, 0, 0);
die if !defined($key);

$semnum = 0;
$semflag = 0;

# Decrement the semaphore count
$semop = -1;
$opstring = pack("sss", $semnum, $semop, $semflag);

semop($key,$opstring) or die "semop: $!";
```

The code above is rather low-level and clunky. A better approach would be to use the IPC::SysV module in CPAN.

Sockets

While sockets were invented under UNIX, nowadays you can find them on many other operating systems (though sometimes as an unbundled product). If you don't have sockets on your machine, you're going to have difficulty cooperating with processes on the Internet. With sockets, you can do both virtual circuits (that is, TCP streams) and datagrams (that is, UDP packets). You may be able to do even more, depending on your system.

The Perl function calls for dealing with sockets have the same names as the corresponding system calls in C, but their arguments tend to differ for two reasons: first, Perl filehandles work differently from C file descriptors, and second, Perl already knows the length of its strings, so you don't need to pass that information. See Chapter 3 for details on each call.

Most of these routines quietly but politely return the undefined value when they fail, instead of causing your program to die right then and there due to an uncaught exception. (Actually, some of the new Socket module conversion functions call croak() on bad arguments.) It is therefore essential that you check the return values of these functions. Always begin your socket programs this way for optimal success (and don't forget to add -T taint checking switch to the shebang line for servers):

```
#!/usr/bin/perl -w
require 5.002;
use strict;
use sigtrap;
use Socket;
```

All the socket routines create system-specific portability problems. As noted elsewhere, Perl is at the mercy of your C libraries for much of its system behavior. It's probably safest to assume broken System V semantics for signals and to stick with simple TCP and UDP socket operations; for example, don't try to pass open file descriptors over a local UDP datagram socket if you want your code to stand a chance of being portable. (Yes, you can really do that on some machines—see BSD in the Glossary.)

One of the major problems with ancient socket code in Perl was that it tended to use hard-coded values for some of the constants, which severely hurt portability. If you ever see code that does anything like explicitly setting $AF_INET = 2, you know you're in for big trouble. An immeasurably superior approach is to use the Socket module, which more reliably grants access to the various constants and functions you'll need.

Below we will present several sample clients and servers without a great deal of explanation, since it would mostly duplicate the descriptions we've already provided in Chapter 3. Besides those descriptions, you should also check out CPAN. Section 5 of the CPAN *modules* file is devoted to "Networking, Device Control (modems), and Interprocess Communication", and refers you to numerous unbundled modules having to do with networking, Chat and Expect operations, CGI programming, DCE, FTP, IPC, NNTP, Proxy, Ptty, RPC, SNMP, SMTP, Telnet, Threads, and ToolTalk—just to name a few.

Internet TCP clients and servers

Use Internet-domain sockets when you want to do client-server communication between different machines.

Here's a sample TCP client using Internet-domain sockets:

```perl
#!/usr/bin/perl -w
require 5.002;
use strict;
use Socket;
my ($remote, $port, $iaddr, $paddr, $proto, $line);

$remote  = shift || 'localhost';
$port    = shift || 2345;  # random port
if ($port =~ /\D/) { $port = getservbyname($port, 'tcp') }
die "No port" unless $port;
$iaddr   = inet_aton($remote)            or die "no host: $remote";
$paddr   = sockaddr_in($port, $iaddr);

$proto   = getprotobyname('tcp');
socket(SOCK, PF_INET, SOCK_STREAM, $proto) or die "socket: $!";
connect(SOCK, $paddr)                    or die "connect: $!";
while ($line = <SOCK>) {
    print $line;
}

close (SOCK)                             or die "close: $!";
exit;
```

And here's a corresponding server to go along with it. The client didn't need to bind an address, but the server does. However, we'll specify the address as INADDR_ANY so that the kernel can choose the appropriate interface on multihomed hosts. If you want to sit on a particular interface (like the external side of a gateway or firewall machine), you should fill this in with your real address instead.

```perl
#!/usr/bin/perl -Tw
require 5.002;
use strict;
BEGIN { $ENV{PATH} = '/usr/ucb:/bin' }
use Socket;
use Carp;
```

```
sub logmsg { print "$0 $$: @_ at ", scalar localtime, "\n" }

my $port = shift || 2345;
my $proto = getprotobyname('tcp');
socket(Server, PF_INET, SOCK_STREAM, $proto) or die "socket: $!";
setsockopt(Server, SOL_SOCKET, SO_REUSEADDR, pack("l", 1))
                                            or die "setsockopt: $!";
bind(Server, sockaddr_in($port, INADDR_ANY)) or die "bind: $!";
listen(Server,SOMAXCONN)                     or die "listen: $!";

logmsg "server started on port $port";

my $paddr;

$SIG{CHLD} = \&REAPER;

for ( ; $paddr = accept(Client,Server); close Client) {
    my($port,$iaddr) = sockaddr_in($paddr);
    my $name = gethostbyaddr($iaddr,AF_INET);

    logmsg "connection from $name [",
            inet_ntoa($iaddr), "] at port $port";

    print CLIENT "Hello there, $name, it's now ",
                scalar localtime, "\n";
}
```

And here's a multi-threaded version. It's multi-threaded in the sense that, like most typical servers, it spawns (forks) a slave server to handle the client request so that the master server can quickly go back to service the next client.

```
#!/usr/bin/perl -Tw
require 5.002;
use strict;
BEGIN { $ENV{PATH} = '/usr/ucb:/bin' }
use Socket;
use Carp;
use FileHandle;

sub spawn;  # forward declaration
sub logmsg { print "$0 $$: @_ at ", scalar localtime, "\n" }

my $port = shift || 2345;
my $proto = getprotobyname('tcp');
socket(Server, PF_INET, SOCK_STREAM, $proto) or die "socket: $!";
setsockopt(Server, SOL_SOCKET, SO_REUSEADDR, pack("l", 1))
                                            or die "setsockopt: $!";
bind(Server, sockaddr_in($port, INADDR_ANY)) or die "bind: $!";
listen(Server,SOMAXCONN)                     or die "listen: $!";

logmsg "server started on port $port";

my $waitedpid = 0;
my $paddr;
```

```perl
sub REAPER {
    $waitedpid = wait;
    $SIG{CHLD} = \&REAPER;  # if you don't have sigaction(2)
    logmsg "reaped $waitedpid" . ($? ? " with exit $?" : "");
}
$SIG{CHLD} = \&REAPER;

for ( ; $paddr = accept(Client,Server); close Client) {
    my($port,$iaddr) = sockaddr_in($paddr);
    my $name = gethostbyaddr($iaddr,AF_INET);

    logmsg "connection from $name [",
            inet_ntoa($iaddr), "] at port $port";

    spawn sub {
        print "Hello there, $name, it's now ", scalar localtime, "\n";
        exec '/usr/games/fortune'
            or confess "can't exec fortune: $!";
    };

}

sub spawn {
    my $coderef = shift;

    unless (@_ == 0 && $coderef && ref($coderef) eq 'CODE') {
        confess "usage: spawn CODEREF";
    }

    my $pid;
    if (!defined($pid = fork)) {
        logmsg "cannot fork: $!";
        return;
    } elsif ($pid) {
        logmsg "begat $pid";
        return; # i'm the parent
    }
    # else i'm the child -- go spawn

    open(STDIN,  "<&Client")   or die "can't dup client to stdin";
    open(STDOUT, ">&Client")   or die "can't dup client to stdout";
    STDOUT->autoflush();
    exit &$coderef();
}
```

As mentioned, this server takes the trouble to clone off a child version via **fork** for each incoming request. That way it can handle many requests at once, as long as you can create more processes. (You might want to limit this.) Even if you don't fork, the **listen** will allow up to SOMAXCONN (usually five or more) pending connections. Each connection uses up some resources, although not as much as a process. Forking servers also have to be particularly careful about cleaning up their dead children (called zombies in UNIX), because otherwise they'd quickly fill up your process table. The REAPER code above will take care of that for you.

If you're running on a system without restartable system calls (or if you want to be really careful in case you might someday run on such a system), you'll have to write a more elaborate **for** loop. That's because the act of collecting the zombie child process may cause the **accept** to fail and return the undefined value, making your loop fail prematurely. Here's a work-around:

```
for ( $waitedpid = 0;
      ($paddr = accept(Client,Server)) || $waitedpid;
      $waitedpid = 0, close Client)
{
    next if $waitedpid and not $paddr;   # or check $! == EINTR
    # the rest is the same...
```

We suggest that you use the **-T** switch to enable taint checking (see "Cooperating with Strangers" and "Cooperating with Other Languages" later in this chapter) even if you aren't running setuid or setgid. This is always a good idea for servers and other programs (like CGI scripts) that run on behalf of someone else, because it lessens the chances that people from the outside will be able to compromise your system.

Let's look at another TCP client. This one connects to the TCP "time" service on a number of different machines and shows how far their clocks differ from the system on which the client is being run:

```
#!/usr/bin/perl -w
require 5.002;
use strict;
use Socket;

my $SECS_of_70_YEARS = 2208988800;
sub ctime { scalar localtime(shift) }

my $iaddr = gethostbyname('localhost');
my $proto = getprotobyname('tcp');
my $port = getservbyname('time', 'tcp');
my $paddr = sockaddr_in(0, $iaddr);
my($host);

$| = 1;
printf "%-24s %8s %s\n", "localhost", 0, ctime(time());

foreach $host (@ARGV) {
    printf "%-24s ", $host;
    my $hisiaddr = inet_aton($host)      or die "unknown host";
    my $hispaddr = sockaddr_in($port, $hisiaddr);
    socket(SOCKET, PF_INET, SOCK_STREAM, $proto)
                                         or die "socket: $!";
    connect(SOCKET, $hispaddr)           or die "bind: $!";
    my $rtime = '    ';
    read(SOCKET, $rtime, 4);
    close(SOCKET);
```

```
        my $histime = unpack("N", $rtime) - $SECS_of_70_YEARS ;
        printf "%8d %s\n", $histime - time, ctime($histime);
}
```

UNIX-domain clients and servers

That's all fine for Internet-domain clients and servers, but what about local communications? While you can just pretend that your local machine is remote, sometimes you don't want to. UNIX-domain sockets are local to the current host, and are often used internally to implement pipes. They tend to be a little more efficient than Internet-domain sockets. Unlike Internet-domain sockets, UNIX domain sockets can show up in the file system with an *ls*(1) listing.

```
$ ls -l /dev/log
srw-rw-rw-  1 root              0 Oct 31 07:23 /dev/log
```

You can test for these with Perl's -S file test:

```
unless ( -S '/dev/log' ) {
    die "something's wicked with the print system";
}
```

Here's a sample UNIX-domain client:

```
#!/usr/bin/perl -w
require 5.002;
use Socket;
use strict;
my ($rendezvous, $line);

$rendezvous = shift || '/tmp/catsock';
socket(SOCK, PF_UNIX, SOCK_STREAM, 0)        or die "socket: $!";
connect(SOCK, sockaddr_un($rendezvous))      or die "connect: $!";
while ($line = <SOCK>) {
    print $line;
}
exit;
```

And here's a corresponding server.

```
#!/usr/bin/perl -Tw
require 5.002;
use strict;
use Socket;
use Carp;

BEGIN { $ENV{PATH} = '/usr/ucb:/bin' }

my $NAME = '/tmp/catsock';
my $uaddr = sockaddr_un($NAME);
my $proto = getprotobyname('tcp');

socket(Server,PF_UNIX,SOCK_STREAM,0)        or die "socket: $!";
```

```
    unlink($NAME);
    bind  (Server, $uaddr)                        or die "bind: $!";
    listen(Server,SOMAXCONN)                      or die "listen: $!";

    logmsg "server started on $NAME";

    $SIG{CHLD} = \&REAPER;

    for ( ; $paddr = accept(Client,Server); close Client) {
        logmsg "connection on $NAME";
        spawn sub {
            print "Hello there, it's now ", scalar localtime, "\n";
            exec '/usr/games/fortune';
            die "can't exec fortune: $!";
        };
    }
```

As you see, it's remarkably similar to the Internet-domain TCP server, so much so, in fact, that we've omitted several duplicate functions—spawn(), logmsg(), ctime(), and REAPER()—which are exactly the same as in the other server.

So why would you ever want to use a UNIX domain socket instead of a FIFO? Because a FIFO doesn't give you sessions. You can't tell one process's data from another's. With socket programming, you get a separate session for each client—that's why **accept** takes two arguments.

For example, let's say that you have a long-running database server daemon that you want folks from the World Wide Web to be able to access, but only if they go through a CGI interface. You'd have a small, simple CGI program that does whatever checks and logging you feel like, and then acts as a UNIX-domain client and proxies the request to your private server.

UDP: message passing

Another kind of client-server setup is one that uses not connections, but messages, or datagrams. UDP communications involve much lower overhead but also provide less reliability, since there are no promises that messages will arrive at all, let alone in order and unmangled. Still, UDP offers some advantages over TCP, including being able to broadcast or multicast to a whole bunch of destination hosts at once (usually on your local subnet). If you find yourself overly concerned about reliability and start building checks into your message system, then you probably should just use TCP to start with.

Here's a UDP program similar to the sample Internet TCP client given above. However, instead of checking one host at a time, the UDP version will check many of them asynchronously by simulating a multicast and then using **select** to do a timed-out wait for I/O. To do something similar with TCP, you'd have to use a different socket handle for each host.

```perl
#!/usr/bin/perl -w
use strict;
require 5.002;
use Socket;
use Sys::Hostname;

my ( $count, $hisiaddr, $hispaddr, $histime,
     $host, $iaddr, $paddr, $port, $proto,
     $rin, $rout, $rtime, $SECS_of_70_YEARS);

$SECS_of_70_YEARS      = 2208988800;

$iaddr = gethostbyname(hostname());
$proto = getprotobyname('udp');
$port = getservbyname('time', 'udp');
$paddr = sockaddr_in(0, $iaddr); # 0 means let kernel pick

socket(SOCKET, PF_INET, SOCK_DGRAM, $proto)   or die "socket: $!";
bind(SOCKET, $paddr)                          or die "bind: $!";

$| = 1;
printf "%-12s %8s %s\n",  "localhost", 0, scalar localtime time;
$count = 0;
for $host (@ARGV) {
    $count++;
    $hisiaddr = inet_aton($host)              or die "unknown host";
    $hispaddr = sockaddr_in($port, $hisiaddr);
    defined(send(SOCKET, 0, 0, $hispaddr))    or die "send $host: $!";
}

$rin = "";
vec($rin, fileno(SOCKET), 1) = 1;

# timeout after 10.0 seconds
while ($count && select($rout = $rin, undef, undef, 10.0)) {
    $rtime = "";
    ($hispaddr = recv(SOCKET, $rtime, 4, 0))  or die "recv: $!";
    ($port, $hisiaddr) = sockaddr_in($hispaddr);
    $host = gethostbyaddr($hisiaddr, AF_INET);
    $histime = unpack("N", $rtime) - $SECS_of_70_YEARS ;
    printf "%-12s ", $host;
    printf "%8d %s\n", $histime - time, scalar localtime($histime);
    $count--;
}
```

Cooperating with Strangers

Whether you're dealing with a user sitting at the keyboard typing commands, or someone sending information across the network, you need to be careful about the data coming into your programs, since the other person may, either maliciously or accidentally, send you data that will do more harm than good. Perl provides a mechanism to isolate tainted data so that you won't use it to do something you didn't intend to do. For instance, if you mistakenly trust a tainted filename, you might end up appending an entry to your *passwd* file when you thought you were appending to a log file.

And if the data you get from a stranger happens to be a bit of program to execute, you need to be even more careful. Perl provides a method of dealing with that, too. But first we'll talk about ordinary tainted data.

Handling Insecure Data

Perl is designed to make it easy to program securely even when your program is being used by someone with fewer privileges than the program itself. That is, some programs need to grant some extra privileges to their users, without giving away other privileges that they didn't intend to give away. Setuid and setgid programs fall into this category, as do many network servers, and the programs the servers themselves run, such as CGI scripts. At a fundamental level, Perl is easy to program securely because it's straightforward and self-contained. Unlike most command-line shells, which are based on multiple mysterious substitution passes on each line of the script, Perl uses a more conventional evaluation scheme with fewer hidden snags. Additionally, because the language has more built-in functionality, it can rely less upon external (and possibly untrustworthy) programs to accomplish its purposes.

But beyond that, Perl automatically enables a special security-checking mechanism called *taint mode* whenever it detects its program running with differing real and effective user or group IDs.[*] You can also enable taint mode explicitly by using the −T command line switch. This is suggested for server programs and any program run on behalf of someone else, such as a CGI script.

While in this mode, Perl takes special precautions called *taint checks* to prevent both obvious and subtle traps. Some of these checks are reasonably simple, such as verifying that path directories aren't writable by others; careful programmers have always used checks like these. Other checks, however, are best supported by the language itself, and it is these checks especially that contribute to making a setuid Perl program more secure than the corresponding C program.

The principle is simple: you may not use data derived from outside your program to affect something else outside your program—at least, not by accident. All command-line arguments, environment variables, and file input are marked as tainted.

---

[*] The setuid bit in UNIX permissions is mode 04000, and the setgid bit is 02000; either or both may be set to grant the user of the program some of the privileges of the owner (or owners) of the program. Other operating systems may confer special privileges on programs in other ways, but the principle is the same.

Tainted data may not be used directly or indirectly in any command that invokes a subshell, nor in any command that modifies files, directories, or processes. Any variable set within an expression that has previously referenced a tainted value becomes tainted itself, even if it is logically impossible for the tainted value to influence the variable. Because taintedness is associated with each scalar value, some elements of an array or hash might be tainted and others not.

The following code illustrates how tainting would work if you executed all these statements in order:

```
$arg = shift;              # $arg is tainted
$hid = "$arg, 'bar'";      # $hid is also tainted
$line = <>;                # Tainted
$path = $ENV{PATH};        # Tainted, but see below
$mine = 'abc';             # Not tainted
$shout = `echo abc`;       # Tainted
$shout = `echo $shout`;    # Insecure

system "echo $arg";        # Insecure (uses sh)
system "/bin/echo", $arg;  # OK (doesn't use sh)
system "echo $mine";       # Insecure until PATH set
system "echo $hid";        # Insecure two ways

$path = $ENV{PATH};        # $path tainted

$ENV{PATH} = '/bin:/usr/bin';
$ENV{IFS} = "" if $ENV{IFS} ne "";

$path = $ENV{PATH};        # $path now NOT tainted
system "echo $mine";       # OK, is secure now!
system "echo $hid";        # Insecure via $hid still

open(OOF, "< $arg");       # OK (read-only file)
open(OOF, "> $arg");       # Insecure (trying to write)

open(OOF, "echo $arg|");   # Insecure via $arg, but...
open(OOF,"-|")
    or exec 'echo', $arg;  # Considered OK

$shout = `echo $arg`;      # Insecure via $arg

unlink $mine, $arg;        # Insecure via $arg
umask $arg;                # Insecure via $arg

exec "echo $arg";          # Single arg to exec or system is insecure
exec "echo", $arg;         # Considered OK (doesn't use the shell)
exec "sh", '-c', $arg;     # Considered OK, but isn't really
```

If you try to do something insecure, you get a fatal error saying something like "Insecure dependency" or "Insecure $ENV{PATH}". You can still write an insecure **system** or **exec**, but only by explicitly doing something like the last example. If you pass a *LIST* to **system** or **exec**, you are presumed to know what you're doing.

Detecting and laundering tainted data

To test whether a variable contains tainted data, you can use the following
is_tainted() function.

```
sub is_tainted {
    not eval {
        join("",@_), kill 0;
        1;
    };
}
```

This function makes use of the obscure fact that the **kill** function tests for taintedness even when no process IDs are supplied to send the signal to. More important, the function also depends on the fact that using tainted data anywhere within
an expression renders the entire expression tainted. It would be inefficient for
every operator to test every argument for taintedness. Instead, a slightly more efficient and conservative approach is used: if any tainted value has been accessed
within the same expression, the whole expression is considered tainted.

But testing for taintedness only gets you so far. Usually you know perfectly well
which variables contain tainted data—you just have to clear the data's taintedness.
The only way to bypass the tainting mechanism is by referencing subpattern variables set by an earlier regular expression match. The presumption is that if you
reference a substring using **$1**, **$2**, and so on, you knew what you were doing
when you wrote the pattern, and wrote it to weed out anything dangerous. So you
need to give it a bit of thought—don't just blindly untaint anything, or you defeat
the entire mechanism. Also, it's better to verify that the variable has only good
characters rather than checking whether it has any bad characters. That's because
it's far too easy to miss bad characters that you never thought of.

For example, here's a test to make sure $addr contains nothing but "word" charac-
ters (alphabetics, numerics, and underscores), or a hyphen, an @ sign, or a dot.

```
if ($addr =~ /^([-\@\w.]+)$/) {
    $addr = $1;                    # $addr now untainted
}
else {
    die "Bad data in $addr";       # log this somewhere
}
```

This is fairly secure since /\w+/ doesn't normally match shell metacharacters, nor
are dot, hyphen, or "at" going to mean anything special to the shell. Had we used
/(.+)/ instead, it would have been insecure because that pattern lets everything
through. But Perl doesn't check for that. So when untainting, you must be exceed-
ingly careful with your patterns. Laundering data using regular expressions is the
only internal mechanism for untainting dirty data. (But see "Cleaning Up Your
Path" later, about forking a child of lesser privilege.)

Cleaning up your path

When you run a program from within Perl, whether you're using the ` . . . `, **glob**, **system**, **exec**, or **open** commands, Perl checks to make sure your PATH environment variable is secure. If you get the "Insecure $ENV{PATH}" message, you need to set $ENV{PATH} to a known value, and each directory in the path must be non-writable by anyone other than the directory's owner and group. You may be surprised to get this message even when the filename of your executable is absolute (that is, fully qualified from the root of your filesystem). True, when you supply an absolute filename, the PATH isn't used to locate the executable. However, Perl doesn't trust the program you're running not to turn right around and execute some other program using the insecure PATH. So it forces you to set a secure PATH anyway.

Perl has its own notion of which operations are dangerous, but it's still possible to get into trouble with other operations that don't care whether they use tainted values. Make judicious use of the file tests in dealing with any user-supplied filename. When possible, do your **open** operations and such after setting $> = $<. (Remember that under UNIX you have group IDs, too!) Perl doesn't prevent you from opening tainted filenames for reading, so be careful what you print out. The tainting mechanism is intended to prevent stupid mistakes, not to remove the need for thought.

You may recall that **system** never calls the shell when you pass it a list of arguments, but only when you pass it a string containing shell metacharacters. (The same applies to **exec**.) Since you can explicitly bypass the shell by passing a list of arguments, this form is not considered a dangerous operation. Unfortunately, the **open**, **glob**, and backtick functions provide no such alternate calling convention, so more subterfuge will be required.

Perl provides a reasonably safe way to open a file or pipe from within a setuid or setgid program: just create a child process with reduced privilege who does the dirty work for you. First, fork a child using the special **open** syntax that connects the parent and child by a pipe. Now the child resets its user and group IDs (and any other per-process attributes, like environment variables, umasks, current working directories) back to the originals or known safe values. Then the child process, which no longer has any special permissions, does the **open** or other system call. Finally, the child passes whatever data it managed to access back to the parent. Since the file or pipe was opened in the child while running under less privilege than the parent, the child is unlikely to be tricked into doing something it shouldn't.

For example, here's how you might emulate backticks in reasonable safety. Notice how the **exec** is not called with a string that the shell could expand. This is by far the best way to call something that might be subjected to shell escapes: just never call the shell at all. By the time we get to the **exec**, tainting is turned off, however, so be careful what you call and what you pass it.

```
use English;
die unless defined($pid = open(KID, "-|"));
if ($pid) {              # parent
    while (<KID>) {
        # do something
    }
    close KID;
}
else {
    $EUID = $UID;
    $EGID = $GID;     # XXX: initgroups() not called
    $ENV{PATH} = "/bin:/usr/bin";
    exec 'myprog', 'arg1', 'arg2';
    die "can't exec myprog: $!";
}
```

A similar strategy would work for wildcard expansion via **glob**.

Security bugs

Beyond the obvious problems that stem from giving special privileges to interpreters as flexible and inscrutable as shells, many versions of UNIX have the additional difficulty that any setuid script is inherently insecure before it ever gets to the interpreter. That is, the problem is not the script itself, but a race condition in the way kernel invokes an interpreter mentioned on the #! line. (The bug doesn't exist on machines that don't recognize #! in the kernel.) Between the time the kernel opens the file to see which interpreter to run and the time the (now-setuid) interpreter starts up and reopens the file to interpret it, the file in question may have changed, especially if your system supports symbolic links.

Fortunately, sometimes this kernel "feature" can be disabled. Unfortunately, there are two ways to disable it. The system can outlaw scripts with the setuid bit set, which doesn't help much. Alternately, it can ignore the setuid bit on scripts. If the latter is true, Perl can emulate the setuid and setgid mechanism when it notices the (otherwise useless) setuid/gid bits on Perl scripts. It does this via a special executable called *suidperl*, which is automatically invoked for you if it's needed.

However, if the kernel setuid script feature *isn't* disabled, Perl will complain loudly that your setuid script is insecure. You'll need to either disable the kernel setuid script feature,[*] or put a C wrapper around the script. A C wrapper is just a compiled program that does nothing except call your Perl program. Compiled programs are not subject to the kernel bug that plagues setuid scripts.

---

[*] This may be difficult if your kernel vendor manifests the typical degree of deafness.

Here's a simple wrapper, written in C:

```
#define REAL_FILE "/path/to/script"
main(ac, av)
    char **av;
{
    execv(REAL_FILE, av);
}
```

Compile this wrapper into a binary executable and then make *it* rather than your script setuid or setgid. Be sure to use an absolute filename, since C isn't smart enough to do taint checking on your PATH.

See the program *wrapsuid* in the *eg* directory of your Perl distribution for a convenient way to do this automatically for all your setuid Perl programs. It renames your setuid scripts to have a dot on the front, and then compiles a wrapper like the one above for each of them. It gives each wrapper the name of the script it replaces.

In recent years, some vendors have begun to supply systems free of this inherent security bug. On such systems, when the kernel passes the name of the setuid script to open to the interpreter, it no longer passes a filename subject to meddling, but instead passes */dev/fd/3*. This is a special file already opened on the script, so that there can be no race condition for evil scripts to exploit. On these systems, Perl should be compiled with -DSETUID_SCRIPTS_ARE_SECURE_NOW. The *Configure* program that builds Perl tries to figure this out for itself, so you should never have to specify this yourself. Most modern releases of SysVr4 and BSD 4.4 use this approach to avoid the kernel race condition.

Prior to release 5.003 of Perl, a bug in the code of *suidperl* could introduce a security hole in systems compiled with strict POSIX compliance. If you must run an earlier version of *suidperl*, please see CERT advisory CA-96.12.

Handling Insecure Code

Taint checking is useful when you trust yourself to write honest code, but don't necessarily trust whoever's feeding you data not to try to trick you into doing something bad. Taint checking is the sort of security blanket that's useful for setuid programs and programs launched on someone else's behalf, like CGI programs.

It's quite another matter when you don't even trust the writer of the code you're running. What if you fetch an applet off the Net and it contains a virus, or a time bomb, or a Trojan horse? Taint checking is useless here, because the code itself may be tainted, while the data you're feeding it presumably is not. You're placing yourself in the position of someone who receives a mysterious device from a stranger, with a note that says, "Just hold this to your head and pull the trigger." Maybe you think it will dry your hair, but you might not think so for very long.

In this realm, prudence is synonymous with paranoia. What you want is a system in which you can impose a quarantine on suspicious code. The code can continue to exist, and even perform certain functions, but you don't let it wander around doing anything it feels like doing. In Perl, you can impose a kind of quarantine using the Safe module.

Safe

The Safe module allows the programmer to set up special compartments in which all system operations are trapped and namespace access is carefully controlled. The technical details of this module are explained in Chapter 7. Here we'll take a more philosophical approach.

At the most basic level, a Safe object is like a safe, except the idea is to keep the bad people in, not out. In the UNIX world, there is a system call known as *chroot*(2) that can permanently consign a process to run only in a subdirectory of the directory structure, in its own private little hell, if you will. Once the process is put there, there is no way whatsoever for it to reach anything outside, because there's no way for it to name anything outside. A Safe object is a little like that, except that instead of being restricted to a subset of the directory structure, it's restricted to a subset of Perl's package structure, which is hierarchical just as the directory structure is. It suffices to give the Safe object its own "main package", so that it can't influence the rest of your program.

The other important thing about a Safe object is that it limits the operations available to the tainted code. The details of this aren't important here, but what is important is that this is under the control of your code. And since you can create multiple Safe objects in your program, you can confer various degrees of trust upon various chunks of code, depending on where you got them from. Or more importantly, on whom you got them from. This leads us to the notion of Penguin.

Penguin

If you're going to bestow more than the minimal amount of trust on the code you get from someone (and you have to, if you think about it), you must also trust the mechanism by which the trustworthy code is delivered to you. In the good old days, of course, we just ignored the problem, but these days if you do that you get infected by a virus. So we're moving toward the day in which most software will be delivered with an encrypted seal guaranteeing that it comes from where you think it comes from, and that it hasn't been tampered with in the meanwhile.

Penguin is a Perl module that allows you to send encrypted, digitally signed Perl code (termed "executable content" in Marketese) to a remote machine to be executed. At the other end, it lets you receive code and, depending on who signed it, execute it within the constraints of an arbitrarily secure Safe object. You'll note that we didn't say which end was the client and which end was the server. This was intentional, because it doesn't really matter.

Penguin thus enables you to perform Internet commerce safely, write mobile information-gathering agents, distribute "live content" web-browser helper applications, perform distributed load-balanced computation, update remote software, administer distant machines, propagate content-based information, build Internet-wide shared-data applications and network application builders, and so on. And it's completely non-proprietary.

As its author, Felix Gallo, puts it:

> Penguin-as-a-concept grew from early thinking about agent-tcl, a language I made up during a heated discussion with the safe-tcl people. Tcl proved to be an inappropriate implementation language. Soon after I stopped trying, Sun's Java language arrived on the scene, purporting to solve many of the issues I had thought were important. However, although superior to tcl, Java is also an inappropriate and difficult implementation language. Hence Perl, hence Penguin.
>
> Penguin, with its vastly simplified, superior, and innate methods of ensuring safety and security, may become a very interesting tool in the repertoires of the many thousands of Perl programmers already extant on the Internet. Once people discover the glass walls of Java and the inconsistencies and insecurities engendered in the other solutions, we may begin to live in interesting times.

Hmm, we seem to be slipping into a competitive frame of mind here. Ah, well. The next section should help with that.

As of this writing, Penguin is still developing fast enough that it is not yet included as part of the standard Perl distribution. That doesn't mean we don't like it. As usual, consult CPAN for the latest details.

Cooperating with Other Languages

Just as there are many levels on which languages can compete, so too there are many levels on which languages can cooperate. Here we'll talk primarily about generation, translation and embedding (via linking).

Program Generation

Almost from the time people first figured out that they could write programs, they started writing programs that write other programs. These are called *program generators*. (If you're a history buff, you might know that RPG stood for Report

Program Generator long before it stood for Role Playing Game.) Now, anyone who has written a program generator knows that it can make your eyes go crossed even when you're wide awake. The problem is simply that much of your program's data looks like real code, but isn't (at least not yet). The same text file contains both stuff that does something and similar looking stuff that doesn't. Perl has various features that make it easier to mix it together with other languages, textually speaking.

Of course, these features also make it easier to write Perl in Perl, but it's rather expected that Perl would cooperate with itself.

Generating other languages in Perl

Perl is, of course, a text-processing language, and most computer languages are textual. Beyond that, the lack of arbitrary limits together with the various quoting and interpolation mechanisms make it pretty easy to visually isolate the code of the other language you're spitting out. For example, here is a small chunk of *s2p*, the *sed*-to-*perl* translator:

```
print &q(<<"EOT");
:        #!$bin/perl
:        eval 'exec $bin/perl -S \$0 \${1+"\$@"}'
:              if \$running_under_some_shell;
:
EOT
```

Here the enclosed text happens to be legal in two languages, both Perl and shell. We've used the trick of putting a colon and a tab on the front of every line, which visually isolates the enclosed code. One variable, $bin, is interpolated in the multi-line quote in two places, and then the string is passed through a function to strip the colon and tab.

Of course, you aren't required to use multi-line quotes. One often sees CGI scripts containing millions of **print** statements, one per line. It seems a bit like driving to church in an F-16, but hey, if it gets you there....

When you are embedding a large, multi-line quote containing some other language (such as HTML), it's sometimes helpful to pretend you're enclosing Perl into the other language instead:

```
print <<"END";
stuff
blah blah blah ${ \( EXPR ) } blah blah blah
blah blah blah @{[ LIST ]} blah blah blah
nonsense
END
```

You can use either of those two tricks to interpolate the value of any scalar *EXPR* or *LIST* into a longer string.

Generating Perl in other languages

Perl can easily be generated in other languages because it's both concise and malleable. You can pick your quotes not to interfere with the other language's quoting mechanisms. You don't have to worry about indentation, or where you put your line breaks, or whether to backslash your backslashes yet again. You aren't forced to define a package as a single string in advance, since you can slide into your package's namespace repeatedly, whenever you want to evaluate more code in that package.

Translation from Other Languages

One of the very first Perl applications was the *sed*-to-*perl* translator, *s2p*. In fact, Larry delayed the initial release of Perl in order to complete *s2p* and *awk-to-perl* (*a2p*), because he thought they'd improve the acceptance of Perl. Hmm, maybe they did.

s2p

The *s2p* program takes a *sed* script specified on the command line (or from standard input) and produces a comparable Perl script on the standard output.

Options include:

-D*number*
> Sets debugging flags.

-n

> Specifies that this *sed* script was *always* invoked as *sed -n*. Otherwise a switch parser is prepended to the front of the script.

-p

> Specifies that this *sed* script was *never* invoked as *sed -n*. Otherwise a switch parser is prepended to the front of the script.

The Perl script produced looks very *sed*-like, and there may very well be better ways to express what you want to do in Perl. For instance, *s2p* does not make any use of the **split** operator, but you might want to.

The Perl script you end up with may be either faster or slower than the original *sed* script. If you're only interested in speed you'll just have to try it both ways. Of course, if you want to do something *sed* doesn't do, you have no choice. It's often possible to speed up the Perl script by various methods, such as deleting all references to $\ and **chop**.

a2p

The *a2p* program takes an *awk* script specified on the command line (or from standard input) and produces a comparable Perl script on the standard output.

Options include:

-D*number*
> Sets debugging flags.

-F*character*
> Tells *a2p* that this *awk* script is always invoked with a **-F** switch specifying *character*.

-n*fieldlist*
> Specifies the names of the input fields if input does not have to be split into an array for some programmatic reason. If you were translating an *awk* script that processes the password file, you might say:
>
> ```
> a2p -7 -nlogin.password.uid.gid.gcos.shell.home
> ```
>
> Any delimiter may be used to separate the field names.

-*number*
> Causes *a2p* to assume that input will always have that many fields.

a2p cannot do as good a job translating as a human would, but it usually does pretty well. There are some areas where you may want to examine the Perl script produced and tweak it some. Here are some of them, in no particular order.

There is an *awk* idiom of putting `int(...)` around a string expression to force numeric interpretation, even though the argument is always an integer anyway. This is generally unneeded in Perl, but *a2p* can't tell if the argument is always going to be an integer, so it leaves it in. You may wish to remove it.

Perl differentiates numeric comparison from string comparison. *awk* has one operator for both that decides at run-time which comparison to do. *a2p* does not try to do a complete job of *awk* emulation at this point. Instead it guesses which one you want. It's almost always right, but it can be spoofed. All such guesses are marked with the comment `#???`. You should go through and check them. You might want to run at least once with Perl's **-w** switch, which warns you if you use `==` where you should have used **eq**.

It would be possible to emulate *awk*'s behavior in selecting string versus numeric operations at run-time by inspection of the operands, but it would be gross and inefficient. Besides, *a2p* almost always guesses right.

Perl does not attempt to emulate the behavior of *awk* in which nonexistent array elements spring into existence simply by being referenced. If somehow you are relying on this mechanism to create null entries for a subsequent for...in, they won't be there in Perl.

If *a2p* makes a **split** command that assigns to a list of variables that looks like ($Fld1, $Fld2, $Fld3 . . .) you may want to rerun *a2p* using the -n option mentioned above. This will let you name the fields throughout the script. If it splits to an array instead, the script is probably referring to the number of fields somewhere.

The "exit" statement in *awk* doesn't necessarily exit; it goes to the END block if there is one. *awk* scripts that do contortions within the END block to bypass the block under such circumstances can be simplified by removing the conditional in the END block and just exiting directly from the Perl script.

Perl has two kinds of arrays, numerically indexed and associative. *awk* arrays are usually translated to associative arrays, but if you happen to know that the index is always going to be numeric, you could change the { . . . } to [. . .]. Remember that iteration over an associative array is done using the **keys** function, but iteration over a numeric array isn't. You might need to modify any loop that is iterating over the array in question.

awk starts by assuming OFMT has the value %.6g. Perl starts by assuming its equivalent, $#, to have the value %.20g. You'll want to set $# explicitly if you use the default value of OFMT. (Actually, you probably don't want to set $#, but rather put in **printf** formats everywhere it matters.)

Near the top of the line loop will be the **split** operator that is implicit in the *awk* script. There are times when you can move this operator down past some conditionals that test the entire record, so that the **split** is not done as often.

For aesthetic reasons you may wish to change the array base $[from 1 back to Perl's default of 0, but remember to change all array subscripts and all **substr** and **index** operations to match.

Cute comments that say:

```
# Here's a workaround because awk is so dumb.
```

are, of course, passed through unmodified.

awk scripts are often embedded in a shell script that pipes stuff into and out of *awk.* Often the shell script wrapper can be incorporated into the Perl script, since Perl can start up pipes into and out of itself, and can do other things that *awk* can't do by itself.

Scripts that refer to the special variables RSTART and RLENGTH can often be simplified by referring to the variables $`, $&, and $', as long as they are within the scope of the pattern match that sets them.

The produced Perl script may have subroutines defined to deal with *awk*'s semantics regarding "getline" and "print". Since *a2p* usually picks correctness over efficiency, it is almost always possible to rewrite such code to be more efficient by discarding the semantic sugar.

ARGV[0] translates to $0, but ARGV[n] translates to $ARGV[$n]. A loop that tries to iterate over ARGV[0] won't find it.

NOTE   Storage for the *awk* syntax tree is currently static, and can run out.
              You'll need to recompile *a2p* if that happens.

---

find2perl

The *find2perl* program is really easy to understand if you already understand the UNIX *find*(1) program. Just type *find2perl* instead of *find*, and give it the same arguments you would give to *find*. It will spit out an equivalent Perl script.

There are a couple of options you can use that your ordinary *find*(1) command probably doesn't support:

-tar *tarfile*
    Outputs a tar file much like the -cpio switch of some versions of *find*.

-eval *string*
    Evaluates the string as a Perl expression, and continues if true.

Source filters

The notion of a source filter started with the idea that a script or module should be able to decrypt itself on the fly, like this:

```
#!/usr/bin/perl
use MyDecryptFilter;
@*x$]`0uN&k^Zx02jZ^X{.?s!(f;9Q/^A^@~~8H]|,%@^P:q-=
...
```

But the idea grew from there, and now a source filter can be defined to do any transformation on the input text you like. One can now even do things like this:

```
#!/usr/bin/perl
use Filter::exec "a2p";
1,30{print $1}
```

Put that together with the notion of the **-x** switch mentioned at the beginning of this chapter, and you have a general mechanism for pulling any chunk of program out of an article and executing it, regardless of whether it's written in Perl or not. Now that's cooperation.

The Filter module is available from CPAN.

Translation to Other Languages

Historically, the Perl interpreter has been rather self-contained. When Perl was redesigned for Version 5, however, one of the requirements was that it be possible to write extension modules that could traverse the parsed syntax tree and emit code in other languages, either low-level or high-level. This has now come to pass.

More precisely, this is now coming to pass. Malcolm Beattie has been developing a "real compiler" for Perl. As of this writing, it's in Alpha 2 state, which means it mostly works, except for the really hard bits. The compiler consists of an ordinary Perl parser and interpreter (since you need to be able to execute BEGIN blocks to compile Perl), plus a set of modules under the name of B, which is short for both "Backend" and "Beattie". You don't actually invoke the B module directly though. Instead you invoke a particular backend via the O module, which pulls in the B module for you. Typically you invoke the O module right on the command line with the **-M** switch, so a compilation command might look like this:

```
perl -MO=C foo.pl >foo.c
```

There are three backends at the moment. The C backend rather woodenly spits out C calls into the ordinary Perl interpreter, but it can translate almost anything except the most egregious abuses of the dynamic capabilities of the interpreter. The Bytecode module is also fairly complete, and spits out an external Perl byte-code representation, which can then be read back in and executed by a suitably clued version of Perl. Finally, the CC backend attempts to translate into more idiomatic C with a lot of optimization. Obviously, that's a bit harder to do than the other thing. Nevertheless, it already works on a majority of the Perl regression tests. It's possible with some care to get C code that runs considerably faster than Perl 5's interpreter, which is no slouch to begin with. And Malcolm hasn't put in all the optimizations he wants to yet.

This is an ongoing topic of research, but you'll want to keep track of it. You are quite likely to be using this someday soon, if you aren't already. Look for it on CPAN of course, if it's not already a part of the standard Perl distribution by the time you read this.

Embedding Perl in C and C++

Another part of the design of Perl 5 was that it be possible to embed a Perl interpreter in a C or C++ program. And in fact, the ordinary *perl* executable pretends to
have an embedded interpreter in it; the main() function essentially does this:

```
PerlInterpreter *my_perl;

int main(int argc, char **argv)
{
    int exitstatus;

    my_perl = perl_alloc();
    perl_construct( my_perl );

    exitstatus = perl_parse( my_perl, xs_init, argc, argv,
                                     (char **) NULL );
    if (exitstatus)
        exit( exitstatus );

    exitstatus = perl_run( my_perl );

    perl_destruct( my_perl );
    perl_free( my_perl );

    exit(exitstatus);
}
```

The important parts are the calls to perl_parse() and perl_run(), which respectively compile and run the program. If you were embedding Perl in your own program, you might replace the call to perl_run() with calls to perl_call_sv()
function, which calls individual subroutines rather than the program as a whole.
Or you can do both, if the main script contains initialization code as well as subroutine definitions.

There are many other useful entry points into the interpreter, such as
perl_eval_sv(), which evaluates a string, but this chapter is already getting pretty
long, and the fact of the matter is that there is extensive online documentation for
the internals of Perl. To include it here would make this book even more
unwieldy than it is, and most people who would be embedding Perl aren't scared
of online documentation. See the *perlembed*(3) manpage for more on embedding
Perl interpreters in your program.

A number of programs in the real world already have Perl embedded in them—
the authors know of several proprietary products shipping with embedded Perl
interpreters. There are also a couple of modules for the *Apache* HTTP servers that
use an embedded Perl interpreter to avoid process startup costs on CGI-like
scripting. And then there's the version of Berkeley's *nvi* editor with a Perl engine
in it. Watch out, *emacs*, you've got company. :-)

Embedding C and C++ in Perl

If a respectable number of programs embed a Perl interpreter, then a veritable flood of extension modules embed C and C++ into Perl. Again, the Perl distribution itself does this with many of its standard extension modules, including DB_File, DynaLoader, Fcntl, FileHandle, GDBM_File, NDBM_File, ODBM_File, POSIX, Safe, SDBM_File, and Socket. And many of the modules on CPAN do this. So if you decide to do it yourself, you won't feel like you're researching a Ph.D. dissertation.

And again, we only have space to give you teasers for the online documentation, which is exhaustively extensive. We recommend you start with the *perlxstut*(3) manpage, which is a tutorial on the XS language, a preprocessor that spits out the glue routines you need to do the "impedance matching" between Perl and C or C++. You'll also be interested in *perlxs*(3), *perlguts*(3), and *perlcall*(3).

And once again, let us reiterate that your best resource is the Perl community itself. They invented a lot of this stuff, and are emotionally committed to making you like it, whether you like it or not. You'd better cooperate.

7

The Standard
Perl Library

This chapter describes the collection of Perl code that comes along with the Perl distribution. If you use this library and then share your program with others, they will not have to take special steps to execute the program, because the same library is available to Perl programs everywhere.

You'll save some time if you make the effort to get familiar with the standard library. There's no point in reinventing the wheel. You should be aware, however, that the library contains a wide range of material. While some modules may be extremely helpful, others may be completely irrelevant to your needs. For example, some are useful only if you are creating extensions to Perl. We offer below a rough classification of the library modules to aid you in browsing.

First, however, let's untangle some terminology:

package

> A *package* is a simple namespace management device, allowing two different parts of a Perl program to have a (different) variable named $fred. These namespaces are managed with the **package** declaration, described in Chapter 5, *Packages, Modules, and Object Classes*.

library

> A *library* is a set of subroutines for a particular purpose. Often the library declares itself a separate package so that related variables and subroutines can be kept together, and so that they won't interfere with other variables in your program. Generally, a library is placed in a separate file, often ending in " *.pl*", and then pulled into the main program via **require**. (This mechanism has largely been superseded by the module mechanism, so nowadays we often use the term "library" to talk about the whole system of modules that come with Perl. See the title of this chapter, for instance.)

module

A *module* is a library that conforms to specific conventions, allowing the file to be brought in with a **use** directive at compile time. Module filenames end in "*.pm*", because the **use** directive insists on that. (It also translates the sub-package delimiter :: to whatever your subdirectory delimiter is; it is / on UNIX.) Chapter 5 describes Perl modules in greater detail.

pragma

A *pragma* is a module that affects the compilation phase of your program as well as the execution phase. Think of them as hints to the compiler. Unlike modules, pragmas often (but not always) limit the scope of their effects to the innermost enclosing block of your program. The names of pragmas are by convention all lowercase.

For easy reference, this chapter is arranged alphabetically. If you wish to look something up by functional grouping, Tables 7–1 through 7–11 display an (admittedly arbitrary) listing of the modules and pragmas described in this chapter.

Table 7–1: General Programming: Miscellaneous

Module	Function
Benchmark	Check and compare running times of code
Config	Access Perl configuration information
Env	Import environment variables
English	Use English or *awk* names for punctuation variables
Getopt::Long	Extended processing of command-line options
Getopt::Std	Process single-character switches with switch clustering
lib	Manipulate @INC at compile time
Shell	Run shell commands transparently within Perl
strict	Restrict unsafe constructs
Symbol	Generate anonymous globs; qualify variable names
subs	Predeclare subroutine names
vars	Predeclare global variable names

Table 7–2: General Programming: Error Handling and Logging

Module	Function
Carp	Generate error messages
diagnostics	Force verbose warning diagnostics
sigtrap	Enable stack backtrace on unexpected signals
Sys::Syslog	Perl interface to UNIX *syslog*(3) calls

Table 7-3: General Programming: File Access and Handling

Module	Function
Cwd	Get pathname of current working directory
DirHandle	Supply object methods for directory handles
File::Basename	Parse file specifications
File::CheckTree	Run many tests on a collection of files
File::Copy	Copy files or filehandles
File::Find	Traverse a file tree
File::Path	Create or remove a series of directories
FileCache	Keep more files open than the system permits
FileHandle	Supply object methods for filehandles
SelectSaver	Save and restore selected filehandle

Table 7-4: General Programming: Text Processing and Screen Interfaces

Module	Function
Pod::Text	Convert POD data to formatted ASCII text
Search::Dict	Search for key in dictionary file
Term::Cap	Terminal capabilities interface
Term::Complete	Word completion module
Text::Abbrev	Create an abbreviation table from a list
Text::ParseWords	Parse text into a list of tokens
Text::Soundex	The Soundex Algorithm described by Knuth
Text::Tabs	Expand and unexpand tabs
Text::Wrap	Wrap text into a paragraph

Table 7-5: Database Interfaces

Module	Function
AnyDBM_File	Provide framework for multiple DBMs
DB_File	Tied access to Berkeley DB
GDBM_File	Tied access to GDBM library
NDBM_File	Tied access to NDBM files
ODBM_File	Tied access to ODBM files
SDBM_File	Tied access to SDBM files

Table 7–6: Mathematics

Module	Function
integer	Do arithmetic in integer instead of double
Math::BigFloat	Arbitrary-length floating-point math package
Math::BigInt	Arbitrary-length integer math package
Math::Complex	Complex numbers package

Table 7– 7: Networking and Interprocess Communication

Module	Function
IPC::Open2	Open a process for both reading and writing
IPC::Open3	Open a process for reading, writing, and error handling
Net::Ping	Check whether a host is online
Socket	Load the C *socket.h* defines and structure manipulators
Sys::Hostname	Try every conceivable way to get hostname

Table 7–8: Time and Locale

Module	Function
Time::Local	Efficiently compute time from local and GMT time
I18N::Collate	Compare 8-bit scalar data according to the current locale

Table 7–9: For Developers: Autoloading and Dynamic Loading

Module	Function
AutoLoader	Load functions only on demand
AutoSplit	Split a module for autoloading
Devel::SelfStubber	Generate stubs for a SelfLoading module
DynaLoader	Automatic dynamic loading of Perl modules
SelfLoader	Load functions only on demand

Table 7–10: For Developers: Language Extensions and Platform Development Support

Module	Function
ExtUtils::Install	Install files from here to there
ExtUtils::Liblist	Determine libraries to use and how to use them
ExtUtils::MakeMaker	Create a *Makefile* for a Perl extension
ExtUtils::Manifest	Utilities to write and check a *MANIFEST* file
ExtUtils::Miniperl	Write the C code for *perlmain.c*

Table 7–10: For Developers: Language Extensions and Platform Development Support (continued)

Module	Function
ExtUtils::Mkbootstrap	Make a bootstrap file for use by DynaLoader
ExtUtils::Mksymlists	Write linker option files for dynamic extension
ExtUtils::MM_OS2	Methods to override UNIX behavior in ExtUtils::MakeMaker
ExtUtils::MM_Unix	Methods used by ExtUtils::MakeMaker
ExtUtils::MM_VMS	Methods to override UNIX behavior in ExtUtils::MakeMaker
Fcntl	Load the C *fcntl.h* defines
POSIX	Interface to IEEE Std 1003.1
Safe	Create safe namespaces for evaluating Perl code
Test::Harness	Run Perl standard test scripts with statistics

Table 7–11: For Developers: Object-Oriented Programming Support

Module	Function
Exporter	Default import method for modules
overload	Overload Perl's mathematical operations
Tie::Hash	Base class definitions for tied hashes
Tie::Scalar	Base class definitions for tied scalars
Tie::StdHash	Base class definitions for tied hashes
Tie::StdScalar	Base class definitions for tied scalars
Tie::SubstrHash	Fixed-table-size, fixed-key-length hashing

Beyond the Standard Library

If you don't find an entry in the standard library that fits your needs, it's still quite possible that someone has written code that will be useful to you. There are many superb library modules that are not included in the standard distribution, for various practical, political, and pathetic reasons. To find out what is available, you can look at the Comprehensive Perl Archive Network (CPAN). See the discussion of CPAN in the Preface.

Here are the major categories of modules available from CPAN:

- Archiving and Compression
- Authentication, Security and Encryption
- Control Flow Utilities (callbacks, exceptions, and so on)

- Data Types and Data Type Utilities

- Database Interfaces

- Development Support

- Filehandle and Input/Output Stream Utilities

- File Names, File Systems and File Locking

- Images, Pixmap and Bitmap Manipulation, Drawing and Graphing

- Interfaces to/Emulations of Other Programming Languages

- Internationalization and Locale

- Language Extensions and Documentation Tools

- Mail and Usenet News

- Miscellaneous Modules

- Networking, Device Control (modems) and Inter-process Communication

- Operating System Interfaces

- Option, Argument, Parameter and Configuration File Processing

- Server and Daemon Utilities

- String Processing, Language Text Processing, Parsing and Searching

- User Interfaces

- World Wide Web, HTML, HTTP, CGI, MIME

Allow us again to reiterate once more that these things are in a state of flux, and you will certainly find more and better stuff on CPAN than we can possibly describe here. The Perl of Great Price has outgrown its oyster, so to speak, because Perl is truly a community effort these days—see John 14:12.

Library Modules

As mentioned earlier, the following library modules are arranged in alphabetical order, for easy reference.

AnyDBM_File—Provide Framework for Multiple DBMs

```
use AnyDBM_File;
```

This module is a "pure virtual base class"—it has nothing of its own. It's just there to inherit from the various DBM packages. By default it inherits from NDBM_File for compatibility with earlier versions of Perl. If it doesn't find NDBM_File, it looks for DB_File, GDBM_File, SDBM_File (which is always there—it comes with Perl), and finally ODBM_File.

Perl's **dbmopen** function (which now exists only for backward compatibility) actually just calls **tie** to bind a hash to AnyDBM_File. The effect is to bind the hash to one of the specific DBM classes that AnyDBM_File inherits from.

You can override the defaults and determine which class **dbmopen** will tie to. Do this by redefining @**ISA**:

```
@AnyDBM_File::ISA = qw(DB_File GDBM_File NDBM_File);
```

Note, however, that an explicit **use** takes priority over the ordering of @**ISA**, so that:

```
use GDBM_File;
```

will cause the next **dbmopen** to tie your hash to GDBM_File.

You can tie hash variables directly to the desired class yourself, without using **dbmopen** or AnyDBM_File. For example, by using multiple DBM implementations, you can copy a database from one format to another:

```
use Fcntl;          # for O_* values
use NDBM_File;
use DB_File;
tie %oldhash, "NDBM_File", $old_filename, O_RDWR;
tie %newhash, "DB_File",   $new_filename, O_RDWR|O_CREAT|O_EXCL, 0644;
while (($key,$val) = each %oldhash) {
    $newhash{$key} = $val;
}
```

DBM comparisons

Here's a table of the features that the different DBMish packages offer:

Feature	ODBM	NDBM	SDBM	GDBM	BSD-DB
Linkage comes with Perl	Yes	Yes	Yes	Yes	Yes
Source bundled with Perl	No	No	Yes	No	No
Source redistributable	No	No	Yes	GPL	Yes
Often comes with UNIX	Yes	Yes[a]	No	No	No
Builds OK on UNIX	N/A	N/A	Yes	Yes	Yes[b]
Code size	Varies[c]	Varies[c]	Small	Big	Big
Disk usage	Varies[c]	Varies[c]	Small	Big	OK[d]
Speed	Varies[c]	Varies[c]	Slow	OK	Fast
FTPable	No	No	Yes	Yes	Yes
Easy to build	N/A	N/A	Yes	Yes	OK[e]

Feature	ODBM	NDBM	SDBM	GDBM	BSD-DB
Block size limits	1k	4k	1k[f]	None	None
Byte-order independent	No	No	No	No	Yes
User-defined sort order	No	No	No	No	Yes
Wildcard lookups	No	No	No	No	Yes

[a] On mixed-universe machines, may be in the BSD compatibility library, which is often shunned.
[b] Providing you have an ANSI C compiler.
[c] Depends on how much your vendor has "tweaked" it.
[d] Can be trimmed if you compile for one access method.
[e] See the DB_File library module. Requires symbolic links.
[f] By default, but can be redefined (at the expense of compatibility with older files).

See also

Relevant library modules include: DB_File, GDBM_File, NDBM_File, ODBM_File, and SDBM_File. Related manpages: *dbm*(3), *ndbm*(3). Tied variables are discussed extensively in Chapter 5, and the **dbmopen** entry in Chapter 3, *Functions*, may also be helpful. You can pick up the unbundled modules from the *src/misc/* directory on your nearest CPAN site. Here are the most popular ones, but note that their version numbers may have changed by the time you read this:

```
http://www.perl.com/CPAN/src/misc/db.1.85.tar.gz
http://www.perl.com/CPAN/src/misc/gdbm-1.7.3.tar.gz
```

AutoLoader — Load Functions Only on Demand

```
package GoodStuff;
use Exporter;
use AutoLoader;
@ISA = qw(Exporter AutoLoader);
```

The AutoLoader module provides a standard mechanism for delayed loading of functions stored in separate files on disk. Each file has the same name as the function (plus a *.al*), and comes from a directory named after the package (with the *auto/* directory). For example, the function named GoodStuff::whatever() would be loaded from the file *auto/GoodStuff/whatever.al*.

A module using the AutoLoader should have the special marker __END__ prior to the actual subroutine declarations. All code before this marker is loaded and compiled when the module is used. At the marker, Perl stops parsing the file.

When a subroutine not yet in memory is called, the AUTOLOAD function attempts to locate it in a directory relative to the location of the module file itself. As an example, assume *POSIX.pm* is located in */usr/local/lib/perl5/POSIX.pm*. The AutoLoader will look for the corresponding subroutines for this package in */usr/local/lib/perl5/auto/POSIX/*.al*.

Lexicals declared with **my** in the main block of a package using the AutoLoader will not be visible to autoloaded functions, because the given lexical scope ends at the __END__ marker. A module using such variables as file-scoped globals will not work properly under the AutoLoader. Package globals must be used instead. When running under use strict, the use vars pragma may be employed in such situations as an alternative to explicitly qualifying all globals with the package name. Package variables predeclared with this pragma will be accessible to any autoloaded routines, but of course will not be invisible outside the module file.

The AutoLoader is a counterpart to the SelfLoader module. Both delay the loading of subroutines, but the SelfLoader accomplishes this by storing the subroutines right there in the module file rather than in separate files elsewhere. While this avoids the use of a hierarchy of disk files and the associated I/O for each routine loaded, the SelfLoader suffers a disadvantage in the one-time parsing of the lines after __DATA__, after which routines are cached. The SelfLoader can also handle multiple packages in a file.

AutoLoader, on the other hand, only reads code as it is requested, and in many cases should be faster. But it requires a mechanism like AutoSplit to be used to create the individual files.

On systems with restrictions on file name length, the file corresponding to a subroutine may have a shorter name than the routine itself. This can lead to conflicting filenames. The AutoSplit module will warn of these potential conflicts when used to split a module.

See the discussion of autoloading in Chapter 5. Also see the AutoSplit module, a utility that automatically splits a module into a collection of files for autoloading.

AutoSplit — Split a Module for Autoloading

```
# from a program
use AutoSplit;
autosplit_modules(@ARGV)

# or from the command line
perl -MAutoSplit -e 'autosplit(FILE, DIR, KEEP, CHECK, MODTIME)' ...

# another interface
perl -MAutoSplit -e 'autosplit_lib_modules(@ARGV)' ...
```

This function splits up your program or module into files that the AutoLoader module can handle. It is mainly used to build autoloading Perl library modules, especially complex ones like POSIX. It is used by both the standard Perl libraries and by the MakeMaker module to automatically configure libraries for autoloading.

The autosplit() interface splits the specified *FILE* into a hierarchy rooted at the directory *DIR*. It creates directories as needed to reflect class hierarchy. It then creates the file *autosplit.ix*, which acts as both a forward declaration for all package routines and also as a timestamp for when the hierarchy was last updated.

The remaining three arguments to autosplit() govern other options to the autosplitter. If the third argument, *KEEP*, is false, then any pre-existing .*al* files in the autoload directory are removed if they are no longer part of the module (obsoleted functions). The fourth argument, *CHECK*, instructs autosplit() to check the module currently being split to ensure that it really does include a **use** specification for the AutoLoader module, and skips the module if AutoLoader is not detected. Lastly, the *MODTIME* argument specifies that autosplit() is to check the modification time of the module against that of the *autosplit.ix* file, and only split the module if it is newer.

Here's a typical use of AutoSplit by the MakeMaker utility via the command line:

```
perl -MAutoSplit -e 'autosplit($ARGV[0], $ARGV[1], 0, 1, 1)'
```

MakeMaker defines this as a *make* macro, and it is invoked with file and directory arguments. The autosplit() function splits the named file into the given directory and deletes obsolete .*al* files, after checking first that the module does use the AutoLoader and ensuring that the module isn't already split in its current form.

The autosplit_lib_modules() form is used in the building of Perl. It takes as input a list of files (modules) that are assumed to reside in a directory *lib/* relative to the current directory. Each file is sent to the autosplitter one at a time, to be split into the directory *lib/auto/*.

In both usages of the autosplitter, only subroutines defined following the Perl special marker __END__ are split out into separate files. Routines placed prior to this marker are not autosplit, but are forced to load when the module is first required.

Currently, AutoSplit cannot handle multiple package specifications within one file.

AutoSplit will inform the user if it is necessary to create the top-level directory specified in the invocation. It's better if the script or installation process that invokes AutoSplit has created the full directory path ahead of time. This warning may indicate that the module is being split into an incorrect path.

AutoSplit will also warn the user of subroutines whose names cause potential naming conflicts on machines with severely limited (eight characters or less) filename length. Since the subroutine name is used as the filename, these warnings can aid in portability to such systems.

Warnings are issued and the file skipped if AutoSplit cannot locate either the
__END__ marker or a specification of the form package Name;. AutoSplit will also
complain if it can't create directories or files.

Benchmark — Check and Compare Running Times of Code

```
use Benchmark;

# timeit():  run $count iterations of the given Perl code, and time it
$t = timeit($count, 'CODE');  # $t is now a Benchmark object

# timestr():  convert Benchmark times to printable strings
print "$count loops of 'CODE' took:", timestr($t), "\n";

# timediff():  calculate the difference between two times
$t = timediff($t1 - $t2);

# timethis():  run "code" $count times with timeit(); also, print out a
#      header saying "timethis $count: "
$t = timethis($count, "CODE");

# timethese():  run timethis() on multiple chunks of code
@t = timethese($count, {
    'Name1' => '...CODE1...',
    'Name2' => '...CODE2...',
});

# new method:  return the current time
$t0 = new Benchmark;
# ... your CODE here ...
$t1 = new Benchmark;
$td = timediff($t1, $t0);
print "the code took: ", timestr($td), "\n";

# debug method:  enable or disable debugging
Benchmark->debug(1);
$t = timeit(10, ' 5 ** $Global ');
Benchmark->debug(0);
```

The Benchmark module encapsulates a number of routines to help you figure out
how long it takes to execute some code a given number of times within a loop.

For the timeit() routine, $count is the number of times to run the loop. *CODE* is a
string containing the code to run. timeit() runs a null loop with $count iterations,
and then runs the same loop with your code inserted. It reports the difference
between the times of execution.

For `timethese()`, a loop of `$count` iterations is run on each code chunk separately, and the results are reported separately. The code to run is given as a hash with keys that are names and values that are code. `timethese()` is handy for quick tests to determine which way of doing something is faster. For example:

```
$ perl -MBenchmark -Minteger
timethese(100000, { add => '$i += 2', inc => '$i++; $i++' });
__END__
Benchmark: timing 1000000 iterations of add, inc...
      add:  4 secs ( 4.52 usr  0.00 sys =  4.52 cpu)
      inc:  6 secs ( 5.32 usr  0.00 sys =  5.32 cpu)
```

The following routines are exported into your namespace if you use the Benchmark module:

```
timeit()
timethis()
timethese()
timediff()
timestr()
```

The following routines will be exported into your namespace if you specifically ask that they be imported:

```
clearcache()       # clear just the cache element indexed by $key
clearallcache()    # clear the entire cache
disablecache()     # do not use the cache
enablecache()      # resume caching
```

Notes

Code is executed in the caller's package.

The null loop times are cached, the key being the number of iterations. You can control caching with calls like these:

```
clearcache($key);
clearallcache();
disablecache();
enablecache();
```

Benchmark inherits only from the Exporter class.

The elapsed time is measured using *time*(2) and the granularity is therefore only one second. Times are given in seconds for the whole loop (not divided by the number of iterations). Short tests may produce negative figures because Perl can appear to take longer to execute the empty loop than a short test.

The user and system CPU time is measured to millisecond accuracy using *times*(3). In general, you should pay more attention to the CPU time than to elapsed time, especially if other processes are running on the system. Also, elapsed times of five seconds or more are needed for reasonable accuracy.

Because you pass in a string to be **eval**ed instead of a closure to be executed, lexical variables declared with **my** outside of the **eval** are not visible.

Carp — Generate Error Messages

```
use Carp;
carp "Be careful!";          # warn of errors (from perspective of caller)
croak "We're outta here!";   # die of errors (from perspective of caller)
confess "Bye!";              # die of errors with stack backtrace
```

carp() and croak() behave like **warn** and **die**, respectively, except that they report the error as occurring not at the line of code where they are invoked, but at a line in one of the calling routines. Suppose, for example, that you have a routine goo() containing an invocation of carp(). In that case—and assuming that the current stack shows no callers from a package other than the current one—carp() will report the error as occurring where goo() was called. If, on the other hand, callers from different packages are found on the stack, then the error is reported as occurring in the package immediately preceding the package in which the carp() invocation occurs. The intent is to let library modules act a little more like built-in functions, which always report errors where you call them from.

confess() is like **die** except that it prints out a stack backtrace. The error is reported at the line where confess() is invoked, not at a line in one of the calling routines.

Config — Access Perl Configuration Information

```
use Config;
if ($Config{cc} =~ /gcc/) {
    print "built by gcc\n";
}

use Config qw(myconfig config_sh config_vars);
print myconfig();
print config_sh();
config_vars(qw(osname archname));
```

The Config module contains all the information that the *Configure* script had to figure out at Perl build time (over 450 values).[*]

---

[*] Perl was written in C, not because it's a portable language, but because it's a ubiquitous language. A bare C program is about as portable as Chuck Yeager on foot.

Shell variables from the *config.sh* file (written by *Configure*) are stored in a read-only hash, %Config, indexed by their names. Values set to the string "undef" in *config.sh* are returned as undefined values. The Perl **exists** function should be used to check whether a named variable exists.

myconfig

> Returns a textual summary of the major Perl configuration values. See also the explanation of Perl's **-V** command-line switch in Chapter 6, *Social Engineering*.

config_sh

> Returns the entire Perl configuration information in the form of the original *config.sh* shell variable assignment script.

config_vars(@names)

> Prints to STDOUT the values of the named configuration variables. Each is printed on a separate line in the form:

```
name='value';
```

> Names that are unknown are output as name='UNKNOWN';.

Here's a more sophisticated example using %Config:

```
use Config;

defined $Config{sig_name} or die "No sigs?";
foreach $name (split(' ', $Config{sig_name})) {
    $signo{$name} = $i;
    $signame[$i] = $name;
    $i++;
}

print "signal #17 = $signame[17]\n";
if ($signo{ALRM}) {
    print "SIGALRM is $signo{ALRM}\n";
}
```

Because configuration information is not stored within the Perl executable itself, it is possible (but unlikely) that the information might not relate to the actual Perl binary that is being used to access it. The Config module checks the Perl version number when loaded to try to prevent gross mismatches, but can't detect subsequent rebuilds of the same version.

Cwd — Get Pathname of Current Working Directory

```
use Cwd;
$dir = cwd();            # get current working directory safest way

$dir = getcwd();         # like getcwd(3) or getwd(3)
```

```
$dir = fastcwd();          # faster and more dangerous

use Cwd 'chdir';           # override chdir; keep PWD up to date
chdir "/tmp";
print $ENV{PWD};           # prints "/tmp"
```

cwd() gets the current working directory using the most natural and safest form for the current architecture. For most systems it is identical to `pwd` (but without the trailing line terminator).

getcwd() does the same thing by re-implementing *getcwd*(3) or *getwd*(3) in Perl.

fastcwd() looks the same as getcwd(), but runs faster. It's also more dangerous because you might **chdir** out of a directory that you can't **chdir** back into.

It is recommended that one of these functions be used in *all* code to ensure portability because the *pwd* program probably only exists on UNIX systems.

If you consistently override your **chdir** built-in function in all packages of your program, then your PWD environment variable will automatically be kept up to date. Otherwise, you shouldn't rely on it. (Which means you probably shouldn't rely on it.)

DB_File — Access to Berkeley DB

```
use DB_File;

# brackets in following code indicate optional arguments
[$X =] tie %hash,  "DB_File", $filename [, $flags, $mode, $DB_HASH];
[$X =] tie %hash,  "DB_File", $filename, $flags, $mode, $DB_BTREE;
[$X =] tie @array, "DB_File", $filename, $flags, $mode, $DB_RECNO;

$status = $X->del($key [, $flags]);
$status = $X->put($key, $value [, $flags]);
$status = $X->get($key, $value [, $flags]);
$status = $X->seq($key, $value [, $flags]);
$status = $X->sync([$flags]);
$status = $X->fd;

untie %hash;
untie @array;
```

DB_File is the most flexible of the DBM-style tie modules. It allows Perl programs to make use of the facilities provided by Berkeley DB (not included). If you intend to use this module you should really have a copy of the Berkeley DB manual page at hand. The interface defined here mirrors the Berkeley DB interface closely.

Berkeley DB is a C library that provides a consistent interface to a number of database formats. DB_File provides an interface to all three of the database (file) types currently supported by Berkeley DB.

The file types are:

DB_HASH

> Allows arbitrary key/data pairs to be stored in data files. This is equivalent to the functionality provided by other hashing packages like DBM, NDBM, ODBM, GDBM, and SDBM. Remember, though, the files created using DB_HASH are not binary compatible with any of the other packages mentioned. A default hashing algorithm that will be adequate for most applications is built into Berkeley DB. If you do need to use your own hashing algorithm, it's possible to write your own and have DB_File use it instead.

DB_BTREE

> The btree format allows arbitrary key/data pairs to be stored in a sorted, balanced binary tree. It is possible to provide a user-defined Perl routine to perform the comparison of keys. By default, though, the keys are stored in lexical order. This is useful for providing an ordering for your hash keys, and may be used on hashes that are only in memory and never go to disk.

DB_RECNO

> DB_RECNO allows both fixed-length and variable-length flat text files to be manipulated using the same key/value pair interface as in DB_HASH and DB_BTREE. In this case the key will consist of a record (line) number.

How does DB_File interface to Berkeley DB?

DB_File gives access to Berkeley DB files using Perl's **tie** function. This allows DB_File to access Berkeley DB files using either a hash (for DB_HASH and DB_BTREE file types) or an ordinary array (for the DB_RECNO file type).

In addition to the **tie** interface, it is also possible to use most of the functions provided in the Berkeley DB API.

Differences from Berkeley DB

Berkeley DB uses the function *dbopen*(3) to open or create a database. Below is the C prototype for *dbopen*(3).

```
DB *
dbopen (const char *file, int flags, int mode,
        DBTYPE type, const void *openinfo)
```

The type parameter is an enumeration selecting one of the three interface methods, DB_HASH, DB_BTREE or DB_RECNO. Depending on which of these is actually chosen, the final parameter, openinfo, points to a data structure that allows tailoring of the specific interface method.

This interface is handled slightly differently in DB_File. Here is an equivalent call using DB_File.

```
tie %array, "DB_File", $filename, $flags, $mode, $DB_HASH;
```

The `filename`, `flags`, and `mode` parameters are the direct equivalent of their *dbopen*(3) counterparts. The final parameter `$DB_HASH` performs the function of both the `type` and `openinfo` parameters in *dbopen*(3).

In the example above `$DB_HASH` is actually a reference to a hash object. DB_File has three of these predefined references. Apart from `$DB_HASH`, there are also `$DB_BTREE` and `$DB_RECNO`.

The keys allowed in each of these predefined references are limited to the names used in the equivalent C structure. So, for example, the `$DB_HASH` reference will only allow keys called `bsize`, `cachesize`, `ffactor`, `hash`, `lorder`, and `nelem`.

To change one of these elements, just assign to it like this:

```
$DB_HASH->{cachesize} = 10_000;
```

Array offsets

In order to make `RECNO` more compatible with Perl, the array offset for all `RECNO` arrays begins at 0 rather than 1 as in Berkeley DB.

In-memory databases

Berkeley DB allows the creation of in-memory databases by using `NULL` (that is, a (char *)0 in C) in place of the filename. `DB_File` uses **undef** instead of `NULL` to provide this functionality.

```
use strict;
use Fcntl;
use DB_File;

my ($k, $v, %hash);

tie(%hash, 'DB_File', undef, O_RDWR|O_CREAT, 0, $DB_BTREE)
    or die "can't tie DB_File: $!":

foreach $k (keys %ENV) {
    $hash{$k} = $ENV{$k};
}

# this will now come out in sorted lexical order
# without the overhead of sorting the keys
while  (($k,$v) = each %hash) {
    print "$k=$v\n";
}
```

Using the Berkeley DB interface directly

In addition to accessing Berkeley DB using a tied hash or array, you can also make direct use of most functions defined in the Berkeley DB documentation.

To do this you need to remember the return value from **tie**, or use the **tied** function to get at it yourself later on.

```
$db = tie %hash, "DB_File", "filename";
```

Once you have done that, you can access the Berkeley DB API functions directly.

```
$db->put($key, $value, R_NOOVERWRITE);  # invoke the DB "put" function
```

All the functions defined in the *dbopen*(3) manpage are available except for `close()` and `dbopen()` itself. The DB_File interface to these functions mirrors the way Berkeley DB works. In particular, note that all these functions return only a status value. Whenever a Berkeley DB function returns data via one of its parameters, the DB_File equivalent does exactly the same thing.

All the constants defined in the *dbopen* manpage are also available.

Below is a list of the functions available. (The comments only tell you the differences from the C version.)

get

> The $flags parameter is optional. The value associated with the key you request is returned in the $value parameter.

put

> As usual the flags parameter is optional. If you use either the R_IAFTER or R_IBEFORE flags, the $key parameter will be set to the record number of the inserted key/value pair.

del

> The $flags parameter is optional.

fd

> No differences encountered.

seq

> The $flags parameter is optional. Both the $key and $value parameters will be set.

sync

> The $flags parameter is optional.

Examples

Here are a few examples. First, using $DB_HASH:

```
use DB_File;
use Fcntl;

tie %h,  "DB_File", "hashed", O_RDWR|O_CREAT, 0644, $DB_HASH;

# Add a key/value pair to the file
$h{apple} = "orange";

# Check for value of a key
print "No, we have some bananas.\n" if $h{banana};

# Delete
delete $h{"apple"};
untie %h;
```

Here is an example using $DB_BTREE. Just to make life more interesting, the default comparison function is not used. Instead, a Perl subroutine, Compare(), does a case-insensitive comparison.

```
use DB_File;
use Fcntl;

sub Compare {
    my ($key1, $key2) = @_;
    "\L$key1" cmp "\L$key2";
}

$DB_BTREE->{compare} = 'Compare';
tie %h,  'DB_File', "tree", O_RDWR|O_CREAT, 0644, $DB_BTREE;

# Add a key/value pair to the file
$h{Wall}  = 'Larry';
$h{Smith} = 'John';
$h{mouse} = 'mickey';
$h{duck}  = 'donald';

# Delete
delete $h{duck};

# Cycle through the keys printing them in order.
# Note it is not necessary to sort the keys as
# the btree will have kept them in order automatically.
while ($key = each %h) { print "$key\n" }

untie %h;
```

The preceding code yields this output:

```
mouse
Smith
Wall
```

Next, an example using $DB_RECNO. You may access a regular textfile as an array of lines. But the first line of the text file is the zeroth element of the array, and so on. This provides a clean way to seek to a particular line in a text file.

```
my(@line, $number);
$number = 10;
use Fcntl;
use DB_File;
tie(@line, "DB_File", "/tmp/text", O_RDWR|O_CREAT, 0644, $DB_RECNO)
    or die "can't tie file: $!";
$line[$number - 1] = "this is a new line $number";
```

Here's an example of updating a file in place:

```
use Fcntl;
use DB_File;
tie(@file, 'DB_File', "/tmp/sample", O_RDWR, 0644, $DB_RECNO)
    or die "can't update /tmp/sample: $!";
print "line #3 was ", $file[2], "\n";
$file[2] = `date`;
untie @file;
```

Note that the tied array interface is incomplete, causing some operations on the resulting array to fail in strange ways. See the discussion of tied arrays in Chapter 5. Some object methods are provided to avoid this. Here's an example of reading a file backward:

```
use DB_File;
use Fcntl;
$H = tie(@h, "DB_File", $file, O_RDWR, 0640, $DB_RECNO)
        or die "Cannot open file $file: $!\n";
# print the records in reverse order
for ($i = $H->length - 1; $i >= 0; --$i) {
    print "$i: $h[$i]\n";
}
untie @h;
```

Locking databases

Concurrent access of a read-write database by several parties requires that each use some kind of locking. Here's an example that uses the fd() method to get the file descriptor, and then a careful **open** to give something Perl will **flock** for you. Run this repeatedly in the background to watch the locks granted in proper order. You have to call the sync() method to ensure that the writes make it to disk between access, or else the library would normally hold some in its own cache.

```perl
use Fcntl;
use DB_File;

use strict;

sub LOCK_SH { 1 }
sub LOCK_EX { 2 }
sub LOCK_NB { 4 }
sub LOCK_UN { 8 }

my($oldval, $fd, $db_obj, %db_hash, $value, $key);

$key   = shift || 'default';
$value = shift || 'magic';

$value .= " $$";

$db_obj = tie(%db_hash, 'DB_File', '/tmp/foo.db', O_CREAT|O_RDWR, 0644)
                    or die "dbcreat /tmp/foo.db $!";
$fd = $db_obj->fd;
print "$$: db fd is $fd\n";
open(DB_FH, "+<&=$fd") or die "fdopen $!";

unless (flock (DB_FH, LOCK_SH | LOCK_NB)) {
    print "$$: CONTENTION; can't read during write update!
                Waiting for read lock ($!) ....";
    unless (flock (DB_FH, LOCK_SH)) { die "flock: $!" }
}
print "$$: Read lock granted\n";

$oldval = $db_hash{$key};
print "$$: Old value was $oldval\n";
flock(DB_FH, LOCK_UN);

unless (flock (DB_FH, LOCK_EX | LOCK_NB)) {
    print "$$: CONTENTION; must have exclusive lock!
                Waiting for write lock ($!) ....";
    unless (flock (DB_FH, LOCK_EX)) { die "flock: $!" }
}

print "$$: Write lock granted\n";
$db_hash{$key} = $value;
sleep 10;

$db_obj->sync();                 # to flush
flock(DB_FH, LOCK_UN);
undef $db_obj;                   # removing the last reference to the DB
                                 # closes it. Closing DB_FH is implicit.
untie %db_hash;
print "$$: Updated db to $key=$value\n";
```

See also

Related manpages: *dbopen*(3), *hash*(3), *recno*(3), *btree*(3).

Berkeley DB is available from these locations:

* *ftp://ftp.cs.berkeley.edu/ucb/4bsd/db.1.85.tar.gz*

* *http://www.perl.com/CPAN/src/misc/db.1.85.tar.gz*

Devel::SelfStubber — Generate Stubs for a SelfLoading Module

```
use Devel::SelfStubber;

$modulename = "Mystuff::Grok";   # no .pm suffix or slashes
$lib_dir = "";                   # defaults to current directory
Devel::SelfStubber->stub($modulename, $lib_dir);   # stubs only

# to generate the whole module with stubs inserted correctly
use Devel::SelfStubber;
$Devel::SelfStubber::JUST_STUBS = 0;
Devel::SelfStubber->stub($modulename, $lib_dir);
```

Devel::SelfStubber supports inherited, autoloaded methods by printing the stubs you need to put in your module before the __DATA__ token. A subroutine stub looks like this:

```
sub moo;
```

The stub ensures that if a method is called, it will get loaded. This is best explained using the following example:

Assume four classes, A, B, C, and D. A is the root class, B is a subclass of A, C is a subclass of B, and D is another subclass of A.

If D calls an autoloaded method moo() which is defined in class A, then the method is loaded into class A, and executed. If C then calls method moo(), and that method was reimplemented in class B, but set to be autoloaded, then the lookup mechanism never gets to the AUTOLOAD mechanism in B because it first finds the moo() method already loaded in A, and so erroneously uses that. If the method moo() had been stubbed in B, then the lookup mechanism would have found the stub, and correctly loaded and used the subroutine from B.

So, to get autoloading to work right with classes and subclasses, you need to make sure the stubs are loaded.

The SelfLoader can load stubs automatically at module initialization with:

```
SelfLoader->load_stubs();
```

But you may wish to avoid having the stub-loading overhead associated with your initialization.[*] In this case, you can put the subroutine stubs before the __DATA__ token. This can be done manually, by inserting the output of the first call to the stub() method above. But the module also allows automatic insertion of the stubs. By default the stub() method just prints the stubs, but you can set the global $Devel::SelfStubber::JUST_STUBS to 0 and it will print out the entire module with the stubs positioned correctly, as in the second call to stub().

At the very least, this module is useful for seeing what the SelfLoader thinks are stubs; in order to ensure that future versions of the SelfStubber remain in step with the SelfLoader, the SelfStubber actually uses the SelfLoader to determine which stubs are needed.

diagnostics — Force Verbose Warning Diagnostics

```
# As a pragma:
use diagnostics;
use diagnostics -verbose;

enable  diagnostics;
disable diagnostics;

# As a program:
$ perl program 2>diag.out
$ splain [-v] [-p] diag.out
```

The diagnostics module extends the terse diagnostics normally emitted by both the Perl compiler and the Perl interpreter, augmenting them with the more explicative and endearing descriptions found in Chapter 9, *Diagnostic Messages*. It affects the compilation phase of your program rather than merely the execution phase.

To use in your program as a pragma, merely say:

```
use diagnostics;
```

at the start (or near the start) of your program. (Note that this enables Perl's -w flag.) Your whole compilation will then be subject to the enhanced diagnostics. These are still issued to STDERR.

---

[*] Although note that the load_stubs() method will be called sooner or later, at latest when the first subroutine is being autoloaded—which may be too late, if you're trying to moo().

Due to the interaction between run-time and compile-time issues, and because it's probably not a very good idea anyway, you may *not* use:

```
no diagnostics
```

to turn diagnostics off at compile time. However, you can turn diagnostics on or off at run-time by invoking diagnostics::enable() and diagnostics::disable(), respectively.

The -verbose argument first prints out the *perldiag*(1) manpage introduction before any other diagnostics. The $diagnostics::PRETTY variable, if set in a BEGIN block, results in nicer escape sequences for pagers:

```
BEGIN { $diagnostics::PRETTY = 1 }
```

The standalone program

While apparently a whole other program, *splain* is actually nothing more than a link to the (executable) *diagnostics.pm* module. It acts upon the standard error output of a Perl program, which you may have treasured up in a file, or piped directly to *splain*.

The –v flag has the same effect as:

```
use diagnostics -verbose
```

The –p flag sets $diagnostics::PRETTY to true. Since you're post-processing with *splain*, there's no sense in being able to enable() or disable() diagnostics.

Output from *splain* (unlike the pragma) is directed to STDOUT.

Examples

The following file is certain to trigger a few errors at both run-time and compile-time:

```
use diagnostics;
print NOWHERE "nothing\n";
print STDERR "\n\tThis message should be unadorned.\n";
warn "\tThis is a user warning";
print "\nDIAGNOSTIC TESTER: Please enter a <CR> here: ";
my $a, $b = scalar <STDIN>;
print "\n";
print $x/$y;
```

If you prefer to run your program first and look at its problems afterward, do this while talking to a Bourne-like shell:

```
perl -w test.pl 2>test.out
./splain < test.out
```

If you don't want to modify your source code, but still want on-the-fly warnings, do this:

```
perl -w -Mdiagnostics test.pl
```

If you want to control warnings on the fly, do something like this. (Make sure the **use** comes first, or you won't be able to get at the **enable()** or **disable()** methods.)

```
use diagnostics; # checks entire compilation phase
print "\ntime for 1st bogus diags: SQUAWKINGS\n";
print BOGUS1 'nada';
print "done with 1st bogus\n";

disable diagnostics; # only turns off run-time warnings
print "\ntime for 2nd bogus: (squelched)\n";
print BOGUS2 'nada';
print "done with 2nd bogus\n";

enable diagnostics; # turns back on run-time warnings
print "\ntime for 3rd bogus: SQUAWKINGS\n";
print BOGUS3 'nada';
print "done with 3rd bogus\n";

disable diagnostics;
print "\ntime for 4th bogus: (squelched)\n";
print BOGUS4 'nada';
print "done with 4th bogus\n";
```

DirHandle — Supply Object Methods for Directory Handles

```
use DirHandle;

my $d = new DirHandle ".";    # open the current directory
if (defined $d) {
    while (defined($_ = $d->read)) { something($_); }
    $d->rewind;
    while (defined($_ = $d->read)) { something_else($_); }
}
```

DirHandle provides an alternative interface to Perl's **opendir**, **closedir**, **readdir**, and **rewinddir** functions.

The only objective benefit to using DirHandle is that it avoids name-space pollution by creating anonymous globs to hold directory handles. Well, and it also closes the DirHandle automatically when the last reference goes out of scope. But since most people only keep a directory handle open long enough to slurp in all the filenames, this is of dubious value. But hey, it's object-oriented.

DynaLoader — Automatic Dynamic Loading of Perl Modules

```
package YourModule;
require DynaLoader;
@ISA = qw(... DynaLoader ...);

bootstrap YourModule;
```

This module defines the standard Perl interface to the dynamic linking mechanisms available on many platforms. A common theme throughout the module system is that *using* a module should be easy, even if the module itself (or the installation of the module) is more complicated as a result. This applies particularly to the DynaLoader. To use it in your own module, all you need are the incantations listed above in the synopsis. This will work whether YourModule is statically or dynamically linked into Perl. (This is a *Configure* option for each module.) The `bootstrap()` method will either call YourModule's bootstrap routine directly if YourModule is statically linked into Perl, or if not, YourModule will inherit the `bootstrap()` method from DynaLoader, which will do everything necessary to load in your module, and then call YourModule's `bootstrap()` method for you, as if it were there all the time and you called it yourself. Piece of cake, of the have-it-and-eat-it-too variety.

The rest of this description talks about the DynaLoader from the viewpoint of someone who wants to extend the DynaLoader module to a new architecture. The *Configure* process selects which kind of dynamic loading to use by choosing to link in one of several C implementations, which must be linked into *perl* statically. (This is unlike other C extensions, which provide a single implementation, which may be linked in either statically or dynamically.)

The DynaLoader is designed to be a very simple, high-level interface that is sufficiently general to cover the requirements of SunOS, HP-UX, NeXT, Linux, VMS, Win-32, and other platforms. By itself, though, DynaLoader is practically useless for accessing non-Perl libraries because it provides almost no Perl-to-C "glue". There is, for example, no mechanism for calling a C library function or supplying its arguments in any sort of portable form. This job is delegated to the other extension modules that you may load in by using DynaLoader.

Internal interface summary

```
Variables:
    @dl_library_path
    @dl_resolve_using
    @dl_require_symbols
    $dl_debug
```

```
Subroutines:
   bootstrap($modulename);
   @filepaths = dl_findfile(@names);
   $filepath = dl_expandspec($spec);
   $libref   = dl_load_file($filename);
   $symref   = dl_find_symbol($libref, $symbol);
   @symbols  = dl_undef_symbols();
   dl_install_xsub($name, $symref [, $filename]);
   $message = dl_error;
```

The `bootstrap()` and `dl_findfile()` routines are standard across all platforms, and so are defined in *DynaLoader.pm*. The rest of the functions are supplied by the particular *.xs* file that supplies the implementation for the platform. (You can examine the existing implementations in the *ext/DynaLoader/*.xs* files in the Perl source directory. You should also read *DynaLoader.pm*, of course.) These implementations may also tweak the default values of the variables listed below.

@dl_library_path

The default list of directories in which `dl_findfile()` will search for libraries. Directories are searched in the order they are given in this array variable, beginning with subscript 0. `@dl_library_path` is initialized to hold the list of "normal" directories (*/usr/lib* and so on) determined by the Perl installation script, *Configure*, and given by `$Config{'libpth'}`. This is to ensure portability across a wide range of platforms. `@dl_library_path` should also be initialized with any other directories that can be determined from the environment at run-time (such as `LD_LIBRARY_PATH` for SunOS). After initialization, `@dl_library_path` can be manipulated by an application using **push** and **unshift** before calling `dl_findfile()`. **unshift** can be used to add directories to the front of the search order either to save search time or to override standard libraries with the same name. The load function that `dl_load_file()` calls might require an absolute pathname. The `dl_findfile()` function and `@dl_library_path` can be used to search for and return the absolute pathname for the library/object that you wish to load.

@dl_resolve_using

A list of additional libraries or other shared objects that can be used to resolve any undefined symbols that might be generated by a later call to `dl_load_file()`. This is only required on some platforms that do not handle dependent libraries automatically. For example, the Socket extension shared library (*auto/Socket/Socket.so*) contains references to many socket functions that need to be resolved when it's loaded. Most platforms will automatically know where to find the "dependent" library (for example, */usr/lib/libsocket.so*).

A few platforms need to be told the location of the dependent library explicitly. Use `@dl_resolve_using` for this. Example:

```
@dl_resolve_using = dl_findfile('-lsocket');
```

`@dl_require_symbols`

A list of one or more symbol names that are in the library/object file to be dynamically loaded. This is only required on some platforms.

`dl_error`

```
$message = dl_error();
```

Error message text from the last failed DynaLoader function. Note that, similar to errno in UNIX, a successful function call does not reset this message. Implementations should detect the error as soon as it occurs in any of the other functions and save the corresponding message for later retrieval. This will avoid problems on some platforms (such as SunOS) where the error message is very temporary (see, for example, *dlerror*(3)).

`$dl_debug`

Internal debugging messages are enabled when `$dl_debug` is set true. Currently, setting `$dl_debug` only affects the Perl side of the DynaLoader. These messages should help an application developer to resolve any DynaLoader usage problems. `$dl_debug` is set to `$ENV{'PERL_DL_DEBUG'}` if defined. For the DynaLoader developer and porter there is a similar debugging variable added to the C code (see *dlutils.c*) and enabled if Perl was built with the -DDEBUGGING flag. This can also be set via the PERL_DL_DEBUG environment variable. Set to 1 for minimal information or higher for more.

`dl_findfile`

```
@filepaths = dl_findfile(@names)
```

Determines the full paths (including file suffix) of one or more loadable files, given their generic names and optionally one or more directories. Searches directories in `@dl_library_path` by default and returns an empty list if no files were found. Names can be specified in a variety of platform-independent forms. Any names in the form -lname are converted into *libname.**, where .* is an appropriate suffix for the platform. If a name does not already have a suitable prefix or suffix, then the corresponding file will be sought by trying prefix and suffix combinations appropriate to the platform: *$name.o*, *lib$name.** and *$name*. If any directories are included in `@names`, they are searched before `@dl_library_path`. Directories may be specified as -Ldir. Any other names are treated as filenames to be searched for. Using arguments of the form `-Ldir` and `-lname` is recommended. Example:

```
@dl_resolve_using = dl_findfile(qw(-L/usr/5lib -lposix));
```

dl_expandspec

```
$filepath = dl_expandspec($spec)
```

Some unusual systems such as VMS require special filename handling in order to deal with symbolic names for files (that is, VMS's Logical Names). To support these systems a `dl_expandspec()` function can be implemented either in the *dl_*.xs* file or code can be added to the autoloadable `dl_expandspec()` function in *DynaLoader.pm.*

dl_load_file

```
$libref = dl_load_file($filename)
```

Dynamically load `$filename`, which must be the path to a shared object or library. An opaque "library reference" is returned as a handle for the loaded object. `dl_load_file()` returns the undefined value on error. (On systems that provide a handle for the loaded object such as SunOS and HP-UX, the returned handle will be `$libref`. On other systems `$libref` will typically be `$filename` or a pointer to a buffer containing `$filename`. The application should not examine or alter `$libref` in any way.) Below are some of the functions that do the real work. Such functions should use the current values of `@dl_require_symbols` and `@dl_resolve_using` if required.

```
SunOS:   dlopen($filename)
HP-UX:   shl_load($filename)
Linux:   dld_create_reference(@dl_require_symbols); dld_link($filename)
NeXT:    rld_load($filename, @dl_resolve_using)
VMS:     lib$find_image_symbol($filename, $dl_require_symbols[0])
```

dl_find_symbol

```
$symref = dl_find_symbol($libref, $symbol)
```

Returns the address of the symbol `$symbol`, or the undefined value if not found. If the target system has separate functions to search for symbols of different types, then `dl_find_symbol()` should search for function symbols first and then search for other types. The exact manner in which the address is returned in `$symref` is not currently defined. The only initial requirement is that `$symref` can be passed to, and understood by, `dl_install_xsub()`. Here are some current implementations:

```
SunOS:   dlsym($libref, $symbol)
HP-UX:   shl_findsym($libref, $symbol)
Linux:   dld_get_func($symbol) and/or dld_get_symbol($symbol)
```

```
NeXT:    rld_lookup("_$symbol")
VMS:     lib$find_image_symbol($libref, $symbol)
```

dl_undef_symbols

```
@symbols = dl_undef_symbols()
```

Returns a list of symbol names which remain undefined after `dl_load_file()`.
It returns `()` if these names are not known. Don't worry if your platform does
not provide a mechanism for this. Most platforms do not need it and hence do
not provide it; they just return an empty list.

dl_install_xsub

```
dl_install_xsub($perl_name, $symref [, $filename])
```

Creates a new Perl external subroutine named `$perl_name` using `$symref` as a
pointer to the function that implements the routine. This is simply a direct call
to `newXSUB()`. It returns a reference to the installed function. The `$filename`
parameter is used by Perl to identify the source file for the function if required
by **die**, **caller**, or the debugger. If `$filename` is not defined, then *DynaLoader*
will be used.

bootstrap()

```
bootstrap($module);
```

This is the normal entry point for automatic dynamic loading in Perl.

It performs the following actions:

- Locates an *auto/$module* directory by searching `@INC`

- Uses `dl_findfile()` to determine the filename to load

- Sets `@dl_require_symbols` to `("boot_$module")`

- Executes an *auto/$module/$module.bs* file if it exists (typically used to
  add to `@dl_resolve_using` any files that are required to load the module
  on the current platform)

- Calls `dl_load_file()` to load the file

- Calls `dl_undef_symbols()` and warns if any symbols are undefined

- Calls `dl_find_symbol()` for "boot_$module"

- Calls `dl_install_xsub()` to install it as `${module}::bootstrap`

- Calls `&{"${module}::bootstrap"}` to bootstrap the module (actually it uses
  the function reference returned by `dl_install_xsub()` for speed)

English — Use English or awk Names for Punctuation Variables

```
use English;
...
if ($ERRNO =~ /denied/) { ... }
```

This module provides aliases for the built-in "punctuation" variables. Variables with side effects that get triggered merely by accessing them (like $0) will still have the same effects under the aliases.

For those variables that have an *awk*(1) version, both long and short English alternatives are provided. For example, the $/ variable can be referred to either as $RS or as $INPUT_RECORD_SEPARATOR if you are using the English module.

Here is the list of variables along with their English alternatives:

Perl	English	Perl	English
@_	@ARG	$?	$CHILD_ERROR
$_	$ARG	$!	$OS_ERROR
$&	$MATCH	$!	$ERRNO
$`	$PREMATCH	$@	$EVAL_ERROR
$'	$POSTMATCH	$$	$PROCESS_ID
$+	$LAST_PAREN_MATCH	$$	$PID
$.	$INPUT_LINE_NUMBER	$<	$REAL_USER_ID
$.	$NR	$<	$UID
$/	$INPUT_RECORD_SEPARATOR	$>	$EFFECTIVE_USER_ID
$/	$RS	$>	$EUID
$|	$OUTPUT_AUTOFLUSH	$(	$REAL_GROUP_ID
$,	$OUTPUT_FIELD_SEPARATOR	$(	$GID
$,	$OFS	$)	$EFFECTIVE_GROUP_ID
$\	$OUTPUT_RECORD_SEPARATOR	$)	$EGID
$\	$ORS	$0	$PROGRAM_NAME
$"	$LIST_SEPARATOR	$]	$PERL_VERSION
$;	$SUBSCRIPT_SEPARATOR	$^A	$ACCUMULATOR
$;	$SUBSEP	$^D	$DEBUGGING
$%	$FORMAT_PAGE_NUMBER	$^F	$SYSTEM_FD_MAX
$=	$FORMAT_LINES_PER_PAGE	$^I	$INPLACE_EDIT
$-	$FORMAT_LINES_LEFT	$^P	$PERLDB
$~	$FORMAT_NAME	$^T	$BASETIME
$^	$FORMAT_TOP_NAME	$^W	$WARNING
$:	$FORMAT_LINE_BREAK_CHARACTERS	$^X	$EXECUTABLE_NAME
$^L	$FORMAT_LINEFEED	$^O	$OSNAME

Env — Import Environment Variables

```
use Env;                    # import all possible variables
use Env qw(PATH HOME TERM);  # import only specified variables
```

Perl maintains environment variables in a pseudo-associative array named %ENV. Since this access method is sometimes inconvenient, the Env module allows environment variables to be treated as simple variables.

The Env::import() routine ties environment variables to global Perl variables with the same names. By default it ties suitable, existing environment variables (that is, variables yielded by keys %ENV). An environmental variable is considered suitable if its name begins with an alphabetic character, and if it consists of nothing but alphanumeric characters plus underscore.

If you supply arguments when invoking use Env, they are taken to be a list of environment variables to tie. It's OK if the variables don't yet exist.

After an environment variable is tied, you can use it like a normal variable. You may access its value:

```
@path = split(/:/, $PATH);
```

or modify it any way you like:

```
$PATH .= ":.";
```

To remove a tied environment variable from the environment, make it the undefined value:

```
undef $PATH;
```

Note that the corresponding operation performed directly against %ENV is not **undef**, but **delete**:

```
delete $ENV{PATH};
```

Exporter — Default Import Method for Modules

```
# in module YourModule.pm:
package YourModule;
use Exporter ();
@ISA = qw(Exporter);

@EXPORT = qw(...);            # Symbols to export by default.
@EXPORT_OK = qw(...);         # Symbols to export on request.
%EXPORT_TAGS = (tag => [...]); # Define names for sets of symbols.

# in other files that wish to use YourModule:
use YourModule;               # Import default symbols into my package.
use YourModule qw(...);       # Import listed symbols into my package.
use YourModule ();            # Do not import any symbols!
```

Any module may define a class method called import(). Perl automatically calls a module's import() method when processing the **use** statement for the module. The module itself doesn't have to define the import() method, though. The Exporter module implements a default import() method that many modules choose to inherit instead. The Exporter module supplies the customary import semantics, and any other import() methods will tend to deviate from the normal import semantics in various (hopefully documented) ways. Now we'll talk about the normal import semantics.

Specialized import lists

Ignoring the class name, which is always the first argument to a class method, the arguments that are passed into the import() method are known as an *import list*. Usually the import list is nothing more than a list of subroutine or variable names, but occasionally you may want to get fancy. If the first entry in an import list begins with !, :, or /, the list is treated as a series of specifications that either add to or delete from the list of names to import. They are processed left to right. Specifications are in the form:

Symbol	Meaning
[!]*name*	This *name* only
[!]:DEFAULT	All names in @EXPORT
[!]:*tag*	All names in $EXPORT_TAGS{*tag*} anonymous list
[!]/*pattern*/	All names in @EXPORT and @EXPORT_OK that match *pattern*

A leading ! indicates that matching names should be deleted from the list of names to import. If the first specification is a deletion, it is treated as though preceded by :DEFAULT. If you just want to import extra names in addition to the default set, you will still need to include :DEFAULT explicitly.

For example, suppose that *YourModule.pm* says:

```
@EXPORT      = qw(A1 A2 A3 A4 A5);
@EXPORT_OK   = qw(B1 B2 B3 B4 B5);
%EXPORT_TAGS = (
    T1 => [qw(A1 A2 B1 B2)],
    T2 => [qw(A1 A2 B3 B4)]
);
```

Individual names in EXPORT_TAGS must also appear in @EXPORT or @EXPORT_OK. Note that you cannot use the tags directly within either @EXPORT or @EXPORT_OK (though you could preprocess tags into either of those arrays, and in fact, the export_tags() and export_ok_tags() functions below do precisely that).

An application using YourModule can then say something like this:

```
use YourModule qw(:DEFAULT :T2 !B3 A3);
```

The :DEFAULT adds in A1, A2, A3, A4, and A5. The :T2 adds in only B3 and B4, since A1 and A2 were already added. The !B3 then deletes B3, and the A3 does nothing because A3 was already included. Other examples include:

```
use Socket qw(!/^[AP]F_/ !SOMAXCONN !SOL_SOCKET);
use POSIX  qw(:errno_h :termios_h !TCSADRAIN !/^EXIT/);
```

Remember that most patterns (using //) will need to be anchored with a leading ^, for example, /^EXIT/ rather than /EXIT/.

You can say:

```
BEGIN { $Exporter::Verbose=1 }
```

in order to see how the specifications are being processed and what is actually being imported into modules.

Module version checking

The Exporter module will convert an attempt to import a number from a module into a call to $module_name->require_version($value). This can be used to validate that the version of the module being used is greater than or equal to the required version. The Exporter module also supplies a default require_version() method, which checks the value of $VERSION in the exporting module.

Since the default require_version() method treats the $VERSION number as a simple numeric value, it will regard version 1.10 as lower than 1.9. For this reason it is strongly recommended that the module developer use numbers with at least two decimal places; for example, 1.09.

Prior to release 5.004 or so of Perl, this only worked with modules that use the Exporter module; in particular, this means that you can't check the version of a class module that doesn't require the Exporter module.

Managing unknown symbols

In some situations you may want to prevent certain symbols from being exported. Typically this applies to extensions with functions or constants that may not exist on some systems.

The names of any symbols that cannot be exported should be listed in the @EXPORT_FAIL array.

If a module attempts to import any of these symbols, the Exporter will give the module an opportunity to handle the situation before generating an error. The Exporter will call an export_fail() method with a list of the failed symbols:

```
@failed_symbols = $module_name->export_fail(@failed_symbols);
```

If the export_fail() method returns an empty list, then no error is recorded and all requested symbols are exported. If the returned list is not empty, then an error is generated for each symbol and the export fails. The Exporter provides a default export_fail() method that simply returns the list unchanged.

Uses for the export_fail() method include giving better error messages for some symbols and performing lazy architectural checks. Put more symbols into @EXPORT_FAIL by default and then take them out if someone actually tries to use them and an expensive check shows that they are usable on that platform.

Tag handling utility functions

Since the symbols listed within %EXPORT_TAGS must also appear in either @EXPORT or @EXPORT_OK, two utility functions are provided that allow you to easily add tagged sets of symbols to @EXPORT or @EXPORT_OK:

```
%EXPORT_TAGS = (Bactrian => [qw(aa bb cc)], Dromedary => [qw(aa cc dd)]);

Exporter::export_tags('Bactrian');       # add aa, bb and cc to @EXPORT
Exporter::export_ok_tags('Dromedary'); # add aa, cc and dd to @EXPORT_OK
```

Any names that are not tags are added to @EXPORT or @EXPORT_OK unchanged, but will trigger a warning (with -w) to avoid misspelt tag names being silently added to @EXPORT or @EXPORT_OK. Future versions may regard this as a fatal error.

ExtUtils::Install — Install Files from Here to There

```
use ExtUtils::Install;
install($hashref, $verbose, $nonono);
uninstall($packlistfile, $verbose, $nonono);
```

install() and uninstall() are specific to the way ExtUtils::MakeMaker handles the platform-dependent installation and deinstallation of Perl extensions. They are not designed as general-purpose tools. If you're reading this chapter straight through (brave soul), you probably want to take a glance at the MakeMaker entry first. (Or just skip over everything in the ExtUtils package until you start writing an Ext.)

install() takes three arguments: a reference to a hash, a verbose switch, and a don't-really-do-it switch. The hash reference contains a mapping of directories;

each key/value pair is a combination of directories to be copied. The key is a directory to copy from, and the value is a directory to copy to. The whole tree below the "from" directory will be copied, preserving timestamps and permissions.

There are two keys with a special meaning in the hash: `"read"` and `"write"`. After the copying is done, install will write the list of target files to the file named by `$hashref->{write}`. If there is another file named by `$hashref->{read}`, the contents of this file will be merged into the written file. The read and the written file may be identical, but on the Andrew File System (AFS) it is fairly likely that people are installing to a different directory than the one where the files later appear.

`uninstall()` takes as first argument a file containing filenames to be unlinked. The second argument is a verbose switch, the third is a no-don't-really-do-it-now switch (useful to know what will happen without actually doing it).

ExtUtils::Liblist — Determine Libraries to Use and How to Use Them

```
require ExtUtils::Liblist;
ExtUtils::Liblist::ext($potential_libs, $Verbose);
```

This utility takes a list of libraries in the form -llib1 -llib2 -llib3 and returns lines suitable for inclusion in a Perl extension *Makefile* on the current platform. Extra library paths may be included with the form -L/another/path. This will affect the searches for all subsequent libraries.

`ExtUtils::Liblist::ext()` returns a list of four scalar values, which Makemaker will eventually use in constructing a *Makefile*, among other things. The values are:

EXTRALIBS

List of libraries that need to be linked with *ld*(1) when linking a Perl binary that includes a static extension. Only those libraries that actually exist are included.

LDLOADLIBS

List of those libraries that can or must be linked when creating a shared library using *ld*(1). These may be static or dynamic libraries.

LD_RUN_PATH

A colon-separated list of the directories in LDLOADLIBS. It is passed as an environment variable to the process that links the shared library.

BSLOADLIBS

List of those libraries that are needed but can be linked in dynamically with the DynaLoader at run-time on this platform. This list is used to create a *.bs* (bootstrap) file. SunOS/Solaris does not need this because *ld*(1) records the information (from LDLOADLIBS) into the object file.

Portability

This module deals with a lot of system dependencies and has quite a few architecture-specific ifs in the code.

ExtUtils::MakeMaker — Create a Makefile for a Perl Extension

```
use ExtUtils::MakeMaker;
WriteMakefile( ATTRIBUTE => VALUE, ... );

# which internally is really more like...
%att = (ATTRIBUTE => VALUE, ...);
MM->new(\%att)->flush;
```

When you build an extension to Perl, you need to have an appropriate *Makefile*[*] in the extension's source directory. And while you could conceivably write one by hand, this would be rather tedious. So you'd like a program to write it for you.

Originally, this was done using a shell script (actually, one for each extension) called *Makefile.SH*, much like the one that writes the *Makefile* for Perl itself. But somewhere along the line, it occurred to the perl5-porters that, by the time you want to compile your extensions, there's already a bare-bones version of the Perl executable called *miniperl*, if not a fully installed *perl*. And for some strange reason, Perl programmers prefer programming in Perl to programming in shell. So they wrote MakeMaker, just so that you can write *Makefile.PL* instead of *Makefile.SH*.

MakeMaker isn't a program; it's a module (or it wouldn't be in this chapter). The module provides the routines you need; you just need to **use** the module, and then call the routines. As with any programming job, there are many degrees of freedom; but your typical *Makefile.PL* is pretty simple. For example, here's *ext/POSIX/Makefile.PL* from the Perl distribution's POSIX extension (which is by no means a trivial extension):

```
use ExtUtils::MakeMaker;
WriteMakefile(
    NAME         => 'POSIX',
    LIBS         => ["-lm -lposix -lcposix"],
    MAN3PODS     => ' ',     # Pods will be built by installman.
    XSPROTOARG   => '-noprototypes',     # XXX remove later?
    VERSION_FROM => 'POSIX.pm',
);
```

---

[*] If you don't know what a *Makefile* is, or what the *make*(1) program does with one, you *really* shouldn't be reading this section. We will be assuming that you know what happens when you type a command like `make foo`.

Several things are apparent from this example, but the most important is that the WriteMakefile() function uses named parameters. This means that you can pass many potential parameters, but you're only required to pass the ones you want to be different from the default values. (And when we say "many", we mean "many"—there are about 75 of them. See the Attributes section later.)

As the synopsis above indicates, the WriteMakefile() function actually constructs an object. This object has attributes that are set from various sources, including the parameters you pass to the function. It's this object that actually writes your *Makefile*, meshing together the demands of your extension with the demands of the architecture on which the extension is being installed. Like many craftily crafted objects, this MakeMaker object delegates as much of its work as possible to various other subroutines and methods. Many of these may be overridden in your *Makefile.PL* if you need to do some fine tuning. (Generally you don't.)

But let's not lose track of the goal, which is to write a *Makefile* that will know how to do anything to your extension that needs doing. Now as you can imagine, the *Makefile* that MakeMaker writes is quite, er, full-featured. It's easy to get lost in all the details. If you look at the POSIX *Makefile* generated by the bit of code above, you will find a file containing about 122 macros and 77 targets. You will want to go off into a corner and curl up into a little ball, saying, "Never mind, I didn't really want to know."

Well, the fact of the matter is, you really *don't* want to know, nor do you have to. Most of these items take care of themselves—that's what MakeMaker is there for, after all. We'll lay out the various attributes and targets for you, but you can just pick and choose, like in a cafeteria. We'll talk about the *make* targets first, because they're the actions you eventually want to perform, and then work backward to the macros and attributes that feed the targets.

But before we do that, you need to know just a few more architectural features of MakeMaker to make sense of some of the things we'll say. The targets at the end of your *Makefile* depend on the macro definitions that are interpolated into them. Those macro definitions in turn come from any of several places. Depending on how you count, there are about five sources of information for these attributes. Ordered by increasing precedence and (more or less) decreasing permanence, they are:

- Platform-specific values in Perl's Config module, provided by the *Configure* program that was run when Perl was installed on this machine.

- The WriteMakefile() function call arguments in *Makefile.Pl*, supplied by the extension writer. (You saw some of those above.)

- Platform-specific hints in the extension's *hints/* directory, also provided by extension writer. We'll talk about those later.

- Overriding values from the command line for *Makefile.PL* script, supplied by the person who runs the script. These look like KEY=VALUE.

- Overriding values from the command line for *make* itself, supplied by the person who runs the *make*. These also look like KEY=VALUE.

The first four of these turn into attributes of the object we mentioned, and are eventually written out as macro definitions in your *Makefile*. In most cases, the names of the values are consistent from beginning to end. (Except that the Config database keeps the names in lowercase, as they come from Perl's *config.sh* file. The names are translated to uppercase when they become attributes of the object.) In any case, we'll tend to use the term *attributes* to mean both attributes and the *Makefile* macros derived from them.

The *Makefile.PL* and the *hints* may also provide overriding methods for the object, if merely changing an attribute isn't good enough.

The hints files are expected to be named like their counterparts in *PERL_SRC/hints*, but with a *.pl* filename extension (for example, *next_3_2.pl*), because the file consists of Perl code to be evaluated. Apart from that, the rules governing which hintsfile is chosen are the same as in *Configure*. The hintsfile is **eval**ed within a routine that is a method of our MakeMaker object, so if you want to override or create an attribute, you would say something like:

```
$self->{LIBS} = ['-ldbm -lucb -lc'];
```

By and large, if your *Makefile* isn't doing what you want, you just trace back the name of the misbehaving attribute to its source, and either change it there or override it downstream.

Extensions may be built using the contents of either the Perl source directory tree or the installed Perl library. The recommended way is to build extensions after you have run *make install* on Perl itself. You can then build your extension in any directory on your hard disk that is not below the Perl source tree. The support for extensions below the *ext/* directory of the Perl distribution is only good for the standard extensions that come with Perl.

If an extension is being built below the *ext/* directory of the Perl source, then MakeMaker will set PERL_SRC automatically (usually to ../..). If PERL_SRC is defined and the extension is recognized as a standard extension, then other variables default to the following:

```
PERL_INC     = PERL_SRC
PERL_LIB     = PERL_SRC/lib
PERL_ARCHLIB = PERL_SRC/lib
```

```
INST_LIB    = PERL_LIB
INST_ARCHLIB = PERL_ARCHLIB
```

If an extension is being built away from the Perl source, then MakeMaker will leave PERL_SRC undefined and default to using the installed copy of the Perl library. The other variables default to the following:

```
PERL_INC    = $archlibexp/CORE
PERL_LIB    = $privlibexp
PERL_ARCHLIB = $archlibexp
INST_LIB    = ./blib/lib
INST_ARCHLIB = ./blib/arch
```

If Perl has not yet been installed, then PERL_SRC can be defined as an override on the command line.

Targets

Far and away the most commonly used *make* targets are those used by the installer to install the extension. So we aim to make the normal installation very easy:

```
perl Makefile.PL  # generate the Makefile
make              # compile the extension
make test         # test the extension
make install      # install the extension
```

This assumes that the installer has dynamic linking available. If not, a couple of additional commands are also necessary:

```
make perl         # link a new perl statically with this extension
make inst_perl    # install that new perl appropriately
```

Other interesting targets in the generated *Makefile* are:

```
make config       # check whether the Makefile is up-to-date
make clean        # delete local temp files (Makefile gets renamed)
make realclean    # delete derived files (including ./blib)
make ci           # check in all files in the MANIFEST file
make dist         # see the "Distribution Support" section below
```

Now we'll talk about some of these commands, and how each of them is related to MakeMaker. So we'll not only be talking about things that happen when you invoke the *make* target, but also about what MakeMaker has to do to generate that *make* target. So brace yourself for some temporal whiplash.

Running MakeMaker

This command is the one most closely related to MakeMaker because it's the one in which you actually run MakeMaker. No temporal whiplash here. As we mentioned earlier, some of the default attribute values may be overridden by adding arguments of the form KEY=VALUE. For example:

```
perl Makefile.PL PREFIX=/tmp/myperl5
```

To get a more detailed view of what MakeMaker is doing, say:

```
perl Makefile.PL verbose
```

Making whatever is needed

A *make* command without arguments performs any compilation needed and puts any generated files into staging directories that are named by the attributes INST_LIB, INST_ARCHLIB, INST_EXE, INST_MAN1DIR, and INST_MAN3DIR. These directories default to something below *./blib* if you are *not* building below the Perl source directory. If you *are* building below the Perl source, INST_LIB and INST_ARCHLIB default to *../../lib*, and INST_EXE is not defined.

Running tests

The goal of this command is to run any regression tests supplied with the extension, so MakeMaker checks for the existence of a file named *test.pl* in the current directory and, if it exists, adds commands to the **test** target of the *Makefile* that will execute the script with the proper set of Perl –I options (since the files haven't been installed into their final location yet).

MakeMaker also checks for any files matching glob("t/*.t"). It will add commands to the **test** target that execute all matching files via the Test::Harness module with the –I switches set correctly. If you pass TEST_VERBOSE=1, the **test** target will run the tests verbosely.

Installing files

Once the installer has tested the extension, the various generated files need to get put into their final resting places. The **install** target copies the files found below each of the INST_* directories to their INSTALL* counterparts.

INST_LIB	→	INSTALLPRIVLIB[a] or INSTALLSITELIB[b]
INST_ARCHLIB	→	INSTALLARCHLIB[a] or INSTALLSITEARCH[b]
INST_EXE	→	INSTALLBIN
INST_MAN1DIR	→	INSTALLMAN1DIR
INST_MAN3DIR	→	INSTALLMAN3DIR

[a] if INSTALLDIRS set to "perl"
[b] if INSTALLDIRS set to "site"

The INSTALL* attributes in turn default to their %Config counterparts, $Config{installprivlib}, $Config{installarchlib}, and so on.

If you don't set INSTALLARCHLIB or INSTALLSITEARCH, MakeMaker will assume you want them to be subdirectories of INSTALLPRIVLIB and INSTALLSITELIB, respectively. The exact relationship is determined by *Configure*. But you can usually just go with the defaults for all these attributes.

The PREFIX attribute can be used to redirect all the INSTALL* attributes in one go. Here's the quickest way to install a module in a nonstandard place:

```
perl Makefile.PL PREFIX=~ \
```

The value you specify for PREFIX replaces one or more leading pathname components in all INSTALL* attributes. The prefix to be replaced is determined by the value of $Config{prefix}, which typically has a value like */usr*. (Note that the tilde expansion above is done by MakeMaker, not by *perl* or *make*.)

If the user has superuser privileges and is not working under the Andrew File System (AFS) or relatives, then the defaults for INSTALLPRIVLIB, INSTALLARCHLIB, INSTALLBIN, and so on should be appropriate.

By default, *make install* writes some documentation of what has been done into the file given by $(INSTALLARCHLIB)/perllocal.pod. This feature can be bypassed by calling *make pure_install*.

If you are using AFS, you must specify the installation directories, since these most probably have changed since Perl itself was installed. Do this by issuing these commands:

```
perl Makefile.PL INSTALLSITELIB=/afs/here/today
    INSTALLBIN=/afs/there/now INSTALLMAN3DIR=/afs/for/manpages
make
```

Be careful to repeat this procedure every time you recompile an extension, unless you are sure the AFS installation directories are still valid.

Static linking of a new Perl binary

The steps above are sufficient on a system supporting dynamic loading. On systems that do not support dynamic loading, however, the extension has to be linked together statically with everything else you might want in your *perl* executable. MakeMaker supports the linking process by creating appropriate targets in the *Makefile*. If you say:

```
make perl
```

it will produce a new *perl* binary in the current directory with all extensions linked in that can be found in INST_ARCHLIB, SITELIBEXP, and PERL_ARCHLIB. To do that,

MakeMaker writes a new *Makefile*; on UNIX it is called *Makefile.aperl*, but the name may be system-dependent. When you want to force the creation of a new *perl*, we recommend that you delete this *Makefile.aperl* so the directories are searched for linkable libraries again.

The binary can be installed in the directory where Perl normally resides on your machine with:

```
make inst_perl
```

To produce a Perl binary with a different filename than *perl*, either say:

```
perl Makefile.PL MAP_TARGET=myperl
make myperl
make inst_perl
```

or say:

```
perl Makefile.PL
make myperl MAP_TARGET=myperl
make inst_perl MAP_TARGET=myperl
```

In either case, you will be asked to confirm the invocation of the inst_perl target, since this invocation is likely to overwrite your existing Perl binary in INSTALLBIN.

By default *make inst_perl* documents what has been done in the file given by $(INSTALLARCHLIB)/perllocal.pod. This behavior can be bypassed by calling *make pure_inst_perl*.

Sometimes you might want to build a statically linked Perl even though your system supports dynamic loading. In this case you may explicitly set the linktype:

```
perl Makefile.PL LINKTYPE=static
```

Attributes you can set

The following attributes can be specified as arguments to WriteMakefile() or as NAME=VALUE pairs on the command line. We give examples below in the form they would appear in your *Makefile.PL*, that is, as though passed as a named parameter to WriteMakefile() (including the comma that comes after it).

C

A reference to an array of *.c filenames. It's initialized by doing a directory scan and by derivation from the values of the xs attribute hash. This is not currently used by MakeMaker but may be handy in *Makefile.PLs*.

CONFIG

An array reference containing a list of attributes to fetch from %Config. For example:

```
CONFIG => [qw(archname manext)],
```

defines ARCHNAME and MANEXT from *config.sh*. MakeMaker will automatically add the following values to CONFIG:

ar	dlext	ldflags	ranlib
cc	dlsrc	libc	sitelibexp
cccdlflags	ld	lib_ext	sitearchexp
ccdlflags	lddlflags	obj_ext	so

CONFIGURE

A reference to a subroutine returning a hash reference. The hash may contain further attributes, for example, {LIBS => . . . }, that have to be determined by some evaluation method. Be careful, because any attributes defined this way will override hints and WriteMakefile() parameters (but not command-line arguments).

DEFINE

An attribute containing additional defines, such as -DHAVE_UNISTD_H.

DIR

A reference to an array of subdirectories containing *Makefile.PLs*. For example, SDBM_FILE has:

```
DIR => ['sdbm'],
```

MakeMaker will automatically do recursive MakeMaking if subdirectories contain *Makefile.PL* files. A separate MakeMaker class is generated for each subdirectory, so each MakeMaker object can override methods using the fake MY:: class (see below) without interfering with other MakeMaker objects. You don't even need a *Makefile.PL* in the top level directory if you pass one in via –M and –e:

```
perl -MExtUtils::MakeMaker -e 'WriteMakefile()'
```

DISTNAME

Your name for distributing the package (by *tar* file). This defaults to NAME below.

DL_FUNCS

A reference to a hash of symbol names for routines to be made available as universal symbols. Each key/value pair consists of the package name and an array of routine names in that package. This attribute is used only under AIX (export lists) and VMS (linker options) at present. The routine names supplied will be expanded in the same way as XSUB names are expanded by the XS attribute.

The default key/value pair looks like this:

```
"$PKG" => ["boot_$PKG"]
```

For a pair of packages named RPC and NetconfigPtr, you might, for example, set it to this:

```
DL_FUNCS => {
    RPC          => [qw(boot_rpcb rpcb_gettime getnetconfigent)],
    NetconfigPtr => ['DESTROY'],
},
```

DL_VARS

An array of symbol names for variables to be made available as universal symbols. It's used only under AIX (export lists) and VMS (linker options) at present. Defaults to []. A typical value might look like this:

```
DL_VARS => [ qw( Foo_version Foo_numstreams Foo_tree ) ],
```

EXE_FILES

A reference to an array of executable files. The files will be copied to the INST_EXE directory. A *make realclean* command will delete them from there again.

FIRST_MAKEFILE

The name of the *Makefile* to be produced. Defaults to the contents of MAKE-FILE, but can be overridden. This is used for the second *Makefile* that will be produced for the MAP_TARGET.

FULLPERL

A Perl binary able to run this extension.

H

A reference to an array of **.h* filenames. Similar to C.

INC

Directories containing include files, in **-I** form. For example:

```
INC => "-I/usr/5include -I/path/to/inc",
```

INSTALLARCHLIB

Used by *make install*, which copies files from INST_ARCHLIB to this directory if INSTALLDIRS is set to "perl".

INSTALLBIN

Used by *make install*, which copies files from INST_EXE to this directory.

INSTALLDIRS

Determines which of the two sets of installation directories to choose: *install-privlib* and *installarchlib* versus *installsitelib* and *installsitearch*. The first pair is chosen with INSTALLDIRS=perl, the second with INSTALLDIRS=site. The default is "site".

INSTALLMAN1DIR

> This directory gets the command manpages at *make install* time. It defaults to $Config{installman1dir}.

INSTALLMAN3DIR

> This directory gets the library manpages at *make install* time. It defaults to $Config{installman3dir}.

INSTALLPRIVLIB

> Used by *make install*, which copies files from INST_LIB to this directory if INSTALLDIRS is set to "perl".

INSTALLSITELIB

> Used by *make install*, which copies files from INST_LIB to this directory if INSTALLDIRS is set to "site" (default).

INSTALLSITEARCH

> Used by *make install*, which copies files from INST_ARCHLIB to this directory if INSTALLDIRS is set to "site" (default).

INST_ARCHLIB

> Same as INST_LIB, but for architecture-dependent files.

INST_EXE

> Directory where executable scripts should be staged during running of *make*. Defaults to ./blib/bin, just to have a dummy location during testing. *make install* will copy the files in INST_EXE to INSTALLBIN.

INST_LIB

> Directory where we put library files of this extension while building it.

INST_MAN1DIR

> Directory to hold the command manpages at *make* time.

INST_MAN3DIR

> Directory to hold the library manpages at *make* time

LDFROM

> Defaults to $(OBJECT) and is used in the *ld*(1) command to specify what files to link/load from. (Also see dynamic_lib later for how to specify *ld* flags.)

LIBPERL_A

> The filename of the Perl library that will be used together with this extension. Defaults to *libperl.a*.

LIBS

> An anonymous array of alternative library specifications to be searched for (in order) until at least one library is found.

For example:

```
LIBS => ["-lgdbm", "-ldbm -lfoo", "-L/path -ldbm.nfs"],
```

Note that any element of the array contains a complete set of arguments for the *ld* command. So do not specify:

```
LIBS => ["-ltcl", "-ltk", "-lX11"],
```

See *NDBM_File/Makefile.PL* for an example where an array is needed. If you specify a scalar as in:

```
LIBS => "-ltcl -ltk -lX11",
```

MakeMaker will turn it into an array with one element.

LINKTYPE

"static" or "dynamic" (the latter is the default unless usedl=undef in *config.sh*). Should only be used to force static linking. (Also see linkext, later in this chapter).

MAKEAPERL

Boolean that tells MakeMaker to include the rules for making a Perl binary. This is handled automatically as a switch by MakeMaker. The user normally does not need it.

MAKEFILE

The name of the *Makefile* to be produced.

MAN1PODS

A reference to a hash of POD-containing files. MakeMaker will default this to all EXE_FILES files that include POD directives. The files listed here will be converted to manpages and installed as requested at *Configure* time.

MAN3PODS

A reference to a hash of *.pm* and *.pod* files. MakeMaker will default this to all *.pod* and any *.pm* files that include POD directives. The files listed here will be converted to manpages and installed as requested at *Configure* time.

MAP_TARGET

If it is intended that a new Perl binary be produced, this variable holds the name for that binary. Defaults to *perl*.

MYEXTLIB

If the extension links to a library that it builds, set this to the name of the library (see SDBM_File).

NAME

Perl module name for this extension (for example, DBD::Oracle). This will default to the directory name, but should really be explicitly defined in the *Makefile.PL*.

NEEDS_LINKING

MakeMaker will figure out whether an extension contains linkable code anywhere down the directory tree, and will set this variable accordingly. But you can speed it up a very little bit if you define this Boolean variable yourself.

NOECHO

Governs *make*'s @ (echoing) feature. By setting NOECHO to an empty string, you can generate a *Makefile* that echos all commands. Mainly used in debugging MakeMaker itself.

NORECURS

A Boolean that inhibits the automatic descent into subdirectories (see DIR above). For example:

```
NORECURS => 1,
```

OBJECT

A string containing a list of object files, defaulting to $(BASEEXT)$(OBJ_EXT). But it can be a long string containing all object files. For example:

```
OBJECT => "tkpBind.o tkpButton.o tkpCanvas.o",
```

PERL

Perl binary for tasks that can be done by *miniperl*.

PERLMAINCC

The command line that is able to compile *perlmain.c*. Defaults to $(CC).

PERL_ARCHLIB

Same as PERL_LIB for architecture-dependent files.

PERL_LIB

The directory containing the Perl library to use.

PERL_SRC

The directory containing the Perl source code. Use of this should be avoided, since it may be undefined.

PL_FILES

A reference to hash of files to be processed as Perl programs. By default MakeMaker will turn the names of any *.PL* files it finds (except *Makefile.PL*) into keys, and use the basenames of these files as values. For example:

```
PL_FILES => {'whatever.PL' => 'whatever'},
```

This turns into a Makefile entry resembling:

```
all :: whatever

whatever :: whatever.PL
        $(PERL) -I$(INST_ARCHLIB) -I$(INST_LIB) \
                -I$(PERL_ARCHLIB) -I$(PERL_LIB) whatever.PL
```

You'll note that there's no I/O redirection into *whatever* there. The *.*PL* files are expected to produce output to the target files themselves.

PM

A reference to a hash of *.pm* files and *.pl* files to be installed. For example:

```
PM => {'name_of_file.pm' => '$(INST_LIBDIR)/install_as.pm'},
```

By default this includes *.*pm* and *.*pl*. If a *lib/* subdirectory exists and is not listed in DIR (above) then any *.*pm* and *.*pl* files it contains will also be included by default. Defining PM in the *Makefile.PL* will override PMLIBDIRS.

PMLIBDIRS

A reference to an array of subdirectories that contain library files. Defaults to:

```
PMLIBDIRS => [ 'lib', '$(BASEEXT)' ],
```

The directories will be scanned and any files they contain will be installed in the corresponding location in the library. A libscan() method may be used to alter the behavior. Defining PM in the *Makefile.PL* will override PMLIBDIRS.

PREFIX

May be used to set the three INSTALL* attributes in one go (except for probably INSTALLMAN1DIR if it is not below PREFIX according to %Config). They will have PREFIX as a common directory node and will branch from that node into lib/, lib/ARCHNAME or whatever *Configure* decided at the build time of your Perl (unless you override one of them, of course).

PREREQ

A placeholder, not yet implemented. Will eventually be a hash reference: the keys of the hash are names of modules that need to be available to run this extension (for example, Fcntl for SDBM_File); the values of the hash are the desired versions of the modules.

SKIP

An array reference specifying the names of sections of the *Makefile* not to write. For example:

```
SKIP => [qw(name1 name2)],
```

TYPEMAPS

A reference to an array of typemap filenames. (Typemaps are used by the XS preprocessing system.) Use this when the typemaps are in some directory other than the current directory or when they are not named *typemap*. The last typemap in the list takes precedence. A typemap in the current directory has highest precedence, even if it isn't listed in TYPEMAPS. The default system typemap has lowest precedence.

VERSION

Your version number for distributing the package. This number defaults to 0.1.

VERSION_FROM

Instead of specifying the VERSION in the *Makefile.PL*, you can let MakeMaker parse a file to determine the version number. The parsing routine requires that the file named by VERSION_FROM contain one single line to compute the version number. The first line in the file that contains the regular expression:

```
/(\$[\w:]*\bVERSION)\b.*=/
```

will be evaluated with **eval** and the value of the named variable after the **eval** will be assigned to the VERSION attribute of the MakeMaker object. The following lines will be parsed satisfactorily:

```
$VERSION = '1.00';
( $VERSION ) = '$Revision: 1.51 $ ' =~ /\$Revision:\s+([^\s]+)/;
$FOO::VERSION = '1.10';
```

but these will fail:

```
my $VERSION = '1.01';
local $VERSION = '1.02';
local $FOO::VERSION = '1.30';
```

The file named in VERSION_FROM is added as a dependency to the *Makefile* in order to guarantee that the *Makefile* contains the correct VERSION attribute after a change of the file.

XS

A hash reference of *.xs* files. MakeMaker will default this. For example:

```
XS => {'name_of_file.xs' => 'name_of_file.c'},
```

The **.c* files will automatically be included in the list of files deleted by a *make clean*.

XSOPT

A string of options to pass to *xsubpp* (the XS preprocessor). This might include -C++ or -extern. Do not include typemaps here; the TYPEMAP parameter exists for that purpose.

XSPROTOARG

May be set to an empty string, which is identical to -prototypes, or -noprototypes. MakeMaker defaults to the empty string.

XS_VERSION

Your version number for the *.xs* file of this package. This defaults to the value of the VERSION attribute.

Additional lowercase attributes

There are additional lowercase attributes that you can use to pass parameters to the methods that spit out particular portions of the *Makefile*. These attributes are not normally required.

clean

Extra files to clean.

```
clean => {FILES => "*.xyz foo"},
```

depend

Extra dependencies.

```
depend => {ANY_TARGET => ANY_DEPENDENCY, ...},
```

dist

Options for distribution (see "Distribution Support" below).

```
dist => {
    TARFLAGS => 'cvfF',
    COMPRESS => 'gzip',
    SUFFIX => 'gz',
    SHAR => 'shar -m',
    DIST_CP => 'ln',
},
```

If you specify COMPRESS, then SUFFIX should also be altered, since it is needed in order to specify for *make* the target file of the compression. Setting DIST_CP to "ln" can be useful if you need to preserve the timestamps on your files. DIST_CP can take the values "cp" (copy the file), "ln" (link the file), or "best" (copy symbolic links and link the rest). Default is "best".

`dynamic_lib`

  Options for dynamic library support.

```
dynamic_lib => {
    ARMAYBE => 'ar',
    OTHERLDFLAGS => '...',
    INST_DYNAMIC_DEP => '...',
},
```

`installpm`

  Some installation options having to do with AutoSplit.

```
{SPLITLIB => '$(INST_LIB)' (default) or '$(INST_ARCHLIB)'}
```

`linkext`

  Linking style.

```
linkext => {LINKTYPE => 'static', 'dynamic', or ""},
```

  Extensions that have nothing but *.pm* files used to have to say:

```
linkext => {LINKTYPE => ""},
```

  with Pre-5.0 MakeMakers. With Version 5.00 of MakeMaker such a line can be
  deleted safely. MakeMaker recognizes when there's nothing to be linked.

`macro`

  Extra macros to define.

```
macro => {ANY_MACRO => ANY_VALUE, ...},
```

`realclean`

  Extra files to really clean.

```
{FILES => '$(INST_ARCHAUTODIR)/*.xyz'}
```

Useful Makefile macros

Here are some useful macros that you probably shouldn't redefine because they're
derivative.

`FULLEXT`

  Pathname for extension directory (for example, *DBD/Oracle*).

`BASEEXT`

  Basename part of FULLEXT. May be just equal to FULLEXT.

`ROOTEXT`

  Directory part of FULLEXT with leading slash (for example, */DBD*)

INST_LIBDIR

    $(INST_LIB)$(ROOTEXT)

INST_AUTODIR

    $(INST_LIB)/auto/$(FULLEXT)

INST_ARCHAUTODIR

    $(INST_ARCHLIB)/auto/$(FULLEXT)

Overriding MakeMaker methods

If you cannot achieve the desired *Makefile* behavior by specifying attributes, you may define private subroutines in the *Makefile.PL*. Each subroutine returns the text it wishes to have written to the *Makefile*. To override a section of the *Makefile* you can use one of two styles. You can just return a new value:

```
sub MY::c_o { "new literal text" }
```

or you can edit the default by saying something like:

```
sub MY::c_o {
    my $self = shift;
    local *c_o;
    $_=$self->MM::c_o;
    s/old text/new text/;
    $_;
}
```

Both methods above are available for backward compatibility with older *Makefile.PIs*.

If you still need a different solution, try to develop another subroutine that better fits your needs and then submit the diffs to either *perl5-porters@nicoh.com* or *comp.lang.perl.modules* as appropriate.

Distribution support

For authors of extensions, MakeMaker provides several *Makefile* targets. Most of the support comes from the ExtUtils::Manifest module, where additional documentation can be found. Note that a *MANIFEST* file is basically just a list of filenames to be shipped with the kit to build the extension.

make distcheck

    Reports which files are below the build directory but not in the *MANIFEST* file and vice versa. (See `ExtUtils::Manifest::fullcheck()` for details.)

make skipcheck

Reports which files are skipped due to the entries in the *MANIFEST.SKIP* file. (See `ExtUtils::Manifest::skipcheck()` for details).

make distclean

Does a *realclean* first and then the *distcheck*. Note that this is not needed to build a new distribution as long as you are sure that the *MANIFEST* file is OK.

make manifest

Rewrites the *MANIFEST* file, adding all remaining files found. (See `ExtUtils::Manifest::mkmanifest()` for details.)

make distdir

Copies all files that are in the *MANIFEST* file to a newly created directory with the name `$(DISTNAME)-$(VERSION)`. If that directory exists, it will be removed first.

make disttest

Makes *distdir* first, and runs *perl Makefile.PL, make,* and *make test* in that directory.

make tardist

First does a command `$(PREOP)`, which defaults to a null command. Does a *make distdir* next and runs *tar*(1) on that directory into a tarfile. Then deletes the *distdir*. Finishes with a command `$(POSTOP)`, which defaults to a null command.

make dist

Defaults to `$(DIST_DEFAULT)`, which in turn defaults to *tardist*.

make uutardist

Runs a *tardist* first and *uuencode*s the tarfile.

make shdist

First does a command `$(PREOP)`, which defaults to a null command. Does a *distdir* next and runs *shar* on that directory into a sharfile. Then deletes the *distdir*. Finishes with a command `$(POSTOP)`, which defaults to a null command. Note: for *shdist* to work properly, a *shar* program that can handle directories is mandatory.

make ci

Does a `$(CI)` and a `$(RCS_LABEL)` on all files in the *MANIFEST* file.

Customization of the distribution targets can be done by specifying a hash reference to the `dist` attribute of the `WriteMakefile()` call. The following parameters are recognized:

Parameter	Default
CI	(′ci -u′)
COMPRESS	(′compress′)
POSTOP	(′@ :′)
PREOP	(′@ :′)
RCS_LABEL	(′rcs -q -Nv$(VERSION_SYM):′)
SHAR	(′shar′)
SUFFIX	(′Z′)
TAR	(′tar′)
TARFLAGS	(′cvf′)

An example:

```
WriteMakefile( ′dist′ => { COMPRESS=>"gzip", SUFFIX=>"gz" })
```

ExtUtils::Manifest — Utilities to Write and Check a MANIFEST File

```
require ExtUtils::Manifest;

ExtUtils::Manifest::mkmanifest();
ExtUtils::Manifest::manicheck();
ExtUtils::Manifest::filecheck();
ExtUtils::Manifest::fullcheck();
ExtUtils::Manifest::skipcheck();
ExtUtild::Manifest::manifind();
ExtUtils::Manifest::maniread($file);
ExtUtils::Manifest::manicopy($read, $target, $how);
```

These routines automate the maintenance and use of a *MANIFEST* file. A *MANIFEST* file is essentially just a list of filenames, one per line, with an optional comment on each line, separated by whitespace (usually one or more tabs). The idea is simply that you can extract the filenames by saying:

```
awk ′{print $1}′ MANIFEST
```

mkmanifest() writes the names of all files in and below the current directory to a file named in the global variable $ExtUtils::Manifest::MANIFEST (which defaults to *MANIFEST*) in the current directory. As the counterpart to the *awk* command above, it works much like:

```
find . -type f -print > MANIFEST
```

except that it also checks the existing *MANIFEST* file (if any) and copies over any comments that are found there. Also, all filenames that match any regular expression in a file *MANIFEST.SKIP* (if such a file exists) are ignored.

manicheck() checks whether all files listed in a *MANIFEST* file in the current directory really do exist.

`filecheck()` finds files below the current directory that are not mentioned in the *MANIFEST* file. An optional *MANIFEST.SKIP* file will be consulted, and any filename matching a regular expression in such a file will not be reported as missing in the *MANIFEST* file.

`fullcheck()` does both a `manicheck()` and a `filecheck()`.

`skipcheck()` lists all files that are skipped due to your *MANIFEST.SKIP* file.

`manifind()` returns a hash reference. The keys of the hash are the files found below the current directory. The values are null strings, representing all the *MANIFEST* comments that aren't there.

`maniread($file)` reads a named *MANIFEST* file (defaults to *MANIFEST* in the current directory) and returns a hash reference, the keys of which are the filenames, and the values of which are the comments that *are* there. Er, which may be null if the comments aren't there. . . .

`manicopy($read, $target, $how)` copies the files that are the keys in the hash `%$read` to the named target directory. The hash reference `$read` is typically returned by the `maniread()` function. `manicopy()` is useful for producing a directory tree identical to the intended distribution tree. The third parameter `$how` can be used to specify a different method of "copying". Valid values are "`cp`", which actually copies the files, "`ln`", which creates hard links, and "`best`", which mostly links the files but copies any symbolic link to make a tree without any symbolic link. "`best`" is the default, though it may not be the best default.

Ignoring files

The *MANIFEST.SKIP* file may contain regular expressions of files that should be ignored by `mkmanifest()` and `filecheck()`. The regular expressions should appear one on each line. A typical example:

```
\bRCS\b
^MANIFEST\.
(?i)^makefile$
~$
\.html$
\.old$
^blib/
^MakeMaker-\d
```

Exportability

`mkmanifest()`, `manicheck()`, `filecheck()`, `fullcheck()`, `maniread()`, and `manicopy()` are exportable.

Global variables

$ExtUtils::Manifest::MANIFEST defaults to MANIFEST. Changing it results in both a different *MANIFEST* and a different *MANIFEST.SKIP* file. This is useful if you want to maintain different distributions for different audiences (say a user version and a developer version including RCS).

$ExtUtils::Manifest::Quiet defaults to 0. You can set it to a true value to get all the functions to shutup already.

Diagnostics

All diagnostic output is sent to STDERR.

Not in MANIFEST: *file*
> A file excluded by a regular expression in *MANIFEST.SKIP* was missing from the *MANIFEST* file.

No such file: *file*
> A file mentioned in a *MANIFEST* file does not exist.

MANIFEST: *$!*
> The *MANIFEST* file could not be opened.

Added to MANIFEST: *file*
> Reported by mkmanifest() if $Verbose is set and a file is added to *MANIFEST*. $Verbose is set to 1 by default.

See also

The *ExtUtils::MakeMaker* library module generates a *Makefile* with handy targets for most of this functionality.

ExtUtils::Miniperl — Write the C Code for perlmain.c

```
use ExtUtils::Miniperl;
writemain(@directories);
```

writemain() takes an argument list of directories containing archive libraries that are needed by Perl modules and that should be linked into a new Perl binary. It correspondingly writes to STDOUT a file intended to be compiled as *perlmain.c* that contains all the bootstrap code to make the modules associated with the libraries available from within Perl.

The typical usage is from within a *Makefile* generated by ExtUtils::MakeMaker. So under normal circumstances you won't have to deal with this module directly.

WARNING   This entire module is automatically generated from a script called
              minimod.PL when Perl itself is built. So if you want to patch it,
              please patch *minimod.PL* in the Perl distribution instead.

ExtUtils::Mkbootstrap — Make a Bootstrap File for Use by DynaLoader

```
use ExtUtils::Mkbootstrap;
mkbootstrap();
```

mkbootstrap() typically gets called from an extension's *Makefile*. It writes a **.bs* file
that is needed by some architectures to do dynamic loading. It is otherwise unre-
markable, and MakeMaker usually handles the details. If you need to know more
about it, you've probably already read the module.

ExtUtils::Mksymlists — Write Linker Option Files for Dynamic Extension

```
use ExtUtils::Mksymlists;

Mksymlists( NAME     => $name,
            DL_FUNCS => { $pkg1 => [$func1, $func2], $pkg2 => [$func3] },
            DL_VARS  => [$var1, $var2, $var3]);
```

ExtUtils::Mksymlists() produces files used by the linker under some OSes during
the creation of shared libraries for dynamic extensions. It is normally called from a
MakeMaker-generated *Makefile* when the extension is built. The linker option file
is generated by calling the function Mksymlists(), which is exported by default
from ExtUtils::Mksymlists. It takes one argument, a list of key/value pairs, in which
the following keys are recognized:

NAME

> This gives the name of the extension (for example, Tk::Canvas) for which the
> linker option file will be produced.

DL_FUNCS

> This is identical to the DL_FUNCS attribute available via MakeMaker, from which
> it is usually taken. Its value is a reference to a hash, in which each key is the
> name of a package, and each value is a reference to an array of function
> names, which should be exported by the extension. So, one might say:

```
DL_FUNCS => {
    Homer::Iliad   => [ qw(trojans greeks) ],
    Homer::Odyssey => [ qw(travelers family suitors) ],
},
```

The function names should be identical to those in the XSUB code; Mksym-lists() will alter the names written to the linker option file to match the changes made by *xsubpp*. In addition, if none of the functions in a list begins with the string "boot_", Mksymlists() will add a bootstrap function for that package, just as *xsubpp* does. (If a boot_*pkg* function is present in the list, it is passed through unchanged.) If DL_FUNCS is not specified, it defaults to the bootstrap function for the extension specified in NAME.

DL_VARS

This is identical to the DL_VARS attribute available via MakeMaker, and, like DL_FUNCS, it is usually specified via MakeMaker. Its value is a reference to an array of variable names that should be exported by the extension.

FILE

This key can be used to specify the name of the linker option file (minus the OS-specific extension) if for some reason you do not want to use the default value, which is the last word of the NAME attribute (for example, for Tk::Canvas, FILE defaults to Canvas).

FUNCLIST

This provides an alternate means to specify function names to be exported from the extension. Its value is a reference to an array of function names to be exported. These names are passed through unaltered to the linker options file.

DLBASE

This item specifies the name by which the linker knows the extension, which may be different from the name of the extension itself (for instance, some linkers add an "_" to the name of the extension). If it is not specified, it is derived from the NAME attribute. It is presently used only by OS/2.

When calling Mksymlists(), one should always specify the NAME attribute. In most cases, this is all that's necessary. In the case of unusual extensions, however, the other attributes can be used to provide additional information to the linker.

ExtUtils::MM_OS2 — Methods to Override UNIX Behavior in ExtUtils::MakeMaker

```
use ExtUtils::MM_OS2; # Done internally by ExtUtils::MakeMaker if needed
```

See ExtUtils::MM_Unix for documentation of the methods provided there. This package overrides the implementation of the methods, not the interface.

ExtUtils::MM_Unix — Methods Used by ExtUtils::MakeMaker

```
require ExtUtils::MM_Unix;
```

The methods provided by this package (and by the other MM_* packages) are designed to be used in conjunction with ExtUtils::MakeMaker. You will never **require** this module yourself. You would only define methods in this or a similar module if you're working on improving the porting capabilities of MakeMaker. Nevertheless, this is a laudable goal, so we'll talk about it here.

When MakeMaker writes a *Makefile*, it creates one or more objects that inherit their methods from package MM. MM itself doesn't provide any methods, but it inherits from the ExtUtils::MM_Unix class. However, for certain platforms, it also inherits from an OS-specific module such as MM_VMS, and it does this *before* it inherits from the MM_Unix module in the **@ISA** list. The inheritance tree of MM therefore lets the OS-specific package override any of the methods listed here. In a sense, the MM_Unix package is slightly misnamed, since it provides fundamental methods on non-UNIX systems too, to the extent that the system is like UNIX.

MM methods

We've avoided listing deprecated methods here, as well as any private methods you're unlikely to want to override.

catdir *LIST*

> Concatenates two or more directory names to form a complete path ending with a directory. On UNIX it just glues it together with a / character.

catfile *LIST*

> Concatenates one or more directory names and a filename to form a complete path ending with a filename. Also uses / on UNIX.

dir_target

> Takes an array of directories that need to exist and returns a *Makefile* entry for a *.exists* file in these directories. Returns nothing if the entry has already been processed. We're helpless, though, if the same directory comes as $(FOO) and as bar. Both of them get an entry; that's why we use "::".

file_name_is_absolute *FILENAME*

> Takes as argument a path and returns true if it is an absolute path.

`find_perl` *VERSION, NAMES, DIRS, TRACE*

Searches for an executable Perl that is at least the specified *VERSION*, named by one of the entries in *NAMES* (an array reference), and located in one of the entries of *DIRS* (also an array reference). It prints debugging info if *TRACE* is true.

`guess_name`

Guesses the name of this package by examining the working directory's name. MakeMaker calls this only if the developer has not supplied a NAME attribute. Shame on you.

`has_link_code`

Returns true if C, XS, MYEXTLIB or similar objects exist within this object that need a compiler. Does not descend into subdirectories as `needs_linking()` does.

`libscan` *FILENAME*

Takes a path to a file that is found by `init_dirscan()` and returns false if we don't want to include this file in the library. It is mainly used to exclude *RCS/*, *CVS/*, and *SCCS/* directories from installation.

`lsdir` *DIR, REGEXP*

Takes as arguments a directory name and a regular expression. Returns all entries in the directory that match the regular expression.

`maybe_command_in_dirs`

Method under development. Not yet used.

`maybe_command` *FILENAME*

Returns true if the argument is likely to be a command.

`needs_linking`

Does this module need linking? Looks into subdirectory objects, if any. (See also `has_link_code()`.)

`nicetext` *TARGET*

(A misnamed method.) The MM_Unix version of the method just returns the argument without further processing. On VMS, this method ensures that colons marking targets are preceded by space. Most UNIX *makes* don't need this, but it's necessary under VMS to distinguish the target delimiter from a colon appearing as part of a filespec.

`path`

Takes no argument. Returns the environment variable PATH as an array.

`perl_script` *FILENAME*

> Returns true if the argument is likely to be a Perl script. With MM_Unix this is true for any ordinary, readable file.

`prefixify` *ATTRNAME, OLDPREFIX, NEWPREFIX*

> Processes a path attribute in `$self->{ `*ATTRNAME*` }`. First it looks it up for you in `%Config` if it doesn't have a value yet. Then it replaces (in-place) the *OLD-PREFIX* with the *NEWPREFIX* (if it matches).

`replace_manpage_separator` *FILENAME*

> Takes the filename of a package, which if it's a nested package will have a name of the form "`Foo/Bar`" (under UNIX), and replaces the subdirectory delimiter with "`::`". Returns the altered name.

Methods to produce chunks of text for the Makefile

When MakeMaker thinks it has all its ducks in a row, it calls a special sequence of methods to produce the Makefile for a given MakeMaker object. The list of methods it calls is specified in the array `@ExtUtils::MakeMaker::MM_Sections`, one method per section. Since these routines are all called the same way, we won't document each of them separately, except to list them.

By far the most accurate and up-to-date documentation for what each method does is actually the *Makefile* that MakeMaker produces. Each section of the file is labeled with the name of the method that produces it, so once you see how you want to change the *Makefile*, it's a trivial matter to work back from the proposed change and find the method responsible for it.

You've plowed through a lot of ugly things to get here, but since you've read this far, we'll reward you by pointing out something incredibly beautiful in Make-Maker. The arguments (if any) that are passed to each method are simply the pseudo-attributes of the same name that you already saw documented under "Additional Lowercase Attributes" in the section on ExtUtils::MakeMaker. You'll recall that those pseudo-attributes were specified as anonymous hashes, which Just Happen to have exactly the same syntax inside as named parameters. Fancy that. So the arguments just come right into your method as ordinary named parameters. Assign the arguments to a hash, and off you go. And it's completely forward and backward compatible. Even if you override a method that didn't have arguments before, there's no problem. Since it's all driven off the method name, just name your new pseudo-attribute after your method, and your method will get its arguments.

The return values are also easy to understand: each method simply returns the string it wants to put into its section of the *Makefile*.

Two special methods are `post_initialize()` and `postamble()`, each of which returns an empty string by default. You can define them in your *Makefile.PL* to insert customized text near the beginning or end of the *Makefile*.

Here are the methods. They're called in this order (reading down the columns):

`post_initialize()`	`top_targets()`	`realclean()`
`const_config()`	`linkext()`	`dist_basics()`
`constants()`	`dlsyms()`	`dist_core()`
`const_loadlibs()`	`dynamic()`	`dist_dir()`
`const_cccmd()`	`dynamic_bs()`	`dist_test()`
`tool_autosplit()`	`dynamic_lib()`	`dist_ci()`
`tool_xsubpp()`	`static()`	`install()`
`tools_other()`	`static_lib()`	`force()`
`dist()`	`installpm()`	`perldepend()`
`macro()`	`installpm_x()`	`makefile()`
`depend()`	`manifypods()`	`staticmake()`
`post_constants()`	`processPL()`	`test()`
`pasthru()`	`installbin()`	`test_via_harness()`
`c_o()`	`subdirs()`	`test_via_script()`
`xs_c()`	`subdir_x()`	`postamble()`
`xs_o()`	`clean()`	

See also

ExtUtils::MakeMaker library module.

ExtUtils::MM_VMS — Methods to Override UNIX Behavior in ExtUtils::MakeMaker

```
use ExtUtils::MM_VMS; # Done internally by ExtUtils::MakeMaker if needed
```

See ExtUtils::MM_Unix for documentation of the methods provided there. This package overrides the implementation of the methods, not the interface.

Fcntl — Load the C fcntl.h Defines

```
use Fcntl;

$nonblock_flag = O_NDELAY();
$create_flag = O_CREAT();
$read_write_flag = O_RDWR();
```

This module is just a translation of the C *fcntl.h* file. Unlike the old mechanism which required a translated *fcntl.ph* file, *fcntl* uses the *h2xs* program (see the Perl source distribution) and your native C compiler. This means that it has a much better chance of getting the numbers right.

Note that only #define symbols get translated; you must still correctly pack up your own arguments to pass as arguments for locking functions and so on.

The following routines are exported by default, and each routine returns the value of the #define that is the same as the routine name:

FD_CLOEXEC	F_DUPFD	F_GETFD	F_GETFL	F_GETLK	F_RDLCK
F_SETFD	F_SETFL	F_SETLK	F_SETLKW	F_UNLCK	F_WRLCK
O_APPEND	O_CREAT	O_EXCL	O_NDELAY	O_NOCTTY	
O_NONBLOCK	O_RDONLY	O_RDWR	O_TRUNC	O_WRONLY	

File::Basename — Parse File Specifications

```
use File::Basename;

($name, $path, $suffix) = fileparse($fullname, @suffixlist)
fileparse_set_fstype($os_string);  # $os_string specifies OS type
$basename = basename($fullname, @suffixlist);
$dirname = dirname($fullname);

($name, $path, $suffix) = fileparse("lib/File/Basename.pm", '\.pm');
fileparse_set_fstype("VMS");
$basename = basename("lib/File/Basename.pm", ".pm");
$dirname = dirname("lib/File/Basename.pm");
```

These routines allow you to parse file specifications into useful pieces using the syntax of different operating systems.

fileparse_set_fstype

> You select the syntax via the routine fileparse_set_fstype(). If the argument passed to it contains one of the substrings "VMS", "MSDOS", or "MacOS", the file specification syntax of that operating system is used in future calls to fileparse(), basename(), and dirname(). If it contains none of these substrings, UNIX syntax is used. This pattern matching is case-insensitive. If you've selected VMS syntax and the file specification you pass to one of these routines contains a /, it assumes you are using UNIX emulation and applies the UNIX syntax rules instead for that function call only. If you haven't called fileparse_set_fstype(), the syntax is chosen by examining the osname entry from the Config package according to these rules.

fileparse

> The fileparse() routine divides a file specification into three parts: a leading *path*, a file *name*, and a *suffix*. The *path* contains everything up to and including the last directory separator in the input file specification. The remainder of the input file specification is then divided into *name* and *suffix* based on the

optional patterns you specify in `@suffixlist`. Each element of this list is interpreted as a regular expression, and is matched against the end of *name*. If this succeeds, the matching portion of *name* is removed and prepended to *suffix*. By proper use of `@suffixlist`, you can remove file types or versions for examination. You are guaranteed that if you concatenate *path*, *name*, and *suffix* together in that order, the result will be identical to the input file specification. Using UNIX file syntax:

```
($name, $path, $suffix) = fileparse('/virgil/aeneid/draft.book7',
                                     '\.book\d+');
```

would yield:

```
$name   eq 'draft'
$path   eq '/virgil/aeneid',
$suffix eq '.book7'
```

(Note that the suffix pattern is in single quotes. You'd have to double the backslashes if you used double quotes, since double quotes do backslash interpretation.) Similarly, using VMS syntax:

```
($name, $path, $suffix) = fileparse('Doc_Root:[Help]Rhetoric.Rnh', '\..*');
```

would yield:

```
$name   eq 'Rhetoric'
$path   eq 'Doc_Root:[Help]'
$suffix eq '.Rnh'
```

basename

The `basename()` routine returns the first element of the list produced by calling `fileparse()` with the same arguments. It is provided for compatibility with the UNIX shell command *basename*(1).

dirname

The `dirname()` routine returns the directory portion of the input file specification. When using VMS or MacOS syntax, this is identical to the second element of the list produced by calling `fileparse()` with the same input file specification. When using UNIX or MS-DOS syntax, the return value conforms to the behavior of the UNIX shell command *dirname*(1). This is usually the same as the behavior of `fileparse()`, but differs in some cases. For example, for the input file specification `lib/`, `fileparse()` considers the directory name to be *lib/*, while `dirname()` considers the directory name to be . (dot).

File::CheckTree — Run Many Tests on a Collection of Files

```
use File::CheckTree;

$warnings += validate( q{
    /vmunix            -e || die
    /boot              -e || die
    /bin               cd
        csh            -ex
        csh            !-ug
        sh             -ex
        sh             !-ug
    /usr               -d || warn "What happened to $file?\n"
});
```

The `validate()` routine takes a single multi-line string, each line of which contains a filename plus a file test to try on it. (The file test may be given as "cd", causing subsequent relative filenames to be interpreted relative to that directory.) After the file test you may put "|| die" to make it a fatal error if the file test fails. The default is:

```
|| warn
```

You can reverse the sense of the test by prepending "!". If you specify "cd" and then list some relative filenames, you may want to indent them slightly for readability. If you supply your own **die** or **warn** message, you can use $file to interpolate the filename.

File tests may be grouped: -rwx tests for all of -r, -w, and -x. Only the first failed test of the group will produce a warning.

`validate()` returns the number of warnings issued, presuming it didn't **die**.

File::Copy — Copy Files or Filehandles

```
use File::Copy;

copy("src-file", "dst-file");
copy("Copy.pm", \*STDOUT);

use POSIX;
use File::Copy 'cp';

$fh = FileHandle->new("/dev/null", "r");
cp($fh, "dst-file");'
```

The Copy module provides one function, `copy()`, that takes two parameters: a file to copy from and a file to copy to. Either argument may be a string, a FileHandle reference, or a FileHandle glob. If the first argument is a filehandle of some sort, it will be read from; if it is a filename, it will be opened for reading. Likewise, the second argument will be written to (and created if need be).

An optional third parameter is a hint that requests the buffer size to be used for copying. This is the number of bytes from the first file that will be held in memory at any given time, before being written to the second file. The default buffer size depends upon the file and the operating system, but will generally be the whole file (up to 2Mb), or 1kb for filehandles that do not reference files (for example, sockets).

When running under VMS, this routine performs an RMS copy of the file, in order to preserve file attributes, indexed file structure, and so on. The buffer size parameter is ignored.

You may use the syntax:

```
use File::Copy "cp"
```

to get at the cp() alias for the copy() function. The syntax is exactly the same.

copy() returns 1 on success, 0 on failure; $! will be set if an error was encountered.

File::Find — Traverse a File Tree

```
use File::Find;
find(\&wanted, 'dir1', 'dir2'...);
sub wanted { ... }

use File::Find;
finddepth(\&wanted, 'dir1', 'dir2'...);  # traverse depth-first
sub wanted { ... }
```

find() is similar to the UNIX *find*(1) command in that it traverses the specified directories, performing whatever tests or other actions you request. However, these actions are given in the subroutine, wanted(), which you must define (but see *find2perl* below). For example, to print out the names of all executable files, you could define wanted() this way:

```
sub wanted {
    print "$File::Find::name\n" if -x;
}
```

$File::Find::dir contains the current directory name, and $_ the current filename within that directory. $File::Find::name contains "$File::Find::dir/$_". You are

chdired to $File::Find::dir when find() is called. You can set
$File::Find::prune to true in wanted() in order to prune the tree; that is, find()
will not descend into any directory when $File::Find::prune is set.

This library is primarily for use with the *find2perl*(1) command, which is supplied
with the standard Perl distribution and converts a *find*(1) invocation to an appropriate wanted() subroutine. The command:

```
find2perl / -name .nfs\* -mtime +7 \
            -exec rm -f {} \; -o -fstype nfs -prune
```

produces something like:

```
sub wanted {
    /^\.nfs.*$/ &&
    (($dev, $ino, $mode, $nlink, $uid, $gid) = lstat($_)) &&
    int(-M _) > 7 &&
    unlink($_)
    ||
    ($nlink || (($dev, $ino, $mode, $nlink, $uid, $gid) = lstat($_))) &&
    $dev < 0 &&
    ($File::Find::prune = 1);
}
```

Set the variable $File::Find::dont_use_nlink if you're using the AFS.

finddepth() is just like find(), except that it does a depth-first search.

Here's another interesting wanted() function. It will find all symbolic links that
don't resolve:

```
sub wanted {
    -l and not -e and print "bogus link: $File::Find::name\n";
}
```

File::Path — Create or Remove a Series of Directories

```
use File::Path;

mkpath(['/foo/bar/baz', 'blurfl/quux'], 1, 0711);
rmtree(['/foo/bar/baz', 'blurfl/quux'], 1, 1);
```

The mkpath() function provides a convenient way to create directories, even if
your *mkdir*(2) won't create more than one level of directory at a time. mkpath()
takes three arguments:

- The name of the path to create, or a reference to a list of paths to create

- A Boolean value, which if true will cause mkpath() to print the name of each
  directory as it is created (defaults to false)

- The numeric mode to use when creating the directories (defaults to 0777)

It returns a list of all directories created, including intermediate directories, which are assumed to be delimited by the UNIX path separator, /.

Similarly, the `rmtree()` function provides a convenient way to delete a subtree from the directory structure, much like the UNIX *rm -r* command. `rmtree()` takes three arguments:

- The root of the subtree to delete, or a reference to a list of roots. All of the files and directories below each root, as well as the roots themselves, will be deleted.

- A Boolean value, which if true will cause `rmtree()` to print a message each time it examines a file, giving the name of the file and indicating whether it's using *rmdir*(2) or *unlink*(2) to remove it, or whether it's skipping it. (This argument defaults to false.)

- A Boolean value, which if true will cause `rmtree()` to skip any files to which you do not have delete access (if running under VMS) or write access (if running under another operating system). This will change in the future when a criterion for "delete permission" under operating systems other than VMS is settled. (This argument defaults to false.)

`rmtree()` returns the number of files successfully deleted. Symbolic links are treated as ordinary files.

FileCache — Keep More Files Open Than the System Permits

```
use FileCache;

cacheout $path;          # open the file whose path name is $path
print $path "stuff\n";   # print stuff to file given by $path
```

The `cacheout()` subroutine makes sure that the file whose name is $path is created and accessible through the filehandle also named $path. It permits you to write to more files than your system allows to be open at once, performing the necessary opens and closes in the background. By preceding each file access with:

```
cacheout $path;
```

you can be sure that the named file will be open and ready to do business. However, you do not need to invoke `cacheout()` between successive accesses to the same file.

`cacheout()` does not create directories for you. If you use it to open an existing file that FileCache is seeing for the first time, the file will be truncated to zero length with no questions asked. (However, in its opening and closing of files in the background, cacheout() keeps track of which files it has opened before and does not overwrite them, but appends to them instead.)

cacheout() checks the value of NOFILE in *sys/param.h* to determine the number of open files allowed. This value is incorrect on some systems, in which case you should set $FileCache::maxopen to be four less than the correct value for NOFILE.

FileHandle — Supply Object Methods for Filehandles

```
use FileHandle;

$fh = new FileHandle;
if ($fh->open "< file") {
    print <$fh>;
    $fh->close;
}

$fh = new FileHandle "> file";
if (defined $fh) {
    print $fh "bar\n";
    $fh->close;
}

$fh = new FileHandle "file", "r";
if (defined $fh) {
    print <$fh>;
    undef $fh;       # automatically closes the file
}

$fh = new FileHandle "file", O_WRONLY|O_APPEND;
if (defined $fh) {
    print $fh "stuff\n";
    undef $fh;       # automatically closes the file
}

$pos = $fh->getpos;
$fh->setpos($pos);

$fh->setvbuf($buffer_var, _IOLBF, 1024);

($readfh, $writefh) = FileHandle::pipe;

autoflush STDOUT 1;
```

new

Creates a FileHandle, which is a reference to a newly created symbol (see the Symbol library module). If it receives any parameters, they are passed to open(). If the open fails, the FileHandle object is destroyed. Otherwise, it is returned to the caller.

new_from_fd

> Creates a FileHandle like new() does. It requires two parameters, which are passed to fdopen(); if the fdopen() fails, the FileHandle object is destroyed. Otherwise, it is returned to the caller.

open

> Accepts one parameter or two. With one parameter, it is just a front end for the built-in **open** function. With two parameters, the first parameter is a filename that may include whitespace or other special characters, and the second parameter is the open mode in either Perl form (">", "+<", and so on) or POSIX form ("w", "r+", and so on).

fdopen

> Like open() except that its first parameter is not a filename but rather a filehandle name, a FileHandle object, or a file descriptor number.

getpos

> If the C functions *fgetpos*(3) and *fsetpos*(3) are available, then getpos() returns an opaque value that represents the current position of the FileHandle, and setpos() uses that value to return to a previously visited position.

setvbuf

> If the C function *setvbuf*(3) is available, then setvbuf() sets the buffering policy for the FileHandle. The calling sequence for the Perl function is the same as its C counterpart, including the macros _IOFBF, _IOLBF, and _IONBF, except that the buffer parameter specifies a scalar variable to use as a buffer.

WARNING	A variable used as a buffer by setvbuf() must not be modified in any way until the FileHandle is closed or until setvbuf() is called again, or memory corruption may result!

The following supported FileHandle methods are just front ends for the corresponding built-in Perl functions:

clearerr	getc
close	gets
eof	seek
fileno	tell

The following supported FileHandle methods correspond to Perl special variables:

autoflush	format_page_number
format_formfeed	format_top_name
format_line_break_characters	input_line_number
format_lines_left	input_record_separator
format_lines_per_page	output_field_separator
format_name	output_record_separator

Furthermore, for doing normal I/O you might need these methods:

$fh->print

> See Perl's built-in **print** function.

$fh->printf

> See Perl's built-in **printf** function.

$fh->getline

> This method works like Perl's <FILEHANDLE> construct, except that it can be safely called in an array context, where it still returns just one line.

$fh->getlines

> This method works like Perl's <FILEHANDLE> construct when called in an array context to read all remaining lines in a file. It will also croak() if accidentally called in a scalar context.

Bugs

Due to backward compatibility, all filehandles resemble objects of class FileHandle, or actually classes derived from that class. But they aren't. Which means you can't derive your own class from FileHandle and inherit those methods.

While it may look as though the filehandle methods corresponding to the built-in variables are unique to a particular filehandle, currently some of them are not, including the following:

input_line_number()
input_record_separator()
output_record_separator()

GDBM_File — Tied Access to GDBM Library

```
use GDBM_File;

tie (%hash, "GDBM_File", $filename, &GDBM_WRCREAT, 0644);
# read/writes of %hash are now read/writes of $filename
untie %hash;
```

GDBM_File is a module that allows Perl programs to make use of the facilities provided by the GNU *gdbm* library. If you intend to use this module, you should have a copy of the *gdbm*(3) manpage at hand.

Most of the *libgdbm.a* functions are available as methods of the GDBM_File interface.

Availability

gdbm is available from any GNU archive. The master site is prep.ai.mit.edu, but you are strongly urged to use one of the many mirrors. You can obtain a list of mirror sites by issuing the command, *finger fsf@prep.ai.mit.edu*. A copy is also stored on CPAN:

```
http://www.perl.com/CPAN/src/misc/gdbm-1.7.3.tar.gz
```

See also

DB_File library module.

Getopt::Long — Extended Processing of Command-Line Options

```
use Getopt::Long;
$result = GetOptions(option-descriptions);
```

The Getopt::Long module implements an extended function called GetOptions(). This function retrieves and processes the command-line options with which your Perl program was invoked, based on the description of valid options that you provide.

GetOptions() adheres to the POSIX syntax for command-line options, with GNU extensions. In general, this means that options have long names instead of single letters, and are introduced with a double hyphen --. (A single hyphen can also be used, but implies restrictions on functionality. See later in the chapter.) There is no bundling of command-line options, as was the case with the more traditional single-letter approach. For example, the UNIX *ps*(1) command can be given the command-line argument:

```
-vax
```

which means the combination of -v, -a and -x. With the Getopt::Long syntax, -vax would be a single option.

Command-line options can be used to set values. These values can be specified in one of two ways:

```
--size 24
--size=24
```

GetOptions() is called with a list of option descriptions, each of which consists of two elements: the option specifier and the option linkage. The option specifier defines the name of the option and, optionally, the value it can take. The option linkage is usually a reference to a variable that will be set when the option is used. For example, the following call to GetOptions():

```
&GetOptions("size=i" => \$offset);
```

will accept a command-line option "size" that must have an integer value. With a command line of --size 24 this will cause the variable $offset to be assigned the value 24.

Alternatively, the first argument to GetOptions may be a reference to a hash describing the linkage for the options. The following call is equivalent to the example above:

```
%optctl = (size => \$offset);
&GetOptions(\%optctl, "size=i");
```

Linkage may be specified using either of the above methods, or both. The linkage specified in the argument list takes precedence over the linkage specified in the hash.

The command-line options are implicitly taken from array @ARGV. Upon completion of GetOptions(), @ARGV will contain only the command-line arguments that were not options. (But see below for a way to process non-option arguments.) Each option specifier handed to GetOptions() designates the name of an option, possibly followed by an argument specifier. Values for argument specifiers are:

<none>

Option does not take an argument. If the user invokes the option, the option variable will be set to 1.

!

Option does not take an argument and may be negated, that is, prefixed by "no". For example, foo! will allow --foo (with value 1 being assigned to the option variable) and -nofoo (with value 0).

`=s`

Option takes a mandatory string argument. This string will be assigned to the option variable. Even if the string argument starts with - or --, it will be assigned to the option variable rather than taken as a separate option.

`:s`

Option takes an optional string argument. This string will be assigned to the option variable. If the string is omitted from the command invocation, `""` (an empty string) will be assigned to the option variable. If the string argument starts with - or --, it will be taken as another option rather than assigned to the option variable.

`=i`

Option takes a mandatory integer argument. This value will be assigned to the option variable. Note that the value may start with - to indicate a negative value.

`:i`

Option takes an optional integer argument. This integer value will be assigned to the option variable. If the optional argument is omitted, the value 0 will be assigned to the option variable. The value may start with - to indicate a negative value.

`=f`

Option takes a mandatory floating-point argument. This value will be assigned to the option variable. Note that the value may start with - to indicate a negative value.

`:f`

Option takes an optional floating-point argument. This value will be assigned to the option variable. If the optional argument is omitted, the value 0 will be assigned to the option variable. The value may start with - to indicate a negative value.

A lone hyphen - is considered an option; the corresponding option name is the empty string.

A lone double hyphen -- terminates the processing of options and arguments. Any options following the double hyphen will remain in `@ARGV` when `GetOptions()` returns.

If an argument specifier concludes with `@` (as in `=s@`), then the option is treated as an array. That is, multiple invocations of the same option, each with a particular value, will result in the list of values being assigned to the option variable, which is an array. See the following section for an example.

Linkage specification

The linkage specifier is optional. If no linkage is explicitly specified but a hash reference is passed, GetOptions() will place the value in the hash. For example:

```
%optctl = ();
&GetOptions (\%optctl, "size=i");
```

will perform the equivalent of the assignment:

```
$optctl{"size"} = 24;
```

For array options, a reference to an anonymous array is generated. For example:

```
%optctl = ();
&GetOptions (\%optctl, "sizes=i@");
```

with command-line arguments:

```
-sizes 24 -sizes 48
```

will perform the equivalent of the assignment:

```
$optctl{"sizes"} = [24, 48];
```

If no linkage is explicitly specified and no hash reference is passed, GetOptions() will put the value in a global variable named after the option, prefixed by opt_. To yield a usable Perl variable, characters that are not part of the syntax for variables are translated to underscores. For example, --fpp-struct-return will set the variable $opt_fpp_struct_return. (Note that this variable resides in the namespace of the calling program, not necessarily main.) For example:

```
&GetOptions ("size=i", "sizes=i@");
```

with command line:

```
-size 10 -sizes 24 -sizes 48
```

will perform the equivalent of the assignments:

```
$opt_size = 10;
@opt_sizes = (24, 48);
```

A lone hyphen (-) is considered an option; the corresponding identifier is $opt_ .

The linkage specifier can be a reference to a scalar, a reference to an array, or a reference to a subroutine:

- If a scalar reference is supplied, the new value is stored in the referenced variable. If the option occurs more than once, the previous value is overwritten.

- If an array reference is supplied, the new value is appended (pushed) to the referenced array.

- If a code reference is supplied, the referenced subroutine is called with two arguments: the option name and the option value. The option name is always the true name, not an abbreviation or alias.

Aliases and abbreviations

The option specifier may actually include a "|"-separated list of option names:

```
foo|bar|blech=s
```

In this example, foo is the true name of the option. If no linkage is specified, options -foo, -bar and -blech all will set $opt_foo.

Options may be invoked as unique abbreviations, depending on configuration variable $Getopt::Long::autoabbrev.

Non-option callback routine

A special option specifier <> can be used to designate a subroutine to handle non-option arguments. For example:

```
&GetOptions(..."<>", \&mysub...);
```

In this case GetOptions() will immediately call &mysub for every non-option it encounters in the options list. This subroutine gets the name of the non-option passed. This feature requires $Getopt::Long::order to have the value of the predefined and exported variable, $PERMUTE. See also the examples.

Option starters

On the command line, options can start with - (traditional), -- (POSIX), and + (GNU, now being phased out). The latter is not allowed if the environment variable POSIXLY_CORRECT has been defined.

Options that start with -- may have an argument appended, following an equals sign (=). For example: --foo=bar.

Return value

A return status of 0 (false) indicates that the function detected one or more errors.

Configuration variables

The following variables can be set to change the default behavior of GetOptions():

$Getopt::Long::autoabbrev
>   If true, then allow option names to be invoked with unique abbreviations. Default is 1 unless environment variable POSIXLY_CORRECT has been set.

$Getopt::Long::getopt_compat
>   If true, then allow "+" to start options. Default is 1 unless environment variable POSIXLY_CORRECT has been set.

$Getopt::Long::order
>   If set to $PERMUTE, then non-options are allowed to be mixed with options on the command line. If set to $REQUIRE_ORDER, then mixing is not allowed. Default is $REQUIRE_ORDER if environment variable POSIXLY_CORRECT has been set, $PERMUTE otherwise. Both $PERMUTE and $REQUIRE_ORDER are defined in the library module and automatically exported. $PERMUTE means that:
>
>   -foo arg1 -bar arg2 arg3
>
>   is equivalent to:
>
>   -foo -bar arg1 arg2 arg3
>
>   If a non-option callback routine is specified, @ARGV will always be empty upon successful return of GetOptions() since all options have been processed, except when -- is used. So, for example:
>
>   -foo arg1 -bar arg2 -- arg3
>
>   will call the callback routine for arg1 and arg2, and then terminate, leaving arg3 in @ARGV. If $Getopt::Long::order is $REQUIRE_ORDER, option processing terminates when the first non-option is encountered.
>
>   -foo arg1 -bar arg2 arg3
>
>   is equivalent to:
>
>   -foo -- arg1 -bar arg2 arg3

$Getopt::Long::ignorecase
>   If true, then ignore case when matching options. Default is 1.

$Getopt::Long::VERSION
>   The version number of this Getopt::Long implementation is in the format major.minor. This can be used to have Exporter check the version. Example:
>
>   use Getopt::Long 2.00;
>
> $Getopt::Long::major_version and $Getopt::Long::minor_version may be inspected for the individual components.

`$Getopt::Long::error`

Internal error flag. May be incremented from a callback routine to cause options parsing to fail.

`$Getopt::Long::debug`

Enable copious debugging output. Default is 0.

Examples

If the option specifier is `one:i` (which takes an optional integer argument), then the following situations are handled:

```
-one -two          # $opt_one = "", -two is next option
-one -2            # $opt_one = -2
```

Also, assume specifiers `foo=s` and `bar:s`:

```
-bar -xxx          # $opt_bar = "", -xxx is next option
-foo -bar          # $opt_foo = '-bar'
-foo --            # $opt_foo = '--'
```

In GNU or POSIX format, option names and values can be combined:

```
+foo=blech         # $opt_foo = 'blech'
--bar=             # $opt_bar = ""
--bar=--           # $opt_bar = '--'
```

Example using variable references:

```
$ret = &GetOptions ('foo=s', \$foo, 'bar=i', 'ar=s', \@ar);
```

With command-line options `-foo blech -bar 24 -ar xx -ar yy` this will result in:

```
$opt_foo = 'blech'
$opt_bar = 24
@ar = ('xx', 'yy')
```

Example of using the `<>` option specifier:

```
@ARGV = qw(-foo 1 bar -foo 2 blech);
&GetOptions("foo=i", \$myfoo, "<>", \&mysub);
```

Results:

```
&mysub("bar") will be called (with $myfoo being 1)
&mysub("blech") will be called (with $myfoo being 2)
```

Compare this with:

```
@ARGV = qw(-foo 1 bar -foo 2 blech);
&GetOptions("foo=i", \$myfoo);
```

This will leave the non-options in @ARGV:

```
$myfoo becomes 2
@ARGV becomes qw(bar blech)
```

If you're using the use strict pragma, which requires you to employ only lexical variables or else globals that are fully declared, you will have to use the double-colon package delimiter or else the use vars pragma. For example:

```
use strict;
use vars qw($opt_rows $opt_cols);
use Getopt::Long;
```

Getopt::Std — Process Single-Character Options with Option Clustering

```
use Getopt::Std;

getopt('oDI');     # -o, -D & -I take arg.  Sets opt_* as a side effect.
getopts('oif:');   # -o & -i are boolean flags, -f takes an argument.
                   # Sets opt_* as a side effect.
```

The getopt() and getopts() functions give your program simple mechanisms for processing single-character options. These options can be clustered (for example, -bdLc might be interpreted as four single-character options), and you can specify individual options that require an accompanying argument. When you invoke getopt() or getopts(), you pass along information about the kinds of options your program expects. These functions then analyze @ARGV, extract information about the options, and return this information to your program in a set of variables. The processing of @ARGV stops when an argument without a leading "-" is encountered, if that argument is not associated with a preceding option. Otherwise, @ARGV is processed to its end and left empty.

For each option in your program's invocation, both getopt() and getopts() define a variable $opt_x where x is the option name. If the option takes an argument, then the argument is read and assigned to $opt_x as its value; otherwise, a value of 1 is assigned to the variable.

Invoke getopt() with one argument, which should contain all options that require a following argument. For example:

```
getopt('dV');
```

If your program is then invoked as:

```
myscr -bfd January -V 10.4
```

then these variables will be set in the program:

```
$opt_b = 1;
$opt_f = 1;
$opt_d = "January";
$opt_V = 10.4;
```

Space between an option and its following argument is unnecessary. The previous command line could have been given this way:

```
myscr -bfdJanuary -V10.4
```

In general, your program can be invoked with options given in any order. All options not "declared" in the invocation of getopt() are assumed to be without accompanying argument.

Where getopt() allows any single-character option, getopts() allows only those options you declare explicitly. For example, this invocation:

```
getopts('a:bc:');
```

legitimizes only the options -a, -b, and -c. The colon following the a and c means that these two options require an accompanying argument; b is not allowed to have an argument. Accordingly, here are some ways to invoke the program:

```
myscr -abc            # WRONG unless bc is really the argument to -a
myscr -a -bc          # WRONG, with same qualification
myscr -a foo -bc bar  # $opt_a = "foo"; $opt_b = 1; $opt_c = "bar"
myscr -bafoo -cbar    # same as previous
```

getopts() returns false if it encounters errors during option processing. However, it continues to process arguments and assign values as best it can to $opt_x variables. You should always check for errors before assuming that the variables hold meaningful values.

getopt() does not return a meaningful value.

Remember that both getopt() and getopts() halt argument processing upon reading an argument (without leading "-") where none was called for. This is not considered an error. So a user might invoke your program with invalid arguments, without your being notified of the fact. However, you can always check to see whether @ARGV has been completely emptied or not—that is, whether all arguments have been processed. If you're using the use strict pragma, which requires you to employ only lexical variables or else globals that are fully declared, you will have to use the double-colon package delimiter or else the use vars pragma. For example:

```
use strict;
use vars qw($opt_o $opt_i $opt_D);
use Getopt::Std;
```

I18N::Collate — Compare 8-bit Scalar Data According to the Current Locale

```
use I18N::Collate;

setlocale(LC_COLLATE, $locale);          # uses POSIX::setlocale
$s1 = new I18N::Collate "scalar_data_1";
$s2 = new I18N::Collate "scalar_data_2";
```

This module provides you with objects that can be collated (ordered) according to your national character set, provided that Perl's POSIX module and the POSIX *setlocale*(3) and *strxfrm*(3) functions are available on your system. $locale in the setlocale() invocation shown above must be an argument acceptable to *setlocale*(3) on your system. See the *setlocale*(3) manpage for further information. Available locales depend upon your operating system.

Here is an example of collation within the standard 'C' locale:

```
use I18N::Collate;

setlocale(LC_COLLATE, 'C');
$s1 = new I18N::Collate "Hello";
$s2 = new I18N::Collate "Goodbye";
# following line prints "Hello comes before Goodbye"
print "$$s1 comes before $$s2" if $s2 le $s1;
```

The objects returned by the new() method are references. You can get at their values by dereferencing them—for example, $$s1 and $$s2. However, Perl's built-in comparison operators are overloaded by I18N::Collate, so that they operate on the objects returned by new() without the necessity of dereference. The **print** line above dereferences $s1 and $s2 to access their values directly, but does not dereference the variables passed to the **le** operator. The comparison operators you can use in this way are the following:

```
<   <=  >   >=  ==  !=  <=>
lt  le  gt  ge  eq  ne  cmp
```

I18N::Collate uses POSIX::setlocale() and POSIX::strxfrm() to perform the collation. Unlike strxfrm(), however, I18N::Collate handles embedded NULL characters gracefully.

To determine which locales are available with your operating system, check whether the command:

```
locale -a
```

lists them. You can also check the *locale*(5) or *nlsinfo* manpages, or look at the filenames within one of these directories (or their subdirectories): */usr/lib/nls*,

/usr/share/lib/locale, or */etc/locale*. Not all locales your vendor supports are necessarily installed. Please consult your operating system's documentation and possibly your local system administrator.

integer — Do Arithmetic in Integer Instead of Double

```
use integer;

$x = 10/3;    # $x is now 3, not 3.33333333333333333
```

This module tells the compiler to use integer operations from here to the end of the enclosing block. On many machines, this doesn't matter a great deal for most computations, but on those without floating point hardware, it can make a big difference.

This pragma does not automatically cast everything to an integer; it only forces integer operations on arithmetic. For example:

```
use integer;
print sin(3);          # 0.141120008059867
print sin(3) + 4;      # 4
```

You can turn off the integer pragma within an inner block by using the `no integer` directive.

IPC::Open2 — Open a Process for Both Reading and Writing

```
use IPC::Open2;

# with named filehandles
$pid = open2(\*RDR, \*WTR, $cmd_with_args);
$pid = open2(\*RDR, \*WTR, $cmd, "arg1", "arg2", ...);

# with object-oriented handles
use FileHandle;
my($rdr, $wtr) = (FileHandle->new, FileHandle->new);
$pid = open2($rdr, $wtr, $cmd_with_args);
```

The `open2()` function forks a child process to execute the specified command. The first two arguments represent filehandles, one way or another. They can be FileHandle objects, or they can be references to typeglobs, which can either be explicitly named as above, or generated by the Symbol package, as in the example below. Whichever you choose, they represent handles through which your program can read from the command's standard output and write to the command's standard input, respectively. `open2()` differs from Perl's built-in **open** function in that it allows your program to communicate in both directions with the child process.

open2() returns the process ID of the child process. On failure it reports a fatal error.

Here's a simple use of open2() by which you can give the program user interactive access to the *bc*(1) command. (*bc* is an arbitrary-precision arithmetic package.) In this case we use the Symbol module to produce "anonymous" symbols:

```
use IPC::Open2;
use Symbol;

$WTR = gensym();  # get a reference to a typeglob
$RDR = gensym();  # and another one

$pid = open2($RDR, $WTR, 'bc');

while (<STDIN>) {             # read commands from user
    print $WTR $_;           # write a command to bc(1)
    $line = <$RDR>;          # read the output of bc(1)
    print STDOUT "$line";    # send the output to the user
}
```

open2() establishes unbuffered output for $WTR. However, it cannot control buffering of output from the designated command. Therefore, be sure to heed the following warning.

WARNING   It is extremely easy for your program to hang while waiting to read the next line of output from the command. In the example just shown, *bc* is known to read and write one line at a time, so it is safe. But utilities like *sort*(1) that read their entire input stream before offering any output will cause a deadlock when used in the manner we have illustrated. You might do something like this instead:

```
$pid = open2($RDR, $WTR, 'sort');

while (<STDIN>) {
    print $WTR $_;
}
close($WTR);    # finish sending all output to sort(1)

while (<$RDR>) {    # now read the output of sort(1)
    print STDOUT "$_";
}
```

More generally, you may have to use **select** to determine which file descriptors are ready to read, and then **sysread** for the actual reading.

See also

The IPC::open3 module shows an alternative that handles STDERR as well.

IPC::Open3 — Open a Process for Reading, Writing, and Error Handling

```
use IPC::Open3;

$pid = open3($WTR, $RDR, $ERR, $cmd_with_args);
$pid = open3($WTR, $RDR, $ERR, $cmd, "arg1", "arg2", ...);
```

IPC::Open3 works like IPC::Open2, with the following differences:

- The first two arguments ($WTR and $RDR) are given in reverse order compared to IPC::Open2.

- A third filehandle can be given, for standard error. If this argument is given as "", then STDERR and STDOUT for $cmd will be on the same filehandle.

- If $WTR begins with <&, then the leading <& is stripped from the name and the remainder is assumed to be a regular filehandle for an open file, rather than a reference to a typeglob. open3() opens this file as STDIN for $cmd and closes it in the parent. Likewise, if $RDR or $ERR begins with >&, then $cmd directs STDOUT or STDERR directly to that file rather than to the parent.

Warnings given for IPC::Open2 regarding possible program hangs apply to IPC::Open3 as well.

lib — Manipulate @INC at Compile-Time

```
use lib LIST;
no lib LIST;
```

This module simplifies the manipulation of Perl's special @INC variable at compile-time. It is used to add extra directories to Perl's search path so that later **use** or **require** statements will find modules not located along Perl's default search path.

Adding directories

Directories itemized in *LIST* are added to the start of the Perl search path. Saying:

```
use lib LIST;
```

is *almost* the same as saying:

```
BEGIN { unshift(@INC, LIST) }
```

The difference is that, for each directory in *LIST* (called $dir here), the lib module also checks to see whether a directory called $dir/$archname/*auto* exists, where $archname is derived from Perl's configuration information:

```
use Config;
$archname = $Config{'archname'};
```

If so, the $dir/$archname directory is assumed to be an architecture-specific directory and is added to @INC in front of $dir.

If *LIST* includes both $dir and $dir/$archname, then $dir/$archname will be added to @INC twice (assuming $dir/$archname/*auto* exists).

Deleting directories

You should normally only add directories to @INC. If you need to delete directories from @INC, take care to delete only those you yourself added. Otherwise, be certain that the directories you delete are not needed by other modules directly or indirectly invoked by your script. Other modules may have added directories they need for correct operation.

By default the statement:

```
no lib LIST
```

deletes the first instance of each named directory from @INC. To delete multiple instances of the same name from @INC you can specify the name multiple times.

To delete all instances of all the specified names from @INC you can specify :ALL as the first parameter of *LIST*. For example:

```
no lib qw(:ALL .);
```

For each directory in *LIST* (called $dir here) the lib module also checks to see whether a directory called $dir/$archname/*auto* exists. If so, the $dir/$archname directory is assumed to be a corresponding architecture-specific directory and is also deleted from @INC.

If *LIST* includes both $dir and $dir/$archname then $dir/$archname will be deleted from @INC twice (assuming $dir/$archname/*auto* exists).

Restoring the original directory list

When the lib module is first loaded, it records the current value of @INC in an array @lib::ORIG_INC. To restore @INC to that value you can say:

```
@INC = @lib::ORIG_INC;
```

See also

The AddINC module (not in the standard Perl library, but available from CPAN) deals with paths relative to the source file.

Math::BigFloat—Arbitrary-Length, Floating-Point Math Package

```
use Math::BigFloat;

$f = Math::BigFloat->new($string);

# NSTR is a number string; SCALE is an integer value.
# In all following cases $f remains unchanged.
# All methods except fcmp() return a number string.
$f->fadd(NSTR);            # return sum of NSTR and $f
$f->fsub(NSTR);            # return $f minus NSTR
$f->fmul(NSTR);            # return $f multiplied by NSTR
$f->fdiv(NSTR[,SCALE]);    # return $f divided by NSTR to SCALE places
$f->fneg();                # return negative of $f
$f->fabs();                # return absolute value of $f
$f->fcmp(NSTR);            # compare $f to NSTR; see below for return value
$f->fround(SCALE);         # return rounded value of $f to SCALE digits
$f->ffround(SCALE);        # return rounded value of $f at SCALEth place
$f->fnorm();               # return normalization of $f
$f->fsqrt([SCALE]);        # return sqrt of $f to SCALE places
```

This module allows you to use floating-point numbers of arbitrary length. For example:

```
$float = new Math::BigFloat "2.1231231231231231231231231231231231231231233123123";
```

Number strings (*NSTRs*) have the form, `/[+-]\d*\.?\d*E[+-]\d+/`. Embedded white space is ignored, so that the number strings used in the following two lines are identical:

```
$f = Math::BigFloat->new("-20.0    0732");
$g = $f->fmul("-20.00732");
```

The return value NaN indicates either that an input parameter was "Not a Number", or else that you tried to divide by zero or take the square root of a negative number. The fcmp() method returns -1, 0, or 1 depending on whether $f is less than, equal to, or greater than the number string given as an argument. If the number string is undefined or null, the undefined value is returned.

If *SCALE* is unspecified, division is computed to the number of digits given by:

```
max($div_scale, length(dividend)+length(divisor))
```

A similar default scale value is computed for square roots.

When you use this module, Perl's basic math operations are overloaded with routines from Math::BigFloat. Therefore, you don't have to employ the methods shown above to multiply, divide, and so on. You can rely instead on the usual operators. Given this code:

```
$f = Math::BigFloat->new("20.00732");
$g = Math::BigFloat->new("1.7");
```

the following six lines all yield the corresponding values for $h:

```
$h = 20.00732 * 1.7;     # 34.012444 (ordinary math--$h is not an object)
$h = $f * $g;            # "34.012444" ($h is now a BigFloat object)
$h = $f * 1.7;           # "34.012444" ($h is now a BigFloat object)
$h = 20.00732 * $g;      # "34.012444" ($h is now a BigFloat object)
$h = $f->fmul($g);       # "+34012444E-6" ($h is now a BigFloat object)
$h = $f->fmul(1.7);      # "+34012444E-6" ($h is now a BigFloat object)
```

Math::BigInt — Arbitrary-Length Integer Math Package

```
use Math::BigInt;

$i = Math::BigInt->new($string);

# BINT is a big integer string; in all following cases $i remains unchanged.
# All methods except bcmp() return a big integer string, or strings.
$i->bneg;          # return negative of $i
$i->babs           # return absolute value of $i
$i->bcmp(BINT)     # compare $i to BINT; see below for return value
$i->badd(BINT)     # return sum of BINT and $i
$i->bsub(BINT)     # return $i minus BINT
$i->bmul(BINT)     # return $i multiplied by BINT
$i->bdiv(BINT)     # return $i divided by BINT; see below for return value
$i->bmod(BINT)     # return $i modulus BINT
$i->bgcd(BINT)     # return greatest common divisor of $i and BINT
$i->bnorm          # return normalization of $i
```

This module allows you to use integers of arbitrary length. Integer strings (*BINT*s) have the form /^\s*[+-]?[\d\s]+$/. Embedded whitespace is ignored. Output values are always in the canonical form: /^[+-]\d+$/ . For example:

```
'+0'               # canonical zero value
'   -123 123 123'  # canonical value:  '-123123123'
'1 23 456 7890'    # canonical value:  '+1234567890'
```

The return value NaN results when an input argument is not a number, or when a divide by zero is attempted. The bcmp() method returns –1, 0, or 1 depending on whether $f is less than, equal to, or greater than the number string given as an argument. If the number string is undefined or null, the undefined value is returned. In a list context the bdiv() method returns a two-element array containing the quotient of the division and the remainder; in a scalar context only the quotient is returned.

When you use this module, Perl's basic math operations are overloaded with routines from Math::BigInt. Therefore, you don't have to employ the methods shown above to multiply, divide, and so on. You can rely instead on the usual operators. Given this code:

```
$a = Math::BigInt->new("42 000 000 000 000");
$b = Math::BigInt->new("-111111");
```

the following five lines yield these string values for $c:

```
$c = 42000000000000 - -111111;
                            # 42000000111111; ordinary math--$c is a double
$c = $a - $b;               # "+42000000111111"; $c is now a BigInt object
$c = $a - -111111;·         # "+42000000111111"; $c is now a BigInt object
$c = $a->bsub($b);          # "+42000000111111"; $c is just a string
$c = $a->bsub(-111111);     # "+42000000111111"; $c is just a string
```

Math::Complex — Complex Numbers Package

```
use Math::Complex;
$cnum = new Math::Complex;
```

When you use this module, complex numbers declared as:

```
$cnum = Math::Complex->new(1, 1);
```

can be manipulated with overloaded math operators. The operators:

```
+ - * / neg ~ abs cos sin exp sqrt
```

are supported, and return references to new objects. Also,

```
"" (stringify)
```

is available to convert complex numbers to strings. In addition, the methods:

```
Re Im arg
```

are available. Given a complex number, $cnum:

```
$cnum = Math::Complex->new($x, $y);
```

then $cnum->Re() returns $x, $cnum->Im() returns $y, and $cnum->arg() returns atan2($y, $x).

sqrt(), which should return two roots, returns only one.

NDBM_File — *Tied Access to NDBM Files*

```
use Fcntl;
use NDBM_File;

tie(%hash, NDBM_File, 'Op.dbmx', O_RDWR|O_CREAT, 0644);
# read/writes of %hash are now read/writes of the file, Op.dmx.pag
untie %hash;
```

See Perl's built-in **tie** function. Also see under DB_File in this chapter for a description of a closely related module.

Net::Ping — *Check Whether a Host Is Online*

```
use Net::Ping;

$hostname = 'elvis';        # host to check
$timeout = 10;              # how long to wait for a response
print "elvis is alive\n"    if pingecho($hostname, $timeout);
```

pingecho() uses a TCP echo (not an ICMP one) to determine whether a remote host is reachable. This is usually adequate to tell whether a remote host is available to *rsh*(1), *ftp*(1), or *telnet*(1).

The parameters for pingecho() are:

hostname
    The remote host to check, specified either as a hostname or as an IP address.

timeout
    The timeout in seconds. If not specified it will default to 5 seconds.

WARNING   pingecho() uses **alarm** to implement the timeout, so don't set another
             alarm while you are using it.

ODBM_File — *Tied Access to ODBM Files*

```
use Fcntl;
use ODBM_File;

tie(%hash, ODBM_File, 'Op.dbmx', O_RDWR|O_CREAT, 0644);
# read/writes of %hash are now read/writes of the file, Op.dmx
untie %hash;
```

See Perl's built-in **tie** function. Also see under DB_File in this chapter for a description of a closely related module.

overload—Overload Perl's Mathematical Operations

```
# In the SomeThing module:
package SomeThing;

use overload
    '+' => \&myadd,
    '-' => \&mysub;

# In your other code:
use SomeThing;

$a = SomeThing->new(57);
$b=5+$a;

if (overload::Overloaded $b) {...}    # is $b subject to overloading?

$strval = overload::StrVal $b;
```

Caveat Scriptor: This interface is the subject of ongoing research. Feel free to play with it, but don't be too surprised if the interface changes subtly (or not so subtly) as it is developed further. If you rely on it for a mission-critical application, please be sure to write some good regression tests. (Or perhaps in this case we should call them "progression" tests.)

This module allows you to substitute class methods or your own subroutines for standard Perl operators. For example, the code:

```
package Number;
use overload
    "+"  => \&add,
    "*=" => "muas";
```

declares function add() for addition, and method muas() in the Number class (or one of its base classes) for the assignment form *= of multiplication.

Arguments to use overload come in key/value pairs. Legal values are values permitted inside a &{ ... } call, so the name of a subroutine, a reference to a subroutine, or an anonymous subroutine will all work. Legal keys are listed below.

The subroutine add() will be called to execute $a+$b if $a is a reference to an object blessed into the package Number, or if $a is not an object from a package with overloaded addition, but $b is a reference to a Number. It can also be called in other situations, like $a+=7, or $a++. See the section on "Autogeneration".

Calling conventions for binary operations

The functions specified with the use overload directive are typically called with three arguments. (See the "No Method" section later in this chapter for the four-argument case.) If the corresponding operation is binary, then the first two arguments are the two arguments of the operation. However, due to general object-calling conventions, the first argument should always be an object in the package, so in the situation of 7+$a, the order of the arguments gets interchanged before the method is called. It probably does not matter when implementing the addition method, but whether the arguments are reversed is vital to the subtraction method. The method can query this information by examining the third argument, which can take three different values:

false (0)
> The order of arguments is as in the current operation.

true (1)
> The arguments are reversed.

undefined
> The current operation is an assignment variant (as in $a+=7), but the usual function is called instead. This additional information can be used to generate some optimizations.

Calling conventions for unary operations

Unary operations are considered binary operations with the second argument being **undef**. Thus the function that overloads {"++"} is called with arguments ($a, undef, "") when $a++ is executed.

Overloadable operations

The following operations can be specified with use overload:

- *Arithmetic operations*

```
+     -     *    /    %    **     <<     >>    x    .
+=    -=    *=   /=   %=   **=    <<=    >>=   x=   .=
```

  For these operations a substituted non-assignment variant can be called if the assignment variant is not available. Methods for operations "+", "–", "+=", and "–=" can be called to automatically generate increment and decrement methods. The operation "–" can be used to autogenerate missing methods for unary minus or abs().

- *Comparison operations*

```
<     <=    >    >=    ==    !=    <=>
lt    le    gt   ge    eq    ne    cmp
```

The <=> operator can substitute for any of the other numeric compare operators, and **cmp** can substitute for any missing string compare operators. When using **sort** on arrays, cmp is used to compare values subject to use overload.

- *Bit and unary operations*

        &   ^ | neg   !   ~

  "neg" stands for unary minus. If the method for neg is not specified, it can be autogenerated using the method for subtraction.

- *Increment and decrement*

        ++   --

  If undefined, addition and subtraction methods can be used instead. These operations are called both in prefix and postfix form.

- *Transcendental functions*

        atan2   cos   sin   exp   abs   log   sqrt

  If abs is unavailable, it can be autogenerated using methods for "<" or "<=>" combined with either unary minus or subtraction.

- *Boolean, string and numeric conversion*

        bool   ""   0+

  (Yes, that really is two double-quotes in a row.) If one or two of these operations are unavailable, the remaining ones can be used instead. bool is used in the flow control operators (like **while** and **if**) and for the trinary "?:" operation. These functions can return any arbitrary Perl value. If the corresponding operation for this value is overloaded, too, then that operation will be called again with this value.

- *Special*

        nomethod   fallback   =

  The following sections provide explanation.

Three keys are recognized by Perl that are not covered by the above descriptions: "nomethod", "fallback", and "=".

No method

"nomethod" should be followed by a reference to a function of four parameters. If defined, it is called when the overloading mechanism cannot find a method for some operation. The first three arguments of this function coincide with the arguments for the corresponding method if it were found; the fourth argument is the symbol corresponding to the missing method. If several methods are tried, the last one is used.

For example, 1-$a can be equivalent to:

```
&nomethodMethod($a, 1, 1, "-")
```

if the pair "nomethod" => "nomethodMethod" was specified in the use overload directive.

If some operation cannot be resolved and there is no function assigned to "nomethod", then an exception will be raised via **die** unless "fallback" was specified as a key in a use overload directive.

Fallback

The "fallback" key governs what to do if a method for a particular operation is not found. Three different cases are possible depending on the value of "fallback":

undefined

Perl tries to use a substituted method (see the section later on "Autogeneration". If this fails, it then tries to call the method specified for "nomethod"; if missing, an exception will be raised.

true

The same as for the undefined value, but no exception is raised. Instead, Perl silently reverts to what it would have done were there no use overload present.

defined, but false

No autogeneration is tried. Perl tries to call the method specified for "nomethod", and if this is missing, raises an exception.

Copy constructor

The value for "=" is a reference to a function with three arguments; that is, it looks like the other values in use overload. However, it does not overload the Perl assignment operator. This would rub Camel hair the wrong way.

This operation is called when a *mutator* is applied to a reference that shares its object with some other reference, such as:

```
$a=$b;
$a++;
```

In order to change $a but not $b, a copy of $$a is made, and $a is assigned a reference to this new object. This operation is done during execution of the $a++, and not during the assignment, (so before the increment $$a coincides with $$b). This is only done if ++ is expressed via a method for "++" or "+=". Note that if this operation is expressed via "+" (a nonmutator):

```
$a=$b;
$a=$a+1;
```

then $a does not reference a new copy of $$a, since $$a does not appear as an lvalue when the above code is executed.

If the copy constructor is required during the execution of some mutator, but a method for "=" was not specified, it can be autogenerated as a string copy if the object is a plain scalar.

As an example, the actually executed code for:

```
$a=$b;
# Something else which does not modify $a or $b...
++$a;
```

may be:

```
$a=$b;
# Something else which does not modify $a or $b...
$a = $a->clone(undef, "");
$a->incr(undef, "");
```

This assumes $b is subject to overloading, "++" was overloaded with \&incr, and "=" was overloaded with \&clone.

Autogeneration

If a method for an operation is not found, and the value for "fallback" is true or undefined, Perl tries to autogenerate a substitute method for the missing operation based on the defined operations. Autogenerated method substitutions are possible for the following operations:

Assignment forms of arithmetic operations
    $a+=$b can use the method for "+" if the method for "+=" is not defined.

Conversion operations
    String, numeric, and Boolean conversion are calculated in terms of one another if not all of them are defined.

Increment and decrement
    The ++$a operation can be expressed in terms of $a+=1 or $a+1, and $a-- in terms of $a-=1 and $a-1.

abs($a)
    Can be expressed in terms of $a<0 and -$a (or 0-$a).

Unary minus

Can be expressed in terms of subtraction.

Concatenation

Can be expressed in terms of string conversion.

Comparison operations

Can be expressed in terms of its three-valued counterpart: either <=> or cmp:

```
<,  >,  <=, >=, ==, !=    in terms of <=>
lt, gt, le, ge, eq, ne    in terms of cmp
```

Copy operator

Can be expressed in terms of an assignment to the dereferenced value if this value is a scalar and not a reference.

WARNING   One restriction for the comparison operation is that even if, for example, cmp returns a blessed reference, the autogenerated lt function will produce only a standard logical value based on the numerical value of the result of cmp. In particular, a working numeric conversion is needed in this case (possibly expressed in terms of other conversions).

Similarly, .= and x= operators lose their overloaded properties if the string conversion substitution is applied.

When you **chop** an object that is subject to overloaded operations, the object is promoted to a string and its overloading properties are lost. The same can happen with other operations as well.

Run-time overloading

Since all **use** directives are executed at compile-time, the only way to change overloading during run-time is:

```
eval 'use overload "+" => \&addmethod';
```

You can also say:

```
eval 'no overload "+", "--", "<="';
```

although the use of these constructs during run-time is questionable.

Public functions

The overload module provides the following public functions:

overload::StrVal(*arg*)

Gives string value of *arg* if stringify overloading is absent.

overload::Overloaded(*arg*)

  Returns true if *arg* is subject to overloading of some operations.

overload::Method(*obj*, *op*)

  Returns the undefined value or a reference to the method that implements *op*.

Diagnostics

When Perl is run with the -Do switch or its equivalent, overloading induces diagnostic messages.

Bugs

Because it is used for overloading, the per-package associative array %OVERLOAD now has a special meaning in Perl.

Overloading is not yet inherited via the @ISA tree, though individual methods may be.

POSIX—Perl Interface to IEEE Std 1003.1

```
use POSIX;                     # import all symbols
use POSIX qw(setsid);          # import one symbol
use POSIX qw(:errno_h :fcntl_h);  # import sets of symbols

printf "EINTR is %d\n", EINTR;

$sess_id = POSIX::setsid();

$fd = POSIX::open($path, O_CREAT|O_EXCL|O_WRONLY, 0644);
# note: $fd is a filedescriptor, *NOT* a filehandle
```

The POSIX module permits you to access all (or nearly all) the standard POSIX 1003.1 identifiers. Many of these identifiers have been given Perl-ish interfaces.

This description gives a condensed list of the features available in the POSIX module. Consult your operating system's manpages for general information on most features. Consult the appropriate Perl built-in function whenever a POSIX routine is noted as being identical to the function.

The "Classes" section later in this chapter describes some classes for signal objects, TTY objects, and other miscellaneous objects. The "Functions" section later in this chapter describes POSIX functions from the 1003.1 specification. The remaining sections list various constants and macros in an organization that roughly follows IEEE Std 1003.1b-1993.

WARNING   A few functions are not implemented because they are C-specific.[*] If
              you attempt to call one of these functions, it will print a message
              telling you that it isn't implemented, and will suggest using the Perl
              equivalent, should one exist. For example, trying to access the
              setjmp() call will elicit the message: "setjmp() is C-specific: use
              eval {} instead".

              Furthermore, some vendors will claim 1003.1 compliance without
              passing the POSIX Compliance Test Suites (PCTS). For example, one
              vendor may not define EDEADLK, or may incorrectly define the seman-
              tics of the *errno* values set by *open*(2). Perl does not attempt to ver-
              ify POSIX compliance. That means you can currently say "use POSIX"
              successfully, and then later in your program find that your vendor
              has been lax and there's no usable ICANON macro after all. This could
              be construed to be a bug. Whose bug, we won't venture to guess.

Classes

POSIX::SigAction

new

> Creates a new POSIX::SigAction object that corresponds to the C struct
> sigaction. This object will be destroyed automatically when it is no longer
> needed. The first parameter is the fully qualified name of a subroutine which
> is a signal handler. The second parameter is a POSIX::SigSet object. The third
> parameter contains the sa_flags.
>
> ```
> $sigset = POSIX::SigSet->new;
> $sigaction = POSIX::SigAction->new('main::handler', $sigset,
>                 &POSIX::SA_NOCLDSTOP);
> ```
>
> This POSIX::SigAction object should be used with the POSIX::sigaction() func-
> tion.

POSIX::SigSet

new

> Creates a new SigSet object. This object will be destroyed automatically when
> it is no longer needed. Arguments may be supplied to initialize the set. Create
> an empty set:
>
> ```
> $sigset = POSIX::SigSet->new;
> ```

---

[*] The 1003.1 standard wisely recommends that other language bindings should avoid duplicating the
idiosyncracies of C. This is something we were *glad* to comply with.

Create a set with SIGUSR1:

```
$sigset = POSIX::SigSet->new(&POSIX::SIGUSR1);
```

addset

Adds a signal to a SigSet object. Returns **undef** on failure.

```
$sigset->addset(&POSIX::SIGUSR2);
```

delset

Removes a signal from the SigSet object. Returns **undef** on failure.

```
$sigset->delset(&POSIX::SIGUSR2);
```

emptyset

Initializes the SigSet object to be empty. Returns **undef** on failure.

```
$sigset->emptyset();
```

fillset

Initializes the SigSet object to include all signals. Returns **undef** on failure.

```
$sigset->fillset();
```

ismember

Tests the SigSet object to see whether it contains a specific signal.

```
if ($sigset->ismember(&POSIX::SIGUSR1 ) ){
    print "contains SIGUSR1\n";
}
```

POSIX::Termios

new

Creates a new Termios object. This object will be destroyed automatically when it is no longer needed.

```
$termios = POSIX::Termios->new;
```

getattr

Gets terminal control attributes for a given *fd*, 0 by default. Returns **undef** on failure. Obtain the attributes for standard input:

```
$termios->getattr()
```

Obtain the attributes for standard output:

```
$termios->getattr(1)
```

getcc

> Retrieves a value from the c_cc field of a Termios object. The c_cc field is an array, so an index must be specified.

```
$c_cc[1] = $termios->getcc(&POSIX::VEOF);
```

getcflag

> Retrieves the c_cflag field of a Termios object.

```
$c_cflag = $termios->getcflag;
```

getiflag

> Retrieves the c_iflag field of a Termios object.

```
$c_iflag = $termios->getiflag;
```

getispeed

> Retrieves the input baud rate.

```
$ispeed = $termios->getispeed;
```

getlflag

> Retrieves the c_lflag field of a Termios object.

```
$c_lflag = $termios->getlflag;
```

getoflag

> Retrieves the c_oflag field of a Termios object.

```
$c_oflag = $termios->getoflag;
```

getospeed

> Retrieves the output baud rate.

```
$ospeed = $termios->getospeed;
```

setattr

> Sets terminal control attributes for a given *fd*. Returns **undef** on failure. The following sets attributes immediately for standard output.

```
$termios->setattr(1, &POSIX::TCSANOW);
```

setcc

> Sets a value in the c_cc field of a Termios object. The c_cc field is an array, so an index must be specified.

```
$termios->setcc(&POSIX::VEOF, 4);
```

setcflag

> Sets the c_cflag field of a Termios object.

```
$termios->setcflag(&POSIX::CLOCAL);
```

setiflag

> Sets the c_iflag field of a Termios object.

> $termios->setiflag(&POSIX::BRKINT);

setispeed

> Sets the input baud rate. Returns **undef** on failure.

> $termios->setispeed(&POSIX::B9600);

setlflag

> Sets the c_lflag field of a Termios object.

> $termios->setlflag(&POSIX::ECHO);

setoflag

> Set the c_oflag field of a Termios object.

> $termios->setoflag(&POSIX::OPOST);

setospeed

> Sets the output baud rate. Returns **undef** on failure.

> $termios->setospeed(&POSIX::B9600);

Baud rate values

> B0 B50 B75 B110 B134 B150 B200 B300 B600 B1200 B1800 B2400 B4800 B9600 B19200 B38400

Terminal interface values

> TCSADRAIN TCSANOW TCOON TCIOFLUSH TCOFLUSH TCION TCIFLUSH TCSAFLUSH TCIOFF TCOOFF

c_cc index values

> VEOF VEOL VERASE VINTR VKILL VQUIT VSUSP VSTART VSTOP VMIN VTIME NCCS

c_cflag field values

> CLOCAL CREAD CSIZE CS5 CS6 CS7 CS8 CSTOPB HUPCL PARENB PARODD

c_iflag field values

> BRKINT ICRNL IGNBRK IGNCR IGNPAR INLCR INPCK ISTRIP IXOFF IXON PARMRK

c_lflag field values

> ECHO ECHOE ECHOK ECHONL ICANON IEXTEN ISIG NOFLSH TOSTOP

c_oflag field values

> OPOST

While these constants are associated with the Termios class, note that they are actually symbols in the POSIX package.

Here's an example of a complete program for getting unbuffered, single-character input on a POSIX system:

```perl
#!/usr/bin/perl -w
use strict;
$| = 1;
for (1..4) {
    my $got;
    print "gimme: ";
    $got = getone();
    print "--> $got\n";
}
exit;

BEGIN {
    use POSIX qw(:termios_h);

    my ($term, $oterm, $echo, $noecho, $fd_stdin);

    $fd_stdin = fileno(STDIN);

    $term     = POSIX::Termios->new();
    $term->getattr($fd_stdin);
    $oterm    = $term->getlflag();

    $echo     = ECHO | ECHOK | ICANON;
    $noecho   = $oterm & ~$echo;

    sub cbreak {
        $term->setlflag($noecho);
        $term->setcc(VTIME, 1);
        $term->setattr($fd_stdin, TCSANOW);
    }

    sub cooked {
        $term->setlflag($oterm);
        $term->setcc(VTIME, 0);
        $term->setattr($fd_stdin, TCSANOW);
    }

    sub getone {
        my $key = "";
        cbreak();
        sysread(STDIN, $key, 1);
        cooked();
        return $key;
    }

}

END { cooked() }
```

Functions

Table 7-12: Functions

Function Name	Definition
_exit	Identical to the C function *_exit*(2).
abort	Identical to the C function *abort*(3).
abs	Identical to Perl's built-in **abs** function.

access	Determines the accessibility of a file. Returns **undef** on failure.
	
	``
	if (POSIX::access("/", &POSIX::R_OK)){
	    print "have read permission\n";
	}
	``

acos	Identical to the C function *acos*(3).
alarm	Identical to Perl's built-in **alarm** function.
asctime	Identical to the C function *asctime*(3).
asin	Identical to the C function *asin*(3).
assert	Similar to the C macro *assert*(3).
atan	Identical to the C function *atan*(3).
atan2	Identical to Perl's built-in **atan2** function.
atexit	C-specific: use **END** {} instead.
atof	C-specific.
atoi	C-specific.
atol	C-specific.
bsearch	Not supplied. You should probably be using a hash anyway.
calloc	C-specific.
ceil	Identical to the C function *ceil*(3).
chdir	Identical to Perl's built-in **chdir** function.
chmod	Identical to Perl's built-in **chmod** function.
chown	Identical to Perl's built-in **chown** function.
clearerr	Use method `FileHandle::clearerr()` instead.
clock	Identical to the C function *clock*(3).
close	Closes a file. This uses file descriptors such as those obtained by calling `POSIX::open()`. Returns **undef** on failure. ``` $fd = POSIX::open("foo", &POSIX::O_RDONLY); POSIX::close($fd); ```
closedir	Identical to Perl's built-in **closedir** function.
cos	Identical to Perl's built-in **cos** function.
cosh	Identical to the C function *cosh*(3).

Table 7-12: Functions (continued)

Function Name	Definition

creat	Creates a new file. This returns a file descriptor like the ones returned by POSIX::open(). Use POSIX::close() to close the file.
	
	`$fd = POSIX::creat("foo", 0611);`
	`POSIX::close($fd);`

ctermid	Generates the path name for the controlling terminal. `$path = POSIX::ctermid();`
ctime	Identical to the C function *ctime*(3)
cuserid	Gets the character login name of the user. `$name = POSIX::cuserid();`
difftime	Identical to the C function *difftime*(3).
div	C-specific.
dup	Similar to the C function *dup*(2). Uses file descriptors such as those obtained by calling POSIX::open(). Returns **undef** on failure.
dup2	Similar to the C function *dup2*(2). Uses file descriptors such as those obtained by calling POSIX::open(). Returns **undef** on failure.
errno	Returns the value of *errno*. `$errno = POSIX::errno();`
execl	C-specific; use Perl's **exec** instead.
execle	C-specific; use Perl's **exec** instead.
execlp	C-specific; use Perl's **exec** instead.
execv	C-specific; use Perl's **exec** instead.
execve	C-specific; use Perl's **exec** instead.
execvp	C-specific; use Perl's **exec** instead.
exit	Identical to Perl's built-in **exit** function.
exp	Identical to Perl's built-in **exp** function.
fabs	Identical to Perl's built-in **abs** function.
fclose	Use method FileHandle::close() instead.
fcntl	Identical to Perl's built-in **fcntl** function.
fdopen	Use method FileHandle::new_from_fd() instead.
feof	Use method FileHandle::eof() instead.

Table 7–12: Functions (continued)

Function Name	Definition
ferror	Use method `FileHandle::error()` instead.
fflush	Use method `FileHandle::flush()` instead.
fgetc	Use method `FileHandle::getc()` instead.
fgetpos	Use method `FileHandle::getpos()` instead.
fgets	Use method `FileHandle::gets()` instead.
fileno	Use method `FileHandle::fileno()` instead.
floor	Identical to the C function *floor*(3).
fmod	Identical to the C function *fmod*(3).
fopen	Use method `FileHandle::open()` instead.
fork	Identical to Perl's built-in **fork** function.

fpathconf	Retrieves the value of a configurable limit on a file or directory. This uses file descriptors such as those obtained by calling `POSIX::open()`. Returns **undef** on failure. The following will determine the maximum length of the longest allowable pathname on the filesystem that holds */tmp/foo*.
	
	```$fd = POSIX::open("/tmp/foo", &POSIX::O_RDONLY);```
	```$path_max = POSIX::fpathconf($fd, &POSIX::_PC_PATH_MAX);```

fprintf	C-specific; use Perl's built-in **printf** function instead.
fputc	C-specific; use Perl's built-in **print** function instead.
fputs	C-specific; use Perl's built-in **print** function instead.
fread	C-specific; use Perl's built-in **read** function instead.
free	C-specific
freopen	C-specific; use Perl's built-in **open** function instead.
frexp	Returns the mantissa and exponent of a floating-point number. ```($mantissa, $exponent) = POSIX::frexp(3.14);```
fscanf	C-specific; use <> and regular expressions instead.
fseek	Use method `FileHandle::seek()` instead.
fsetpos	Use method `FileHandle::setpos()` instead.

fstat	Gets file status. This uses file descriptors such as those obtained by calling `POSIX::open()`. The data returned is identical to the data from Perl's built-in **stat** function. Odd how that happens...
	
	```$fd = POSIX::open("foo", &POSIX::O_RDONLY);```
	```@stats = POSIX::fstat($fd);```

ftell	Use method `FileHandle::tell()` instead.

Table 7–12: Functions (continued)

Function Name	Definition
fwrite	C-specific; use Perl's built-in **print** function instead.
getc	Identical to Perl's built-in **getc** function.
getchar	Returns one character from STDIN.
getcwd	Returns the name of the current working directory.
getegid	Returns the effective group ID (gid).
getenv	Returns the value of the specified environment variable.
geteuid	Returns the effective user ID (uid).
getgid	Returns the user's real group ID (gid).
getgrgid	Identical to Perl's built-in **getgrgid** function.
getgrnam	Identical to Perl's built-in **getgrnam** function.
getgroups	Returns the ids of the user's supplementary groups.
getlogin	Identical to Perl's built-in **getlogin** function.
getpgrp	Identical to Perl's built-in **getpgrp** function.
getpid	Returns the process's ID (pid).
getppid	Identical to Perl's built-in **getppid** function.
getpwnam	Identical to Perl's built-in **getpwnam** function.
getpwuid	Identical to Perl's built-in **getpwuid** function.
gets	Returns one line from STDIN.
getuid	Returns the user's ID (uid).
gmtime	Identical to Perl's built-in **gmtime** function.
isalnum	Identical to the C function, except that it can apply to a single character or to a whole string. (If applied to a whole string, all characters must be of the indicated category.)
isalpha	Identical to the C function, except that it can apply to a single character or to a whole string.
isatty	Returns a Boolean indicating whether the specified filehandle is connected to a TTY.
iscntrl	Identical to the C function, except that it can apply to a single character or to a whole string.
isdigit	Identical to the C function, except that it can apply to a single character or to a whole string.
isgraph	Identical to the C function, except that it can apply to a single character or to a whole string.
islower	Identical to the C function, except that it can apply to a single character or to a whole string.
isprint	Identical to the C function, except that it can apply to a single character or to a whole string.

Table 7–12: Functions (continued)

Function Name	Definition
ispunct	Identical to the C function, except that it can apply to a single character or to a whole string.
isspace	Identical to the C function, except that it can apply to a single character or to a whole string.
isupper	Identical to the C function, except that it can apply to a single character or to a whole string.
isxdigit	Identical to the C function, except that it can apply to a single character or to a whole string.
kill	Identical to Perl's built-in **kill** function.
labs	C-specific; use Perl's built-in **abs** function instead.
ldexp	Identical to the C function *ldexp*(3).
ldiv	C-specific; use the division operator / and Perl's built-in **int** function instead.
link	Identical to Perl's built-in **link** function.

localeconv	Gets numeric formatting information. Returns a reference to a hash containing the current locale formatting values. The database for the de (Deutsch or German) locale:
	
	`$loc = POSIX::setlocale(&POSIX::LC_ALL, "de");`
	`print "Locale = $loc\n";`
	`$lconv = POSIX::localeconv();`
	`print "decimal_point     = ", $lconv->{decimal_point},     "\n";`
	`print "thousands_sep     = ", $lconv->{thousands_sep},     "\n";`
	`print "grouping          = ", $lconv->{grouping},          "\n";`
	`print "int_curr_symbol   = ", $lconv->{int_curr_symbol},   "\n";`
	`print "currency_symbol   = ", $lconv->{currency_symbol},   "\n";`
	`print "mon_decimal_point = ", $lconv->{mon_decimal_point}, "\n";`
	`print "mon_thousands_sep = ", $lconv->{mon_thousands_sep}, "\n";`
	`print "mon_grouping      = ", $lconv->{mon_grouping},      "\n";`
	`print "positive_sign     = ", $lconv->{positive_sign},     "\n";`
	`print "negative_sign     = ", $lconv->{negative_sign},     "\n";`
	
	`print "int_frac_digits   = ", $lconv->{int_frac_digits},   "\n";`
	`print "frac_digits       = ", $lconv->{frac_digits},       "\n";`
	`print "p_cs_precedes     = ", $lconv->{p_cs_precedes},     "\n";`
	`print "p_sep_by_space    = ", $lconv->{p_sep_by_space},    "\n";`
	`print "n_cs_precedes     = ", $lconv->{n_cs_precedes},     "\n";`
	`print "n_sep_by_space    = ", $lconv->{n_sep_by_space},    "\n";`
	`print "p_sign_posn       = ", $lconv->{p_sign_posn},       "\n";`
	`print "n_sign_posn       = ", $lconv->{n_sign_posn},       "\n";`

localtime	Identical to Perl's built-in **localtime** function.
log	Identical to Perl's built-in **log** function.

Table 7-12: Functions (continued)

Function Name	Definition
log10	Identical to the C function *log10*(3).
longjmp	C-specific; use Perl's built-in **die** function instead.
lseek	Moves the read/write file pointer. This uses file descriptors such as those obtained by calling POSIX::open(). $fd = POSIX::open("foo", &POSIX::O_RDONLY); $off_t = POSIX::lseek($fd, 0, &POSIX::SEEK_SET); Returns **undef** on failure.
malloc	C-specific.
mblen	Identical to the C function *mblen*(3).
mbstowcs	Identical to the C function *mbstowcs*(3).
mbtowc	Identical to the C function *mbtowc*(3).
memchr	C-specific; use Perl's built-in **index** instead.
memcmp	C-specific; use **eq** instead.
memcpy	C-specific; use **=** instead.
memmove	C-specific; use **=** instead.
memset	C-specific; use **x** instead.
mkdir	Identical to Perl's built-in **mkdir** function.
mkfifo	Similar to the C function *mkfifo*(2). Returns **undef** on failure.
mktime	Converts date/time information to a calendar time. Returns **undef** on failure. Synopsis: mktime(*sec, min, hour, mday, mon, year, wday* = 0, *yday* = 0, *isdst* = 0) The month (*mon*), weekday (*wday*), and yearday (*yday*) begin at zero. That is, January is 0, not 1; Sunday is 0, not 1; January 1st is 0, not 1. The year (*year*) is given in years since 1900. That is, the year 1995 is 95; the year 2001 is 101. Consult your system's *mktime*(3) manpage for details about these and the other arguments. Calendar time for December 12, 1995, at 10:30 am. $time_t = POSIX::mktime(0, 30, 10, 12, 11, 95); print "Date = ", POSIX::ctime($time_t);
modf	Returns the integral and fractional parts of a floating-point number. ($fractional, $integral) = POSIX::modf(3.14);
nice	Similar to the C function *nice*(3). Returns **undef** on failure.
offsetof	C-specific.

Table 7-12: Functions (continued)

Function Name	Definition

open	Opens a file for reading or writing. This returns file descriptors, not Perl filehandles. Returns **undef** on failure. Use POSIX::close() to close the file. Open a file read-only:
	
	```\n$fd = POSIX::open("foo");\n```
	Open a file for reading and writing:
	
	```\n$fd = POSIX::open("foo", &POSIX::O_RDWR);\n```
	Open a file for writing, with truncation:
	
	```\n$fd = POSIX::open("foo", &POSIX::O_WRONLY | &POSIX::O_TRUNC);\n```
	Create a new file with mode 0644; set up the file for writing:
	
	```\n$fd = POSIX::open("foo", &POSIX::O_CREAT | &POSIX::O_WRONLY,\n 0644);\n```

opendir	Opens a directory for reading. Returns **undef** on failure. ```\n$dir = POSIX::opendir("/tmp");\n@files = POSIX::readdir($dir);\nPOSIX::closedir($dir);\n```
pathconf	Retrieves the value of a configurable limit on a file or directory. Returns **undef** on failure. The following will determine the maximum length of the longest allowable pathname on the filesystem that holds */tmp*: ```\n$path_max = POSIX::pathconf("/tmp", &POSIX::_PC_PATH_MAX);\n```
pause	Similar to the C function *pause*(3). Returns **undef** on failure.
perror	Identical to the C function *perror*(3).
pipe	Creates an interprocess channel. Returns file descriptors like those returned by POSIX::open(). ```\n($fd0, $fd1) = POSIX::pipe();\nPOSIX::write($fd0, "hello", 5);\nPOSIX::read($fd1, $buf, 5);\n```
pow	Computes $x raised to the power $exponent. ```\n$ret = POSIX::pow($x, $exponent);\n```
printf	Prints the specified arguments to STDOUT.
putc	C-specific; use Perl's built-in **print** function instead.

Table 7–12: Functions (continued)

Function Name	Definition
putchar	C-specific; use Perl's built-in **print** function instead.
puts	C-specific; use Perl's built-in **print** function instead.
qsort	C-specific; use Perl's built-in **sort** function instead.
raise	Sends the specified signal to the current process.
rand	Non-portable; use Perl's built-in **rand** function instead.

read	Reads from a file. This uses file descriptors such as those obtained by calling POSIX::open(). If the buffer $buf is not large enough for the read, then Perl will extend it to make room for the request. Returns **undef** on failure.
	
	    $fd = POSIX::open("foo", &POSIX::O_RDONLY);
	    $bytes = POSIX::read($fd, $buf, 3);

readdir	Identical to Perl's built-in **readdir** function.
realloc	C-specific.
remove	Identical to Perl's built-in **unlink** function.
rename	Identical to Perl's built-in **rename** function.
rewind	Seeks to the beginning of the file.
rewinddir	Identical to Perl's built-in **rewinddir** function.
rmdir	Identical to Perl's built-in **rmdir** function.
scanf	C-specific; use <> and regular expressions instead.
setgid	Sets the real group id for this process, like assigning to the special variable $(.
setjmp	C-specific; use **eval {}** instead.
setlocale	Modifies and queries program's locale. The following will set the traditional UNIX system locale behavior. $loc = POSIX::setlocale(&POSIX::LC_ALL, "C");
setpgid	Similar to the C function *setpgid*(2). Returns **undef** on failure.
setsid	Identical to the C function *setsid*(8).
setuid	Sets the real user ID for this process, like assigning to the special variable $<.
sigaction	Detailed signal management. This uses POSIX::SigAction objects for the $action and $oldaction arguments. Consult your system's *sigaction*(3) manpage for details. Returns **undef** on failure. POSIX::sigaction($sig, $action, $oldaction)
siglongjmp	C-specific; use Perl's built-in **die** function instead.

Table 7–12: Functions (continued)

Function Name	Definition
sigpending	Examine signals that are blocked and pending. This uses POSIX::SigSet objects for the `$sigset` argument. Consult your system's *sigpending*(2) manpage for details. Returns **undef** on failure. POSIX::sigpending($sigset)
sigprocmask	Changes and/or examines this process's signal mask. This uses POSIX::SigSet objects for the `$sigset` and `$oldsigset` arguments. Consult your system's *sigprocmask*(2) manpage for details. Returns **undef** on failure. POSIX::sigprocmask($how, $sigset, $oldsigset)
sigsetjmp	C-specific; use **eval** {} instead.
sigsuspend	Install a signal mask and suspend process until signal arrives. This uses POSIX::SigSet objects for the `$signal_mask` argument. Consult your system's *sigsuspend*(2) manpage for details. Returns **undef** on failure. POSIX::sigsuspend($signal_mask)
sin	Identical to Perl's built-in **sin** function.
sinh	Identical to the C function *sinh*(3).
sleep	Identical to Perl's built-in **sleep** function.
sprintf	Identical to Perl's built-in **sprintf** function.
sqrt	Identical to Perl's built-in **sqrt** function.
srand	Identical to Perl's built-in **srand** function.
sscanf	C-specific; use regular expressions instead.
stat	Identical to Perl's built-in **stat** function.
strcat	C-specific; use .= instead.
strchr	C-specific; use **index** instead.
strcmp	C-specific; use **eq** instead.
strcoll	Identical to the C function *strcoll*(3).
strcpy	C-specific; use = instead.
strcspn	C-specific; use regular expressions instead.
strerror	Returns the error string for the specified *errno*.

Table 7–12: Functions (continued)

Function Name	Definition

strftime	Converts date and time information to string. Returns the string.
	
	strftime(*fmt, sec, min, hour, mday, mon, year,*
	          wday = 0, *yday* = 0, *isdst* = 0)
	
	The month (*mon*), weekday (*wday*), and yearday (*yday*) begin at zero. That is, January is 0, not 1; Sunday is 0, not 1; January 1st is 0, not 1. The year (*year*) is given in years since 1900. That is, the year 1995 is 95; the year 2001 is 101. Consult your system's *strftime*(3) manpage for details about these and the other arguments. The string for Tuesday, December 12, 1995:
	
	`$str = POSIX::strftime("%A, %B %d, %Y", 0, 0, 0, 12,`
	`                            11, 95, 2);`
	`print "$str\n";`

strlen	C-specific; use **length** instead.
strncat	C-specific; use .= and/or **substr** instead.
strncmp	C-specific; use **eq** and/or **substr** instead.
strncpy	C-specific; use = and/or **substr** instead.
strpbrk	C-specific.
strrchr	C-specific; use **rindex** and/or **substr** instead.
strspn	C-specific.
strstr	Identical to Perl's built-in **index** function.
strtod	C-specific.
strtok	C-specific.
strtol	C-specific.
strtoul	C-specific.
strxfrm	String transformation. Returns the transformed string. `$dst = POSIX::strxfrm($src);`
sysconf	Retrieves values of system configurable variables. Returns **undef** on failure. The following will get the machine's clock speed. `$clock_ticks = POSIX::sysconf(&POSIX::_SC_CLK_TCK);`
system	Identical to Perl's built-in **system** function.
tan	Identical to the C function *tan*(3).
tanh	Identical to the C function *tanh*(3).
tcdrain	Similar to the C function *tcdrain*(3). Returns **undef** on failure.
tcflow	Similar to the C function *tcflow*(3). Returns **undef** on failure.

Table 7–12: Functions (continued)

Function Name	Definition
tcflush	Similar to the C function *tcflush*(3). Returns **undef** on failure.
tcgetpgrp	Identical to the C function *tcgetpgrp*(3).
tcsendbreak	Similar to the C function *tcsendbreak*(3). Returns **undef** on failure.
tcsetpgrp	Similar to the C function *tcsetpgrp*(3). Returns **undef** on failure.
time	Identical to Perl's built-in **time** function.
times	Returns elapsed realtime since some point in the past (such as system startup), user and system times for this process, and user and system times for child processes. All times are returned in clock ticks. `($realtime, $user, $system, $cuser, $csystem) = POSIX::times();` Note: Perl's built-in **times** function returns four values, measured in seconds.
tmpfile	Use method `FileHandle::new_tmpfile()` instead.
tmpnam	Returns a name for a temporary file. `$tmpfile = POSIX::tmpnam();`
tolower	Identical to Perl's built-in **lc** function.
toupper	Identical to Perl's built-in **uc** function.
ttyname	Identical to the C function *ttyname*(3).

tzname	Retrieves the time conversion information from the `tzname` variable.
	
	    `POSIX::tzset();`
	    `($std, $dst) = POSIX::tzname();`

tzset	Identical to the C function *tzset*(3).
umask	Identical to Perl's built-in **umask** function.

uname	Gets name of current operating system.
	
	    `($sysname, $nodename, $release,`
	        `$version, $machine) = POSIX::uname();`

ungetc	Use method `FileHandle::ungetc()` instead.
unlink	Identical to Perl's built-in **unlink** function.
utime	Identical to Perl's built-in **utime** function.
vfprintf	C-specific.
vprintf	C-specific.
vsprintf	C-specific.
wait	Identical to Perl's built-in **wait** function.

Table 7–12: Functions (continued)

Function Name	Definition
waitpid	Wait for a child process to change state. This is identical to Perl's built-in **waitpid** function. ```\n$pid = POSIX::waitpid(-1, &POSIX::WNOHANG);\nprint "status = ", ($? / 256), "\n";\n```
wcstombs	Identical to the C function *wcstombs*(3).
wctomb	Identical to the C function *wctomb*(3).
write	Writes to a file. Uses file descriptors such as those obtained by calling POSIX::open(). Returns **undef** on failure. ```\n$fd = POSIX::open("foo", &POSIX::O_WRONLY);\n$buf = "hello";\n$bytes = POSIX::write($b, $buf, 5);\n```

Pathname constants

_PC_CHOWN_RESTRICTED	_PC_LINK_MAX	_PC_MAX_CANON
_PC_MAX_INPUT	_PC_NAME_MAX	_PC_NO_TRUNC
_PC_PATH_MAX	_PC_PIPE_BUF	_PC_VDISABLE

POSIX constants

_POSIX_ARG_MAX	_POSIX_CHILD_MAX	_POSIX_CHOWN_RESTRICTED
_POSIX_JOB_CONTROL	_POSIX_LINK_MAX	_POSIX_MAX_CANON
_POSIX_MAX_INPUT	_POSIX_NAME_MAX	_POSIX_NGROUPS_MAX
_POSIX_NO_TRUNC	_POSIX_OPEN_MAX	_POSIX_PATH_MAX
_POSIX_PIPE_BUF	_POSIX_SAVED_IDS	_POSIX_SSIZE_MAX
_POSIX_STREAM_MAX	_POSIX_TZNAME_MAX	_POSIX_VDISABLE
_POSIX_VERSION		

System configuration

_SC_ARG_MAX	_SC_CHILD_MAX	_SC_CLK_TCK	_SC_JOB_CONTROL
_SC_NGROUPS_MAX	_SC_OPEN_MAX	_SC_SAVED_IDS	_SC_STREAM_MAX
_SC_TZNAME_MAX	_SC_VERSION		

Error constants

E2BIG	EACCES	EAGAIN	EBADF	EBUSY	ECHILD	EDEADLK
EDOM	EEXIST	EFAUL	EFBIG	EINTR	EINVAL	EIO
EISDIR	EMFILE	EMLINK	ENAMETOOLONG	ENFILE	ENODE	ENOENT
ENOEXEC	ENOLCK	ENOMEM	ENOSPC	ENOSYS	ENOTDIR	ENOTEMPTY
ENOTTY	ENXIO	EPERM	EPIPE	ERANGE	EROFS	ESPIPE
ESRCH	EXDEV					

File control constants

FD_CLOEXEC	F_DUPFD	F_GETFD	F_GETFL	F_GETLK	F_OK
F_RDLCK	F_SETFD	F_SETFL	F_SETLK	F_SETLKW	F_UNLCK
F_WRLCK	O_ACCMODE	O_APPEND	O_CREAT	O_EXCL	O_NOCTTY
O_NONBLOCK	O_RDONLY	O_RDWR	O_TRUNC	O_WRONLY	

Floating-point constants

DBL_DIG	DBL_EPSILON	DBL_MANT_DIG	DBL_MAX
DBL_MAX_10_EXP	DBL_MAX_EXP	DBL_MIN	DBL_MIN_10_EXP
DBL_MIN_EXP	FLT_DIG	FLT_EPSILON	FLT_MANT_DIG
FLT_MAX	FLT_MAX_10_EXP	FLT_MAX_EXP	FLT_MIN
FLT_MIN_10_EXP	FLT_MIN_EXP	FLT_RADIX	FLT_ROUNDS
LDBL_DIG	LDBL_EPSILON	LDBL_MANT_DIG	LDBL_MAX
LDBL_MAX_10_EXP	LDBL_MAX_EXP	LDBL_MIN	LDBL_MIN_10_EXP
LDBL_MIN_EXP			

Limit constants

ARG_MAX	CHAR_BIT	CHAR_MAX	CHAR_MIN	CHILD_MAX
INT_MAX	INT_MIN	LINK_MAX	LONG_MAX	LONG_MIN
MAX_CANON	MAX_INPUT	MB_LEN_MAX	NAME_MAX	NGROUPS_MAX
OPEN_MAX	PATH_MAX	PIPE_BUF	SCHAR_MAX	SCHAR_MIN
SHRT_MAX	SHRT_MIN	SSIZE_MAX	STREAM_MAX	TZNAME_MAX
UCHAR_MAX	UINT_MAX	ULONG_MAX USHRT_MAX		

Locale constants

LC_ALL	LC_COLLATE	LC_CTYPE	LC_MONETARY	LC_NUMERIC	LC_TIME

Math constants

HUGE_VAL

Signal constants

SA_NOCLDSTOP	SIGABRT	SIGALRM	SIGCHLD	SIGCONT	SIGFPE
SIGHUP	SIGILL	SIGINT	SIGKILL	SIGPIPE	SIGQUIT
SIGSEGV	SIGSTOP	SIGTERM	SIGTSTP	SIGTTIN	SIGTTOU
SIGUSR1	SIGUSR2	SIG_BLOCK	SIG_DFL	SIG_ERR	SIG_IGN
SIG_SETMASK	SIG_UNBLOCK				

Stat constants

S_IRGRP	S_IROTH	S_IRUSR	S_IRWXG	S_IRWXO	S_IRWXU	S_ISGID
S_ISUID	S_IWGRP	S_IWOTH	S_IWUSR	S_IXGRP	S_IXOTH	S_IXUSR

Stat macros

S_ISBLK	S_ISCHR	S_ISDIR	S_ISFIFO	S_ISREG

Stdlib constants

EXIT_FAILURE	EXIT_SUCCESS	MB_CUR_MAX	RAND_MAX

Stdio constants

BUFSIZ	EOF	FILENAME_MAX	L_ctermid	L_cuserid	L_tmpname	TMP_MAX

Time constants

CLK_TCK	CLOCKS_PER_SEC

Unistd constants

R_OK	SEEK_CUR	SEEK_END	SEEK_SET	STDIN_FILENO
STDOUT_FILENO	STRERR_FILENO	W_OK	X_OK	

Wait constants

WNOHANG	WUNTRACED

Wait macros

```
WIFEXITED   WEXITSTATUS   WIFSIGNALED   WTERMSIG   WIFSTOPPED   WSTOPSIG
```

Pod::Text — Convert POD Data to Formatted ASCII Text

```
use Pod::Text;

pod2text("perlfunc.pod", *filehandle);   # send formatted output to file
$text = pod2text("perlfunc.pod");        # assign formatted output to $text
```

Pod::Text converts documentation in the POD format (such as can be found throughout the Perl distribution) into formatted ASCII text. Termcap is optionally supported for boldface/underline, and can be enabled with:

```
$Pod::Text::termcap=1
```

If termcap is not enabled, backspaces are used to simulate bold and underlined text.

The pod2text() subroutine can take one or two arguments. The first is the name of a file to read the POD from, or "<&STDIN" to read from STDIN. The second argument, if provided, is a filehandle glob where output should be sent. (Use *STDOUT to write to STDOUT.)

A separate *pod2text* program is included as part of the standard Perl distribution. Primarily, a wrapper for Pod::Text, it can be invoked this way:

```
pod2text < input.pod
```

Safe — Create Safe Namespaces for Evaluating Perl Code

```
use Safe;
$cpt = new Safe;   # create a new safe compartment
```

The Safe extension module allows the creation of compartments in which untrusted Perl code can be evaluated. Each compartment provides a new namespace and has an associated operator mask.

The root of the namespace (that is, main::) is changed to a different package, and code evaluated in the compartment cannot refer to variables outside this namespace, even with run-time glob lookups and other tricks. Code that is compiled outside the compartment can choose to place variables into (or share variables with) the compartment's namespace, and only that data will be visible to code evaluated in the compartment.

By default, the only variables shared with compartments are the underscore variables $_ and @_ (and, technically, the much less frequently used %_, the _ filehandle and so on). This is because otherwise Perl operators that default to $_ would not work and neither would the assignment of arguments to @_ on subroutine entry.

Each compartment has an associated operator mask with which you can exclude particular Perl operators from the compartment. (The mask syntax is explained below.) Recall that Perl code is compiled into an internal format before execution. Evaluating Perl code (for example, via eval STRING or do FILE) causes the code to be compiled into an internal format and then, provided there was no error in the compilation, executed. Code evaluated in a compartment is compiled subject to the compartment's operator mask. Attempting to evaluate compartmentalized code that contains a masked operator will cause the compilation to fail with an error. The code will not be executed.

By default, the operator mask for a newly created compartment masks out all operations that give access to the system in some sense. This includes masking off operators such as **system**, **open**, **chown**, and **shmget**, but operators such as **print**, **sysread**, and **<FILEHANDLE>** are not masked off. These file operators are allowed since, in order for the code in the compartment to have access to a filehandle, the code outside the compartment must have explicitly placed the filehandle variable inside the compartment.

Since it is only at the compilation stage that the operator mask applies, controlled access to potentially unsafe operations can be achieved by having a handle to a wrapper subroutine (written outside the compartment) placed into the compartment. For example:

```
$cpt = new Safe;
sub wrapper {
    ;# vet arguments and perform potentially unsafe operations
}
$cpt->share('&wrapper');   # see share method below
```

An operator mask exists at user-level as a string of bytes of length MAXO, each of which is either 0x00 or 0x01. Here, MAXO is the number of operators in the current version of Perl. The subroutine MAXO (available for export by package Safe) returns the number of operators in the currently running Perl executable. The presence of a 0x01 byte at offset n of the string indicates that operator number n should be masked (that is, disallowed). The Safe extension makes available routines for converting from operator names to operator numbers (and vice versa) and for converting from a list of operator names to the corresponding mask (and vice versa).

Methods in class Safe

To create a new compartment, use:

```
$cpt = new Safe NAMESPACE, MASK;
```

where *NAMESPACE* is the root namespace to use for the compartment (defaults to Safe::Root000000000, auto-incremented for each new compartment). *MASK* is the operator mask to use. Both arguments are optional.

The following methods can then be used on the compartment object returned by the above constructor. The object argument is implicit in each case.

root(*NAMESPACE*)
> A get-or-set method for the compartment's namespace. With the *NAMESPACE* argument present, it sets the root namespace for the compartment. With no *NAMESPACE* argument present, it returns the current root namespace of the compartment.

mask(*MASK*)
> A get-or-set method for the compartment's operator mask. With the *MASK* argument present, it sets the operator mask for the compartment. With no *MASK* argument present, it returns the current operator mask of the compartment.

trap(*OP*, . . .)
> Sets bits in the compartment's operator mask corresponding to each operator named in the list of arguments. Each *OP* can be either the name of an operation or its number. See *opcode.h* or *opcode.pl* in the main Perl distribution for a canonical list of operator names.

untrap(*OP*, . . .)
> Resets bits in the compartment's operator mask corresponding to each operator named in the list of arguments. Each *OP* can be either the name of an operation or its number. See *opcode.h* or *opcode.pl* in the main Perl distribution for a canonical list of operator names.

share(*VARNAME*, . . .)
> Shares the variables in the argument list with the compartment. Each *VARNAME* must be a string containing the name of a variable with a leading type identifier included. Examples of legal variable names are $foo for a scalar, @foo for an array, %foo for a hash, &foo for a subroutine and *foo for a typeglob. (A typeglob results in the sharing of all symbol table entries associated with foo, including scalar, array, hash, subroutine, and filehandle.)

varglob(*VARNAME*)

>   Returns a typeglob for the symbol table entry of *VARNAME* in the package of the
>   compartment. *VARNAME* must be the name of a variable without any leading
>   type marker. For example:

```
$cpt = new Safe 'Root';
$Root::foo = "Hello world";
# Equivalent version which doesn't need to know $cpt's package name:
${$cpt->varglob('foo')} = "Hello world";
```

reval(*STRING*)

>   Evaluates *STRING* as Perl code inside the compartment. The code can only see
>   the compartment's namespace (as returned by the root() method). Any
>   attempt by code in *STRING* to use an operator which is in the compartment's
>   mask will cause an error (at run-time of the main program, but at compile-
>   time for the code in *STRING*). If the code in *STRING* includes an **eval** (and the
>   **eval** operator is permitted) then the error can occur at run-time for *STRING*
>   (although it is at compile-time for the **eval** within *STRING*). The error is of the
>   form "%s trapped by operation mask operation...." If an operation is
>   trapped in this way, then the code in *STRING* will not be executed. If such a
>   trapped operation occurs, or if any other compile-time or return error occurs,
>   then $@ is set to the error message, just as with an **eval**. If there is no error,
>   then the method returns the value of the last expression evaluated, or a return
>   statement may be used, just as with subroutines and **eval**.

rdo(*FILENAME*)

>   Evaluates the contents of file *FILENAME* inside the compartment. See the
>   reval() method earlier for further details.

Subroutines in package Safe

The Safe package contains subroutines for manipulating operator names and operator masks. All are available for export by the package. The canonical list of operator names is contained in the array op_name defined and initialized in file
opcode.h of the Perl source distribution.

ops_to_mask(*OP,* ...)

>   Takes a list of operator names and returns an operator mask with precisely
>   those operators masked.

mask_to_ops(*MASK*)

>   Takes an operator mask and returns a list of operator names corresponding to
>   those operators which are masked in *MASK*.

`opcode(OP, . . . )`

> Takes a list of operator names and returns the corresponding list of opcodes (which can then be used as byte offsets into a mask).

`opname(OP, . . . )`

> Takes a list of opcodes and returns the corresponding list of operator names.

`fullmask`

> Returns a mask with all operators masked. It returns the string `"\001" x MAXO()`.

`emptymask`

> Returns a mask with all operators unmasked. It returns the string `"\0" x MAXO()`. This is useful if you want a compartment to make use of the name-space protection features but do not want the default restrictive mask.

`MAXO`

> This returns the number of operators (hence the length of an operator mask).

`op_mask`

> This returns the operator mask that is actually in effect at the time the invocation to the subroutine is compiled. This is probably not terribly useful.

SDBM_File — Tied Access to SDBM Files

```
use Fcntl;
use SDBM_File;

tie(%hash, SDBM_File, 'Op.dbmx', O_RDWR|O_CREAT, 0644);
# read/writes of %hash are now read/writes of the file, Op.dmx.pag
untie %h;
```

See Perl's built-in **tie** function. Also see the DB_File module in this chapter for a description of a closely related module.

Search::Dict — Search for Key in Dictionary File

```
use Search::Dict;
look *FILEHANDLE, $key, $dict, $fold;
```

The `look()` routine sets the file position in FILEHANDLE to be the first line greater than or equal (stringwise) to `$key`. It returns the new file position, or -1 if an error occurs.

If `$dict` is true, the search is in dictionary order (ignoring everything but word characters and whitespace). If `$fold` is true, then case is ignored. The file must be sorted into the appropriate order, using the **-d** and **-f** flags of UNIX *sort*(1), or the equivalent command on non-UNIX machines. Unpredictable results will otherwise ensue.

SelectSaver — Save and Restore Selected Filehandle

```
use SelectSaver;

select $fh_old;
{
    my $saver = new SelectSaver($fh_new); # selects $fh_new
}
# block ends; object pointed to by "my" $saver is destroyed
# previous handle, $fh_old is now selected

# alternative invocation, without filehandle argument
my $saver = new SelectSaver; # selected filehandle remains unchanged
```

A SelectSaver object contains a reference to the filehandle that was selected when the object was created. If its `new()` method is given a filehandle as an argument, then that filehandle is selected; otherwise, the selected filehandle remains unchanged.

When a SelectSaver object is destroyed, the filehandle that was selected immediately prior to the object's creation is re-selected.

SelfLoader — Load Functions Only on Demand

```
package GoodStuff;
use SelfLoader;

[initializing code]
__DATA__
sub {...};
```

This module is used for delayed loading of Perl functions that (unlike AutoLoader functions) are packaged within your script file. This gives the *appearance* of faster loading.

In the example above, SelfLoader tells its user (GoodStuff) that functions in the GoodStuff package are to be autoloaded from after the __DATA__ token.

The __DATA__ token tells Perl that the code for compilation is finished. Everything after the __DATA__ token is available for reading via the filehandle Good-Stuff::DATA, where GoodStuff is the name of the current package when the __DATA__ token is reached. This token works just the same as __END__ does in package main, except that data after __END__ is retrievable only in package main, whereas data after __DATA__ is retrievable in whatever the current package is.

Note that it is possible to have __DATA__ tokens in the same package in multiple files, and that the last __DATA__ token in a given package that is encountered by the compiler is the one accessible by the filehandle. That is, whenever the

__DATA__ token is parsed, any DATA filehandle previously open in the current package (opened in a different file, presumably) is closed so that the new one can be opened. (This also applies to __END__ and the main::DATA filehandle: main::DATA is reopened whenever __END__ is encountered, so any former association is lost.)

SelfLoader autoloading

The SelfLoader will read from the GoodStuff::DATA filehandle to get definitions for functions placed after __DATA__, and then **eval** the requested subroutine the first time it's called. The costs are the one-time parsing of the data after __DATA__, and a load delay for the first call of any autoloaded function. The benefits are a speeded up compilation phase, with no need to load functions that are never used.

You can use __END__ after __DATA__. The SelfLoader will stop reading from DATA if it encounters the __END__ token, just as you might expect. If the __END__ token is present, and is followed by the token DATA, then the SelfLoader leaves the Good-Stuff::DATA filehandle open on the line after that token.

The SelfLoader exports the AUTOLOAD subroutine to the package using the Self-Loader, and this triggers the automatic loading of an undefined subroutine out of its DATA portion the first time that subroutine is called.

There is no advantage to putting subroutines that will always be called after the __DATA__ token.

Autoloading and file-scoped lexicals

A my $pack_lexical statement makes the variable $pack_lexical visible *only* up to the __DATA__ token. That means that subroutines declared elsewhere cannot see lexical variables. Specifically, autoloaded functions cannot see such lexicals (this applies to both the SelfLoader and the Autoloader). The use vars pragma (see later in this chapter) provides a way to declare package-level globals that will be visible to autoloaded routines.

SelfLoader and AutoLoader

The SelfLoader can replace the AutoLoader—just change use AutoLoader to use SelfLoader[*] and the __END__ token to __DATA__.

There is no need to inherit from the SelfLoader.

---

[*] Be aware, however, that the SelfLoader exports an AUTOLOAD function into your package. But if you have your own AUTOLOAD and are using the AutoLoader too, you probably know what you're doing.

The SelfLoader works similarly to the AutoLoader, but picks up the subroutine definitions from after the __DATA__ instead of in the *lib/auto/* directory. SelfLoader needs less maintenance at the time the module is installed, since there's no need to run AutoSplit. And it can run faster at load time because it doesn't need to keep opening and closing files to load subroutines. On the other hand, it can run slower because it needs to parse the code after the __DATA__. Details of the AutoLoader and another view of these distinctions can be found in that module's documentation.

How to read DATA from your Perl program

(This section is only relevant if you want to use the GoodStuff::DATA together with the SelfLoader.)

The SelfLoader reads from wherever the current position of the GoodStuff::DATA filehandle is, until EOF or the __END__ token. This means that if you want to use that filehandle (and *only* if you want to), you should either

- Put all your subroutine declarations immediately after the __DATA__ token and put your own data after those declarations, using the __END__ token to mark the end of subroutine declarations. You must also ensure that the SelfLoader first reads its stubs by calling SelfLoader->load_stubs();, or by using a function which is selfloaded; or

- You should read the GoodStuff::DATA filehandle first, leaving the handle open and positioned at the first line of subroutine declarations.

You could even conceivably do both.

Classes and inherited methods

This section is only relevant if your module is a class, and has methods that could be inherited.

A subroutine stub (or forward declaration) looks like:

```
sub stub;
```

That is, it is a subroutine declaration without the body of the subroutine. For modules that aren't classes, there is no real need for stubs as far as autoloading is concerned.

For modules that *are* classes, and need to handle inherited methods, stubs are needed to ensure that the method inheritance mechanism works properly. You can load the stubs into the module at **require** time, by adding the statement SelfLoader->load_stubs(); to the module to do this.

The alternative is to put the stubs in before the __DATA__ token before releasing the module, and for this purpose the Devel::SelfStubber module is available. However this does require the extra step of ensuring that the stubs are in the module. If you do this, we strongly recommended that you do it before releasing the module and *not* at install time.

Multiple packages and fully qualified subroutine names

Subroutines in multiple packages within the same file are supported—but you should note that this requires exporting SelfLoader::AUTOLOAD to every package which requires it. This is done automatically by the SelfLoader when it first loads the subs into the cache, but you should really specify it in the initialization before the __DATA__ by putting a use SelfLoader statement in each package.

Fully qualified subroutine names are also supported. For example:

```
__DATA__
sub foo::bar {23}
package baz;
sub dob {32}
```

will all be loaded correctly by the SelfLoader, and the SelfLoader will ensure that the packages "foo" and "baz" correctly have the SelfLoader::AUTOLOAD method when the data after __DATA__ is first parsed.

See the discussion of autoloading in Chapter 5. Also see the AutoLoader module, a utility that handles modules that have been into a collection of files for autoloading.

Shell — Run Shell Commands Transparently Within Perl

```
use Shell qw(date cp ps);  # list shell commands you want to use

$date = date();   # put the output of the date(1) command into $date
cp("-p" "/etc/passwd", "/tmp/passwd");  # copy password file to a tmp file
print ps("-ww");  # print the results of a "ps -ww" command
```

This module allows you to invoke UNIX utilities accessible from the shell command line as if they were Perl subroutines. Arguments (including switches) are passed to the utilities as strings.

The Shell module essentially duplicates the built-in backtick functionality of Perl. The module was written so that its implementation could serve as a demonstration of autoloading. It also shows how function calls can be mapped to subprocesses.

sigtrap—Enable Stack Backtrace on Unexpected Signals

```
use sigtrap;       # initialize default signal handlers
use sigtrap LIST;  # LIST example:  qw(BUS SEGV PIPE SYS ABRT TRAP)
```

The sigtrap pragma initializes a signal handler for the signals specified in *LIST*, or (if no list is given) for a set of default signals. The signal handler prints a stack dump of the program and then issues a (non-trapped) ABRT signal.

In the absence of *LIST*, the signal handler is set up to deal with the ABRT, BUS, EMT, FPE, ILL, PIPE, QUIT, SEGV, SYS, TERM, and TRAP signals.

Socket—Load the C socket.h Defines and Structure Manipulators

```
use Socket;

$proto = getprotobyname('udp');
socket(Socket_Handle, PF_INET, SOCK_DGRAM, $proto);
$iaddr = gethostbyname('hishost.com');
$port = getservbyname('time', 'udp');
$sin = sockaddr_in($port, $iaddr);
send(Socket_Handle, 0, 0, $sin);

$proto = getprotobyname('tcp');
socket(Socket_Handle, PF_INET, SOCK_STREAM, $proto);
$port = getservbyname('smtp');
$sin = sockaddr_in($port, inet_aton("127.1"));
$sin = sockaddr_in(7, inet_aton("localhost"));
$sin = sockaddr_in(7, INADDR_LOOPBACK);
connect(Socket_Handle, $sin);

($port, $iaddr) = sockaddr_in(getpeername(Socket_Handle));
$peer_host = gethostbyaddr($iaddr, AF_INET);
$peer_addr = inet_ntoa($iaddr);

socket(Socket_Handle, PF_UNIX, SOCK_STREAM, 0);
unlink('/tmp/usock');
$sun = sockaddr_un('/tmp/usock');
bind(Socket_Handle, $sun);
```

This module is just a translation of the C *socket.h* file. Unlike the old mechanism of requiring a translated *socket.ph* file, this uses the *h2xs* program (see the Perl source distribution) and your native C compiler. This means that it has a far more likely chance of getting the numbers right. This includes all of the commonly used preprocessor-defined constants like AF_INET, SOCK_STREAM, and so on.

In addition, some structure manipulation functions are available:

inet_aton *HOSTNAME*

> Takes a string giving the name of a host, and translates that to a four-byte, packed string (structure). Takes arguments of both the rtfm.mit.edu and 18.181.0.24 types. If the host name cannot be resolved, returns the undefined value.

inet_ntoa *IP_ADDRESS*

> Takes a four-byte IP address (as returned by inet_aton()) and translates it into a string of the form *d.d.d.d* where the *d*s are numbers less than 256 (the normal, readable, dotted-quad notation for Internet addresses).

INADDR_ANY

> Note: This function does not return a number, but a packed string. Returns the four-byte wildcard IP address that specifies any of the host's IP addresses. (A particular machine can have more than one IP address, each address corresponding to a particular network interface. This wildcard address allows you to bind to all of them simultaneously.) Normally equivalent to inet_aton('0.0.0.0').

INADDR_LOOPBACK

> Note: does not return a number, but a packed string. Returns the four-byte loopback address. Normally equivalent to inet_aton('localhost').

INADDR_NONE

> Note: does not return a number, but a packed string. Returns the four-byte invalid IP address. Normally equivalent to inet_aton('255.255.255.255').

sockaddr_in *PORT, ADDRESS*

sockaddr_in *SOCKADDR_IN*

> In a list context, unpacks its *SOCKADDR_IN* argument and returns a list consisting of (*PORT, ADDRESS*). In a scalar context, packs its (*PORT, ADDRESS*) arguments as a *SOCKADDR_IN* and returns it. If this is confusing, use pack_sockaddr_in() and unpack_sockaddr_in() explicitly.

pack_sockaddr_in *PORT, IP_ADDRESS*

> Takes two arguments, a port number and a four-byte *IP_ADDRESS* (as returned by inet_aton()). Returns the sockaddr_in structure with those arguments packed in with AF_INET filled in. For Internet domain sockets, this structure is normally what you need for the arguments in **bind**, **connect**, and **send**, and is also returned by **getpeername**, **getsockname**, and **recv**.

unpack_sockaddr_in *SOCKADDR_IN*

> Takes a `sockaddr_in` structure (as returned by `pack_sockaddr_in()`) and returns a list of two elements: the port and the four-byte IP address. This function will croak if the structure does not have AF_INET in the right place.

sockaddr_un *PATHNAME*

sockaddr_un *SOCKADDR_UN*

> In a list context, it unpacks its *SOCKADDR_UN* argument and returns a list consisting of (*PATHNAME*). In a scalar context, it packs its *PATHNAME* argument as a *SOCKADDR_UN* and returns it. If this is confusing, use `pack_sockaddr_un()` and `unpack_sockaddr_un()` explicitly. These functions are only supported if your system has <*sys/un.h*>.

pack_sockaddr_un *PATH*

> Takes one argument, a pathname. Returns the `sockaddr_un` structure with that path packed in with AF_UNIX filled in. For UNIX domain sockets, this structure is normally what you need for the arguments in **bind**, **connect**, and **send**, and is also returned by **getpeername**, **getsockname** and **recv**.

unpack_sockaddr_un *SOCKADDR_UN*

> Takes a `sockaddr_un` structure (as returned by `pack_sockaddr_un()`) and returns the pathname. Will croak if the structure does not have AF_UNIX in the right place.

strict — Restrict Unsafe Constructs

```
use strict;        # apply all possible restrictions

use strict 'vars'; # restrict unsafe use of variables for rest of block
use strict 'refs'; # restrict unsafe use of references for rest of block
use strict 'subs'; # restrict unsafe use of barewords for rest of block

no strict 'vars';  # relax restrictions on variables for rest of block
no strict 'refs';  # relax restrictions on references for rest of block
no strict 'subs';  # relax restrictions on barewords for rest of block
```

If no import list is given to **use strict**, all possible restrictions upon unsafe Perl constructs are imposed. (This is the safest mode to operate in, but is sometimes too strict for casual programming.) Currently, there are three possible things to be strict about: refs, vars, and subs.

In all cases the restrictions apply only until the end of the immediately enclosing block.

strict 'refs'

> This generates a run-time error if you use symbolic references.

```
use strict 'refs';
$ref = \$foo;
print $$ref;        # ok
$ref = "foo";
print $$ref;        # run-time error; normally ok
```

strict 'vars'

This generates a compile-time error if you access a variable that wasn't declared via **my**, or fully qualified, or imported.

```
use strict 'vars';
use vars '$foe';
$SomePack::fee = 1;  # ok, fully qualified
my $fie = 10;        # ok, my() var
$foe = 7;            # ok, pseudo-imported by 'use vars'
$foo = 9;            # blows up--did you mistype $foe maybe?
```

The last line generates a compile-time error because you're touching a global name without fully qualifying it. Since the purpose of this pragma is to encourage use of **my** variables, using **local** on a variable isn't good enough to declare it. You can, however, use **local** on a variable that you declared with **use vars**.

strict 'subs'

This generates a compile-time error if you try to use a bareword identifier that's not a predeclared subroutine.

```
use strict 'subs';

$SIG{PIPE} = Plumber;     # blows up (assuming Plumber sub not declared yet)
$SIG{PIPE} = "Plumber";   # okay, means "main::Plumber" really
$SIG{PIPE} = \&Plumber;   # preferred form
```

The **no strict 'vars'** statement negates any preceding **use strict vars** for the remainder of the innermost enclosing block. Likewise, **no strict 'refs'** negates any preceding invocation of **use strict refs**, and **no strict 'subs'** negates **use strict 'subs'**.

The arguments to **use strict** are sometimes given as barewords—that is, without surrounding quotes. Be aware, however, that the following sequence will not work:

```
use strict;      # or just: use strict subs;
...
no strict subs;  # WRONG!  Should be: no strict 'subs';
...
```

The problem here is that giving **subs** as a bareword is no longer allowed after the **use strict** statement. :-)

subs — Predeclare Subroutine Names

```
use subs qw(sub1 sub2 sub3);
sub1 $arg1, $arg2;
```

This predeclares the subroutines whose names are in the list, allowing you to use them without parentheses even before they're defined. It has the additional benefit of allowing you to override built-in functions, since you may only override built-ins via an import, and this pragma does a pseudo-import.

See also the vars module.

Symbol — Generate Anonymous Globs; Qualify Variable Names

```
use Symbol;

$sym = gensym;
open($sym, "filename");
$_ = <$sym>;

ungensym $sym;          # no effect

print qualify("x");              # "main::x"
print qualify("x", "FOO");       # "FOO::x"
print qualify("BAR::x");         # "BAR::x"
print qualify("BAR::x", "FOO");  # "BAR::x"
print qualify("STDOUT", "FOO");  # "main::STDOUT" (global)
print qualify(\*x);              # \*x--for example: GLOB(0x99530)
print qualify(\*x, "FOO");       # \*x--for example: GLOB(0x99530)
```

gensym() creates an anonymous glob and returns a reference to it. Such a glob reference can be used as a filehandle or directory handle.

For backward compatibility with older implementations that didn't support anonymous globs, ungensym() is also provided. But it doesn't do anything.

qualify() turns unqualified symbol names into qualified variable names (for example, myvar becomes MyPackage::myvar). If it is given a second parameter, qualify() uses it as the default package; otherwise, it uses the package of its caller. Regardless, global variable names (for example, STDOUT, %ENV, %SIG) are always qualified with main::.

Qualification applies only to symbol names (strings). References are left unchanged under the assumption that they are glob references, which are qualified by their nature.

Sys::Hostname—Try Every Conceivable Way to Get Hostname

```
use Sys::Hostname;
$host = hostname();
```

Attempts several methods of getting the system hostname and then caches the result. It tries syscall(SYS_gethostname), `hostname`, `uname -n`, and the file */com/host*. If all that fails, it croak()s.

All nulls, returns, and newlines are removed from the result.

Sys::Syslog—Perl Interface to UNIX syslog(3) Calls

```
use Sys::Syslog;

openlog $ident, $logopt, $facility;
syslog $priority, $mask, $format, @args;
$oldmask = setlogmask $mask_priority;
closelog;
```

Sys::Syslog is an interface to the UNIX *syslog*(3) program. Call syslog() with a string priority and a list of **printf** args just like *syslog*(3). Sys::Syslog needs *syslog.ph*, which must be created with *h2ph* by your system administrator.

Sys::Syslog provides these functions:

openlog $ident, $logopt, $facility
> $ident is prepended to every message. $logopt contains one or more of the words pid, ndelay, cons, nowait. $facility specifies the part of the system making the log entry.

syslog $priority, $mask, $format, @args
> If $priority and $mask permit, logs a message formed as if by sprintf($format, @args), with the addition that %m is replaced with "$!" (the latest error message).

setlogmask $mask_priority
> Sets log mask to $mask_priority and returns the old mask.

closelog
> Closes the log file.

Examples

```
openlog($program, 'cons, pid', 'user');
syslog('info', 'this is another test');
syslog('mail|warning', 'this is a better test: %d', time);
closelog();
```

```
syslog('debug', 'this is the last test');
openlog("$program $$", 'ndelay', 'user');
syslog('notice', 'fooprogram: this is really done');

$! = 55;
syslog('info', 'problem was %m'); # %m == $! in syslog(3)
```

Term::Cap — Terminal Capabilities Interface

```
require Term::Cap;

$terminal = Tgetent Term::Cap { TERM => undef, OSPEED => $ospeed };
$terminal->Trequire(qw/ce ku kd/);
$terminal->Tgoto('cm', $col, $row, $FH);
$terminal->Tputs('dl', $count, $FH);
```

These are low-level functions to extract and use capabilities from a terminal capability (termcap) database. For general information about the use of this database, see the *termcap*(5) manpage.

The "new" function of Term::Cap is Tgetent(), which extracts the termcap entry for the specified terminal type and returns a reference to a terminal object. If the value associated with the TERM key in the Tgetent() argument list is false or undefined, then it defaults to the environment variable TERM.

Tgetent() looks in the environment for a TERMCAP variable. If it finds one, and if the value does not begin with a slash and looks like a termcap entry in which the terminal type name is the same as the environment string TERM, then the TERMCAP string is used directly as the termcap entry and there is no search for an entry in a termcap file somewhere.

Otherwise, Tgetent() looks in a sequence of files for the termcap entry. The sequence consists of the filename in TERMCAP, if any, followed by either the files listed in the TERMPATH environment variable, if any, or otherwise the files *$HOME/.termcap*, */etc/termcap*, and */usr/share/misc/termcap*, in that order. (Filenames in TERMPATH may be separated by either a colon or a space.) Whenever multiple files are searched and a tc field occurs in the requested entry, the entry named in the tc field must be found in the same file or one of the succeeding files. If there is a tc field in the TERMCAP environment variable string, Tgetent() continues searching as indicated above.

OSPEED is the terminal output bit rate (often mistakenly called the baud rate). OSPEED can be specified as either a POSIX termios/SYSV termio speed (where 9600 equals 9600) or an old BSD-style speed (where 13 equals 9600). See the next section, "Getting Terminal Output Speed", for code illustrating how to obtain the output speed.

Tgetent() returns a reference to a blessed object ($terminal in the examples above). The actual termcap entry is available as $terminal->{TERMCAP}. Failure to find an appropriate termcap entry results in a call to Carp::croak().

Once you have invoked Tgetent(), you can manage a terminal by sending control strings to it with Tgoto() and Tputs(). You can also test for the existence of particular terminal capabilities with Trequire().

Trequire() checks to see whether the named capabilities have been specified in the terminal's termcap entry. For example, this line:

```
$terminal->Trequire(qw/ce ku kd/);
```

checks whether the ce (clear to end of line), ku (keypad up-arrow), and kd (keypad down-arrow) capabilities have been defined. Any undefined capabilities will result in a listing of those capabilities and a call to Carp::croak().

Tgoto() produces a control string to move the cursor relative to the screen. For example, to move the cursor to the fifth line and forty-fifth column on the screen, you can say:

```
$row = 5; $col = 45;
$terminal->Tgoto('cm', $row, $col, STDOUT);
```

The first argument in this call must always be cm. If a file handle is given as the final argument, then Tgoto() sends the appropriate control string to that handle. With or without a handle, the routine returns the control string, so you could achieve the same effect this way:

```
$str = $terminal->Tgoto('cm', $row, $col);
print STDOUT $str;
```

Tgoto() performs the necessary % interpolation on the control strings. (See the *termcap*(5) manpage for details.)

The Tputs() routine allows you to exercise other terminal capabilities. For example, the following code deletes one line at the cursor's present position, and then turns on the bold text attribute:

```
$count = 1;
$terminal->Tputs('dl', $count, $FILEHANDLE);  # delete one line
$terminal->Tputs('md', $count, $FILEHANDLE);  # turn on bold attribute
```

Again, Tputs() returns the terminal control string, and the file handle can be omitted. The $count for such calls should normally be 1, unless padding is required. (Padding involves the output of "no-op" characters in order to effect a delay required by the terminal device. It is most commonly required for hardcopy devices.) A count greater than 1 is taken to specify the amount of padding. See the *termcap*(5) manpage for more about padding.

Tputs() does *not* perform % interpolation. This means that the following will not work:

```
$terminal->Tputs('DC', 1, $FILEHANDLE);  # delete one character (WRONG!)
```

If the terminal control string requires numeric parameters, then you must do the interpolation yourself:

```
$str = $terminal->Tputs('DC', 1);
$str =~ s/%d/7/;
print STDOUT $str;         # delete seven characters
```

The output strings for Tputs() are cached for counts of 1. Tgoto() does not cache. $terminal->{_xx} is the raw termcap data and $terminal->{xx} is the cached version (where *xx* is the two-character terminal capability code).

Getting terminal output speed

You can use the POSIX module to get your terminal's output speed for use in the Tgetent() call:

```
require POSIX;
my $termios = new POSIX::Termios;
$termios->getattr;
my $ospeed = $termios->getospeed;
```

The method using *ioctl*(2) works like this:

```
require 'ioctl.pl';
ioctl(TTY, $TIOCGETP, $sgtty);
($ispeed, $ospeed) = unpack('cc', $sgtty);
```

Term::Complete — Word Completion Module

```
use Term::Complete;

$input = Complete('prompt_string', \@completion_list);
$input = Complete('prompt_string', @completion_list);
```

The Complete() routine sends the indicated prompt string to the currently selected filehandle, reads the user's response, and places the response in $input. What the user types is read one character at a time, and certain characters result in special processing as follows:

TAB

> The tab character causes Complete() to match what the user has typed so far against the list of strings in @completion_list. If the user's partial input uniquely matches one of these strings, then the rest of the matched string is

output. However, input is still not finished until the user presses the return key. If the user's partial input does not uniquely match one string in @comple-tion_list when the tab character is pressed, then the partial input remains unchanged and the bell character is output.

CTRL-D

If the user types CTRL-D, the current matches between the user's partial input string and the completion list are printed out. If the partial input string is null, then the entire completion list is printed. In any case, the prompt string is then reissued, along with the partial input. You can substitute a different character for CTRL-D by defining $Term::Complete::complete. For example:

```
$Term::Complete::complete = "\001";  # use ctrl-a instead of ctrl-d
```

CTRL-U

Typing CTRL-U erases any partial input. You can substitute a different character for CTRL-U by defining $Term::Complete::kill.

DEL, BS

The delete and backspace characters both erase one character from the partial input string. You can redefine them by assigning a different character value to $Term::Complete::erase1 and $Term::Complete::erase2.

The user is not prevented from providing input that differs from all strings in the completion list, or from adding to input that has been completed from the list. The final input (determined when the user presses the return key) is the string returned by Complete().

The TTY driver is put into raw mode using the system command stty raw -echo and restored using stty -raw echo. When Complete() is called multiple times, it offers the user's immediately previous response as the default response to each prompt.

Test::Harness — Run Perl Standard Test Scripts with Statistics

```
use Test::Harness;
runtests(@tests);
```

This module is used by MakeMaker. If you're building a Perl extension and if you have test scripts with filenames matching *t/*.t* in the extension's subdirectory, then you can run those tests by executing the shell command, make test.

runtests(@tests) runs all test scripts named as arguments and checks standard output for the expected "ok *n*" strings. (Standard Perl test scripts print "ok *n*" for each single test, where *n* is an integer incremented by one each time around.) After all tests have been performed, runtests() prints some performance statistics that are computed by the Benchmark module.

runtests() is exported by Test::Harness by default.

The test script output

The first line output by a standard test script should be 1..*m* with *m* being the number of tests that the test script attempts to run. Any output from the test script to standard error is ignored and bypassed, and thus will be seen by the user. Lines written to standard output that look like Perl comments (starting with /^\s*\#/) are discarded. Lines containing /^(not\s+)?ok\b/ are interpreted as feedback for runtests().

The global variable $Test::Harness::verbose is exportable and can be used to let runtests() display the standard output of the script without altering the behavior otherwise.

It is tolerated if the script omits test numbers after ok. In this case Test::Harness maintains its own counter. So the following script output:

```
1..6
not ok
ok
not ok
ok
ok
not ok
```

will generate:

```
FAILED tests 1, 3, 6
Failed 3/6 tests, 50.00% okay
```

Diagnostics

All tests successful.\nFiles=%d, Tests=%d, %s
: If all tests are successful, some statistics about the performance are printed.

FAILED tests %s\n\tFailed %d/%d tests, %.2f%% okay.
: For any single script that has failing subtests, these statistics are printed.

Test returned status %d (wstat %d)
: Scripts that return a non-zero exit status, both $?>>8 and $?, are printed in a message similar to the above.

```
Failed 1 test, %.2f%% okay.
```

```
Failed %d/%d tests, %.2f%% okay.
```

If not all tests were successful, the script dies with one of the above messages.

Notes

Test::Harness uses $^X to determine which Perl binary to run the tests with. Test scripts running via the shebang (#!) line may not be portable because $^X is not consistent for shebang scripts across platforms. This is no problem when Test::Harness is run with an absolute path to the Perl binary or when $^X can be found in the path.

Text::Abbrev — Create an Abbreviation Table from a List

```
use Text::Abbrev;

%hash = ();
abbrev(*hash, LIST);
```

The abbrev() routine takes each string in *LIST* and constructs all unambiguous abbreviations (truncations) of the string with respect to the other strings in *LIST*. Each such truncation (including the null truncation consisting of the entire string) is used as a key in %hash for which the associated value is the non-truncated string.

So, if good is the only string in *LIST* beginning with g, the following key/value pairs will be created:

```
g     => good,
go    => good,
goo   => good,
good  => good
```

If, on the other hand, the string go is also in the list, then good yields these key/value pairs:

```
goo   => good,
good  => good
```

and go yields only:

```
go => go
```

Text::ParseWords — Parse Text into a List of Tokens

```
use Text::ParseWords;
@words = quotewords($delim, $keep, @lines);
```

quotewords() accepts a delimiter (which can be a regular expression) and a list of lines, and then breaks those lines up into a list of delimiter-separated words. It ignores delimiters that appear inside single or double quotes.

The $keep argument is a Boolean flag. If it is false, then quotes are removed from the list of words returned by quotewords(); otherwise, quotes are retained.

The value of $keep also affects the interpretation of backslashes. If $keep is true, then backslashes are fully preserved in the returned list of words. Otherwise, a single backslash disappears and a double backslash is returned as a single backslash. (Be aware, however, that, regardless of the value of $keep, a single backslash occurring within quotes causes a Perl syntax error—presumably a bug.)

Text::Soundex — The Soundex Algorithm Described by Knuth

```
use Text::Soundex;

$code = soundex $string;   # get soundex code for a string
@codes = soundex @list;    # get list of codes for list of strings

# set value to be returned for strings without soundex code
$soundex_nocode = 'Z000';
```

This module implements the soundex algorithm as described by Donald Knuth in Volume 3 of *The Art of Computer Programming*. The algorithm is intended to hash words (in particular surnames) into a small space using a simple model that approximates the sound of the word when spoken by an English speaker. Each word is reduced to a four-character string, the first character being an uppercase letter and the remaining three being digits.

If there is no soundex code representation for a string, then the value of $soundex_nocode is returned. This variable is initially set to the undefined value, but many people seem to prefer an unlikely value like Z000. (How unlikely this is depends on the data set being dealt with.) Any value can be assigned to $soundex_nocode.

In a scalar context soundex() returns the soundex code of its first argument, and in an array context a list is returned in which each element is the soundex code for the corresponding argument passed to soundex().

For example:

```
@codes = soundex qw(Mike Stok);
```

leaves @codes containing ('M200', 'S320').

Here are Knuth's examples of various names and the soundex codes they map to:

Names	Code
Euler, Ellery	E460
Gauss, Ghosh	G200
Hilbert, Heilbronn	H416
Knuth, Kant	K530
Lloyd, Ladd	L300
Lukasiewicz, Lissajous	L222

So we have:

```
$code = soundex 'Knuth';              # $code contains 'K530'
@list = soundex qw(Lloyd Gauss);      # @list contains 'L300', 'G200'
```

As the soundex algorithm was originally used a *long* time ago in the United States, it considers only the English alphabet and pronunciation.

As it is mapping a large space (arbitrary-length strings) onto a small space (single letter plus three digits), no inference can be made about the similarity of two strings that end up with the same soundex code. For example, both Hilbert and Heilbronn end up with a soundex code of H416.

Text::Tabs — Expand and Unexpand Tabs

```
use Text::Tabs;

$tabstop = 8;                         # set tab spacing to 8 (default)
print expand("Hello\tworld");         # convert tabs to spaces in output
print unexpand("Hello,        world");  # convert spaces to tabs in output
$tabstop = 4;                         # set tab spacing to 4
print join("\n", expand(split(/\n/,
           "Hello\tworld, \nit's a nice day.\n")));
```

This module expands tabs into spaces and "unexpands" spaces into tabs, in the manner of the UNIX *expand*(1) and *unexpand*(1) programs. All tabs and spaces—not only leading ones—are subject to being expanded and unexpanded.

Both expand() and unexpand() take as argument an array of strings, which are returned with tabs or spaces transformed. Newlines may not be included in the strings, and should be used to split strings into separate elements before they are passed to expand() and unexpand().

expand(), unexpand(), and $tabstop are imported into your program when you **use** this module.

Text::Wrap — Wrap Text into a Paragraph

```
use Text::Wrap;

$Text::Wrap::columns = 20; # default is 76
$pre1 = "\t";             # prepend this to first line of paragraph
$pre2 = "";               # prepend this to subsequent lines
print wrap($pre1, $pre2, "Hello, world, it's a nice day, isn't it?");
```

This module is a simple paragraph formatter that wraps text into a paragraph and indents each line. The single exported function, wrap(), takes three arguments: a string to prepend to the first output line; a string to prepend to each subsequent output line; and the text to be wrapped.

$columns is exported on request.

Tie::Hash, Tie::StdHash — Base Class Definitions for Tied Hashes

```
package NewHash;
require Tie::Hash;

@ISA = (Tie::Hash);

sub DELETE { ... }        # Provides additional method
sub CLEAR { ... }         # Overrides inherited method

package NewStdHash;
require Tie::Hash;

@ISA = (Tie::StdHash);

sub DELETE { ... }

package main;

tie %new_hash, "NewHash";
tie %new_std_hash, "NewStdHash";
```

This module provides some skeletal methods for hash-tying classes. (See Chapter 5 for a list of the functions required in order to tie a hash to a package.) The basic Tie::Hash package provides a new() method, as well as methods TIEHASH(), EXISTS() and CLEAR(). The Tie::StdHash package provides most methods required for hashes. It inherits from Tie::Hash, and causes tied hashes to behave exactly like standard hashes, allowing for selective overloading of methods. The new() method is provided as grandfathering in case a class forgets to include a TIEHASH() method.

For developers wishing to write their own tied hashes, the required methods are briefly defined below. (Chapter 5 not only documents these methods, but also has sample code.)

TIEHASH *ClassName, LIST*

> The method invoked by the command:

> ```
> tie %hash, ClassName, LIST
> ```

> Associates a new hash instance with the specified class. *LIST* would represent additional arguments (along the lines of AnyDBM_File and compatriots) needed to complete the association.

STORE *this, key, value*

> Store *value* into *key* for the tied hash *this*.

FETCH *this, key*

> Retrieve the value associated with *key* for the tied hash *this*.

FIRSTKEY *this*

> Return the key/value pair for the first key in hash *this*.

NEXTKEY *this, lastkey*

> Return the next key/value pair for the hash.

EXISTS *this, key*

> Verify that *key* exists with the tied hash *this*.

DELETE *this, key*

> Delete *key* from the tied hash *this*.

CLEAR *this*

> Clear all values from the tied hash *this*.

Chapter 5 includes a method called DESTROY() as a "necessary" method for tied hashes. However, it is not actually required, and neither Tie::Hash nor Tie::StdHash defines a default for this method.

See also

The library modules relating to various DBM-related implementations (DB_File, GDBM_File, NDBM_File, ODBM_File, and SDBM_File) show examples of general tied hashes, as does the Config module. While these modules do not utilize Tie::Hash, they serve as good working examples.

Tie::Scalar, Tie::StdScalar — Base Class Definitions for Tied Scalars

```
package NewScalar;
require Tie::Scalar;

@ISA = (Tie::Scalar);

sub FETCH { ... }          # Provides additional method
sub TIESCALAR { ... }      # Overrides inherited method

package NewStdScalar;
require Tie::Scalar;

@ISA = (Tie::StdScalar);

sub FETCH { ... }

package main;

tie $new_scalar, "NewScalar";
tie $new_std_scalar, "NewStdScalar";
```

This module provides some skeletal methods for scalar-tying classes. (See Chapter 5 for a list of the functions required in tying a scalar to a package.) The basic Tie::Scalar package provides a new() method, as well as methods TIESCALAR(), FETCH() and STORE(). The Tie::StdScalar package provides all methods specified in Chapter 5. It inherits from Tie::Scalar and causes scalars tied to it to behave exactly like the built-in scalars, allowing for selective overloading of methods. The new() method is provided as a means of grandfathering for classes that forget to provide their own TIESCALAR() method.

For developers wishing to write their own tied-scalar classes, methods are summarized below. (Chapter 5 not only documents these, but also has sample code.)

TIESCALAR *ClassName*, *LIST*
> The method invoked by the command:

>   tie $scalar, ClassName, *LIST*

> Associates a new scalar instance with the specified class. *LIST* would represent additional arguments (along the lines of the AnyDBM_File library module and associated modules) needed to complete the association.

FETCH *this*
> Retrieve the value of the tied scalar referenced by *this*.

STORE *this, value*

    Store *value* in the tied scalar referenced by *this*.

DESTROY *this*

    Free the storage associated with the tied scalar referenced by *this*. This is rarely needed, since Perl manages its memory well. But the option exists, should a class wish to perform specific actions upon the destruction of an instance.

See also

Chapter 5 has a good example using tied scalars to associate process IDs with priority.

Tie::SubstrHash — Fixed-table-size, Fixed-key-length Hashing

```
require Tie::SubstrHash;
tie %myhash, "Tie::SubstrHash", $key_len, $value_len, $table_size;
```

The Tie::SubstrHash package provides a hash table–like interface to an array of determinate size, with constant key size and record size.

Upon tying a new hash to this package, the developer must specify the size of the keys that will be used, the size of the value fields that the keys will index, and the size of the overall table (in terms of the number of key/value pairs, not hard memory). *These values will not change for the duration of the tied hash.* The newly allocated hash table may now have data stored and retrieved. Efforts to store more than $table_size elements will result in a fatal error, as will efforts to store a value not exactly $value_len characters in length, or to reference through a key not exactly $key_len characters in length. While these constraints may seem excessive, the result is a hash table using much less internal memory than an equivalent freely allocated hash table.

Because the current implementation uses the table and key sizes for the hashing algorithm, there is no means by which to dynamically change the value of any of the initialization parameters.

Time::Local — Efficiently Compute Time from Local and GMT Time

```
use Time::Local;

$time = timelocal($sec, $min, $hours, $mday, $mon, $year);
$time = timegm($sec, $min, $hours, $mday, $mon, $year);
```

These routines take a series of arguments specifying a local (`timelocal()`) or Greenwich (`timegm()`) time, and return the number of seconds elapsed between January 1, 1970, and the specified time. The arguments are defined like the corresponding arguments returned by Perl's **gmtime** and **localtime** functions.

The routines are very efficient and yet are always guaranteed to agree with the **gmtime** and **localtime** functions. That is, if you pass the value returned by **time** to **localtime**, and if you then pass the values returned by **localtime** to `timelocal()`, the returned value from `timelocal()` will be the same as the value originally returned from **time**.

Both routines return −1 if the integer limit is hit. On most machines this applies to dates after January 1, 2038.

vars — Predeclare Global Variable Names

```
use vars qw($frob @mung %seen);
```

This module predeclares all variables whose names are in the list, allowing you to use them under **use strict**, and disabling any typo warnings.

Packages such as the AutoLoader and SelfLoader that delay loading of subroutines within packages can create problems with file-scoped lexicals defined using **my**. This is because they move the subroutines outside the scope of the lexical variables. While the **use vars** pragma cannot duplicate the effect of file-scoped lexicals (total transparency outside of the file), it can act as an acceptable substitute by pre-declaring global symbols, ensuring their availability to the routines whose loading was delayed.

See also the **subs** module.

8

Other Oddments

Did you ever have a junk drawer? You know, one of those drawers where you put everything important enough to keep (like the spare key to the back door), but not important enough to have a place of its own (like the back door itself).

Well, this chapter is the junk drawer of the book. We stuffed many important (and a few not-so-important) things in this chapter. Read on.

The Perl Debugger

First of all, have you tried using the **-w** switch?

If you invoke Perl with the **-d** switch, your script runs under the Perl debugger. This works like an interactive Perl environment, prompting for debugger commands that let you examine source code, set breakpoints, dump out your function-call stack, change the values of variables, and so on. Any command not recognized by the debugger[*] is directly executed (**eval**'d) as Perl code in the current package.[†] This is so wonderfully convenient that you often fire up the debugger all by itself just to test out Perl constructs interactively to see what they do. Here's a common way to get that:

```
perl -d -e 42
```

In Perl, the debugger is not a separate program as it usually is in a typical programming environment. Instead, the **-d** flag tells the compiler to insert source information into the parse trees it's about to hand off to the interpreter. That

---

[*] Leading whitespace before a command would cause the debugger to think it's *not* a command for it, but rather for Perl, so be careful not to do that.

[†] The debugger uses the DB package for its own state information.

means your code must first compile correctly for the debugger to work on it. Then when the interpreter starts up, it pre-loads a Perl library file containing the debugger itself.

Debugger Commands

The debugger understands the following commands:

h [*command*]

> Prints out a help message.

> If you supply another debugger command as an argument to the h command, it prints out the description for just that command. The command "h h" produces a more compact help listing designed to fit on one screen. If the output of the h command (or any command, for that matter) scrolls past your screen, just precede the command with a leading pipe symbol so it's run through your pager:

```
DB<1> |h
```

p *expr*

> Same as "print DB::OUT *expr*" in the current package. In particular, since this is just Perl's own **print** function, this means that nested data structures and objects are not dumped, unlike with the x command. The DB::OUT handle is opened to */dev/tty* (or perhaps an editor window) no matter where standard output may have been redirected to.

x *expr*

> Evals its expression in a list context and dumps out the result in a pretty-printed fashion. Nested data structures are printed out recursively, unlike with the print command above.

V [*pkg* [*vars*]]

> Display all (or some) variables in package (defaulting to the main package) using a data pretty-printer. (Hashes show their keys and values so you see what's what, control characters are made printable, nested data structures print out in a legible fashion, and so on.) Make sure you type the identifiers without a type specifier such as $ or @, like this:

```
V DB filename line
```

> In place of a variable name, you can use ~*pattern* or !*pattern* to print existing variables whose names either match or don't match the specified regular expression.

X [*vars*]

> Same as V *currentpackage* [*vars*].

T

> Produce a stack backtrace. See below for details on its output.

s [*expr*]

> Single step. Executes until it reaches the beginning of another statement, descending into subroutine calls. If an expression is supplied that includes function calls, it, too, will be single-stepped.

n

> Next. Executes over subroutine calls, until it reaches the beginning of the next statement at this same level.

<CR>

> Repeat last n or s command.

c [*line*]

> Continue, optionally inserting a one-time-only breakpoint at the specified line.

l

> List next few lines.

l *min+incr*

> List *incr*+1 lines starting at *min*.

l *min-max*

> List lines *min* through *max*.

l *line*

> List a single line.

l *subname*

> List first few lines from subroutine.

−

> List previous few lines.

w [*line*]

> List window (a few lines) around the given *line*, or the current one if no *line* is supplied.

.

> Return debugger pointer to the last-executed line and print it out.

f *filename*

> Switch to viewing a different file.

/pattern/

Search forward for *pattern*; final / is optional.

?pattern?

Search backward for *pattern*; final ? is optional.

L

List all breakpoints and actions for the current file.

S [[!]*pattern*]

List subroutine names matching (or not matching with "!") *pattern*. If no *pattern* is given, all subroutines are listed.

t

Toggle trace mode.

t *expr*

Trace through execution of *expr*.

b [*line*] [*condition*]

Set a breakpoint at *line*. If *line* is omitted, set a breakpoint on the line that is about to be executed. *condition*, if given, is evaluated each time the statement is reached, and a breakpoint is taken only if *condition* is true. Breakpoints may only be set on lines that begin an executable statement. Conditions don't use if:

```
b 237 $x > 30
b 33 /pattern/i
```

b *subname* [*condition*]

Set a (possibly conditional) breakpoint at the first line of the named subroutine.

d [*line*]

Delete a breakpoint at the specified *line*. If *line* is omitted, deletes the breakpoint on the line that is about to be executed.

D

Delete all installed breakpoints.

a [*line*] *command*

Set an action to be done before the *line* is executed. The sequence of steps taken by the debugger is:

- Check for a breakpoint at this line.

- Print the line if necessary (tracing).

- Do any actions associated with that line.

- Prompt the user if at a breakpoint or in single-step.
- Evaluate the line.

For example, this will print out $foo every time line 53 is passed:

```
a 53 print "DB FOUND $foo\n"
```

A

Delete all installed actions.

O [*opt*[=*val*]]

Set or query values of options. *val* defaults to 1. *opt* can be abbreviated to the shortest unique string, which is why some options are uppercase and others are lowercase. Options are:

Option	Value
recallCommand ShellBang	The characters used to recall command or spawn shell. By default, these are both set to "!" (see below).
pager	Program to use for output of pager-piped commands (those beginning with a | character). By default, $ENV{PAGER} will be used.
PrintRet	Enables printing of return value after r command.
frame	Enables printing messages on entry and exit from subroutines.

The following options affect what happens with V, X, and x commands:

Option	Value
arrayDepth hashDepth	Print only to depth *n* ("" for all).
compactDump veryCompact	Change style of array and hash dump.
globPrint	Whether to print contents of globs.
DumpDBFiles	Dump arrays holding debugged files.
DumpPackages	Dump symbol tables of packages.
quote HighBit undefPrint	Change style of string dump.
tkRunning	Run Tk while prompting (with ReadLine).[a]
signalLevel warnLevel dieLevel	Level of verbosity.

[a] A Perl application is usually frozen when sitting at the debugger prompt. Tk support keeps the event loop of Tk running while reading the prompt.

During startup, options are initialized from $ENV{PERLDB_OPTS}. You can put additional initialization options TTY, noTTY, ReadLine, and NonStop there. Here's an example using the $ENV{PERLDB_OPTS} variable:

```
$ PERLDB_OPTS="N f=2" perl -d myprogram
```

This will run the script myprogram without human intervention, printing out the call tree with entry and exit points. Note that "N f=2" is equivalent to "Non-Stop=1 frame=2".

< *command*

Set an action to happen before every debugger prompt. A multi-line *command* may be entered by backslashing the newlines. *command* should be Perl code.

> *command*

Set an action to happen after the prompt when you've just given a command to return to executing the script. A multi-line *command* may be entered by back-slashing the newlines. *command* should be Perl code.

! *number*

Redo a previous command (defaults to previous command).

! -*number*

Redo *number*'th-to-last command.

! *pattern*

Redo last command that started with *pattern*. See "O recallCommand", too.

!! *cmd*

Run *cmd* in a subprocess (which will read from DB::IN, write to DB::OUT). See "O shellBang", too.

H -*number*

Display last *number* commands. Only commands longer than one character are listed. If *number* is omitted, lists them all.

q or ^D

Quit. ("quit" doesn't quite work for this.)

R

Restart the debugger by **exec**ing a new session. It tries to maintain your history across this, but internal settings and command line options may be lost.

| *dbcmd*

Run debugger command, piping DB::OUT to $ENV{PAGER}.

| | *dbcmd*

Same as | *dbcmd* but DB::OUT is temporarily **select**ed as well. Often used with commands that would otherwise produce long output, such as

    |V main

= [*alias value*]

Define a command alias, or list current aliases.

command

Execute *command* as a Perl statement. A semicolon is not needed at the end.

Using the Debugger

If you have any compile-time executable statements (code within a BEGIN block or a use statement), they will not be stopped by the debugger, although **require**s will.

The debugger prompt is something like:

```
DB<8>
```

or even:

```
DB<<17>>
```

where that number is the command number. A *csh*-like history mechanism allows you to access previous commands by number. For example, !17 would repeat command number 17. The number of angle brackets indicates the depth of the debugger. You get more than one set of brackets, for example, if you're already at a breakpoint and then print out the result of a function call that itself also has a breakpoint.

If you want to enter a multi-line command, such as a subroutine definition with several statements, you may escape the newline that would normally end the debugger command with a backslash. Here's an example:

```
DB<1> for (1..4) {            \
    cont:      print "ok\n";     \
    cont: }
    ok
    ok
    ok
    ok
```

Note that this business of escaping a newline is specific to interactive commands typed into the debugger.

Let's say you want to fire up the debugger on a little program of yours (let's call it *camel_flea*), and stop it as soon as it gets down to a function named infested. Here's how you'd do that:

```
shell_prompt% perl -d camel_flea
Stack dump during die enabled outside of evals.

Loading DB routines from perl5db.pl patch level 0.94
Emacs support available.
```

```
Enter h or 'h h' for help.

main::(camel_flea:3):   $a = 1;
   DB<1>
```

The debugger halts your program right before the first run-time executable statement (but see above regarding compile-time statements) and asks you to enter a command. Contrary to popular expectations, whenever the debugger stops to show you a line of code, it displays the line it's *about* to execute, not the one it just executed.

Now, you'd like to stop as soon as your program gets to the infested function, so you enter a breakpoint there like so:

```
DB<1> b infested
DB<2> c
```

The debugger now continues until it hits that function, at which point it does this:

```
main::infested(camel_flea:12):      my bugs;
```

It might be nice to look at a window of source code around the breakpoint, so you use the w command:

```
DB<2> w
9:       }
10:
11:      sub infested {
12==>b       my $bugs;
13:          return 3.5;
14:      }
DB<2>
```

As you see, your current line is line 12, and it has a breakpoint on it.

Now, you'd like to see who called whom, so you ask for a stack backtrace:

```
DB<2> T
$ = main::infested called from file 'Ambulation.pm' line 10
@ = Ambulation::legs(1, 2, 3, 4) called from file 'camel_flea' line 7
$ = main::pests('bactrian', 4) called from file 'camel_flea' line 4
```

The left-hand character up there ($ or @) tells whether the function was called in a scalar or list context (we bet you can tell which is which). There are three lines because you were three functions deep when you ran the stack backtrace. Here's what each line means:

• Line number one says you were in the function main::infested when you ran the stack dump. It tells you the function was called in a scalar context from line 10 of the file *Ambulation.pm*. It also shows that it was called without any arguments whatsoever, meaning it was called as &infested.

- Line number two shows that the function Ambulation::legs was called in a list context from the *camel_flea* file with four arguments.

- Line number three shows that main::pests was called in a scalar context, also from *camel_flea*, but from line 4.

Limited control over the Perl debugger can also be managed from within your Perl script itself. You might do this, for example, to set an automatic breakpoint at a certain subroutine whenever a particular program is run under the debugger. Setting $DB::single to 1 will stop at the next statement as though you'd used the debugger's s command. If you set $DB::single to 2, it's equivalent to having just typed the n command. The $DB::trace variable can be set to 1 to simulate having typed the t command.

Debugger Customization

To modify the debugger, copy *perl5db.pl* from the Perl library to another file and modify it as necessary. You'll also want to set your PERL5DB environment variable to say something like this:

```
BEGIN { require "myperl5db.pl" }
```

You can do some customization by setting up a *.perldb* file with initialization code. For instance, you could make aliases like these (the last one is one people expect to be there):

```
$DB::alias{'len'}  = 's/^len(.*)/p length($1)/';
$DB::alias{'stop'} = 's/^stop (at|in)/b/';
$DB::alias{'ps'}   = 's/^ps\b/p scalar /';
$DB::alias{'quit'} = 's/^quit\b.*/exit/';
```

Readline Support

As shipped, the only command-line history mechanism supplied is a simplistic one that checks for leading exclamation points. This is fine for casual use. However, if you install the Term::ReadKey and Term::ReadLine modules from CPAN, you will have full editing capabilities much like GNU *readline*(3) provides. Look for these in the *modules/by-module/Term* directory on CPAN.

Editor Support for Debugging

If you have GNU *emacs* installed on your system, it can interact with the Perl debugger to provide an integrated software development environment reminiscent of its interactions with C debuggers.

Perl is also delivered with a start file for making *emacs* act like a syntax-directed editor that understands (some of) Perl's syntax. Look in the *emacs/* directory of the Perl source distribution.

(Historically, a similar setup for interacting with *vi* and the X11 window system had also been available, but at the time of this writing, no debugger support for *vi* currently exists.)

Debugger Internals

When you call the **caller** function from package DB, Perl sets the @DB::args array to the arguments that stack frame was called with. It also maintains other magical internal variables, such as @DB::dbline, an array of the source code lines for the currently selected (with the debugger's f command) file. Perl effectively inserts a call to the function DB::DB(*linenum*) in front of every place that can have a break-point. Instead of a subroutine call it calls DB::sub, setting $DB::sub to the name of the called subroutine. It also inserts a BEGIN {require 'perl5db.pl'} before the first line, since no subroutine call is possible until &DB::sub is defined (for subroutines defined outside this file). In fact, the same is true if $DB::deep (how many levels of recursion deep into the debugger you are) is not defined.

At the start, the debugger reads your config file (*./.perldb* or *˜/.perldb* under UNIX), which can set important options. This file may define a subroutine &afterinit to be executed after the debugger is initialized.

After the config file is processed, the debugger consults the environment variable PERLDB_OPTS and parses it as arguments to the O *opt=val* debugger command.

The following options can only be specified at startup. To set them in your config file, call &parse_options("*opt=val*").

TTY
> The TTY to use for debugging I/O.

noTTY
> If set, goes in NonStop mode. On an interrupt, if TTY is not set, it uses the value of noTTY or */tmp/perldbtty$$* to find TTY using Term::Rendezvous. The current variant is to have the name of TTY in this file.

ReadLine
> If false, a dummy ReadLine is used so that you can debug ReadLine applications.

NonStop

> If true, no interaction is performed until an interrupt.

LineInfo

> File or pipe to print line number info to. If it's a pipe, then a short, *emacs*-like message is used. Example config file:

```
&parse_options("NonStop=1 LineInfo=db.out");
sub afterinit { $trace = 1; }
```

> The script will run without human intervention, putting trace information into the file *db.out*. (If you interrupt it, you had better reset `LineInfo` to something "interactive"!)

Debugger Bugs

If your program **exits** or **dies**, so too does the debugger.

You cannot get the stack frame information or otherwise debug functions that were not compiled by Perl, such as C or C++ extensions.

If you alter your @_ arguments in a subroutine (such as with **shift** or **pop**), the stack backtrace will not show the original values.

Alternative Debuggers: The Perl Profiler

If you wish to supply an alternative debugger for Perl to run, just invoke your script with the –d: *module* switch. One of the most popular alternative debuggers for Perl is DProf, the Perl profiler. As of this writing, DProf was not included with the standard Perl distribution, but it is expected to be included "real soon now."

Meanwhile, you can fetch the Devel::DProf module from CPAN. Assuming it's properly installed on your system, you can use it to profile the Perl program in *mycode.pl* by typing:

```
perl -d:DProf mycode.pl
```

When the script terminates, the profiler will dump the profile information to a file called *tmon.out*. A tool like *dprofpp* (also supplied with the Devel::DProf package) interprets the profile.

Other Debugging Resources

You did try the **-w** switch, didn't you?

Common Goofs for Novices

The biggest goof of all is forgetting to use the **-w** switch, which points out many errors. The second biggest goof is not using use strict when it's appropriate.

Apart from those, there are certain traps that almost everyone falls into, and other traps you'll fall into only if you come from a particular culture. We've separated these out in the following sections.

Universal Blunders

- Putting a comma after the filehandle in a **print** statement. Although it looks extremely regular and pretty to say:

  ```
  print STDOUT, "goodbye", $adj, "world!\n";    # WRONG
  ```

  this is nonetheless incorrect, because of that first comma. What you want instead is:

  ```
  print STDOUT "goodbye", $adj, "world!\n";     # ok
  ```

  The syntax is this way so that you can say:

  ```
  print $filehandle "goodbye", $adj, "world!\n";
  ```

  where $filehandle is a scalar holding the name of a filehandle at run-time. This is distinct from:

  ```
  print $notafilehandle, "goodbye", $adj, "world!\n";
  ```

  where $notafilehandle is simply a string that is added to the list of things to be printed. See Indirect Object in the glossary.

- Using == instead of **eq** and != instead of **ne**. The == and != operators are *numeric* tests. The other two are *string* tests. The strings "123" and "123.00" are equal as numbers, but not equal as strings. Also, any non-numeric string is numerically equal to zero. Unless you are dealing with numbers, you almost always want the string comparison operators instead.

- Forgetting the trailing semicolon. Every statement in Perl is terminated by a semicolon or the end of a block. Newlines aren't statement terminators as they are in *awk* or Python.

- Forgetting that a *BLOCK* requires braces. Naked statements are not *BLOCK*s. If you are creating a control structure such as a **while** or an **if** that requires one or more *BLOCK*s, you *must* use braces around each *BLOCK*.

- Not saving **$1**, **$2**, and so on, across regular expressions. Remember that every new m/atch/ or s/ubsti/tute/ will set (or clear, or mangle) your **$1**, **$2**... variables, as well as **$`**, **$'**, and **$&**. One way to save them right away is to evaluate the match within a list context, as in:

  ```
  ($one,$two) = /(\w+) (\w+)/;
  ```

- Not realizing that a **local** also changes the variable's value within other subroutines called within the scope of the local. It's easy to forget that **local** is a runtime statement that does dynamic scoping, because there's no equivalent in languages like C. See **local** in Chapter 3, *Functions*. Usually you wanted a **my** anyway.

- Losing track of brace pairings. A good text editor will help you find the pairs. Get one.

- Using loop control statements in do {} while. Although the braces in this control structure look suspiciously like part of a loop *BLOCK*, they aren't.

- Saying @foo[1] when you mean $foo[1]. The @foo[1] reference is an array *slice*, and means an array consisting of the single element $foo[1]. Sometimes, this doesn't make any difference, as in:

  ```
  print "the answer is @foo[1]\n";
  ```

  but it makes a big difference for things like:

  ```
  @foo[1] = <STDIN>;
  ```

  which will slurp up all the rest of STDIN, assign the *first* line to $foo[1], and discard everything else. This is probably not what you intended. Get into the habit of thinking that $ means a single value, while @ means a list of values, and you'll do okay.

- Forgetting to select the right filehandle before setting **$^**, **$~**, or **$|**. These variables depend on the currently selected filehandle, as determined by select(*FILEHANDLE*). The initial filehandle so selected is STDOUT. You should really be using the filehandle methods from the FileHandle module instead. See Chapter 7, *The Standard Perl Library*.

Frequently Ignored Advice

Practicing Perl Programmers should take note of the following:

- Remember that many operations behave differently in a list context than they do in a scalar one. Chapter 3 has all the details.

- Avoid barewords if you can, especially all lowercase ones. You can't tell just by looking at it whether a word is a function or a bareword string. By using quotes on strings and parentheses around function call arguments, you won't ever get them confused. In fact, the pragma use strict at the beginning of your program makes barewords a compile-time error—probably a good thing.

- You can't tell just by looking which built-in functions are unary operators (like **chop** and **chdir**), which are list operators (like **print** and **unlink**), and which are argumentless (like **time**). You'll want to learn them from Chapter 2, *The Gory Details*. Note also that user-defined subroutines are by default list operators, but can be declared as unary operators with a prototype of ($).

- People have a hard time remembering that some functions default to $_, or @ARGV, or whatever, while others do not. Take the time to learn which are which, or avoid default arguments.

- *<FH>* is not the name of a filehandle, but an angle operator that does a line-input operation on the handle. This confusion usually manifests itself when people try to **print** to the angle operator:

```
print <FH> "hi";    # WRONG, omit angles
```

- Remember also that data read by the angle operator is assigned to $_ only when the file read is the sole condition in a **while** loop:

```
while (<FH>)      { }
while ($_ = <FH>) { }..
<FH>;  # data discarded!
```

- Remember not to use = when you need =~; the two constructs are quite different:

```
$x =  /foo/;  # searches $_, puts result in $x
$x =~ /foo/;  # searches $x, discards result
```

- Use **my** for local variables whenever you can get away with it (but see "Formats" in Chapter 2 for where you can't). Using **local** actually gives a local value to a global variable, which leaves you open to unforeseen side effects of dynamic scoping.

- Don't localize a module's exported variables. If you localize an exported variable, its exported value will not change. The local name becomes an alias to a new value but the external name is still an alias for the original.

Awk Traps

Accustomed *awk* users should take special note of the following:

- The English module, loaded via

  ```
  use English;
  ```

  allows you to refer to special variables (like $RS) using their *awk* names; see the end of Chapter 2 for details.

- Semicolons are required after all simple statements in Perl (except at the end of a block). Newline is not a statement delimiter.

- Braces are required on **if** and **while** blocks.

- Variables begin with $ or @ in Perl.

- Arrays index from 0, as do string positions in **substr** and **index**.

- You have to decide whether your array has numeric or string indices.

- You have to decide whether you want numeric or string comparisons.

- Hash values do not spring into existence upon reference.

- Reading an input line does not split it for you. You get to split it yourself to an array. And the **split** operator has different arguments than you might guess.

- The current input line is normally in $_, not $0. It generally does not have the newline stripped. ($0 is the name of the program executed.) See Chapter 2.

- $1, $2, and so on, do not refer to fields—they refer to substrings matched by the last pattern match.

- The **print** operator does not add field and record separators unless you set $,, and $\. ($OFS and $ORS if you're using English.)

- You must **open** your files before you **print** to them.

- The range operator is .. rather than comma. The comma operator works (more or less) as in does C.

- The match binding operator is =~, not ~. (~ is the 1's complement operator, as in C.)

- The exponentiation operator is **, not ^. ^ is the bitwise XOR operator, as in C. (You know, one could get the feeling that *awk* is basically incompatible with C.)

- The concatenation operator is dot (.), not "nothing". (Using "nothing" as an operator would render /pat/ /pat/ unparsable, since the third slash would be interpreted as a division operator—the tokener is in fact slightly context sensitive for operators like /, ?, and <. And, in fact, a dot itself can be the beginning of a number.)

- The **next**, **exit**, and **continue** keywords work differently.
- The following variables work differently:

awk	Perl
ARGC	$#ARGV or scalar @ARGV
ARGV[0]	$0
FILENAME	$ARGV
FNR	$. - something
FS	(whatever you like)
NF	$#Fld, or some such
NR	$.
OFMT	$#
OFS	$,
ORS	$\
RLENGTH	length($&)
RS	$/
RSTART	length($`)
SUBSEP	$;

- You cannot set $RS to a pattern, only a string.
- When in doubt, run the *awk* construct through *a2p* and see what it gives you.

C Traps

Cerebral C programmers should take note of the following:

- Curlies are required for **if** and **while** blocks.
- You must use **elsif** rather than "else if" or "elif". Syntax like:

```
if (expression) {
    block;
}
else if (another_expression) {
    another_block;
}
```

is illegal. The **else** part is always a block, and a naked **if** is not a block. You mustn't expect Perl to be exactly the same as C. What you want instead is:

```
if (expression) {
    block;
}
elsif (another_expression) {
    another_block;
}
```

Note also that "elif" is "file" spelled backward. Only Algol-ers would want a keyword that was the same as another word spelled backward.

- The `break` and `continue` keywords from C become in Perl **last** and **next**, respectively. Unlike in C, these do *not* work within a `do { } while` construct.

- There's no switch statement. (But it's easy to build one on the fly; see "Bare Blocks and Case Structures" in Chapter 2.)

- Variables begin with $, @, or % in Perl.

- **printf** does not implement the * format for interpolating field widths, but it's trivial to use interpolation of double-quoted strings to achieve the same effect.

- Comments begin with #, not /*.

- You can't take the address of anything, although a similar operator in Perl is the backslash, which creates a reference.

- `ARGV` must be capitalized. `$ARGV[0]` is C's `argv[1]`, and C's `argv[0]` ends up in `$0`.

- Functions such as **link**, **unlink**, and **rename** return true for success, not 0.

- Signal handlers deal with signal names, not numbers.

Sed Traps

Seasoned *sed* programmers should take note of the following:

- Backreferences in substitutions use $ rather than \.

- The pattern matching metacharacters (,), and | do not have backslashes in front. The corresponding literal characters do.

- The range operator in Perl is ... rather than a comma.

Shell Traps

Sharp shell programmers should take note of the following:

- Variables are prefixed with $ or @ on the left side of the assignment as well as the right. A shellish assignment like:

```
camel='dromedary';      # WRONG
```

won't be parsed the way you expect. You need:

```
$camel='dromedary';      # ok
```

- The loop variable of a **foreach** also requires a $. Although *csh* likes:

```
foreach hump (one two)
stuff_it $hump
end
```

in Perl this is written as:

```
foreach $hump ("one", "two") {
    stuff_it($hump);
}
```

- The backtick operator does variable interpretation without regard to the presence of single quotes in the command.

- The backtick operator does no translation of the return value. In Perl, you have to trim the newline explicitly, like this:

```
chop($thishost = `hostname`);
```

- Shells (especially *csh*) do several levels of substitution on each command line. Perl does substitution only within certain constructs such as double quotes, backticks, angle brackets, and search patterns.

- Shells tend to interpret scripts a little bit at a time. Perl compiles the entire program before executing it (except for BEGIN blocks, which execute at compile time).

- The arguments are available via **@ARGV**, not **$1**, **$2**, and so on.

- The environment is not automatically made available as separate scalar variables. But see the Env module.

Previous Perl Traps

Penitent Perl 4 (and Prior) Programmers should take note of the following changes between Release 4 and Release 5 that might affect old scripts:

- @ now always interpolates an array in double-quotish strings. Some programs may now need to use backslash to protect any @ that shouldn't interpolate.

- Barewords that used to look like strings to Perl will now look like subroutine calls if a subroutine by that name is defined before the compiler sees them. For example:

```
sub SeeYa { die "Hasta la vista, baby!" }
$SIG{'QUIT'} = SeeYa;
```

In prior versions of Perl, that code would set the signal handler. Now, it actually calls the function! You may use the **-w** switch to find such risky usage.

- Symbols starting with "_" are no longer forced into package main, except for $_ itself (and @_, and so on).

- Double-colon is now a valid package separator in an identifier. Thus, the statement:

  ```
  print "$a::$b::$c\n";
  ```

  now parses $a:: as the variable reference, where in prior versions only the $a was considered to be the variable reference. Similarly,

  ```
  print "$var::abc::xyz\n";
  ```

  is now interpreted as a single variable $var::abc::xyz, whereas in prior versions, the variable $var would have been followed by the constant text ::abc::xyz.

- s'lhs'rhs' now does no interpolation on either side. It used to interpolate $lhs but not $rhs.

- The second and third arguments of **splice** are now evaluated in scalar context (as documented) rather than list context.

- These are now semantic errors because of precedence:

  ```
  shift @list + 20; # now parses like shift(@list + 20), illegal!
  $n = keys %map + 20; # now parses like keys(%map + 20), illegal!
  ```

  Because if those were to work, then this couldn't:

  ```
  sleep $dormancy + 20;
  ```

- The precedence of assignment operators is now the same as the precedence of assignment. Previous versions of Perl mistakenly gave them the precedence of the associated operator. So you now must parenthesize them in expressions like

  ```
  /foo/ ? ($a += 2) : ($a -= 2);
  ```

  Otherwise:

  ```
  /foo/ ? $a += 2 : $a -= 2;
  ```

  would be erroneously parsed as:

  ```
  (/foo/ ? $a += 2 : $a) -= 2;
  ```

  On the other hand,

  ```
  $a += /foo/ ? 1 : 2;
  ```

  now works as a C programmer would expect.

- open FOO || die is now incorrect. You need parentheses around the filehandle, because **open** has the precedence of a list operator.

- The elements of argument lists for formats are now evaluated in list context. This means you can interpolate list values now.

- You can't do a **goto** into a block that is optimized away. Darn.

- It is no longer syntactically legal to use whitespace as the name of a variable, or as a delimiter for any kind of quote construct. Double darn.

- The **caller** function now returns a false value in a scalar context if there is no caller. This lets library modules determine whether they're being required or run directly.

- m//g now attaches its state to the searched string rather than the regular expression. See "Regular Expressions" in Chapter 2 for further details.

- reverse is no longer allowed as the name of a **sort** subroutine.

- *taintperl* is no longer a separate executable. There is now a –**T** switch to turn on tainting when it isn't turned on automatically.

- Double-quoted strings may no longer end with an unescaped $ or @.

- The archaic **if** *BLOCK BLOCK* syntax is no longer supported.

- Negative array subscripts now count from the end of the array.

- The comma operator in a scalar context is now guaranteed to give a scalar context to its arguments.

- The ** operator now binds more tightly than unary minus. It was documented to work this way before, but didn't.

- Setting $#array lower now discards array elements immediately.

- **delete** is not guaranteed to return the deleted value for **tie**d arrays, since this capability may be onerous for some modules to implement.

- The construct "this is $$x", which used to interpolate the pid at that point, now tries to dereference $x. **$$** by itself still works fine, however.

- The meaning of **foreach** has changed slightly when it is iterating over a list which is not an array. This used to assign the list to a temporary array, but for efficiency it no longer does so. This means that you'll now be iterating over the actual values, not over copies of the values. Modifications to the loop variable can change the original values. To retain prior Perl semantics you'd need to assign your list explicitly to a temporary array and then iterate over that. For example, you might need to change:

  ```
  foreach $var (grep /x/, @list) { ... }
  ```

  to:

```
foreach $var (my @tmp = grep /x/, @list) { ... }
```

Otherwise changing $var will clobber the values of @list. (This most often happens when you use $_ for the loop variable, and call subroutines in the loop that don't properly localize $_.)

- Some error messages will be different.

- Some bugs may have been inadvertently removed.[*]

Efficiency

While most of the work of programming may be simply getting a program working properly, you may find yourself wanting more bang for the buck out of your Perl program. Perl's rich set of operators, datatypes, and control constructs are not necessarily intuitive when it comes to speed and space optimization. Many trade-offs were made during Perl's design, and such decisions are buried in the guts of the code. In general, the shorter and simpler your code is, the faster it runs, but there are exceptions. This section attempts to help you make it work just a wee bit better.

(If you want it to work a lot better, you can play with the new Perl-to-C translation modules, or rewrite your inner loop as a C extension.)

You'll note that sometimes optimizing for time may cost you in space or programmer efficiency (indicated by conflicting hints below). Them's the breaks. If programming were easy, they wouldn't need something as complicated as a human being to do it, now would they?

Time Efficiency

- Use hashes instead of linear searches. For example, instead of searching through @keywords to see if $_ is a keyword, construct a hash with:

```
my %keywords;
for (@keywords) {
    $keywords{$_}++;
}
```

Then, you can quickly tell if $_ contains a keyword by testing $keyword{$_} for a non-zero value.

- Avoid subscripting when a **foreach** or list operator will do. Subscripting sometimes forces conversion from floating point to integer, and there's often a better way to do it. Consider using **foreach**, **shift**, and **splice** operations. Consider saying use integer.

---

[*] Much to the consternation of Perl poets.

- Avoid **goto**. It scans outward from your current location for the indicated label.

- Avoid **printf** if **print** will work. Quite apart from the extra overhead of **printf**, some implementations have field length limitations that **print** gets around.

- Avoid **$&**, **$`**, and **$'**. Any occurrence in your program causes all matches to save the searched string for possible future reference. (However, once you've blown it, it doesn't hurt to have more of them.)

- Avoid using **eval** on a string. An **eval** of a string (not of a *BLOCK*) forces recompilation every time through. The Perl parser is pretty fast for a parser, but that's not saying much. Nowadays there's almost always a better way to do what you want anyway. In particular, any code that uses **eval** merely to construct variable names is obsolete, since you can now do the same directly using symbolic references:

  ```
  ${$pkg . '::' . $varname} = &{ "fix_" . $varname }($pkg);
  ```

- Avoid string **eval** inside a loop. Put the loop into the **eval** instead, to avoid redundant recompilations of the code. See the **study** operator in Chapter 3 for an example of this.

- Avoid run-time-compiled patterns. Use the /*pattern*/o (once only) pattern modifier to avoid pattern recompilation when the pattern doesn't change over the life of the process. For patterns that change occasionally, you can use the fact that a null pattern refers back to the previous pattern, like this:

  ```
  "foundstring" =~ /$currentpattern/;       # Dummy match (must succeed).
  while (<>) {
      print if //;
  }
  ```

  You can also use **eval** to recompile a subroutine that does the match (if you only recompile occasionally).

- Short-circuit alternation is often faster than the corresponding regular expression. So:

  ```
  print if /one-hump/ || /two/;
  ```

  is likely to be faster than:

  ```
  print if /one-hump|two/;
  ```

  at least for certain values of one-hump and two. This is because the optimizer likes to hoist certain simple matching operations up into higher parts of the syntax tree and do very fast matching with a Boyer-Moore algorithm. A complicated pattern defeats this.

- Reject common cases early with next if. As with simple regular expressions, the optimizer likes this. And it just makes sense to avoid unnecessary work. You can typically discard comment lines and blank lines even before you do a split or chop:

```
while (<>) {
    next if /^#/;
    next if /^$/;
    chop;
    @piggies = split(/,/);
    ...
}
```

- Avoid regular expressions with many quantifiers, or with big {*m,n*} numbers on parenthesized expressions. Such patterns can result in exponentially slow backtracking behavior unless the quantified subpatterns match on their first "pass".

- Try to maximize the length of any non-optional literal strings in regular expressions. This is counterintuitive, but longer patterns often match faster than shorter patterns. That's because the optimizer looks for constant strings and hands them off to a Boyer-Moore search, which benefits from longer strings. Compile your pattern with the -Dr debugging switch to see what Perl thinks the longest literal string is.

- Avoid expensive subroutine calls in tight loops. There is overhead associated with calling subroutines, especially when you pass lengthy parameter lists, or return lengthy values. In increasing order of desperation, try passing values by reference, passing values as dynamically scoped globals, inlining the subroutine, or rewriting the whole loop in C.

- Avoid getc for anything but single-character terminal I/O. In fact, don't use it for that either. Use sysread.

- Use readdir rather than <*>. To get all the non-dot files within a directory, say something like:

```
opendir(DIR,".");
@files = sort grep(!/^\./, readdir(DIR));
closedir(DIR);
```

- Avoid frequent substr on long strings.

- Use pack and unpack instead of multiple substr invocations.

- Use **substr** as an lvalue rather than concatenating substrings. For example, to replace the fourth through sixth characters of $foo with the contents of the variable $bar, don't do:

  ```
  $foo = substr($foo,0,3) . $bar . substr($foo,6);
  ```

  Instead, simply identify the part of the string to be replaced, and assign into it, as in:

  ```
  substr($foo,3,3) = $bar;
  ```

  But be aware that if $foo is a huge string, and $bar isn't exactly 3 characters long, this can do a lot of copying too.

- Use s/// rather than concatenating substrings. This is especially true if you can replace one constant with another of the same size. This results in an in-place substitution.

- Use modifiers and equivalent **and** and **or**, instead of full-blown conditionals. Statement modifiers and logical operators avoid the overhead of entering and leaving a block. They can often be more readable too.

- Use $foo = $a || $b || $c. This is much faster (and shorter to say) than:

  ```
  if ($a) {
      $foo = $a;
  }
  elsif ($b) {
      $foo = $b;
  }
  elsif ($c) {
      $foo = $c;
  }
  ```

  Similarly, set default values with:

  ```
  $pi ||= 3;
  ```

- Group together any tests that want the same initial string. When testing a string for various prefixes in anything resembling a switch structure, put together all the /^a/ patterns, all the /^b/ patterns, and so on.

- Don't test things you know won't match. Use **last** or **elsif** to avoid falling through to the next case in your switch statement.

- Use special operators like **study**, logical string operations, pack 'u' and unpack '%' formats.

- Beware of the tail wagging the dog. Misstatements resembling (<STDIN>)[0] and 0 .. 2000000 can cause Perl much unnecessary work. In accord with UNIX philosophy, Perl gives you enough rope to hang yourself.

- Factor operations out of loops. The Perl optimizer does not attempt to remove invariant code from loops. It expects you to exercise some sense.

- Slinging strings can be faster than slinging arrays.

- Slinging arrays can be faster than slinging strings. It all depends on whether you're going to reuse the strings or arrays, and on which operations you're going to perform. Heavy modification of each element implies that arrays will be better, and occasional modification of some elements implies that strings will be better. But you just have to try it and see.

- **my** variables are normally faster than **local** variables.

- Sorting on a manufactured key array may be faster than using a fancy sort subroutine. A given array value may participate in several sort comparisons, so if the sort subroutine has to do much recalculation, it's better to factor out that calculation to a separate pass before the actual sort.

- `tr/abc//d` is faster than `s/[abc]//g`.

- **print** with a comma separator may be faster than concatenating strings. For example:

```
print $fullname{$name} . " has a new home directory " .
    $home{$name} . "\n";
```

has to glue together the two hashes and the two fixed strings before passing them to the low-level print routines, whereas:

```
print $fullname{$name}, " has a new home directory ",
    $home{$name}, "\n";
```

doesn't. On the other hand, depending on the values and the architecture, the concatenation may be faster. Try it.

- Prefer `join("", ...)` to a series of concatenated strings. Multiple concatenations may cause strings to be copied back and forth multiple times. The **join** operator avoids this.

- **split** on a fixed string is generally faster than **split** on a pattern. That is, use `split(/ /, ...)` rather than `split(/ +/, ...)` if you know there will only be one space. However, the patterns `/\s+/`, `/^/` and `/ /` are specially optimized, as is the **split** on whitespace.

- Pre-extending an array or string can save some time. As strings and arrays grow, Perl extends them by allocating a new copy with some room for growth and copying in the old value. Pre-extending a string with the **x** operator or an array by setting `$#array` can prevent this occasional overhead, as well as minimize memory fragmentation.

- Don't **undef** long strings and arrays if they'll be reused for the same purpose. This helps prevent reallocation when the string or array must be re-extended.

- Prefer `"\0" x 8192` over `unpack("x8192",())`.

- `system("mkdir...")` may be faster on multiple directories if *mkdir*(2) isn't available.

- Avoid using **eof** if return values will already indicate it.

- Cache entries from passwd and group (and so on) that are apt to be reused. For example, to cache the return value from **gethostbyaddr** when you are converting numeric addresses (like 198.112.208.11) to names (like "www.ora.com"), you can use something like:

```
sub numtoname {
    local($_) = @_;
    unless (defined $numtoname{$_}) {
        local(@a) = gethostbyaddr(pack('C4', split(/\./)),2);
        $numtoname{$_} = @a > 0 ? $a[0] : $_;
    }
    $numtoname{$_};
}
```

- Avoid unnecessary system calls. Operating system calls tend to be rather expensive. So for example, don't call the **time** operator when a cached value of $now would do. Use the special _ filehandle to avoid unnecessary *stat*(2) calls. On some systems, even a minimal system call may execute a thousand instructions.

- Avoid unnecessary **system** calls. The **system** operator has to fork a subprocess and execute the program you specify. Or worse, execute a shell to execute the program you specify. This can easily execute a million instructions.

- Worry about starting subprocesses, but only if they're frequent. Starting a single *pwd*, *hostname*, or *find* process isn't going to hurt you much—after all, a shell starts subprocesses all day long. We do occasionally encourage the toolbox approach, believe it or not.

- Keep track of your working directory yourself rather than calling *pwd* repeatedly. (A package is provided in the standard library for this. See the Cwd module in Chapter 7.)

- Avoid shell metacharacters in commands—pass lists to **system** and **exec** where appropriate.

- Set the sticky bit on the Perl interpreter on machines without demand paging.

      chmod +t /usr/bin/perl

- Using defaults doesn't make your program faster.

Space Efficiency

- Use **vec** for compact integer array storage.
- Prefer numeric values over string values—they require little additional space over that allocated for the scalar header structure.
- Use **substr** to store constant-length strings in a longer string.
- Use the Tie::SubstrHash module for very compact storage of a hash array, if the key and value lengths are fixed.
- Use __END__ and the DATA filehandle to avoid storing program data as both a string and an array.
- Prefer **each** to **keys** where order doesn't matter.
- Delete or **undef** globals that are no longer in use.
- Use some kind of DBM to store hashes.
- Use temp files to store arrays.
- Use pipes to offload processing to other tools.
- Avoid list operations and file slurps.
- Avoid using tr///, each of which must store a translation table of 256 short integers (not characters, since we have to remember which characters are to be deleted).
- Don't unroll your loops or inline your subroutines.

Programmer Efficiency

- Use defaults.
- Use funky shortcut command-line switches like –a, –n, –p, –s, –i.
- Use **for** to mean **foreach**.
- Sling UNIX commands around with backticks.
- Use <*> and such.
- Use run-time-compiled patterns.

- Use patterns with lots of *, +, and {}.
- Sling whole arrays and slurp entire files.
- Use **getc**.
- Use $&, $`, and $'.
- Don't check error values on **open**, since *<HANDLE>* and print *HANDLE* will simply no-op when given an invalid handle.
- Don't **close** your files—they'll be closed on the next **open**.
- Pass subroutine arguments as globals.
- Don't name your subroutine parameters. You can access them directly as $_[*EXPR*].
- Use whatever you think of first.

Maintainer Efficiency

- Don't use defaults.
- Use **foreach** to mean **foreach**.
- Use meaningful loop labels with **next** and **last**.
- Use meaningful variable names.
- Use meaningful subroutine names.
- Put the important thing first on the line using **and**, **or**, and statement modifiers.
- Close your files as soon as you're done with them.
- Use packages, modules, and classes to hide your implementation details.
- Pass arguments as subroutine parameters.
- Name your subroutine parameters using **my**.
- Parenthesize for clarity.
- Put in lots of (useful) comments.
- Write the script as its own POD document.

Porter Efficiency

- Wave a handsome tip under his nose.
- Avoid functions that aren't implemented everywhere. You can use **eval** tests to see what's available.

- Don't expect native float and double to **pack** and **unpack** on foreign machines.
- Use network byte order when sending binary data over the network.
- Don't send binary data over the network.
- Check $] to see if the current version supports all the features you use.
- Don't use $]: use **require** with a version number.
- Put in the `eval exec` hack even if you don't use it.
- Put the `#!/usr/bin/perl` line in even if you don't use it.
- Test for variants of UNIX commands. Some *finds* can't handle *-xdev*, for example.
- Avoid variant UNIX commands if you can do it internally. UNIX commands don't work too well on MS-DOS or VMS.
- Use the Config module or the `$^O` variable to find out what kind of machine you're running on.
- Put all your scripts and manpages into a single NFS filesystem that's mounted everywhere.

User Efficiency

- Avoid forcing prompt order—pop users into their favorite editor with a form.
- Better yet, use a GUI like the Perl Tk extension, where users can control the order of events.
- Put up something for users to read while you continue doing work.
- Use autoloading so that the program *appears* to run faster.
- Give the option of helpful messages at every prompt.
- Give a helpful usage message if users don't give correct input.
- Display the default action at every prompt, and maybe a few alternatives.
- Choose defaults for beginners. Allow experts to change the defaults.
- Use single character input where it makes sense.
- Pattern the interaction after other things the user is familiar with.
- Make error messages clear about what needs fixing. Include all pertinent information such as filename and `errno`, like this:

```
open(FILE, $file) or die "$0: Can't open $file for reading: $!\n";
```

- Use **fork** and **exit** to detach when the rest of the script is batch processing.

- Allow arguments to come either from the command line or via standard input.

- Use text-oriented network protocols.

- Don't put arbitrary limitations into your program.

- Prefer variable-length fields over fixed-length fields.

- Be vicariously lazy.

- Be nice.

Programming with Style

Each programmer will, of course, have his or her own preferences in regards to formatting, but there are some general guidelines that will make your programs easier to read, understand, and maintain.

The most important thing is to run your programs under the **–w** flag at all times. You may turn it off explicitly for particular portions of code via the **$^W** variable if you must. You should also always run under use strict or know the reason why not. The use sigtrap and even the use diagnostics pragmas may also prove of benefit.

Regarding aesthetics of code layout, about the only thing Larry cares strongly about is that the closing brace of a multi-line *BLOCK* should line up in the same column as the start of the keyword that started the construct. Beyond that, he has other preferences that aren't so strong. Examples in this book (should) all follow these coding conventions.

- Four-column indent.

- An opening brace should be put on the same line as its preceding keyword, if possible; otherwise, line them up vertically.

```
while ($condition) {      # for short ones, align with keywords
    # do something
}

# if the condition wraps, line up the  braces with each other
while ($this_condition and $that_condition
        and $this_other_long_condition)
{
    # do something
}
```

- Put space before the opening brace of a multi-line *BLOCK*.
- A one-line *BLOCK* may be put on one line, including braces.
- Do not put space before a semicolon.
- Omit the semicolon in a short, one-line *BLOCK*.
- Surround most operators with space.
- Surround a "complex" subscript (inside brackets) with space.
- Put blank lines between chunks of code that do different things.
- Put a newline between a closing brace and **else**.
- Do not put space between a function name instance and its opening parenthesis.
- Put space after each comma.
- Break long lines after an operator (but before **and** and **or**).
- Line up corresponding items vertically.
- Omit redundant punctuation as long as clarity doesn't suffer.

Larry has his reasons for each of these things, but he doesn't claim that everyone else's mind works the same as his does.

Here are some other, more substantive style issues to think about:

- Just because you *can* do something a particular way doesn't mean you *should* do it that way. Perl is designed to give you several ways to do anything, so consider picking the most readable one. For instance:

    ```
    open(FOO,$foo) || die "Can't open $foo: $!";
    ```

  is better than:

    ```
    die "Can't open $foo: $!" unless open(FOO,$foo);
    ```

  because the second way hides the main point of the statement in a modifier. On the other hand

    ```
    print "Starting analysis\n" if $verbose;
    ```

  is better than:

    ```
    $verbose && print "Starting analysis\n";
    ```

  since the main point isn't whether the user typed **-v** or not.

  Similarly, just because an operator lets you assume default arguments doesn't mean that you have to make use of the defaults. The defaults are there for lazy systems programmers writing one-shot programs. If you want your program to be readable, consider supplying the argument.

Along the same lines, just because you *can* omit parentheses in many places doesn't mean that you ought to:

```
return print reverse sort num values %array;
return print(reverse(sort num (values(%array))));
```

When in doubt, parenthesize. At the very least it will let some poor schmuck bounce on the % key in *vi*.

Even if *you* aren't in doubt, consider the mental welfare of the person who has to maintain the code after you, and who will probably put parentheses in the wrong place.

- Don't go through silly contortions to exit a loop at the top or the bottom. Perl provides the **last** operator so you can exit in the middle. Just "outdent" it to make it more visible:

```
LINE:
    for (;;) {
        statements;
      last LINE if $foo;
        next LINE if /^#/;
        statements;
    }
```

- Don't be afraid to use loop labels—they're there to enhance readability as well as to allow multi-level loop breaks. See the example just given.

- Avoid using **grep**, **map**, or backticks in a void context; that is, when you just throw away their return values. Those functions all have return values, so use them. Otherwise, use a **foreach** loop or the **system** function.

- For portability, when using features that may not be implemented on every machine, test the construct in an **eval** to see whether it fails. If you know the version or patchlevel of a particular feature, you can test **$]** ($PERL_VERSION in the English module) to see whether the feature is there. The Config module will also let you interrogate values determined by the *Configure* program when Perl was installed.

- Choose mnemonic identifiers. If you can't remember what mnemonic means, you've got a problem.

- While short identifiers like $gotit are probably OK, use underscores to separate words. It is generally much easier to read $var_names_like_this than $VarNamesLikeThis, especially for non-native speakers of English. Besides, the same rule works for $VAR_NAMES_LIKE_THIS.

Package names are sometimes an exception to this rule. Perl informally reserves lowercase module names for pragmatic modules like integer and strict. Other modules should begin with a capital letter and use mixed case, but probably without underscores due to name-length limitations of some primitive filesystems.

- You may find it helpful to use letter case to indicate the scope or nature of a variable. For example:

```
$ALL_CAPS_HERE   # constants only (beware clashes with Perl vars!)
$Some_Caps_Here  # package-wide global/static
$no_caps_here    # function scope my() or local() variables
```

Function and method names seem to work best as all lowercase. For example, `$obj->as_string()`.

You can use a leading underscore to indicate that a variable or function should not be used outside the package that defined it.

- If you have a really hairy regular expression, use the **/x** modifier and put in some whitespace to make it look a little less like line noise.

- Don't use slash as a delimiter when your regexp has slashes or backslashes.

- Don't use quotes as a delimiter when your string contains that same quote. Use the `q//`, `qq//`, or `qx//` pseudofunctions instead.

- Use the **and** and **or** operators to avoid having to parenthesize list operators so much, and to reduce the incidence of punctuational operators like `&&` and `||`. Call your subroutines as if they were functions or list operators to avoid excessive ampersands and parentheses.

- Use "here" documents instead of repeated **print** statements.

- Line up corresponding things vertically, especially if they're too long to fit on one line anyway.

```
$IDX = $ST_MTIME;
$IDX = $ST_ATIME       if $opt_u;
$IDX = $ST_CTIME       if $opt_c;
$IDX = $ST_SIZE        if $opt_s;

mkdir $tmpdir, 0700 or die "can't mkdir $tmpdir: $!";
chdir($tmpdir)       or die "can't chdir $tmpdir: $!";
mkdir 'tmp',    0777 or die "can't mkdir $tmpdir/tmp: $!";
```

- That which I tell you three times is true:

Always check the return codes of system calls.
Always check the return codes of system calls.
ALWAYS CHECK THE RETURN CODES OF SYSTEM CALLS!

Error messages should go to STDERR, and should say which program caused
the problem and what the failed system call and arguments were. Most
importantly, they should contain the standard system error message for what
went wrong. Here's a simple but sufficient example:

```
opendir(D, $dir)    or die "can't opendir $dir: $!";
```

- Line up your translations when it makes sense:

```
tr [abc]
   [xyz];
```

- Think about reusability. Why waste brainpower on a one-shot script when you
  might want to do something like it again? Consider generalizing your code.
  Consider writing a module or object class. Consider making your code run
  cleanly with use strict and -w in effect. Consider giving away your code.
  Consider changing your whole world view. Consider . . . oh, never mind.

- Be consistent.

- Be nice.

Distribution and Installation

You should see the Preface of this book for how to fetch and build a Perl kit for
your system. Specific installation instructions come in the *README* file of the Perl
distribution kit. Typically, you'll get the Perl kit either as a *tar* file or as a set of
shar (shell archive) scripts.* A *.Z* extension indicates you need to *uncompress* the
file first. A *.gz* extension indicates you need to *gunzip* the file first. You then
unpack the file as appropriate, read the *README* file and run a massive shell
script called *Configure*, which tries to figure out everything about your system.
After this is done, you do a series of "makes" to find header file dependencies, to
compile Perl (and *a2p*), to run regression tests, and to install Perl in your system
directories.

It's possible you'll get a copy of Perl that is already compiled. You'll have to make
sure you get *suidperl*, *a2p*, and *s2p* as well, and the Perl library routines (see
Chapter 7). Install these files in the directories that your version was compiled for.
Note: binary distributions of Perl are made available because they're handy, not
because you are restricted from getting the source and compiling it yourself. The
people who give you the binary distribution ought to provide you with some form
of access to the source, if only a pointer to where *they* got the source from. See
the *Copying* file in the distribution for more information.

---

* Operating systems other than UNIX may have special instructions, in which case you should follow
them instead of what's in this section. Look for a file named *README.xxx*, where *xxx* is your OS name.

Translation from Awk and Sed

Along with the Perl distribution come three translators: *a2p*, which translates *awk*(1) (not necessarily *nawk*(1)) scripts to Perl; *s2p*, which translates *sed*(1) scripts to Perl; and *find2perl*, which translates *find*(1) commands to Perl. These translators don't necessarily produce idiomatic Perl, but you can use the output as a starting place. The translators can also help you see how the features of other languages map into those of Perl.

The *a2p* translator is written in C, so it is compiled and installed automatically along with Perl. The *s2p* and *find2perl* translators are themselves written in Perl, so no further compilation is necessary. They are installed automatically when Perl is installed. They are described more fully in Chapter 6, *Social Engineering*.

Examples

The Perl source distribution comes with some sample scripts in the *eg/* subdirectory. Feel free to browse among them and use them. They are not installed automatically, however, so you'll need to copy them to the appropriate directory, and possibly fix the #! line to point to the right interpreter.

The files in the *t/* and *lib/* subdirectories, although incredibly arcane in spots, can also serve as examples.

The examples in this book are also available for anonymous FTP from *ftp.ora.com* and the *scripts* subdirectory of CPAN. (See the Preface for more information about CPAN.)

Patches

Since Perl is constantly being honed and improved, Larry occasionally posts patches through CPAN. Your distribution is likely to have had most of the patches applied already—check the output of *perl -v* to see the current patchlevel of your distribution.

Bug reports may be reported by invoking the *perlbug* command, included with the Perl distribution.

Patches are sent out with complete instructions on how to apply them. You'll want to have the *patch* program handy. (This program was written in self-defense by Larry when he couldn't persuade people to apply (in order and by hand) all his *rn* patches, resulting in cascading chaotic catastrophes around the world.) The *patch* program is available from the GNU project, because they have taken over the maintenance (the patching of *patch*, how quaint) after Larry got a little more busy with Perl.

Perl Poetry

The forgery in the attendant sidebar appeared on Usenet on April Fool's Day, 1990. It is presented here without comment, merely to show how disgusting the metaphors of a typical programming language really are. So much for anything resembling literary value. Larry is particularly relieved that "Black Perl", originally written for Perl 3, no longer parses under Perl 5.

Larry's, er, corpus has fortunately been overshadowed by that of the reigning Perl Poet, Sharon Hopkins. She has written quite a few Perl poems, as well as a paper on Perl poetry that she presented at the Usenix Winter 1992 Technical Conference, entitled "Camels and Needles: Computer Poetry Meets the Perl Programming Language". (The paper is available as *misc/poetry.ps* on CPAN.) Besides being the most prolific Perl poet, Sharon is also the most widely published, having had the following poem published in both the *Economist* and the *Guardian*:

```
#!/usr/bin/perl

APPEAL:

listen (please, please);

    open yourself, wide;
        join (you, me),
    connect (us,together),

tell me.

do something if distressed;

        @dawn, dance;
        @evening, sing;
        read (books,$poems,stories) until peaceful;
        study if able;

        write me if-you-please;

sort your feelings, reset goals, seek (friends, family, anyone);

            do*not*die (like this)
            if sin abounds;

keys (hidden), open (locks, doors), tell secrets;
    do not, I-beg-you, close them, yet.

                            accept (yourself, changes),
                            bind (grief, despair);

    require truth, goodness if-you-will, each moment;

select (always), length(of-days)

# listen (a perl poem)
# Sharon Hopkins
# rev. June 19, 1995
```

Perl Poetry

Article 970 of comp.lang.perl:
Path: jpl-devvax!pl-dexxav!lwall
From: lwall@jpl-dexxav.JPL.NASA.GOV (Larry Wall)
Newsgroups: news.groups,rec.arts.poems,comp.lang.perl
Subject: CALL FOR DISCUSSION: comp.lang.perl.poems
Message-ID: <0401@jpl-devvax.JPL.NASA.GOV>
Date: 1 Apr 90 00:00:00 GMT
Reply-To: lwall@jpl-devvax.JPL.NSAS.GOV (Larry Wall)
Organization: Jet Prepulsion Laboratory, Pasadena, CA
Lines: 61

It has come to my attention that there is a crying need for a place for people to express both their emotional and technical natures simultaneously. Several people have sent me some items which don't fit into any newsgroup. Perhaps it's because I recently posted to both comp.lang.perl and to rec.arts.poems, but people seem to be writing poems in Perl, and they're asking me where they should post them. Here is a sampling:

From a graduate student (in finals week), the following haiku:

```
study, write, study,
do review (each word) if time.
close book. sleep? what's that?
```

And someone writing from Fort Lauderdale writes:

```
sleep, close together,
sort of sin each spring & wait;
50% die
```

A person who wishes to remain anonymous wrote the following example of "Black Perl". (The Pearl poet would have been shocked, no.doubt.)

```
BEFOREHAND: close door, each window & exit; wait until time.
    open spellbook, study, read (scan, select, tell us);
write it, print the hex while each watches,
    reverse its length, write again;
        kill spiders, pop them, chop, split, kill them.
            unlink arms, shift, wait & listen (listening, wait),
sort the flock (then, warn the "goats" & kill the "sheep");
    kill them, dump qualms, shift moralities,
        values aside, each one;
            die sheep! die to reverse the system
                you accept (reject, respect);
next step,
    kill the next sacrifice, each sacrifice,
        wait, redo ritual until "all the spirits are pleased";
    do it ("as they say").
do it(*everyone***must***participate***in***forbidden**s*e*x*).
return last victim; package body;
    exit crypt (time, times & "half a time") & close it,
        select (quickly) & warn your next victim;
AFTERWORDS: tell nobody.
    wait, wait until time;
        wait until next year, next decade;
            sleep, sleep, die yourself,
                die at last
```

I tried that, and it actually parses in Perl. It doesn't appear to do anything useful, however. I think I'm glad, actually... I hereby propose the creation of comp.lang.perl.poems as a place for such items, so we don't clutter the perl or poems newsgroups with things that may be of interest to neither. Or, alternately, we should create rec.arts.poems.perl for items such as those above which merely parse, and don't do anything useful. (There is precedent in rec.arts.poems, after all.) Then also create comp.lang.perl.poems for poems that actually do something, such as this haiku of my own:

```
print STDOUT q
Just another Perl hacker,
unless $spring
```

Larry Wall   lwall@jpl-devvax.jpl.nasa.gov

History Made Practical

In order to understand why Perl is defined the way it is (or isn't), one must first understand why Perl even exists. So, let's drag out the old dusty history book. ...

Way back in 1986, Larry was a systems programmer on a project that was developing multi-level-secure wide-area networks. He was in charge of an installation consisting of three Vaxen and three Suns on the West Coast, connected over an encrypted, 1200-baud serial line to a similar configuration on the East Coast. Since Larry's primary job was support (he wasn't a programmer on the project, just the system guru), he was able to exploit his three virtues (laziness, impatience, and hubris) to develop and enhance all sorts of useful tools—such as *rn*, *patch*, and *warp*. *

One day, after Larry had just finished ripping *rn* to shreds, leaving it in pieces on the floor of his directory, the great Manager came to him and said, "Larry, we need a configuration management and control system for all six Vaxen and all six Suns. We need it in a month. Go to it!"

So, Larry, never being one to shirk work, asked himself what was the best way to have a bi-coastal CM system, without writing it from scratch, that would allow viewing of problem reports on both coasts, with approvals and control. The answer came to him in one word: B-news.

Larry went off and installed news on these machines, and added two control commands: an "append" command to append to an existing article, and a "synchronize" command to keep the article numbers the same on both coasts. CM would be done using RCS, and approvals and submissions would be done using news and *rn*. Fine so far.

Then the great Manager asked him to produce reports. News was maintained in separate files on a master machine, with lots of cross references between files. Larry's first thought was "Let's use *awk*." Unfortunately, the *awk* of that day couldn't handle opening and closing of multiple files based on information in the files. Larry didn't want to have to code a special-purpose tool. As a result, a new language was born.

This new tool wasn't originally called Perl. Larry bandied about a number of names with his officemates and cohorts (Dan Faigin, who wrote this history, and Mark Biggar, his brother-in-law, who also helped greatly with the initial design).

---

* It was about this time that Larry latched onto the phrase "feeping creaturism" in a desperate attempt to justify on the basis of biological necessity his overwhelming urge to add "just one more feature". After all, if Life Is Simply Too Complicated, why not programs too? Especially programs like *rn* that really ought to be treated as advanced Artificial Intelligence projects so that they can read your news for you. Of course, some people say that the *patch* program is already *too* smart.

Larry actually considered and rejected every three or four letter word in the dictionary. One of the earliest names was "Gloria", after his sweetheart (and wife).

He soon decided that this would cause too much domestic confusion. The name then became "Pearl", which mutated into our present-day "Perl", partly because Larry saw a reference to a graphics language called "pearl", but mostly because he's too lazy to type five letters all the time. And, of course, so that Perl could be used as a four letter word. (You'll note, however, the vestiges of the former spelling in the acronym's gloss: "Practical Extraction *And* Report Language".)

This early Perl lacked many of the features of today's Perl. Pattern matching and filehandles were there, scalars were there, and formats were there, but there were very few functions, no associative arrays, and only a crippled implementation of regular expressions, borrowed from *rn*. The manpage was only 15 pages long. But Perl was faster than *sed* and *awk*, and began to be used on other applications on the project.

But Larry was needed elsewhere. Another great Manager came over one day and said "Larry, support R&D." And Larry said, OK. He took Perl with him and discovered that it was turning into a good tool for system administration. He borrowed Henry Spencer's beautiful regular expression package and butchered it into something Henry would prefer not to think about during dinner. Then Larry added most of the goodies he wanted, and a few goodies other people wanted. He released it on the network.[*] The rest, as they say, is history.[†]

---

[*] More astonishingly, he kept on releasing it as he went to work at Jet Propulsion Lab, then at NetLabs, Seagate, and now O'Reilly & Associates (a small company that publishes pamphlets about computers and stuff).

[†] And this, so to speak, is a footnote to history. When Perl was started, *rn* had just been ripped to pieces in anticipation of a major rewrite. Since he started work on Perl, Larry hasn't touched *rn*. It is still in pieces. Occasionally Larry threatens to rewrite *rn* in Perl.

9

Diagnostic Messages

These messages are classified as follows (listed in increasing order of desperation):

Class	Meaning
(W)	A warning (optional)
(D)	A deprecation (optional)
(S)	A severe warning (mandatory)
(F)	A fatal error (trappable)
(P)	An internal error (panic) that you should never see (trappable)
(X)	A very fatal error (non-trappable)
(A)	An alien error message (not generated by Perl)

Optional warnings are enabled by using the **–w** switch. Warnings may be captured by setting `$SIG{__WARN__}` to a reference to a routine that will be called on each warning before printing it. Trappable errors may be trapped using **eval**. You can also capture control before a trappable error "dies" by setting `$SIG{__DIE__}` to a subroutine reference, but if you don't call **die** within that handler, the fatal exception is still thrown when you return from it. In other words, you're not allowed to "de-fatalize" an exception that way. You must use an **eval** wrapper for that.

In the following messages *%s* stands for an interpolated string that is determined only when the message is generated. (Similarly, *%d* stands for an interpolated number—think **printf** formats, but we use *%d* to mean a number in any base here.) Note that some messages begin with *%s* —which means that listing them alphabetically is problematical. You should search among these messages if the one you are looking for does not appear in the expected place. The symbols `" % - ? @` sort before alphabetic characters, while `[` and `\` sort after.

References of the form, "See **unpack**," refer to entries in Chapter 3, *Functions*.

If you decide a bug is a Perl bug and not your bug, you should try to reduce it to a minimal test case and then report it with the *perlbug* program that comes with Perl.

`"my" variable %s can't be in a package`
> (F) Lexically scoped variables aren't in a package, so it doesn't make sense to try to declare one with a package qualifier on the front. Use **local** if you want to localize a package variable.

`"no" not allowed in expression`
> (F) The **no** keyword is recognized and executed at compile time, and returns no useful value.

`"use" not allowed in expression`
> (F) The **use** keyword is recognized and executed at compile time, and returns no useful value.

`% may only be used in unpack`
> (F) You can't pack a string by supplying a checksum, since the checksumming process loses information, and you can't go the other way. See **unpack**.

`%s ( . . . ) interpreted as function`
> (W) You've run afoul of the rule that says that any list operator followed by parentheses turns into a function, with all the list operator's arguments found inside the parens. See the section "Terms and List Operators (Leftward)" in Chapter 2, *The Gory Details*.

`%s argument is not a HASH element`
> (F) The argument to **delete** or **exists** must be a hash element, such as

```
$foo{$bar}
$ref->[12]->{"susie"}
```

`%s did not return a true value`
> (F) A **required** (or **used**) file must return a true value to indicate that it compiled correctly and ran its initialization code correctly. It's traditional to end such a file with a "`1;`", though any true value would do. See **require**.

`%s found where operator expected`
> (S) The Perl lexer knows whether to expect a term or an operator. If it sees what it knows to be a term when it was expecting to see an operator, it gives you this warning. Usually it indicates that an operator or delimiter was omitted, such as a semicolon.

`%s had compilation errors.`
> (F) The final summary message when a *perl -c* command fails.

%s has too many errors.

(F) The parser has given up trying to parse the program after 10 errors. Further error messages would likely be uninformative.

%s matches null string many times

(W) The pattern you've specified would be an infinite loop if the regular expression engine didn't specifically check for that.

%s never introduced

(S) The symbol in question was declared but somehow went out of scope before it could possibly have been used.

%s syntax OK

(F) The final summary message when a *perl -c* command succeeds.

%s: Command not found.

(A) You've accidentally run your script through *csh* instead of *perl*. Check the #! line, or manually feed your script into *perl* yourself.

%s: Expression syntax.

(A) You've accidentally run your script through *csh* instead of *perl*. Check the #! line, or manually feed your script into *perl* yourself.

%s: Undefined variable.

(A) You've accidentally run your script through *csh* instead of *perl*. Check the #! line, or manually feed your script into *perl* yourself.

%s: not found

(A) You've accidentally run your script through the Bourne shell instead of *perl*. Check the #! line, or manually feed your script into *perl* yourself.

-P not allowed for setuid/setgid script

(F) The script would have to be opened by the C preprocessor by name, which provides a race condition that breaks security.

-T and -B not implemented on filehandles

(F) Perl can't peek at the stdio buffer of filehandles when it doesn't know about your kind of stdio. You'll have to use a filename instead.

500 Server error

See Server error.

?+* follows nothing in regexp

(F) You started a regular expression with a quantifier. Backslash it if you meant it literally.

`@ outside of string`

(F) You had a **pack** template that specified an absolute position outside the string being unpacked. See **pack**.

`accept() on closed fd`

(W) You tried to do an **accept** on a closed socket. Did you forget to check the return value of your **socket** call? See **accept**.

`Allocation too large:` *%d*

(F) You can't allocate more than 64K on an MS-DOS machine.

`Arg too short for msgsnd`

(F) **msgsnd** requires a string at least as long as `sizeof(long)`.

`Ambiguous use of` *%s* `resolved as` *%s*

(W)(S) You said something that may not be interpreted the way you thought. Normally it's pretty easy to disambiguate it by supplying a missing quote, operator, pair of parentheses, or declaration.

`Args must match #! line`

(F) The setuid emulator requires that the switches *perl* was invoked with match the switches specified on the `#!` line.

`Argument "`*%s*`" isn't numeric`

(W) The indicated string was fed as an argument to an operator that expected a numeric value instead. If you're fortunate the message will identify which operator was so unfortunate.

`Array @`*%s* `missing the @ in argument` *%d* `of` *%s*`()`

(D) Really old Perl let you omit the `@` on array names in some spots. This is now heavily deprecated.

`assertion botched:` *%s*

(P) The *malloc*(3) package that comes with Perl had an internal failure.

`Assertion failed: file "`*%s*`"`

(P) A general assertion failed. The file in question must be examined.

`Assignment to both a list and a scalar`

(F) If you assign to a conditional operator, the second and third arguments must either both be scalars or both be lists. Otherwise Perl won't know which context to supply to the right side.

`Attempt to free non-arena SV:` *%d*

(P) All SV objects are supposed to be allocated from arenas that will be garbage collected upon exit. An SV was discovered to be outside any of those arenas. This probably means that someone screwed up in a C extension module.

`Attempt to free temp prematurely`

(W) Mortalized values are supposed to be freed by the internal `free_tmps()` routine. This indicates that something else is freeing the SV before the `free_tmps()` routine gets a chance, which means that the `free_tmps()` routine will be freeing an unreferenced scalar when it does try to free it.

`Attempt to free unreferenced glob pointers`

(P) The reference counts got screwed up on symbol aliases.

`Attempt to free unreferenced scalar`

(W) Perl went to decrement the reference count of a scalar to see if it would go to 0, and discovered that it had already gone to 0 earlier, and should have been freed, and in fact, probably was freed. This could indicate that `SvREFCNT_dec()` was called too many times, or that `SvREFCNT_inc()` was called too few times, or that the SV was mortalized when it shouldn't have been, or that memory has been corrupted. In any event, it's likely a problem with the C extension module you're developing.

`Bad arg length for %s, is %d, should be %d`

(F) You passed a buffer of the wrong size to one of **msgctl**, **semctl** or **shmctl**. In C parlance, the correct sizes are `sizeof(struct msqid_ds *)`, `sizeof(struct semid_ds *)` and `sizeof(struct shmid_ds *)`, respectively.

`Bad associative array`

(P) One of the internal hash routines was passed a null HV pointer.

`Bad filehandle: %s`

(F) A symbol was passed to something wanting a filehandle, but the symbol has no filehandle associated with it. Perhaps you didn't do an **open**, or did it in another package.

`Bad free() ignored`

(S) An internal routine called *free*(3) on something that had never been *malloc*(3)ed in the first place.

`Bad name after %s::`

(F) You started to name a symbol by using a package prefix, and then didn't finish the symbol. In particular, you can't interpolate outside of quotes, so

```
$var = 'myvar';
$sym = mypack::$var;
```

is not the same as

```
$var = 'myvar';
$sym = "mypack::$var";
```

`Bad symbol for array`

(P) An internal request asked to add an array entry to something that wasn't a symbol table entry.

`Bad symbol for filehandle`

(P) An internal request asked to add a filehandle entry to something that wasn't a symbol table entry.

`Bad symbol for hash`

(P) An internal request asked to add a hash entry to something that wasn't a symbol table entry.

`Badly placed ()'s`

(A) You've accidentally run your script through *csh* instead of *perl*. Check the `#!` line, or manually feed your script into *perl* yourself.

`BEGIN failed--compilation aborted`

(F) An untrapped exception was raised while executing a BEGIN subroutine. Compilation stops immediately and the interpreter is exited.

`bind() on closed fd`

(W) You tried to do a **bind** on a closed socket. Did you forget to check the return value of your **socket** call? See **bind**.

`Bizarre copy of %s in %s`

(P) Perl detected an attempt to copy an internal value that is not copiable.

`Callback called exit`

(F) A subroutine invoked from an external package via `perl_call_sv()` exited by calling **exit**.

`Can't "last" outside a block`

(F) A **last** statement was executed to break out of the current block, except that there's this itty bitty problem called there isn't a current block. See note on the next entry.

`Can't "next" outside a block`

(F) A **next** statement was executed to reiterate the current block, but there isn't a current block. Note that an **if** or **else** block doesn't count as a "loopish" block. You can usually double the curly brackets to get the same effect though, since the inner brackets will be considered a block that loops once. See **last**.

`Can't "redo" outside a block`

(F) A **redo** statement was executed to restart the current block, but there isn't a current block. See note on the previous entry.

Can't bless non-reference value

(F) Only hard references may be blessed. This is how Perl "enforces" encapsulation of objects.

Can't break at that line

(S) A debugger warning indicating the line number specified wasn't the location of a statement that could be stopped at.

Can't call method "*%s*" in empty package "*%s*"

(F) You called a method correctly, and it correctly indicated a package functioning as a class, but that package doesn't have anything at all defined in it, let alone methods.

Can't call method "*%s*" on unblessed reference

(F) A method call must know what package it's supposed to run in. It ordinarily finds this out from the object reference you supply, but you didn't supply an object reference in this case. A reference isn't an object reference until it has been blessed.

Can't call method "*%s*" without a package or object reference

(F) You used the syntax of a method call, but the slot filled by the object reference or package name contains an expression that returns neither an object reference nor a package name. (Perhaps it's null?) Something like this will reproduce the error:

```
$BADREF = undef;
process $BADREF 1,2,3;
$BADREF->process(1,2,3);
```

Can't chdir to *%s*

(F) You called perl -x/foo/bar, but */foo/bar* is not a directory that you can *chdir*(2) to, possibly because it doesn't exist.

Can't coerce *%s* to integer in *%s*

(F) Certain types of SVs, in particular real symbol table entries (type GLOB), can't be forced to stop being what they are. So you can't say things like:

```
*foo += 1;     # ERROR
```

You *can* say

```
$foo = *foo;   # make a "fake" glob value
$foo += 1;
```

but then $foo no longer contains a glob.

Can't coerce %s to number in %s

> (F) Certain types of SVs, in particular real symbol table entries (type GLOB), can't be forced to stop being what they are. See preceding entry.

Can't coerce %s to string in %s

> (F) Certain types of SVs, in particular real symbol table entries (type GLOB), can't be forced to stop being what they are. See previous two entries.

Can't create pipe mailbox

> (P) An error peculiar to VMS. The process is suffering from exhausted quotas or other plumbing problems.

Can't declare %s in my

> (F) Only scalar, array and hash variables may be declared as lexical variables. They must have ordinary identifiers as names, since lexical variables don't live in a symbol table, and can't be package qualified.

Can't do inplace edit on %s: %s

> (S) The creation of the new file failed for the indicated reason.

Can't do inplace edit without backup

> (F) You're on a system such as MS-DOS that gets confused if you try reading from a deleted (but still opened) file. You have to use the switch, -i.bak, or some such.

Can't do inplace edit: %s > 14 characters

> (S) There isn't enough room in the filename to make a backup name for the file. Perhaps you should get a system with longer filenames. :-)

Can't do inplace edit: %s is not a regular file

> (S) You tried to use the -i switch on a special file, such as a file in */dev*, or a FIFO. The file was ignored.

Can't do setegid!

> (P) The setegid() call failed for some reason in the setuid emulator of *suidperl*.

Can't do seteuid!

> (P) The setuid emulator of *suidperl* failed for some reason.

Can't do setuid

> (F) This typically means that ordinary *perl* tried to exec *suidperl* to do setuid emulation, but couldn't exec it. If you're running */usr/local/bin/perl5.003*, it looks for a corresponding */usr/local/bin/sperl5.003*. (Note the "s".) If the file is there, check the execute permissions. If it isn't, ask your sysadmin why he and/or she removed it.

Can't do waitpid with flags

(F) This machine doesn't have either *waitpid*(2) or *wait4*(2), so only **waitpid** without flags is emulated.

Can't do {n,m} with n > m

(F) Minima must be less than or equal to maxima. If you really want your regular expression to match something 0 times, just put {0}.

Can't emulate -*%s* on #! line

(F) The #! line specifies a switch that doesn't make sense at this point. For example, it'd be kind of silly to put a -x on the #! line.

Can't exec "*%s*": *%s*

(W) A **system**, **exec** or piped **open** call could not execute the named program for the indicated reason. Typical reasons include: the permissions were wrong on the file, the file wasn't found in $ENV{PATH}, the executable in question was compiled for another architecture, or the #! line in a script points to an interpreter that can't be run for similar reasons. (Or maybe your system doesn't support #! at all.)

Can't exec *%s*

(F) Perl was trying to execute the indicated program for you because that's what the #! line said. If that's not what you wanted, you may need to mention "perl" on the #! line somewhere.

Can't execute *%s*

(F) You used the -S switch, but the script to execute could not be found in the PATH, or at least not with the correct permissions.

Can't find label *%s*

(F) You said to **goto** a label that isn't mentioned anywhere that it's possible for us to go to. See **goto**.

Can't find string terminator *%s* anywhere before EOF

(F) Perl strings can stretch over multiple lines. This message means that the closing delimiter was omitted. Since bracketed quotes count nesting levels, the following is missing its final parenthesis:

```
print q(The character '(' starts a s(n)ide comment.)
```

Can't fork

(F) A fatal error occurred while trying to fork while opening a pipeline.

Can't get filespec - stale stat buffer?

(S) A warning peculiar to VMS. This arises because of the difference between access checks under VMS and under the UNIX model Perl assumes. Under VMS, access checks are done by filename, rather than by bits in the stat buffer, so that ACLs and other protections can be taken into account. Unfortunately, Perl assumes that the stat buffer contains all the necessary information, and passes it, instead of the filespec, to the access-checking routine. It will try to retrieve the filespec using the device name and FID present in the stat buffer, but this works only if you haven't made a subsequent call to the CRTL stat routine, since the device name is overwritten with each call. If this warning appears, the name lookup failed, and the access-checking routine gave up and returned FALSE, just to be conservative. (Note: The access-checking routine knows about the Perl **stat** operator and file tests, so you shouldn't ever see this warning in response to a Perl command; it arises only if some internal code takes stat buffers lightly.)

`Can't get pipe mailbox device name`

(P) An error peculiar to VMS. After creating a mailbox to act as a pipe, Perl can't retrieve its name for later use.

`Can't get SYSGEN parameter value for MAXBUF`

(P) An error peculiar to VMS. Perl asked `$GETSYI` how big you want your mailbox buffers to be, and didn't get an answer.

`Can't goto subroutine outside a subroutine`

(F) The deeply magical goto *SUBROUTINE* call can only replace one subroutine call for another. It can't manufacture one out of whole cloth. In general you should only be calling it out of an AUTOLOAD routine anyway. See **goto**.

`Can't localize a reference`

(F) You said something like `local $$ref`, which is not allowed because the compiler can't determine whether `$ref` will end up pointing to anything with a symbol table entry, and a symbol table entry is necessary to do a **local**.

`Can't localize lexical variable %s`

(F) You used **local** on a variable name that was previous declared as a lexical variable using **my**. This is not allowed. If you want to localize a package variable of the same name, qualify it with the package name.

`Can't locate %s in @INC`

(F) You said to use (or **require**, or **do**) a file that couldn't be found in any of the libraries mentioned in `@INC`. Perhaps you need to set the PERL5LIB environment variable to say where the extra library is, or maybe the script needs to add the library name to `@INC` with the use lib directive. Or maybe you just misspelled the name of the file. See **require**.

`Can't locate object method "%s" via package "%s"`

(F) You called a method correctly, and it correctly indicated a package functioning as a class, but the package doesn't define that method name, nor do any of its base classes (which is why the message says "via" rather than "in").

Can't locate package %s for @%s::ISA

(W) The @ISA array contained the name of another package that doesn't seem to exist.

Can't mktemp()

(F) The mktemp routine failed for some reason while trying to process a -e switch. Maybe your */tmp* partition is full, or clobbered.

Can't modify %s in %s

(F) You aren't allowed to assign to the item indicated, or otherwise try to change it, such as with an autoincrement.

Can't modify non-existent substring

(P) The internal routine that does assignment to a **substr** was handed a NULL pointer.

Can't msgrcv to readonly var

(F) The target of a **msgrcv** must be modifiable in order to be used as a receive buffer.

Can't open %s: %s

(S) An inplace edit couldn't open the original file for the indicated reason. Usually this is because you don't have read permission for the file.

Can't open bidirectional pipe

(W) You tried to say open(CMD, "|cmd|"), which is not supported. You can try any of several modules in the Perl library to do this, such as Open2. Alternately, direct the pipe's output to a file using ">", and then read it in under a different filehandle.

Can't open error file %s as stderr

(F) An error peculiar to VMS. Perl does its own command-line redirection, and couldn't open for writing the file specified after 2> or 2>> on the command line.

Can't open input file %s as stdin

(F) An error peculiar to VMS. Perl does its own command-line redirection, and couldn't open for reading the file specified after < on the command line.

Can't open output file %s as stdout

(F) An error peculiar to VMS. Perl does its own command-line redirection, and couldn't open for writing the file specified after > or >> on the command line.

Can't open output pipe (name: %s)

(P) An error peculiar to VMS. Perl does its own command-line redirection, and couldn't open the pipe into which to send data destined for STDOUT.

`Can't open perl script "`*%s*`": `*%s*

(F) The script you specified can't be opened for the indicated reason.

`Can't rename `*%s*` to `*%s*`: `*%s*`, skipping file`

(S) The rename done by the **-i** switch failed for some reason, probably because you don't have write permission to the directory.

`Can't reopen input pipe (name: `*%s*`) in binary mode`

(P) An error peculiar to VMS. Perl thought STDIN was a pipe, and tried to reopen it to accept binary data. Alas, it failed.

`Can't reswap uid and euid`

(P) The **setreuid** call failed for some reason in the setuid emulator of *suidperl*.

`Can't return outside a subroutine`

(F) The **return** statement was executed in mainline code, that is, where there was no subroutine call to return out of.

`Can't stat script "`*%s*`"`

(P) For some reason you can't *fstat*(2) the script even though you have it open already. Bizarre.

`Can't swap uid and euid`

(P) The **setreuid** call failed for some reason in the setuid emulator of *suidperl*.

`Can't take log of `*%d*

(F) Logarithms are only defined on positive real numbers.

`Can't take sqrt of `*%d*

(F) For ordinary real numbers, you can't take the square root of a negative number. There's a Complex module available for Perl, though, if you really want to do that.

`Can't undef active subroutine`

(F) You can't undefine a routine that's currently running. You can, however, redefine it while it's running, and you can even **undef** the redefined subroutine while the old routine is running. Go figure.

`Can't unshift`

(F) You tried to **unshift** an "unreal" array that can't be unshifted, such as the main Perl stack.

`Can't upgrade that kind of scalar`

(P) The internal sv_upgrade() routine adds "members" to an SV, making it into a more specialized kind of SV. The top several SV types are so specialized, however, that they cannot be interconverted. This message indicates that such a conversion was attempted.

Can't upgrade to undef

(P) The undefined SV is the bottom of the totem pole, in the scheme of upgradability. Upgrading to undef indicates an error in the code calling sv_upgrade().

Can't use "my %s" in sort comparison

(F) The global variables $a and $b are reserved for sort comparisons. You mentioned $a or $b in the same line as the <=> or **cmp** operator, and the variable had earlier been declared as a lexical variable. Either qualify the sort variable with the package name, or rename the lexical variable.

Can't use %s for loop variable

(F) Only a simple scalar variable may be used as a loop variable on a **foreach**.

Can't use %s ref as %s ref

(F) You've mixed up your reference types. You have to dereference a reference of the type needed. You can use the **ref** function to test the type of the reference, if need be.

Can't use \1 to mean $1 in expression

(W) In an ordinary expression, backslash is a unary operator that creates a reference to its argument. The use of backslash to indicate a backreference to a matched substring is only valid as part of a regular expression pattern. Trying to do this in ordinary Perl code produces a value that prints out looking like SCALAR(0xdecaf). Use the $1 form instead.

Can't use string ("%s") as %s ref while "strict refs" in use

(F) Only hard references are allowed by **use strict refs**. Symbolic references are disallowed.

Can't use an undefined value as %s reference

(F) A value used as either a hard reference or a symbolic reference must be a defined value. This helps to de-lurk some insidious errors.

Can't use global %s in "my"

(F) You tried to declare a magical variable as a lexical variable. This is not allowed, because the magic can only be tied to one location (namely the global variable) and it would be incredibly confusing to have variables in your program that looked like magical variables but weren't.

Can't use subscript on %s

(F) The compiler tried to interpret a bracketed expression as a subscript, but to the left of the brackets was an expression that didn't look like an array reference, or anything else subscriptable.

`Can't write to temp file for -e: %s`

(F) The *write*(2) routine failed for some reason while trying to process a **-e** switch. Maybe your */tmp* partition is full, or clobbered.

`Can't x= to readonly value`

(F) You tried to repeat a constant value (perhaps the undefined value) with an assignment operator, which implies modifying the value itself. Perhaps you need to copy the value to a temporary, and repeat that.

`Cannot open temporary file`

(F) The *creat*(2) routine failed for some reason while trying to process a **-e** switch. Maybe your */tmp* partition is full, or clobbered.

`chmod: mode argument is missing initial 0`

(W) A novice will sometimes say

```
chmod 777, $filename
```

not realizing that 777 will be interpreted as a decimal number, equivalent to 01411. Octal constants are introduced with a leading 0 in Perl, as in C.

`Close on unopened file %s`

(W) You tried to **close** a filehandle that was never opened.

`connect() on closed fd`

(W) You tried to do a **connect** on a closed socket. Did you forget to check the return value of your **socket** call? See **connect**.

`Corrupt malloc ptr %d at %d`

(P) The *malloc*(3) package that comes with Perl had an internal failure.

`corrupted regexp pointers`

(P) The regular expression engine got confused by what the regular expression compiler gave it.

`corrupted regexp program`

(P) The regular expression engine got passed a regular expression program without a valid magic number.

`Deep recursion on subroutine "%s"`

(W) This subroutine has called itself (directly or indirectly) 100 more times than it has returned. This probably indicates an infinite recursion, unless you're writing strange benchmark programs, in which case it indicates something else.

`Did you mean &%s instead?`

(W) You probably referred to an imported subroutine &FOO as $FOO or some such.

Did you mean $ or @ instead of %?

> (W) You probably said %hash{$key} when you meant $hash{$key} or @hash{@keys}. On the other hand, maybe you just meant %hash and got carried away.

Do you need to predeclare *%s*?

> (S) This is an educated guess made in conjunction with the message "*%s found where operator expected*". It often means a subroutine or module name is being referenced that hasn't been declared yet. This may be because of ordering problems in your file, or because of a missing **sub**, **package**, **require**, or **use** statement. If you're referencing something that isn't defined yet, you don't actually have to define the subroutine or package before the current location. You can use an empty sub foo; or package FOO; to enter a "forward" declaration.

Don't know how to handle magic of type '*%s*'

> (P) The internal handling of magical variables has been cursed.

do_study: out of memory

> (P) This should have been caught by safemalloc() instead.

Duplicate free() ignored

> (S) An internal routine has called free() on something that had already been freed.

elseif should be elsif

> (S) There is no keyword **elseif** in Perl because Larry thinks it's ugly. Your code will be interpreted as an attempt to call a method named elseif() for the class returned by the following block. This is unlikely to do what you want.

END failed--cleanup aborted

> (F) An untrapped exception was raised while executing an END subroutine. The interpreter is immediately exited.

Error converting file specification *%s*

> (F) An error peculiar to VMS. Since Perl may have to deal with file specifications in either VMS or UNIX syntax, it converts them to a single form when it must operate on them directly. Either you've passed an invalid file specification to Perl, or you've found a case the conversion routines don't handle. Drat.

Execution of *%s* aborted due to compilation errors.

> (F) The final summary message when a Perl compilation fails.

Exiting eval via *%s*

> (W) You are exiting an **eval** by unconventional means, such as a **goto**, or a loop control statement.

Exiting subroutine via %s

(W) You are exiting a subroutine by unconventional means, such as a **goto**, or a loop control statement.

Exiting substitution via %s

(W) You are exiting a substitution by unconventional means, such as a **return**, a **goto**, or a loop control statement.

Fatal VMS error at %s, line %d

(P) An error peculiar to VMS. Something untoward happened in a VMS system service or RTL routine; Perl's exit status should provide more details. The filename in *%s* and the line number in *%d* tell you which section of the Perl source code is distressed.

fcntl is not implemented

(F) Your machine apparently doesn't implement *fcntl*(2). What is this, a PDP-11 or something?

Filehandle %s never opened

(W) An I/O operation was attempted on a filehandle that was never initialized. You need to do an **open** or a **socket** call, or call a constructor from the FileHandle package.

Filehandle %s opened only for input

(W) You tried to write on a read-only filehandle. If you intended it to be a read-write filehandle, you needed to open it with +< or +> or +>> instead of with < or nothing. If you only intended to write the file, use > or >>. See **open**.

Filehandle only opened for input

(W) You tried to write on a read-only filehandle. If you intended it to be a read-write filehandle, you needed to open it with +< or +> or +>> instead of with < or nothing. If you only intended to write the file, use > or >>. See **open**.

Final $ should be \$ or $name

(F) You must now decide whether the final $ in a string was meant to be a literal dollar sign, or was meant to introduce a variable name that happens to be missing. So you have to add either the backslash or the name.

Final @ should be \@ or @name

(F) You must now decide whether the final @ in a string was meant to be a literal "at" sign, or was meant to introduce a variable name that happens to be missing. So you have to add either the backslash or the name.

`Format %s redefined`

(W) You redefined a format. To suppress this warning, say

```
{
    local $^W = 0;
    eval "format NAME =...";
}
```

`Format not terminated`

(F) A format must be terminated by a line with a solitary dot. Perl got to the end of your file without finding such a line. If you think you have such a line, make sure there are no spaces or tabs on either side of the dot.

`Found = in conditional, should be ==`

(W) You said

```
if ($foo = 123)
```

when you meant

```
if ($foo == 123)
```

(or something like that).

`gdbm store returned %d, errno %d, key "%s"`

(S) A warning from the GDBM_File extension module that a `store()` failed.

`gethostent not implemented`

(F) Your C library apparently doesn't implement *gethostent*(3), probably because if it did, it'd feel morally obligated to return every hostname on the Internet. DNS tends to give machines a sense of grandeur.

`get{sock,peer}name() on closed fd`

(W) You tried to get a socket or peer socket name on a closed socket. Did you forget to check the return value of your **socket** call?

`getpwnam returned invalid UIC %d for user "%s"`

(S) A warning peculiar to VMS. The call to `sys$getuai` underlying the **getpwnam** function returned an invalid UIC.

`Glob not terminated`

(F) The lexer saw a left angle bracket in a place where it was expecting a term, so it's looking for the corresponding right angle bracket, and not finding it. Chances are you left out some needed parentheses earlier in the line, and you really meant a "less than".

`Global symbol "%s" requires explicit package name`

> (F) You've said use strict vars, which indicates that all variables must either be lexically scoped (using **my**), or explicitly qualified to say which package the global variable is in (using ::).

`goto must have label`

> (F) Unlike **next** or **last**, you're not allowed to **goto** an unspecified destination, the opinions of Elizabethans nothwithstanding. Go to **goto**.

`Had to create %s unexpectedly`

> (S) A routine asked for a symbol from a symbol table that ought to have existed already, but for some reason it didn't, and had to be created on an emergency basis to prevent a core dump. This probably indicates a typo in an extension module.

`Hash %%s missing the % in argument %d of %s()`

> (D) Really old Perl let you omit the % on hash names in some spots. This is now heavily deprecated.

`Illegal division by zero`

> (F) You tried to divide a number by 0. Either something was wrong in your logic, or you need to put a conditional in to guard against meaningless input. Maybe both.

`Illegal modulus zero`

> (F) You tried to divide a number by 0 to get the remainder. Most numbers don't take to this kindly.

`Illegal octal digit`

> (F) You used an 8 or 9 in a octal number.

`Illegal octal digit ignored`

> (W) You may have tried to use an 8 or 9 in a octal number. Interpretation of the octal number stopped before the 8 or 9.

`Insecure dependency in %s`

> (F) You tried to do something that the tainting mechanism didn't like. The tainting mechanism is turned on when you're running setuid or setgid, or when you specify –T to turn it on explicitly. The tainting mechanism labels all data that's derived directly or indirectly from the user, who is considered to be unworthy of your trust. If any such data is used in a "dangerous" operation, you get this error.

`Insecure directory in %s`

> (F) You can't use **system**, **exec**, or a piped **open** in a setuid or setgid script if $ENV{PATH} contains a directory that is writable by the world.

Insecure PATH

(F) You can't use **system**, **exec**, or a piped **open** in a setuid or setgid script if $ENV{PATH} is derived from data supplied (or potentially supplied) by the user. The script must set the path to a known value, using trustworthy data.

Internal inconsistency in tracking vforks

(S) A warning peculiar to VMS. Perl keeps track of the number of times you've called **fork** and **exec**, in order to determine whether the current call to **exec** should affect the current script or a subprocess (see **exec**). Somehow, this count has become scrambled, so Perl is making a guess and treating this **exec** as a request to terminate the Perl script and execute the specified command.

internal disaster in regexp

(P) Something went badly wrong in the regular expression parser.

internal urp in regexp at /%s/

(P) Something went badly awry in the regular expression parser.

invalid [] range in regexp

(F) The range specified in a character class had a minimum character greater than the maximum character.

ioctl is not implemented

(F) Your machine apparently doesn't implement *ioctl*(2), which is pretty strange for a machine that supports C.

junk on end of regexp

(P) The regular expression parser is confused.

Label not found for "last %s"

(F) You named a loop to break out of, but you're not currently in a loop of that name, not even if you count where you were called from. See **last**.

Label not found for "next %s"

(F) You named a loop to continue, but you're not currently in a loop of that name, not even if you count where you were called from. See **last**.

Label not found for "redo %s"

(F) You named a loop to restart, but you're not currently in a loop of that name, not even if you count where you were called from. See **last**.

listen() on closed fd

(W) You tried to do a **listen** on a closed socket. Did you forget to check the return value of your **socket** call? See **listen**.

`Literal @`*`%s`* `now requires backslash`

(F) It used to be that Perl would try to guess whether you wanted an array interpolated or a literal `@`. It did this when the string was first used at run-time. Now strings are parsed at compile time, and ambiguous instances of `@` must be disambiguated, either by putting a backslash to indicate a literal, or by declaring (or using) the array within the program before the string (lexically). (Someday it will simply assume that any unbackslashed `@` interpolates an array.)

`Method for operation` *`%s`* `not found in package` *`%s`* `during blessing`

(F) An attempt was made to specify an entry in an overloading table that somehow doesn't point to a valid method.

`Might be a runaway multi-line` *`%s`* `string starting on line` *`%d`*

(S) This is an advisory indicating that the previously reported error may have been caused by a missing delimiter on a string or pattern, because it eventually ended earlier on the current line.

`Misplaced _ in number`

(W) An underline in a decimal constant wasn't on a three-digit boundary.

`Missing $ on loop variable`

(F) Apparently you've been programming in *csh* too much. Scalar variables are always introduced with a $ in Perl, unlike in the shells, where it can vary from one line to the next.

`Missing comma after first argument to` *`%s`* `function`

(F) While certain functions allow you to specify a filehandle or an "indirect object" before the argument list, this ain't one of 'em.

`Missing operator before` *`%s`*`?`

(S) This is an educated guess made in conjunction with the message "*%s* `found where operator expected`". Often the missing operator is a comma.

`Missing right bracket`

(F) The lexer counted more opening curly brackets (braces) than closing ones. Hint: you'll find the missing one near the place you were last editing.

`Missing semicolon on previous line?`

(S) This is an educated guess made in conjunction with the message "*%s* `found where operator expected`". Don't automatically put a semicolon on the previous line just because you saw this message.

Modification of a read-only value attempted

(F) You tried, directly or indirectly, to change the value of a constant. You didn't, of course, try 2 = 1, since the compiler catches that. But an easy way to do the same thing is:

```
sub mod { $_[0] = 1 }
mod(2);
```

Another way is to assign to a **substr** that's off the end of the string.

Modification of non-creatable array value attempted, subscript *%d*

(F) You tried to make an array value spring into existence, and the subscript was probably negative, even counting from end of the array backwards.

Modification of non-creatable hash value attempted, subscript "*%s*"

(F) You tried to make a hash value spring into existence, and it couldn't be created for some peculiar reason.

Module name must be constant

(F) Only a bare module name is allowed as the first argument to a **use**. If you want to get fancier than that, call **require** within a BEGIN block.

msg*%s* not implemented

(F) You don't have System V message IPC on your system.

Multidimensional syntax *%s* not supported

(W) Multidimensional arrays aren't written like $foo[1,2,3]. They're written like $foo[1][2][3], as in C.

Negative length

(F) You tried to do a **read/write/send/recv** operation with a buffer length that is less than 0. This is difficult to imagine.

nested *?+ in regexp

(F) You can't quantify a quantifier without intervening parens. So things like ** or +* or ?* are illegal, because you can't match things as many times as you want.

Note, however, that the minimal matching quantifiers, *?, +?, and ??, appear to be nested quantifiers, but aren't.

No #! line

(F) The setuid emulator requires that scripts have a well-formed #! line even on machines that don't support the #! construct.

No *%s* allowed while running setuid

(F) Certain operations are deemed to be too insecure for a setuid or setgid script to even be allowed to attempt. Generally speaking there will be another way to do what you want that is, if not secure, at least securable.

No -e allowed in setuid scripts

(F) A setuid script can't be specified by the user.

No comma allowed after *%s*

(F) A list operator that has a filehandle or "indirect object" is not allowed to have a comma between that and the following arguments. Otherwise it'd be just another one of the arguments.

No command into which to pipe on command line

(F) An error peculiar to VMS. Perl handles its own command-line redirection, and found a | at the end of the command line, so it doesn't know whither to pipe the output from this command.

No DB::DB routine defined

(F) The currently executing code was compiled with the **-d** switch, but for some reason the *perl5db.pl* file (or some facsimile thereof) didn't define a routine to be called at the beginning of each statement. Which is odd, because the file should have been **require**d automatically, and should have blown up the **require** if it didn't parse right.

No dbm on this machine

(P) This is counted as an internal error, because every machine should supply dbm nowadays, since Perl comes with SDBM.

No DBsub routine

(F) The currently executing code was compiled with the **-d** switch, but for some reason the *perl5db.pl* file (or some facsimile thereof) didn't define a DB::sub routine to be called at the beginning of each ordinary subroutine call.

No error file after 2> or 2>> on command line

(F) An error peculiar to VMS. Perl handles its own command-line redirection, and found a 2> or a 2>> on the command line, but can't find the name of the file to which to write data destined for STDERR.

No input file after < on command line

(F) An error peculiar to VMS. Perl handles its own command-line redirection, and found a < on the command line, but can't find the name of the file from which to read data for STDIN.

No output file after > on command line

(F) An error peculiar to VMS. Perl handles its own command-line redirection, and found a lone > at the end of the command line, so it doesn't know whither you wanted to redirect STDOUT.

No output file after > or >> on command line

(F) An error peculiar to VMS. Perl handles its own command-line redirection, and found a > or a >> on the command line, but can't find the name of the file to which to write data destined for STDOUT.

No Perl script found in input

(F) You called perl -x, but no line was found in the file beginning with #! and containing the word "perl".

No setregid available

(F) *Configure* didn't find anything resembling the *setregid*(2) call for your system.

No setreuid available

(F) *Configure* didn't find anything resembling the *setreuid*(2) call for your system.

No space allowed after -I

(F) The argument to -I must follow the -I immediately with no intervening space.

No such pipe open

(P) An error peculiar to VMS. The internal routine my_pclose() tried to close a pipe that hadn't been opened. This should have been caught earlier as an attempt to close an unopened filehandle.

No such signal: SIG*%s*

(W) You specified a signal name as a subscript to %SIG that was not recognized. Say kill -l in your shell to see the valid signal names on your system.

Not a CODE reference

(F) Perl was trying to evaluate a reference to a code value (that is, a subroutine), but found a reference to something else instead. You can use the **ref** function to find out what kind of reference it really was.

Not a format reference

(F) I'm not sure how you managed to generate a reference to an anonymous format, but this indicates you did, and that it didn't exist.

Not a GLOB reference

(F) Perl was trying to evaluate a reference to a typeglob (that is, a symbol table entry that looks like `*foo`), but found a reference to something else instead. You can use the **ref** function to find out what kind of reference it really was.

Not a HASH reference

(F) Perl was trying to evaluate a reference to a hash value, but found a reference to something else instead. You can use the **ref** function to find out what kind of reference it really was.

Not a perl script

(F) The setuid emulator requires that scripts have a well-formed `#!` line even on machines that don't support the `#!` construct. The line must mention "perl".

Not a SCALAR reference

(F) Perl was trying to evaluate a reference to a scalar value, but found a reference to something else instead. You can use the **ref** function to find out what kind of reference it really was.

Not a subroutine reference

(F) Perl was trying to evaluate a reference to a code value (that is, a subroutine), but found a reference to something else instead. You can use the **ref** function to find out what kind of reference it really was.

Not a subroutine reference in %OVERLOAD

(F) An attempt was made to specify an entry in an overloading table that somehow doesn't point to a valid subroutine.

Not an ARRAY reference

(F) Perl was trying to evaluate a reference to an array value, but found a reference to something else instead. You can use the **ref** function to find out what kind of reference it really was.

Not enough arguments for %s

(F) The function requires more arguments than you specified.

Not enough format arguments

(W) A format specified more picture fields than the subsequent values line supplied.

Null filename used

(F) You can't **require** the null filename, especially since on many machines that means the current directory! See **require**.

NULL OP IN RUN

(P) Some internal routine called run() with a null opcode pointer.

Null realloc

(P) An attempt was made to *realloc*(3) NULL.

NULL regexp argument

(P) The internal pattern-matching routines blew it bigtime.

NULL regexp parameter

(P) The internal pattern-matching routines are out of their gourd.

Odd number of elements in hash list

(S) You specified an odd number of elements to a hash list, which is odd, since hash lists come in key/value pairs.

oops: oopsAV

(S) An internal warning that the grammar is screwed up.

oops: oopsHV

(S) An internal warning that the grammar is screwed up.

Operation `%s' %s: no method found

(F) An attempt was made to use an entry in an overloading table that somehow no longer points to a valid method.

Operator or semicolon missing before %s

(S) You used a variable or subroutine call where the parser was expecting an operator. The parser has assumed you really meant to use an operator, but this is highly unlikely to be correct. For example, if you say *foo *foo it will be interpreted as if you said *foo * 'foo'.

Out of memory for yacc stack

(F) The *byacc* parser wanted to grow its stack so it could continue parsing, but *realloc*(3) wouldn't give it more memory, virtual or otherwise.

Out of memory!

(X) *malloc*(3) returned 0, indicating there was insufficient remaining memory (or virtual memory) to satisfy the request.

page overflow

(W) A single call to **write** produced more lines than can fit on a page.

panic: ck_grep

(P) Failed an internal consistency check trying to compile a **grep**.

panic: ck_split

(P) Failed an internal consistency check trying to compile a **split**.

panic: corrupt saved stack index

(P) The savestack was requested to restore more localized values than there are in the savestack.

panic: die %s

(P) We popped the context stack to an **eval** context, and then discovered it wasn't an **eval** context.

panic: do_match

(P) The internal pp_match() routine was called with invalid operational data.

panic: do_split

(P) Something terrible went wrong in setting up for the **split**.

panic: do_subst

(P) The internal pp_subst() routine was called with invalid operational data.

panic: do_trans

(P) The internal do_trans() routine was called with invalid operational data.

panic: goto

(P) We popped the context stack to a context with the specified label, and then discovered it wasn't a context we know how to do a **goto** in.

panic: INTERPCASEMOD

(P) The lexer got into a bad state at a character case modifier like \u.

panic: INTERPCONCAT

(P) The lexer got into a bad state parsing a string with brackets.

panic: last

(P) We popped the context stack to a block context, and then discovered it wasn't a block context.

panic: leave_scope clearsv

(P) A writable lexical variable became read-only somehow within the scope.

panic: leave_scope inconsistency

(P) The savestack probably got out of sync. At any rate, there was an invalid enum on the top of it.

panic: malloc

(P) Something requested a negative number of bytes of *malloc*(3).

`panic: mapstart`

(P) The compiler is screwed up with respect to the **map** function.

`panic: null array`

(P) One of the internal array routines was passed a null AV pointer.

`panic: pad_alloc`

(P) The compiler got confused about which scratchpad it was allocating and freeing temporaries and lexicals from.

`panic: pad_free curpad`

(P) The compiler got confused about which scratchpad it was allocating and freeing temporaries and lexicals from.

`panic: pad_free po`

(P) An invalid scratchpad offset was detected internally.

`panic: pad_reset curpad`

(P) The compiler got confused about which scratchpad it was allocating and freeing temporaries and lexicals from.

`panic: pad_sv po`

(P) An invalid scratchpad offset was detected internally.

`panic: pad_swipe curpad`

(P) The compiler got confused about which scratchpad it was allocating and freeing temporaries and lexicals from.

`panic: pad_swipe po`

(P) An invalid scratchpad offset was detected internally.

`panic: pp_iter`

(P) The **foreach** iterator got called in a non-loop context frame.

`panic: realloc`

(P) Something requested a negative number of bytes of *realloc*(3).

`panic: restartop`

(P) Some internal routine requested a **goto** (or something like it), and didn't supply the destination.

`panic: return`

(P) We popped the context stack to a subroutine or **eval** context, and then discovered it wasn't a subroutine or **eval** context.

`panic: scan_num`

(P) `scan_num()` got called on something that wasn't a number.

`panic: sv_insert`

> (P) The `sv_insert()` routine was told to remove more string than there was string.

`panic: top_env`

> (P) The compiler attempted to do a **goto**, or something weird like that.

`panic: yylex`

> (P) The lexer got into a bad state while processing a character case modifier like \u.

`Parens missing around "`*%s*`" list`

> (W) You said something like
>
> ```
>     my $foo, $bar = @_;
> ```
>
> when you meant
>
> ```
>     my ($foo, $bar) = @_;
> ```
>
> Remember that **my** and **local** bind closer than comma.

`Perl `*%s*` required--this is only version `*%s*`, stopped`

> (F) The module in question uses features of a version of Perl more recent than the currently running version. How long has it been since you upgraded, anyway? See **require**.

`Permission denied`

> (F) The setuid emulator in *suidperl* decided you were up to no good.

`pid `*%d*` not a child`

> (W) A warning peculiar to VMS. **waitpid** was asked to wait for a process which isn't a subprocess of the current process. While this is fine from VMS's perspective, it's probably not what you intended.

`POSIX getpgrp can't take an argument`

> (F) Your C compiler uses POSIX *getpgrp*(2), which takes no argument, unlike the BSD version, which takes a *pid*.

`Possible memory corruption: `*%s*` overflowed 3rd argument`

> (F) An *ioctl*(2) or *fcntl*(2) returned more than Perl was bargaining for. Perl guesses a reasonable buffer size, but puts a sentinel byte at the end of the buffer just in case. This sentinel byte got clobbered, and Perl assumes that memory is now corrupted. You can try to trap this with **eval**, but remember your *malloc* arena may have been clobbered. Expect your program to dump core soon. If you're lucky, it won't set fire to the laser printer first. See **ioctl**.

`Precedence problem: open` *%s* `should be open(` *%s* `)`

(S) The old irregular construct

```
open FOO || die;
```

is now misinterpreted as

```
open(FOO || die);
```

because of the strict regularization of Perl 5's grammar into unary and list operators. (The old **open** was a little of both.) You must put parens around the filehandle, or use the new **or** operator instead of ||.

`print on closed filehandle` *%s*

(W) The filehandle you're printing on got itself closed sometime before now. Check your logic flow. It may have flowed away.

`printf on closed filehandle` *%s*

(W) The filehandle you're writing to got itself closed sometime before now. Check your logic flow. See previous joke.

`Probable precedence problem on` *%s*

(W) The compiler found a bare word where it expected a conditional, which often indicates that an || or && was parsed as part of the last argument of the previous construct, for example:

```
open FOO || die;
```

`Prototype mismatch: (` *%s* `) vs (` *%s* `)`

(S) The subroutine being defined had a predeclared (forward) declaration with a different function prototype. The prototypes must match.

`Read on closed filehandle <` *%s* `>`

(W) The filehandle you're reading from got itself closed sometime before now. Check your logic flow. Don't see the previous joke.

`Reallocation too large:` *%d*

(F) You can't allocate more than 64K on an MS-DOS machine.

`Recompile perl with -DDEBUGGING to use -D switch`

(F) You can't use the **-D** option unless the code to produce the desired output is compiled into *perl*, which entails some overhead, which is why it's currently left out of your copy.

`Recursive inheritance detected`

(F) More than 100 levels of inheritance were used. Probably indicates an unintended loop in your inheritance hierarchy. Use **-Do** to trace object method lookups. (But see previous entry.)

Reference miscount in sv_replace()

> (W) The internal sv_replace() function was handed a new SV with a reference count of other than 1.

regexp memory corruption

> (P) The regular expression engine got confused by what the regular expression compiler gave it.

regexp out of space

> (P) A "can't happen" error, because safemalloc() should have caught it earlier. If it didn't, your Perl is misconfigured.

regexp too big

> (F) The current implementation of regular expression uses 16-bit shorts as address offsets within a string. Unfortunately this means that if the regular expression compiles to longer than 32767 bytes, it'll blow up. Usually when you want a regular expression this big, there is a better way to do it with multiple statements.

Reversed %s= operator

> (W) You wrote your assignment operator backward. The = must always come last, to avoid ambiguity with subsequent unary operators.

Runaway format

> (F) Your format contained the ~~ repeat-until-blank sequence, but it produced 200 lines at once, and the 200th line looked exactly like the 199th line. Apparently you didn't arrange for the arguments to exhaust themselves, either by using ^ instead of @ (for scalar variables), or by shifting or popping (for array variables).

Scalar value @%s[%s] better written as $%s[%s]

> (W) You've used an array slice (indicated by @) to select a single value of an array. Generally it's better to ask for a scalar value (indicated by $). The difference is that $foo[&bar] always behaves like a scalar, both when assigning to it and when evaluating its argument, while @foo[&bar] behaves like a list when you assign to it, and provides a list context to its subscript, which can do weird things if you're only expecting one subscript. On the other hand, if you were actually hoping to treat the array element as a list, you need to look into how references work, since Perl will not magically convert between scalars and lists for you.

Script is not setuid/setgid in suidperl

> (F) Oddly, the *suidperl* program was invoked on a script with its setuid or setgid bit unset. This doesn't make much sense.

Search pattern not terminated

(F) The lexer couldn't find the final delimiter of a `//` or `m{}` construct. Remember that bracketing delimiters count nesting level.

seek() on unopened file

(W) You tried to use the **seek** function on a filehandle that was either never opened or has been closed since.

select not implemented

(F) This machine doesn't implement the *select*(2) system call.

sem%s not implemented

(F) You don't have System V semaphore IPC on your system.

semi-panic: attempt to dup freed string

(S) The internal newSVsv() routine was called to duplicate a scalar that had previously been marked as free.

Semicolon seems to be missing

(W) A nearby syntax error was probably caused by a missing semicolon, or possibly some other missing operator, such as a comma.

Send on closed socket

(W) The filehandle you're sending to got itself closed sometime before now. Check your logic flow.

Sequence (?#... not terminated

(F) A regular expression comment must be terminated by a closing parenthesis. Embedded parentheses aren't allowed. But with the **/x** modifier you can use an ordinary comment starting with #, which doesn't care.

Sequence (?%s...) not implemented

(F) A proposed regular expression extension has the character reserved but has not yet been written.

Sequence (?%s...) not recognized

(F) You used a regular expression extension that doesn't make sense.

Server error

(A) Also known as "500 Server error". This is a CGI error, not a Perl error. You need to make sure your script is executable, is accessible by the user CGI is running the script under (which is probably not the user account you tested it under), does not rely on any environment variables (like PATH) from the user it isn't running under, and isn't in a location where the CGI server can't find it, basically, more or less.

`setegid() not implemented`

(F) You tried to assign to $), and your operating system doesn't support the *setegid*(2) system call (or equivalent), or at least *Configure* didn't think so.

`seteuid() not implemented`

(F) You tried to assign to $>, and your operating system doesn't support the *seteuid*(2) system call (or equivalent), or at least *Configure* didn't think so.

`setrgid() not implemented`

(F) You tried to assign to $(, and your operating system doesn't support the *setrgid*(2) system call (or equivalent), or at least *Configure* didn't think so.

`setruid() not implemented`

(F) You tried to assign to $<, and your operating system doesn't support the *setruid*(2) system call (or equivalent), or at least *Configure* didn't think so.

`Setuid/gid script is writable by world`

(F) The setuid emulator won't run a script that is writable by the world, because the world might have written on it already.

`shm%s not implemented`

(F) You don't have System V shared memory IPC on your system.

`shutdown() on closed fd`

(W) You tried to do a **shutdown** on a closed socket. Seems a bit superfluous.

`SIG%s handler "%s" not defined.`

(W) The signal handler named in **%SIG** doesn't, in fact, exist. Perhaps you put it into the wrong package?

`sort is now a reserved word`

(F) An ancient error message that almost nobody ever runs into anymore. But before **sort** was a keyword, people sometimes used it as a filehandle.

`Sort subroutine didn't return a numeric value`

(F) A **sort** comparison routine must return a number. You probably blew it by not using <=> or **cmp**, or by not using them correctly. See **sort**.

`Sort subroutine didn't return single value`

(F) A **sort** comparison subroutine may not return a list value with more or less than one element. See **sort**.

`Split loop`

(P) The **split** was looping infinitely. (Obviously, a **split** shouldn't iterate more times than there are characters of input, which is what happened.) See **split**.

`Stat on unopened file %s`

(W) You tried to use the **stat** function (or an equivalent file test) on a filehandle that was either never opened or has been closed since.

`Statement unlikely to be reached`

(W) You did an **exec** with some statement after it other than a **die**. This is almost always an error, because **exec** never returns unless there was a failure. You probably wanted to use **system** instead, which does return. To suppress this warning, put the **exec** in a block by itself. Or put a **die** after it.

`Subroutine %s redefined`

(W) You redefined a subroutine. To suppress this warning, say

```
{
    local $^W = 0;
    eval "sub name { ... }";
}
```

`Substitution loop`

(P) The substitution was looping infinitely. (Obviously, a substitution shouldn't iterate more times than there are characters of input, which is what happened.) See the discussion of substitution in the section "Pattern-Matching Operators" in Chapter 2.

`Substitution pattern not terminated`

(F) The lexer couldn't find the interior delimiter of an `s///` or `s{}{}` construct. Remember that bracketing delimiters count nesting level.

`Substitution replacement not terminated`

(F) The lexer couldn't find the final delimiter of an `s///` or `s{}{}` construct. Remember that bracketing delimiters count nesting level.

`substr outside of string`

(W) You tried to reference a **substr** that pointed outside of a string. That is, the absolute value of the offset was larger than the length of the string. See **substr**.

`suidperl is no longer needed since . . .`

(F) Your *perl* was compiled with –DSETUID_SCRIPTS_ARE_SECURE_NOW, but a version of the setuid emulator somehow got run anyway.

`syntax error`

(F) Probably means you had a syntax error. Common reasons include:

- A keyword is misspelled.

- A semicolon is missing.

- A comma is missing.

- An opening or closing parenthesis is missing.

- An opening or closing brace is missing.

- A closing quote is missing.

Often there will be another error message associated with the syntax error giving more information. (Sometimes it helps to turn on **-w**.) The error message itself often tells you where it was in the line when it decided to give up. Sometimes the actual error is several tokens before this, since Perl is good at understanding random input. Occasionally the line number may be misleading, and once in a blue moon the only way to figure out what's triggering the error is to call *perl -c* repeatedly, chopping away half the program each time to see if the error went away. Sort of the cybernetic version of 20 Questions.

syntax error at line %d: `%s' unexpected
> (A) You've accidentally run your script through the Bourne shell instead of *perl*. Check the #! line, or manually feed your script into *perl* yourself.

System V IPC is not implemented on this machine
> (F) You tried to do something with a function beginning with **sem**, **shm** or **msg**. See **semctl**, for example.

Syswrite on closed filehandle
> (W) The filehandle you're writing to got itself closed sometime before now. Check your logic flow. If you're tired of that, check someone else's.

tell() on unopened file
> (W) You tried to use the **tell** function on a filehandle that was either never opened or has been closed since.

Test on unopened file %s
> (W) You tried to invoke a file test operator on a filehandle that isn't open. Check your logic.

That use of $[is unsupported
> (F) Assignment to $[is now strictly circumscribed, and interpreted as a compiler directive. You may only say one of
>
> ```
> $[ = 0;
> $[ = 1;
> ...
> local $[ = 0;
> local $[ = 1;
> ...
> ```
>
> This is to prevent the problem of one module changing the array base out from under another module inadvertently. See the section on $[in Chapter 2.

The %s function is unimplemented
> (F) The function indicated isn't implemented on this architecture, according to the probings of *Configure*.

The crypt() function is unimplemented due to excessive paranoia.
> (F) *Configure* couldn't find the *crypt*(3) function on your machine, probably because your vendor didn't supply it, probably because they think the U.S. government thinks it's a secret, or at least that they will continue to pretend that it is. And if you quote me on that, I will deny it.

The stat preceding -l _ wasn't an lstat
> (F) It makes no sense to test the current stat buffer for symbolic linkhood if the last **stat** that wrote to the stat buffer already went past the symlink to get to the real file. Use an actual filename instead.

times not implemented
> (F) Your version of the C library apparently doesn't do *times*(3). I suspect you're not running on UNIX.

Too few args to syscall
> (F) There has to be at least one argument to **syscall** to specify the system call to call, silly dilly.

Too many ('s

Too many)'s
> (A) You've accidentally run your script through *csh* instead of *perl*. Check the #! line, or manually feed your script into *perl* yourself.

Too many args to syscall
> (F) Perl supports a maximum of 14 args to **syscall**.

Too many arguments for %s
> (F) The function requires fewer arguments than you specified.

trailing \ in regexp
> (F) The regular expression ends with an unbackslashed backslash. Backslash it.

Translation pattern not terminated
> (F) The lexer couldn't find the interior delimiter of a tr/// or tr[][] construct.

Translation replacement not terminated
> (F) The lexer couldn't find the final delimiter of a tr/// or tr[][] construct.

truncate not implemented
> (F) Your machine doesn't implement a file truncation mechanism that *Configure* knows about.

Type of arg *%d* **to** *%s* **must be** *%s* **(not** *%s***)**

> (F) This function requires the argument in that position to be of a certain type. Arrays must be `@NAME` or `@{EXPR}`. Hashes must be `%NAME` or `%{EXPR}`. No implicit dereferencing is allowed—use the `{EXPR}` forms as an explicit dereference.

umask: argument is missing initial 0

> (W) A umask of 222 is incorrect. It should be 0222, since octal literals always start with 0 in Perl, as in C.

Unable to create sub named "*%s***"**

> (F) You attempted to create or access a subroutine with an illegal name.

Unbalanced context: *%d* **more PUSHes than POPs**

> (W) The exit code detected an internal inconsistency in how many execution contexts were entered and left.

Unbalanced saves: *%d* **more saves than restores**

> (W) The exit code detected an internal inconsistency in how many values were temporarily localized.

Unbalanced scopes: *%d* **more ENTERs than LEAVEs**

> (W) The exit code detected an internal inconsistency in how many blocks were entered and left.

Unbalanced tmps: *%d* **more allocs than frees**

> (W) The exit code detected an internal inconsistency in how many mortal scalars were allocated and freed.

Undefined format "*%s***" called**

> (F) The **format** indicated doesn't seem to exist. Perhaps it's really in another package?

Undefined sort subroutine "*%s***" called**

> (F) The **sort** comparison routine specified doesn't seem to exist. Perhaps it's in a different package? See **sort**.

Undefined subroutine &*%s* **called**

> (F) The subroutine indicated hasn't been defined, or if it was, it has since been undefined.

Undefined subroutine called

> (F) The anonymous subroutine you're trying to call hasn't been defined, or if it was, it has since been undefined.

Undefined subroutine in sort

(F) The **sort** comparison routine specified is declared but doesn't seem to have been defined yet. See **sort**.

Undefined top format "%s" called

(F) The **format** indicated doesn't seem to exist. Perhaps it's really in another package?

unexec of %s into %s failed!

(F) The **unexec()** routine failed for some reason. See your local FSF representative, who probably put it there in the first place.

Unknown BYTEORDER

(F) There are no byteswapping functions for a machine with this byte order.

unmatched () in regexp

(F) Unbackslashed parentheses must always be balanced in regular expressions. If you're a *vi* user, the **%** key is valuable for finding the matching parenthesis.

Unmatched right bracket

(F) The lexer counted more closing curly brackets (braces) than opening ones, so you're probably missing an opening bracket. As a general rule, you'll find the missing one (so to speak) near the place you were last editing.

unmatched [] in regexp

(F) The brackets around a character class must match. If you wish to include a closing bracket in a character class, backslash it or put it first.

Unquoted string "%s" may clash with future reserved word

(W) You used a bareword that might someday be claimed as a reserved word. It's best to put such a word in quotes, or capitalize it somehow, or insert an underbar into it. You might also declare it as a subroutine.

Unrecognized character \%d ignored

(S) A garbage character was found in the input, and ignored, in case it's a weird control character on an EBCDIC machine, or some such.

Unrecognized signal name "%s"

(F) You specified a signal name to the **kill** function that was not recognized. Say **kill -l** in your shell to see the valid signal names on your system.

Unrecognized switch: -%s

(F) You specified an illegal option to *perl.* Don't do that. (If you think you *didn't* do that, check the **#!** line to see if it's supplying the bad switch on your behalf.)

`Unsuccessful %s on filename containing newline`

(W) A file operation was attempted on a filename, and that operation failed, probably because the filename contained a newline, probably because you forgot to **chop** or **chomp** it off. See **chop**.

`Unsupported directory function "%s" called`

(F) Your machine doesn't support *opendir*(3) and *readdir*(3).

`Unsupported function %s`

(F) This machine doesn't implement the indicated function, apparently. At least, *Configure* doesn't think so.

`Unsupported socket function "%s" called`

(F) Your machine doesn't support the Berkeley socket mechanism, or at least that's what *Configure* thought.

`Unterminated <> operator`

(F) The lexer saw a left angle bracket in a place where it was expecting a term, so it's looking for the corresponding right angle bracket, and not finding it. Chances are you left out some needed parentheses earlier in the line, and you really meant a "less than".

`Use of $# is deprecated`

(D) This was an ill-advised attempt to emulate a poorly defined *awk* feature. Use an explicit **printf** or **sprintf** instead.

`Use of $* is deprecated`

(D) This variable magically turned on multiline pattern matching, both for you and for any luckless subroutine that you happen to call. You should use the new /m and /s modifiers now to do that without the dangerous action-at-a-distance effects of **$***.

`Use of %s in printf format not supported`

(F) You attempted to use a feature of **printf** that is accessible only from C. This usually means there's a better way to do it in Perl.

`Use of %s is deprecated`

(D) The construct indicated is no longer recommended for use, generally because there's a better way to do it, and also because the old way has bad side effects.

`Use of bare << to mean <<"" is deprecated`

(D) You are now encouraged to use the explicitly quoted form if you wish to use a blank line as the terminator of the here-document.

`Use of implicit split to @_ is deprecated`

(D) It makes a lot of work for the compiler when you clobber a subroutine's argument list, so it's better if you assign the results of a **split** explicitly to an array (or list).

`Use of uninitialized value`

(W) An undefined value was used as if it were already defined. It was interpreted as a `""` or a 0, but maybe it was a mistake. To suppress this warning, assign an initial value to your variables.

`Useless use of %s in void context`

(W) You did something without a side effect in a context that does nothing with the return value, such as a statement that doesn't return a value from a block, or the left side of a scalar comma operator. Very often this points not to stupidity on your part, but a failure of Perl to parse your program the way you thought it would. For example, you'd get this if you mixed up your C precedence with Python precedence and said

```
$one, $two = 1, 2;
```

when you meant to say

```
($one, $two) = (1, 2);
```

Another common error is to use ordinary parentheses to construct a list reference when you should be using square or curly brackets, for example, if you say

```
$array = (1,2);
```

when you should have said

```
$array = [1,2];
```

The square brackets explicitly turn a list value into a scalar value, while parentheses do not. So when a parenthesized list is evaluated in a scalar context, the comma is treated like C's comma operator, which throws away the left argument, which is not what you want.

`Variable "%s" is not exported`

(F) While use **strict** in effect, you referred to a global variable that you thought was imported from another module, because something else of the same name (usually a subroutine) is exported by that module. It usually means you put the wrong funny character on the front of your variable.

`Variable name "%s::%s" used only once: possible typo`

(W) Typographical errors often show up as unique names. If you had a good reason for having a unique name, then just mention it again somehow to suppress the message. You might consider declaring the variable with use **vars**.

Variable syntax.

(A) You've accidentally run your script through *csh* instead of *perl*. Check the #! line, or manually feed your script into *perl* yourself.

Warning: unable to close filehandle %s properly.

(S) The implicit **close** done by an **open** got an error indication on the **close**. This usually indicates your filesystem ran out of disk space.

Warning: Use of "%s" without parens is ambiguous

(S) You wrote a unary operator followed by something that looks like a binary operator that could also have been interpreted as a term or unary operator. For instance, if you know that the **rand** function has a default argument of 1.0, and you write

```
rand + 5;
```

you may *think* you wrote the same thing as

```
rand() + 5;
```

but in actual fact, you got

```
rand(+5);
```

So put in parentheses to say what you really mean.

Write on closed filehandle

(W) The filehandle you're writing to got itself closed sometime before now. Check your logic flow.

X outside of string

(F) You had a **pack** template that specified a relative position before the beginning of the string being unpacked. See **pack**.

x outside of string

(F) You had a **pack** template that specified a relative position after the end of the string being unpacked. See **pack**.

Xsub "%s" called in sort

(F) The use of an external subroutine as a **sort** comparison is not yet supported.

Xsub called in sort

(F) The use of an external subroutine as a **sort** comparison is not yet supported.

You can't use -l on a filehandle

(F) A filehandle represents an opened file, and when you opened the file it already went past any symlink you are presumably trying to look for. Use a filename instead.

YOU HAVEN'T DISABLED SET-ID SCRIPTS IN THE KERNEL YET!

(F) And you probably never will, since you probably don't have the sources to your kernel, and your vendor probably doesn't give a rip about what you want. Your best bet is to use the wrapsuid script in the *eg/* directory to put a setuid C wrapper around your script.

You need to quote "*%s*"

(W) You assigned a bareword as a signal handler name. Unfortunately, you already have a subroutine of that name declared, which means that Perl 5 will try to call the subroutine when the assignment is executed, which is probably not what you want. (If it IS what you want, put an & in front.)

[gs]etsockopt() on closed fd

(W) You tried to get or set a socket option on a closed socket. Did you forget to check the return value of your **socket** call? See **getsockopt**.

\1 better written as $1

(W) Outside of patterns, backreferences live on as variables. The use of backslashes is grandfathered on the righthand side of a substitution, but stylistically it's better to use the variable form because other Perl programmers will expect it, and it works better if there are more than nine backreferences.

'|' and '<' may not both be specified on command line

(F) An error peculiar to VMS. Perl does its own command-line redirection, and found that STDIN was a pipe, and that you also tried to redirect STDIN using <. Only one STDIN stream to a customer, please.

'|' and '>' may not both be specified on command line

(F) An error peculiar to VMS. Perl does its own command-line redirection, and thinks you tried to redirect STDOUT both to a file and into a pipe to another command. You need to choose one or the other, though nothing's stopping you from piping into a program or Perl script which "splits" output into two streams, such as

```
open(OUT,">$ARGV[0]") or die "Can't write to $ARGV[0]: $!";
while (<STDIN>) {
    print STDOUT;
    print OUT;
}
close OUT;
```

Glossary

actual arguments

The *scalar values* that you supply to a *function* or *subroutine* when you call it. For instance, when you call `piglatin("bingo")`, the string `"bingo"` is the actual argument. See also *argument*[*] and *formal arguments*.

address operator

A language construct for manipulating the actual location of an object in your computer's memory. Strictly speaking, there are no such operators in Perl, since it handles all that for you automatically. You tell Perl that you want a new *thingy*, and Perl worries about creating, moving, and destroying the thingy for you. Not so strictly speaking, the backslash operator returns a reference to a thingy, which works much like an address. See also *network address*.

alternatives

A list of possible choices from which you may select only one, as in "Would you like door A, B, or C?" Alternatives in regular expressions are separated with a vertical bar: |. Alternatives in normal Perl expressions are separated with a double vertical bar: ||. You might say there are two alternatives for alternatives. (Then again, you might not. Your choice.)

---

* When we italicize a word or phrase in here, it usually means you can find it defined elsewhere in the Glossary. Think of them as hyperlinks.

anonymous

Used to describe a *thingy* that is not directly accessible through a named *variable*. Such a thingy must be indirectly accessible through at least one *hard reference*. When the last hard reference goes away, the anonymous thingy is destroyed without pity.

architecture

The kind of computer you're working on, where one "kind" of computer means all those computers that can run the same *binary* program. Since Perl scripts are text files, not binaries, a Perl script is much less sensitive to the architecture it's running on than programs in other languages (such as C) that are compiled into machine code. See also *operating system*.

argument

A piece of data supplied as input to a *program*, *subroutine*, or *function* when it is invoked to tell it what it's supposed to do. Also called a "parameter".

ARGV

The name of the array containing the *argument* "vector" from the *command line*. If you use the empty <> operator, **ARGV** is both the name of the *filehandle* used to traverse the arguments, and of the *scalar* containing the name of the current input file. It's also what you say to your dentist when the Novocaine isn't working.

arithmetic operator

A symbol such as + or ** that tells Perl to do arithmetic. In addition, see *operator*.

array

A named list of values, each of which has a unique *key* to identify it. In a normal array, the key is numeric (an integer, in fact). In a *hash* (an associative array), the key is a string.

array context

A quaint, archaic expression used by people who have read the first edition of this book. Nowadays called *list context*.

array literal

Strictly, a comma-separated, parenthesized LIST of *scalar literals*. Used loosely to refer to any parenthesized LIST even if it contains *variables* or *expressions*.

array value

Another archaic phrase. See *list value*.

array variable

A named list that may be processed by *functions* such as **shift** and **splice** that require an array name as the first *argument*.

ASCII

Used roughly to mean the American Standard Code for Information Interchange (a 7-bit character set), and any international extensions based on it.

assignment

An operation whose mission in life is to change the value of a *variable*.

assignment operator

A compound operator composed of an ordinary assignment together with some other operator, that changes the value of a variable in place, that is, relative to its old value. For example, $a += 2 adds 2 to $a.

associative array

See *hash*.

associativity

Determines whether you do the left *operator* first or the right *operator* first, when you have "A *operator* B *operator* C", if the two operators are of the same precedence. Operators like + are left associative, while operators like ** are

right associative. See the section "Operators" in Chapter 2, *The Gory Details*, for a list of associativity.

autoincrement

To add one to something automatically. Usually used to describe the ++ operator.

autosplit

To split a string automatically on *whitespace*, such as the **-a** switch does in order to emulate *awk*.

AV

Short for "array value", which refers to one of Perl's internal data types. (Not to be confused with *array value*, by which people usually mean *list value*.) An AV is a kind of *SV*.

awk

Descriptive editing term—short for "awkward". Also coincidentally refers to a venerable text processing language from which Perl derived some of its ideas.

backtracking

The practice of saying, "If I had to do it all over, I'd do it differently," and then actually going back and doing it all over differently. Mathematically speaking, it's returning from an unsuccessful recursion on a tree of possibilities. Backtracking happens in Perl when it attempts to match patterns with a *regular expression*, and its earlier guesses don't pan out.

base class

A generic *object class* from which other more specific classes are derived genetically by *inheritance*. Also called a "superclass" by people who respect their ancestors.

BASIC/PLUS

Another ancient language, from which Perl derived exactly one idea. OK, maybe two.[*]

big-endian

From Swift: someone who eats boiled eggs big end first. Also used of computers that store the most significant *byte* of a word at a lower byte address than the least significant byte. Often

---

[*] BASIC/PLUS is a registered trademark of Digital Equipment Corporation. And the answers are: statement modifiers and maybe formats.

considered superior to little-endian machines. See also *little-endian*.

binary

Having to do with numbers represented in base two. That means there are basically two numbers, zero and one. Some people think in binary, as shown by the kinds of questions they ask: "Should we all use Perl or Java?" Also used to describe a non-text file, presumably because such a file makes full use of all the binary bits in its bytes.

bit

A very small piece of litter. Also a number in the range zero to one, inclusive.

bit shift

The movement of bits left or right in a computer word, which has the effect of multiplying or dividing by a power of two.

bless

In corporate life, to grant official approval to a thing, as in, "The VP of Engineering has blessed our WebCruncher project." Similarly in Perl, to grant official approval to a *thingy* so that it can function as a WebCruncher *object*. See the **bless** function in Chapter 3, *Functions*.

block

What a *process* does when it has to wait for something: "My process blocked waiting for the disk." As an unrelated noun, it refers to a large chunk of data, of a size that the *operating system* likes to deal with (normally a power of two such as 512 or 8192). Typically refers to a chunk of data that's coming from or going to a disk file.

BLOCK

A syntactic construct consisting of a sequence of Perl *statements* bounded by braces. The if and while statements are defined in terms of BLOCKs. Sometimes we also say "block" to mean a sequence of statements that act like a BLOCK, such as within an **eval** or a file, even though the statements aren't bounded by braces.

block buffering

A method of making input and output efficient by doing it a block at a time. By default, Perl does block buffering to disk files. See *buffer* and *command buffering*.

Boolean context

A special kind of *scalar context* in which the program is expecting to decide whether the *scalar value* returned by an expression is *true* or *false*. See *context*.

breakpoint

A spot in your program where you've told the debugger to stop *execution* so you can poke around and see whether anything is wrong yet.

BSD

A psychoactive drug, popular in the 80s, probably developed at U. C. Berkeley or thereabouts. Similar in many ways to the prescription-only medication called "System V", but infinitely more useful. (Or, at least, more fun.) The full chemical name is "Berkeley Standard Distribution".

buffer

A temporary holding location for data. *Block buffering* means that the data is passed on to its destination whenever the buffer is full. *Line buffering* means that it's passed on whenever a complete line is received. *Command buffering* means that it's passed on after every print command. If your output is unbuffered, every byte is transmitted separately, without passing through a holding area.

byte

A piece of data worth eight *bits* in most places.

bytecode

A pidgin-like language spoken among 'droids when they don't wish to reveal their orientation (see *endian*). Named after some similar languages spoken (for similar reasons) between compilers and interpreters in the late twentieth century. These languages are characterized by representing everything as a non-architecture-dependent sequence of bytes.

C

A language beloved by many for its inside-out type definitions, inscrutable precedence rules, and heavy *overloading* of the function-call mechanism. (Well, actually, people first switched to C because they found lower-case identifiers easier to read than upper.) The Perl *interpreter* is written in C, so it's not surprising that Perl borrowed a few ideas from it.

C preprocessor

The typical C compiler's first pass, which processes lines beginning with '# for conditional compilation and macro definition, and does various manipulations of the program text based on the current definitions. Also known as *cpp*(1).

call by reference

An *argument*-passing mechanism in which the *formal arguments* refer directly to the *actual arguments*, and the *subroutine* can change the actual arguments by changing the formal arguments. See also *call by value*.

call by value

An *argument*-passing mechanism in which the *formal arguments* refer to a copy of the *actual arguments*, and the *subroutine* cannot change the actual arguments by changing the formal arguments. (See also *call by reference*).

character

A small pattern of *bits* (usually seven, eight, or sixteen in number) that is the machine's representation of a unit of orthography. Americans typically confuse characters with *bytes*. So does Perl.

character class

A square-bracketed list of characters used in a *regular expression* to indicate that any character of the set may occur at this point.

class

A *package* that either defines *methods* (*subroutines*) that deal with *objects* of your class, or that derives methods from other packages that know how to deal with objects of your class. (Or think they know how.) See also *inheritance*.

class method

A *method* that treats the whole *class* as an *object*. One sort of class method is a *constructor*. (A class method is also known as a "static" method in C++ terminology.)

client

In networking, a *process* that initiates contact with a *server* process in order to exchange data with it and perhaps receive a service.

closure

An *anonymous* subroutine that, when generated at run-time, keeps track of the identities of externally visible *lexical variables* even after those lexical variables have supposedly gone out of *scope*. They're called "closures" because this sort of behavior gives mathematicians a sense of closure.

CODE

The word "CODE" is returned by the **ref** function when you apply it to a CV. See *CV*.

collating sequence

The order that characters sort into. This is used by string comparison routines to decide, for example, where in this glossary to put "collating sequence".

command

In *shell* programming, the syntactic combination of a program name with its arguments. More loosely, anything you type to a shell (a command interpreter) that starts it doing something. In Perl programming, a *statement*, which might start with a *label*, and typically ends with a semicolon.

command buffering

An option in Perl that lets you store up the output of each Perl command and then flush it out as a single request to the *operating system*. It's enabled by setting the $| variable to a non-zero value. It's used when you don't want data sitting around not going where it's supposed to, which may happen because the default on a *file* or *pipe* is to use block buffering. See also *buffer*.

command-line arguments

The *values* you supply along with a program name when you tell a *shell* to execute a command. These values are passed to a Perl script through @**ARGV**.

command name

The name of the program currently executing, as typed on the command line. In C the command name is passed to the program as the first command-line argument. In Perl, it comes in separately as $0.

comment

A remark that doesn't affect the meaning of the program. In Perl, a comment is introduced by a '# character and continues to the end of the line.

compile-time

The time when Perl is trying to make sense of your program, as opposed to when it thinks it knows what your program means and is merely trying to do what it thinks your program says to do. See also *run-time*.

compiler

Strictly speaking, a program that munches up another program and spits out yet another file containing the program in a more executable form, typically containing native machine instructions. The *perl* program is not a compiler by this definition, but it does contain a compiler that takes a program and turns it into a more executable form (*syntax trees*) within the *perl* process itself, which the *interpreter* then interprets. There are, however, extension *modules* to get Perl to act more like a real compiler.

composer

A "constructor" for a *thingy* that isn't really an *object*, like an array or a hash. For example, a pair of braces acts as a composer for a hash, and a pair of brackets acts as a composer for an array. See "Creating Hard References" in Chapter 4, *References and Nested Data Structures*.

concatenation

The process of gluing one cat's nose to another cat's tail. Also, a similar operation on two strings.

conditional

Something "iffy".

connection

In telephony, the temporary electrical circuit between the caller's and the callee's phone. In networking, the same kind of temporary circuit between a *client* and a *server*.

construct

As a noun, a piece of syntax made up of smaller pieces. As a transitive verb, to create an *object* using a *constructor*.

constructor

A special *class method* that constructs an *object* and returns it. Sometimes we use the term loosely to mean a *composer*.

context

The surroundings, or environment. The context given by the surrounding code determines what kind of data a particular *expression* is expected to return. The two primary contexts are *list context* and *scalar context*. Scalar context is sometimes subdivided into *Boolean context*, *numeric context*, and *string context*. There's also a "don't care" context (which is dealt with in Chapter 2, if you care).

continuation

The treatment of more than one physical *line* as a single logical line. Makefile lines are continued by putting a backslash before the *newline*. Internet message headers are continued by putting a space or tab *after* the newline. Perl lines do not need any form of continuation mark, because *whitespace* (including newline) is gleefully ignored. Usually.

core dump

The corpse of a *process*, in the form of a file left in the *working directory* of the process, usually as a result of certain kinds of fatal error.

CPAN

Comprehensive Perl Archive Network. (See the Preface for more details.)

current package

Which *package* the current statement is compiled in. Scan backward in the text of your program until you find a package declaration at the same *block* level, or in an enclosing block. That's your current package name.

current working directory

See *working directory*.

currently selected output channel

The last *filehandle* that was designated with select(FILEHANDLE); the default is STDOUT, if no filehandle has been selected.

CV

An internal "code value" typedef. A CV is a kind of *SV*.

dangling statement

A bare, single *statement*, without any braces, hanging off an **if** or **while** conditional. C allows them. Perl doesn't.

data flow

What your program looks like from the perspective of a particular piece of data from the time it enters your program to the time it leaves or is combined with some other data to make new data.

data reduction

The process of extracting only the most interesting tidbits because the boss can't read fast enough.

data structure

How your various pieces of data relate to each other, and what shape they make when you put them all together, as in a rectangular table, or a triangular-shaped tree.

data type

A set of possible values, together with all the operations that know how to deal with those values. For example, a numeric data type has a certain set of numbers that you can work with, and it has various mathematical operations you can do on the numbers that would make little sense on, say, a string such as "Kilroy". Strings have their own operations, such as *concatenation*. Compound types made of a number of smaller pieces generally have operations to compose and decompose them, and perhaps to rearrange them. Objects that model things in the real world often have operations that correspond to real activities. For instance, if you model an elevator, your elevator object might have an open_door() method.

DBM

Stands for "Data Base Management" routines, a set of routines that emulate an *associative array* using disk files. The routines use a dynamic hashing scheme to locate any entry with only two disk accesses. DBM files allow a Perl script to keep a persistent *hash* across multiple invocations. You can use **tie** your hash variables to various DBM implementations—see Chapter 5, *Packages, Modules, and Object Classes*.

declaration

An assertion you make that something exists and perhaps what it's like, without any commitment as to how or where you'll use it. A declaration is like the part of your recipe that says, "two cups flour, one large egg, four or five tadpoles . . . ." See *statement* for its opposite. Note that some declarations also function as statements.

decrement

To subtract one from something.

default

A value that is chosen for you if you don't supply a value of your own.

defined

Having a meaning. Perl thinks that some of the things people try to do are devoid of meaning; in particular, making use of variables that have never been given a *value*, and performing certain operations on data that isn't there. For example, if you try to read data past the end of a file, Perl will hand you back an *undefined* value. See also *false*.

delimiter

Some *character* or *string* that sets bounds to an arbitrarily-sized textual object.

dereference

A fancy computer science term meaning "to follow a *reference* to what it points to". The "de" part of it refers to the fact that you're taking away one level of *indirection*.

derived class

A *class* that defines some of its *methods* in terms of a more generic class, called a *base class*. Note that classes aren't classified exclusively into base classes or derived classes: a class can function as both a derived class and a base class simultaneously.

destroy

To deallocate the memory of a *thingy*.

destructor

A special *method* that is called when an *object* is thinking about *destroying* itself.

device

A whiz-bang hardware gizmo (like a disk or tape drive) attached to your computer that the *operating system* tries to make look like a file (or a bunch of files). Under UNIX, these fake files tend to live in the */dev* directory.

directory

A place where you find files, and perhaps other directories. Some *operating systems* call these "folders", "drawers", or "catalogs".

directory handle

A name that represents a particular instance of opening a directory to read it, until you close it.

dump

A Perl *statement* that is one of the many ways to get a Perl program to produce a *core dump*. Most of the others are undocumented.

dynamic scoping

Making variables visible throughout the rest of the *block* in which they are first used, as well as within any *subroutines* that are called by the rest of the block. Dynamically scoped variables can have their values temporarily changed (and implicitly restored later) by a **local** statement. Compare *Lexical Scoping*. Used more loosely to mean how a subroutine that is in the middle of calling another subroutine "contains" that subroutine at run-time.

eclectic

Derived from many sources. Some would say *too* many.

element

A basic building block. When you're talking about an *array*, it's one of the items that make up the array.

endian

See *little-endian* and *big-endian*.

environment

The collective set of *environment variables* your *process* inherits from its parent. Accessed via %ENV.

environment variable

A mechanism by which some high-level agent such as a user can pass its preferences down to child *processes*, grandchild processes, great-grandchild processes, and so on. Each environment variable is a *key/value* pair, like one element of a *hash*.

EOF

End of File. Sometimes used metaphorically as the trailing *delimiter* of a *here document*.

errno

The error number returned by a UNIX *system call* when it fails. Perl refers to the error by the name $! (or $OS_ERROR if you use the English module).

exception

A fancy term for an error. See *fatal error*.

exception handling

The way a program responds to an error. The exception handling mechanism in Perl is the **eval** construct.

executable file

A *file* that is specially marked to tell the *operating system* that it's OK to run this file as a program. Abbreviated to "executable".

execute

To run a program or subroutine. (Has nothing to do with the **kill** command, unless you're trying to run a *signal handler*.)

execute bit

The special mark that tells the operating system it can run this program. There are actually three execute bits under UNIX, and which bit gets used depends on whether you own the file singularly, collectively, or not at all.

exit status

See *status*.

exponent

The part of a *floating-point* number that says where to put the decimal point in the other part. See *mantissa*.

export

To make symbols from your *module* available for *import* by other modules.

expression

Anything you can legally say in a spot where a *value* is required. Typically composed of *literals*, *variables*, *operators*, *functions*, and *subroutine* calls.

false

In Perl, any value that would look like "" or "0" if evaluated in a string context. Since undefined values evaluate to "", all undefined values are false, but not all false values are undefined.

fatal error

An error that causes termination of the *process* after printing a nasty message on your *standard error* stream. "Fatal" errors that happen inside an **eval** aren't fatal to the whole program, just to that particular **eval**. The nasty message then shows up in the $@ variable. You can cause a fatal error with the **die** operator. This is also known as throwing or raising an *exception*.

field

A single piece of numeric or string data that is part of a longer *string, record,* or *line.* Variable-width fields are usually separated by *delimiters* (so use **split** to extract the fields), while fixed-width fields are usually at fixed positions (so use **unpack**).

file

A named collection of data, usually stored on a disk in a *directory.* Roughly like a document, if you're into office metaphors. In some *operating systems* like UNIX, you can actually give a file more than one name.

file descriptor

The little number the *operating system* uses to keep track of which opened *file* you're talking about. Perl hides the file descriptor inside a *standard I/O* stream, and then attaches the stream to a *filehandle.*

file glob

A "wildcard" match on *filenames.*

file test operator

A built-in Perl operator that you use to determine whether something is *true* about a file, such as whether you could open it if you tried.

filehandle

What you pick up a file with. Or, a name (not necessarily related to the real name of a file) that represents a particular instance of opening a file until you close it. Thus if you're going to open and close several different files in succession, it's possible to open each of them with the same filehandle, so you don't have to write out separate code to process each file. It's like the game show host calling someone "Contestant #1" so that he doesn't have to remember too many names from day to day.

filename

The name for a file. This name is listed in a *directory,* and you can use it in an **open** statement to tell the *operating system* exactly which file you want to open.

filesystem

A set of *directories* and *files* residing on a partition of the disk. You can move a file around from directory to directory within a filesystem without actually moving the file itself, at least under UNIX.

floating point

A method of storing numbers in scientific notation, such that the precision of the number is independent of its magnitude (the decimal point "floats"). Perl does its numeric work with floating-point numbers, when it can't get away with using *integers.*

flush

The act of emptying a *buffer,* often before it's full.

fork

To create a child *process* identical to the parent process, at least until it gets ideas of its own.

formal arguments

Generic names a *subroutine* knows its *arguments* by. In many languages, formal arguments are always given individual names, but in Perl they are passed via *arrays.* The formal arguments to a Perl program are $ARGV[0], $ARGV[1], and so on. The formal arguments to a Perl subroutine are $_[0], $_[1], and so on. You may give the arguments individual names by assigning the values to a **local** or **my** list.

format

A specification of how many spaces and digits and things to put somewhere so that whatever you're printing comes out nice and pretty.

freely available

Means you don't have to pay money to get it, but the copyright on it may still belong to someone else (like Larry).

freely redistributable

Means you're not in trouble if you give a bootleg copy of it to your friends (hint).

function

Mathematically, a mapping of each of a set of input values to a particular output value. In computers, refers to a *subroutine* or *operation* that returns a *value.* It may or may not have input values (called *arguments*).

garbage collection

A misnamed feature of some programming languages—it should be called "expecting your mother to pick up after you". Strictly speaking, Perl doesn't do this, but relies on a reference counting mechanism to keep things tidy. However, when your interpreter thread exits, a kind of garbage collector runs to make sure everything is cleaned up if you've been messy with circular references and such.

GID

Group ID—in UNIX, the numeric group ID that the *operating system* uses to identify you and members of your *group*.

glob

Strictly, the shell's * character, which will match a "glob" of characters when you're trying to generate a list of filenames. Loosely, the act of using globs and similar symbols to do pattern matching.

global

Something you can see from anywhere, usually used of *variables* and *subroutines* that are visible everywhere in your program. In Perl, only certain special variables are truly global—most variables (and all subroutines) are local to the current *package*.

group

A set of users that you're a member of. In some operating systems (like UNIX), you can give certain file access permissions to other members of your group.

GV

An internal "glob value", meaning a *typeglob*. A GV is a kind of *SV*.

hard reference

A *scalar* value containing the actual address of a *thingy*, such that the thingy's *reference* count accounts for it. (Some hard references are held internally, such as the implicit reference from one of a *typeglob*'s variable slots to its corresponding thingy.) A hard reference is different from a *symbolic reference*.

has-a

A relationship between two *objects* that is more tenuous than an *is-a* relationship, and that can be modeled by containment of one object in another (which in Perl means containment of a *reference* to the contained object.) You generally don't want to use *inheritance* to model the *has-a* relationship because *methods* that make sense on the contained object probably don't make sense on the object as a whole. Just because your car *has-a* brake pedal doesn't mean you should stomp on your car.

hash

A named list of *key/value* pairs, arranged such that you can easily use any key to find its associated value; a binary relation, to database users. This glossary is like a hash, where the word to be defined is the key, and the definition is the value. A hash is also sometimes called an "associative array". (Which is a good reason for calling it a hash instead.)

hash table

A method used internally by Perl for implementing associative arrays (hashes) efficiently.

header file

A file containing certain required definitions that you must include "ahead" of the rest of your program to do certain obscure operations. A C header file has a *.h* extension. A Perl header file has a *.ph* extension. See the **require** operator in Chapter 3. (Header files have been superseded by the *module* mechanism.)

here document

So called because of a similar construct in *shells* which pretends that the *lines* "right here" following the *command* are a separate *file* to be fed to the command, up to some trailing *delimiter* string. In Perl, however, it's just a fancy form of quoting.

hexadecimal

A number in base sixteen, "hex" for short. The digits for ten through sixteen are customarily represented by the letters a through f. Hexadecimal constants in Perl start with 0x.

home directory

The directory you are placed into when you log in. On a UNIX system, the name is often placed into $ENV{HOME} or $ENV{LOGDIR} by the login program, but you can also find it with (getpwuid($<))[7].

host

The computer on which a program or other data resides.

hubris

Excessive pride, the sort of thing Zeus zaps you for. Also the quality that makes you write (and maintain) programs that other people won't want to say bad things about. Hence, the third great virtue of a programmer. See also *laziness* and *impatience*.

HV

Short for "hash value," which refers to one of Perl's internal data types. An HV is a kind of *SV.*

identifier

A legally formed name for most anything in which a computer program might be interested. Many languages (including Perl) allow identifiers that start with a letter and contain letters and digits. Perl also counts the underscore character as a valid letter.

impatience

The anger you feel when the computer is being lazy. This makes you write programs that don't just react to your needs, but actually anticipate them. Or at least that pretend to. Hence, the second great virtue of a programmer. See also *laziness* and *hubris.*

import

Gain access to symbols that are exported from another module. See the **use** operator in Chapter 3.

increment

To add one to something.

indexing

Formerly, the act of looking up a *key* in an index (like the phone book), but now merely the act of using any kind of key or position to find the corresponding *value*, even if no index is involved. Things have degenerated to the point that Perl's **index** function merely locates the position (index) of one string in another.

indirect object

In English grammar, a short noun phrase between a verb and its direct object indicating the beneficiary or recipient of the action. In Perl, can be understood as *verb indirect-object object* where 'STDOUT is the recipient of the 'print action, and class *method*, you might say:

```
% perl
sub Bob::give { shift; print
    "Thanks for the @_!\n"; }
give Bob memories
^D
Thanks for the memories!
```

indirection

When Randal says, "I don't know the answer . . . go ask Larry." Similarly, if something in a program isn't the answer, but indicates where the answer is, that's indirection. This can be done with *symbolic* or *hard references.*

inheritance

What you get from your ancestors, genetically or otherwise. If you happen to be a *class*, your ancestors are called *base classes* and your descendants are called *derived classes.* See *single inheritance* and *multiple inheritance.*

integer

Number with no fractional part; whole number.

interpolation

The insertion of one piece of text somewhere in the middle of another piece of text. The inserted piece may derive from a variable or other indirect source.

interpreter

Strictly speaking, a program that reads a second program and does what the second program says directly without turning the program into a different form first, which is what *compilers* do. Perl is not an interpreter by this definition, because it contains a kind of compiler that takes a program and turns it into a more executable form (*syntax trees*) within the Perl process itself, which the Perl *run-time* system then interprets.

invocation

The act of calling up a program, subroutine, or function to do what it's supposed to do.

IPC

Short for Inter-Process Communication. Sometimes a *process* just needs to talk to some other process.

is-a

A relationship between two *objects* in which one object is considered to be a more specific version of the other generic object: "A camel is a mammal." Since the generic object really only exists in a platonic sense, we usually add a little abstraction to the notion of objects and think of the relationship as being between a generic *base class* and a specific *derived class.* Oddly enough, platonic classes don't always have platonic relationships—see *inheritance.*

iteration

Doing something again and again and again and again and again and . . . . Usually this is done until you're loopy, which is why they call them loops.*

iterator

A special programming gizmo that keeps track for you of where you are in something that you're trying to iterate over. The **foreach** loop in Perl contains an iterator.

key

A special kind of data, such as your Social Security number, that can be used to locate other data. The other data may be considered the *value* associated with the key.

keyword

See *reserved word*.

label

A kind of *key* you can give to a statement so that you can talk about that statement elsewhere in the program.

laziness

The quality that makes you go to great effort to reduce overall energy expenditure. It makes you write labor-saving programs that other people will find useful, and document what you wrote so you don't have to answer so many questions about it. Hence, the first great virtue of a programmer. Also hence, this book. See also *impatience* and *hubris*.

left shift

A *bit shift* that multiplies the number by some power of two.

lexical scoping

Looking at your *Oxford English Dictionary* through a microscope. (Also known as *static* scoping, because dictionaries don't change very fast.) Similarly, looking at variables that are stored in a private dictionary for each subroutine, which are visible only from their point of declaration down to the end of the block in

which they are declared. —Syn. *static scoping*. —Ant. *dynamic scoping*. [< Gk]

library

A collection of procedures. In ancient days, referred to a collection of subroutines in a *.pl* file. In modern times, refers often to the entire collection of Perl modules on your system.

line

In UNIX, a sequence of zero or more nonnewline characters terminated with a *newline* character. On non-UNIX machines, this is emulated even if the underlying *operating system* has different ideas.

line buffering

Used by a *standard I/O* output stream that flushes its *buffer* after every *newline*. Many standard I/O libraries automatically set this up on output that is going to the terminal.

line number

The number of lines read prior to this one, plus 1. Perl keeps a separate line number for each script or input file it opens. The current script line number is represented by `__LINE__`. The current input line number (for the file that was most recently read from via <>) is represented by the `$.` variable. Many error messages report both values, if available.

link

In UNIX, a name in a directory, representing a file. A given file can have multiple links to it. It's like having the same phone number listed in the phone directory under different names.

list

An ordered set of values.

LIST

A syntactic construct representing a comma-separated list of expressions, evaluated to produce a *list value*. Each *expression* in a *LIST* is evaluated in a *list context*.

list context

The situation in which an *expression* is expected by its surroundings (the code calling it) to return a list of values rather than a single value. Functions that want a *LIST* of arguments tell those arguments that they should produce a list value. See also *context*.

---

* We'd put in the usual joke referring you back to *Iteration*, but that trick has been iterated too often already, and is no longer funny. Look for the joke under *Loop* instead. Also look for a similar joke under *Recursion*, which is still funny at some level or other.

list operator

Generally, an *operator* that does something with a list of values. Specifically, those operators (such as **print**, **unlink**, and **system**) that do not require parentheses around their *argument* list.

list value

An unnamed list of scalar values that may be passed around within a program and passed to any function that provides a *list context*.

literal

Often means "figurative", as in "I'm literally scared to death." More literally, a symbol in a programming language like a number or *string* that gives you an actual *value* instead of merely representing possible values like a *variable*.

little-endian

From Swift: someone who eats boiled eggs little end first. Also used of computers that store the least significant *byte* of a word at a lower byte address than the most significant byte. Often considered superior to big-endian machines. See also *big-endian*.

local

Not meaning the same thing everywhere. A *variable* in Perl can be localized inside a *block* or a *package*. See *scope*.

logical operator

Symbols representing the concepts "and", "or", and "not".

loop

A construct that performs something repeatedly, like a roller coaster. (Go to the next entry if you're tired of riding this one.) See *loop*.

loop control statement

Any statement within the body of a loop that can make a loop stop looping or skip an *iteration*. See the middle sentence of the previous entry. Generally you shouldn't try this on roller coasters without a parachute.

loop label

A kind of key or name attached to a loop so that loop control statements can talk about which loop they want to control.

lvalue

Term used by language-lawyers for a location you can assign a new *value* to, such as a

variable or an element of an *array*. The "l" is short for "left", as in the left side of an assignment, a typical place for lvalues.

magical increment

An *increment* operator that knows how to add 1 to alphanumeric strings as well as to numbers.

magical variables

Special variables that have side effects when you access them or assign to them. For example, in Perl, changing elements of the %ENV array also changes the corresponding environment variables that subprocesses will use. Reading the $! variable gives you the current UNIX error number or message.

manpage

A "page" from the UNIX manuals, typically accessed online via the *man*(1) command. A manpage contains a synopsis, a description, a list of bugs, and so on, and is typically longer than a page. There are manpages documenting *commands, system calls, library functions, devices, protocols, files,* and such.

mantissa

The part of a *floating-point* number that gives the digits of the number without saying where the decimal point really belongs. See *exponent*.

matching

See *pattern matching*.

metacharacter

A *character* that is not supposed to be treated normally. Which characters are to be treated specially as metacharacters varies greatly from context to context. Your *shell* will have certain metacharacters, double-quoted Perl strings have other metacharacters, and patterns have all the double-quote metacharacters plus some extra ones. In addition, people sometimes use this term to describe characters that have the eighth bit set.

method

A kind of action that an *object* can take if you direct it to.

minimalism

The belief that "small is beautiful." Paradoxically, if you say something in a small language, it turns out big, and if you say it in a big language, it turns out small. Go figure.

mode

In the context of the *stat*(2) system call, refers to the word holding the permissions and the type of the file.

modifier

A *conditional* or *loop* that you put after the *statement* instead of before, if you know what I mean.

module

A *file* that defines a *package* of (almost) the same name, which can either *export* symbols or function as an *object class*. The unit of reusability in Perl. See the **use** operator.

modulus

A divisor, when you're interested in the remainder instead of the quotient.

multi-dimensional array

An array with multiple subscripts for finding a single element. Perl does them with *references*—see Chapter 4.

multiple inheritance

The features you got from your mother and father, mixed together unpredictably. (See also *inheritance*, and *single inheritance*.) In computer languages (including Perl), the notion that a given class may have multiple direct ancestors or *base classes*.

namespace

A domain of names. You needn't worry whether the names in one such domain have been used in another. See *package*.

network address

The most important attribute of a socket, like your telephone's telephone number.

newline

A single character that represents the end of a line, with the ASCII value of 012 octal under UNIX (but 015 on a Mac), and represented by \n in Perl strings. For certain physical devices like terminals, this gets translated to a line feed and a carriage return.

null character

A character with the ASCII value of zero. It's used by C and some UNIX system calls to terminate strings, but Perl allows strings to contain a null.

null list

A *list value* with zero elements, represented in Perl by ().

null string

A *string* not containing any characters, not to be confused with a string containing a *null character*, which has a positive length.

numeric context

The situation in which an expression is expected by its surroundings (the code calling it) to return a number. See also *context* and *string context*.

nybble

Half a byte, equivalent to one hexadecimal digit.

object

Something that "knows" what kind of thing it is, and what it can do because of what kind of thing it is. Your program can request an object to do things, but the object gets to decide whether it wants to do it or not.

octal

A number in base eight. Only the digits zero through seven are allowed. Octal constants in Perl start with zero, as in 013.

offset

How many things you have to skip over when moving from the beginning of a string or array to a specific position within it. Thus, the minimum offset is zero, not one, because you don't skip anything to get to the first item.

operand

You, after you dial the operator on your phone. Or, an expression that gives a *value* that an operator operates on. See also *precedence*.

operating system

A special program that runs on the bare machine and hides the gory details of managing *processes* and *devices*. It is usually used in a looser sense to indicate a particular culture of programming. The loose sense can be used at varying levels of specificity. At one extreme, you might say that all versions of UNIX and UNIX-lookalikes are the same operating system (upsetting many people, especially some lawyers). At the other extreme, this particular version of this particular vendor's operating system is different than any other version of this or any other vendor's operating system. Perl is much more portable across operating systems than many other languages. See also *architecture*.

operator

A *function*, generally one that is built into a language, often with a special syntax or symbol. A given operator may have specific expectations about what *types* of data you give as its arguments (operands) and what type of data you want back from it.

operator overloading

A kind of *overloading* that you can do on the built-in *operators* to make them work (syntactically) on *objects* as if they were ordinary scalar values, but with the actual semantics supplied by the object class. This is set up with the overload *pragma*—see Chapter 7, *The Standard Perl Library*.

options

See *switches*.

overloading

Giving additional meanings to a symbol or construct. Actually, all languages do overloading to one extent or another, since people are good at figuring out things from *context*. If you look in your dictionary, you will find that the meaning of the word "single" is not single.

overriding

Hiding or invalidating some other definition of the same name. (Not to be confused with *overloading*, which only adds definitions.) To confuse the issue further, we use the word with two overloaded definitions: to describe how you can define your own *subroutine* that hides a built-in *function* of the same name, and also to describe how you can define a replacement *method* in a *derived class* that hides a *base class*'s method of the same name. You'll find both of these usages in Chapter 5.

owner

The one user (apart from the superuser) who has absolute control over a *file*. A file may also have a *group* of users that may exercise joint ownership if the real owner permits them. See *permission flags*.

package

A quantity of code that values its privacy, and tries to keep other code from trespassing upon its *namespace* by fencing all of its private belongings (*variables* and *subroutines*) into its own area. A variable or subroutine mentioned in the package belongs only to that package, even if there's another variable or subroutine with an identical name in some other package.

package local

A *variable* or *subroutine* belonging to a package and not visible to anyone else. At least, not without peeking. See *namespace*.

parameter

See *argument*.

parsing

The subtle but sometimes brutal art of attempting to turn your possibly malformed program into a valid *syntax tree*.

PATH

The list of *directories* the system looks in to find a program you want to *execute*. The list is stored as one of your *environment variables*, accessible in Perl as $ENV{PATH}.

pathname

A fully qualified filename such as */usr/bin/perl* or *C:\my_apps\perl.exe*. Sometimes confused with PATH.

pattern matching

Taking a pattern, expressed as a *regular expression*, and trying the pattern various ways on a string to see if there's any way to make it fit. Often used to pick interesting tidbits out of a file.

permission flags

Bits that the *owner* of a file sets or unsets in order to allow or disallow access to other people. These flags are part of the *mode* word returned by the **stat** operator when you ask about a file. On UNIX systems you can check the *ls*(1) manpage for more information about the permission flags.

Pern

What you get when you do Perl++ twice. Increment it only once, and your hair curls. Increment it three times, and you get a tasty beverage that isn't Java. See also *slice*.

pipe

A direct *connection* that carries the output of one *process* to the input of another without the necessity of an intermediate temporary file. Once the pipe is set up, the two processes in question can mostly read and write as if they were talking to a normal file.

pipeline

A series of *processes* all in a row, linked by *pipes*, where each passes its output to the next.

pointer

A *variable* in a language like C that contains the exact memory location of some other item. Perl handles pointers internally so you don't have to worry about them. Instead, you just use symbolic pointers in the form of *keys* and *variable* names, or *hard references*, which aren't pointers (but act like pointers, and do in fact contain pointers).

port

The part of the address of a TCP or UDP socket that directs packets to the correct process after finding the right machine, something like the phone extension number you give when you reach the company operator.

pragma

A library module whose practical hints and suggestions are received (and possibly ignored) by the compiler. [< Gr]

precedence

The rules of conduct that, in the absence of other guidance, determine what should happen first (i.e., in the absence of parentheses, you always do multiplication before addition).

preprocessing

What some other helper *process* did to transform the incoming data into a form more suitable for the current process. Often done with an incoming *pipe*. See also *C preprocessor*.

procedure

A *subroutine*.

process

An instance of a running program. Under multitasking systems like UNIX, two or more separate processes could be running the same program independently at the same time—in fact, the **fork** function is designed to bring about this

happy state of affairs. Under other operating systems processes are sometimes called "tasks" or "jobs".

protocol

In networking, an agreed-upon way of sending messages back and forth so that neither correspondent will get too confused.

pseudo literal

An *operator* that looks something like a *literal*, such as the output-grabbing operator, `` `command` ``.

pseudo terminal

A thing that looks like an ordinary terminal to the computer, but instead of being attached to a real terminal, is really attached to another computer program, which is doing the pseudotyping.

public domain

Something not owned by anybody. Perl is copyrighted, and is thus *not* in the public domain—it's just *freely available* and *freely redistributable*.

PV

A "pointer value", which is Perl Internals Talk for a **char***.

qualified

Possessing an explicit package name. The symbol **$ex::loser** is qualified; **$loser** is unqualified.

readable

With regard to files, one that has the proper permission bit set to let you access the file. With regard to computer programs, one that's well enough written that someone can come back later and have a chance of figuring out what it's trying to do. Who knows, you might even have to come back and figure out your own program.

record

A set of related data values in a *file* or stream, often associated with a unique *key* field. In UNIX, often commensurate with a *line*, or a blank-line-delimited set of lines (a "paragraph"). Each line of the */etc/passwd* file is a record, keyed on login name, containing information about that user.

recursion

The art of defining something (at least partly) in terms of itself by means of *recursion*, which is a naughty no-no in dictionaries.

reference

A place you look to find a pointer to information stored somewhere else. (See *indirection*.) References come in two flavors, *symbolic references*, and *hard references*.

regular expression

A single entity with various interpretations, like an elephant. To a computer scientist, it's a grammar for a little language in which some strings are legal and others aren't. To normal people, it's a pattern that you can use to find what you're looking for when it varies from case to case. Example of a regular expression:

    /Oh s.*t./

This pattern will match strings like "Oh say can you see by the dawn's early light," and "Oh sit!". See the section "Regular Expressions" in Chapter 2.

regular file

A *file* that's not a *directory*, a *device*, a named *pipe* or *socket*, or a *symbolic link*. Perl uses the -f *file test operator* to identify regular files.

relation

Jargon used by relational database folks to mean a *file*—albeit a particular sort of file, tabular in form, in which all the tuples (*records*) are of the same kind, each containing the same domains (*keys*) and ranges (*fields*). The UNIX */etc/passwd* file is a relation keyed on login name. It's called a relation because it relates keys and fields in much the same way as an hash associates keys and values.

relational operator

An operator that says whether a particular ordering relationship is *true* about a pair of operands. Perl has both numeric and string relational operators. See *collating sequence*.

reserved words

A word with a specific, built-in meaning to a *compiler*, such as **if** or **delete**. In many languages (not Perl) it's illegal to use reserved words to name anything else. (Which is why they're reserved, after all.) In Perl, you just can't

use them to name *labels* or *filehandles*. Also called "keywords".

return value

The *value* produced by a *subroutine* or *expression* when evaluated. In Perl, a return value may be either a *list* or a *scalar* value. The subroutine call piglatin('bingo') returns the value "ingobay".

right shift

A *bit shift* that divides a number by some power of two.

run-time

The time when Perl is actually doing what your script says to do, as opposed to the earlier period of time when it was trying to figure out whether what you said made any sense whatsoever. See also *compile-time*.

run-time pattern

A pattern that contains one or more variables to be interpolated before parsing the pattern as a *regular expression*, and that therefore cannot be analyzed at compile time, but must be re-analyzed each time the pattern match operator is evaluated. Run-time patterns are useful but expensive.

rvalue

A *value* that you might find on the right side of an *assignment*. See also *lvalue*.

scalar

A simple value, such as a number or string.

scalar context

The situation in which an *expression* is expected by its surroundings (the code calling it) to return a single *value* rather than a *list* of values. See also *context* and *list context*. A scalar context sometimes imposes additional constraints on the return value—see *string context* and *numeric context*. Sometimes we talk about a *Boolean context* inside conditionals, but this imposes no additional constraints, since any scalar value, whether numeric or *string*, is already true or false.

scalar literal

A number or quoted *string*—an actual *value* in the text of your program, as opposed to a *variable*.

scalar value

A value that happens to be a *scalar* as opposed to a *list*.

scalar variable

A *variable* prefixed with $ that holds a single value.

scope

How far away you can see a variable from, looking through one. Perl has two visibility mechanisms: it does *dynamic scoping* of **local** *variables*, meaning that the rest of the *block*, and any *subroutines* that are called by the rest of the block, can see the variables that are local to the block. Perl does *lexical scoping* of **my** variables, meaning that the rest of the block can see the variable, but other subroutines called by the block *cannot* see the variable.

script

A text *file* that is a program intended to be *executed* directly rather than *compiled* to another form of file before execution.

sed

A venerable stream editor from which Perl derives some of its ideas.

server

In networking, a *process* that either advertises a *service* or just hangs around at a known location and waits for *clients* who need service to get in touch with it.

service

Something you do for someone else to make them happy, like giving them the time of day (or of their life). On some UNIX machines, well-known services are listed by the **getservent** function.

setgid

Same as setuid, only having to do with giving away *group* privileges.

setuid

Said of a program that runs with the privileges of its *owner* rather than (as is usually the case) the privileges of whoever is running it. Also describes the bit in the mode word (*permission flags*) that implements the feature. This bit must be explicitly set by the owner to implement this feature, and the program must be written not to give away more privileges than it ought.

shell

A *command-line interpreter.* The program that interactively gives you a prompt, accepts one or more *lines* of input, and executes the programs you mentioned, feeding each of them their proper *arguments* and input data. Shells can also execute scripts containing such commands. Under the UNIX *operating system*, typical shells are the Bourne shell (*/bin/sh*), the C shell (*/bin/csh*), and the Korn shell (*/bin/ksh*). Perl is not strictly a shell because it's not interactive (although Perl programs can be interactive).

side effects

Something extra that happens when you evaluate an *expression.* Nowadays it can refer to almost anything. For example, evaluating a simple assignment statement typically has the "side effect" of assigning a value to a variable. (And you thought assigning the value was your primary intent in the first place!) Likewise, assigning a value to the special variable $| has the side effect of forcing a flush after every **write** or **print** on the currently selected filehandle.

signal handler

A *subroutine* that, instead of being content to be called in the normal fashion, sits around waiting for a bolt out of the blue before it will deign to *execute.* Under UNIX, bolts out of the blue are called signals, and you send them with a **kill** command.

single inheritance

The features you got from your mother, if she told you you don't have a father. (See also *inheritance*, and *multiple inheritance*.) In computer languages, the notion that *classes* reproduce asexually, so that a given class can only have one direct ancestor or *base class*. Perl enforces no such restriction.

slice

A selection of *array elements.*

socket

An endpoint for network communication between two *processes*, that works much like a telephone. The most important thing about a socket is its *network address* (like a phone number). Different kinds of sockets have different kinds of addresses—some look like filenames, and some don't.

soft reference

See *symbolic reference*.

standard error

The default output stream for making nasty remarks that don't belong in *standard output*. Represented within a Perl program by the *filehandle* STDERR. You can use this stream explicitly, but the operators **die** and **warn** write to your standard error stream automatically.

standard I/O

A standard C library for doing *buffered* input and output to the *operating system*. (The "standard" of standard I/O is only marginally related to the "standard" of standard input and output.) In general, Perl relies on whatever implementation of standard I/O a given operating system supplies, so the buffering characteristics of a Perl program on one machine may not exactly match those on another machine. Normally this only influences efficiency, not semantics. If your standard I/O package is doing block buffering and you want it to *flush* the buffer more often, just set the $| variable to a nonzero value.

standard input

The default input stream for your program, which if possible shouldn't care where its data is coming from. Represented within a Perl program by the *filehandle* STDIN.

standard output

The default output stream for your program, which if possible shouldn't care where its data is going. Represented within a Perl program by the *filehandle* STDOUT.

stat structure

A special internal buffer in which Perl keeps the information about the last *file* you requested information on.

statement

A *command* to the computer about what to do next, like a step in a recipe: "Add marmalade to batter and mix until mixed." Not to be confused with a *declaration*, which doesn't tell the computer to do anything, but just to learn something.

static

Varying slowly, compared to something else. (Unfortunately, everything is relatively stable compared to something else, except for certain elementary particles, and we're not so sure about them.) In computers, where things are supposed to vary rapidly, "static" has a derogatory connotation, indicating a slightly dysfunctional *variable*, *subroutine*, or *method*. In Perl culture, the word is considered to be politically incorrect.

static method

See *class method*.

static scoping

Same as *lexical scoping*.

status

The *value* returned to the parent *process* when one of its child processes dies. This value is placed in the special variable $?. Its upper eight *bits* are the exit status of the defunct process, and its lower eight bits identify the signal (if any) that the process died from. On UNIX systems, this status value is the same as the status word returned by *wait*(2). See **system** in Chapter 3.

STDERR

See *standard error*.

STDIN

See *standard input*.

STDIO

See *standard I/O*.

STDOUT

See *standard output*.

string

A sequence of characters such as "He said !@#*&%@#*?\n." A string does not have to be entirely printable.

string context

The situation in which an expression is expected by its surroundings (the code calling it) to return a *string*. See also *context* and *numeric context*.

struct

C keyword introducing a structure definition or name.

structure

See *data structure*.

subclass

See *derived class*.

subroutine

A named piece of program that can be invoked from elsewhere in the program in order to accomplish some sub-goal of the program. A subroutine is often parameterized to accomplish different but related things depending on its input *arguments*. If the subroutine returns a meaningful *value*, it is also called a *function*.

subscript

A *value* that indicates the position of a particular *array element* in an array.

substring

A portion of a *string*, starting at a certain *character* position (*offset*), and proceeding for a certain number of characters.

superclass

See *base class*.

superuser

The person whom the *operating system* will let do almost anything. Typically your system administrator or someone pretending to be your system administrator. On UNIX systems, the *root* user.

SV

Short for "scalar value". But within the Perl interpreter every *thingy* is treated as a kind of SV, in an object-oriented sort of way. Every *value* inside Perl is passed around as an SV* pointer in C. The SV *struct* knows its own "thingy type", and the code is smart enough (we hope) not to try to call a *hash* function on a *subroutine*.

switch

An option you give on a command line to influence the way your program works. In UNIX, these are usually introduced with a minus sign. The word is also used as a nickname for a *switch statement*.

switch clustering

The combining of multiple command line switches –a –b –c into one switch –abc. In Perl, any switch with an additional *argument* must be the last switch in a cluster.

switch statement

A program construct that lets you evaluate an *expression* and, based on the expression's value, do a multi-way branch to the appropriate piece of code for that value. Also called a "case structure", after the similar Pascal construct.

symbol table

Where a *compiler* remembers symbols. A program like Perl must somehow remember all the names of all the *variables*, *filehandles*, and *subroutines* you've used. It does this by placing the names in a symbol table, which is implemented in Perl using a *hash table*. There is a separate symbol table for each *package*, to give each package its own *namespace*.

symbolic debugger

A program that lets you step through the *execution* of your program, stopping or printing things out here and there to see if anything has gone wrong, and if so, what. The "symbolic" part just means that you can talk to the debugger using the same symbols in which your program is written.

symbolic link

An alternate filename that points to the real *filename*. Whenever the *operating system* is trying to parse a pathname containing a symbolic link, it merely substitutes the real name and continues parsing.

symbolic reference

A variable whose value is the name of another variable or subroutine. By *dereferencing* the first variable, you can get at the second one.

syntax

From Greek, "with-arrangement". How things (particularly symbols) are put together with each other.

syntax tree

An internal representation of your program wherein lower-level *constructs* dangle off the higher-level constructs enclosing them.

system call

A *subroutine* call directly to the *operating system*. Many of the important subroutines and functions you use aren't direct system calls, but are built up in one or more layers above the system call level. In general, Perl users don't need to worry about the distinction.

tainted

Said of data that might be derived from the grubby hands of a user, and thus unsafe for a secure program to rely on. Perl does taint checks if you run a *setuid* program or use the -T switch.

TCP

Short for Transmission Control Protocol. A protocol wrapped around the Internet Protocol to make an unreliable packet transmission mechanism appear to the application program to be a reliable stream of bytes. (Well, usually.)

text

Normally, a *string* or *file* containing primarily printable characters. The word has been usurped in some UNIX circles to mean the portion of your *process* that contains machine code to be executed.

thingy

Something sort of like an object, that you may or may not know the name of, but that you can refer to with circumlocutions like "that hangy-down thingy that dangles in the back of your throat". Similarly in Perl, a value that is sort of like an object, that you may or may not know the name of, but that you can refer to via references from which the thingy dangles, metaphorically speaking. Specifically, the sort of value that your reference points to when you create a reference to a variable. See *anonymous*, *hard reference*, and *object*, not necessarily in that order.

thread

An instance of running a program, but lighter weight than a process, in that a process could have multiple threads running around in it, all sharing the same process's resources. (If you're a dragonrider, see *Pern*.)

tie

The bond between a magical variable and its implementation class. See the **tie** function in Chapters 3 and 5.

tokenizing

Splitting up a program text into its separate words and symbols, each of which is called a token. Also known as "lexing", in which case you get "lexemes" instead of tokens.

toolbox approach

The notion that, with a complete set of simple tools that work well together, you can build almost anything you want. Which is fine if you're assembling a tricycle, but if you're building a defranishizing comboflux, you really want your own machine shop to build special tools in. Perl is sort of a machine shop.

true

See *false*. (And hold it up to a mirror for the secret message.)

tuple

In the lingo of relational databases, a *record* or *line* containing fields. See *relation*.

type

See *data type*.

type casting

Converting data explicitly from one type to another. C permits this. Perl does not need it.

typeglob

Used of a single identifier, prefaced with * (for example, *name), to stand for any or all of $name, @name, %name, &name, or just name. How you use it determines whether it is interpreted as all of those, or only one of them. See "Typeglobs and Filehandles" in Chapter 2.

UID

A User ID. Often used in the context of file ownership.

unary operator

An operator with only one *operand*, like ! or **chdir**. Unary operators are usually prefix operators, that is, they precede their operand. The ++ and -- operators can be either prefix or postfix. (Of course, that *does* change their meaning.)

undefined

Nobody has ever given this a reasonable definition. See also *defined*.

UNIX

A very large and constantly evolving language with several alternate and largely incompatible syntaxes, in which anyone can define anything any way they choose, and usually do. Speakers of this language think it's easy to learn because it's so easily twisted to one's own ends, but dialectical differences make tribal intercommunication nearly impossible, and travelers are often reduced to a pidgin-like subset of the language. To be universally understood, a UNIX shell programmer must spend years of study in the art. Many have abandoned this discipline and now communicate via an Esperanto-like language called Perl. In ancient times UNIX was also used to refer to some code that a couple of people at Bell Labs wrote to make use of a PDP-7 computer that wasn't doing much of anything else at the time.

unqualified

See *qualified*.

value

This is hard to define. It's something like real data—the actual numbers and strings that wander around in your program. But we don't really need to define it. If you didn't know a value when you see it, you wouldn't have this book. :-)

variable

A named storage location that can hold any of various values, as your program sees fit.

variable interpolation

See *interpolation*.

vector

Mathematical jargon for a list of *scalar values*.

warning

A message printed to the STDERR stream to the effect that something might be wrong but it isn't worth blowing up over. See the **warn** operator in Chapter 3.

whitespace

A *character* that moves your cursor around but doesn't otherwise put anything on your screen. Typically refers to any of the following: space, tab, line feed, carriage return, form feed, or vertical tab.

word

In normal "computerese", the piece of data of the size most efficiently dealt with by your computer, typically 32 bits or so, give or take a few powers of two. In UNIX culture, it more often refers to an alphanumeric identifier, or to a string of non-whitespace characters bounded by whitespace or line boundaries.

working directory

Your current *directory*, from which relative pathnames are interpreted by the *operating system*. The operating system knows your current directory because you told it with a **chdir**, or because you started out in the same place where your parent *process* was when you were born.

wrapper

A program that runs some other program for you, modifying some of its input or output to better suit your purposes. More generally, just about anything that wraps things up. And that just about wraps things up, except for the excess.

XS

An extraordinarily exported, expeditiously excellent, expressly eXternal Subroutine, executed in existing C or C++, or in an exciting new extension language called (exasperatingly) XS. Examine Chapter 6, *Social Engineering*, for the exact explanation. *Exeunt*.

Index

Punctuation in the index is sorted in the alphabetical order of each symbol's English equivalent: "ampersand", "asterisk", "at sign", "backslash", etc. Entries that consist only of punctuation are listed at the front of the index. Variable names beginning with $ and consisting only of punctuation, such as $_ and $^, are combined under the heading "$ variables", starting on the second page of the index. Terms with initial punctuation followed by alphanumeric characters, such as "%INC hash", are sorted by their alphanumeric characters (e.g., "INChash").

About the Authors

Larry Wall is one of the associates of O'Reilly & Associates; in his copious free time :-) he has authored some of the most popular free programs available for UNIX, including the *rn* news reader, the ubiquitous *patch* program, and the Perl programming language. He's also known for *metaconfig*, a program that writes *Configure* scripts, and for the *warp* space-war game, the first version of which was written in BASIC/PLUS at Seattle Pacific University. By training Larry is actually a linguist, having wandered about both U.C. Berkeley and U.C.L.A. as a grad student. (Oddly enough, while at Berkeley, he had nothing to do with the UNIX development going on there.)

Over the course of years, he has spent time at Unisys, JPL, NetLabs, and Seagate, playing with everything from discrete event simulators to network-management systems, with the occasional spacecraft thrown in. (He also plays with his four kids every now and then, but they win too often.) It was at Unisys, while trying to glue together a bicoastal configuration management system over a 1200 baud encrypted link using a hacked-over version of Netnews, that Perl was born.

Tom Christiansen is a freelance consultant specializing in Perl training and writing. After working for several years for TSR Hobbies (of Dungeons and Dragons fame), he set off for college where he spent a year in Spain and five in America dabbling in music, linguistics, programming, and some half-dozen different spoken languages. Tom finally escaped UW-Madison with BAs in Spanish and Computer Science and an MS in Computer Science.

He then spent five years at Convex as a jack-of-all-trades working on everything from system administration to utility and kernel development, with customer support and training thrown in for good measure. Tom also served two terms on the USENIX Association Board of Directors.

With over fifteen year's experience in UNIX system administration and programming, Tom presents seminars internationally. Living in the foothills above Boulder, Colorado, surrounded by mule deer, skunks, and the occasional mountain lion and black bear, Tom takes summers off for hiking, hacking, birding, music making, and gaming.

Randal L. Schwartz is an eclectic tradesman and entrepreneur, making his living through software design, technical writing and training, system administration, security consultation, and video production. He is known internationally for his prolific, humorous, and occasionally incorrect spatterings on Usenet—especially his "Just another perl hacker" signoffs in *comp.lang.perl*.

Randal honed his many crafts through seven years of employment at Tektronix, ServioLogic, and Sequent. Since 1985, he has owned and operated Stonehenge Consulting Services in his home town of Portland, Oregon.

Colophon

Our look is the result of reader comments, our own experimentation, and distribution channels. Distinctive covers complement our distinctive approach to technical topics, breathing personality and life into potentially dry subjects. UNIX and its attendant programs can be unruly beasts. Nutshell Handbooks help you tame them.

The animal featured on the cover of *Programming Perl* is a camel (one-hump dromedary). Camels are large ruminant mammals, weighing between 1,000 and 1,600 pounds and standing six to seven feet tall at the shoulders. They are well known for their use as draft and saddle animals in the desert regions, especially of Africa and Asia. Camels can go for days without water. If food is scarce, they will eat anything, even their owner's tent. Camels live up to 50 years.

Edie Freedman designed the cover of this book, using a 19th-century engraving from the Dover Pictorial Archive. The cover layout was produced with Quark XPress 3.3 using the ITC Garamond font. Whenever possible, our books use RepKover™, a durable and flexible lay-flat binding. If the page count exceeds RepKover's limit, perfect binding is used.

The inside layout was designed by Edie Freedman, Jennifer Niederst, and Nancy Priest. Text was prepared by Erik Ray in SGML using the DocBook 2.4 DTD. The print version of this book was created by translating the SGML source into a set of gtroff macros using a filter developed at ORA by Norman Walsh. Steve Talbott designed and wrote the underlying macro set on the basis of the GNU gtroff -gs macros; Lenny Muellner adapted them to SGML and implemented the book design. The GNU groff text formatter version 1.09 was used to generate PostScript output.

How to stay in touch with O'Reilly

1. Visit Our Award-Winning Web Site

http://www.oreilly.com/

★ "Top 100 Sites on the Web" —*PC Magazine*
★ "Top 5% Web sites" —*Point Communications*
★ "3-Star site" —*The McKinley Group*

Our web site contains a library of comprehensive product information (including book excerpts and tables of contents), downloadable software, background articles, interviews with technology leaders, links to relevant sites, book cover art, and more. File us in your Bookmarks or Hotlist!

2. Join Our Email Mailing Lists

New Product Releases

To receive automatic email with brief descriptions of all new O'Reilly products as they are released, send email to:
listproc@online.oreilly.com
Put the following information in the first line of your message (*not* in the Subject field):
subscribe oreilly-news

O'Reilly Events

If you'd also like us to send information about trade show events, special promotions, and other O'Reilly events, send email to:
listproc@online.oreilly.com
Put the following information in the first line of your message (*not* in the Subject field):
subscribe oreilly-events

3. Get Examples from Our Books via FTP

There are two ways to access an archive of example files from our books:

Regular FTP

- ftp to:
  ftp.oreilly.com
  (login: anonymous
  password: your email address)
- Point your web browser to:
  ftp://ftp.oreilly.com/

FTPMAIL

- Send an email message to:
  ftpmail@online.oreilly.com
  (Write "help" in the message body)

4. Contact Us via Email

order@oreilly.com
To place a book or software order online. Good for North American and international customers.

subscriptions@oreilly.com
To place an order for any of our newsletters or periodicals.

books@oreilly.com
General questions about any of our books.

software@oreilly.com
For general questions and product information about our software. Check out O'Reilly Software Online at **http://software.oreilly.com/** for software and technical support information. Registered O'Reilly software users send your questions to: **website-support@oreilly.com**

cs@oreilly.com
For answers to problems regarding your order or our products.

booktech@oreilly.com
For book content technical questions or corrections.

proposals@oreilly.com
To submit new book or software proposals to our editors and product managers.

international@oreilly.com
For information about our international distributors or translation queries. For a list of our distributors outside of North America check out:
http://www.oreilly.com/www/order/country.html

5. Work with Us

Check out our website for current employment opportunites:
www.jobs@oreilly.com
Click on "Work with Us"

O'Reilly & Associates, Inc.
101 Morris Street, Sebastopol, CA 95472 USA
TEL   707-829-0515 or 800-998-9938
        (6am to 5pm PST)
FAX   707-829-0104

International Distributors

UK, EUROPE, MIDDLE EAST AND AFRICA (EXCEPT FRANCE, GERMANY, AUSTRIA, SWITZERLAND, LUXEMBOURG, LIECHTENSTEIN, AND EASTERN EUROPE)

INQUIRIES
O'Reilly UK Limited
4 Castle Street
Farnham
Surrey, GU9 7HS
United Kingdom
Telephone: 44-1252-711776
Fax: 44-1252-734211
Email: josette@oreilly.com

ORDERS
Wiley Distribution Services Ltd.
1 Oldlands Way
Bognor Regis
West Sussex PO22 9SA
United Kingdom
Telephone: 44-1243-779777
Fax: 44-1243-820250
Email: cs-books@wiley.co.uk

FRANCE

INQUIRIES
Éditions O'Reilly
18 rue Séguier
75006 Paris, France
Tel: 33-1-40-51-52-30
Fax: 33-1-40-51-52-31
Email: france@editions-oreilly.fr

ORDERS
GEODIF
61, Bd Saint-Germain
75240 Paris Cedex 05, France
Tel: 33-1-44-41-46-16 (French books)
Tel: 33-1-44-41-11-87 (English books)
Fax: 33-1-44-41-11-44
Email: distribution@eyrolles.com

GERMANY, SWITZERLAND, AUSTRIA, EASTERN EUROPE, LUXEMBOURG, AND LIECHTENSTEIN

INQUIRIES & ORDERS
O'Reilly Verlag
Balthasarstr. 81
D-50670 Köln
Germany
Telephone: 49-221-973160-91
Fax: 49-221-973160-8
Email: anfragen@oreilly.de (inquiries)
Email: order@oreilly.de (orders)

CANADA (FRENCH LANGUAGE BOOKS)

Les Éditions Flammarion ltée
375, Avenue Laurier Ouest
Montréal (Québec) H2V 2K3
Tel: 00-1-514-277-8807
Fax: 00-1-514-278-2085
Email: info@flammarion.qc.ca

HONG KONG

City Discount Subscription Service, Ltd.
Unit D, 3rd Floor, Yan's Tower
27 Wong Chuk Hang Road
Aberdeen, Hong Kong
Tel: 852-2580-3539
Fax: 852-2580-6463
Email: citydis@ppn.com.hk

KOREA

Hanbit Media, Inc.
Sonyoung Bldg. 202
Yeksam-dong 736-36
Kangnam-ku
Seoul, Korea
Tel: 822-554-9610
Fax: 822-556-0363
Email: hant93@chollian.dacom.co.kr

PHILIPPINES

Mutual Books, Inc.
429-D Shaw Boulevard
Mandaluyong City, Metro
Manila, Philippines
Tel: 632-725-7538
Fax: 632-721-3056
Email: mbikikog@mnl.sequel.net

TAIWAN

O'Reilly Taiwan
No. 3, Lane 131
Hang-Chow South Road
Section 1, Taipei, Taiwan
Tel: 886-2-23968990
Fax: 886-2-23968916
Email: taiwan@oreilly.com

CHINA

O'Reilly Beijing
Room 2410
160, FuXingMenNeiDaJie
XiCheng District
Beijing, China PR 100031
Tel: 86-10-66412305
Fax: 86-10-86631007
Email: beijing@oreilly.com

INDIA

Computer Bookshop (India) Pvt. Ltd.
190 Dr. D.N. Road, Fort
Bombay 400 001 India
Tel: 91-22-207-0989
Fax: 91-22-262-3551
Email: cbsbom@giasbm01.vsnl.net.in

JAPAN

O'Reilly Japan, Inc.
Kiyoshige Building 2F
12-Bancho, Sanei-cho
Shinjuku-ku
Tokyo 160-0008 Japan
Tel: 81-3-3356-5227
Fax: 81-3-3356-5261
Email: japan@oreilly.com

ALL OTHER ASIAN COUNTRIES

O'Reilly & Associates, Inc.
101 Morris Street
Sebastopol, CA 95472 USA
Tel: 707-829-0515
Fax: 707-829-0104
Email: order@oreilly.com

AUSTRALIA

WoodsLane Pty., Ltd.
7/5 Vuko Place
Warriewood NSW 2102
Australia
Tel: 61-2-9970-5111
Fax: 61-2-9970-5002
Email: info@woodslane.com.au

NEW ZEALAND

Woodslane New Zealand, Ltd.
21 Cooks Street (P.O. Box 575)
Waganui, New Zealand
Tel: 64-6-347-6543
Fax: 64-6-345-4840
Email: info@woodslane.com.au

LATIN AMERICA

McGraw-Hill Interamericana
Editores, S.A. de C.V.
Cedro No. 512
Col. Atlampa
06450, Mexico, D.F.
Tel: 52-5-547-6777
Fax: 52-5-547-3336
Email: mcgraw-hill@infosel.net.mx

O'REILLY®